POLICE ADMINISTRATION
STRUCTURES, PROCESSES, AND BEHAVIOR

EIGHTH EDITION

Charles R. Swanson
University of Georgia

Leonard Territo
Saint Leo University

Robert W. Taylor
The University of Texas at Dallas

PEARSON

Boston Columbus Indianapolis New York San Francisco Upper Saddle River
Amsterdam Cape Town Dubai London Madrid Milan Munich Paris Montreal Toronto
Delhi Mexico City São Paulo Sydney Hong Kong Seoul Singapore Taipei Tokyo

Editorial Director: *Vernon Anthony*
Senior Acquisitions Editor: *Eric Krassow*
Development Editor: *Megan Moffo*
Editorial Assistant: *Lynda Cramer*
Director of Marketing: *David Gesell*
Marketing Manager: *Adam Kloza*
Senior Marketing Coordinator: *Alicia Wozniak*
Senior Marketing Assistant: *Les Roberts*
Senior Managing Editor: *JoEllen Gohr*
Project Manager: *Jessica H. Sykes*
Senior Operations Supervisor: *Pat Tonneman*

Senior Art Director: *Diane Ernsberger*
Text and Cover Designer: *Suzanne Behnke*
Cover Art: *Getty One*
Media Editor: *Michelle Churma*
Lead Media Project Manager: *Karen Bretz*
Full-Service Project Management: *Lynn Steines,*
    S4Carlisle Publishing Services
Composition: *S4Carlisle Publishing Services*
Printer/Binder: *Courier Kendallville*
Cover Printer: *Lehigh-Phoenix Color/Hagerstown*
Text Font: *Adobe Garamond*

Library of Congress Cataloging-in-Publication Data

Swanson, Charles R.
    Police administration: structures, processes, and behavior / Charles R. Swanson,
Leonard Territo, Robert W. Taylor.—8th ed.
        p. cm.
    ISBN-13: 978-0-13-512103-0
    ISBN-10: 0-13-512103-5
    1. Police administration.   I. Territo, Leonard.   II. Taylor, Robert W.   III. Title.
HV7935.S95 2012
363.2068—dc22

                                                                    2011011144

10 9 8 7 6 5
V011

ISBN-10:   0-13-512103-5
ISBN-13: 978-0-13-512103-0

For our daughter, Maggie, forever in our hearts.

—Mike Swanson

For my wife, Elena, the kindest and sweetest woman I have ever known,
and our children, Lorraine, Kseniya, and Illia, and grandchildren,
Matthew and Branden.

—Leonard Territo

For my wonderful and beautiful wife, Mary, and our children, Matt,
Scott, Laura, and Shawna, and our grandchildren, Olivia, Auggie,
and Brody and the many more to come.

—Bob Taylor

brief contents

contents

12

Financial Management   511

part four
Organizational Issues   541

13

Stress and Police Personnel   542

14

Legal Aspects of Police Administration   586

Preface

The field of police administration is dynamic and ever changing. Laws are modified, new problems occur, and administrative practices that were once accepted as gospel are challenged, modified, and, in some cases, discarded. For instance, in the early morning hours of September 11, 2001, our country was attacked in a manner that will forever change the way we look at police and security in this country. The terrorist attacks on the World Trade Center and the Pentagon have hailed the development of a completely new federal branch—the Department of Homeland Security. Local police officers now have a significant role in the detection and prevention of terrorist attacks through expanded, yet controversial, roles posed by the USA Patriot Act. The primary mission of police in local communities has become somewhat blurred as community policing efforts from the last decade fade to the emergence of security checks, intelligence gathering, and participation in joint terrorism task forces. In this edition, as with the previous seven editions, we have tried to provide the most current and useful information to readers in an effort to help them deal with these dynamic changes. This edition has posed significant challenges as local, state, and federal governments try to cope with the new threats of terrorism while still addressing the core issues of crime rates and social disorder in many of our largest urban areas.

Collectively, the three authors of this text have been police officers, detectives, administrators, and educators for over 100 years. We have studied, practiced, researched, taught, and consulted on police administration, and an inevitable by-product of these experiences is the development of certain perspectives. It is these perspectives that form the rationale for this book.

New to This Edition

This is the most wide-ranging revision of *Police Administration*. A number of chapters have been totally or entirely re-written. The authors and editors have also developed pedagogical aids to help students maximize their learning experience and to simplify the understanding of complex issues.

Chapter 1: The Evolution of Police Administration

- Updated content on the Civil Rights movement and the 9/11 attacks

Chapter 2: Policing Today

- New, detailed, and current material on zero-tolerance policing, community policing and CompStat, particularly focused on crime reduction and neighborhood improvement by increasing feelings of safety among residents
- A review of the Chicago Alternative Policing Strategy (CAPS) and its success from a basic community policing methodology to an innovative and sophisticated cooperation between local police and the people and neighborhoods they serve to combat crime

- Detailed discussion on policing strategies today focusing on intelligence-led policing, evidence-based policing, hot-spots policing, directed and saturation patrol, and predictive policing
- Exciting material on the impact of new technologies in law enforcement, including crime analysis, geographic information systems, expert systems, and artificial intelligence as applied to strategies aimed at reducing crime and improving police-community relationships

Chapter 3: Intelligence, Terrorism, and Homeland Security

- New material focusing on intelligence, the intelligence process and cycle, and the role of fusion centers in preventing terrorism
- Expanded direction on how local and state police departments can improve their intelligence collection and analysis methodology aimed at preventing terrorism
- A new critical analysis aimed at fusion centers and other law enforcement responses to terrorism based on recent governmental reports to Congress
- Discussion on the changes in the U.S. Department of Homeland Security since the election of President Barack Obama, with a special focus on Arizona's new law on immigration and its potential impact on local and state police
- Detailed discussion on defining and conceptualizing terrorism and terrorist events, as well as expanded discussion on the continuing threat from al-Qaeda, and other radical Islamic groups
- A completely new case study detailing recent "homegrown" terrorist attacks
- New material on HAMAS and Hezbollah and their role in supporting the war against the United States in Iraq and Afghanistan
- New material on narco-terrorism and the U.S.-Mexico border, including a discussion of the various Mexican cartels active in using violence and murder in their war for power
- Discussion of the various right-wing extremist groups in the United States
- Expanded material on hate crimes and the spread of hate via the Internet

Chapter 4: Politics and Police Administration

- New material on public interest organizations and their involvement with police departments, including the involvement of such groups as the American Civil Liberties Union (ACLU) and the National Association for the Advancement of Colored People (NAACP)
- New content on police brutality and its political and operational consequences, especially as it relates to minority citizens
- A discussion of the history of alleged law enforcement racial profiling and media accounts of racial profiling

- New material on the recently passed Arizona immigration law, its political implications, and the reluctance of some police chiefs and sheriffs to become involved in the enforcement of federal immigration laws because of its potential negative effects on police community relations

Chapter 5: Organizational Theory

- New content includes resource dependency theory, population ecology, neo-institutional theory, networked and virtual organization, and a case study of the DC sniper case

Chapter 6: Organizational Design

- New and exciting material on the structure of police organizations today, including discussions on decentralization, performance measurement, and the impact of intelligence-led policing
- Discussion on the unique organizational structure and features of sheriff's offices

Chapter 7: Leadership

- New sections include Leaders and Managers, Bureaucracy and Decision Space, and a discussion of the police as street-level bureaucrats
- New material on the re-emergence of the traits approach
- New discussion that covers emotional and social intelligence, organizational citizenship, leadership neutralizers, and substitutes and other new topics
- New material on leadership from born concept to charismatic, servant, spiritual, authentic, and ethical

Chapter 8: Planning and Decision Making

- New material on planning police responses to disasters
- Detailed and comprehensive discussion outlining three over-arching models for decision making: the rational comprehensive model by Herbert Simon, the incremental-muddling through model by Charles E. Lindblom, and the heuristic model by William Gore.
- Presentation of new alternative decision-making methodologies, including operational modeling, naturalistic modeling and recognition-primed decision making (RPD), and 'thin slicing' by Malcolm Gladwell
- Important new discussion on police response to "active shooter" situations, particularly focused on response to school shootings using the Quick Action Deployment (QUAD) or Advanced Law Enforcement Rapid Response Training (ALERRT) tactical philosophies
- Focused material on the assets and liabilities of group decision making including detailed discussion on groupthink, brainstorming, ethics, and the common errors associated with decision making

Chapter 9: Human Resource Management

- Summary of federal laws affecting police personnel management with case law illustrations (e.g., rights of police officers called to active duty)
- Detailed coverage of effective and new recruiting strategies and their cost
- Discussion of the needs of different generations of police officers (e.g., Gen Xers and Yers)
- Material on discipline, early warning systems, progressive discipline, and the disciplinary matrix
- Major section on promotional testing, written and oral boards, assessment centers, types of promotional lists, selecting from promotional lists, and why officers decline to participate in promotional testing

Chapter 10: Organizational and Interpersonal Communication

- An expanded discussion of teleconferencing to more efficiently communicate within the organization
- Material on some of the negative effects associated with the increased use of technology, including police managers unwittingly dropping out of the organizational grapevine and, as a result, possibly missing out on some very important informal communication that takes place within their organizations
- Discussion on communicating across generations

Chapter 11: Labor Relations

- A new and extensive discussion of the impact of police unions on the community, including their impact on discipline and accountability

Chapter 12: Financial Management

- Charts showing advantages and disadvantages of each budget format
- New section on the economy and the police budget

Chapter 13: Stress and Police Personnel

- Updated discussion of diseases of adaptation and recent medical findings
- New cautionary tale about the consequences of police work addiction (the workaholic) on officer health, along with a work addiction self-administered risk test
- Discussion on what actually happens physiologically to the officer during the event, the aftermath, its consequences and what the police department can do to assist officers in working through this very traumatic event.
- Discussion of sleep deprivation as a stress inducer; includes the physiological responses as well as the relationship between sleep deprivation and work-related accidents

Chapter 14: Legal Aspects of Police Administration

- Comprehensive material on negligence and liability arising from police misconduct including discussion on basic types of tort actions, Title 42, U.S. Code, Section 1983, and judicially created Bivens actions
- Focused discussion on vicarious liability assumed by the police administrator relating to negligent hiring, negligent assignment, retention and entrustment, negligent direction and supervision, and negligent training
- Critical discussion on police misuse of firearms and deadly force, police use of force and less-lethal weapons (including TASERS), high-speed pursuits, and the handling of emotionally disturbed persons
- New and important material regarding police officer truthfulness and the growing impact of *Brady v. Maryland* on individual officers (Brady violations) and the importance of officer truthfulness and character
- New and important material regarding officer use of social network sites such as Facebook, YouTube, Twitter, and the like, and a guide for officer postings
- Discussion of issues that involve officer behavior relating to conduct unbecoming an officer, officer personal appearance and grooming habits, sexual conduct and sexual orientation, residency requirements, moonlighting, and alcohol and drug use

Chapter 15: Organizational Change

- New material on the role of the rank and file in organizational change and some of the advantages of involving them in the change process; includes the fact that it heightens morale and commitment, develops democratic skills and habits, and makes for better decisions
- Discussion of why organizational efforts sometimes fail and the ways in which both internal and external changes can be thwarted by those who have their own political and professional agendas
- Material on ways to make organizational change succeed, including a discussion of coaching as a tool to facilitate organizational change, setting flexible priorities, assembling resources, creating opportunities and then following through

Supplements

The following supplements accompany this textbook:

- Instructor's Manual and Test Bank
- PowerPoint
- My Fest

To access supplementary materials online, instructors need to request an instructor access code. Go to www.pearsonhighered.com/irc to register for an instructor access code. Within 48 hours of registering, you will receive a confirming e-mail including an instructor access code. Once you have received your code, locate your text in the online catalog and click on the Instructor Resources button on the left side of the catalog product page. Select a supplement, and a login page will appear. Once you have logged in, you can access instructor material for all Prentice Hall textbooks. If you have any difficulties accessing the site or downloading a supplement, please contact Customer Service at http://247.prenhall.com.

ACKNOWLEDGMENTS

Although it is insufficient compensation for their gracious assistance, we wish to recognize here the individuals and organizations who helped to make this book a reality. Unless asked to do otherwise, we have indicated their organizational affiliation at the time they made their contribution.

We thank Will Aitchison for his extensive contributions to Chapter 11, Labor Relations. He also allowed us to draw from his previous works, and for this we are greatly indebted.

We also wish to thank our long-time secretary, Sharon Ostermann, for typing considerable portions of the 8th edition, as well as providing invaluable assistance in conducting the necessary research to be certain this edition contained the most current and accurate information in policing today. Her pleasant attitude and considerable intelligence made this revision a much easier task.

We would like to thank the following reviewers for their comments and suggestions: Salih Hakan Can, Penn State University, Schuylkill Haven; Stephen A. Morreale, Worcester State College; M. Michael Parker, North Carolina Central University; Michael F. Raymond, NHTI—Concord's Community College; Jeffrey Ian Ross, University of Baltimore; and Robert L. Werling, California State University, Stanislaus.

A special thanks to these individuals: Sal Territo, Maryellin Territo, Jeannie Griffin, Linda Pittman, Dwayne Shumate, and Donna McKnight, who provided typing and research assistance and made innumerable contributions, not only for this edition but for many previous ones as well. Max Bromley was responsible for developing the extensive instructor's manual and accompanying learning tools for this edition.

Many people helped strengthen this book by providing critiques, photographs, and suggestions. We have elected to indicate their organizational affiliation when they helped us, even though some have moved on to other responsibilities. We are grateful for the help of Charlie Rinkevich and Peggy Hayward, Federal Law Enforcement Training Center, Glynco, Georgia; Scott Wofford, Radio Shack, Fort Worth, Texas; the Drug Enforcement Administration; our colleague of 20 years, Jim Campbell, East Carolina University; Chief John Kerns, Sacramento, California, Police Department; U.S. Secret Service; Bureau of Alcohol, Tobacco, Firearms, and Explosives; Deputy Superintendent Jim Finley, Illinois State Police; Drs. Walter Booth and Chris Hornickj, Multidimensional Research Association, Aurora, Colorado; Lieutenant Rick Frey, Broward County, Florida, Sheriff's Office; Captain Lawrence Akley, St. Louis, Missouri, Metro Police Department; Chief Lee McGehee and Captain Glenn Whiteacre, Ocala,

Florida, Police Department; the Maricopa, Arizona, Sheriff's Office; Inspector Vivian Edmond, Michelle Andonian, and Commander Dorothy Knox, Detroit, Michigan, Police Department; Major Herman Ingram, Baltimore, Maryland, Police Department; Commissioner Morgan Elkins and Captain Dennis Goss, Kentucky State Police; St. Paul, Minnesota, Police Department; Thomas J. Deakin, John E. Ott, editor of the *FBI Law Enforcement Bulletin*, all three with the Federal Bureau of Investigation; our good friend, Bill Tafoya, the "father" of futuristics in policing; our lifelong friend, Ron Lynch, University of North Carolina; the California Highway Patrol; Norma Kane, the Kansas City, Missouri, Police Department; the San Diego, California, Police Department; the Texas Department of Public Safety: the Philadelphia Police Department; National Tactical Officers Association; Lieutenant James B. Bolger, Michigan State Police; the Denver Police Department; Colonel Carroll D. Buracker and Scott Boatright, Fairfax County, Virginia, Police Department; Major Dave Sturtz, Ohio State Patrol; the National Consortium for Justice Information and Statistics, Sacramento, California; Phoenix, Arizona, Police and Fire Departments; Lieutenant Mark Stallo, Dallas, Texas Police Department; Mary Ann Wycoff, Police Foundation; Don Fish, Florida Police Benevolent Association; Captain Keith Bushey, Los Angeles, California, Police Department; Deputy Chief Kevin Stoeher, Mt. Lebanon, Pennsylvania, Police Department; Karen Anderson and Lisa Bird, LAN Publications Group; Lieutenant Rex Splitt, Craig, Colorado, Police Department; Chief R. E. Hansen and Cynthia Shaw, Fayetteville, North Carolina, Police Department; Officer David Hoffman, Anchorage, Alaska, Police Department; LaNell Thornton, Chief Paul Annee, and Lieutenant Michael Spears, Indianapolis, Indiana, Police Department; Lexington-Fayette, Kentucky, Urban County Police Department; Environmental Systems Research Institute, Redlands, California; Nancy Brandon, Metro Software, Park City, Utah; Larry Yium, Director of Budget and Finance, Houston, Texas; Lois Roethel and Leslie Doak, Las Vegas, Nevada, Police Department; the Knox County, Maine, Sheriff's Department; Chief Jim Wetherington, a mentor, and Assistant Chief Sam Woodall, Semper Fi, Columbus, Georgia, Police Department; Sergeant Mike Parker, Los Angeles County Sheriff's Office; Major John F. Meeks, Baltimore, Maryland, Police Department; Mary Foss and Chief Randall Gaston, Anaheim, California, Police Department; Captain Tom Brennan, Newark, New Jersey, Police Department; Lieutenant Robert O'Toole, Boston, Massachusetts, Police Department; Commander Tim McBride, Los Angeles, California, Police Department; Sergeant Patrick Melvin, Phoenix, Arizona, Police Department; Officer Matthew Rastovski, Birmingham, Alabama, Police Department; Lieutenant Doug Cain, Baton Rouge, Louisiana, Police Department; Sheriff Leroy D. Baca and Natalie Salazar Macias, Los Angeles County Sheriff's Office; Chief P. Thomas Shanahan and Sergeant James Cifala, Ann Arundel County Police Department, Maryland; Chief Harold L. Hurts, Police Chief Jack Harris, Phoenix, Arizona, Police Department; Amy M. Pich, Seattle, Washington, Police Department; Deputy Chief Raymond D. Schultz, Albuquerque, New Mexico, Police Department; Sheriff Cal Henderson and Detective Herb Metzger,

Hillsborough County Sheriff's Office, Tampa, Florida; Sergeant Robert J. Delaney, Chicago, Illinois, Police Department; a very special thanks to Dr. Eric Fritsch and Professor Peggy Tobolowsky, University of North Texas, for their continued support and willingness to review specific parts of this text; Sergeant Don Pahlke (retired), Portland, Oregon, Police Bureau, Bob's partner in a squad car, who taught Bob what real policing was all about; former Chief David M. Kunkle, Chief David O. Brown, Assistant Chief Floyd Simpson, Deputy Chief Brian Harvey, Lt. Ronald Thomasson, Lt. Dianna Watts, and Mr. Michael Freeman, Dallas, Texas Police Department; retired Chief Lowell Cannaday, Irving, Texas, Police Department; Chief Jimmy Perdue, North Richland Hills, Texas, Police Department; former Chief and good friend, Mr. Darrell Stephens, Charlotte-Mecklenburg, North Carolina Police Department; former Commissioner Paul Evans, Boston Police Department; former Chief Bob Olsen, Minneapolis, Minnesota, Police Department; Mr. Gil Kerlikowske, Director of National Drug Policy; Sheriff Jerry Keller (retired), Las Vegas Metropolitan Police Department; Sheriff Lupe Valdez, Dallas County Sheriff's Office; Dean Victor Strecher (retired), Sam Houston State University; Mr. Bill Hill, former Dallas County District Attorney, Dallas Texas; Chief Greg Allen, Assistant Chief Pete Pacillas, and Ms. Jennifer Callan, El Paso, Texas, Police Department; Mr. Doug Bodrero, Dr. Richard Holden, and Dr. Jonathan White, Institute for Intergovernmental Research, Tallahassee, Florida; Dr. David Carter, Michigan State University; Dr. John Liederbach, Bowling Green State University; Dr. Shelly Greenberg, Johns Hopkins University; Dr. Geoff Alpert, University of South Carolina; Dr. James Marquardt, University of Texas at Dallas; Dr. John Ellis Price, President, University of North Texas at Dallas for his continuing support of the Caruth Police Institute; and our colleagues and friends at the Law Enforcement Training Network (LETN), Mr. Lonnie Wilder and Mr. David Willox.

Lieutenant Stephen Hartnett of the Tampa, Florida, Police Department provided us with material on the psychological testing of police applicants. Chief of Police Ronald Miller and Major Roger Villanueva of the Kansas City, Kansas, Police Department provided us with information on their agency's college incentive and college tuition assistance programs. Chief of Police Bill McCarthy of the City of Des Moines, Iowa, Police Department provided us with information on the agency's salary schedule. Cynthia Brown, publisher of *American Police Beat*, Cambridge, Massachusetts, gave us permission to use numerous articles and photographs in several of our chapters. Melonie Hamilton with *Police Magazine*, Torrence, California, assisted us in obtaining photos in relation to our discussion of assessment centers, as well as our discussion of Internal Affairs investigations.

We would also like to thank Chief Joe Lumpkin of the Athens Clarke County, Georgia, Police Department for his continued good counsel and information on the subject of police administration and Chief Dwayne Orrick of the Cordele, Georgia, Police Department for his continued work as the president of the Georgia Association of Chiefs of Police. We also wish to thank Deanette L. Palmer, Ph.D., a psychologist with the Spokane, Washington, Police Department. We wish to thank Meredith A. Bowman of the Southeastern Public Safety Institute, St. Petersburg

College, St. Petersburg, Florida, and our colleague Jim Sewell, Florida Department of Law Enforcement, who has also contributed to this book. And a very special thanks to Ms. Jennifer Davis-Lamb, Ms. Shayna Luza, and Mr. Gary Sims, Caruth Police Institute, University of North Texas at Dallas for their outstanding research and energy on this project. Their hard work helped improve the overall quality of this book. In addition, a special thank you to Dr. Rick Smith, Caruth Police Institute for his invaluable support during this project. Lastly, we would like to thank our editor, Eric Krassow, for his continued guidance, support, patience, and encouragement. It has been a pleasure working with him.

Charles R. "Mike" Swanson
Leonard Territo
Robert W. Taylor

About the Authors

Charles R. "Mike" Swanson provides promotional testing services to police departments through his firm Swanson and Bracken (Promotionaltesting.com) and has more than 30 years of experience in designing police promotional systems, conducting job analysis, preparing written tests and assessment centers, and training assessors. He has provided promotional consulting services to state police, state patrol, sheriffs, and county and municipal law enforcement agencies.

Mike enlisted in the Marine Corps when he was 17 years old, subsequently working as a patrol officer and detective in the Tampa Police Department. He served in the Florida Governor's Office as a senior police planner and later as deputy director of the Council on Law Enforcement and Criminal Justice. He taught at East Carolina University before accepting a faculty position in the University of Georgia's Carl Vinson Institute of Government, where he rose through the administrative ranks, retiring in 2001 as its interim director.

In addition to co-writing this book, Mike has co-authored four others, including *Criminal Investigation*, and has authored or co-authored numerous conference papers, articles, monographs, and book chapters on various aspects of policing. He holds bachelor's and master's degrees in criminology from Florida State University and a Ph.D. in public administration from the University of Georgia. In addition to other recognition he is the 2001 recipient of the O. W. Wilson Award for Distinguished Police Scholarship, received commendations from the Governors of three states for his contributions to public safety, was the Georgia Association of Chiefs of Police's first hononary chief for his service to the association over a 20-year period, and received the University of Georgia's Walter Bernard Hill award for distinguished service to law enforcement agencies.

Leonard Territo is presently a visiting distinguished professor at Saint Leo University, Saint Leo, Florida, and professor emeritus in the Department of Criminology at the University of South Florida, Tampa, Florida. He was previously the chief deputy (undersheriff) of the Leon County Sheriff's Office in Tallahassee, Florida. He also served for almost 9 years with the Tampa Police Department as a patrol officer, motorcycle officer, and homicide detective. He is the former chairperson of the Department of Police Administration and director of the Florida Institute for Law Enforcement at St. Petersburg Junior College, St. Petersburg, Florida.

In addition to writing nearly 50 articles, book chapters, and technical reports, he has authored and co-authored twelve books, including *Criminal Investigation*, which is in its eleventh edition; *International Sex Trafficking of Women and Children: Understanding the Global Epidemic; The International Trafficking of Human Organs: A Multi-Disciplinary Perspective; Crime and Justice in America*, which is in its sixth edition; *Stress Management in Law Enforcement*, which is in its second edition; *Police Civil Liability;*

College Crime Prevention and Personal Safety Awareness; Stress and Police Personnel; The Police Personnel Selection Process; Hospital and College Security Liability; and a crime novel, *Ivory Tower Cop,* which was inspired by a true story. His books have been used in more than a thousand colleges and universities in all 50 states, and his writings have been used and referenced by both academic and police departments in 14 countries, including Australia, Barbados, Canada, Chile, Czechoslovakia, England, France, Germany, Israel, the Netherlands, Poland, Saudi Arabia, South Korea, and Spain.

His teaching awards include being selected from among 200 criminal justice educators from the state of Florida as the Outstanding Criminal Justice Educator of the Year by the College of Social and Behavioral Sciences at the University of South Florida. He has been given awards by both the Florida Police Chiefs Association and the Tampa Police Academy for his years of teaching and meritorious service; he was given an award for Distinguished Scholarly Publications by Saint Leo University, Saint Leo, Florida; and he has been selected for inclusion in *Who's Who in American Law Enforcement.*

Robert W. Taylor is currently professor and program head for the Public Affairs program at The University of Texas at Dallas. Previous to this appointment, he was the Executive Director of the Caruth Police Institute, Dallas Police Department. The Institute was established through a $9.5 million grant from the Communities Foundation of Texas in January 2008, merging the resources of the University of North Texas and The University of Texas at Dallas for the benefit of the Dallas Police Department. Dr. Taylor was a principal party to the development of the Institute and was appointed the founding director by the University of North Texas System. The primary mission of the Institute is to provide direction and coordination of major training and research projects for the Dallas Police Department. The Institute represents a national "think tank" on policing strategies focused on major urban cities in the United States. Dr. Taylor was professor and chair of the Department of Criminal Justice at the University of North Texas previous to this assignment.

For the past 25 years, Dr. Taylor has studied police administration, police tactics and strategies, and police responses to terrorism. He has traveled extensively throughout the Middle East and Southeast Asia, meeting several heads of state and acting as a consultant to numerous federal agencies on intelligence analysis and terrorism, hostage negotiations, Middle Eastern groups, and the Palestinian-Israeli conflict. Since September 11, 2001, Dr. Taylor has been a consultant to the U.S. Department of Justice, working with the Institute for Intergovernmental Research. He acts as a lead instructor in the State and Local Anti-Terrorism Training (SLATT) program and is responsible for training all law enforcement and other related criminal justice professionals. He also contracts with the U.S. Department of State, Anti-Terrorism Assistance Program.

Dr. Taylor has authored or co-authored over 150 articles, books, and manuscripts. Most of his publications focus on international and domestic terrorism, police administration and management, police procedures, drug trafficking, and criminal justice policy. Dr. Taylor is the senior author of *Juvenile Justice: Policies, Practices and Programs*, third edition and *Digital Crime, Digital Terrorism*, second edition. Further, Dr. Taylor is co-author of the landmark text *Criminal Investigation*, currently in its eleventh edition. Dr. Taylor continues to conduct research in policing and is the recipient of numerous grants and contracts (over $18 million in funded projects). His latest work has concentrated in four areas: (1) international terrorism, especially Middle Eastern groups, and the spread of radical Islam to the rest of the world; (2) intelligence analysis and decision making, particularly during protracted conflict or crisis situations; (3) quality improvement in police agencies through advanced leadership and management practices; and (4) evaluation of various policing strategies including community policing, Compstat, and intelligence-led policing in the United States. In 2004, Dr. Taylor was asked by the International Justice Mission in Washington, D.C., to assist in the training of the Cambodian National Police on child sex slavery and human trafficking as part of a large project funded through the U.S. Department of State. His interest and research in this area has led to a leadership role in designing and developing training efforts in the United States aimed at raising awareness of the human trafficking tragedy for American law enforcement officers, funded through the U.S. Department of Justice. Dr. Taylor focuses on the nexus among human trafficking, drug trafficking, and the financing of terrorist incidents internationally and domestically.

Dr. Taylor has been a consultant to the U.S. Army; U.S. Air Force; U.S. Marine Corps; U.S. Department of Homeland Security; U.S. Department of Treasury; Federal Law Enforcement Training Center; U.S. Secret Service; Bureau of Alcohol, Tobacco, and Firearms; U.S. Department of Justice; Federal Bureau of Investigation; Drug Enforcement Administration; Police Foundation; and Police Executive Research Forum (PERF); as well as numerous state and local municipalities and private corporations. He has also conducted significant training in the United States protectorates of the U.S. Virgin Islands, Guam, and Saipan and the countries of England, France, Switzerland, Thailand, Cambodia, Barbados, Northern Cyprus, Bahrain, United Arab Emirates, Kenya, and Turkey. He is an active member of the Academy of Criminal Justice Sciences (elected national chair of the Police Section—2002) and the American Society of Criminology. In 2008, Dr. Taylor was awarded the prestigious O.W. Wilson Award by the Academy of Criminal Justice Sciences "in recognition of his outstanding contribution to police education, research, and practice."

Dr. Taylor has an extensive background in academic and professional criminal justice, having taught at four major universities and serving as a sworn police officer and major crimes detective (in Portland, Oregon) for over 6 years. Dr. Taylor is a graduate of Michigan State University (Master of Science, 1973) and Portland State University (Doctor of Philosophy, 1981).

part one
Foundations

These first four chapters are foundational in that they tell us how law enforcement got to where it is today, explain current police operational philosophies, describe how national and domestic terrorism have impacted on the role of our police agencies, and discuss the continuing importance of politics. This section also serves to introduce terms and concepts referred to in subsequent chapters.

Chapter 1, "The Evolution of Police Administration" differs from other histories of policing because it has a specific, rather than a general, focus. It explains policing's trials and tribulations as it morphed from a colonial night watchman system into complex organizations testing new philosophies. Also chronicled are the social, political, economic, and technological forces which continuously shape and reshape American policing. The underlying thesis of this chapter is policing is like a sandbar in a river, being shaped and reshaped by the currents of the society in which it is embedded.

The second chapter, "Policing Today," examines in greater detail the shifts in operational philosophies identified in the previous chapter. More specifically, as police departments came to gripes with the limitations of the traditional philosophy of simply responding to an incident, it opened the door to successive waves of delivering law enforcement services in new ways, such as community policing. This chapter provides a strong understanding of the use and limitations of these different operational philosophies and strategies aimed at lowering crime and providing better police services to our communities.

Chapter 3, "Intelligence, Terrorism, and Homeland Security," addresses the significant shifts that have occurred in law enforcement in the wake of the 9/11 attacks on this country, as well as the threats posed by the Mexican drug cartels operating near our border, "homegrown" terrorists, and recent trends in radical Islamic groups. The chapter vividly illustrates the dangers of international terrorism and domestic right-wing hate groups, left-wing anarchists, and ecoterrorists.

"Politics and Police Administration" is the fourth and final chapter in this section. In Chapter 1, the struggle to free law enforcement from politics in the worse sense of the word was discussed. However, because one of the characteristics of a democracy is there are multiple points of access to points of influence and decision making, there is not, nor should there be, a "bright line" separating police administration and politics. This chapter takes a pragmatic view of how politics affect law enforcement agencies.

1

The Evolution of Police Administration

Objectives

- State how events in England influenced the development of unified, full-time police departments in the United States.

- Identify two reasons why the Pinkerton National Detective Agency was so effective in dealing with outlaws.

- Describe the importance of the frontier closing in 1890.

- Define *politics* and give three reasons why it cannot be kept out of police agencies.

- Define and describe machine politics in the 19th century.

- Identify the worst and best things about the patronage/spoils system.

- Explain why the concept of a police profession is so important.

- Discuss the contributions of Chief Gus Vollmer.

- Describe the impact of prohibition on policing.

- Describe the Black Codes and Jim Crow laws.

- State how World War II affected law enforcement.

- Explain the unequal badge problem.

- Identify and discuss the forces that made the 1960s so tumultuous.

- Describe how the police rank and file became isolated in the 1960s.

- Name the events that fostered research on policing during the 1970s.

- Define COP, ZTP, CompStat, and EBP.

OUTLINE

Introduction

Studying the evolution of police administration is crucial because (1) the past is full of important lessons; (2) ignoring these lessons increases the probability that prior mistakes will be repeated and opportunities forfeited; (3) knowledge of the past breeds *esprit de corps,* or pride in the heritage of one's chosen profession; (4) it instills an appreciation that each of us stands on the shoulders of the men and women who served before us with dignity, compassion, and valor; (5) there is a more complete comprehension of where and why a profession is when you know where it has been; (6) concepts in this chapter are part of the vocabulary of policing; and (7) it sets the stage for discussions in some of the chapters that follow.

The Urbanization of American Policing

The earliest American colonists, who were primarily English, depended on volunteer citizen night watchmen, patrolling from dusk to dawn, to alert them to threats, such as fires, crimes, and pirates. Raising an alarm was the collective responsibility of all residents. Other offices familiar to the colonists, such as sheriff, constable, and coroner were subsequently added, although initially their numbers were very small. In 1625, New Amsterdam, now New York City, created the office of sheriff.[1]

In 1833, Philadelphia became the first city in this country to have a paid, full-time day police force.[2] Gradually, the widespread use of volunteer citizens night patrols was replaced by paid night police departments, which were entirely separate from the full-time day police. It was not until 1844, in New York City, that the first unified day-night police force was created (see Figure 1.1).

To no small degree, the rise of unified, full-time police departments in America was influenced by events in England. During the late 17th and early 18th centuries, England's economy made two key shifts: (1) improved agricultural methods provided significant surplus crops to support people living in cities and (2) people were drawn to cities by the industrial revolution (1760–1830),[3] which shifted production from manual labor to machine made, initially in the textile industry and then spreading to other goods. Factories surpassed homes and small workshops as employers.

As the populations of England's cities grew, so did their problems, such as slums, crime, and appalling working conditions. As a result, social unrest escalated. The old ways of dealing with crime and unrest were inadequate. In 1829, Parliament passed the Metropolitan Police Act with the strong support of **Sir Robert Peel** (1788–1850), creating a full-time police agency for London.

New principles, such as officers should be hired on a probationary basis, were articulated for the London Metropolitan Police, stressing the need for professional conduct by the agency and its officers.[4] The effort to create a force in which the public

Figure 1.1
New York City police officers, circa 1865, of the 32nd Precinct, then located at West 135th Street on 10th Avenue. Note that ranking officers wear a double-breasted coat whereas patrolmen's coats are single-breasted.
(Courtesy Alfred J. Young Collection)

Figure 1.2
Satire of police corruption. "Mulberry Ring" refers to the New York City Police Department, then located at 300 Mulberry Street. (Courtesy Library of Congress, Caroline and Erwin Swann collection of caricature & cartoon)

would have confidence and would support produced grim numbers: In the first three years of its existence 5,000 officers were dismissed and another 6,000 resigned, many of them under pressure.[5] American cities selectively drew on the experience of the Metropolitan Police, gradually creating centralized, full-time police departments. However, the majority of American politicians during the 1800s had no interest in hiring quality officers, choosing instead to continue using officers to suit their own purposes: graft, control of elections, and harassment of the opposition party (see Figure 1.2).

In the history and image of America, the "wild and wooly" West looms large (see Figure 1.3), although it spans a scant 90 years, from roughly 1800 to 1890. The acclaimed Pony Express (1860–1861) is a prime example of how quickly things changed in the West. From Missouri to California, relay stations were established every 10 miles, where Pony Express riders could obtain fresh mounts.[6] Despite its success, the Pony Express was out of business in 18 months due to the completion of the transcontinental telegraph (1861).

Factors contributing to the settlement of the West included the discovery of gold at Sutter's Mill, California (1848), the availability of tracts of land to settlers under the Homestead Act (1862), and the conclusion of the Civil War (1861–1865). Although there were already free African Americans in the West, that number was increased after 1865, due to assistance from the federal **Freedmen's Bureau** (1865–1872), flight from the South's repressive laws enacted to keep "Negroes" segregated and powerless, and the brutality of the **Ku Klux Klan (KKK)**, which was formed in 1866 for social purposes, but quickly turned to suppressing African Americans.

Benjamin "Pap" Singleton (1809–1892), a former slave in Tennessee, promoted the idea of forming African American townships in Kansas, leading to the establishment of such townships as Nicodemus (1877; see Figure 1.4). Singlehandedly, Singleton may have been responsible for the migration of 20,000 people out of the South, although other promoters established similar settlements both in Kansas and Oklahoma, perhaps as many as 42.[7] As an organized movement, the exodus was finished by 1872.

The completion of the transcontinental railroad (1869) and the construction of other rail lines provided mass transportation into the West to adventurers and settlers. By the mid-1880s, cattle drives up the Chisholm and other trails from Texas to Abilene,[8] Dodge City, Wichita, and other Kansas "cow towns" were a thing of the past due to the expansion of railroads, settlements, and the commercial availability of barbed wire, which closed off open range.

Figure 1.3
"Big Ned," Con Wagner, and "Ace" Moore were lynched by vigilantes in a partially completed cabin near Laramie, Wyoming (1868). Hoisted just off of the ground with no fall to break their necks, the men slowly strangled.
(Courtesy Denver Public Library, Western History Collection, Arundel Hull, Z-5808)

Figure 1.4
Prosperous African American settlers in Nicodemus, Kansas, 1877.
(Courtesy Library of Congress, Historic Engineering Record)

Figure 1.5
Standing Rock Reservation Lakota (Sioux) officers Red Tomahawk and Eagle Man. These and others attempted to arrest Hunkpapa Sioux spiritual leader Sitting Bull. His officers opened fire, and in the ensuing battle, eight officers and Sitting Bull and seven followers were killed.
(Courtesy of the Denver Public Library, Western History Collection, D. Barry, B-836)

West of the Mississippi, episodic war with Native Americans lasted from 1823 to 1890.[9] Eventually the tribes were forced onto reservations, producing a need for law and order on tribal lands and protection from trespassers. Lacking any appropriated funds to create a reservation law enforcement capability, agents on various reservations scrapped together funds and recruited Native Americans as police officers. The Congress finally began appropriating money for tribal police agencies in 1879 (see Figure 1.5).[10] Tribal enforcement agencies represent an out-of-the-mainstream example of American police administration, as is the United States Mint Police (1792).

Western law enforcement agencies were spread thin, their jurisdiction limited. They lacked a central records system, and there was an abundance of stagecoach and train robbers.[11] It is therefore not surprising that the **Pinkerton National Detective Agency**, Wells Fargo detectives, and Union Pacific operatives developed a strong record in catching or killing these robbers. Unrestricted by jurisdiction, these "lawmen" pursued bandits across jurisdictional lines and were aided by their employers' record systems.

In 1890, the federal government announced the frontier was closed; six states were later admitted to the union.[12] Both Arizona and New Mexico realized that their aspirations for statehood would be impeded by the image of thieves, rustlers, and bandits and created the Arizona Rangers (1901) and the New Mexico Territorial Mounted Police (1905) to curb lawlessness, drawing on the long experience of the Texas Rangers (1823).[13]

The significance of the **frontier closing** in 1890 is that it marks the onset of the swift transition from a rural, agrarian society to an urbanized one in only 30 years; by the time of the Census of 1920, 51 percent of Americans lived in cities. In practical terms, the present consequence of urbanization is that most full-time municipal officers now work in large agencies. The largest of these is the New York City Police Department with 36,000 officers.[14] However, over half of all municipal police departments, 55 percent, have 10 or fewer full-time officers.[15] The 3,067 sheriff's departments follow the same pattern; 65 percent of all full-time deputies work in the 600 largest agencies.[16] The proliferation of agencies means there is a vast difference in capabilities among local law enforcement agencies. It also complicates the task of sharing information and intelligence and makes coordination of effort more difficult.

The events highlighted in this section and those that follow illustrate the most important point of this chapter: policing cannot be understood if examined alone, as though the institution was an island in a lake. The more persuasive analogy is that policing is a

sandbar in a river, subject to being changed continuously by the societal currents in which it is immersed. As a profoundly significant social institution, policing is shaped and reformed repeatedly by a multitude of forces in American society and transnationally.

Politics and Administration in the 19th Century: Ills of the Patronage System/Spoils System

Politics is the process of acquiring and maintaining control over a government, including its policies, administration, and operations. Politics isn't inherently bad or good—these types of descriptions come from how power is used, as opposed to some basic quality of power itself. There is no way to keep politics out of police departments because (1) police departments must be responsive to democratic control, meaning ultimately supervision by elected as opposed to appointed officials; (2) public policy is expressed in the laws, regulations, operating procedures, decisions, and actions taken or not taken by a governmental agency. It is where politics and administration intersect, the method by which governmental agencies are guided and controlled; and (3) as a practical matter, politics flourish in even the smallest agencies. The type of politics we do want to keep out of policing is highly partisan party politics, which has had a long and, most frequently, unhealthy relationship with policing.

During the 1800s, a **political machine** or **machine politics** was often a tightly controlled political party headed by a boss or small autocratic group whose purpose was to repeatedly win elections for personal gain, often though graft and corruption. These parties had a hierarchical structure running from the boss at the top through the precincts to each neighborhood, where block captains make sure supporters "voted right." The phrase "vote early and often" reflects the machine politics spirit. Loyal voters were rewarded with incentives for their support, such as jobs, promotions, transfers to more desirable positions, lucrative contracts, liquor licenses, or helping their recently arrived immigrant relatives gain citizenship and find housing. New York Senator William Marcy (1786–1857) coined the phrase, "to the [election] victor belongs the spoils" [the authority to make patronage appointments and bestow other benefits].

The use of government resources by politicians to reward loyal voters is called **patronage** or the **spoils system**. The worst abuses of the patronage system, when people were rewarded for their loyalty rather than their ability, spanned from 1820 to 1883, when the **Pendleton Act** was passed, establishing the United States Civil Service commission and mandating that some federal employees pass a competitive examination and be appointed on the basis of merit. Even behind this progressive/reform legislation ugliness was at work: momentum for its passage was garnered from the assassination of **President James Garfield** (1881; see Figure 1.6) in Washington, D.C. by Charles Guiteau, a frustrated seeker of a patronage job as ambassador to France.[17]

However, the Pendleton Act initially only covered a small percentage of federal jobs. When **President Benjamin Harrison** (1833–1901) took office (1889),[18] he seized upon this loophole, and 31,000 postmaster jobs changed hands through

Figure 1.6
Artist's sketch of the assassination President Garfield at the Baltimore and Ohio train station in Washington, D.C. His assassin is being apprehended in the background.
(Courtesy Library of Congress)

patronage. This action was at odds with his avowed support for civil service reform and he received substantial criticism for his "prostitution of the public service."[19]

Under the 19th century patronage system, a person seeking employment in a police department usually needed a letter of endorsement from a powerful politician allied with the party in power. The letters were typically written by elected officials, such as members of the city council or county commission, prominent state officials, or the chairman of a county's political party. When a new party came to power, the entire staff of a police agency was dismissed and replaced by patronage appointments.[20]

Machine politics and the ugly side of patronage were enhanced by the absence of an effective secret ballot at the polls in many states during much of the 19th century.[21] Each political party distributed ballot tickets for its own candidates. Because these tickets varied in size and color, carrying a ticket into a polling place made voting a public act and subjected voters to harassment and intimidation.[22] Votes were sold for drinks and money, and states were slowly enacting residency requirements to vote.[23]

According to "Boss" Tweed, the mid-1800s ringleader of the most powerful New York City political machine, ballots didn't make a difference, the counters did.[24] As a final insult to the democratic process, state courts, dominated by patronage judges, consistently ruled that ballots could not be released for investigating and prosecuting abuses, such as using the names of dead people as voters in an election.[25]

Patronage that is not excessive or does not create inefficiency, however, is useful. Elected officials can appoint persons who agree with their policies, making governing easier. Patronage involves more people in the democratic process because they feel their efforts and votes have meaning.

There are examples of resistance to corruption during the 19th century. In 1856, San Francisco citizens, outraged by election corruption, graft, and out-of-control crime, formed the Committee of Vigilance to provide "security for life and property." An earlier Vigilance Committee (1851) had only focused on rampant crime. Even with its own constitution and terms on the committee limited to three months, the committee was nonetheless a vigilante group, executing criminals, forcing corrupt elected officials to resign, and ordering people to leave the state immediately. Because the owner of the San Francisco newspaper supported the committee, its early reputation was excellent. However, as historians looked more closely at the committee, its reputation began to suffer. On the other side of the country, the **Lexow Committee** (1894–1895), named after its chairman, was established by the New York Senate to examine police corruption in the New York City Police Department. Its report, which ran some 10,000 pages, was instrumental in that city electing a reform candidate as mayor.

Figure 1.7
At the beginning of the 20th century, children were still being exploited as a labor source. Here, "coal breaker boys" (circa 1890–1910) take a break from their 14-hour days in the mines, where they separated chunks of coal. Note their lunch pails in the foreground. (Courtesy Library of Congress, Detroit Publishing Company)

Nationally, some reform candidates were occasionally elected, although machine politics usually defeated them in the next election, and from time to time the outrage of decent citizens boiled over, leading them to such activities as sacking brothels protected by politicians and engaging in election day violence. However, real progress was not made until the 20th century.

The Reformation Period

As policing entered the 20th century, our cities were staggering under the burdens of machine politics, rampant patronage, government inefficiency, poverty, corruption, crime, slums, inadequate health care, riots, and the exploitation of woman and children by industries[26] (see Figure 1.7). State and federal governments were similarly dysfunctional and scandalized. Conditions were so intolerable that they finally became the stimulus for change.

Change came in the form of the **reformation period** (1900–1926), which had two immediate needs: (1) arousing the public from its apathy and (2) creating a conceptual cornerstone or model for improvement by separating politics and patronage in the worst sense from the administration of governmental agencies.

Arousing the Public from Its Apathy: The Muckrakers

Author Lincoln Steffens exposed major corruption in Chicago, St. Louis, and other municipalities in *The Shame of the Cities* (1906). He believed that bribery was not an ordinary felony, but an act of treason that subverted democracy. Sinclair's novel,

Figure 1.8
Colonel Roosevelt standing at the middle of his troops on San Juan Hill, Cuba, during the Spanish American War (1898). He previously served as Police Commissioner of New York City (1895–1897), famous there for his "midnight ramble," checking to see that officers were working their assignments.
(Courtesy Library of Congress)

The Jungle (1906), called attention to major abuses in the meat-packing industry, which led to the passage of the Pure Food and Drug Act (1906). Churchill's *Coniston* (1906) addressed political corruption in New Hampshire and Phillips's *The Treason of the Senate* did likewise with that body. It was President Theodore Roosevelt (see Figure 1.8, 1858–1919) who, in a 1906 speech, labeled Steffens, Sinclair, and other writers who exposed social ills, scandals, and corruption as "**muckrakers**." Although he was a popular president, there is also evidence of him being less than fair minded.[27] The muckraker tradition continues into the present day.

The Conceptual Cornerstone

The conceptual cornerstone was provided for by Woodrow Wilson (1856–1924) while he was a faculty member at Bryn Mawr College in Pennsylvania.[28] He later served as president (1913–1921). Wilson called for a dichotomy or separation of politics, in the worst sense of the word, and administration.[29] However impractical that might seem now, the idea was then very progressive.[30]

As the work of the muckrakers and the conceptual cornerstone entwined, rapid progress was made. In 1906, the New York Bureau of Municipal Research was formed. Staunton, Virginia, appointed the first city manager in 1908, placing responsibility for day-to-day operations in the hands of a trained professional not beholding to any political party. Two years later, the **city manager movement** was well underway, and appointees were usually experienced engineers or business managers. Further impetus was created in 1914, when the International City Manager Association was founded and the University of Michigan offered a degree in municipal administration.

In 1916, the National Municipal League issued a model city charter calling for a strict separation of politics and administration, which had a trickle-down effect on the police and other departments with city managers working hard to see that capable persons were appointed to leadership positions. The **Boston Police Strike** of 1919 was seen as incompatible with the new public service, and Massachusetts and other states passed laws forbidding police unionization, killing it until the 1960s (see Chapter 11, Labor Relations).

In 1922, The Cleveland Foundation completed a major study of crime in that city, which at that time was the fifth-largest in the nation.[31] Separate groups worked on different aspects of the criminal justice system. **Raymond Fosdick** (1883–1972) guided the group working on the police department, which was soundly criticized. Fosdick concluded that it was mostly just a larger version of what existed there in 1866—the record system was meager, precincts were too numerous, there was confusion in the lines of authority, and widespread corruption was common. The Cleveland study is noteworthy because it appears to be the model, albeit slowly adopted, of using outside experts to study police agencies.

As the separation of politics and administration gained traction, attention was focused on new ideas. Illustratively, scientific management sought to find the one best way to do things, the bureaucratic model was carefully articulated, and administrative theory formulated generic principles and methods of administration (see Chapter 5, Organizational Theory).

The shift to these new ideas was marked by the publication of White's *Public Administration* (1926) and Willoughby's *Principles of Public Administration* (1927). The politics/administration dichotomy was not abandoned; both authors endorsed the city manager's 1924 code of political neutrality.

However clean the discussion of politics and administration, it endures to this day as an area of practical concern for police executives and even for those farther down the chain of command:

I was selected to attend a prestigious national training program. At the last minute, the newly elected mayor wanted to reward this other detective who turned out a block of voters that swung the election. My division commander called me into his office and said "unpack your bags" because this other guy was going in my slot. It stunk, but who wants to hear a bunch of boo-hoos? There's no virtue in self-pity.

During the Reformation Period, progress was made toward reducing corruption, fraud, waste, and abuse in government; creating a cadre of qualified personnel to hold public jobs; developing the civil service system; emphasizing proper recruitment, selection, training, and promotion of governmental employees; freeing public affairs from highly partisan/machine politics; and developing new theories, models, and practices related to organizations. The Reformation Period is more than history; it was the landmark that unleashed a process of improvement that has been continuous. Chapter 2, Policing Today, covers some of these developments.

Police Professionalization

Profession and Professional

The word **profession** comes from the Latin *pro* (forth) and *fateri* (confess), meaning to announce a belief. At its earliest use, the word referred to public statements or declarations of faith.[32] By 1541, *profession* meant a learned occupation and 25 years later, its meaning was reduced to how a person habitually earned a living. In 1675, there was another shift, professing to be duly qualified. The serious work on professions has centered on specifying what criteria must be met to constitute a profession. Table 1.1 illustrates three different views about such criteria.

The importance to policing of being seen as a profession was fundamental to transforming the public view of officers from corrupt thugs and heavy-handed brutes to something noble—professionals. Every opportunity to develop this view was seized upon. For example, when cars first became available, they were largely purchased by people with a degree of affluence, those thought of as being upper class. Knowing that such people were influential in molding opinions, chiefs quickly assigned their best officers to traffic enforcement duties.

August Vollmer: The Father of Modern Law Enforcement

Beginning in 1829, England's London Metropolitan Police created a full-time paid police force that was "professional" in the sense of that's how officers habitually earned

---

Table 1.1
THREE VIEWS OF THE CRITERIA MAKING UP A PROFESSION[33]

Most Commonly Identified Criteria	Merton's Criteria
1. An organized body of theoretical knowledge.	1. Knowing (systematic knowledge).
2. Advanced study is needed to master knowledge.	2. Doing (trained capacity and technical skill).
3. A code of conduct guides action.	3. Helping (knowing and doing).
4. Prestige.	
5. Standards of admission.	
6. A professional association.	**Becker's Criteria**
7. Altruism is the driving force for wanting to practice the profession.	If you can get people to call you one, you are one.

Figure 1.9
*August Vollmer, seated
second from left.*
(Courtesy of the Berkeley
Police Department)

their living. Similar "professional" officers existed in this country from roughly 1845 onward. However, the genesis of American professional policing was the work of **August (Gus) Vollmer** in Berkley, California, during 1905–1932 (see Figure 1.9). Without detracting from the genius of his efforts, note that his successes closely parallel those of the Reformation Period of 1900–1926.

Carte summarized the work of this giant: Under Chief Vollmer's leadership, the Berkeley Police Department (BPD) became the model for professional policing. He mobilized officers, moving them first to bicycles and then to patrol cars, introduced a police signal system to dispatch calls, established a modern records system, used crime analysis to establish and staff geographical beats, created the first scientific crime laboratory in the United States in 1916, and the first lie detection machine used in investigation was built in the BPD in 1921.[34]

Quick FACTS ▸▸ August "Gus" Vollmer

"Gus" Vollmer (1876–1955) is the father of modern law enforcement. Born in New Orleans to German immigrant parents, his formal education ended in the sixth grade. Gus served with the Marine Corps in the Philippines during the Spanish-American War (1898), fighting 25 engagements with enemy forces. He was elected Berkeley Town Marshall in 1905 and in 1909, the title was changed to Police Chief. In 1921, he was elected President of the International Association of Police Chiefs, Retiring from the Berkeley Police Department in 1932, he remained active as a consultant and writer for many years. Suffering from failing eyesight, Parkinson's disease, and cancer, this extraordinary man ended his own life at 79 years of age.

Quick FACTS ▸▸ O.W. Wilson

Orlando Winfield Wilson (1900–1972) both studied under Vollmer and worked for him as a patrol officer. After graduating from the University of California at Berkeley, O.W. spent the next 14 years serving as Chief of the Fullerton, California, and then the Wichita, Kansas, Police Departments. He advocated many of the things Vollmer did, earning him a reputation as a progressive leader. In 1939, he joined the Berkeley faculty as professor of police administration. From 1943–1947, O.W. served as an Army Colonel in England, Italy, and Germany, often helping to reorganize police agencies. He returned to Berkeley and became the Dean of the School of Criminology (1950–1960). O.W. became Superintendant of Chicago's scandal-ridden police department (1960–1967), earning him a reputation as a fair but tough-minded reformer. Well established as an advocate of professionalism, O. W. Wilson's *Police Administration* (1950) was the final jewel in his crown.

Despite these achievements, Vollmer is better known for his tireless efforts to improve the caliber of personnel. He established police training in 1908, encouraged officers to attend college classes, introduced intelligence and psychological testing for officers, and, around 1919, began recruiting college students.[35] Although they never constituted a majority of officers, the "college cops" set the tone for the BPD over the coming decades. The most influential of these "college cops" was **O.W. Wilson**.[36]

The Pendleton Act of 1883 to the Military Model

The Pendleton Act of 1883 marked the beginning of the end for the ills of the patronage/spoils system. In the three decades following its adoption, state and local governments also adopted similar measures, although the spoils systems lasted well into the 1900s. The federal Hatch Act (1939) placed another wedge between politics and administration by forbidding federal employees from engaging in partisan political activities, which also spurred similar measures, "Little Hatch Acts," by state and local governments.

Although the rise of federal and state civil service systems intuitively is attractive, some observers were not so enthusiastic. Fosdick, writing in 1920, concluded that it sometimes made it difficult to terminate officers who committed serious breaches because the proof did not satisfy civil service safeguards.

Civil service and Vollmer's notion of educated, professional officers also conflicted. The former's emphasis was on keeping politics out of policing, whereas Vollmer's concept of merit was competent performance. Perhaps as much as 80 percent of an agency's budget is spent on personnel and related support costs, so personnel issues continue to be prominent for chiefs today (see Chapter 7, Leadership; Chapter 9, Human Resource Management; and Chapter 12, Financial Management).

While some worked at ending the spoils system, other reformers sought to enhance professionalization by using a new model that presumably would lead to more efficient operations. They concluded the country was besieged by crime and that police, as our front line of defense against it, were analogous to the military.

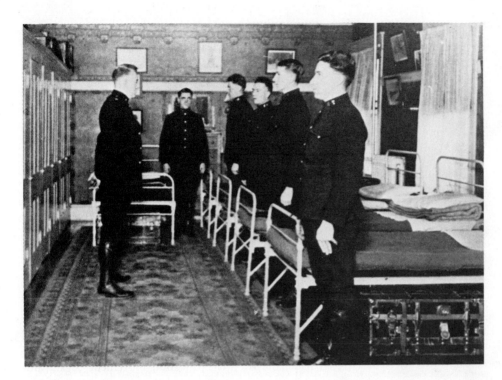

Figure 1.10
The military model at work in policing. A 1906 Pennsylvania State Police barracks inspection. (Courtesy of the Pennsylvania State Police)

The **military model** (see Figure 1.10) resulted in more staff positions to do specialized work, an emphasis on both line inspection of officers and staff inspections of functions, written policies and procedures, enhanced training, increased accountability, and the widespread adoption of the bureaucratic form of organization (see Chapter 5, Organizational Theory), which remains in use today. The implementation of the military model required expanded authority for chiefs, who were then able to put an end to precincts operating so independently that they sometimes looked like completely separate agencies.

The military model was so persuasive that some jurisdictions hired military officers to head their law enforcement agencies. Illustratively, retired Marine Major General Smedley Butler was hired as Director of Public Safety in Philadelphia, serving during 1924–1925. General Butler is among an elite group of 19 men in our nation's history who were awarded two Congressional Medals of Honor for valor.

Prohibition to the 1930s

The Roaring '20s and Prohibition

The 1920s are often referred to as the "roaring '20s" because of the tremendous changes that occurred in America in that decade. Following World War I, military demobilization released hundreds of thousands of young men to work in the rapidly expanding economy as our factories shifted from the production of military

CARRIE NATION

Figure 1.11
The family Bible recorded her name as Carry Nation (1846–1911), although it is habitually misspelled as "Carrie." She referred to herself as "a bulldog running along at the feet of Jesus, barking at what He doesn't like."
(Courtesy Library of Congress, George Grantham Bain Collection)

necessities to consumer goods. Henry Ford made millions of affordable cars. The construction of highways quickly paralleled this development, as did the proliferation of motels, gas stations, cafes, and other businesses catering to travelers. Some state highway patrol agencies were created to foster the safe movement of vehicles along these new road systems. Suburbs, formerly limited to areas served by trolley and train lines, could spring up anywhere there were roads. Some suburbs evolved into towns, resulting in more small police departments, and big-city police agencies added more officers.

Women rebelled at the strict rules for their dress and behavior. A new sound, jazz, swept the nation, abetted by the rapid expansion of radio stations, which also created national sports heroes, such as baseball's Babe Ruth, and golf's Bobby Jones. Also during the second decade of the 20th century, the first "talkie" movie was made, the rural electrification movement began, and telephone service expanded dramatically. Amid all of these changes, the "noble experiment" of **prohibition** was a defining force throughout the 1920s.

In the first half of the 19th century, ministers used their pulpits to denounce drinking, claiming that those who imbibed excessively were sinners who had lost their way with God. Thus, the **temperance movement**, which began in the second half of the 19th century, grew out of churches.

There were substantial reasons to oppose alcohol, drunkenness being made worse by other vices commonly found in saloons, such as prostitution and gambling. Drinking constituted both significant family and public health problems: In the 1800s, deaths by liver cirrhosis and chronic alcoholism were 25 per 100,000 people.[37] Given these problems, the existence of a national prohibition law (1919–1933), can in part be viewed as pro-family legislation.[38]

In the second half of the 18th century, temperance crusaders turned from using moral persuasion to legal coercion.[39] Some 17 states adopted prohibition laws, although by 1903, all but three abandoned them.[40,41]

Making alcohol illegal was preceded by the formation and mutual support of various temperance movement organizations, including the Prohibition Party (1869), which offered candidates for election, and the Woman's Christian Temperance Union (WCTU, 1874). Perhaps the best-known WCTU temperance activist was **Carry Nation** (see Figure 1.11) who went into saloons with a hatchet, ripping kegs open and scolding drinkers. She was arrested more than 30 times for these "hatchitations."

Prohibition was ratified as the 18th Amendment to the Constitution in 1919, the same year Congress passed the **National Prohibition Act**, more commonly known as the **Volstead Act**, as the legal means for enforcing the new amendment. The making, manufacturing, selling, bartering, transporting, importing, exporting, and delivery of alcohol were made illegal, with the exception that 200 gallons of alcohol could be made annually by homeowners for their own consumption. However well intended, national prohibition resulted in a large, illicit market for alcohol that gangsters fought violently to control. They smuggled "booze" from Canada and across the ocean in "rum runner" boats, set up illegal breweries and stills, and hijacked their rival's liquor convoys. Illegal bars called **speakeasies** were established, so named because at their entrances customers spoke the password softly before entering and drinking. In New York City alone, there were an estimated 32,000 speakeasies.[42] "**Bootlegger**" was a flexible term meaning people who made, smuggled, or transported liquor. It was also used to refer to people who had a flask slipped into their boots or held one on their leg by a garter (see Figure 1.12).

The prohibition era is a prime example of the law of unintended consequences. It did more to damage the image and reputation of policing than any other single event. To protect their operations, gangsters bribed police, judges, and other public officials to "look the other way" on a massive scale. The police professionalization movement was hampered and law enforcement suffered a self-inflicted black eye that lingered for decades afterwards. Still, officers of integrity continued to enforce the law (see Figure 1.13). In Chicago, Eliot Ness, a federal Treasury agent, and 10 agents he handpicked, were known as the **untouchables** because they couldn't be "bought."

Prohibition also resulted in 1,300 breweries being closed,[43] causing thousands of people to lose their jobs and fewer tax dollars flowing to governments. Less well recognized is that prohibition created the environment in which organized crime could be invented,[44] or at least systematized, and gain a tenacious grip on public officials. Because prohibition laws were widely flaunted, many people also had diminished regard for the law and authority.

Recognizing the widespread disobedience to the Volstead Act and the many ills associated with it, Congress abolished the Volstead Act in 1931. Two years later, the 21st Amendment repealed the 18th Amendment. Still, the damage done to public esteem for government and its officials lingered on for years, and organized crime continues to plague our society.

Figure 1.12
A 1922 "bootlegger" and "flapper." Tired of the strict roles set for "proper ladies," flappers asserted their independence during the 1920s by challenging conventional notions about how women should behave. "Shockingly," they wore make-up, danced, and dressed "provocatively," wore their hair bobbed, and smoked and drank in speakeasies. (Courtesy Library of Congress, National Photo Company Collection)

Figure 1.13
New York City police pour alcohol seized in a 1921 speakeasy raid into the sewer system.
(Courtesy Library of Congress)

The Lawless Years: Late 1920s to 1930s

Overlapping with the later portion of the prohibition period, the lawless, or gangsters', era lasted from the late 1920s and into the mid-1930s, when criminals filled their pockets with spectacular bank robberies and kidnappings, known as the "**snatch racket**." These bandits operated in the same era as prohibition gangsters, but were independent of them, specializing in robbing "soft targets," small banks, and snatching wealthy people from their unprotected homes.

In the crash of October 1929, the stock market lost 80 percent of its value, wiping out billions of dollars of wealth. Millions of people became unemployed, lost their homes and farms, and consumer spending dried up. The severe droughts in the American prairie states during 1930–1936 created a "**dustbowl**" as fertile topsoil got blown away. More people lost everything and immigrated, seeking a better life elsewhere, many going to California. Collectively, these immigrants were called **Okies** because so many of them, between 400,000 and 500,000, fled Oklahoma; the plight of these families was memorialized in John Steinbeck's *The Grapes of Wrath*[45] (1939; see Figure 1.14.) In response to these migrations, some cities established "**bum blockades**" manned by police officers to turn back everyone who lacked sufficient funds to support themselves[46] so they wouldn't be a drain on local resources. In California, the police sold license plates at the state line

Figure 1.14
Her tough life is carved into the face of this 32-year-old mother. With her seven children, she lived in a migrant pea picker camp near Nipomo, California. Note the condition of the clothes, the kerosene lantern, and the canvas tent. Because the early pea crop failed, the camp is destitute. The parents of this family have just sold the tent in order to buy food for their family. (Courtesy Library of Congress)

blockades as a partial test of finances. The bum blockades also had the affect of souring a portion of that generation on law enforcement for years.

During the depression, as a means to ensure that jobs went to local taxpayers and to help the local tax base, city and county governments enacted **residency requirements** mandating that employees live within the jurisdiction of the employing unit of government and existing employees had to meet the same standard to keep their jobs.[47] Critics of the requirement argue that it places officers in a difficult situation: They must choose between living in better neighborhoods, which they find difficult to afford, or living in lower-income areas where their children may have to attend marginal schools.[48]

However difficult the 1930s, law enforcement, surprisingly, gained some momentum, moving away from its tarnished image and toward increased legitimacy and authority in society. President Hoover appointed the **National Commission on Law Observance and Law Enforcement** in 1929, the first comprehensive study of crime and policing in America's history. It was commonly referred to as the **Wickersham Commission**, taking the name of its chairman. The Wickersham Commission issued its report in 1931, consisting of 14 volumes, much of it written by August Vollmer. Among its recommendations was support for the police having civil service protection and enhanced training and education. Major academic police programs sprang up or expanded at the University of California, Berkeley; the Michigan State University; and Northwestern University.[49]

The importance of separating police and politics gained additional impetus as law enforcement associations were created. In 1934, the International Association of Chiefs of Police (**IACP**) was formed.[50] The IACP issued a newsletter, creating a common perception of what was important to the profession. The FBI established its crime laboratory in 1932, which supported the analysis of evidence submitted from state and local police agencies, and two years afterward, its prestigious National Police Academy (**NA**, 1934) to train police executives, resulting in a core of knowledgeable leaders. As the next decade began in 1940, the National Sheriffs Association (**NSA**) came into being.

Overlapping with the later portion of the prohibition period, the lawless, or gangster, era lasted from the late-1920s and into the mid-1930s, when criminals filled their pockets with spectacular bank robberies and kidnappings, known as the "snatch racket." The kidnapping and murder of the infant son of "Lucky Lindy" Lindbergh, the first man to complete a trans-Atlantic flight, led to the adoption of the Federal Kidnapping Act (1932), which gave the Federal Bureau of Investigation (FBI) some jurisdiction over such crimes.

In some circles, bank robbers achieved celebrity status, with colorful names like "Pretty Boy" Floyd, "Creepy Karpis," and "Handsome Harry" Piermont. Because these bandits moved rapidly from one state to another, frustrating state and local investigators who lacked wider jurisdiction, the Congress passed the federal Bank Robbery Act (1934) and tasked the FBI with its enforcement. Fairly quickly, the FBI apprehended or killed notorious bank robbers resisting arrest, making it a very dangerous occupation. **John Dillinger** (1903–1934), who may have robbed two dozen banks, was killed in a gunfight with FBI agents outside of a Chicago theater, marking the end of the lawless era.[51]

The Ku Klux Klan: Formation to the 1930s

Like the situation in prohibition, the relationship between some law enforcement officers and the Ku Klux Klan (KKK) was toxic, producing effects that have lingered for decades. The KKK was formed in Pulaski, Tennessee in 1866 by Confederate Army veterans who were bored and wanted to create a mysterious stir at parties.[52] They made up names for themselves such as Grand Cyclops and Imperial Wizard, and wore masks and robes made from sheets by the wife of a founding member. However, quite quickly the agenda shifted from fun to repressing former slaves, referred to as freedmen, first by intimidation tactics and then by violence.

The KKK essentially took over some of the duties that **slave patrols** held until the end of the civil war. Those patrols, usually of three to six persons,[53] could enter any plantation and search, without warrant, slave quarters, disperse all slave meetings, hunt down fugitive slaves, and administer impromptu punishments as they saw fit.[54] Many Southerners tolerated or approved of the Klan's activities. Freeing the slaves upset the status quo and created chaos. The KKK repression of African Americans had the potential to maintain white supremacy and "restore order,"[55] warding off feared depredations by them, creating some resemblance to the pre-1865 South.

Southern state and local legislatures quickly adopted **Black Codes** in reaction to losing the Civil War; the codes were intended to keep African Americans "inferior." During 1880–1960, **Jim Crow laws** added more restrictions. The name Jim Crow was taken from a minstrel show character, played by white actors who blackened their faces with burnt cork and presented a grotesque caricature of African Americans.

Together, the Black Codes and Jim Crow laws made a mockery of equality. It was all but impossible for African Americans to vote and they were prohibited from assembling unless a White person was present. Separate facilities, including telephone booths and cemeteries, were mandated, it was illegal to teach Blacks how to read or write, and mixed marriages were forbidden. Enforcement of these laws caused the police to drop even lower in the estimation of African Americans.

To combat the KKK and the Black Codes, the Republican-dominated Congress passed laws to "reconstruct" the south (1865–1877) into something that approximated life in the northern states. Reformists of all types, primarily from New England, flooded the South, many with the selfless intention of helping the South "to raise itself." Others arrived with the intention of simply making profits and gaining power. The "uninvited do-gooders" that came south with their alien ideas were derisively lumped together by southerners as **carpetbaggers**, so called because their luggage was cheaply made of second-hand carpet.

The federal **Forces Act** (1870) was passed in response to the actions of the KKK. Prosecutions under the Act resulted, for the most part, in the disintegration of the Klan, although arguably state and local legislative bodies had substantially achieved White supremacy through the Black Codes. Since the reconstruction following the Civil War, the KKK has reinvented itself several times (see Figure 1.15 and Chapter 3, Intelligence, Terrorism, and Homeland Security).

Lynchings are often associated with the KKK, but were not unique to it. The term is derived from the name of Charles Lynch (1736–1796) of Virginia. During the tumultuous American Revolution, he led a group of people who took the law into their own hands to deal with criminals. At its earliest meaning, **lynching** meant rough justice and often only involved a severe beating. Later, it became synonymous with hanging someone without the legal authority to do so.[56,57,58]

Nationally, lynching was a ferocity that was substantially race-based against African Americans, Chinese, Hispanic, and Native American victims.[59] Before these lynchings, some victims were beaten or tortured.[60] Some of these grisly acts were

Figure 1.15
A KKK parade, circa 1921. The participation of children was intended to indoctrinate them in hate. (Courtesy Library of Congress, National Photo Company Collection)

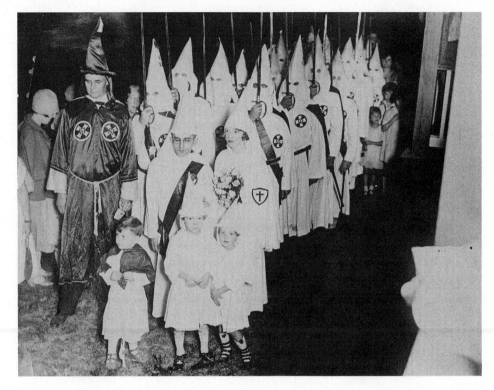

conducted in sight of African American enclaves and their church congregations as a means of intimidation.[61]

Lynchings were often based on mere suspicion or an accusation. At least occasionally, law enforcement officers led the posses that apprehended and lynched the "offender." In other instances, police officials released prisoners to lynch mobs or failed to intervene when mobs seized African Americans and executed them. An ugly truth is that some officers were also Klan members. Lynchings tainted police race relations across generations, creating a hostility toward, and an abiding suspicion of, the police, often manifested by a lack of cooperation.[62]

The 1940s and 1950s: War, Communists, and the Professional Model Reasserted

These two decades were dominated by WW II and the Korean War (1950–1953). The mobilization of all able-bodied men created opportunities for women in policing and the defense industry. The police took on new responsibilities as part of the war effort, the civil rights movement was born, there was substantial fear of communism, and the publication of O.W. Wilson's ***Police Administration*** reaffirmed the professional model of policing.

The 1940s: World War II and Some Progress for Women in Policing

The 1940s were defined by America's involvement in World War II, which lasted some four years after Operation Z, the Japanese attack on Pearl Harbor, Hawaii (December 7, 1941). The men in public safety agencies had no exemptions from compulsory military service and they volunteered and were drafted in great numbers. Departments quickly had two related problems: (1) staffing and (2) as their officers marched off to war, a pool of less physically able officers, who could not meet military standards, was left.

Although small numbers of women had been hired as police officers since 1920, the war opened the door to more of them, although they were often assigned to specialty duties such as dealing with juvenile delinquents and shoplifting. This practice was the norm for several decades thereafter (see Figure 1.16). The **Civil Rights Act of 1964** invalidated Jim Crow laws. Title VII of the Act forbade businesses to discriminate in hiring, promoting, and firing on the basis of sex, race, color, religion, and national origin, but state and local units of government were excluded from this requirement until the passage of the **Equal Employment Opportunity Act of 1972**, which amended Title VII. Functionally, this opened the door for women to be used

Figure 1.16
The door to a police career opened a little wider for these women taking the 1947 New York City Police Department entrance examination. (Courtesy Library of Congress)

in all types of assignments, including patrol, and fostered more minority hirings. Police duties during World War II expanded to civil defense tasks in some jurisdictions as they were tasked with such responsibilities as directing the work of air wardens. Concerned about air raids and shelling from submarines, **air raid warden** units were formed around the country, staffed by women, civic and fraternal groups, Boy Scouts, and other volunteers. Among their duties were checking to make sure no lights were showing, which our enemies could see and use to navigate toward their targets. Downtown areas were dark and windows everywhere were outfitted with dark shades. Nonetheless, a few attacks did occur.[63]

Law enforcement was engaged in combating forged **ration books**, which limited the amount of commodities (e.g., butter, gas, and meat) that the public could buy in order to redirect those good to a rapidly expanding military. Civilians supported the war effort with **victory gardens** (see Figure 1.17), planting vegetables and fruit to meet some of their own food needs.[64]

When the war ended, veterans came home, the domestic market for goods heated up, and jobs were plentiful in an expanding economy. Some numbers of veterans made a smooth transition from the military to police departments because of the preference given to military veterans in hiring and their familiarity with wearing a uniform and a rank hierarchy with authority and responsibility.

Now past the pain of the depression and the war, a new prosperity seemed within the grasp of Americans. New highways were built, and factories that had produced

Figure 1.17
Spring 1943, planting a victory garden for personal consumption at an unspecified location. Even small children were involved in this effort. (Courtesy Library of Congress)

tanks now churned out cars. Many people who suddenly joined the middle class left the cities for the newly developing suburbs, purchased with the help of veterans' benefits. The Levitt brothers built so many suburban homes that a generic name for any suburb became "Levitt Town."

A novelty in the 1940s, television expanded in the 1950s as quickly as radio stations did following World War I. The New York City Police Department rapidly seized on TV for administration purposes and to broadcast lineups of suspects to police precincts located conveniently for victims.

The 1950s: The Korean War, Fear of Communism, and the Professional Model Reasserted

For the most part, interest in the police waned during the 1950s, as new issues came to the fore, including urban congestion and the perception that traditional values were on the decline.[65] O. W. Wilson's *Police Administration* (1950) essentially validated the military model, whose core operational philosophy was R2I: respond to incident. Crime was thought to be prevented and apprehensions made by random, aggressive patrol in all areas of the city at all times. *Police Administration* quickly became the "Bible" for law enforcement executives, who were guided by it as they sought to find the optimum way to organize and staff the units in their agency and achieve the most efficient operations. Written policies and procedures manuals became more common and comprehensive.

On the streets, officers who were combat veterans watched rookie officers closely. The veterans would tolerate rookies who drank too much, ran around on their spouses, and were bill dead-beats,[66] but if a rookie couldn't be counted on in a fight, the veterans would run him off. This value may account for some portion of the belief in police circles that women were ill-equipped for patrol work: physically, they wouldn't be able to do the rough hands-on part of policing.

The Korean War (1950–1953) saw the recall of many World War II veterans, including some law enforcement officers, who had joined or stayed in reserve and National Guard units. Because the Korean War was confined to one peninsula and, thus, was a war fought on a smaller scale, the impact on police staffing was far less than that of World War II.

In 1953, Ethel and Julius Rosenberg were executed for divulging nuclear bomb secrets to the Soviet Union. The Soviet Union beat the United States into space in 1957 with the first satellite, Sputnik, causing concerns about communists using the bomb to rule the world from space. In addition, Castro's rise to power in Cuba (1959) put communism on our doorstep. Senator Joseph McCarthy ran roughshod, searching everywhere for communists, until he was discredited.

Rosa Parks (1913–2005), an African American woman riding a public bus in Montgomery, Alabama, refused to give up her seat up to a White man on December 1, 1955 and was arrested (see Figure 1.18). **Martin Luther King**, Jr., a 26-year-old minister in that city, organized a bus boycott by African Americans

that lasted 381 days and reduced bus revenues by 80 percent.[67] The incident birthed the Civil Rights movement. The next year, federal courts ordered the desegregation of the bus system.

Although African Americans had served as lawmen in the West after the Civil War, their numbers were not large. Some municipalities with large African American populations, including Washington D.C. (1861), Chicago and New Orleans (1872), and Charleston, S.C. (1873), began hiring minorities at the onset and after the Civil War to police their "own kind." During the 1950s, more substantial representation was achieved. In *Brown v. Board of Education* (1954), the Supreme Court ruled that segregation was illegal, although the ruling was more often ignored than followed. Nationally, real progress in the hiring and promotion of African Americans was not made until the succession of civil rights bills previously noted were passed during the 1960s and 1970s.

During the 1950s and extending into the mid-1960s, some southern police departments came to grips with the problem of the "**unequal badge**." In these cities, African American officers were not allowed to arrest a White person because of the fear it might trigger a riot. Often, southern minority officers could not drive patrol cars for a similar same reason; it was believed that White motorists would not accept a ticket

Figure 1.18
Mourners file past the casket of Rosa Parks, the mother of the Civil Rights movement, in the Rotunda of the U.S. Capitol, Washington, D.C. Honoring a private citizen in this manner is rare. Parks is the first woman to be so recognized.
(Courtesy MANDEL NGAN/AFP/Getty Images)

from an African American officer.[68] This resulted in the practice of majority officers dropping their African Americans counterparts off at their walking beats in minority business districts at the beginning of a shift and picking them up afterwards. Minorities subtly retaliated by getting into the back seat when being picked up, making it appear that majority officers were their chauffeurs.

In 1959, the California Peace Officers Standards and Training Commission (**POST**) was legislatively created to set minimum standards for selection and training of police officers. Although some states followed suit during the early 1960s, many POST units were not created until the late 1960s and early 1970s when federal grant funds from the now-defunct federal Law Enforcement Assistance Administration (LEAA) were available. POST units play in an important role in police professionalization. They essentially constitute a professional licensing board and can revoke an officer's certificate to hold a job with any public law enforcement agency in the state that issued it.

The Turbulent 1960s: Riots, Political Protests, Assassinations, and the Isolation of the Rank and File

World War II regained international attention with the trial (1961) of Adolph Eichmann in Israel for his role in the holocaust. Closer to home, the Bay of Pigs, the American-sponsored Cuban invasion (1961), intended to topple Castro, failed. Further concerns about the "commies" controlling outer space were sparked when the Soviet Union launched the first man into orbit (1962). The Soviets ignited the Cuban Missile Crisis in October 1962 by placing nuclear weapons in Cuba, and war seemed terrifyingly imminent. Although Russian Premier Khrushchev quickly removed the weapons, the practical effect was that Castro's hand was strengthened: We agreed not to invade or sponsor further invasions of Cuba.

Domestically, the 1960s was a staggering decade for our society as smoldering racial, social, and economic tensions erupted. In 1965, these tensions boiled over in Los Angeles' Watts neighborhood. A California Highway Patrol majority motorcycle officer stopped Marquette Frye, an African American, for drunk driving. Frye's brother was also in the car and the men's mother soon appeared. Los Angeles officers arrived to assist as African Americans congregated at the scene. Events spiraled out of control, rocks were thrown at the officers and all three Fryes were arrested. Six days of looting, sniping, and arson followed in Watts, 34 people were killed, most of them minorities, and losses amounted to $200 million before an uneasy peace was restored.

Over the next three years, more than two dozen major cities were struck by similar riots. The 1967 Detroit riot could not be controlled by local officers and elements of the state police and Michigan's National Guard. Ultimately, it took the presence of two brigades, one each from the 82nd and 101st Airborne Divisions to restore order. The following year in Washington, D.C., a riot broke out the day the Reverend Martin Luther King was assassinated in Memphis,

Figure 1.19
Army soldier on duty during the 1968 riot in Washington, D.C. The smoldering building in the background is an indicator of the wider damage. (Courtesy Library of Congress)

Tennessee. It was only quelled with the assistance of nearly 14,000 troops (see Figure 1.19), although rioters came within two blocks of the White House before being forced back.

The causes cited across all of these riots were fundamentally the same: high rates of minority unemployment; poor housing; White store owners who took money from the minority communities but showed no reciprocity, such as jobs for them; a segregated and unequal society; and police officers viewed as hostile and repressive, a force of occupation to maintain the status quo.

The first mass murder on an American university campus occurred at the University of Texas in 1966. **Charles Whitman** brought an assortment of firearms, including a scoped rifle, to the 28th floor of a campus building and began shooting. Before he was stopped, Whitman killed 14 people and wounded 32 others. He died a few days later of wounds inflicted by the police. To some degree, the incident helped transform campus security departments from simply being unarmed watchmen to professional police agencies.

In 1967, the first national study of police since the Wickersham Report (1931) was completed. President Johnson's Commission on Law Enforcement and Criminal Justice issued a summary report, ***The Challenge of Crime in a Free Society***. The study was supplemented by task force reports on the police, organized crime, and other topics. The organization of the Commission's report paralleled The Cleveland Foundation's use in 1922 of subordinate working groups to study specific areas. Among the recommendations made was that police officers should have college degrees. The 1968 report from the **National Advisory Commission on Civil**

Disorders, the Kerner Commission, which also took the name of its chair, simply confirmed what everyone knew were the causes of riots. It also acknowledged the confusing demands being placed on law enforcement: One side saw the police as maintaining order at the expense of justice while the other demanded tougher enforcement.[69]

The Kerner Commission didn't start the role debate, but it certainly added credence, as did The *Challenge of Crime in a Free Society*, to the need to have such a discussion. As stated earlier, at the core of the military model was the belief that there was a war on crime led by the police. Their duty was ferreting out crime, conducting investigations, making arrests, and assisting with the prosecution of offenders. Others suggested that the police needed to be something more than that or risk forever being seen as the "bullies" of a culturally divided society. During the 1960s, the police, albeit slowly and under pressure, began a metamorphosis from just being crime fighters. Their role enlarged to being conflict managers, community relations specialists, and a conduit to social welfare agencies.

Meanwhile, other events in the 1960s were also changing the world-view of police officers. There were hippies, psychedelic drugs, massive demonstrations against the Vietnam War, draft evaders and military deserters, civil rights marches and demonstrations, the beginning of open emergence by gays, the burgeoning women's rights movement, the passage of civil rights legislation discussed earlier, and Supreme Court decisions, such as the restrictions placed on police interrogations by *Miranda v. Arizona* (1966). Native Americans sought more control over their lands and **Cesar Chavez** unionized mostly Mexican farm workers in the Southwest to provide them better working conditions and wages.

Chicago police clashed repeatedly with demonstrators at the 1968 Democratic National Convention. Both sides used excessive force. The demonstrators threw apples into which razors had been inserted, vials containing urine, and garbage can lids at the police. Such provocations do not, however, excuse the lack of control exhibited by the police on some occasions.

Further evidence to the police that our society was unraveling during the 1960s were the assassinations of President Kennedy (1917–1963) in Dallas;[70] Robert Kennedy (1925–1968), the dead President's brother, who was campaigning for the presidency in Los Angeles; and the civil rights leader, Reverend Martin Luther King, Jr. (1929–1968), who was supporting a sanitation workers strike in Memphis. On April 4, 1968, the Reverend Martin Luther King, Jr. stepped outside of his hotel room and was shot to death (see Figure 1.20). The day before, in Memphis, he gave perhaps his most notable address, "I've Been to the Mountaintop."

A new world was unfolding that the police did not understand and in which they felt isolated and unsupported. In this milieu, police professionalism took on new urgency. During the 1960s, police departments, as an entry-level educational attainment, commonly required a tenth-grade to a high school degree, or its counterpart, the general equivalency degree (GED). The first major law enforcement agency to require a college degree was the Multnomah County Sheriff's Office (Oregon) in 1965,[71]

Figure 1.20
The Lorraine Hotel, Memphis, Tennessee. Reverend King, a Nobel Peace Prize winner (1964), occupied room 306.
(Courtesy Library of Congress, Highsmith (Carol M.) Archive)

although in most cases, if any college was required it usually amounted to 6 to 12 semester hours. Other departments hired officers with the understanding that they would complete a certain number of hours within a specified time period after appointment or forfeit their jobs. Police lockers rooms were polarized as older, less-educated officers taunted younger, college-attending officers with epithets like "egghead" and "educated idiot." Despite pockets of some sort of college as an entry-level requirement, during much of this era, the vast number of agencies simply required a high school education.

Nonetheless, in policing, "professional" slowly became synonymous with "education" from roughly 1965–1967 onward. Education was seen as a means of improving community relations, which were generally poor before the urban riots and also contributed to their advent, and of reducing police violence, promoting more judicious use of police discretionary decision-making, countering corruption as a competing model, and redefining the role of policing our society.[72] From the late 1960s until the mid-1970s, there was a quick proliferation of police administration and criminal justice programs in community colleges and universities.

Some impetus to college education for officers came in programs adopted by progressive communities. Those officers with college degrees got an additional 5 or 10 percent above the normal salary and those without a degree could work on a degree and get some reimbursement for the cost, based on their final grade.[73] Beginning in 1968, the federal Law Enforcement Education Program (LEEP), an arm of LEAA, provided up to $2,400 a year to help defray college education costs for criminal justice majors. Repayment could be accomplished by a 25 percent loan forgiveness formula for each year of service with a public criminal justice agency, up to a maximum of four years/100 percent.

Character and background checks became more robust and the use of polygraphs and credit checks became more standard. Some psychological screening was done, although it often involved the general practitioner conducting the entry-level physical exam to simply state that no abnormalities were observed. The most important leap in the quality of applicant screening was the result of standards set by emerging POSTs.

The professionalization movement during the 1950s and 1960s shaped the role of the police and created a sense of pride and unity among officers. However, in the second half of the 1960s, police unity was redirected as a result of riots and civil rights demonstrations, Supreme Court decisions "handcuffing" the police, a spiraling crime rate, an increasingly critical press, a perceived lack of public support, and the creation of civilian review boards to investigate allegations of police misconduct. Officers saw administrators as trying to bring unwanted change into their world and dismissed the "bosses" as out of touch with the realities of police work on the street. Together, these events resulted in the police rank and file feeling they were isolated and unsupported, creating a "we against them" mentality that propelled them to join unions as states began passing public sector collective bargaining laws in the 1960s. Unions created a new power center in police departments, exciting officers and alarming administrators.

The 1970s: Research and Experimentation, Rising Transnational Terrorism

Wadman and Allisan wrote, "The 1970s are generally regarded as a period of malaise in American history . . . the Vietnam War ended without a sense of closure [1975], the **Watergate Scandal** intensified distrust of government . . . the economic downturn reduced budgets, limiting the ability of the police to innovate . . . and traditional police professionalism concepts made it difficult for communities to influence police priorities and programs."[74] President Nixon's 1974 resignation while facing impeachment grew out of the burglary of the Democratic National Committee headquarters at the Watergate Office Complex in Washington, D.C. The burglary was initially tied to the Republican Committee to Reelect the President and then to members of President Nixon's staff. As a result of Watergate, 61 percent of Americans expressed distrust of government—a burden on all public agencies, including the police. Prior events may have also fed this distrust, including the killing of four Kent State University students by members of the Ohio National Guard (1970) who fired on the demonstrators[75] and disillusionment with the Vietnam War. Because police officers also tried to control protests, they were often bitterly resented by demonstrators who labeled them "pigs."[76]

Once again, the country seemed to be coming unglued. Two assassination attempts were made on President Ford's life in an 18-day period and presidential candidate George Wallace was shot and paralyzed while campaigning in Maryland.[77] Against this social backdrop, important things were occurring in policing. The previously mentioned *Challenge of Crime in a Free Society* found "There is no subject connected with crime or criminal justice into which further research is unnecessary."[78] Doig reached the same conclusion, declaring that law enforcement was a *terra incognita*, an unknown land.[79] During the 1970s, with grants from LEAA, there was a torrent of research. An early trilogy of major experiments rocked policing: (1) the **Kansas City Preventive Patrol Study**, (2) the **Rand Criminal Investigation Study**, and (3) the **team policing** experiment.

The Kansas City Preventive Patrol Study examined three types of patrol services to see what difference each made:

1. *Reactive districts* received no regular patrol; officers who responded to calls entered and left the district by the shortest routes.
2. *Proactive districts* were saturated with two to three times the normal amount of patrolling.
3. *Control districts* maintained regular or normal patrolling.

The study found no significant differences in reported crime, arrests, traffic accidents, fear of crime, or security measures by citizens were found. As local governmental leaders learned of the results, some refused to fund requests for additional police officers. The findings were controversial and dismissed by police leaders as being a lone and methodologically flawed study.

The Rand (Corporation) Criminal Investigation Study sought to determine what factors contribute to the success of criminal investigations, and just what it is that detectives do. Focusing on serious crimes, the study concluded that the preliminary investigations conducted by patrol officers provided the information that led to the solution of most crimes. Critics of detectives said it confirmed suspicions of their value, while police leaders labeled it "one, unreplicated study." Like the Kansas City Study, the finding became an issue in police budgets for a period of time.

Team policing was a bold reform effort to reshape how police resources were used and to reduce the amount of specialization by using patrol officers in a variety of roles, such as plainclothes assignments.[80] Roughly 20 to 30 officers were formed into teams, under the 24-hour direction of a single commander who controlled how they were deployed. By the end of the 1970s, team policing vanished due to problems of implementation and the opposition of mid-level police managers who correctly saw that it reduced their importance. The experiment increased appreciation of the capabilities of patrol officers and helped set the stage for community policing, which exploded during the 1980s.

Around 1970, there was a movement toward new organizations. In 1969, the International Association of Police Women (**IAPW**), with roots that date back to 1926, adopted its current name. A number of state-level women officers associations belong to IAWP. The National Association of Women Law Enforcement Executives

(**NAWLEE**) also advocates for women's issues in policing. The formation of the federal National Criminal Justice Reference Service (**NCJRS**, 1972) created an easily accessible body of cutting-edge information for criminal justice students, scholars, and practitioners. **HAPCOA**, the Hispanic American Police Command Officers Association, was formed in 1973 to assist in the recruitment, training, and promotion of qualified Hispanic men and women and to advocate for Hispanic law enforcement issues. The Police Executive Research Forum (**PERF**, 1975) was formed by the largest city, county, and state agencies for the purpose of pursuing research and public policy work of particular interest to its members. The National Organization of Black Law Enforcement Executives (**NOBLE**, 1976) focuses on crime in low-income urban areas. The Commission on Accreditation of Law Enforcement Agencies (**CALEA**, 1979) was established with the support of the IACP, NSA, PERF, and NOBLE as an independent accrediting body for law enforcement agencies. CALEA accreditation can reduce liability insurance costs, can be used as a tool in attracting new businesses to a community, and stimulates community pride and confidence in a community's police department. Although its formation falls in a later era, the National Association of Asian American Law Enforcement Commanders (**NAAALEC**) was created in 2002 to promote a positive police image in Asian/Pacific communities and to speak on topics of common concerns for its membership.

The **Greensboro Massacre** (North Carolina, 1979) was one of the most brutal and widely seen assaults on civil rights. Representatives of the Communist Workers Party, then known as the Workers Viewpoint Organization, were attempting to unionize African American workers, when members of a KKK and American Nazi Party (ANP) caravan opened fire, killing 3 and wounding 10. Remarkably, only a police intelligence officer and a police photographer were present and they did not intervene. The incident was recorded by the news media and the nationally distributed pictures provided yet another example that the police would not protect minorities. When all-White juries in both state and federal trials failed to convict the attackers, the judicial process was also stained. Finally, at civil trial, five attackers and the police were found liable.

Although terrorism is an ancient strategy, transnational terrorism began a march toward the present during the 1970s (see Chapter 3, Intelligence, Terrorism, and Homeland Security). On Black Sunday (1970), operatives of the Popular Front for the Liberation of Palestine (**PFLP**) hijacked four planes. The Black September Organization (**BSO**), a Palestinian group, killed 11 Israeli athletes and team officials at the 1972 Olympic Games in Munich, some of whom died in a botched rescue attempt. Four years later, the PFLP, aided by two Germans from the Revolutionary Cells, hijacked an Air France jet and forced it to fly to the Entebbe Airport in Uganda.[81] The hijackers released all non-Jewish passengers but held their Jewish hostages in the terminal. The hijackers demanded the release of 53 Palestinians held in several countries in exchange. The Israel Defense Force Forces (IDF) conducted a spectacular raid, freeing the hostages.[82] The success of the Entebbe raid may have encouraged President Carter to approve a military plan to free 53 American hostages held in Iran for more than a year. The raid failed and played a part in his defeat by Ronald Reagan.[83]

1980s to the 9/11 Attacks: The Community Oriented Policing Era

Innovation in policing strategies occurred at a rapid pace during this 20-year period. The most recent innovations came about as a result of the convergence of several phenomena, including the rise of terrorism on the forefront of American consciousness from threats both foreign (such as Al Qaeda's attack on the World Trade Centers) and domestic (**Timothy McVeigh's** and the Oklahoma City Bombing), as well as a call for more transparency in policing due to high-profile incidents involving law enforcement at **Ruby Ridge** and in **Waco**, Texas. Chapter 8 addresses the impact of police decision-making during critical incidents, such as those observed in protracted terrorist incidents. Technological advances in policing have also played a large role in the development of new strategies in policing. These new paradigms include **community-oriented policing (COP)**, **zero tolerance policing (ZTP)**, CompStat, and **evidence-based policing (EBP)**. COP is the development of police strategies and programs in partnership with communities in order to deliver custom-tailored police services and solutions to problems, as well as a renewed focus on crime prevention rather than crime detection. ZTP was based on the premise that when small infractions of the law are ignored it creates a climate conducive to more serious crimes being committed. The extension of this thinking was ZTP, which required non-discretionary enforcement for all crimes. CompSTAT, which was initially implemented in 1994 in the New York City Police Department, is a management control system designed to develop, analyze, and disseminate information about reported crime and to track efforts to deal with it.[84] Finally, evidence-based policing (EBP) is based on research . . . that is, which strategies in policing provide the most successful outcomes in terms of prevention, detection, and eradication. These new strategies should be then identified as "best practices," and adopted much more widely for use.

Each of these new strategies in policing will be further discussed in detail in Chapter 2, Policing Today, along with other emerging approaches such as directed patrol and intelligence-led policing. However, it should be noted that of all of these approaches, community oriented policing was the fastest and most transformative to policing, having an important impact on not only police operations (such as patrol and investigations), but also on the structure and culture of the police organization. This brief discussion of contemporary strategies sets the stage for our next chapter exploring the continuing evolution of policing strategies today. Certainly, policing has dramatically changed since the days of August Vollmer and O.W. Wilson; policing has become much more proactive, focused on preventing not only crime but terrorism as well. Perhaps, no greater challenge confronts American policing today than the imperative to prevent the next terrorist attack on the American homeland.

CONCLUSION

American colonists, who were primarily English, initially relied on volunteer citizen night watchmen for rudimentary law enforcement services. Over time, they introduced offices that were familiar to them, such as constable, sheriff, and magistrate. Parliament's enactment of the Metropolitan Police Act of 1829 created a full-time police force for London, a development closely watched from this country. English practices have had a strong influence on the shape of American policing.

Machine politics and the grotesque use of patronage resulted in the police being used to further the aims of whichever party was in power. It took decades of effort to separate law enforcement from politics in the worst sense.

Although the "wild west" is a vivid image, it lasted only about 90 years and among its by-products was the rise of tribal law enforcement agencies on reservations. Following the civil war, numbers of African Americans left the deep south and headed west to find better lives. In part, this quest was fermented by the rise of the initially repressive and then murderous KKK, which assumed some of the characteristics of the former slave patrols. Additionally, harsh laws had been quickly passed in southern states to keep the freed slaves "in their place." As settlers, cowboys, and lawmen, African Americans made contributions to the westward movement of this country that are often ignored.

By 1920 most Americans were living in cities, whose explosive growth fostered large municipal police departments. Opportunities there attracted August Vollmer, the Father of American law enforcement, a great innovator and the first advocate of college educated police officers. Prohibition, an ill-advised social experiment, had a terrible effect on policing, resulting in its corruption and giving it a terrible image. The combination of the depression of 1929 and the dustbowl of the Midwest sent people scurrying off to different parts of the country. To protect jobs for tax paying citizens, local governments enacted residency requirements and some had the police operate "bum blockades" that turned back migrants trying to enter their town, further blackening the reputation of the police. The gangster crime era could not be controlled by local law enforcement and the FBI's ultimate success in combating it helped create its reputation for effectiveness.

World War II created a somewhat wider crack for women to enter law enforcement. However, neither women nor minorities made significant headway nationally until the passage of federal job discrimination laws. The 1960s left law enforcement officers feeling isolated and unsupported as a maelstrom of riots, anti-war demonstrators, assassinations, and Supreme Court decisions supporting the rights of accused persons rippled across the country.

The 1970s were largely stagnant in terms of law enforcement, although education for police officers continued to gain traction and the Kansas City Preventive Patrol and Rand Criminal Investigation studies helped set the stage for an explosion of new policing philosophies over the next two decades, including COP, ZTP, CompStat, and EBP. Many departments quickly adopted such innovations and then struggled to find ways to incorporate them with each successive iteration of operational approaches. Beginning in the 1970s there were signs that a new phenomenon, transnational terrorism, was on the near horizon, a lesson driven home by the murderous attacks of 9/11.

CHAPTER REVIEW

1. How did events in 19th century England influence the development of unified, full-time police departments in this country?

2. What two factors made the Pinkerton National Detective Agency very effective in dealing with outlaws?

3. Of what importance is the closing of the frontier in 1890?

4. How is politics defined? Why can't it be kept out of police agencies?

5. What was machine politics in the 19th century?

6. What are the worst and best things about the patronage/spoils system?

7. Why is the concept of a police profession so important?

8. How did Gus Vollmer contribute to policing?

9. In what ways did prohibition affect policing?

10. What were the Black Codes and Jim Crow laws, and what were they intended to accomplish?

11. In what ways did World War II affect law enforcement?

12. The unequal badge problem was institutionalized racism. What was it?

13. What forces made the 1960s so politically and socially tumultuous?

14. How did the police rank and file become isolated in the 1960s?

15. What events led to research on policing during the 1970s?

16. What are COP, ZTP, CompStat, and EBP?

INTERNET ACTIVITIES AND RESOURCES

1. Go to The Wild West, *www.thewildwest.org/cowboys/wildwestoutlawsandlawmen*, to learn about legendary outlaws and lawmen.

2. Visit the **FBI, National Security Branch**, *www.FBI.gov/hq/nsb/nsb.htm*, for an overview of national security operations.

3. To learn more about modern policing on Native American Reservations, see National Congress of American Indians, *www.NCAI.org/LAW-Enforcement-and-Tribal-cou .34.0.html* a related site is National Native American Law Enforcement Association, *www.nnalea.org*.

KEY TERMS

air raid wardens: persons in WWII who patrolled to make sure that during "black outs" no lights were showing that could assist enemy submarines in identifying targets if they shelled our coast. Also used to prevent enemy submarines or aircraft from using lights to assist in their navigation. Police and civic groups shared this duty across the country.

Black Codes: laws quickly adopted in southern states following the Civil War to repress African Americans.

Black September Organization (BSO): terrorist group.

bootlegger: someone who smuggled illegal alcohol during prohibition; also referred to people who hid a flask in their boot or held one to their leg with a garter.

Boston Police Strike: 1919 police strike that killed the possibility of police unionization until the 1960s.

bum blockades: police-staffed blockades established by some cities during the Depression to turn immigrants away at the city limits who would be a drain on local government resources if allowed to enter.

carpetbaggers: Northerners who came to the South following the Civil War, so-called because their suitcases were cheaply made of second-hand carpet.

Challenge of Crime in a Free Society: 1967 government report calling for improvements across the criminal justice system.

Chavez, Cesar: farm worker and later civil rights activist, fought for better working conditions and pay for migrant pickers.

city manager movement: style of city government that began in Stanton, Virginia, in 1908.

Civil Rights Act of 1964: Federal law that invalidated Jim Crow laws; Title 7 forbade discrimination by businesses and unions on the basis of sex, race, color, religion, or national origin in hiring, promoting, and firing. Title 7 did not apply to state and local governments. See Equal Employment Opportunity Act of 1972.

Commission on Accreditation of Law Enforcement Agencies (CALEA): created in 1979 with the support of police associations, this private body accredits law enforcement agencies that meet its list of standards.

community-oriented policing: early 1980s policing philosophy that essentially provided custom-tailored police services to neighborhoods and business districts. Used interchangeably with problem-oriented policing (POP).

Community-Oriented Policing Services (COPS): a federal grant program.

Dillinger, John: bank robber killed in Chicago by FBI agents in 1934, marking the end of the lawless era.

dustbowl: term for dried-out prairie states, where good topsoil blew away; many immigrated from those states to seek a better life. See okies.

Equal Employment Opportunity Act of 1972: law that amended Title 7 of the Civil Rights Act of 1964 to include state and local units of government.

evidence-based policing (EBP): theory of policing that grew out of 1998 article by Larry Sherman, who argued that police practices should be based on the best evidence available.

Forces Act: federal legislation (1870) to combat Ku Klux Klan.

Fosdick, Raymond: author who played a major role in the Cleveland Foundation Study.

Freedmen's Bureau: federal agency that provided assistance to African Americans after the Civil War.

frontier closing: 1890—the official date set by the federal government for the "closing of the frontier," a key point in the transition from a rural to an urban society.

Garfield, President: U.S. president assassinated by frustrated patronage seeker; event gave momentum to passage of Pendleton Act.

Greensboro Massacre (N.C.): brutal and widely seen 1979 attack on African Americans by KKK and American Nazi Party.

Harrison, President: U.S. president accused of "prostitution of the public service."

Hispanic American Police Command Officers Association (HAPCOA): established 1973, HAPCOA provides training and other opportunities for its members.

International Association of Chiefs of Police (IACP): a professional organization of chiefs of international, federal, state, and local police agencies of all sizes.

International Association of Police Women (IAPW): organization founded in 1969, roots in organization date back to 1926.

Jim Crow laws: southern laws that repressed African Americans, enacted 1880–1960, followed the Black Codes.

Kansas City Preventive Patrol Study: part of the trilogy of research and experiments that rocked policing in the early 1970s.

King, Martin Luther Jr., Reverend: distinguished leader in the Civil Rights movement.

KKK: Ku Klux Klan, organization founded as a social club in 1866, quickly turned to terrorizing African Americans.

Lexow Committee: committee that in 1894–1895 examined corruption in the New York Police Department.

lynching: initially a severe beating, later synonymous with illegally hanging someone; initially meant rough justice.

machine politics: see political machine.

McVeigh, Timothy: individual convicted of the Oklahoma City bombing and murders, executed in 2001; he stated he wanted to get revenge for Ruby Ridge and Waco.

military model: police theory that there is a war against crime and the police are front-line soldiers.

muckrakers: journalists and writers who exposed corruption and other abuses.

National Academy (NA): institution founded in 1934 by FBI to train state and local law enforcement officials.

National Advisory Commission on Civil Disorders: government report on riots in 1968; also known as the Kerner Commission after the group's Chair.

National Association of American Asian Law Enforcement Commanders (NAAALEC): founded in 2002, an organization fostering leadership, fraternal enrichment, and advancement.

National Association of Women Law Enforcement Executives (NAWLEE): established to address the unique needs of women holding senior positions in law enforcement.

National Commission on Law Observance and Law Enforcement: first comprehensive national study of police, 1929.

National Criminal Justice Reference Service (NCJRS): on-line reference source for criminal justice students, scholars, practitioners, and the public.

National Organization of Black Law Enforcement Executives (NOBLE): founded in 1976, NOBLE works toward the elimination of racism and bias with the law enforcement field.

National Prohibition Act: see Volstead Act, prohibition.

National Sheriffs Association (NSA): chartered in 1940, the NSA, like other professional organizations provides education, training, and information resources to its members.

Nation, Carry: WCTU activist, gained notoriety for "hatchitations," ripping alcohol kegs open with her axe.

Okies: term for immigrants from dust bowl states, many of them from Oklahoma.

patronage: in the worst sense, rewarding voters for their loyalty rather than their ability; useful in appointing qualified supporters who can help politicians implement their policies.

Peel, Sir Robert: driving force behind the London Metropolitan Police (1829).

Pendleton Act: federal legislation (1883) establishing the U.S. Civil Service Commission.

Police Executive Research Forum (PERF): group formed to do research and public policy work of interest to the larger jurisdictions founding it.

Popular Front for the Liberation of Palestine (PFLP): terrorist organization.

Pinkerton National Detective Agency: a private detective agency that excelled at tracking down outlaws.

Police Administration: book authored by O.W. Wilson, known for many decades as the "Bible" of police administration, reasserted professional model of policing.

political machine: a tightly controlled political party headed by a boss or small autocratic group whose purpose was to repeatedly win elections for personal gain, often through graft and corruption.

Politics: the process of acquiring and maintaining control over a government, including its policies, administration, and operations.

Peace Officer Standards and Training Commissions (POSTs): organizations that played an important role in police professionalization.

profession: several definitions; see Table 1.1.

prohibition: national prohibition officially lasted from 1919 to 1933.

Rand Criminal Investigation Study: part of the trilogy of research and experiments that rocked policing in the early 1970s.

ration books: to divert as much food as possible to support service members fighting in WWII, national food rationing was instituted in the United States in 1942. Each person was issued a book of stamps that established the amounts of various types of foods he/she could have. Also see victory gardens.

reformation period: reformers sought to free policing from political abuses and corruption; had two needs: arouse apathetic public and a conceptual model to drive it.

residency requirements: rules from the Depression era, stating that before hiring, person had to live in a community six months or a year; intent was to protect jobs for local tax-paying residents.

Ruby Ridge: 1992 Idaho standoff involving Weaver family and a friend and federal agents; fatalities on both sides; Weavers were seen by far-right groups as martyrs to federal government.

Singleton, Benjamin "Pap": former Tennessee slave, promoted founding African American townships in Kansas after the Civil War.

slave patrols: groups that hunted down fugitive slaves, administered impromptu punishments as they saw fit, and dispersed slave meetings; continued through the end of the Civil War.

snatch racket: 1920s and 1930s gangster term for kidnappings.

speakeasies: illegal bars during federal prohibition.

spoils system: see patronage.

team policing: an attempt to reshape how police resources were used by reducing specialization and enlarging the role of uniformed patrol officers. Part of the trilogy of research and experiments that rocked policing in the 1970s.

temperance movement: late 19th-century anti-alcohol movement; church based.

unequal badge: term that describes African American officers in some southern communities who, until the early 1960s, only walked beats in African American business and entertainment districts; by custom, African American officers were often not allowed to arrest Caucasians because an "ugly incident" leading to rioting might occur.

untouchables: Treasury agents under Elliot Ness assigned to Chicago who couldn't be corrupted.

victory gardens: small household gardens planted during WW II for personal consumption so more food could be used in war effort.

Vollmer, August (Gus): father of modern law enforcement.

Volstead Act: National Prohibition Act; see prohibition.

Waco: Texas city where, in1993, there was a 51-day federal siege of the Branch Davidian Compound led by David Koresh; ended with federal fatalities and perhaps 75 or more Branch Davidian deaths; federal authorities were sharply criticized, but no wrongdoing was found.

Watergate Scandal: petty burglary that ultimately led to President Nixon's resignation.

Whitman, Charles: man who committed the first mass murders on a college campus at the University of Texas in 1966.

Wickersham Commission: see National Commission on Law Observance and Law Enforcement (1929).

Wilson, O.W.: chief of several jurisdictions; studied under Vollmer; his *Police Administration* has been regarded as the "Bible" of police administration for decades.

zero tolerance policing: ZTP was based on the premise that when small infractions of the law are ignored it creates a climate conducive to more serious crimes being committed. The extension of this thinking was ZTP, which required non-discretionary enforcement for all crimes.

ENDNOTES

[1] New Amersterdam was settled by the Dutch. To be precise, the office they created was schout, their cultural equivalent of a sheriff.

[2] Raymond Fosdick, *American Police Systems* (Montclair, N.J.: Patterson Smith reprint, 1969), pp. 63–64.

[3] These dates are for the first of three successive industrial revolutions in England. Others define the period as 1760–1840 and 1750–1850.

[4] Many sources list these principles, including the New Westminster Police Service (British Columbia, Canada), www.NWpolice.org/Peel.html, January 9, 2010. Also see Douglas Hurd, *Sir Robert Peel: A Biography* (London: Weidenfeld & Nicolson, 2007). Susan Lentz maintains that the principles are the

invention of 20th-century textbook writers, see "The Invention of Peel's Principles," *Journal of Criminal Justice*, Vol. 35, No. 1, pp. 69–79, January 2007.

[5] Melville Lee, *A History of Police in England* (Montclair, N.J.: Patterson Smith reprint, 1971), p. 240.

[6] Despite the perils of the wilderness through which they traveled, the riders could not carry firearms in order to transport more mail. The work was so dangerous that the Pony Express preferred to recruit orphans because they would not be missed if killed.

[7] Perhaps 250,000 former slaves left the South for the West from during the 1870s, so many they were called "exodusters" and Singleton hailed as the "Moses of the Colored Exodus." See Mike Meacham, "The Exoduster Movement," *Western Journal of Black Studies*, Vol. 27, Issue 2, Summer, 2003, pp. 108–117 and The Testimony of Benjamin Singleton Before the Senate Select Committee Investigating the Negro Exodus from the South, Washington, D.C.: April 17, 1880. Sources identify the place of "Pap" Singleton's death alternatively as "someplace in the West" and St. Louis.

[8] At one time or another, three legendary lawmen of the West were employed in Abilene: Bat Masterson, Wyatt Earp, and Wild Bill Hickok.

[9] On January 9, 1918, at Bear Valley the 10th Calvary fought Yaquis Indians who had crossed from Mexico into southern Arizona, raiding ranches. The Yaquis were in revolt against their government, trying to establish a separate territory for themselves. The raids were conducted to obtain goods that would assist them in their struggle. The 10th Calvary was an African American unit, whose valor was well established over a period of decades. Native Americans respectfully referred to African Americans as "Buffalo Soldiers." Thus, although 1890 is traditionally given as the end of warfare with Native Americans in this country, the last battle was actually fought 28 years later at Bear Valley.

[10] For an excellent summary of the development of tribal police systems, see David Etheridge, *Indian Law Enforcement History* (Washington, D.C.: Bureau of Indian Affairs, Division of Law Enforcement Services, February 1, 1975), 80 pp.

[11] Charles Boles robbed 28 Wells Fargo stagecoaches before being arrested. He was fond of leaving poems at scene of his crimes, signed "Black Bart, the PO8"
One read:

> I've labored long and hard for bread,
> For honor and for riches
> But on my corns too long you've tread
> You fine haired sons of bitches

[12] Only Utah (1896), Oklahoma (1907), Arizona and New Mexico (1912), Alaska (1959), and Hawaii (1959) had not yet been granted statehood.

[13] See M. David Desoucy, *Arizona Rangers* (Mount Pleasant, S.C.: Arcadia Publishing, 2008), Chuck Hornung, *Fullerton's Rangers: A History of the Mexico Territorial Mounted Police* (Jefferson, N.C.: McFarland & Company, 2005), and Mike Cox, *The Texas Rangers: Wearing the Cinco Peso, 1821–1900* (New York: Forge Books, 2008). "Texas Ranger" was not used in any legislation until 1874, although the term "Ranger" had been widely used by Texas citizens for many years.

[14] Sixty percent of all full-time municipal law enforcement officers work for the 600 largest departments, employing 100 or more. Brian A. Reaves, *Census of State and Local Law Enforcement Agencies, 2004* (Washington, D.C.: Bureau of Justice Statistics, 2007), p. 4.

[15] Ibid., calculated from the data in Table 5, p.5.

[16] Sixty-five percent of all full-time deputies work in the 351 agencies employing 100 or more deputies while the 929 sheriff's offices with fewer than 10 deputies have only 5,149 full-time deputies. Ibid., Appendix Table 2, p. 9.

[17] The site of the assassination is where the present National Gallery of Art is located, 401 West Constitution Avenue NW.

[18] The Dodge City Cow-Boy Band played at his inauguration. It was a curious choice; the bandleader was prone to tossing his baton away and directing with a loaded revolver. No author, *Band of Buckaroos, Wild West*, Vol. 22, No. 2, p. 16, August 2009.

[19] Editorial, Nation, Vol. 48, Issue 1243, 1889, pp. 338–341.

[20] Thomas A. Reppetto, *The Blue Parade* (New York: Free Press, 1978), pp. 41–42.

[21] Peter H. Argersinger, "New Perspectives on Election Fraud in the Gilded Age," *Political Science Quarterly*, Vol. 100, No. 4, Winter 1985–1986, p. 672.

[22] Ibid., p. 672. This is the reason that in all states today, any political signs or activities on behalf of a party or candidate cannot be displayed or conducted within a specified number of feet of a polling station.

[23] Ibid., p. 672.

[24] Ibid., p. 678.

[25] Ibid., pp. 680–681.

[26] Alice B. Stone and Donald C Stone, "Early Development of Education in Public Administration:" in *American Public Administration: Past, Present, and Future,* edited by Frederick C. Mosher (Tuscaloosa: University of Alabama Press, 1975), pp. 17–18.

[27] In 1906, racial tensions between the residents of Brownsville, Texas and members of the all-black 25th Infantry Regiment, stationed at nearby Fort Brown, were high. One evening, rifle shots were fired, which killed a white bartender. The Mayor blamed the Black soldiers. Despite the fact that every White commander of the regiment swore all of the men were in the barracks that night, President Roosevelt ordered them to be dishonorably discharged on the basis of a "conspiracy of silence" because no one came forward to identify the "guilty." This was done without any hearing, trial, or opportunity of the regiment members to confront their accusers. Years later, on the presentation of a careful study of the matter, President Nixon reversed the dishonorable discharges. For further information on President Roosevelt's tenure as New York City Police Commissioner, see Jay Stuart Berman, *Police Administration and Progressive Reform: Theodore Roosevelt as Police Commissioner of New Yor*k (Santa Barbara: ABC-CLIO, 1987). This work was originally published by Greenwood Press, the title passed through several publishing houses before coming to rest with ABC-CLIO on October 1, 2008.

[28] In Welsh, the name means "big hill." Bryn Mawr was the first institution of higher learning to offer graduate degrees to women. Its first Ph.D was awarded in 1888.

[29] Woodrow Wilson, "The Study of Administration," *Political Science Quarterly* 2 (June 1887), pp. 197–222.

[30] Parenthetically, Woodrow Wilson is the only United States president (1913–1921) to hold an earned Ph.D and signed the legislation making Mother's Day a national holiday.

[31] Raymond Fosdick and Others, edited by Roscoe Pound and Felix Frankfurter, *Criminal Justice in Cleveland, Report of the Cleveland Foundation* (Cleveland: The Cleveland Foundation, 1922). The 81 detectives, supposedly the "cream of the department," were substantially short of that. After administering the Army Alpha Test for Mental Ability to all officers, 25 percent of all detectives were found by Fosdick to have "inferior intelligence," and the personnel in the traffic and mounted patrol units had higher test scores.

[32] E. W. Roddenbury, "Achieving Professionalization," *Journal of Criminal Law, Criminology, and Police Science 44* (May 1953–1954), p. 109.

[33] See Sylvia R. Cruess, Sharon Johnson, and Richard L. Cruess, "Profession," *Teaching and Learning in Medicine,* Vol. 6, No 4, Winter 2004, pp. 74–76, Robert K. Merton, "Some Thoughts on the Professions in American Society (Address before the Brown University Graduate Convocation, Providence, R.I., June 6, 1960), and Howard Becker, "The Nature of a Profession," in the Sixty-First Yearbook of the National Society for the Study of Education (Chicago: National Society for the Study of Education, 1962).

[34] Gene Edward Carte, "August Vollmer and the Origins of Police Professionalism," *Journal of Police Science and Administration l,* No. 3, 1973, p. 274.

[35] Larry T. Hoover ascribes the development of a police academic establishment to O. W. Wilson. See "From Police Administration to Police Science: The Development of a Police Academic Establishment in the United States," *Police Quarterly,* Vol. 8, No. 1 (2005), pp. 8–22.

[36] The Academy of Criminal Justice Sciences Police Section bestows an annual award in Wilson's name for distinguished police scholarship.

[37] Jack S. Blocker, "Did Prohibition Really Work," *American Journal of Public Health,* Vol. 96, No. 2, February 2006, p. 235.

[38] Marcia Yablon, "The Prohibition Hangover," conference paper, Law & Society Annual Meeting, Humboldt University, Berlin, Germany, July 25, 2007.

[39] Holland Webb, "Temperance Movements and Prohibition," *International Social Science Review,* Vol. 74, Issue 1 and 2, 1999, p. 61.

[40] No Author, "Abandoning Prohibition," *The Nation*, May 21, 1930, Volume 76, Issue 1977, pp. 409–410.

[41] Oddly, this was at the same time that Americans began drinking more; between 1900 and 1913 the annual production of alcohol grew dramatically. Beer jumped from 1.2 billion to 2 billion gallons and liquor grew from 97 to 147 million gallons. Blocker, "Did Prohibition Really Work?" p. 235.

[42] Seth Kugel, "Tell Them Seth Sent You," *New York Times*, April 29, 2007.

[43] Ibid., p. 236.

[44] Jack Kelly, "Gangster City," *American Heritage*, Vol. 46, Issue 2, April 1995, p. 65.

[45] Toni Alexander, "Welcome to Old Times: Inserting the Okie Past Into California's San Joaquin Valley Present," *Journal of Cultural Geography*, Vol. 26. No. 1, February 2009, p. 74.

[46] Cecilia Rasmussen, "LAPD Blocked Dust Bowl Migrants at State Borders," *The Los Angeles Times*, March 9, 2003.

[47] Kevin M. O'Brien, "Do Municipal Residency Requirements Affect Labour Market Outcomes?" *Urban Studies*, Vol. 34, Issue 11, November 1997, p. 1159.

[48] Kevin Johnson, "Police, Firefighters Challenge Residency Rules," *USA Today*, October 3, 2006.

[49] Frank J. Remington, "Development of Criminal Justice Education as an Academic Discipline," *Journal of Criminal Justice Education*, Vol. 1. No. 1, March 1990, pp. 9–20.

[50] Its roots are traceable back to the National Chiefs of Police Union (1893), which largely focused on apprehension of fugitives.

[51] In Chicago, Dillinger dated Romanian immigrant Ana Cumpanas, a brothel operator known as Anna Sage. Subsequently, he was involved with one of her employees. Fearing deportation and perhaps stung by being dropped by Dillinger, Sage betrayed him to the FBI. According to FBI records, on July 22, 1934, Sage wore an orange skirt and a white blouse to a movie with Dillinger at the Biograph Theater to help agents identify him. This is in contrast to the numerous media reports stating she wore a red dress, which probably made better reading. Sage's betrayal did her little good. After receiving a $5,000 reward, she was deported to Romania. Annually, gangster buffs hold a ceremony on July 22 at the Biograph, complete with food, drinks, bagpipes, and speakers, to commemorate Dillinger's death. Dary Matera authored the most recent biography of him. See *John Dillinger* (New York: Carroll & Croft, 2005).

[52] Elaine Frantz Parsons, "Midnight Rangers: Costume and Performance in the Reconstruction-Era Ku Klux Klan," Vol. 93, No. 3, *The Journal of American History*, December 2005, p. 812. Some of the founding KKK members may have earlier been part of a musical group, the "Midnight Rangers;" in that era, "rangers" were roaming groups of armed men of dubious legality. Also see, Patrick O'Donnell, *Ku Klux Klan: America's First Terrorists Exposed* (Idea Men Productions: West Orange, N.J., 2006).

[53] Occasionally, women accompanied these patrols although their role is not clear.

[54] The topic of slave patrols has received little attention. See K.B. Turner, David Giacopassi, and Margaret Vandiver, "Ignoring the Past: Coverage of Slave Patrols in Criminal Justice Texts," *Journal of Criminal Justice Education*, Vol. 17. Issue 1, March 2006.

[55] Danial Kato, "Law and (Dis)Order: Why the KKK was So Successful in 1868?" Conference Paper, Western Political Science Association, 2007, Las Vegas, Annual Meeting, 35 pp.

[56] Brundage estimates that following 1865, between 4,000 and 5,000 people were lynched in the South and that 91 percent of the victims were African Americans. W. F. Brundage, "The Ultimate Shame: Lynch-Law in the Post-Civil War American South," *Social Alternatives*, Vol. 25, No. 1, First Quarter, 2006, pp. 28–29.

[57] A more modest number is put forth by Stovel, 1,200. See Katherine Stovel, "Local Sequential Patterns: The Structure of Lynching in the Deep South, 1880-1930," *Social Forces*, Vol. 79, No. 3, 2001, pp. 843–880.

[58] Carrigan and Webb identified 597 Mexican lynchings between 1848 and 1928, a figure that probably is substantially low. See William D. Carrigan and Clive Webb, The Lynching of Persons of Mexican Origin or Descent in the United States, 1848 to 1928, *Journal of Social History*, Vol. 37, No. 2, Winter 2003, p. 413.

[59] Brundage, p. 29.

[60] Ibid., p. 29.

[61] Ibid., p. 29. The first and second Klans not only lynched people, but even more horrifying, also tied their victims to trees with logging chains, stacked wood around it, doused the stack with kerosene, and burning them alive. The National Association for the Advancement of Colored People (NAACP) was founded in 1909, partially in response to lynching incidents.

[62] When the lead coauthor was working as a patrol officer he was dispatched to an African American bar on an aggravated assault call. In addition to the bartender, there were only three patrons—two men and a woman, sitting in a booth together. Nobody knew anything about an assault. One of the men was glassy eyed. When asked to stand up, he fell out of the booth, which was covered in blood from several knife wounds in his back. His assailant was the other man.

[63] In 1942, Japanese submarines shelled the oil installation at Goleta (CA) and also Ft. Stevens (OR). The first attack caused $500 in damage and the second one failed to hit its target. These incidents did start a West Coast fear of imminent Japanese invasion. A seaplane launched from a Japanese sub dropped incendiary bombs in an Oregon forest. The Japanese also deployed incendiary bombs on the Pacific jet stream, which carried them as far as Arizona and Kansas. Although German subs sank American vessels within sight of our coastal cities, the German's primary use of subs to target the United States' mainland was to land groups of saboteurs.

[64] Unimaginable today, families collected their waste fats and grease for cooking; 3 pounds would help make a pound of explosives. Women turned in their hosiery so parachutes and powder bags for naval guns could be made. At scrap metal drives, families turned in every iron pot and aluminum pan they could to help make tanks and airplanes.

[65] Many saw the new rock'n'roll sound popularized by such performers as Little Richard, Elvis Presley, and Jerry Lee Lewis as inspired by the devil to seize the souls of our children. The emergence of doo-wop music in the mid-1950s, a smooth harmonized group sound, provided further "evidence" of the evil of rock'n'roll.

[66] There is one exception to a bill dead-beat being accepted. Historically, many employee credit unions wouldn't issue a loan unless the applicant had co-signers. If an officer defaulted on such a loan and his cosigners had to pay it off, his reputation went to absolute zero and he might find that his backups were slow getting to him, a hint that it was time to find another occupation.

[67] One of the casualties of that boycott was a city of Montgomery White librarian, Juliette Morgan, who wrote a letter printed in the Montgomery Advertiser praising the restraint of African Americans in protesting for equal treatment. The KKK is thought to be responsible for burning a cross on her lawn and invectives were hurled at her from all quarters. Although Juliette Morgan was not a healthy person, the intense hostility displayed toward her must have played a role in her suicide 18 months later. See Mary Stanton, *Journey Toward Justice*: Juliette Hampton Morgan (Athens, Georgia: University of Georgia, 2006).

[68] The lead author on this book was the field training officer for the first African American Tampa Police Department officer trained for general patrol duties in 1964 and witnessed attempts by White motorists to refuse his trainee's traffic citation. Such events were not unusual. See Elliot M. Rudwick, *The Unequal Badge: Negro Policemen in the South* (Atlanta: Southern Relations Council, 1962) and Jack Kuykendall and David E. Burns, "The Black Police Officer: A Historical Perspective," *Journal of Contemporary Criminal Justice,* Vol. 1, No. 4, 1980.

[69] This quote has been restated for succinctness. See U.S. National Advisory Commission on Civil Disorders, Report of the National Advisory Commission on Civil Disorders (Washington, D.C.: U. S. Government Printing Office, 1968), p. 157.

[70] Some believe that it was Castro's retaliation for a Central Intelligence Agency attempted assassination of him in 1961, coordinated by mobster "Handsome Johnny" Roselli (1905–1976). Roselli broke into crime with Capone's outfit in Chicago. The men allegedly involved in the assassination were apprehended and executed in Cuba. Several months after testifying before a Senate committee on this affair, Roselli's decomposing and legless body was found in a steel barrel near Dumfounding Bay, Florida. There is, of course, no shortage of theories about JFK's assassination. The topic continues to command attention; see Amy Zegart, "A Plot to Assassinate Castro Was Approved by CIA Director Allen Dulles," *The New York Times*, January 26, 2007.

[71] Garr Nielsen, Multnomah County, Oregon, *The Police Chief*, Vol. 73, No. 8, August, 2006. Reviewed on-line, no page numbers.

[72] James Q. Wilson, "The Police and Their Problems," *Public Policy*, Vol. 12, 1963, pp. 189–216.

[73] Typically, with a final grade of "A" an officer received 100 percent of the cost of the course, 50 percent for a "B," and 25 percent for a "C."

[74] Robert C. Wadman and William Thomas Allison, *To Serve and Protect* (Prentice Hall: Upper Saddle River, N.J., 2000), p. 151.

[75] By 1973, all major American troop formations were withdrawn from South Vietnam, although advisors remained. The country fell to the North Vietnam communists in 1975.

[76] Vietnam veterans attending college often chose to conceal their service because the anti-war movement, which permeated campuses, would lead to them being spit at or reviled as "baby killers," a shameful reward for their service. At the same time, law enforcement personnel attending universities part-time did not reveal their occupation because of student "paranoia about police spies" investigating anti-war activities or drug use.

[77] His assailant was released from prison in 2007.

[78] Nicholas deB Katzenback, *The Challenge of Crime in a Free Society* (Washington, D.C.: Government Printing Office, 1967), p. 12.

[79] Jameson W. Doig, "Police Problems, Proposals, and Strategies for Change," *Public Administration Review*, 28, September/October 1968, p. 393.

[80] National Research Council of the National Academies, *Fairness and Effectiveness in Policing: The Evidence* (The National Academies Press: Washington, D.C.: 2001), p. 176.

[81] Joe Schwartz, *Israel's Defense, First Things: A Journal of Religion and Public Life*, Issue 191, March 2009, p. 29. His assailant was released from prison in 2007.

[82] After the raid, Ugandan Army officers murdered an Israeli passenger who previously had been taken from the terminal to a hospital.

[83] It also led to U.S. Navy Seal Team 6 (ST6) being designated as a primary counter-terrorism group (1981). Six years later, ST6 was folded into the U.S. Navy Special Warfare Development Group (NSWDG) with responsibility for maritime environment terrorism.

[84] David Weisburd et. al., *CompStat and Organizational Change: A National Assessment* (Washington, D.C.: National Institute of Justice, 2008), p. 5.

2

Policing Today

As society changes, so must policing change to address social, economic, and technological conditions.
—William F. Walsh

Objectives

- Define *community policing.*

- Describe the four-step problem-solving model called SARA.

- Identify the problems commonly associated with traditional policing.

- Define the concept of a *problem* as defined by Herman Goldstein.

- Define the CAPS program.

- Define CompStat and identify the core principles of CompStat as presented in the New York City Police Department model.

- Discuss three newer police strategies, "hot-spot" policing, intelligence-led policing (ILP), and predictive policing.

- List and briefly describe some of the more common crime analysis techniques.

- Describe a geographic information system and explain how such a system enhances police service.

- Explain the impact of information technologies on the police.

OUTLINE

Introduction

Policing has evolved over the last century to encompass not only crime-fighting methodologies, but also an increase in services to the community. It is important to understand this evolution because (1) the traditional model of policing, based on random patrol care responding to individual calls for service, is reactive and ineffective in reducing crime; (2) as a response, police agencies focused on social problems as well as crime in the 1980s, engaging the wider community to assist in curbing crime and disorder; (3) the resulting policing strategy, community policing, still provides a strong philosophical model used by police agencies across the United States today; (4) community policing has been enhanced through a management accountability process called **CompStat**, originally beginning in New York under the leadership of then-Commissioner Bill Bratton; (5) police agencies today employ a variety of policing strategies and models aimed at preventing crime as well as arresting offenders; and (6) police agencies today use new and advanced information technologies to manage operations and to evaluate the various policing strategies used in their communities.

Community Policing

As explained in Chapter 1, the failure of traditional law enforcement methods to curb rising crime rates during the 1970s and 1980s and to reintegrate the police with society gave rise to a new movement, generally referred to as **community oriented policing (COP)** or **community policing**. One of the first major critics of the traditional policing model was Herman Goldstein.[1] In his classic work *Policing a Free Society,* Goldstein questioned the effectiveness of traditional police methods in safeguarding the constitutional rights and privileges celebrated in American society (e.g., freedom of speech and expression, due process, the right to privacy) versus the control of crime and the decay of social order. Goldstein pointed out that these two goals may be incompatible under the traditional police model and called for a closer link between the police and the community.

During the same time period, Wilson and Kelling's "broken windows" thesis emerged as a dominant theme in American policing debate.[2] Arguing that crime seemed to increase dramatically in neighborhoods where visible signs of social decay and disorder were present (e.g., graffiti on bridge structures, unkept lots with overgrown weeds, visible drug and prostitution activities, warehouses with broken windows). Wilson and Kelling argued that areas with these types of crimes are signs of decaying neighborhoods and therefore a breeding ground for more serious crimes. The philosophy of **zero-tolerance policing (ZTP)** focuses on targeting police responses to less serious crimes in these areas, addressing the counter-intuitive argument that disorder may elicit more fear than actual crime.[3] Where adopted, officers are not given any discretion in dealing with minor crimes of disorder; an arrest has to be made. In more recent times, ZTP has been re-labeled as "disorder policing" in some circles.

Although ZTP has been given credit for reducing crime in some jurisdictions, most notably New York City, the empirical evidence of its effectiveness raises some questions,[4] as does the assumed progression from disorder to serious crimes.[5] Moreover, the strategy may have some unintended consequences: in New York City the implementation of ZTP was accompanied by an increase in citizen complainants and lawsuits alleging police misconduct and abuse of force.[6] Still, some policy makers continue to adopt ZTP, which can be used as the dominant strategy in an agency or within the framework of other policing strategies such as community-oriented policing. Others maintain the two strategies are incompatible and that working closely with the community can achieve ZTP results without generating increases in complainants and lawsuits.[7]

Kelling and Coles went on to argue that "broken windows needed fixing" and that the police must be directed to do more than just "crime control."[8] Indeed, they argued that other functions of the police were as important, and maybe more important, than strictly enforcing the law and maintaining order. Police should focus more on a service orientation, building key partnerships with churches, youth centers, and other neighborhood groups in an effort to forge new alliances with the community. Crime was seen not as the sole purview of the police but rather as an entire community responsibility. Police administrators began to look for new techniques and operational strategies that emphasized more service than arrest. Decentralization of services, characterized by storefront operations and neighborhood centers, began to be commonplace in police organizations. Old programs, such as the horse patrol, bike patrol, and the "walking beat" officer, were reintroduced to American policing as ways to bring the police and the community closer together (see Figure 2.1).

Although Braiden[9] argues that community policing was "nothing new under the sun" because it only echoed the ideas expressed by Sir Robert Peel in the early 1800s, community policing did represent a refreshing approach to earlier problems. Community policing embraced the Peelian principle of police as members of the public giving full-time attention to community welfare and existence. Therefore, policing was linked to a myriad of social issues other than simply crime, including poverty, illiteracy, racism, teenage pregnancy, and the like.[10]

Although precise definitions of community policing are hard to find, it generally is an operational and management philosophy that is uniquely identifiable. Primarily, community policing was characterized by ongoing attempts to promote greater community involvement in the police function. For the most part, the movement focused on programs that fostered five elements: (1) a commitment to crime prevention, (2) public scrutiny of the police, (3) accountability of police actions to the public, (4) customized police service, and (5) community organization.[11]

Community policing advocates argue that **traditional policing** is a system of response; that is, the police respond to calls for services *after* the activity occurs. Police response is then reactive and incident driven rather than proactive and preventive. Further, a randomized motor patrol neither lowers crime nor increases the chances of catching suspects. Increasing the number of police, then, has limited impact on the crime rate because improving response time on calls for service has little relevance to preventing the original incident.[12] In addition, the role of the individual police officer is largely limited within the confines of patrol and response.

In present practice, COP is a proactive approach to crime control with three complimentary elements: (1) community partnerships, (2) problem solving, using the SARA model, and (3) organizational transformation (see Figure 2.2). Organizational transformation means changing the police department so it supports COP. For example, because new values and methods are being introduced, the awards and performance appraisal systems must be designed to reinforce COP.[13]

Figure 2.1
Officers interact with community functions in order to provide customized police services appropriate to the city area. In this case, an officer on horseback provides visible patrol for the congested areas of Manhattan.
(© Enigma/Alamy)

Community Policing and Compstat

Although community policing has *not* had the drastic effects its supporters had hoped, the premise behind the philosophy has in turn led to the quality movement within policing: making the police be more efficient and effective. Today, most ambitious police methodology focuses on precisely that concept—CompStat. The word CompStat is derived from "comp," stemming from the word "computer," and "stat," which originates from "statistics." The process was originally developed in New York City by then-Commissioner William Bratton in the mid 1990s,[14] and continues in

Community Policing

Collaborative Community Relationships	Problem Solving: Two Tools	Organizational Transformation
• Other government agencies • Community members & groups • Nonprofits/service providers • Private businesses • News media	• The SARA Model: Scanning for problem Analysis of problem Response: implement solution Assessment: evaluation of impact • The Crime/Problem Analysis Triangle: 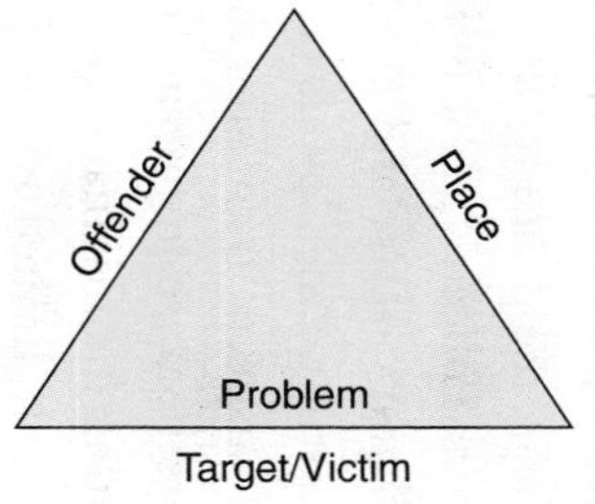 *Place* *Problem* *Offender* Target/Victim	• DEPARTMENT MANAGEMENT Organizational Structure Climate & culture Leadership Plans, policies, and procedures Decision making Evaluation of department performance Transparency/openness • Personnel Train all personnel Reevaluate recruitment and selection criteria New Performance Appraisal system Revise Award System Decrease specialization Officers have stable, geographic area of responsibility • Technology Data robust and accurate Timely access to data

Figure 2.2
Key Components of Community Policing.
Source: Contents of table are drawn from Community Oriented Policing Services, "Definition of Community Policing," WWW.COPS.USDOJ and Center for Problem-Oriented Policing, "The Problem Analysis Triangle," WWW.PopCenter.org, both accessed April 14, 2010.

Quick **FACTS** ▸▸ Review of Research on Traditional Policing

1. Increasing the number of police does not lower the crime rate or increase the proportion of solved crimes.
2. Randomized motor patrol neither lowers crime nor increases the chances of catching suspects.
3. Two-person patrol cars are not more effective than one-person cars in lowering crime rates or catching criminals; they are also no safer.
4. Saturation patrol does not reduce crime; instead, it displaces crime.

5. The kind of crime that terrifies Americans most (mugging, rape, robbery, burglary, and homicide) is rarely encountered by police on patrol.
6. Improving response time on calls has no effect on the likelihood of arresting criminals or even in satisfying involved citizens.
7. Crimes are not solved through criminal investigations conducted by police—they are solved because suspects are immediately apprehended or someone identifies them (name or license number).

Source: Adapted with permission of the Free Press, a Division of Simon & Schuster Adult Publishing Group, from *New Blue Line: Police Innovation in Six American Cities* by Jerome H. Skolnick and David H. Bayley. Copyright © 1986 by Jerome H. Skolnick and David H. Bayley. All rights reserved.

some form today in most major cities. CompStat is a process that looks at the individual needs of the community and then designs proactive strategies to stop or prevent crime. To accomplish this goal, Bratton required his department (New York in the 1990s and Los Angeles in the 2000s) to analyze crime data weekly and required police administrators to meet regularly to share information between divisions and precincts. A key component of CompStat is to force police commanders to address crime and social problems in their areas of responsibility and to address them immediately. Police commanders are then held accountable for the success or failure of their plans and decisions. Combining the two strategies of in-depth analysis with management accountability is the heart of the process.

Essentially, CompStat is a collection of modern management practices, military-like deployment efforts, and strong enforcement strategies all based on the availability of accurate and timely statistical crime data. Four core principles highlight a police department's model of CompStat:

1. *Accurate and timely intelligence and statistical crime information based on geographical settings and/or areas.* High-tech computer systems and geographical mapping programs are most helpful in providing the aggregate and individual data often required for effective CompStat efforts. However, more rudimentary aspects of visual crime analysis can be accomplished through daily pin mapping and bulletins.
2. *Rapid deployment of resources, particularly combining the immediate presence of uniform patrol working in concert with directed undercover operations.* Rapid deployment of other city and governmental resources, such as nuisance and abatement personnel, sanitation workers, and alcoholic beverage and licensing enforcement, is an additional aspect of this principle.
3. *Effective tactics and strategies of enforcement that focus on visible street crimes or "quality-of-life" crimes,* such as loitering, drinking in public, street prostitution, or even jumping subway turnstiles.

4. *Relentless follow-up and assessment,* which include placing accountability and responsibility not only on the individual police officer on the beat but also on individual police managers of traditionally defined areas, such as division heads or precinct captains.[15]

CompStat focuses on using the most accurate and timely information and data available to the police, opening lines of communication both horizontally and vertically within the organization, activating the community at large, and improving the overall efficiency and effectiveness of the police. CompStat is problem-oriented and preventive, and stresses the need to focus on problems rather than on past incidents. In this manner, CompStat significantly departs from the traditional police model by taking a preventive approach rather than a more reactive, incident-driven approach. CompStat meetings tend to focus on an individual area or a community's problems with an eye toward remedying the situation or preventing future crime.

The CompStat process is not limited to large, metropolitan agencies. Indeed, CompStat can be implemented in cities of all sizes with diverse populations and varying crime rates. The process helps police executives clarify their agency's mission and focus its efforts on the most important issues first, identifying problems early and developing effective strategies for remediation and prevention. Most importantly, the CompStat process allows the organization to learn quickly what works and what does not, while providing a flexible methodology to try innovative programs and promising strategies.[16]

Community Policing Models

Many cities have implemented a blend of community policing strategies with CompStat. To understand the merger of these important movements and the evolution of policing today, three historical case studies that highlight the evolution of the community policing philosophy are presented: Newport News, Virginia; Chicago, Illinois; and Minneapolis, Minnesota.

Newport News, Virginia

In 1983, under the direction of a new chief, Darrel Stephens, the Newport News Police Department developed a "problem-oriented" approach to policing. Known as **problem-oriented policing**, this innovative style of community policy focused on the department's traditional response to major, recurring problems. Its goal was to reassess the traditional, incident-driven aspects of police work and fundamentally change the way the Newport News Police Department viewed its mission. The resulting self-analysis yielded an important four-step, problem-solving methodology (commonly referred to as **SARA**) that has become an integral part of daily operations (see Figure 2.3).

Scanning—Instead of relying on broad, law-related concepts, such as robbery, burglary, and auto theft, officers are encouraged to group individual, related

Figure 2.3
The problem-solving system used in Newport News, Virginia, Police Department.
Source: William Speiman and John E. Eck. "Problem Oriented Policing," in *Research in Brief* (Washington, D.C.: National Institute of Justice, October 1988), p. 4.

IN THE NEWS Did Community Policing and Compstat Really Drive Down Crime in New York City?

A recent survey of over 100 retired NYPD captains and senior executives found that they believed crime statistics had been manipulated to portray lower crime rates for the Compstat program under then Commissioner William J. Bratton. The "broken windows" theory, pioneered by George L. Kelling in the 1990s, focuses on "zero-tolerance policing"—that is, aggressive enforcement against minor quality-of-life crimes, like loitering and public intoxication. In a startling revelation, those surveyed said that Compstat does *not* deter repeat offenders and does *not* drive crime down. The management accountability aspect of Compstat is supposed to reinforce a response by the police to, again, drive crime down. Over 500 major police departments use Compstat as a management methodology to help reduce crime, but is it really effective? One researcher, Andrew Karmen, a sociologist from John Jay College of Criminal Justice, indicates that recent studies indicate that after adopting the Compstat model from the NYPD, the results are mixed at best: "Philadelphia is "in the grip of a murder wave," Seattle's homicide rate decline "has flattened out," and the New Orleans Police Department remains as ineffective as it was before Hurricane Katrina. The same dismal trend goes for Minneapolis, Louisville, Boston, and Baltimore." Now, new evidence suggests the NYPD executives may have "cooked the books" in order to show lower crime rates during stressful Compstat meetings—in other words, the Compstat Model originally developed by Bratton in New York City may have been flawed all along. Recent research raises the question as to whether the use of Compstat actually encourages police and district attorneys to manipulate crime statistics and reporting.

(http://assets.nydailynews.com/img/2009/12/24/alg_nypd_police_badge.jpg)

Source: Sewell Chan, "Why Did Crime Fall in New York City," *The New York Times* (August 13, 2007) and Rob Kall, "NYPD Cops Fudged Crime Stats in Compstat Model Program Now Used in Hundreds of US Cities," *OpEdNews.com* (February 7, 2010). See http://www.opednews.com/articles/2/NYPD-Cops-Fudged-Crime-Sta-by-Rob-Kall-100207-650.html

incidents that come to their attention as "problems" and define these problems in more precise and useful terms. For example, an incident that typically would be classified simply as a "robbery" might be seen as part of a pattern of prostitution-related robberies committed by transvestites in center-city hotels. In essence, officers are expected to look for possible problems and accurately define them as part of their daily routine.

Analysis—Officers working on a well-defined problem then collect information from a variety of public and private sources, not just traditional police data, such as criminal records and past offense reports. Officers rely on problem analysis guides that direct officers to examine offenders, victims, the social and physical environment, and previous responses to the problem. The goal is to understand the scope, nature, and causes of the problem and formulate a variety of options for its resolution.

Response—The knowledge gained in the analysis stage is then used to develop and implement solutions. Officers seek the assistance of citizens, businesses, other police units, other public and private organizations, and anyone else who can help develop a program of action. Solutions may go well beyond traditional police responses to include other community agencies and/or municipal organizations.

Assessment—Finally, officers evaluate the impact and the effectiveness of their responses. Were the original problems actually solved or alleviated? They may use the results to revise a response, to collect more data, or even to redefine the problem.[17]

Goldstein[18] further explains this systematic process in his book *Problem-Oriented Policing*. Destined to become a classic in the field, Goldstein's work attempts to give meaning to each of the four steps. For instance, a *problem* is expanded to mean a cluster of similar, related, or recurring incidents rather than a single incident. The assumption is that few incidents are isolated; instead they are part of a wider set of urban social phenomena. Examples of such community problems are the following:

- Disorderly youth who regularly congregate in the parking lot of a specific convenience store
- Street prostitutes and associated "jack roll" robberies of patrons that continually occur in the same area
- Drunk and drinking drivers around the skid-row area of the city
- Panhandlers, vagrants, and other displaced people living on the sidewalk in a business district
- Juvenile runaways, prostitutes, and drug dealers congregating at the downtown bus depot
- Robberies of commercial establishments at major intersections of a main thoroughfare of a suburban area that is a corridor leading out of a large central city[19]

Note that each of these problems incorporates not only a potential or real crime but also a wider community/social issue. Further, each problem has been identified with a specific location. Goldstein[20] emphasizes that the traditional functions of crime analysis under the problem-solving methodology take on much wider and deeper importance. The pooling of data and subsequent analysis provide the basis for problem identification and response strategies. Therefore, the accuracy and timeliness of such information becomes a necessity for the department. However, the ultimate challenge in problem-oriented policing is not the identification of problems but rather the integration of the community with the police in developing effective ways of dealing with them (see Figure 2.4).

Figure 2.4
*Officers focus on prob-
lem solving in tradition-
ally high crime areas,
such as low-income,
densely populated urban
settings. Providing
quality policing and an
improved image are
important parts of the
community policing
movement.*
(Courtesy of Larry Kolvoord/
The Image Works)

Chicago, Illinois

In January 1993, Mayor Richard Daley and then-Police Superintendent Matt L.
Rodriguez announced the first major operational changes to set in place community
policing in the city of Chicago. The new program, the **Chicago Alternative Policing
Strategy (CAPS)**, was designed to move the department from a traditional, reactive,
incident-driven agency to a more proactive and community-oriented department. At
first, CAPS was hailed as a method to combat crime, drugs, and gang activity in the
inner city. However, as the implementation plan unfolded, a much broader mission
statement evolved that focused on a combined effort with the community to "identify
and solve problems of crime and disorder and to improve the quality of life in all of
Chicago's neighborhoods."[21]

As in many large cities implementing community policing, Chicago developed
five prototype districts to serve as "laboratories" for testing new police ideas, innovations, and strategies (see Figure 2.5).

These districts could then refine the successful new programs and hence improve the CAPS model. Essentially, the new CAPS program echoed the methodology for implementing community policing in several other large metropolitan cities
at the time. For instance, in Houston, Texas and New York City, under the direction of then-Commissioner Lee P. Brown, the transition to community policing
occurred only in select neighborhoods or districts and was known as **neighborhood-
oriented policing**. Similar programs evolved in Phoenix, Arizona; Miami, Florida;
Philadelphia, Pennsylvania; and Newark, New Jersey. Only a few cities attempted to
implement community policing strategies on a department-wide basis (Portland,
Oregon and Baltimore, Maryland). Most cities, and particularly large metropolitan

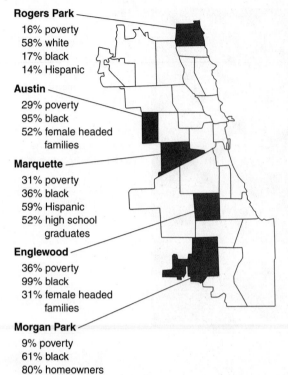

Rogers Park
- 16% poverty
- 58% white
- 17% black
- 14% Hispanic

Austin
- 29% poverty
- 95% black
- 52% female headed families

Marquette
- 31% poverty
- 36% black
- 59% Hispanic
- 52% high school graduates

Englewood
- 36% poverty
- 99% black
- 31% female headed families

Morgan Park
- 9% poverty
- 61% black
- 80% homeowners
- 62% long-term residents

Figure 2.5
Chicago's five experimental districts. Source: Susan M. Harnett and Wesley G. Skogan, "Community Policing: Chicago's Experience," *NIJ Journal* (April 1999): 3.

communities, realized that the implementation of community policing demanded dramatic modification in the existing philosophy, structure, operation, and deployment of police.[22] The gradual evolution toward full-scale adoption essentially continued to redefine both the means and ends of community policing.[23]

CAPS has a number of key features aimed at improving and expanding the overall quality of police services in the city of Chicago, as well as reducing crime.[24] These key features are the following:

- *Crime control and prevention*—CAPS emphasizes both crime control and crime prevention. Vigorous and impartial enforcement of the law, rapid response to serious crimes and life-threatening emergencies, and proactive problem solving with the community are the foundations of the city's policing strategy.
- *Neighborhood orientation*—CAPS gives special attention to the residents and problems of specific neighborhoods, which demands that officers know their beats (i.e., crime trends, hot spots, and community organizations and resources) and develop partnerships with the community to solve problems. Beat officers work the same beat on the same watch every day, so they can more intimately know the beat's residents, its chronic crime problems, and the best strategies for solving those problems.
- *Increased geographic responsibility*—CAPS involves organizing police services so that officers are responsible for crime control in a specific area or beat. A new district organizational structure using rapid-response cars to handle emergency calls allows newly created beat teams to engage in community policing activities. The beat teams share responsibility for specific areas under the leadership of a supervisory beat sergeant.
- *Structured response to calls for police service*—A system of differential responses to citizen calls frees beat team officers from the continuous demands of 911 calls. Emergency calls are handled primarily by rapid-response sector cars, whereas nonemergency and routine calls are handled by beat officers or by telephone call-back contacts. Sector officers also attend to community matters, and sector and beat teams rotate, so that all officers participate in community policing.
- *Proactive, problem-solving approach*—CAPS focuses on the causes of neighborhood problems rather than on discrete incidents of crime or disturbances. Attention is given to the long-term prevention of these problems and to the signs of community disorder and decay that are associated with crime (e.g., "hot spots" such as drug houses, loitering youth, and graffiti).
- *Combined community and city resources for crime prevention and control*—CAPS assumes that police alone cannot solve the crime problem and that they

depend on the community and other city agencies to achieve success. Hence, part of the beat officer's new role is to broker community resources and to draw on other city agencies to identify and respond to local problems. Former Mayor Daley made CAPS a priority of all city agencies. Hence, the mayor's office ensures that municipal agencies are responsive to requests for assistance from beat officers.

- *Emphasis on crime and problem analysis through the CompStat process*—CAPS requires more efficient data collection and analysis to identify crime patterns and to target areas that demand police attention. Emphasis is placed on crime analysis at the district level, and beat information is recorded and shared among officers and across watches or shifts. To accomplish such a task, each district has implemented a local area network of advanced computer workstations employing a crime analysis system called ICAM (Information Collection for Automated Mapping). This new technology allows beat officers and other police personnel to analyze and map crime hot spots, to track other neighborhood problems, and to share this information with the community. The CAPS project also instituted a rigorous CompStat process designed to take CAPS to the next level through management accountability.[25]

- *Training*—The Chicago Police Department has made a significant commitment to training police personnel and the community in the CAPS philosophy and program. Intensive training on problem solving and community partnerships is being provided to district patrol officers and their supervisors. Innovative classroom instruction for the community and a program of joint police–community training have also been developed.

- *Communication and marketing*—The Chicago Police Department is dedicated to communicating the CAPS philosophy to all members of the department and the community. This is a fundamental strategy of the CAPS program. To ensure such communication, an intensive marketing program has been adopted that includes a newsletter, roll-call training, a regular cable television program, information exchanges via computer technology (Internet and fax machines), and various brochures and videos. Feedback is collected through personal interviews, focus groups, community surveys, a CAPS hotline, and several suggestion boxes. The information collected through this marketing program assists in the refinement and development of the CAPS program.

- *Evaluation, strategic planning, and organizational change*—The CAPS program is undergoing one of the most thorough evaluations of any community policing initiative in the United States. A consortium of four major Chicago-area universities (Northwestern, DePaul, Loyola, and the University of Illinois at Chicago) is conducting an evaluation of the process and results in the prototype districts.

Today, CAPS represents one of the largest and most comprehensive community policing initiatives in the country (see Figure 2.6). During its first 10 years of operation,

evaluation findings indicated that major crime and neighborhood problems were reduced, drug and gang problems were reduced, and public perception of the quality of police services was improved.[26] Under this orientation, the community is viewed as a valuable resource from which powerful information and ties can be gathered. It aims "to increase the interaction and cooperation between local police and the people and

Figure 2.6
(a) Chicage community policing at a glance.

Chicago's community policing effort is more extensive and more organized than programs in most other jurisdictions, and it permeates the city to a greater extent than in most others. Below is an "at a glance" description of a typical, more limited program compared to Chicago's program.

Chicago's Community Policing Model

Police

- The entire patrol division is involved.
- The program is fully staffed with permanent officers on regular shifts.
- Extensive training is given to both officers and supervisors.
- All districts and all shifts are involved.
- Program activities are supervised through the regular chain of command and through standard patrol operations.

Residents

- Residents are expected to take an active role in solving problems.
- Residents are encouraged to meet with police regularly to exchange information and report on actions taken.
- Public priorities play an important role in setting beat team priorities.
- Residents receive training in Chicago's problem-solving model.

Municipal Services

- Management systems are in place to trigger a rapid response to service requests.
- Agencies are held accountable by the mayor for the effectiveness of their response.
- Community policing is the entire city's program, not the police department's program.

More Limited Community Policing Model

Police

- Small units are staffed by officers who have volunteered for a community policing assignment.
- Officers work overtime and are usually paid with temporary federal funding.
- Officers work on evening shift only.
- Little training is provided; officers' personal motivation propels the program.
- Officers are assigned only to selected areas.
- Program activities are supervised by the chief's office or from outside the routine command structure.

Residents

- Residents are asked to be the police department's "eyes and ears."
- Surveys or postcards are distributed to residents as a way of gathering information.
- Residents are called to meet occasionally, to publicize the program.
- Residents have no role in setting police priorities or operations.

Municipal Services

- Service agencies have no special responsibility to police or citizen groups.
- Service agencies believe community policing is the police department's program and should be funded by the police department's budget.

(a)

(Continued)

(b)

(b) *Chicago Alternative Policing Strategy (CAPS) Gun Turn-In Event, represents an on-going partnership with the community to curb gang violence.*
Source: http://mayor.cityofchicago.org/mayor/en/photo_galleries/press_room_photo_galleries/201 (retrieved on July 16, 2010).

neighborhoods they serve" to combat crime.[27] Hence, the major goals of community policing are not only to reduce crime but, more significantly, to increase feelings of safety among residents.[28] These two goals appear to be separate but are actually very closely linked in the community policing process. This approach attempts to increase the visibility and accessibility of police to the community. Through this process, police officers are no longer patrol officers enforcing the laws of the state but rather neighborhood officers. These officers infiltrate local neighborhoods, targeting specific areas in need of improvement. By involving themselves within the community, the officers are more available to meet and discuss the specific problems and concerns of each neighborhood and work to develop long-term solutions.[29] These solutions are the root of the proactive approach to policing. By listening to the public, the police will be better informed of the specific problems in each area. As cooperation between police and citizens in solving neighborhood problems increases, residents feel more secure.[30]

Minneapolis, Minnesota

Comparing the core principles of CompStat with the problem-solving model of Newport News, presented earlier, reveals a significant amount of similarity. Indeed, CompStat may well be the natural evolution of the problem-solving model in today's more sophisticated cities. It is important that Chicago's CAPS program incorporated CompStat as a vehicle to enhance crime fighting and management accountability. While a number of jurisdictions, including Los Angeles, Philadelphia, New Oreleans, Albuquerque, Sacramento, Boston, and Dallas, continue to refine the CompStat principles, none has been more successful in implementing the process than the Minneapolis Police Department.

In Minneapolis, the CompStat program is referred to as **CODEFOR** (**C**omputer **O**ptimized **DE**ployment—**F**ocus **O**n **R**esults). This strategy is designed specifically to reduce crime and involves every geographical and structural unit within the Minneapolis Police Department. CODEFOR combines the latest technology in computer applications and geographical mapping with field-proven police techniques. Computer-generated maps identify high-intensity crime areas, and police resources are coordinated to such locations in a timely manner. Each week, police managers gather together and ask directed questions regarding the crime rates in each of their areas. Colorful crime maps are projected on large screens, and computer-generated bulletins are passed out at the meeting (see Figure 2.7)

Departmental executives and commanders grill precinct captains on the crimes in their areas. Precinct captains, while not expected to be able to eliminate crime entirely, are expected to articulate a sensible strategy for reversing a trend or eliminating a hot spot. In many cases, those leaders who repeatedly fail to rise to the occasion—not unlike what might happen to the manager of a struggling department in a corporation—have found themselves promptly reassigned. The process works, as police managers are held accountable for reducing crime in their areas. A more enlightened understanding of why the process works is that it gets the top police managers involved with crime once again. In addition to the solution of internal problems, attendance at community meetings, scheduling, and a myriad of other administrative tasks, managers are forced to direct their efforts to addressing crime in their geographical districts of responsibility. This emphasis on crime awareness and crime fighting has sparked renewed feelings of self-worth among managers as well as an increase in communication between the beat officer and the precinct captain. Everyone realizes that individual performance and success are dependent on their relationship and their interconnectiveness in addressing crime within the precinct. Obviously, a more team-oriented spirit naturally arises that increases morale and supports the primary goals of CompStat under the CODEFOR program.[31]

The Minneapolis Police Department is one of the few departments not only to generate specific crime statistics each week by geographical area but also to use a much more refined process of tabulating success or failure. Interestingly, the reports are also provided over the Internet on a monthly basis for public consumption and evaluation.[32]

The major case studies presented (Newport News, Chicago, and Minneapolis) represent only three attempts to develop community policing and CompStat initiatives in the United States. Policing continues to develop and change; it is organic. As such, cities large and small are experimenting with best practices in attempts to significantly reduce crime and improve the quality of life within their communities.

Minneapolis Calls for Service
Shooting - Sound of Shots Fired - Shotspotter Activations
July 6 - July 12, 2010

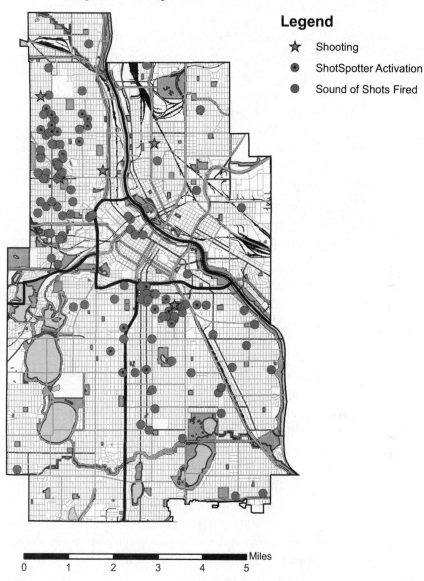

Legend

★ Shooting

● ShotSpotter Activation

● Sound of Shots Fired

Miles
0 1 2 3 4 5

Minneapolis Police Department
Crime Analysis Unit
350 S. 5th St - Room 100
Minneapolis, MN 55415
612-673-2470

Information obtained from 911 CAD System.
NOTE: One incident may be represented by multiple Icons in the map, depending upon the number of callers and location of incoming calls.
**Officers are dispatched to the location where the shooting victim is currently at, which may include the hospital, or location different from the actual shooting incident.

Figure 2.7

Minneapolis' CODEFOR program merges community policing with Compstat. Police executives are held accountable for their strategic response to calls for service and crime. Minneapolis is one of the few departments that shares its crime bulletins and analysis maps with the public on a weekly basis via their website.

Source: http://www.ci.minneapolis.mn.us/police/crime-statistics/codefor/650_MinneapolisShotsFired.pdf, retrieved on July 16, 2010.

Policing Strategies Today

As stated earlier, traditional policing responses appear to be ineffective in reducing crime. Indeed, in his review of what works in policing, Sherman documented the weak empirical support linking random patrols, reactive arrests, and rapid response to significant, if any, decreases in crime.[33] More contemporary policing approaches and strategies, however, have also revealed similar levels of inefficacy. In particular, research has provided little in terms of support for problem-oriented policing as presented through broken windows and zero tolerance.[34] Furthermore, despite the widespread popularity of community policing strategies, most studies evaluating this type of policing have not found that it greatly impacts crime or disorder; at best, community policing reduces citizens' fear of crime,[35] and produces core challenges to police organization as it attempts to restructure and change to adapt to community policing ideologies.[36]

Nevertheless, new policing approaches and tactics are currently being used by police departments in the United States with promising results. Geographic-based and focused policing approaches, such as **hot-spots policing** and directed patrols, represent the most strongly supported policing practices in the United States,[37] aided by the use of geographical information systems (GIS), crime analysis, and artificial intelligence. Similarly, **intelligence-led policing (ILP)** and proactive policing models are also gaining attention as police departments look for ways to do more with fewer resources. Although currently under-researched and new, the geographic-based policing approaches have emerged as innovative strategies for reducing crime and increasing citizen satisfaction with police services. Unfortunately, the sheer number of new and innovative paradigms to combat crime appears to be escalating by the year. Students and scholars alike often have problems segregating and differentiating the various types of policing strategy that may be employed in one city, or for that matter, in one sector of a city. Many of the police strategies employed today are similar, particularly those that are geographically based, with only minor additions or tactical differences. Indeed, many of the "strategies" could be much more easily classified as a police tactic aimed at reducing crime in a specific neighborhood over a specific period of time. The myriad of new names and models has given rise to the thought that the real differences between policing strategies may be more "rhetoric than reality."

Evidence-Based Policing

In recent years, researchers have focused on building a knowledge base as it pertains to what is known about the effectiveness of criminal justice strategies. The ultimate goal is to provide practitioners with sound empirical evidence to help them make informed decisions regarding related policies and programs. **Evidence-based policing** is a reflection of this philosophy. According to Sherman, "evidence-based policing is the use of the best available research on the outcomes of police work to implement guidelines and evaluate agencies, units, and officers."[38] Rather than focusing on "how" to do police work, as in community policing, or utilizing a generalized problem-solving approach to crime, as in problem-oriented policing, evidence-based policing is a paradigm that utilizes the scientific method to identify, implement, evaluate, and modify the methods that are most effective in reducing crime.[39]

Targeted policing illustrates evidence-based policing in practice. It is place-, offense-, offender-, and time-specific; in other words, it forces police officers to focus on the individual incident as opposed to the type of crime.[40] Several individual projects have provided support for the use of target-based interventions in reducing crime and the fear of crime. For instance, the Washington, DC Repeat Offender Project (ROP) was a program implemented in 1982 aimed at increasing the rate of repeat offender arrests. Based on the evidence that a small proportion of individuals commit a disproportionate amount of crime, it was anticipated that arrests of high-rate offenders would impact crime rates. These individuals were proactively identified and targeted by police officers. Results of the two-year study revealed that the likelihood of arrest for repeat offenders increased significantly compared to other groups, and that

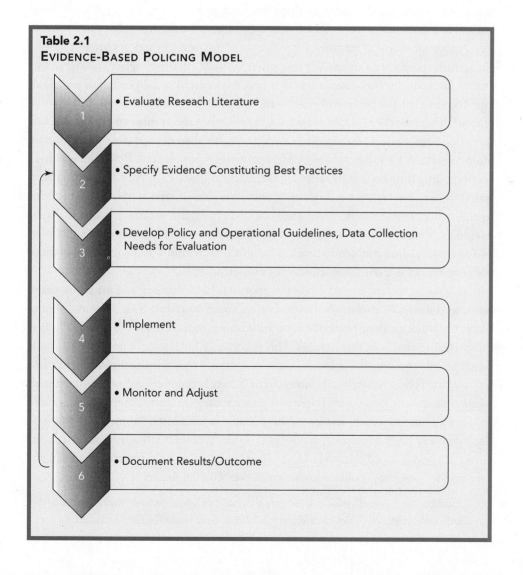

Table 2.1
EVIDENCE-BASED POLICING MODEL

1. • Evaluate Reseach Literature

2. • Specify Evidence Constituting Best Practices

3. • Develop Policy and Operational Guidelines, Data Collection Needs for Evaluation

4. • Implement

5. • Monitor and Adjust

6. • Document Results/Outcome

the arrested individuals had histories of much more serious and chronic offending—crime rates in targeted areas decreased significantly.[41]

The findings from other studies, however, have not been as supportive of this approach. More specifically, the Redlands Second Response Program, also based on targeting repeat offenders, did not observe a reduction in domestic violent victimization.[42] This proactive program was designed with the purpose of educating and providing domestic violence victims with social services to reduce dependency on their abusers. While this type of crime was not reduced within the community under study, the problem may well be with the type of crime rather than the strategy; family violence may be a more difficult crime to deter and prevent than more predatory, stranger-to-stranger crimes.

Hot-Spots Policing

Much like evidence-based policing, hot-spots policing reflects the direct application of empirical data (through various crime analysis and information technologies) that show that crime is *not* randomly dispersed, but rather is concentrated in isolated areas.[43] In their seminal work, Sherman and colleagues found that only a few locations were responsible for a majority of police calls for service and reported crime—particularly predatory crimes like muggings, vehicle thefts, burglary, robbery, and rape.[44] Additionally, they found that all robberies occurred at 2.2 percent of places, all rapes occurred at 1.2 percent of places, and all auto thefts occurred at 2.7 percent of places.[45] These areas or "places" with a higher than average number of crimes are "hot spots," and represent areas that reflect not only higher than normal crime rates, but are often inhabited by lower-income and high-density populations.[46] Similar to these findings, drug distribution also appears to cluster. In Jersey City, New Jersey drug "hot spots" were responsible for a disproportionate number of arrests and calls for service to the police. Furthermore, these areas also experienced a greater amount of issues related to crime and disorder compared to other areas; that is, serious crime, disorder, and street-level drug problems cluster in certain areas within the city. Deploying more police resources to these areas reduces the clustering effect.[47]

Although the concept of crime hot spots has been documented for many years, hot-spot policing is a relatively innovative approach to crime. This type of policing forces the police to identify specific areas with undue concentrations of crime and then direct their resources at those places. This is certainly not a novel idea, and the traditional patrol sergeants of the 1960s could have argued that a map, a few colored pins, and a series of crime reports could have told us "where to send officers" on routine patrol. Again, this appears to be a very important police strategy, particularly in reducing more predatory crimes, recently reinforced by a study in Charlotte, North Carolina. The deployment of street crime units in hot-spot robbery areas not only significantly reduced crime, but also reduced the level of fear expressed by citizens.[48] However, the strongest support for "hot-spots" policing comes from the National Academy of Sciences:

> Studies that focused police resources on crime hot spots provide the strongest
> collective evidence of police effectiveness that is now available. On the basis of a
> series of randomized experimental studies, we conclude that the practice

described as hot-spots policing is effective in reducing crime and disorder and can achieve these reductions without significant displacement of crime control benefits. Indeed, the research evidence suggests that the diffusion of crime control benefits to areas surrounding treated hot spots is stronger than any displacement outcome.[49]

Despite the evidence in support of hot-spots policing, it is uncertain as to what specific tactics have the most influence in problem areas, given the wide array of intervention tactics that are used within the model.[50] For example, hot-spots policing tactics include directed patrols, saturation patrol, aggressive traffic enforcement, zero-tolerance and disorder enforcement, as well as specific drug "buy and bust" programs, even focused problem-oriented policing techniques. In addition, some scholars argue that hot spots do not actually exist in the real world; that is, hot spots are an "amalgam" of different types of locations that simply cluster on a map; they are a product of data construction.[51] These data points could be addresses, buildings, apartment complexes, block faces, census tracks or individual police sectors; however, they are a temporary product of the data world, a logical fallacy that is impossible to operationally identify using agreed upon, replicable, and scientific criteria.[52]

Today, many police departments are utilizing a hot-spots strategy banking on those studies that show that it reduces and prevents crime; however, they are also utilizing a plethora of patrol and arrest techniques that most likely have varying effects on crime in specific places. Future research in this area should focus on parceling-out the various techniques and tactics used in each type of hot spot and measuring the impact of each. Hypothetically, we may well find that it is not one approach, but rather the cumulative impact of visible police patrol and the employment of various arrest tactics that most likely impacts crime the most in a specific area.

Directed and Saturation Patrols

Directed and saturation patrols are tactics commonly used in policing. Although these strategies are considered low on the scale of diverse approaches, they are often used in conjunction with hot-spots policing. While directed patrol usually involves the "directing" of patrol officers to specific locations during their patrol shift, saturation patrol concentrates *additional* officers on specific locations at specific times. The idea is to maximize visible patrol efforts in a specific area. Both types of patrol involve the assignment of officers to problematic areas for proactive enforcement at high-risk times.[53] In theory, increased police presence through directed and saturation patrols in these areas and times is expected to arrest offenders responsible for a great majority of these crimes and generate reductions in crime. It is, however, unknown as to whether crime is actually reduced or simply moved to another location (displaced); when police visibility is increased, offenders often move to other areas of the city.

There is also conflicting evidence that calls into question the effectiveness of directed and saturation patrols as an effective crime control strategy versus more aggressive arrest tactics. Fritsch, Caeti, and Taylor evaluated police strategies aimed at

reducing gang violence in Dallas, Texas.[54] Their initiative targeted five areas that housed seven of the most violent gangs in the city. Officers spent a majority of their time utilizing three suppression tactics, including aggressive curfew enforcement, aggressive truancy enforcement, and saturation patrol, making patrols highly visible in the targeted areas. Although aggressive curfew and truancy enforcement were related to significant reductions in gang violence, saturation patrols did not produce the same effects (see Figure 2.8). Once again, more aggressive arrest techniques in specific areas during specific times aimed at specific predatory crimes may be the most effective tactic in reducing crime.

Intelligence-Led Policing (ILP)

Unlike directed and saturation patrols, intelligence-led policing is not a tactic, nor is it a crime-reduction strategy, but rather a business model for policing. It is "an information-organizing process that allows police agencies to better understand their crime problems and take a measure of the resources available to be able to decide on an enforcement tactic or prevention strategy best designed to control crime."[55] More specifically, intelligence-led policing utilizes criminal intelligence analysis as a means to accomplish crime prevention and reduction through best practices and partnerships with other entities.

There are a number of reasons as to why intelligence-led policing has become popular in recent years. First, widespread recognition of the ineffectiveness of the standard policing model and the difficulty in implementing problem-orienting

Figure 2.8
Officers patrol neighborhoods, focusing on crime control and high-order maintenance activities.
(Courtesy of Dorothy Littell Greco/The Image Works)

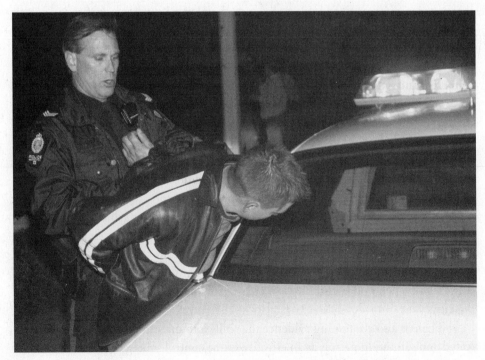

policing has caused police departments to look for alternatives. Second, departments are increasingly faced with financial constraints though demands remain high and the opportunities to employ additional resources and personnel are limited. Third, more sophisticated technologies in information retrieval and analysis of police information have generated interest in systematic approaches to crime.[56]

Although intelligence-led policing emerged in the United States after the September 11th terrorist attacks, the movement toward this approach actually began prior to the 1990s and originated in the United Kingdom.[57] At that time, it was recommended by the Audit Commission that police services should *focus on the offender* rather than focus on reported crime. The British government subsequently passed legislation requiring police departments to adopt the National Intelligence Model, which promoted intelligence-led policing.

It is important to note that intelligence is more than simply data; it also involves information. Whereas data are "identifiable, objective facts about events," information is the addition of context and analysis that puts data into comprehensible forms.[58] Data and information do not become intelligence until they are interpreted, evaluated, and used as a means to inform crime prevention and reduction strategies. In ILP, these objectives are believed to be obtainable primarily through the proactive and objective identification and targeting of the criminal subpopulation.[59]

A recent example of intelligence-led policing in practice is Operation Nine Connect. Ratcliffe and Guidetti report that the New Jersey State Police implemented a gang crackdown in 2008 targeting Nine Trey—a subset of the much larger and well-known "Bloods" gang.[60] Together, officers involved in the crackdown conducted over 8,000 hours of electronic surveillance and more than 2,300 hours of physical surveillance, as well as spent over 1,200 hours transcribing wiretaps and approximately 300 hours developing and maintaining confidential sources. The result was the initial arrest of 60 gang members and the subsequent arrest of at least 30 others.

Despite the popularity and the successes of intelligence-led policing, there are a number of limitations associated with this type of approach, including data entry problems and lack of training in advanced analytic techniques within the police. In addition, Ratcliffe notes the organizational problems of intelligence-led policing, such as the lack of continuity in structure across intelligence units and the confusion over the principles of intelligence-led crime reduction.[61] In addition, as discussed later in Chapter 3, some argue that ILP may well be in conflict with civil and constitutional safeguards that ensure that individuals are "innocent until proven guilty." Focusing on specific individuals as offenders tests this important principle of our democracy.

Predictive Policing

Similar to intelligence-led policing, **predictive policing** is a proactive approach to crime and disorder that uses information and analytical tools to achieve the goal of crime prevention while requiring fewer resources.[62] Not only does predictive policing improve upon intelligence-led policing, it also reflects the principles of problem-oriented, community, and evidence-based policing.[63] According to Beck and McCue, "With new technology, new business processes, and new algorithms, predictive policing is based on directed, information-based patrol; rapid response supported by fact-based prepositioning of assets; and proactive, intelligence-based tactics, strategy, and policy."[64] Consequently, one of the key components of predictive policing is the use of advanced analytics that evaluate and examine data and information through advanced statistics and artificial intelligence. In other words, predictive policing utilizes numerous technologies and techniques such as data mining, crime mapping, and geospatial prediction to plan for and respond to future crime.

Advanced analytics have been used in a variety of capacities from preventing violent crimes to improving deployment, response planning, and policy decision making. For example, police in Richmond, Virginia used advanced analytics and predictive policing to reduce random gunfire on New Year's Eve. Based on information collected from previous years, police were able to predict the time, location, and type of incident most likely to occur on that particular night. In preparation, officers were placed at those locations to prevent and quickly respond to such crimes. The end result was a 47 percent reduction in random gunfire and a significant increase in the number of seized weapons.[65]

Although predictive policing is a new and promising approach, it too has generated a number of questions and concerns. A major criticism is the novelty of predictive policing given its semblance to other policing models, particularly ILP. Moreover, the central tenets of predictive policing closely resemble what crime analysts have been doing for years. Still, others argue that the outcomes of the model are vague and unclear.[66]

Information Technologies in Policing

The evolution of policing strategies has included the development and use of sophisticated information technologies. Today, information technologies assume a new and more vital role. For instance, police operations are incredibly data and information intensive. Rather than utilizing computers for data storage, police departments are now using them as information and knowledge-based systems.[67] This is especially important as police agencies rely more heavily upon intelligence as well as the identification and targeting of crime hot spots and repeat offenders. Crime analysis, geographic information systems (GIS), and artificial intelligence represent the most widely used information technologies in policing today.

Crime Analysis

As the dynamics of policing move toward an information-driven and evidence-based agenda, the need for accurate analyses is becoming increasingly important.

▸▸ Crime Rates Fall in the First Half of 2009

For the third year in a row, crime rates in the United States show that violent crime (down 4.4% overall), property crime (down 6.1% overall, and arson (down 8.2% overall) continue to decline. Researchers point to new policing strategies that impact crime and offending as the primary reason for such dramatic decreases.

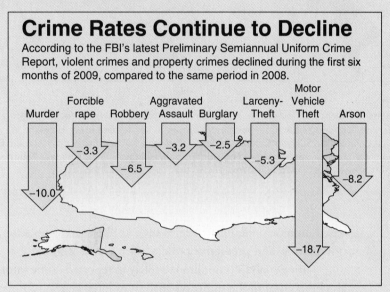

Crime Rates Continue to Decline

According to the FBI's latest Preliminary Semiannual Uniform Crime Report, violent crimes and property crimes declined during the first six months of 2009, compared to the same period in 2008.

Source: http://www.fbi.gov.page2/dec09/crimestats_122109.html (retrieved July 20, 2010).

Consequently, crime analysis has emerged as a means to satisfy this requirement. **Crime analysis** is the process of identifying patterns and relationships between crime data and other relevant data sources to prioritize and target police activity.[68] The uneven distribution of crime in terms of space and place, type of offenders, and victimization theoretically allows analysts to draw inferences from patterns of crime, which can be used as a foundation for allocating police resources. In other words, crime analysis generates associations and relationships between variables (like space, time, offenders, and victims) that are related to crime. The purpose of crime analysis is to organize massive quantities of raw information from data bases used in automated records systems and to forecast specific, future events from the statistical manipulation of these data. In theory, crime analysis provides a thorough and systematic analysis of data on which to make rational decisions regarding past, present, and future actions.[69] Crime analysis is critical when deploying resources

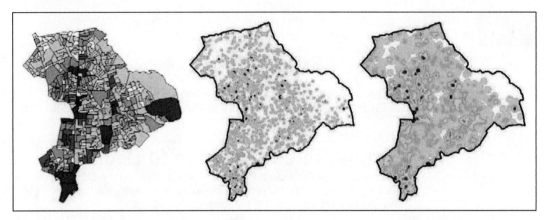

Figure 2.9
*A series of "hot spots" indicating vehicle crimes mapped by census track to varying hot spot thresholds.
Note that "hot spots" become much more apparent as the data used to create the maps are refined.
Source: John E. Eck, Spencer Chaney, James G. Cameron, Michael Leitner, and Ronald E. Wilson, NIJ Special
Report: Mapping Crime: Understanding Hot Spots (Washington, D.C.: National Institute of Justice, August 2005).
See: http://www.ncjrs.gov/pdffiles1/nij/209393.pdf*

based on new policing strategies such as "hot spots" policing, directed and saturation patrols, and predictive policing (see Figure 2.9).

Crime analysis is not limited solely to reported crime information. Attention has
also been given to the statistical analysis of intelligence information. Kinney[70] reports
that criminal intelligence analysis supports investigators, decision makers, and policymakers in their attempts to prevent and control crime. The following are some of the
more common crime analysis techniques:

- *Tactical crime analysis or crime-specific analysis*—a tabular or graphic display of
  reported crimes with a given pattern of time and/or location. It is often used to
  detect patterns of crime (e.g., robberies, burglaries, auto thefts) that cluster in
  specific locations during various time periods. The focus of tactical crime analysis is on recent criminal incidents through the examination of characteristics such
  as how, when, and where the activity has occurred in order to aid suspect identification and case clearance.[71]
- *Strategic crime analysis*—the study of crime and/or social problems in a specific area in an effort to determine long-term patterns of activity as well as to
  evaluate police responses and organizational procedures.[72] Strategic crime
  analysis is often used to determine the effectiveness of police over a given
  period of time, or in the evaluation of specific policing strategies as discussed
  earlier.
- *Link analysis*—a graphic portrayal of associations and relationships among
  people, organizations, events, activities, and locations from a given point in
  time. This technique is a powerful analytic tool used to reveal the hidden
  connections among criminals and the structure of clandestine, organized

criminal entities often found in street gangs, La Cosa Nostra families, white-collar crime syndicates, large drug trafficking cartels, and terrorist organizations. Link analysis is invaluable in complex investigations, particularly those that have a "conspiracy" aspect, as is often found in racketeering and continuing criminal enterprise cases. Link analysis is also a powerful tool used extensively in ILP.

- *Telephone toll analysis*—computerized reports derived from court-ordered long-distance telephone billings of suspects in illegal narcotics trafficking. Reports indicate the number and frequency of calls displayed in numerical, chronological, and geographical order. Link analysis can be used to show the relationship between billing numbers and the numbers called.[73]
- *Visual investigative analysis (VIA)*—charting that depicts key events of criminal activity in chronological order. VIA is used to show the degree of involvement of subjects. This method is especially convincing in conspiracy cases and can also be used as a planning tool to focus the resources of an investigative effort.[74] At a conference focusing on school shootings, a graphical VIA was presented on the Virginia Tech University shooting incident.[75] Interestingly, the VIA effort displayed a horizontal graph, over 60 feet long, with over 1,200 entries.
- *Case analysis and management system (CAMS)*—computerized case management in which large amounts of data are compiled and indexed for each retrieval of specific items. This system is used to clarify relationships and to calculate the probability of associations.[76]
- *Intelligence analysis*—the identification of networks of offenders and criminal activity, often associated with organized crime, gangs, drug traffickers, prostitution rings, and terrorist organizations. Recent interest in intelligence analysis has given rise to the development of large, centralized intelligence processing hubs, referred to as fusion centers (discussed later in Chapter 3, Intelligence, Terrorism, and Homeland Security). Intelligence analysis also becomes the basis for intelligence-led policing.

Crime analysis is a flexible and dynamic process designed primarily to identify trends and patterns associated with crime and social problems. It is designed to be a perpetual and continuous process and to assist law enforcement executives in making more informed decisions in their response to crime. The technology of crime analysis takes advantage of research and statistical methodologies, often in an automated process. It does not necessarily have to be relegated to advanced statistical techniques, but it can be accomplished quite well with a basic understanding of Microsoft Office programs, such as Word and Excel. Indeed, Mark Stallo's inviting work focuses on developing a relatively sophisticated crime analysis model based solely on the application of Microsoft Office products to reported police data.[77]

Geographic Information Systems (GIS)

The use of **geographic information systems (GIS)** in law enforcement to map criminal events coincided with the results of several environmental criminology studies that illustrated crime patterns. Prior to computerized mapping systems, police commonly used pin maps as a means of tracking crime. Unfortunately, this practice has many limitations due to the difficulties in determining clusters and general trends using point data.[78] However, with the advent of sophisticated computerized mapping, researchers have found a widespread adoption of GIS tools across police departments, particularly larger agencies[79] (see Figure 2.10).

There are two types of crime mapping: statistical spatial analysis and spatial modeling. Whereas statistical spatial analysis focuses on the spatial relationship between crime points in a particular area, spatial modeling is concerned with the

Figure 2.10
Geographic information systems (GIS) provide a wide array of maps and diagrams useful for crime analysis and decision making.
(Courtesy of the Dallas Police Department, 2010)

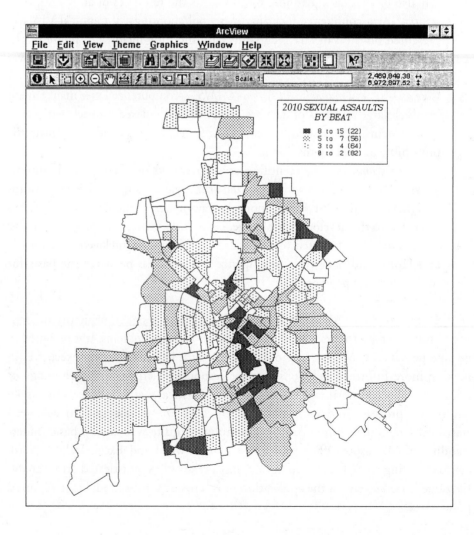

technology and application of data.[80] As previously mentioned, GIS has made these two components of crime mapping easy to use in the realm of policing. Given its functionality, it has become an influential mechanism in hot-spots policing as well as Crime Prevention Through Environmental Design (CPTED), situational policing, directed patrols, and crime analysis. For example, researchers used crime mapping in several of the previously mentioned case studies (the Minneapolis Hot Spots Patrol Project, Jersey City Drug Market Analysis Program, and Jersey City Problem-Oriented Policing at Violent Places) to evaluate the effectiveness of their police strategy. More specifically, analysts mapped official police data to pinpoint street addresses and intersections to be used as cluster areas or "hot spots."

Of course, GIS has a myriad of other uses in policing. Police agencies can use GIS in dispatching police units by providing directions to locations; address histories; and locations of nearby fire and waste hazards, fire hydrants, alarm boxes, high power lines, water lines, and the like. Police managers can not only use GIS to provide graphic analysis of specific crime patterns and to evaluate new policing strategies, but also to track individual officer performance by area.[81] Not surprisingly, GIS have emerged as powerful tools that help police executives make better-informed decisions. Due to its wide range of uses, it is likely that crime mapping and geographic information systems will remain key tools in police operations and in the evaluation of police strategies.

IN THE NEWS   Police Use of Expert Systems

New expert systems are being used in Phoenix, Arizona and Los Angeles, California to solve violent crimes. An expert system's matching and ranking capabilities, combined with the power of enlarging or narrowing the geographical scope of an inquiry, provide powerful tools for investigative analysis. In a crime scene scenario, for instance, with little or no evidence, an expert system can generate a demographic profile of a suspect based on variables such as type of crime, location, time of day, and method of entry (if applicable). The demographic profile can then be used to generate suspect lists while expanding or narrowing a geographical search based on similar criteria. In a like manner, the expert system can use the modus operandi (MO) of a particular crime to identify the set of solved and unsolved crimes with similar MOs. It is the expert system's ability to match the MO of crimes based on similarity that is so powerful, because it can take into account conflicting or incomplete information that conventional computer programs are hard-pressed to deal with effectively. In addition, COPLINK CompStat Analyzer provides a solution that automates data analysis and projection statistics from a myriad of database systems. This capability is critical for the new *Southern California Gang Emergency Operations Center (GEOC)*, a knowledge-based policing project that will connect law enforcement with local government, social services, educational institutions, and community and faith-based organizations focused on reducing gang violence in LA.

Source: Kevin J. Lynch and Frank J. Rogers, "Development of Integrated Criminal Justice Expert System Applications" (2006). See http://ai.arizona.edu/COPLINK/publications/develop/developm.html and Christine Miller, "COPLINK CompStat Analyzer Automates Crime Data Analysis" (2010). See http://www.officer.com/print/Law-Enforcement-Technology/COPLINK-CompStat-Analyzer-automates-crime-data-analysis/1$43834

Artificial Intelligence (AI)

Another type of information system having direct applications in law enforcement is **artificial intelligence (AI)**. Most definitions of AI vary to emphasize the interdisciplinary nature of the subject. Artificial intelligence is a science and a technology based on disciplines such as computer science, biology, psychology, linguistics, mathematics, and engineering. The goal of AI is to develop computers that can think as well as see, hear, walk, talk, and feel.[82] Basically, artificial intelligence can be defined as a shift from mere data processing to an intelligent processing of knowledge. The model for such development is the human body and brain. Artificial intelligence focuses on four major areas of research:

- *Natural language applications*—systems that translate ordinary human commands into language that computer programs can understand and execute; computer programs that read, speak, and understand human languages
- *Robotic applications*—machines that move and relate to objects as humans do; programs that focus on developing visual, tactile, and movement capabilities in machines
- *Computer science applications*—development of more advanced, fifth-generation computers and the replication of physical brain functioning, such as that found in the human cell-computer interfacing and neural networks
- *Cognitive science applications*—programs that mimic the decision-making logic of the human brain, such as that found in expert systems, knowledge-based systems, and logic systems

Figure 2.11 provides a schematic view of the major application domains of AI.

It is this last area of cognitive science applications involving expert systems that police managers find most promising. Basically, expert systems attempt to supplant rather than supplement human efforts in arriving at solutions to complex problems. For instance, the state of Washington used a case analysis expert system to provide suspect profiles in the Green River homicide investigation. The Baltimore, Maryland Police Department uses an expert system (known as ReBES—Residential Burglary Expert System) to assist in solving burglary cases.[83] The system correlates past suspect methods of operation with current burglary events to determine potential trends. About 25 specific items of information relating to a burglary are entered into the AI system, which provides a list of possible suspects, ranked in order of probability.[84] The Los Angeles Sheriff's Department uses a comprehensive database called CHIEFS to aid in homicide investigations. There are other knowledge-based products that link several databases together for easy information retrieval and analysis. One such product is *COPLINK Connect,* which provides one interface for users to access multiple databases. Evaluations of *COPLINK Connect* have been positive, and Chen reports that it directly led to the investigation of several cases in Seattle that would not have been identified if the databases had been accessed separately.[85] Other expert systems are being developed within the FBI's Behavioral Science Unit in

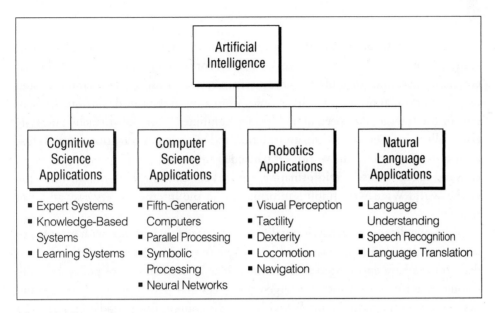

Figure 2.11
The Major application domains of artificial intelligence.
Source: J. A. O'Brien, *Management Information Systems: A Managerial End User Perspective*
[Homewood, Ill: Irwin, 1990], p. 357.

Quantico, Virginia, to support investigations of organized crime, narcotics, arson, and terrorism.[86]

AI development is not limited to traditional criminal investigations. For instance, in Chicago an artificial intelligence program is used to identify traits or behavior patterns shared by officers who have been fired for disciplinary reasons. The program, called "Brainmaker," is being used by the department as an automated "early warning system" intended to flag at-risk officers before they commit acts that could get them fired or arrested.[87]

On a more mundane level, expert systems are also being used to assist local police managers with complex planning and task scheduling. However, their greatest benefit may be in changing the way organizations behave by promoting a different perspective on problem solving. In law enforcement, this approach requires creative and innovative police executives who challenge traditional assumptions concerning the police function and mission. Indeed, with the development of expert systems that attempt to combine textbook guesses about a specific problem, executives need no longer rely on their own intuition or inspiration. What may have worked well in the past may appear foolish when contrasted to solutions based on expert systems.[88]

The future of expert systems and other AI applications holds great promise for law enforcement as the price and power of computer hardware improve and the sophistication of software development increases. The trend is clear. Police administrators will be using more AI-based technology as decision support systems in both operations and management.

The Internet

Clearly, one of the most important technological advantages of the information age is the Internet. The **Internet** is a worldwide network of computer systems and other computer networks that offers the opportunity for sending information to and receiving information from a vast audience from around the world. The unique benefits of the Internet are speed and efficiency combined with global reach. There are essentially no barriers to sending information and receiving information from as close as next door to around the world. Of particular importance to police agencies is the ease and speed with which information can be kept current. With the introduction of the World Wide Web, finding information on the Internet is very easy and user friendly.

Local police agencies have capitalized on the use of the Internet, with most major departments establishing their own home pages (see Figure 2.12). In addition, most departments have encouraged their communities to keep abreast of police activities through the Internet. A list of emergency services and phone numbers, names and descriptions of the most "wanted" fugitives in the community, periodic updates on a specific (usually high-profile) case, employment announcements and opportunities within the department, residential and commercial crime alerts, and even online crime reporting are now available through various departments on the Internet.

As worldwide communication and global reach via the Internet expand, policing will likely experience dramatic changes. For instance, the United Nations recently linked various criminal justice research institutes from different countries, allowing for the first time a free exchange of information among countries on issues impacting the world community (e.g., international terrorism, environmental crime, gangs, and computer fraud). New and combined training sessions, various telecommunication partnerships, and interactive information exchanges (podcasts and webinars) are now commonplace on the Internet. The greater access to information provided by the Internet has made a major difference in the future, not only for police agencies and researchers but also for individual communities addressing wider criminal justice issues. Certainly, the Internet has been one of the strongest catalysts for social, economic, and political change in the world.

The Impact of Information Technologies

Clearly, information technologies in policing have assumed a new and more vital role. They have taken on a new dimension, one that is central to the support of new policing strategies. The new task for information technologies is *analysis,* in addition to the storage and maintenance of information as in the past. The analytic support for various police strategies, however, must permeate the entire organizational structure and not be just a function of the crime analysis division. Information technology functionality must be much more flexible—ranging from support for quick, officer-level field inquiries to longitudinal mapping of a specific neighborhood to

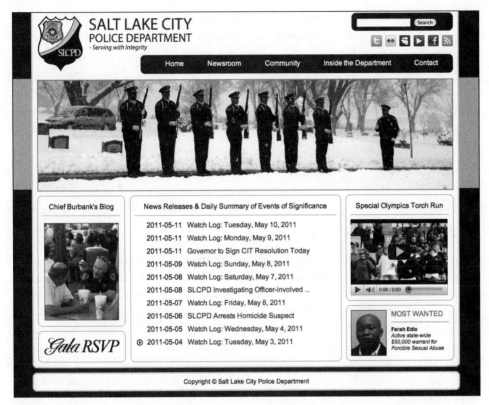

Figure 2.12
Most police departments use the Internet to share important information with their communities, including crime statistics, most wanted, local and homeland security news, recruitment efforts, and chief's messages. Note the linkages to other web portals (Facebook, YouTube, Twitter, Flickr, and MySpace) prominently displayed on the Salt Lake City Police Department Website.
Source: http://www.slcpd.com/ (retrieved on July 18, 2010).

specific managerial performance measurements. Information technologies can no longer be separated from the integral parts of police management and decision making. They can no longer be relegated solely to the storage, maintenance, and retrieval of vast amounts of police data. Most new policing strategies (e.g. community policing, evidence-based policing, predictive policing) are information-based and information-intensive and require the ability to identify problems, suggest specific police responses, and evaluate their effectiveness. This function cannot follow the same information-processing path as before.

Today's police officers must be equipped with information and training. The job still requires the ability to relate to various people under strained conditions in often hostile environments. New policing strategies involve new tactics that call for individual judgment and skill in relating to problems that are both criminal and noncriminal.

The police officer of the future must be able to relate to diverse groups of people in ways that stretch the imagination. To meet this challenge, police executives must ensure that three conditions exist. First, information technology development and design must support the emerging strategies in policing, particularly meeting the analytic demands embraced within such strategies. Second, police officers and executives must manage technology rather than allow themselves to be managed by it. Finally, individual police officers must understand their role in the community as aided by, but not controlled by, information technologies.

CONCLUSION

Although the strategies and techniques discussed in this chapter are promising mechanisms aimed at reducing and preventing crime and increasing the positive relationship between the police and the community, many are under-researched and controversial. This is not a new problem to policing, however. As Weisburd and Eck note, a number of strategies have not been systematically evaluated; this of course makes it difficult to formulate strong conclusions about any one strategy or technique.[89] Additionally, each community and police department is different—what works in Seattle may not be productive in New Orleans or Miami. Consequently, variation in policing interventions is likely to reflect this reality, thereby making evaluations and broad conclusions about policing styles, approaches, and philosophies all the more difficult. Even so, the evidence in support of place-based or hot-spots policing appears to be growing. In fact, Mastrofski and colleagues contend that there is "sufficiently strong and supportive empirical evidence to justify the launch of a national program that focuses on the development and evaluation of hot-spots policing."[90] Regardless of policing approaches, however, information technologies will continue to push law enforcement operations toward more proactive, knowledge-based practices.

CHAPTER REVIEW

1. Define *community policing*.
2. Describe the four-step problem-solving model commonly referred to as SARA.
3. Identify the problems commonly associated with traditional policing.
4. What is Herman Goldstein's definition of a *problem*?
5. What is the CAPS program?
6. Define *CompStat* and identify the core principles of CompStat as presented in the New York Police Department model.
7. Define some of today's new police strategies, such as hot spots policing, intelligence-led policing (ILP), and predictive policing.
8. List and briefly describe some of the more common crime analysis techniques.

9. Describe a geographic information system and explain how such a system enhances police service.

10. What has been the impact of information technologies on the police?

KEY TERMS

artificial intelligence (AI): Computer software systems focused on the intelligent processing of knowledge versus mere data processing; based on scientific disciplines.

CAPS: Chicago Alternative Policing Strategy; one of the largest and most comprehensive community policing initiatives in the United States, conducted by the Chicago Police Department during the 1990s.

CODEFOR: Computer Optimized DEployment—Focus On Results; one of the first experiments in the CompStat process, used in Minneapolis, Minnesota, designed specifically to reduce crime and improve the efficiency and effectiveness of the police department.

community policing: a policing philosophy that focuses on general neighborhood problems as a source of crime; community policing is preventive, proactive, and information-based.

CompStat: a police methodology using the most accurate and timely information to identify crime and social problems within a given geographic area and then to develop strategies designed to stop or prevent them from occurring in the future; CompStat holds police administrators accountable for their decisions, tactics, and strategies aimed at reducing crime.

crime analysis: the organization of massive quantities of raw data and information relating to reported crime in an effort to identify trends and patterns and then to forecast specific events from the statistical manipulation of these data.

directed and saturation patrols: more of a police tactic than a style, directed patrol usually involves the directing of patrol officers to specific locations during their patrol shift; saturation patrol concentrates *additional* officers on specific locations at specific times in an attempt to efficiently deploy officers as well as deter and prevent crime.

evidence-based policing: a style of policing using the best available research to guide, manage, and evaluate police operations within a community.

geographic information systems (GIS): the integration of automated database operations and high-level mapping to analyze, manipulate, and manage spatial data, particularly relevant to crime analysis and forecasting.

hot-spots policing: a geographically based approach to crime-fighting focused on in-depth analysis of "places" and times, and deploying police officers to those locations that account for the majority of calls for service and crime in a community.

intelligence-led policing (ILP): arising from the 9/11 terrorist attacks, ILP is a relatively new policing style focused on offenders, not crime incidents, using intelligence analysis to prevent crime.

Internet: a worldwide network of computer systems and other computer networks that offers the opportunity for sending information to and receiving information from a vast audience from around the world.

neighborhood-oriented policing: a style of community policing fostered by Lee P. Brown in Houston, Texas that focused on crime and social problems in select neighborhoods or districts.

predictive policing: a proactive policing style that uses information and analytical tools to prevent crime while using the fewest police resources possible.

problem-oriented policing: originally branded by Herman Goldstein, this style of policing addresses reoccurring social problems within a community through an innovative, four-step model called SARA.

SARA: a cyclical, four-step problem-solving methodology designed to enhance community policing: Scanning, Analysis, Response, and Assessment.

traditional policing: a style of policing based on response to calls for service after the activity has occurred; traditional policing is reactive and incident driven.

zero-tolerance policing (ZTP): a focused police strategy built on the philosophy that visible signs of social decay often lead to more serious crimes in a specific neighborhood; emphasis then, should be on strict enforcement of the law for even minor crimes of disorder.

ENDNOTES

[1] See Herman Goldstein, *Policing in a Free Society* (Cambridge, Mass.: Ballinger, 1977).

[2] See James Q. Wilson and George L. Kelling, "The Police and Neighborhood Safety: Broken Windows," *Atlantic Monthly,* no. 249 (1982): 29–38.

[3] See Y. Xu, M.L. Fiedler, and K.H. Flaming, "Discovering the Impact of Community Policing," Journal of Research in Crime and Delinquency, Vol. 42, No. 2, 2005, pp. 147–186.

[4] Hyunseok Jang, Larry T. Hoover, and Brian A. Lawton, "Effectiveness of Broken Windows Enforcement on Clearance Rates," *Journal of Criminal Justice*, Vol. 36, Issue 6, November/December 2008, p. 529. See also, National Research Council of the National Academies, *Fairness and Effectiveness in Policing: The Evidence* (The National Academies Press: Washington, D.C.: 2001), pp. 228–230.

[5] B.E. Harcourt and J. Ludwig, "Broken Windows: New Evidence from New York City and a Five City Social Experiment," *University of Chicago Law Review*, Vol. 73, Issue 1, Winter 2006, pp. 271–320. The questioning of this link also appears in the news media; illustratively, see Daniel Brook, "The Cracks in Broken Windows," *The Boston Globe*, on-line, February 19, 2006.

[6] Judith A. Greene, "Zero Tolerance: A Case Study of Police Policies and Practices in New York City," *Crime and Delinquency*, Vol. 45, No. 2, 1999, p. 171–210.

[7] Ibid., p. 171.

[8] George L. Kelling and Catherine M. Coles, *Fixing Broken Windows: Restoring Order and Reducing Crime in Our Communities* (New York: Touchstone Publishing, 1996).

[9] Chris Braiden, "Community Policing: Nothing New under the Sun" (Edmonton, Alberta: Edmonton Police Department, 1987).

[10] Ibid. See Peel's Principle 7, as expressed on p. 2.

[11] Jerome H. Skolnick and David H. Bayley, *Community Policing: Issues and Practices around the World* (Washington, D.C.: U.S. Department of Justice, 1988), pp. 67–70.

[12] A number of researchers have documented the failures of traditional policing methods. Most notably, see A. J. Reiss, *The Police and the Public* (New Haven, Conn.: Yale University Press, 1971); G. L. Kelling, T. Pate, D. Dickman, and C. Brown, *Kansas City Preventive Patrol Experiment* (Washington, D.C.: Police Foundation, 1975); M. T. Farmer, ed., *Differential Police Response Strategies* (Washington, D.C.: Police Executive Research Forum, 1981); L. W. Sherman, P. R. Gartin, and M. E. Buerger, "Hot Spot of Predatory Crime: Routine Activities and the Criminology of Place," *Criminology* 27 (1989): 27–55; and W. H. Bieck, W. Spelman, and T. J. Sweeney, "The Patrol Function," in *Local Government Police Management,* ed. William A. Geller (Washington, D.C.: International City Management Association), pp. 59–95.

[13] David Lilly, "Organizational Values and Police Officer Evaluations: A Content Comparison Between Traditional and and Community Policing Agencies," *Police Quarterly*, Vol. 9, Issue 4, December 2006, pp. 486–513.

[14] For a discussion of CompStat as a new police strategy to reduce crime, see William Bratton and Peter Knobler, *Turnaround: How America's Top Cop Reversed the Crime Epidemic* (New York: Random House, 1998); William Bratton and William Edwards, "What We Have Learned about Policing," *City Journal* (spring 1999): William F. Walsh, "CompStat: An Analysis of an Emerging Police Managerial Paradigm," *Policing: An International Journal of Police Strategies and Management* 24, no. 3, (2001): 347–362; William F. Walsh and Gennaro F. Vito, "The Meaning of CompStat," *Journal of Contemporary Criminal Justice* 20, no. 1 (2004): 51–69; John E. Conklin, *Why Crime Rates Fell* (Boston, Mass.: Pearson Education 2003).

[15] Much of this section has been adapted from Raymond Dussault, "Maps and Management: Comstat Evolves," *Government Technology*, April 2000, pp. 1–2.

[16] William F. Walsh and Gennero F. Vito, "The Meaning of CompStat," *Journal of Contemporary Criminal Justice* 20, no. 1 (2004): 51–69.

[17] The SARA methodology was adapted from William Spelman and John E. Eck, *Newport News Tests Problem-Oriented Policing* (Washington, D.C.: National Institute of Justice, SNI 201, January/February 1987), pp. 2–3, and Spelman and Eck, "Police and Delivery," p. 61.

[18] Herman Goldstein, *Problem-Oriented Policing* (New York: McGraw-Hill, 1990).

[19] This list was adapted, in part, from Goldstein, *Problem-Oriented Policing*, pp. 66–67.

[20] Ibid., pp. 36–37.

[21] City of Chicago, Department of Police, "Fact Sheet—the Chicago Alternative Policing Strategy (CAPS)," July 1995.

[22] Arthur J. Lurigio and Wesley G. Skogan, "Winning the Hearts and Minds of Police Officers: An Assessment of Staff Perceptions of Community Policing in Chicago," *Crime and Delinquency* 40, no. 3 (July 1994): 319.

[23] Mark Moore, "Problem-Solving and Community Policing," in *Modern Policing*, ed. M. Tonry and N. Morris (Chicago: University of Chicago Press, 1992), pp. 99–158.

[24] The key features of the CAPS program presented in this text are adapted from Lurigio and Skogan, "Winning the Hearts and Minds of Police Officers," p. 318, and Chicago Police Department, "Fact Sheet," pp. 1–2.

[25] Wesley G. Skogan and Lynn Steiner, *CAPS at Ten—Community Policing in Chicago: An Evaluation of Chicago's Alternative Policing Strategy* (Northwestern University: Institute for Policy Research for the Chicago Community Policing Evaluation Consortium, January 2004).

[26] Ibid.

[27] Stephen Mastrofski, Roger Parks, and Robert E. Worden, "Community Policing in Action: Lessons from an Observational Study," *Research Preview* (Washington, D.C.: National Institute of Justice, June 1998).

[28] Ibid.

[29] Quint C. Thurman and Jihong Zhao, "Community Policing: Where Are We Now?" *Crime and Delinquency* 43, no. 3 (July 1997): 554–564.

[30] Mastrofski et al., "Community Policing in Action," p. 7.

[31] Interview with Chief Robert K. Olsen, October 7, 2002.

[32] Refer to www.ci.minneapolis.mn.us/citywork/police/index.html

[33] Lawrence W. Sherman, "Policing for Crime Prevention," in L.W. Sherman, D. Gottfredson, D. L. MacKenzie, J. E. Eck, P. Reuter, & S. Bushway (Eds), *Preventing Crime: What Works, What Doesn't, What's Promising—A Report to the Attorney General of the United States* (Washington, DC: United States Department of Justice, Office of Justice Programs, 1997).

[34] D. Weisburd and J. E. Eck, "What can police do to reduce crime, disorder, and fear?" *The Annals of the American Academy of Political and Social Science* 593 (2004), pp. 42–65.

[35] Ibid., and Lawrence W. Sherman, "Policing Communities: What Works?" *Crime and Justice* 8 (1986), pp. 343–386.

[36] See Robert W. Taylor, Eric J. Fritsch, and Tory J. Caeti, "Core Challenges Facing Community Policing: The Emperor *Still* has no Clothes," *ACJS Today*, May-June 1998, Volume XVII: 1, pp. 1–5.

[37] See Larry W. Sherman, "Policing for Crime Prevention," in L.W. Sherman, D. Gottfredson, D.L. MacKenzie, J.E. Eck, P. Reuter, & S. Bushway (Eds), *Preventing Crime: What Works, What Doesn't, What's Promising—A Report to the Attorney General of the United States* (Washington, DC: United States Department of Justice, Office of Justice Programs, 1997).

[38] Larry W. Sherman, "Evidence-Based Policing," *Ideas in American Policing* (Washington, DC: U.S. Department of Justice, Police Foundation, July 1998), pp. 3–4.

[39] Ibid.

[40] A. S. Avdija, "Evidence-Based Policing: A Comparative Analysis of Eight Experimental Studies Focused in the Area of Targeted Policing," *International Journal of Criminal Justice Sciences* 3 (2008), pp. 110–128.

[41] S. E. Martin and L. W. Sherman, *Catching career criminals: The Washington, DC repeat offender project* (Washington, DC: National Institute of Justice, 1986).

[42] R. C. Davis, D. Weisburd, and E. Hamilton, *Preventing Repeat Incidents of Family Violence: A Randomized Field Test of a Second Responder Program in Redlands, California* (Washington, D.C.: Police Foundation, 2007).

[43] David Weisburd, "Hot Spots Policing Experiments and Criminal Justice Research: Lessons from the Field," *Annals of the American Academy of Political and Social Science* 599 (2005), pp. 220–245.

[44] Lawrence W. Sherman, P. R. Gartin, and M. Buerger, "Hot Spots of Predatory Crime: Routine Activities and the Criminology of Place," *Criminology* 27 (1986), pp. 27–55.

[45] Ibid.

[46] John E. Eck, S. Chainey, and J. Cameron, *Mapping Crime: Understanding Hot Spots* (Washington, D.C.: National Institute of Justice, 2005).

[47] David Weisburd and Lorraine G. Mazerolle, "Crime and Disorder in Drug Hot Spots: Implications for Theory and Practice in Policing," *Police Quarterly* 3 (2000), pp. 331–349.

[48] S. L. Rutherford, K. R. Blevins and V. B. Lord, "An Evaluation of the Effects of a Street Crime Unit on Citizens' Fear of Crime," *Professional Issues in Criminal Justice* 3 (2008), pp. 21–36.

[49] Wesley Skogan and Kathleen Frydl (eds), *Fairness and Effectiveness in Policing: The Evidence* (Washington, D.C.: National Academy of Sciences, Committee to Review Research on Police Policy and Practice, 2004), p. 250. See also, Anthony A. Braga, *U.S. COPS Office Crime Prevention Research Review: Police Enforcement Strategies to Prevent Crime in Hot Spot Areas* (Washington, D.C.: U.S. Department of Justice, 2008).

[50] Anthony A. Braga, "The Effects of Hot Spots Policing on Crime," *Annals of the American Academy of Political and Social Sciences* 578 (2001), pp. 104–125.

[51] Ralph B. Taylor, "Hot Spots Do Not Exist and Four Other Fundamental Concerns About Hot Spots Policing," In Natasha A. Frost, J. D. Freilich, and T. R. Clear, *Contemporary Issues in Criminal Justice Policy* (Belmont, CA: Wadsworth Cengage Learning, 2010).

[52] Ibid., p. 272.

[53] C. S. Koper and E. Mayo-Wilson, "Police crackdowns on illegal gun carrying: A systematic review of their impact on gun crime," *Journal of Experimental Criminology* 2 (2006), pp. 227–261.

[54] Eric J. Fritsch, Tory J. Caeti, and Robert W. Taylor, "Gang suppression through saturation patrol, aggressive curfew, and truancy enforcement: A quasi-experimental test of the Dallas anti-gang initiative," *Crime & Delinquency* 45 (2000), pp. 122–139.

[55] Jerry H. Ratcliffe and Robert Guidetti, "State Police Investigative Structure and the Adoption of Intelligence-led Policing. *Policing: An International Journal of Police Strategies and Management* 31 (2008), pp. 111.

[56] Ibid.

[57] Jerry H. Ratcliffe, *Intelligence Led Policing* (Portland, OR: Willan Publishing, 2008).

[58] C. Clarke, "Proactive Policing: Standing on the Shoulders of Community-Based Policing," (2006) *Police Practice and Research,* 7, pp. 3–17.

[59] Jerry H. Ratcliffe and Robert Guidetti, "State Police Investigative Structure and the Adoption of Intelligence-led Policing."

[60] Ibid.

[61] Jerry H. Ratcliffe, "The effectiveness of police intelligence management: A New Zealand case study." *Police Practice and Research* (In Press).

[62] Craig D. Uchida, *A National Discussion on Predictive Policing: Defining our Terms and Mapping Successful Implementation Strategies* (Washington, D.C.: National Institute of Justice, 2010).

[63] Beth Pearsall, "Predictive Policing: The Future of Law Enforcement?" *NIJ Journal* 266 (2010), pp. 16–19.

[64] Charlie Beck and Colleen McCue, "Predictive Policing: What Can We Learn from Wal-Mart and Amazon about Fighting Crime in a Recession?" *The Police Chief* 76 (November 2009). Retrieved from http://policechiefmagazine.org/magazine/ on July 20, 2010.

[65] Beth Pearsall, "Predictive Policing: The Future of Law Enforcement?"

[66] Craig D. Uchida, *A National Discussion on Predictive Policing: Defining our Terms and Mapping Successful Implementation Strategies.*

[67] J. W. Brahan, K. P. Lam, H. Chan, and W. Leung, "AICAMS: Artificial Intelligence Crime Analysis and Management Systems," *Knowledge-Based Systems* 11 *(2009)*, pp. 355–361.

[68] N. Cope, "Intelligence Led Policing or Policing Led Intelligence?" *British Journal of Criminology* 44 (2004), pp. 188–203.

[69] Several scholars have provided definitions of crime analysis. See J. B. Howlett, "Analytical Investigative Techniques," *Police Chief* 47 (December 1980), p. 42; Rachel Boba, *Crime Analysis and Crime Mapping* (Thousand Oaks, Calif.: Sage, 2005), p. 5; S. Gottlieb, S. Arenberg, and R. Singh, *Crime Analysis: From First Report to Final Arrest* (Monclair, Calif.: alpha, 1994); Mark A. Stallo, *Using Microsoft Office to Improve Law Enforcement Operations: Crime Analysis, Community Policing, and Investigations* (Dallas, Tex.: Act, Now, 2010).

[70] J. A. Kinney, "Criminal Intelligence Analysis: A Powerful Weapon," *International Cargo Crime Prevention* (April 1984): p. 4.

[71] Boba, *Crime Analysis and Crime Mapping,* p. 14.

[72] Ibid., pp. 15–16.

[73] D. M. Ross, "Criminal Intelligence Analysis," *Police Product News* (June 1983), p. 45.

[74] Ibid.

[75] Incident occurring on Virginia Tech University, April 16, 2007 resulting in over 30 deaths from gunman, Seung-Hui Cho.

[76] Ross, "Criminal Intelligence Analysis," p. 49.

[77] Mark A. Stallo, *Using Microsoft Office to Improve Law Enforcement Operations.* See http://www .actnowinc.org/books.html (July 20, 2010).

[78] Jerry H. Ratcliffe, "Crime Mapping and the Training Needs of Law Enforcement," *European Journal on Criminal Policy and Research* 10 (2004), pp. 65–83.

[79] David Weisburd and C. Lum, "The Diffusion of Computerized Crime Mapping in Policing: Linking Research and Practice," *Police Practice and Research* 6 (2005), pp. 419–434.

[80] J. R. Battin, "Is Hot Spot Policing Effective Empirically?" *Professional Issues in Criminal Justice* 4 *(2009)*, pp. 35–50.

[81] For more information relating to the applications of GIS technology to policing, see Nancy G. La Vigne and Julie Wartell, *Mapping across Boundaries: Regional Crime Analysis* (Washington, D.C.: Police Executive Research Forum, 2001).

[82] James A. O'Brien, *Management Information Systems: A Managerial End User Perspective* (Homewood, Ill.: Irwin, 1990), p. 356.

[83] W. Coady, "Automated Link Analysis: Artificial Intelligence–Based Tools for Investigators," *Police Chief* 52 (1985), 22–23.

[84] Edward C. Ratledge and Joan E. Jacoby, *Handbook on Artificial Intelligence and Expert Systems in Law Enforcement* (Westport, Conn.: Greenwood, 1989), chap. 8.

[85] H. Chen, J. Schroeder, R. Hauck, L. Ridgeway, H. Atabakhsh, H. Gupta, C. Boarman, and A. Clements, "COPLINK Connect: Information and Knowledge Management for Law Enforcement," *Decision Support Systems* 34 (2002), pp. 271–285.

[86] R. Krause, "The Best and the Brightest," *Law Enforcement Technology* 3 (1986), pp. 25–27.

[87] See "Artificial Intelligence Tackles a Very Real Problem—Police Misconduct Control," *Law Enforcement News,* (September 30): 1994, p. 1.

[88] For more detailed information on this subject, refer to Robert W. Taylor, "Managing Police Information," in *Police and Policing: Contemporary Issues,* ed. Dennis J. Kenney (New York: Praeger, 1989), pp. 257–270.

[89] David Weisburd and John E. Eck, "What can Police do to Reduce Crime, Disorder, and Fear?" *The Annals of the American Academy of Political and Social Science* 593 (2004), pp. 42–65.

[90] Steven D. Mastrofski, David Weisburd and Anthony A. Braga, "Rethinking Policing: The Policy Implications of Hot Spots of Crime." In N. A. Frost, J. D. Freilich, & T. R. Clear (Eds.), *Contemporary Issues in Criminal Justice Policy* (Belmont, CA: Wadsworth-Cengage Learning, 2010), p. 251.

Intelligence, Terrorism, and Homeland Security

It is not the police; it is not the intelligence services that will defeat terrorism. It is communities that will defeat terrorism.
—Ian Blair, Commissioner of Britain's Metropolitan Police

Objectives

- Define *intelligence*.

- Describe the Intelligence Cycle as presented in the *National Criminal Intelligence Sharing Plan (NCISP)*.

- Define a fusion center and briefly list its four primary goals.

- Describe some of the criticisms aimed at fusion centers and other law enforcement responses to terrorism.

- List the four primary areas of responsibility within the Department of Homeland Security.

- Define *terrorism*.

- Briefly describe the concept of jihad and name some of the more radical groups active in the Middle East.

- Describe the concept of a "homegrown" terrorist and briefly discuss recent trends in radical Islamic terrorism.

- Define a *hate crime*.

- Define an *ecoterrorist*.

OUTLINE

Introduction

On September 11, 2001, our world changed forever. For the first time in the past 60 years, America came under attack by an outside and foreign enemy (see Figure 3.1). Our security weaknesses were exploited, our vulnerability was exposed, and our fear became real. For law enforcement and police officers throughout the United States, the attacks on the World Trade Center and the Pentagon posed yet another new challenge to the already difficult task of reducing crime and maintaining order in our communities (see Chapters 1 and 2 for a discussion of the changing role of police in America).

The 9/11 attacks and the ongoing war on terror have demonstrated that terrorism respects no jurisdictional boundaries, whether these attacks take the form of aircraft hijackings, the use of biological agents, or more sophisticated attempts to infiltrate crucial infrastructures. This realization has forced local police administrators to focus considerable attention on the need to improve law enforcement intelligence operations. The notion that state and local law enforcement agencies must enhance their intelligence gathering and analysis capabilities represents a fundamental shift in the strategic dimension of local policing that involves making these agencies "intelligence-led" organizations reminiscent of the military model used for gathering, assessing, and distributing critical information.[1]

While much of the effort to reform intelligence operations after 9/11 focused on the need to restructure and better coordinate the intelligence infrastructure and model at the federal level, there has also been a significant effort to define the role state and local law enforcement agencies play in homeland security.

Figure 3.1
The events of 9/11 changed our world forever . . . characterized as one of the defining moments of the 21st century: 2,752 men, women, and children lost their lives in this horrific terrorist attack. According to former Attorney General John Ashcroft, there is no priority higher than the prevention of terrorism; a role now placed squarely on the shoulders of American police and law enforcement officers.
Source: See http://www.dailymail.co.uk/news/worldnews/article-1249885/New-World-Trade-Center-9-11-aerial-images-ABC-News.html

Intelligence and Terrorism

Historically, the missing dimension in quality intelligence has been analysis.[2] The transformation of raw data, whether acquired through human, technical, or open sources, must be collated, scrutinized, and processed accurately and quickly. The ultimate goal of this analytical process is a finished product more intelligible, accurate, and usable than the data and information drawn on to prepare it. Herein is the definition of **intelligence**—data and information that have been evaluated, analyzed, and produced with careful conclusions and recommendations. Intelligence, then, is a *product* created from systematic and thoughtful examination, placed in context, and provided to law enforcement executives, with facts and alternatives that can inform critical decisions.[3]

There are three major perspectives on the purpose of intelligence and analysis. Each voices a different focus on the ability of intelligence officers and agents to provide sound information on which responsible decision making can be based. The first perspective is associated with the writings of Sherman Kent; it holds that the role of intelligence is to limit surprise from national security policymaking.[4] In other words, the analysis of data (or the making of intelligence) should render facts and figures, identify trends and patterns, and provide statistical support on *past* events. There are no follow-up investigations, postaudits, or continued evaluations concerning the policy implemented in response to the data provided. In essence, this type of analysis provides the facts and leaves the decisions to decision makers.

In the second perspective, analysts not only should be responsible for providing historical data but also should force policymakers and decision makers to confront alternative views of specific events, potential threats, and/or foreign situations. The emphasis is on connecting the political ends with the course of events. Analysts cannot limit themselves simply to giving situational reports and briefings; they must inherently focus on the dynamics of the political arena in order to give meaning to data. This can be particularly true regarding threats (such as terrorism) from foreign sources, in which state and local police executives may be relatively naïve to the geo-global dimensions of a specific region outside the United States. Most important, analysts need to place intelligence into the relevance and perspective of state and local governments. For instance, increased violence in the West Bank may be of little consequence to rural areas in the United States but much more meaningful to areas outside Detroit, Michigan, where nearly 300,000 Palestinians reside.

The final and sharply contrasting perspective concerning the purpose of analysis is somewhat latent. Its emphasis is not on providing past data on which to base decisions or policy; rather, the focus is squarely on the *prediction* of future events. This shift in emphasis can be viewed as an outgrowth of the second perspective as more technological advances have come to pass. With the advent of advanced analytical software and artificial intelligence systems, more robust records management systems, and relatively easy access to huge data banks (see Chapter 2, Policing Today), it should now be possible to provide accurate and reliable predictions concerning specific events.[5] The ultimate goal is twofold: (1) provide accurate information concerning the future in order to avoid decision and policy pitfalls and bureaucratic blunderings and (2) chart out courses of action directly aimed at achieving specific objectives. This, of course, requires a new way of thinking about policing—one that emphasizes prediction and prevention rather than detection and apprehension.

The Intelligence Process and Cycle

The *National Criminal Intelligence Sharing Plan (NCISP),* originally released in 2003 and slightly revised in 2005, contained 28 specific recommendations for major changes in local policing.[6] However, the key concept from the document emphasized the strategic integration of intelligence into the overall mission of the police organization— intelligence-led policing (refer to Chapter 2). Rather than react and respond to past calls for service, the NCISP placed much more emphasis on predictive analysis derived from the discovery of hard facts, information, patterns, intelligence, and good crime analysis. By concentrating on key criminal activities, problems, and individuals targeted through analysis, significant attention could be directed to alleviate the crime problem. In order to protect the civil liberties of all individuals, the intelligence process was developed with key evaluation points aimed at verifying source reliability and validity at the beginning of the collection cycle. The goal was to develop a universal process that would integrate both law enforcement and national security intelligence agendas, while providing mechanisms for securing individual freedoms and allowing law enforcement agencies to be proactive in preventing and deterring crime and terrorism. The end result was the "Intelligence Cycle," presented by the FBI in an effort to bring varied pieces of information together in an effort to draw logical conclusions from a thorough and systematic process (see Figure 3.2). As important, the Intelligence Cycle also provides a means of communicating and sharing intelligence among individuals and agencies through the dissemination process.

Fusion Centers

The transformation of local police agencies into intelligence-led organizations involves four key objectives: (1) the creation of a task and coordination process, (2) the development of core intelligence products to lead the operation, (3) the establishment of standardized training practices, and (4) the development of protocols to facilitate intelligence capabilities. This approach is intended to improve the capability of local law enforcement in regard to responding to terror threats and traditional anti-crime efforts. As indicated in Chapter 2, intelligence-led policing blends community partnerships with crime fighting and police accountability in an effort to maximize police efficiency and effectiveness in terrorism prevention and crime reduction. There is evidence to suggest that this initiative has started to alter the face of traditional policing in the United States. A recent national survey found that a majority of responding local and state police agencies have conducted terrorism threat assessments since 9/11, and about one-third of these agencies have collaborated with the FBI's joint terrorism task force to assist in local crime investigations.[7] The movement to integrate information and develop an overarching process of managing the flow of information and intelligence across all levels and sectors of government and private security has been the impetus to create **fusion centers** (see Figure 3.3) inside local and state police agencies. Fusion centers act as effective and efficient mechanisms for exchanging information and intelligence, maximizing police resources, streamlining public safety operations, and improving the ability to fight crime and terrorism by merging data from a variety of sources.[8] Fusion centers serve as clearinghouses for all potentially relevant homeland security information that can be used to assess local terror threats and aid in the apprehension of more traditional criminal suspects.

Originally launched in New York City under the direction of Raymond Kelly in 2002, the concept of a fusion center blended the power of information technology with terrorism prevention and crime fighting. With a price tag exceeding $11 million, the Real Time Crime Center (RTCC) in New York City combs through tens of millions of criminal complaints, arrest and parole records, and 911 call records dating back a decade in an effort to provide NYPD officers with the information tools necessary to stop a terrorist event or investigate a crime.[9] Fusion centers distribute relevant, actionable, and timely information and intelligence, incorporating a simultaneously vertical (i.e., federal, state, and local) and horizontal (i.e., within the

FEDERAL BUREAU OF INVESTIGATION

SEARCH

Directorate of Intelligence

The Intelligence Cycle

The intelligence cycle is the process of developing unrefined data into polished intelligence for the use of policymakers. The intelligence cycle consists of six steps, described below. The graphic below shows the circular nature of this process, although movement between the steps is fluid. Intelligence uncovered at one step may require going back to an earlier step before moving forward.

Requirements are identified information needs—what we must know to safeguard the nation. Intelligence requirements are established by the Director of National Intelligence according to guidance received from the President and the National and Homeland Security Advisors. Requirements are developed based on critical information required to protect the United States from National Security and criminal threats. The Attorney General and the Director of the FBI participate in the formulation of national intelligence requirements.

Planning and Direction is management of the entire effort, from identifying the need for information to delivering an intelligence product to a consumer. It involves implementation plans to satisfy requirements levied on the FBI, as well as identifying specific collection requirements based on FBI needs. Planning and direction also is responsive to the end of the cycle, because current and finished intelligence, which supports decision-making, generates new requirements. The Executive Assistant Director for the National Security Branch leads intelligence planning and direction for the FBI.

Collection is the gathering of raw information based on requirements. Activities such as interviews, technical and physical surveillances, human source operation, searches, and liaison relationships result in the collection of intelligence.

Processing and Exploitation involves converting the vast amount of information collected into a form usable by analysts. This is done through a variety of methods including decryption, language translations, and data reduction. Processing includes the entering of raw data into databases where it can be exploited for use in the analysis process.

Analysis and Production is the conversion of raw information into intelligence. It includes integrating, evaluating, and analyzing available data, and preparing intelligence products. The information's reliability, validity, and relevance is evaluated and weighed. The information is logically integrated, put in context, and used to produce intelligence. This includes both "raw" and finished intelligence. Raw intelligence is often referred to as "the dots"—individual pieces of information disseminated individually. Finished intelligence reports "connect the dots" by putting information in context and drawing conclusions about its implications.

Dissemination—the last step—is the distribution of raw or finished intelligence to the consumers whose needs initiated the intelligence requirements. The FBI disseminates information in three standard formats: Intelligence Information Reports (IIRs), FBI Intelligence Bulletins, and FBI Intelligence Assessments. FBI intelligence products are provided daily to the Attorney General, the President, and to customers throughout the FBI and in other agencies. These FBI intelligence customers make decisions—operational, strategic, and policy—based on the information. These decisions may lead to the levying of more requirements, thus continuing the FBI intelligence cycle.

Figure 3.3
Fusion centers are high-tech, information-intensive operational centers that analyze and disseminate intelligence relating to terrorism and crime to police officers on the street.
(Courtesy of Jason DeCrow/AP Wide World Photos)

agency, with other local agencies, and across disciplines such as fire, EMS, public works, and private partners) approach within a given jurisdiction. Fusion centers are composed of talented and trained individuals using sophisticated application software in crime analysis and mapping to manage and manipulate information and intelligence into a usable product. The resulting analysis acts as a basis for the deployment of police resources and directed operations in a real-time format—that is, almost immediately. The fusion center not only acts as a centralized host for intelligence information and analysis but also serves as a conduit for passing out critical information to other regional, state, and national authorities. This is a particularly important point that fulfills the National Criminal Intelligence Sharing Plan in protecting the homeland.

Almost every state and several large metropolitan cities have undertaken the development of fusion centers with significant funding assistance from the Department of Homeland Security. For instance, the Chicago Police Department Deployment Operations Center (DOC) was one of the first centers to combine real-time intelligence analysis with the deployment process. In Los Angeles, both the city and the county have well-developed fusion centers, and in Dallas, Texas, the Metropolitan Operations and Analytical Intelligence Center (MOSAIC) provides real-time tactical information to officers on the street 24/7.

The goals of a fusion center are fourfold:

1. Fusion centers support the broad range of activities undertaken by a police department relating to the detection, examination, and investigation of a potential terrorist and/or criminal activity. Ideally, the center serves as a hub of anti-terrorist and anti-crime operations in a specific region, focusing on the recognition of patterns, indications and warnings, source development, interdiction, and the coordination of critical criminal justice resources. These are critical activities for any police agency attempting to be proactive and intelligence-led to be successful in deterring, detecting, disrupting, investigating, and apprehending suspects involved in terrorist and criminal activity directly related to homeland security. Figure 3.4 represents one of several information technology solutions that are commonly used in fusion centers to help identify patterns and indicators associated with terrorism and/or crime.

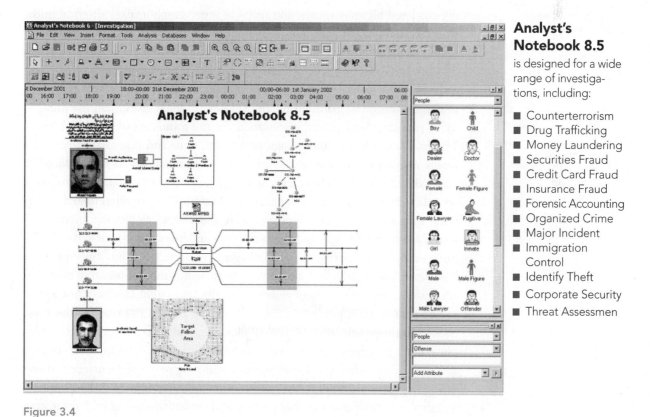

Analyst's Notebook 8.5 is designed for a wide range of investigations, including:

- Counterterrorism
- Drug Trafficking
- Money Laundering
- Securities Fraud
- Credit Card Fraud
- Insurance Fraud
- Forensic Accounting
- Organized Crime
- Major Incident
- Immigration Control
- Identify Theft
- Corporate Security
- Threat Assessmen

Figure 3.4

Application Programs

Since 1990, i2 Corporation has been a worldwide leader of visual investigative analysis software for law enforcement, intelligence, military, and Fortune 500 organizations. The application software performs an array of sophisticated analytical techniques, including social network analysis, commodity flow, telephone record analysis, link analysis, and the like, often used in real-time fusion centers to convey analytical findings in intuitive charts that organize support data.
(Courtesy of i2, Inc., McLean, VA, 2010. Visit www.i2group.com)

2. Fusion centers support operations that protect **critical infrastructure and key resources (CI/KRs)** in a given region, support major incident operations, support specialized units charged with interdiction and investigative operations, and assist in emergency operations and planning. The aim of a fusion center is to reduce the vulnerability of the high-value and high-risk targets identified within a jurisdiction. For example, in any major city there are several important CI/KRs—bank buildings, corporate headquarters, bridges and overpasses, water supply tanks and systems, electronic switching hubs, rail and subway stations, and a myriad of other important infrastructure entities. Fusion centers maintain huge databases that are immediately retrievable for use in thwarting an attack or dealing with an emergency. For instance, the Los Angeles Police Department has implemented the "Archangel Project," aimed at developing a large database for all CI/KRs in the region. Its primary purpose is to maintain as much accessible and critical data as possible on any one given piece of critical infrastructure, so that during an emergency or a potentially threatening event, police resources can be directed appropriately. Hence, building schematics and event histories, alternative road and highway routes, and maps of water supply mains, electrical grids, switching stations, and the like are maintained and accessible within the fusion center. Fusion centers are **all-hazard** in scope—that is, they are developed to support operations during an emergency that is either human-made, such as a terrorist event, or natural, such as a hurricane, flood, or tornado.

3. Fusion centers often maintain public "tip lines," which gives them the capability to promote more public involvement in and awareness of terrorist threats. The goal is to identify and recognize warning signs and potential threats in a timely manner in order to pre-empt potential terrorist attacks and reduce the vulnerability of the CI/KRs in a given region. Fusion centers accomplish this task on a daily basis, focusing on the analysis of crimes that are often linked to terrorist cells and activity for funding, such as narcotics trafficking, credit card abuse, armament and gun theft, prostitution, and human trafficking, by distributing information relating to these linkages to all agencies within a given region. The timeliness of gathering, analyzing, and disseminating information is vital to successfully preventing acts of violence and threats to homeland security.

4. Fusion centers assist police executives in making better-informed decisions, especially during emergencies or critical incidents. Fusion centers are ongoing deployment operations centers with the real-time ability to monitor critical resources. This includes real-time status monitoring of major events, communicating with area medical facilities and trauma units, coordinating the allocation and deployment of multi-agency personnel resources (including military reserve units), monitoring changing weather conditions, and directing all support services through a centralized operations center.

Fusion centers embody the core of collaboration between agencies in law enforcement, as well as members of private security and the general public. The National

Governors Associated Center for Best Practices revealed that states ranked the development of intelligence fusion centers as one of their highest priorities in reducing crime and preventing terrorism in the homeland.[10] Clearly, the 9/11 attacks transformed the role of police in our country. Police executives need to recognize that the public, and federal officials, will increasingly expect local police to take a broader and more important role in safeguarding their communities against terrorists.[11]

Policing Terrorism

According to well-known policing scholar George Kelling and former LAPD Chief Bill Bratton, cities must create a hostile environment for terrorists by instilling effective intelligence gathering and analysis into the everyday workings of local police departments.[12] This theme is echoed and certainly reinforced by federal authorities as presented in the late 2008 report presented by the U.S. Department of Justice, Office of Community Oriented Policing Services, acting as a police chief's guide to policing terrorism.[13] Central to this document and the mission of policing in preventing terrorism and reducing crime must be the systematic collection, analysis, and sharing of intelligence information between agencies. Several important steps for any local police department to consider in developing its intelligence collection methodology and enhancing its role to prevent terrorism include:

- Create an intelligence unit that focuses on counterterrorism and/or appoint a terrorist liaison officer.
- Send officers for training in intelligence gathering, analysis, and sharing. Know the legal and privacy issues surrounding police use of intelligence information.
- Join the local Joint Terrorism Task Force (JTTF) sponsored by the FBI field office in the local jurisdiction. Depending on the size of the department, this may not always be feasible or cost-effective since the FBI provides pay for only overtime and equipment; officer salaries are continued by the home department. Therefore, smaller agencies may wish to only designate an officer to coordinate information between the department and the nearest task force.
- Develop an information-sharing environment between agencies of law enforcement within and across jurisdictions. Implement fusion centers when appropriate to analyze and funnel terrorist information to appropriate authorities.
- Participate in the National SAR Initiative (NSI),which is focused on developing and using the Suspicious Activity Reporting System (SARS). In accordance with the National Criminal Intelligence Sharing Plan and the National Strategy for Information Sharing (NSIS), developed within the U.S. Department of Justice, this system promotes an Information Sharing Environment (ISE) important to establishing the timely sharing of SAR information with law enforcement agencies, fusion centers, and the Joint Terrorism Task Forces (JTTF)[14] (see Figure 3.5).
- Promote intelligence-led policing and implement community policing efforts with immigrant communities, especially immigrant Muslim communities.

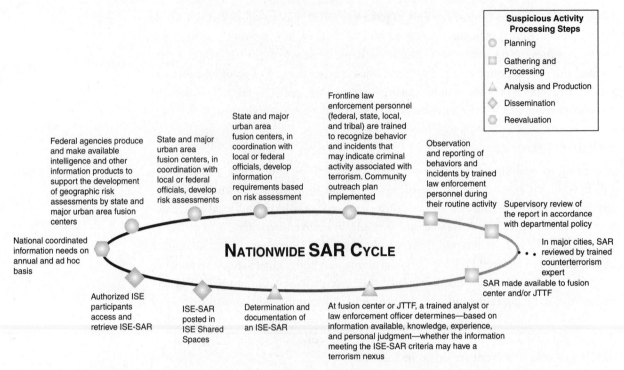

Figure 3.5
The SAR Cycle Chart. This diagram focuses on activities of local, state, and tribal agencies. By following these steps, agencies can be assured that their SAR activities are in alignment with and can support crucial information sharing. This diagram will also help identify gaps in an agency's current process that may need to be addressed and/or corrected.
Source: Suspicious Activity Reporting: Process Implementation Checklist, p. 4. See http://it.ojp.gov/docdownloader.aspx?ddid=1147

Criticisms Aimed at Fusion Centers and Other Law Enforcement Responses to Terrorism

As with any new direction, there have certainly been setbacks and problems that have plagued not only the development and transition of the Department of Homeland Security, but also befuddled the government's response to terrorism. For instance, there continue to be problems relating to the sharing of information between local law enforcement and the FBI. In 2005, the Portland (Oregon) Police Department pulled out of the joint terrorism task force over a dispute regarding top-secret clearances. The FBI would not grant a top-secret clearance to the mayor (Tom Potter) even though he was the chief of police previous to his election.[15] While this situation was remedied and the incidents surrounding this issue appear to be lessening, the problem of sharing top-secret information (as to potential suspects and threats) between the FBI and local police agencies still remains as a "thorn-in-the-side" of many local agencies. One local fusion center director noted that information flow appears to be one way—from the local agency to the FBI.[16]

Fusion centers have also not been without their detractors. Monahan and Palmer note, after an exhausting and comprehensive analysis from 2002 to 2008, that three primary concerns continue to plague these information and intelligence hubs.[17] First, fusion centers are expensive and almost any cost-benefit analysis will reveal significant money spent for very little, tangible evidence of success. The effectiveness of fusion centers, particularly given their financial outlay, is seriously questioned. Few terrorist incidents have actually been prevented due to the work of fusion centers. Second, many fusion centers appear to suffer from "mission creep"; that is, because there are few cases focused on terrorism, many centers have expanded their role to include crime fighting and reduction. According to Monahan and Palmer, the expansion of fusion centers into this mission is well beyond the initial intention of funding "all-hazard" centers for the coordination of intelligence and information to prevent terrorism. And finally, fusion centers come desperately close to violating the civil liberties of people, especially relating to racial and ethnic profiling and breaches of privacy. The American Civil Liberties Union (ACLU) has also highlighted possible privacy and individual infringements stemming from fusion centers.[18]

Fusion centers have access to an enormous amount of personal information regarding individuals. Data banks involving criminal and arrest records, financial records, civil litigation, credit reports, water bills, and even Internet sites such as Facebook and MySpace are now available to police personnel. Quoting a spotty historical past by police relating to intelligence gathering and analysis, the ACLU suggests a number of important potential improvements:

Eliminate ambiguous lines of authority—In many cases, there appears to be a blurred line between the federal government and individual states or local agencies housing fusion centers. There simply is not a clear portrait of who is actually in charge of fusion centers. Although individual fusion centers were developed by state and local governments, the federal government provided much of the original funding and dispatches its own intelligence officers to work alongside state/local officials. Most state/local agencies cannot access classified information, and, hence, must rely on the DHS employee or the FBI to provide this intelligence.

Eliminate private sector involvement in the fusion process—Private sector participation in fusion centers is designed to encourage a number of public safety, transportation, social service, and private sector entities to join together in the fusion process. Because one of the goals of fusion centers is to protect the nation's critical infrastructure—85 percent of which is owned by private interests—fusion centers are strongly encouraged to seek information from "nontraditional sources" (e.g., private corporations, hospitals, transportation companies). Allowing private sector corporations access to classified materials and other sensitive law enforcement information may violate individual Constitutional and personal rights. Police and law enforcement entities undergo rigorous training, are sworn to objectively serve their community, and are paid through public salaries, whereas private companies and their employees are motivated to maximize profits. In short, the availability for personal information to be shared between public and private officials, for the sake of forging public and private partnerships, may be a violation of individual rights to privacy guaranteed by our Constitution.

Eliminate military participation in the fusion process—The Posse Comitatus Act of 1878 clearly prohibits the United States military from acting in a law enforcement capacity on American soil, except under express authority from Congress. Hence, fusion centers should be prohibited from using active-duty military personnel. However, many fusion centers incorporate the National Guard and the Coast Guard, and are a bridge between military and civilian intelligence centers. At least one center in North Dakota is actually located within National Guard facilities. The ACLU argues that military personnel operating in a law enforcement capacity (fusion centers) would erode not only the Posse Comitatus Act, but reduce the Constitutional barriers between the military and American citizenry.

Eliminate illegal data mining in the fusion process—Data fusion can lead to illegal data mining; that is, accessing private sector databases that are not controlled or authenticated. This action clearly jeopardizes an individual's Constitutional right to privacy, as well as subjects the individual to unwarranted scrutiny by the police *without* probable cause. Intelligence gathering and fusion center processes include anticipating, identifying, monitoring, and preventing future criminal and terrorist activities without probable cause. How police agencies focus on one group versus another, and who becomes the target of an investigation, are key questions concerning this issue.

Eliminate excessive secrecy—A fusion center's ability to gather vast amounts of personal information on individuals, with very little oversight, not only undercuts the function and purpose of the intelligence process, but also increases the danger that incompetence and malfeasance will flourish. Fusion centers must be held accountable and transparent to public scrutiny.

Clearly, the power struggle between federal and state/local agencies continues today. Despite the lessons learned from 9/11, there are still major issues in this area. Further, while over $380 million have been spent to improve the nation's ability to thwart terrorist attacks, the Congressional Research Service (CRS) Reports for Congress indicates that fusion centers are ineffective and continue to suffer from lack of interoperability and a host of political power issues between government levels.[19] The CRS reports that while fusion centers were primarily designed to "fuse" federal, state, and local intelligence regarding potential terrorist attacks, they have gravitated more toward collecting and analyzing information on criminals and offenders in local regions—precisely the concern of the ACLU. The CRS document supports the ACLU stance that fusion centers pose significant risks of civil liberty and privacy incursion. Indeed, fusion centers can serve a significant purpose in detecting and investigating terrorists, but their current practices are in need of constant monitoring and supervision.

Homeland Security

In November 2002, President George W. Bush ushered in the largest federal bureaucratic shuffle in 55 years to create the cabinet-level Department of Homeland Security (DHS). Headed by the former governor of Pennsylvania, Tom Ridge, the new department focused the anti-terrorism effort in the United States, absorbing many of the enforcement agencies within the Departments of Treasury and Transportation (Transportation Security Administration; U.S. Coast Guard; U.S. Customs; Bureau of Alcohol, Tobacco, and Firearms; U.S. Secret Service; and Federal Emergency Management Administration [FEMA]). In addition, the department created a division to analyze intelligence gathered by the FBI, CIA, and other police and military agencies. There are four primary areas of responsibility within the Department of Homeland Security:

- Border security and transportation
- Emergency preparedness and response
- Chemical, biological, radiological, and nuclear countermeasures
- Intelligence analysis and infrastructure protection

The building of the department has been slow, with a variety of changes and setbacks coming from changes in leadership and severe criticism stemming from poor agency responses to several national emergencies. For instance, FEMA's lackluster response to the city of New Orleans during Hurricane Katrina in 2005 was eclipsed in 2010 with, again, a very slow and poor response to the largest oil leak in U.S. history crippling the Gulf Coast of Louisiana (British Petroleum's Deep Horizon oil rig explosion and resulting oil spill).

Homeland Security and the Election of President Barack Obama

On January 20, 2009, Senator Barack Obama from the state of Illinois was sworn in as the 44th President of the United States. One of his first duties was to appoint then Governor of Arizona, Janet Napolitano, as the third Secretary of the Department of Homeland Security. Napolitano had received praise in her role as governor in the areas of terrorism and immigration reform.[20] As Secretary of the Department of Homeland Security, Napolitano has played an integral role in bolstering border security by increasing forces along the border, and, in addition, increasing resources and technology to aid in the fight against terrorism.

The Department of Homeland Security is the third-largest department and has the ninth-largest budget in the federal government, boasting over 216,000 employees and a budget that exceeds $55 billion (FY 2010), with an additional $15 billion earmarked for grants aimed at funding anti-terror and border security initiatives at the state and local levels (see Figure 3.6). Much of this money will be provided to local and state law enforcement agencies for the development of programs that address one of the four primary responsibilities of DHS.

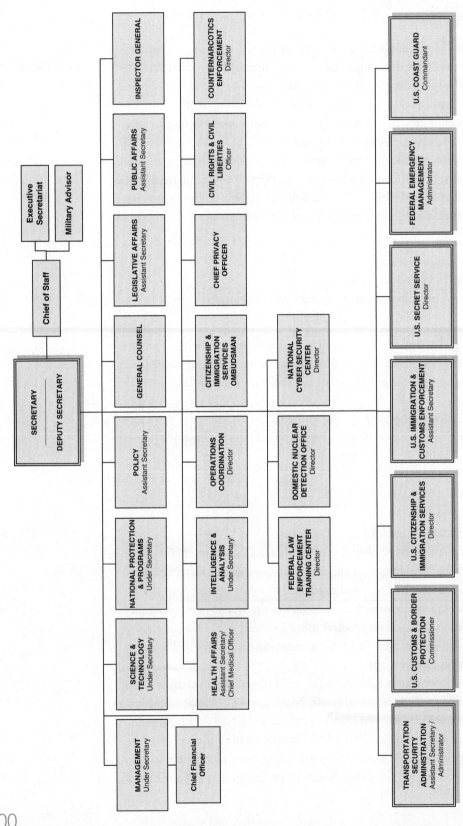

Figure 3.6
U.S. Department of Homeland Security.
Source: U.S. Department of Homeland Security.
*Under Secretary for Intelligence & Analysis title created by Public Law 110-53, Aug. 3rd, 2007 Approved 3/20/2008

Beyond the ultimate mission of ensuring the nation's safety and preventing terrorism, DHS is responsible for immigration policy, airport security, and the protection of the president. Immigration reform is a major hot topic of discussion as it relates to homeland security.

IN THE NEWS   Arizona's New Law on Immigration: Police Caught in the Middle

In April 2010, Arizona's Governor Jan Brewer signed into law legislation making it a state crime to be in the United States illegally. The law further directed local and state police to question people about their immigration status and demand to see appropriate immigration documents if reasonable suspicion existed that the person was indeed in the nation illegally. The new measure also toughened restrictions on hiring illegal immigrants for day labor and knowingly transporting illegal aliens. The law quickly became the centerpiece of controversy, placing the police in the middle of one of the most divisive issues in America. Proponents of the law applauded Arizona's attempt to succeed where the federal government has failed, particularly in securing the state's border with Mexico, which is a major gateway for human, drug, and arms smuggling, as well as a potential transportation route for terrorists from other countries to enter the United States illegally. On the other hand, opponents argued that the law was unconstitutional because it was an attempt by a state to make state and local police agencies responsible for enforcing federal laws. Further, critics argue that the law was unreasonable and leads directly to racial profiling, especially against Hispanic persons. The law was modified to address some of these concerns. Police were barred from using race or ethnicity as the sole basis for stopping and questioning individuals, and police could investigate only those people who they have stopped, detained, or arrested for another violation or crime.

Protestors rallied against Arizona's new immigration law making it a state crime (enforceable by local and state police) to be in the country illegally.
(Courtesy of Newscom)

(Continued)

The law is being challenged by several lawsuits, and Arizona is suffering economically from various boycotts; however, the state has remained steadfast on the passage of the law. With an estimated 460,000 illegal immigrants and the most illegal documented border crossings in 2009 by U.S. Immigration authorities, lawmakers in Arizona are intent to secure their border with Mexico. Interestingly, several other states have developed bills modeled after the Arizona statute including Florida, Iowa, Oklahoma, and Texas.

Immigration reform continues to be a controversial and divisive subject in America, placing the police squarely in the middle. While the Arizona statute is aimed at securing the border against potential terrorists entering our country, and stopping the thousands of illegal immigrants entering the United States primarily from Mexico and South America, it has a profound secondary effect of polarizing Americans. In reality, the state statute will most likely not stop undocumented and illegal immigrants from entering the United States. As long as economic opportunities in the United States exist, Mexicans and other Latin Americans will most likely continue to cross the border in search of jobs and prosperity. Second, the law might divert precious law enforcement resources away from fighting crime and terrorism and alienate a large portion of the U.S. population—Hispanics—against the police. Third, the law may well negatively impact state as well as the U.S. economy as a backlash from Hispanic and Latin American communities who boycott tourism and other business ventures. And finally, some critics argue that the law is morally wrong and profoundly un-American. Our country was founded on immigrants searching for a better life—how can we now bar others from seeking similar objectives in the "land of opportunity"?[1] The arguments relating to Arizona's law, as well as the precarious position of local and state police, will continue to rage until comprehensive immigration reform is addressed within the country.

[1]For an interesting debate on immigration reform and the police, see L. M. Seghetti, K. Ester, and M. J. Garcia, *Enforcing Immigration Law: The Role of State and Local Law Enforcement* (Washington, D.C.: *Congressional Research Service, March* 2009), pp. 1–30. See also ANDRES OPPENHEIMER, "FIVE DEAL BREAKERS IN ARIZONA'S NEW IMMIGRATION LAW" *MIAMI HERALD*, APRIL 27, 2010 AND MICHAEL MISHAK, "SHERIFF JOE ARPAIO DEFENDS ARIZONA'S NEW IMMIGRATION LAW," *LAS VEGAS SUN*, MAY 7, 2010 FOR TWO OPPOSING ISSUES ON IMMIGRATION REFORM AND THE ARIZONA LAW.

Political Violence and Terrorism

The events of 9/11 and continuing incidents of mass violence in America have had a profound impact on federal, state, and local law enforcement agencies, as police administrators are confronted with the most pressing and significant external issue of their careers: how to investigate, interdict, and prevent terrorism. Police departments around the country have had to address new threats of violence that are sometimes the result of federal actions or international foreign policy actions in which they have no authority. For instance, since 9/11, virtually every large metropolitan police department has been placed on the highest alert. Operational demands required police agencies to perform new activities, including increasing infrastructure security around critical buildings and airports, building anti-terrorism barriers, beefing up intelligence gathering and analysis functions, monitoring activity in Middle Eastern communities, and participating in joint terrorism task forces. Even though an extensive federal structure has been developed to counter the terrorist threat, the first level of prevention (and response) remains with uniformed police officers on the street.

The federal structure came under considerable criticism after 9/11 for failing to coordinate anti-terrorism activity, assess and analyze accurate intelligence information, and act quickly to prevent terrorist activities. Since that horrible day, the pressure to reorganize federal efforts has been the focus of national debate and action.[21] At the center of the controversy was the Federal Bureau of Investigation (FBI). In 1992, Agent Coleen Rowley went before Congress to blow the whistle on an agency she described as too big, too slow, and too set in its ways to effectively combat terrorism.[22] According to Rowley, the structure of the FBI was archaic and in need of significant repair. However, it was the closed subculture that existed within the FBI that Rowley hammered during her testimony before Congress, focusing not only on the top-heavy and cumbersome bureaucratic structure but also on the close-minded, egotistical, and noncooperative attitude that existed throughout the ranks of the FBI.[23] Accordingly, FBI Director Robert Mueller has promised to reform the organization. However, criticism aimed at the FBI continues to grab the headlines of most major news agencies.[24] In 2004, a blistering report from a bipartisan presidential commission faulted the FBI for being too ambitious, directly leading to unnecessary new turf battles with the CIA. And a Justice Department report (in 2005) cited "rapid turnover" among counterterrorism managers at FBI headquarters and a failure to retain knowledgeable experts about terrorism as central issues still confounding the FBI's ability to deal effectively with the terrorist threat. The FBI also continues to complete the development of its "next generation" electronic information management system focused on preventing crime and terrorism. In 2005, the FBI was severely criticized, as a newly $170 million computerized case-management system—Virtual Case File (VCF)—developed by Science Applications International Corporation (SAIC) was scraped due to its inoperability. Much of the criticism was been laid at the door of Director Robert Mueller, who took full responsibility for the debacle. The FBI has begun development on yet another information management system—Sentinel. The primary contractor for this system is Lockheed Martin and the final product, including the FBI's updated counterterrorism database, is being implemented in four phases. The $451 million system has been delayed, once again, but is expected to be completed and operational in 2011.[25]

Nowhere was the case for inefficiency and inoperability between agencies and intelligence systems more apparent than in the case of the 2009 Christmas Day bomber. The U.S. State Department, National Security Agency, and the CIA all had significant information on the primary suspect, Umar Farouk Abdulmutallab from Nigeria. He had sent Internet text messages preaching his vile hatred of America and his father had visited the U.S. Embassy in Nigeria to report his son's radical Islamic beliefs and connections to al-Qaeda in Yemen. The information was sent to the National Counterterrorism Center in Washington, and Abdulmutallab was placed on the terrorist watch list. However, he was *not placed* on the FBI's 400,000-name Terrorist Screening Database, the terrorist watch list that feeds both the 14,000-name Secondary Screening Selectee list and the 4,000-name No Fly List, nor was his U.S. visa revoked.[26] This intelligence breakdown allowed Abdulmutallab to board a U.S. airliner (Northwest flight 253) in Amsterdam on Christmas Day, 2009, bound for Detroit, with the apparent intent of blowing up the plane before landing. Federal intelligence and law enforcement agencies simply "dropped the ball" and failed to connect the disparate pieces of information already in their computer databases, allowing a known radical Islamic terrorist to board a flight to the United States armed with plastic explosives in his underwear. Fortunately, the bombing attack was prevented—the explosives only ignited a small fire that was easily controlled and passengers subdued Abdulmutallab until authorities could take him into custody upon landing in the United States (see Figure 3.7).

Defining Terrorism

In the popular mind, terrorism is viewed as the illegitimate and violent actions of specific groups that violate the authority of rightfully established governments. **Terrorism** encompasses the threat of and/or use of violence to achieve a specific set of political objectives or goals.[27] Historically, defining terrorism has been a very difficult venture, shaped and altered by a number of factors, including our own national interests, government interpretations, the news media, hidden political agendas, and emotional human rights rhetoric.[28] Such phrases as "guerrilla warfare," "revolutionary movement,"

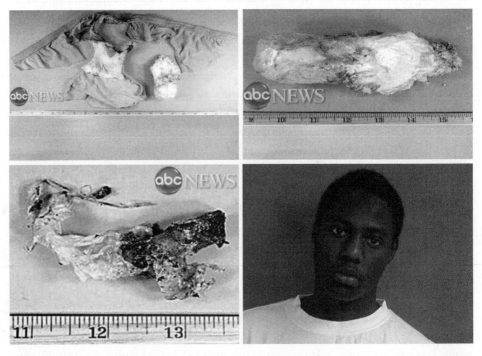

Figure 3.7

Farouk Abdulmutallab attempted to blow-up Northwest Airlines Flight 253 from Amsterdam to Detroit, Michigan on Christmas Day, 2009, by using approximoately 80 gram of explosive material in his underpants. While the material did not explode, it did ignite causing injuries to Abdulmutallab's leg and the inside of the aircraft liner.

(Photographs a, b, and c courtesy of J.B. Nicholas/Splash News/Newscom; d courtesy of U.S. Marshals/Splash News/Newscom) "communist-supported terrorism," and "radical fundamentalist" only heighten ideological sentiment and play to emotion rather than intellect. Hence, we find the cliché that one person's terrorist is another person's freedom fighter to be truly an observation based on perspective and perception.[29] This is certainly the case in the United States, as some actions, such as the first attack on the World Trade Center (1993), the bombing of the Alfred P. Murrah Federal Building in Oklahoma City (1995), the downing of TWA flight 800 (1996), the attacks on 9/11 (2001), and the killing of 13 soldiers at Fort Hood, Texas (2009) are "terrorist," whereas the sporadic bombings at abortion centers or mosques across the country are not.

Large, high-profile terrorist events greatly impact how members of society interact. Random acts of terrorism upset the framework of society, leaving only futile questions without rational answers. Essentially, terrorism tests the basic social structure of dependence and trust. If random bombings and acts of violence occur on a frequent basis at the most secure institutions of a society (e.g., federal buildings, police departments, churches, synagogues, and hospitals), then people tend to lose faith in the existing social and government structure. Safety and security are severely compromised and questioned. Terrorism destroys the solidarity, cooperation, and interdependence on which social functioning is based and substitutes insecurity and distrust.

Terrorism, then, plays to emotion, not intellect.[30] It strikes at the very heart of who we are as Americans. For the first time in modern history (9/11), the United States was rocked by an attack on its own land. People were afraid as their daily lives were impacted and changed forever. The privileges and lifestyle that we so enjoyed in this country appeared to be jeopardized. The ability to travel freely was restricted. Few of us can recall where we were on September 2, 2001, but almost all of us can give vivid details of where we were and what we were doing in the morning hours of September 11, 2001.

The overwhelming question plaguing so many of us was, why? We are a great nation that has helped almost every other nation in need. We give billions of dollars away each year in foreign aid. And we consistently stand for the human rights of all people, emphasizing the dignity of the human spirit and integrity of all people to live free, so why were we the victims of such rage on September 11, 2001, and continuing today, from a group of people that few of us even knew?

Interestingly, the answer may be found in the question. Historically, we have known little about the Middle East. This view is confirmed by the late Osama bin Laden and the al-Qaeda group announcements to the world that one of the primary reasons for the attack was our lack of knowledge about the true political and economic conditions of the Middle East. Indeed, bin Laden made it very clear that they believed our goals in the Middle East were much more motivated by our own self-interest and quest for oil than in safeguarding the human rights of the people in that land. These may be particularly stinging remarks, considering the wars in Iraq and Afghanistan. He maintained that the stationing of American troops in the Middle East—in particular, near the holy city of Mecca (in Saudi Arabia)—was an egregious affront to his religion. He maintained that the people of the Middle

East suffer under puppet governments supported by the United States and that these governments practice state terrorism against their own people. Today, we hear similar reasons given for attacks against the United States, only the focus is much more anti-American regarding our involvement in Iraq, Afghanistan, and other parts of the Middle East.

Here we see quite profoundly the perspective that terrorism can be different things to different people. Theoretically, scholars have been debating the definition of terrorism for the past 25 years.[31] The goal here is to provide a conceptual framework on which to classify and understand terrorism, particularly in the Middle East. The work of Edward Mickolus provides such a framework.[32]

Terrorism is situationally defined—that is, a number of factors play on the difficulty of defining terrorism, including competing political agendas, national interests, economic security, the news media, fundamental cultural and religious beliefs, and the use of misinformation. By exploiting any one of these, it is possible to distort the facts. Even more disturbing and most compromising is the moral judgment passed on those who are labeled terrorists, for we in America assume that terrorism is "what the bad guys do." Hence, what better way is there to distort the sovereign interest of people than to associate them with illegitimate action or sources? In the Middle East, all of these factors are at play, making for a very complicated and difficult analysis. Those perpetrating terrorism against the United States do not view themselves as criminals. Indeed, many are at war and may well be agents provocateur and within the employ of a foreign government. This is an audience that American law enforcement has had little experience with, and these groups pose special challenges to the everyday police officer now charged with thwarting attacks against our homeland and with securing our infrastructure. Conceptualizing terrorism from a different perspective provides us with an opportunity to learn about our adversaries and hopefully exploit their weaknesses. Mickolus conceptualizes terrorism in four distinct typologies, based on actors:

- *International terrorism*—Actions conducted in the international arena by individuals that are members of a nation state. This usually includes members of intelligence and secret services employed by governments, such as the Cuban DGI, the old Soviet KGB, the Syrian Secret Police, the British M-9, the Israili Mossad, and even the CIA.
- *Transnational terrorism*—Actions conducted in the international arena by individuals that have no nation-state. The predominate groups for the past 60 years are associated with the Palestinian cause (e.g., Popular Front for the Liberation of Palestine [PFLP], al-Fatah, Black June, Black September Organization, and Abu Nidal). However, other groups have also been active in the Middle East, such as the Kurdish Workers Party (PKK), the Armenians, and various groups from the breakaway lands of the former Soviet Union. The radical Islamic groups, such as al-Qaeda, HAMAS, and Hezbollah, are also classified in this typology.

- *Domestic terrorism*—Actions conducted by groups within a nation, usually against the government or specific groups within the nation-state. This may be one of the most difficult aspects of attempting to define the concept of terrorism. When do the rights of a government to control splinter elements within its own country end and the rights of the people to rebel become legitimate? This is a difficult question and one most often "flavored" by the myriad of factors already discussed. In any event, within the United States, groups associated with an extremist perspective (whether from the far left, the far right, or single issue) often fall within this typology. Examples of such groups include the Weather Underground, the Earth Liberation Front, the Animal Liberation Front, the Ku Klux Klan, the Neo-Nazis, the National Alliance, many of the radical militias (e.g., the Republic of Texas Militia and the Hutaree Militia of Eastern Michigan), and a myriad of anarchist groups sprouting up in our largest cities. In the Middle East, Israel commonly refers to the Palestinian elements as terrorists acting within Israel's borders, and the Egyptian government has been plagued by radical Islamic extremists influenced by Sheik Abdul Omar Rahman (the Muslim Brotherhood), Osama bin Laden, and American-born Islamic cleric Anwar al-Awlaki.

- *State terrorism*—Actions conducted by governments against their own population. Unfortunately, history is replete with suppressive governments that victimize their own populations. Certainly, the regimes of Adolph Hitler, Joseph Stalin, and Pol Pot represent these types of regimes, often characterized by ethnic and political cleansing. More recently, we have seen these types of activities in smaller countries throughout the Far East and Latin America. In the Middle East, Saddam Hussein in Iraq and Haffez Assad in Syria represented these types of entities. Interestingly, many (including the deceased Osama bin Laden) in the Middle East refer to the governments of Israel, Jordan, Kuwait, Egypt, and Saudi Arabia as suppressive regimes controlled by rich elites that suppress the legitimate rights of their people through the use of kidnapping, death squads, and brutal police tactics. By proxy, the same people also argue that the United States is guilty of state terrorism because it financially and militarily supports these governments. They are quick to point to the military use of power against the Palestinian people in the West Bank and Gaza by the Israelis, the use of armed soldiers in Jordan and Egypt to quell mass demonstrations, and the huge differential between classes in Saudi Arabia. Again, and to re-emphasize, the Middle East is a hodge-podge of cultural, religious, and ethnic groups, all struggling for power and recognition. Precisely defining the terrorist and placing moral judgment is a very difficult task, at best.[33]

From a law enforcement perspective, it is important to understand this conceptualization of terrorism. It provides a framework on which to understand the motivations behind people's actions, particularly in the Middle East and for those

Quick
FACTS ▸▸ Terrorist Attacks Since the 2008 Election of President Barack Obama

Since the election of President Barack Obama on November 4, 2008, attempted terrorist attacks by both Muslim and non-Muslim groups have risen.[1, 2] As of early 2010, there have been 13 attempted terrorist attacks by Muslim groups since President Obama's election, accounting for 39 percent of all attacks by Muslim groups since 9/11. In addition, there have been 28 attempted terrorist attacks by non-Muslim groups since President Obama's election, which accounts for 50 percent of attempted terrorist attacks by these groups since 9/11.[3] This could be caused by two important variables. First, transnational terrorist groups such as al-Qaeda may see a change in administration as an opportunity to coax an overreaction to a terrorist attack in order to maintain public opinion, thus triggering more Muslim anger;[4] or such groups may see this transition as a weak point in America's defense. The second important issue is that some domestic terrorist groups and militias (from the far right) may see the election of an African American President as an offense, or President Obama's progressive social policies as a threat to the status quo.[5] Rises in terrorism often follow elections due to the perceived weakness or shaky transition periods following the election of a new administration, so this could be simply a continuing trend. However, the numbers of attacks within the United States since 2008 are staggering (refer to the following chart).

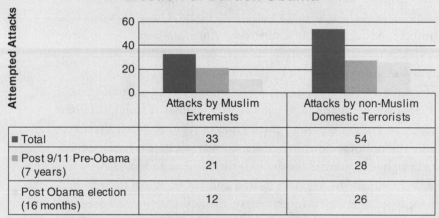

Attempted Terrorist Attacks Pre- and Post-Election of Barack Obama

	Attacks by Muslim Extremists	Attacks by non-Muslim Domestic Terrorists
■ Total	33	54
■ Post 9/11 Pre-Obama (7 years)	21	28
Post Obama election (16 months)	12	26

The rise in terror attacks from both domestic groups and Muslim extremists since the election of President Barack Obama

[1] http://blog.newsweek.com/blogs/thegaggle/archive/2010/02/18/joseph-stack-and-right-wing-terror-isolated-incidents-or-worrying-trend.aspx

[2] http://religiondispatches.org/archive/religionandtheology/2432/

[3] MPAC Data on Post-9/11 Terrorism in the United States, Beutel, A.J. (2010).

[4] http://www.brookings.edu/opinions/2008/1022_terrorism_benjamin.aspx

[5] http://religiondispatches.org/archive/religionandtheology/2432/

Source: A. J. Beutel, "Homegrown Terrorists: A Growing Terrorist Threat?" *MPAC Data on Post-9/11 Terrorism in the United States* (Washington, D.C.: Muslim Public Affairs Council, 2010) and Rick "Ozzie" Nelson, and Arnaud de Borchgrave, "Assessing 'Homegrown Extremism' in the United States." *Center for International and Strategic Studies*, (March 8, 2010). Available at: www.csis.org/files/publication/100304_Nelson_GrowingTerrorist Threat_Web.pdf. and http://religiondispatches.org/archive/religionandtheology/2432/ (June 15, 2010).

expressing a radical Islamic philosophy. Further, it provides a basis on which to develop a conversation or an interview with members of Middle Eastern communities living within the United States, some of whom may be sympathetic to the causes of specific Middle Eastern or radical Islamic groups.

Radical Islamic Terrorism

The list of potential international terrorist threats against the United States is almost unlimited, considering the numerous political conflicts continuing in the international arena. Many of these threats are fueled by political, religious, and/or ideologically motivated causes. Certainly, terrorism from various Middle Eastern groups has posed significant problems to American law enforcement. Historically, the root of conflict in the Middle East was the establishment of Israel in 1948 and the subsequent U.S. support provided to that country. While peace between the two major groups (Israelis and Palestinians) was formally established in 1995, both sides still have major radical movements opposing the process. These groups often act out in the international arena, with the United States being a potential target. Confirmed activities by members of the Jewish Defense League (JDL), the Popular Front for the Liberation of Palestine (PFLP), the Fatah Revolutionary Council, and a host of other splinter groups have caused concern to law enforcement.

However, the most significant activities against the United States in the past 15 years have been led by fundamental Islamic groups acting from clandestine areas in Afghanistan, Iraq, Lebanon, Yemen, and Iran. The first major incident witnessed in the United States connected to fundamental Islam was the bombing of the World Trade Center on February 26, 1993, which killed six people. FBI experts contend that, if the bomb had been just slightly larger and more skillfully placed, the entire building may have collapsed, causing untold devastation and death. Unfortunately, this was just a preview of the horrible events to come just 8 years later. Linkages to Islamic fundamentalist groups in Egypt were developed, resulting in several indictments of Arab nationals living in the United States. One of those convicted was the blind cleric Sheik Abdul Omar Rahman, a spiritual leader and scholar who helped spawn a number of other groups.

The most infamous of these groups is the **al-Qaeda** organization formally led by Osama bin Laden and Ayman al-Zawarahi. It is actually a network of many different fundamental Islamic groups in diverse countries. Their ideology is based primarily on the writings of Sayyid Muhammad Qubt and Ibn Wahhab, two early Islamic scholars calling for a violent purification movement throughout the Middle East and the greater Islamic world. This religious movement is commonly called "Wahhabism" and can be traced back to the early 1920s in Egypt. According to these radical philosophers, the Middle East must be purged of Western influence. To this end, leaders call for a "holy war," or **jihad**, calling on everyday Muslims to join in their fight against the West. Bin Laden and other members of the al-Qaeda network perverted parts of the Koran to justify their philosophy and do not represent mainstream Islam. It is important to understand that Islam is the world's second-largest religion, with over 1 billion peaceful followers, living primarily in Africa, Asia, and Europe. The actions of radical fundamentalists such as Rahman and bin Laden represent not the true path of Islam but rather only a fraction (less than 1 percent) of all Islam.

Unfortunately, the movement has flourished in Egypt and Saudi Arabia for the past 50 years, countries where American influence is easily observed. Members of the al-Qaeda organization are politically motivated to overthrow the "heretic govern-ments" that they see as puppets of Western influence and replace them with Islamic governments based on the rule of the Shariah (the first book of the Koran, strictly regulating all aspects of life).

Osama bin Laden (1957–2011), the son of a wealthy building contractor in Saudi Arabia, rose to power within the fundamental Islamic movement as a student of Ayman al-Zawarahi (see Figure 3.8). However, it was not until the 1979–1989 Soviet–Afghan War that bin Laden actually took a recognized leadership role in the organization. Triumphant over the Soviets and enlisting the aid of American interests in Afghanistan, bin Laden amassed a number of hardened mujahideen (holy warriors) fighters. He became obsessed with Western influence in the Middle East and declared a holy war on the United States in 1996.[34] Fueled by Middle Eastern oil wealth and an increasing radicalization of Islam, bin Laden set out to destroy those entities that he believes have adulterated his homeland. The activities of al-Qaeda have been significant and numerous, culminating on September 11, with the attacks on the World Trade Center and the Pentagon. Their activities include the following:

1996: Bin Laden issues a declaration of war against the "Great Satan" (the United States).

1998: Suicide bombings of the U.S. embassies in Kenya and Tanzania kill 224 people.

2000: Suicide bombing of the USS *Cole* in Yemen kills 17 American sailors.

2001: Attacks on the World Trade Center and the Pentagon kill more than 2,800.

Since Operation Enduring Freedom, which first sent troops to Afghanistan in 2001, and the current wars in Iraq and Afghanistan (2003–today), most scholars and government officials have believed that the stability and operational capability

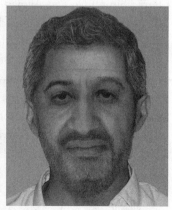

Figure 3.8
Digitally enhanced photographs of Osama bin Laden account for a decade of age and possible changes in facial hair. There was a $25 million bounty on bin Laden's head for the September 11, 2001 attacks and the 1998 U.S. embassy bombings in Tanzania and Kenya. In 2011, members of the Navy's super-secretive SEAL Team Six killed bin Laden in Pakistan.
(a courtesy of AP photo; b and c courtesy of U.S. State Department)

of al-Qaeda has been diminished in the international arena. Certainly, the leadership has been dismantled and most are on the run. Much of the operational capability of al-Qaeda as a single group has also been destroyed. However, al-Qaeda continues to flourish as a *movement* rather than a single group. American soldiers are being attacked in Iraq and Afghanistan on a daily basis by those fighting the "holy jihad." Indeed, the number of deaths of U.S. soldiers over the past several years has continued to climb each year due primarily to the explosion of violence in Iraq and Afghanistan.[35] Suicide bombers expressing the same sentiment have conducted attacks in Riyadh, Istanbul, Madrid, and London with the hallmarks of previous al-Qaeda attacks. The movement adapted from targeting aviation to hitting softer targets, such as mass transit hubs (subway systems) and bus terminals. Notwithstanding the above, it is important to note that the Christmas Day 2009 bomber (Farouk Abdulmutallab) who attempted to blow up a Northwest Airlines flight from Amsterdam to Detroit, Michigan was an active member of al-Qaeda on the Arabian Peninsula (AQAP), a group that subsequently took credit for the attempt. Remnants of the original al-Qaeda group still remain and pose a significant threat to the United States.

Although al-Qaeda may be diminished as a single group, their movement continues to be successful in recruiting new members. From website announcements and flyers to the recruitment of new fighters in the Middle East, the movement continues to grow in sustained acts of violence against Western interests. Most alarming are the number of attacks being planned or those implemented over the past two years from U.S.-born, radical Islamic terrorists.

"Homegrown" Islamic Terrorism

A recent trend observed in the radical Islamic terrorist movement is the development of **"homegrown" terrorism**; that is, instances where U.S. citizens and residents convert to radical Islamic extremism, plot and commit terrorist acts, or fight for the jihadist movement both inside the United States and in foreign counties. In 2009, a number of these instances made national headlines and, once again, threatened the American homeland:

July 2009—A North Carolina man, Daniel Boyd, along with six other individuals, were arrested for operating a terrorist training camp in North Carolina.[36] Daniel Boyd, a U.S. citizen, his two sons, and four others had allegedly been training in their rural lakeside home for "violent jihad." Boyd and his brother had lengthy ties to radical Islamic groups, having been arrested in 1991 in Pakistan on bank robbery charges, and were found with identification indicating they were members of the Islamic terrorist group Hezbollah.[37] Further, Boyd had traveled to the Middle East nearly 20 years prior to train at terrorist camps in Pakistan and Afghanistan, and fought the Soviets (in the Soviet-Afghan War) for three years before returning to the United States.[38] Members of his group also traveled to Israel in 2007 with the intent of joining the Palestinian Islamic jihad movement in that country, but later returned without incident. The seven men were charged with providing material support to terrorists.

September 2009—A 19-year old Jordanian citizen, Hosam Maher Husein (Sam) Smadi, was arrested by the Federal Bureau of Investigation in downtown Dallas, Texas for attempting to detonate an inert/inactive device. The Jordanian had been living and working in Italy, Texas illegally on an expired tourist visa.[39] He had been under constant surveillance by the FBI, and had placed what he believed to be an active car bomb under the Fountain Building in downtown Dallas, a 60-story, glass skyscraper.[40] The decoy device and all materials had been supplied to him by the FBI, who kept him under constant surveillance after discovering him as a potential terrorist in an on-line chat room with a group of extremists. Smadi was subsequently charged with attempting to use a weapon of mass destruction and pleaded guilty to this charge in June 2010.[41]

September 2009—Najibullah Zazi, an Afghan citizen and U.S. legal resident living in Colorado, was arrested on charges of conspiring to use weapons of mass destruction with others against the United States.[42] It was later reported that Zazi had traveled to Pakistan to receive weapons and explosives, and for training in their use and tactics. Zazi pleaded guilty to terrorism charges including conspiracy to use weapons of mass destruction, conspiracy to commit murder overseas, and providing material support for a terrorist organization.[43] He admitted to planning to use explosives when he arrived in New York in September 2009 to make a political statement about civilian killings in Afghanistan.[44] Law enforcement authorities were alerted to Zazi while monitoring various on-line chat rooms. Zazi actually planned his attack on the web and communicated it with others on-line.

October 2009—David Coleman Headley, a U.S. citizen of Pakistani descent, was arrested for plotting the attacks in Mumbai, India that killed 170 people, including 6 Americans. Headley, whose original name is Daood Gilani, had his name changed in order to make his overseas traveling easier.[45] Headley actively scouted targets in Mumbai before the attacks and has admitted to planning and scouting targets against a Danish newspaper that printed images of Muhammad in 2005, an attack that was never carried out.[46] The Chicago native pled guilty to conspiring to bomb public places in India, murder people in India and Denmark, and to providing material support to terrorist groups.[47]

November 2009—Five young men from Virginia (all born in the United States) were arrested in Pakistan for attempting to join Jihadist terrorist groups, specifically Al Qaeda.[48] They had been reported missing by their parents in Virginia on the advice of the local Muslim community after the men had traveled to the Middle East without informing their parents.[49] The "Virginia 5" were reported to have been arrested in a safe house of an anti-India terrorist group in possession of Jihadist literature. They were also reported to be building schematics and maps of local areas. Officials believe they were in the planning stages of a major attack in Pakistan.

November 2009—Major Nidal Malik Hassan, a psychiatrist for the U.S. Army, killed 13 people and wounded 30 others at Ft. Hood, Texas in a Soldier Processing Center. Major Hassan was reportedly unhappy about the continuing wars in the Middle East and feared an approaching deployment to Afghanistan to assist in the

Figure 3.9
Major Nidal Malik Hassan was a mild-mannered Army major and psychiatrist opposed to the war in Iraq and Afghanistan. His apparent "jihad" against these wars was manifested in a shooting massacre at Ft. Hood, Texas on November 5, 2009 claiming 13 lives and wounding 32 others.
(a courtesy of Getty Images; b courtesy of AP Photo/Rodolfo Gonzalez)

war against his fellow Muslims.[50] Major Hassan had showed signs through his career of resistance to the war effort in the Middle East, as well as many disagreements about U.S. foreign policy. Hassan had even been in contact with the radical Muslim cleric Anwar al-Awlaki.[51] Army officials cited numerous failures in supervision and information sharing to recognize these signs and connect the dots that should have produced increased vigilance on Hassan's mental state and potential terrorist activities[52] (see Figure 3.9).

March 2010—Colleen LaRose, more commonly known as "Jihad Jane," was a U.S. citizen born in 1963 and living in Philadelphia. She was apprehended for conspiracy to provide material support to terrorists, conspiracy to kill in a foreign country, attempted identity theft, and making false statements to a government official.[53] Ms. LaRose had been exchanging emails for years in an attempt to recruit fighters for "violent jihad" in South Asia and Europe. Her U.S. citizenship and Caucasian appearance made her appealing to Islamic extremists who used her within the United States.[54] She had also made posts on various on-line message boards and blogs expressing sympathy with various terrorist groups and movements, and a desire to help in any way possible, including fighting and killing, to help ease the suffering of the Muslim people during their jihad or "holy war." LaRose even traveled to South Asia to marry a known and active jihadist in that area. She supplied her American boyfriend's passport to her new "husband" in an attempt to avoid travel restrictions in the United States and Europe.[55] She planned to use her European looks to blend into the Swedish population and to kill a Swedish artist who depicted the face of Mohammed on a dog in 2007[56] (see Figure 3.10).

Figure 3.10
With blonde hair, a fair complexion, and an excellent command of the English language, Colleen LaRose, aka "Jihad Jane" represented the perfect 'homegrown' Islamic extremist. (a courtesy of z03/Zuma Press/Newscom; b courtesy of AFP/Getty Images Newscom)

The case of "Jihad Jane" represents an excellent example of American citizens as terrorists. She was truly a "homegrown" terrorist and attempted to use her unsuspecting looks and American citizenship to further the violent cause of radical Islam. In addition, LaRose's extensive use of the Internet in the form of video posting, email communication, and message board posting illustrated an important mechanism of communication for terrorists worldwide; an electronic avenue that historically has been a method for discussing and planning actual terrorist events.

A Re-Cap of Important New Trends in Radical Islamic Terrorism

Many of the previously mentioned incidents have common associations and methodologies that are worth noting:

Use of the Internet —Almost all of the previously mentioned cases had some linkage with the Internet. Either the suspect used the Internet to contact other individuals involved in the same brand of radicalism, or actually planned the attack over the Internet. Some of the suspects (like Smadi and Jihad Jane) were actually discovered by police authorities because of their extensive Internet usage. Unfortunately, the World Wide Web is fast becoming the new recruiting tool for younger, second-generation Muslim youths living in America, some even born in our country. A report by the National Counterterrorism Center further indicates increased recruitment of Americans and Western Europeans on the Web to conduct terrorist operations within their own country.[57]

Method of Operation (MO)—Almost all of the potential terrorist incidents mentioned in 2009 were focused on large-scale bombings or at least the use of explosives aimed at disrupting communication and/or transportation hubs (like airports, subways systems, and rail systems), causing significant infrastructure failure, and/or the destruction of specific targets such as airplanes or buildings. The suspects trained for their events and in some cases rehearsed for their actions. The events were well planned and specific in nature, designed to inflict mass human casualties.

Common Motive—Many of the suspects came from the "fringe" of radical Islamic thought fueled by discontent toward American policy, particularly focused on the Iraq and Afghan Wars. They were not quiet about their beliefs and shared their thoughts quite openly with others via conversation and the Internet. The basic concept of violent jihad toward America appears to be a common theme. Some of the suspects were recruited by foreign entities also involved in the radical Islamic movement. Recruiting native-born Americans to plan and execute domestic attacks is much easier when the suspect speaks English, and is culturally American, capable of freely moving about the United States without notice. Certainly, this was the case with Jihad Jane.

Anwar al-Awaiki—Several of the suspects had a common association with a U.S.-born, radical cleric named Anwar al-Awaiki (see Figure 3.11). Al-Awaiki is directly tied to al-Qaeda through various intelligence agencies and reports. Further, his use of the Internet to recruit new terrorists and encourage the use of violence within the

Figure 3.11

Anwar al-Awiaki is one of the world's leading radical Islamic ideologues. He is very charismatic and uses the Internet to attract Muslim youth living in the West. He encourages them to use "violent jihad" to accomplish their goals. Al-Awiaki represents the new breed of "homegrown" Islamic radicals; he was born in New Mexico in 1971.

(Courtesy of AFP/Getty Images/Newscom)

radical jihadist movement is well-documented. Al-Awaiki was the past leader of the Islamic Society of North America, an organization linked with the Holy Land Foundation for Relief and Development (Dallas, Texas), and disbanded in 2009 after several of its leaders and executives were sentenced for providing financial aid to terrorist groups in the Middle East (see the following material on Hamas). Al-Awaiki speaks eloquent Arabic and English and is a very charismatic teacher. Umar Farouk Abdulmutallab was Al-Awaiki's student. In addition, Major Nidal Hasan met with al-Awaiki while in Washington, D.C., and several members of the Virginia 5 admit to visiting al-Awaiki's website and conversing with him via the Internet.[58] His excellent English and frequent use of the Internet provide al-Awaiki with a large following, including large groups of disenfranchised youth living in America. He spreads a strong, anti-U.S. agenda, encouraging a violent jihad within America. He currently resides in Yemen.

HAMAS

HAMAS is the largest and most influential Palestinian militant movement today. Its ideology is focused on Israeli–Palestinian conflict and expresses an escalation of armed conflict and terrorism against Israel and its allies (e.g., the United States). HAMAS represent an outgrowth of the Muslim Brotherhood and Wahhabism as expressed by earlier revolutionary writers. It has been a legally registered group in Israel since 1978 and was originally founded by Sheik Ahmed Yassin, the movement's spiritual leader. Yassin was assassinated by the Israeli government as he left prayer service from a mosque in Jerusalem on March 22, 2004, sparking significant violence, yet a quell in suicide bombings. In Arabic, the word "HAMAS" means zeal. But it is also an Arabic acronym for "**H**arakat **A**l-**M**uqawama **A**l-i**S**lamiya," or Islamic Resistance Movement. It is primarily located in the Gaza Strip and the West Bank.

The image of HAMAS in the Middle East is unique in that the group has attempted to rebuild much of the destroyed infrastructure of the Palestinian community while being responsible for 90 percent of the suicide bombings throughout Israel for the past several years. It is an interesting dichotomy: building roads, schools, and social services in the territories of the West Bank and Gaza and wreaking havoc with random suicide bombings against Israel. Hamas has developed strong financial support from unofficial bodies in Saudi Arabia and Iran. In addition, HAMAS makes use of an extensive network of charity associations developed throughout the world, including the United States. This network often serves as a facade for covert activities, including worldwide association with other radical leaders, the transfer of funds to field operatives, and the identification of potential recruits for suicide bombings and other acts of terrorism. Several of these charities operate in larger cities throughout the United States (e.g., New York, Portland, Detroit, Chicago, and Dallas) and have come under the scrutiny of law enforcement. For instance, in late 2002, local police officers and federal agents raided an organization in Richardson, Texas (a suburb of Dallas), seizing records and financial documents, freezing bank accounts, and arresting leaders within the organization. Five leaders of the U.S.-based Muslim charity, Holy Land

Foundation for Relief and Development, were charged with funneling over $12 million to a known terrorist group—that group being HAMAS. Testimony during the various trials indicated that the parent organization for the Holy Land Foundation was the Muslim Brotherhood, a well-known Muslim extremist group stemming from Egypt. In 2008, the five primary leaders of the Holy Land Foundation were convicted of all 108 charges of providing financial support to a known terrorist group, money laundering, and tax fraud. The case remains the single largest and most successful case against terrorism financing in the United States.

In January 2006, HAMAS won the Palestinian Authority's (PA's) general legislative elections, defeating Fatah, the party of the PA's president, Mahmoud Abbas, and setting the stage for a power struggle. Since attaining power, HAMAS has continued its refusal to recognize the state of Israel, leading to severe economic sanctions and naval blockades against the Palestinian Authority, severing the Gaza Strip from outside contact. Attacks on both sides have been documented since 2008 and, finally, in 2010, tensions peaked as the Israeli Defense Forces (IDF) boarded a Turkish freighter bound for Gaza. During the ensuing actions, a Turkish sailor was killed, sparking an international outrage; however, the IDF found a huge shipment of explosives and weapons on the ship, apparently bound for HAMAS to continue their war against Israel. While Israel has eased its naval blockade of the area, the conflict between HAMAS and Israel does not appear to be lessoning.[59]

Hezbollah

Historically, Arab and Iranian (formerly Persian) factions have not collaborated well on issues of political debate. Each sees the other as a major threat in the Middle East. For instance, several wars have been fought between Iran and its neighbors (e.g., Iraq) over border disputes. However, common enemies and philosophies have, unfortunately, united several radical terrorist groups. Their ideology expresses the destruction of Israel and the liberation of Jerusalem as a religious obligation for all Muslims. It justifies the use of terror as a weapon in the hands of the weak and oppressed against the strong, aggressive, and imperialistic activities of Israel and the United States.

Hezbollah, or "Party of God," is based primarily in Lebanon, Syria, and Iran. The basis of Hezbollah is to develop a pan-Islamic republic throughout the Middle East headed by religious clerics in Iran. The group rose to international prominence in 1983 with its involvement in the bombing of the U.S. Marine barracks in Beirut, Lebanon, killing 241 soldiers. For the most part, Hezbollah has been very active throughout the Middle East, targeting U.S. interests abroad. To date, the group has not conducted direct attacks on American soil.

However, since August 2006, Hezbollah has become much more active in the international arena and in the United States. Stemming from its emotionally charged leader, Hassan Nasrallah, and its "victory" over Israel in Lebanon (2006), Hezbollah has garnered significant financial support from Iran. This is particularly distressing as the relationship between the United States and Iran continues to worsen over Iranian President Mahmoud Ahmadinejad's intense verbal attack against the West and his insistence on obtaining

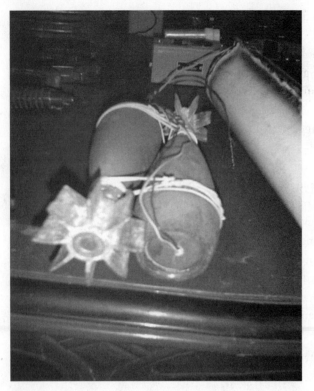

Figure 3.12
Improvised Explosive Devises (IEDs) are used to cause significant bodily damage or death. Many have been found in Iraq and Afghanistan and have been linked back to their manufacturing points in Iran. Hezbollah represents the primary and largest single terrorist group funded by Iran; IEDs were first observed extensively in Lebanon during the 1983 war involving U.S. troops against Hezbollah factions in that country. (Courtesy U.S. Army)

nuclear power for Iran. Further, the increasing number of **improvised explosive devises (IEDs)**, bombs, and other weapons from Iran used in Iraq and Afghanistan against U.S. troops also continues to escalate the situation (see Figure 3.12). In addition, there have been several cases in the United States indicating that profits garnered through illegal activities (e.g., fraud, narcotic trafficking) as well as legitimate business operations have been funneled to the terrorist organization. Several of these cases have arisen in areas of the United States where large concentrations of Lebanese Shiite Muslims reside, such as Charlotte, North Carolina; New York City; and Detroit/Dearborn, Michigan.

In the coming decade, Middle Eastern politics will continue to be combustible and relations with the West more severely strained. As Islamic populations continue to grow in the countries of the former Soviet Union, China, India, Europe, and the United States, it will become more imperative to deal with political realities dispassionately and to transcend stereotypes.[60] Islam is not synonymous with violence, and thus not every Muslim is a terrorist.[61]

Other International Threats

Certainly, the Middle East is not the only area ripe with terrorist activity aimed at the United States. Indeed, the huge growth of Islam in Southeast Asia (e.g., Thailand, Indonesia, Malaysia, the Philippines) continues to also spawn radical movements aimed at destroying Western interests in the area. Jemaah Islamiya (JI) continues to be an active radical Islamic group in Southeast Asia under the leadership of Abu Bakar Bashir (recently released from his Indonesian prison for participation in bombings in Jakarta [2003] and Bali [2002]). And terrorism on the left appears to be escalating throughout Western Europe, fueled in part by the current downtown in the global economy, causing high unemployment and a reduction of government benefits to various populations. Incidents in Germany, Italy, and France have indicated a "reawakening" of the Red Brigades, the Greens, and other cell groups expressing a left-wing, Marxist orientation.[62]

Then, too, a relatively new phenomenon called "**narco-terrorism**" continues to plague American police agencies as well as the international community. The most illustrative cases are seen in South America surrounding the highly lucrative cocaine business. Drug lords in the Medellin and Cali cartels continue to be allied with the M-19 group in Colombia and Sendero Luminoso (Shining Path) in Peru for protection in cultivating and trafficking cocaine to the United States. Similar arrangements between drug dealers and anti-Western political groups (or states) have been observed in Cuba, Nicaragua, Panama, Bulgaria, and Burma.[63] One of the most successful of these collaborations is the development of the notorious street gang Mara Salvatrucha (MS-13).

Originally composed of former soldiers and fighters from civil wars in El Salvador and Honduras during the 1970s and 1980s, MS-13 has become a violent and sophisticated gang associated with drug and human trafficking from Latin America. More problematic to local police agencies is the connection between ethnic drug dealers (Haitians, Jamaicans, and Cubans) and foreign governments, which results in significant financing and armament supplying in support of drug trafficking to the United States.[64]

The Mexican Cartels

Violence along the U.S.-Mexican border has dramatically increased in the last 5 years, so much so, that it has been the focus of most U.S. agencies tasked with preventing terrorism within the United States. For instance, in Ciudad Juarez, the most dangerous city in the world (across the Rio Grande River from El Paso, Texas), over 2,660 people were killed in criminal violence in 2009; that's an average of over 7 people killed every day![65] Most of these murders can be attributed to narco-terrorism and violence between cartels vying for control of the primary transportation routes for billions of dollars worth of illegal drugs entering the United States from Mexico annually. The primary groups operating on the border are the Tijuana Cartel; the Vicente Carrillo Fuentes Organization, also known as the Juarez Cartel; the Gulf Cartel; and the Sinaloa Cartel, composed of several smaller groups including the Guzman-Loera Cartel and the Pacific Cartel. These primary narco-trafficking cartels have direct linkages to Hispanic street gangs operating within the United States (such as the Mexican Mafia, La Familia, and the MS-13 gang), used for street trafficking and enforcement. A rival group operating on the border, Los Zetas, are a group of highly select assassins who deserted from the Mexican Army after extensive training. While originally hired as "enforcers" for the Gulf Cartel, Los Zetas have also become violent leaders in the narco-trafficking business along the U.S.-Mexico border.[66] This gang's brand of narco-terrorism is particularly vicious, often marked by mass murders and mutilated bodies set for display in an effort to frighten rival groups (see Figure 3.13).

Most disturbing are the nearly 400 women in Ciudad Juarez who have also fallen victim to sexual homicide during this same period of time.[67] Since 1993, an estimated 1,000 homicides in Juarez remain unsolved. Many scholars blame the continuing violence and terrorism between trafficking cartels, along with extensive government corruption and poverty, for the significant unrest in Mexico.[68] In an effort to curb the violence, President Filipe Calderon has deployed over 45,000 federal troops and police to 18 states in Mexico. To date, they have had only a limited impact on stopping the violence and have not focused their attention on the myriad of female homicides also accompanying the insurgency. Clearly, the violence in Mexico and particularly along the border will remain a top priority for intelligence agencies and American law enforcement. The violence does not appear to be spilling over into major U.S. cities. During 2009, El Paso reported only 14 murders, and significant drops in murder rates were also reported in Dallas, San Diego, Tucson, and Phoenix during this same period of time.[69] Most interesting, in El Paso, just a stone's throw from the most dangerous city in the world, Juarez, police report only one homicide in the first 6 months of 2010.[70]

Figure 3.13
A murder scene in Ciudad Juarez, Mexico where a police officer was killed reflecting the brutal impact of narco-terrorism. Mexican drug trafficking cartels represent a significant threat to the United States as they wage violence along the U.S.-Mexican border.
(Jesus Alcazar/AFP/Getty Images)

Right-Wing Extremism

The resurgence of right-wing, white supremacist groups across the country was highlighted in the bombing of the Alfred P. Murrah Federal Building in Oklahoma City on April 19, 1995. The blast killed 169 people, including 19 children, and injured more than 500 others. Convicted and sentenced to death, Timothy James McVeigh held "extreme right-wing views and hated the federal government."[71] According to the FBI, the former army sergeant often wore military fatigues, sold weapons at gun shows, and attended militia meetings.[72]

The bombing focused attention on a number of right-wing groups and state militias that have traditionally expressed strong anti-government and White-supremacist propaganda. These groups have also supported violence against minorities (African Americans, Asians, and Jews), homosexuals, and members of the U.S. government (Bureau of Alcohol, Tobacco and Firearms and the Internal Revenue Service). While the number of members of each of these groups is relatively small, they pose a significant threat because of their ability to communicate and coordinate activities. The groups have multiple names and members, publish regular newsletters, maintain websites, and operate automated bulletin board systems. In some cases, documented collusion between these groups and local law enforcement officials has posed a significant threat. Many people are attracted to these groups because they identify themselves with fundamentalist Christianity. Much of their rhetoric focuses on patriotism as interpreted by their leaders, usually using a perversion of the Constitution or the Bible. These groups consist of well-armed ideologues who possess the potential for increased terrorism, at least in geographical pockets throughout the United States.[73]

Quick FACTS ▸▸ Major Right-Wing Militant Groups in the United States

Aryan Nation—This is a White-supremacist organization with strong separatist ideology, founded by Richard Butler of Hayden Lake, Idaho, a major figure in the Christian Identity Church, a pseudoreligious justification for White supremacy. The Nations recruits members from White prison gangs. Their goal is to develop an all-White homeland, to be called the "Northwest Mountain Republic," in Washington, Oregon, Idaho, Montana, and Wyoming. In September 2000, a jury awarded $6.3 million to a mother and son who were assaulted by Aryan Nations guards outside their Idaho compound.[1] The Aryan Nations were forced to sell the land on which the compound was built. With the death of Richard Butler in 2004, the group and its philosophical position continue; however, its numbers have dwindled and the group's future is filled with uncertainty.

Covenant, Sword and Arm of the Lord—This paramilitary group operated primarily in Texas, Arkansas, and Missouri. Eight members were arrested with illegal weapons, explosives, land mines, and an anti-tank rocket launcher in 1985. They were extreme Christian fundamentalist with survivalist mentalities.

Ku Klux Klan (KKK)—This is primarily a southern states organization, with the largest memberships in Alabama, Georgia, Kentucky, South and North Carolina, and Mississippi. Several of the chapters have forgone the traditional cross burning and hooded robes in favor of automatic weapons, paramilitary training camps, and camouflage uniforms. In 2008, a jury awarded $1.5 million in compensatory damages and $1 million in punitive damages to plaintiff Jordan Gruever, represented by the Southern Poverty Law Center against the KKK.[2] The jury found that five KKK members had brutally beaten Gruver, then a 16-year-old of American Indian descent, at a Kentucky county fair. The case, similar to the one against the Aryan Nations in 2000, had a significant impact on the Klan, as its numbers and donations fell dramatically. Current estimates of KKK membership hover around 5,000; however, increases in splinter groups appear to be growing since the election of President Barack Obama in 2008. The group still maintains the White-supremacist and anti-Semitic beliefs prominently characterizing the KKK historically.

Minutemen—This paramilitary organization was strongest during the 1960s. Small enclaves still exist that express strong anti-communist rhetoric and violence against liberals. Their insignia of the crosshairs of a rifle scope usually earmarks this group from other right-wing extremists.

National Alliance—This is a Neo-Nazi group founded by William L. Pierce, who started a new White enclave in rural West Virginia. Pierce was the author of *The Turner Diaries*, the saga of a family that survives the impending race war against African Americans and retreats to the mountains for safety. Pierce's death in 2002 heralded the rise of Erich Gliebe as national chairman. His primary goal has been to foster international membership expressing the White supremacy doctrines of the past, particularly those stemming from Nazi Germany. Significant in-fighting for top leadership positions within the group has greatly diminished membership and finances.

Posse Comitatus—This is a loose-knit group attracting rural farmers. Strong anti-government sentiment claims that the Federal Reserve System and income tax are unconstitutional. Posse leaders have fused tax-protest doctrine with virulent anti-Semitism. Leader Gordon Kahl murdered two U.S. marshals in North Dakota and was subsequently killed in a shootout in 1983.

Skinheads—This is a violence-prone, Neo-Nazi youth gang whose members are noted for their shaved heads. They express a strong White-supremacist, racist, and anti-Semitic ideology and have close linkages to the Ku Klux Klan.

The Order—This is the most violent of the Neo-Nazi groups, with several ties to the Aryan Nations. It is responsible for the murder of a Jewish radio personality in Denver in 1984; at least two armored car robberies totaling $4 million in Seattle, Washington, and Ukiah, California; and a large bombing attempt in Coeur d'Alene, Idaho. The Order has been very quiet during the last decade.

White Aryan Resistance (WAR)—This is the main White-supremacist group in California, headed by Tom Metzger, former Grand Dragon of the California Ku Klux Klan. It currently produces *Race and Reason*, a White-supremacist program shown on public access cable television.

White Revolution—This group was founded in September 2002 by Billy Roper after he was expelled from the National Alliance during a power struggle with Erich Gliebe. The Arkansas-based White Revolution is a racist organization that promotes cooperation between White supremacist groups in the United States and in Europe.

State militias—Active paramilitary organizations exist in almost every state (e.g., the Michigan Militia, the Republic of Texas Militia, and the Arizona Vipers), expressing a strong white,

[1]*Keenan v. Aryan Nations,* CV 99-441, September 8, 2000.
[2]See *Gruver v. Imperial Klans of America,* Civil Action Number 07-CI-00082, November 14, 2008.

(C

Protestant, local constitutionalist perspective of government. They conduct a variety of paramilitary camps and are preparing for an "impending race war." Many groups have legitimate firearms licenses allowing automatic weapons and explosives. One group in Arizona is known to have purchased a World War II–era tank. Strong linkages to local police agencies have been documented. Members are strong gun owner advocates with a superpatriotism and anti-federal government sentiment. In 2009–2010, their financial strength and membership rolls have grown apparently due to deep-seeded conflict over immigration reform. The Southern Poverty Law Center estimates that there are close to 150 militia groups active in the United States. None are more potentially violent than the *Hutaree or Christian Warrior Militia* based in eastern Michigan's Lenawee County. Established in 2008, the group was heavily para-military, participating in extensive training for a future war "preparing for the end time battles" with forces of the anti-Christ.[3] Nine members of the group (located in Michigan, Ohio, and Indiana) were indicted by a grand jury in Detroit for conspiring to murder police officers and civilians using explosives and firearms.[4] Their intent was apparently to "replace" all factions of the government, starting with police officers.

[3]See http://hutaree.com/

[4]See *United States v. Hutaree Members,* copy of federal indictment (see: http://commons.wikimedia.org/wiki/File:Federal-hutaree-indictment-mar-2010.pdf) June 10, 2010.

Source: Adapted from several law enforcement intelligence reports.

Hate Crimes

Right-wing extremist groups represent a movement that promotes Whites, especially northern Europeans and their descendants, as intellectually and morally superior to other races.[74] It is not coincidental that, as these groups have grown in strength, so have the number of reported hate crimes. **Hate crimes** are harms inflicted on a victim by an offender whose motivation derives primarily from hatred directed at a perceived characteristic of the victim (e.g., the person's race, religion, ethnicity, gender, and/or sexual orientation). These crimes are particularly heinous because of their unique impact on victims as well as on the community. Victims often suffer from the suspect's underlying criminal behavior, such as the physical injury caused by violence or the property damage associated with vandalism. In addition, they are victims by the thought that such acts were *not* random, that at least some people in our society detest them because of who they are: African American, Jewish, Islamic, Catholic, Irish, gay-lesbian-transgender, and so on. Hate crimes are often brutal and injurious, and victims are not only physically hurt but also emotionally traumatized and terrified. Others in the community who share the victim's characteristic may also feel vulnerable, and this may escalate the conflict as they attempt to retaliate for the original offense.

In the past, police officers have not been adequately trained to handle such incidents, treating them as routine assaults or vandalism. However, recently enacted federal legislation has resulted in the development of the National Institutes Against Hate Crimes and Terrorism, located at the Simon Wiesenthal Center in Los Angeles, California. The institute provides training for teams of criminal justice professionals from the same jurisdiction to combat hate crimes. Its goal is to provide new strategic approaches to combating hate crimes based on an understanding of the unique elements that differentiate such crimes from other acts. The center has been highly successful in training over 500 participants and providing an ongoing support center for follow-up communication, program evaluation, and professional development via website updates and videoconferences.[75]

Legal definitions of hate crimes vary. The federal definition addresses civil rights violations under 18 U.S.C. Section 245. A hate crime is a criminal offense committed against persons, property, or society that is motivated, in whole or in part, by an offender's bias against an individual's or a group's perceived race, religion, ethnic/national origin, gender, age, disability, or sexual orientation.[76] Most states have a hate crime statute that provides enhanced penalties for crimes in which victims are selected because of the perpetrator's bias against the victims' perceived race, religion, or ethnicity. Some states also classify as hate crimes those in which a victim is selected on the basis of a perception of his or her sexual orientation, gender, or disability. In some states, the passage of hate crime statutes has been controversial as politicians have debated the constitutionality of enhanced penalties based on a suspect's association with an extremist group or the inclusion of homosexuality as a protected class.

Digital Hate

Many White-supremacist groups have used the Internet to recruit potential members and spread their message of hate. Over 1,500 websites can be identified and attributed to extremist organizations that incite racial hatred and religious intolerance as well as terrorism and bomb making. More disturbing is the directed effort by many of these groups to attract young people into their ranks. Based in part on links to other social youth movements involving music and dress (e.g., Skinheads, Black cults, and heavy-metal music), aggressive recruitment on college campuses and the development of web pages designed to attract young people are now quite common. In addition, White-power rock concerts are often sponsored by extremist groups, such as the National Alliance and the World Church of the Creator. These concerts provide face-to-face opportunities for meeting and recruitment.

White-supremacist groups have also created sophisticated computer games aimed at attracting teenagers. *Ethnic Cleansing*, the most high-tech game of its kind, encourages players to kill Blacks, Jews, and Hispanics as they run through urban ghettos and subway environments. In the game, players can dress in Ku Klux Klan robes and carry a noose. Every time a Black enemy is shot, he emits a monkeylike squeal, while Jewish characters shout, "Oy vey!" when they are killed.[77] Quite predictably, the game has spurred significant controversy between game developers and censor advocates. However, very little can be done to ban the game, since many other video games are designed to allow enthusiasts to create new levels and characters, while free software tools enable programmers to build new platforms easily.

These types of games and directed recruitment efforts have been effective tools in swelling the ranks of some extremist organizations.[78] According to one Skinhead source, young people represent the future—"they are the frontline warriors in the battle for white supremacy."[79]

Ecoterrorists and Animal Rights Groups

Many of the single-issue terrorist groups, such as the **Earth Liberation Front (ELF)** and the **Animal Liberation Front (ALF)**, arose from relatively peaceful movements and call for a renewal of the planet's geophysical and biological environment. The notable difference between the terrorist group and the more passive movements (e.g., Earth First and People for the Ethical Treatment of Animals [PETA]) is in the advocacy of violence and destruction to accomplish their ends. Single-issue groups, such as ELF and ALF, pose one of the most significant new threats in domestic terrorism. Both organizations work in small groups with no central hierarchy. They have no formal membership lists, and they work independently in a cell-structured manner similar to other violent groups. The ELF and ALF declared solidarity in 1993 and members of either group usually carry out acts on behalf of both groups. To date, most of their activity has been aimed at the destruction of property and vandalism.

Both groups began in England and migrated to the United States during the 1980s. Like so many other groups, ELF was inspired by the fictional writings of one author, Edward Abbey, whose 1975 novel, *The Monkey Wrench Gang,* told the story of a group of ecologists who were fed up with industrial development in the West. In the novel, environmental activists travel through the western United States spiking trees, burning billboards, sabotaging bulldozers, and damaging the property of people they deem to be destroying the environment. This type of low-level activity has become so popular that, among activists, the term "monkey wrenching" has become a key touchstone for ecoterrorism.[80] The FBI designated ELF a terrorist organization in January 2001. This action was based primarily on the arson attack of a ski resort under construction near Vail, Colorado, in 2001. ELF burned three buildings and caused the destruction of four ski lifts. The group quickly claimed responsibility for the attack, which caused an estimated $12 million in damages. Ironically, the fire almost swept through the adjoining forest and would have destroyed the very habitat ELF was attempting to "save" for the preservation of wildlife. Of course, this was not the only attack from ELF, but it does represent one of the most financially destructive incidents directly attributed to the group.

ALF grew substantially during the 1990s and took on a much more destructive perspective. Instead of just tossing blood or spray-painting individuals wearing furs, the group began a campaign to "free" animals from cages and destroy animal-linked farms, business, and laboratories. Breeding companies were attacked when the animals were released from their cages and the surrounding areas destroyed by fire and/or vandalism. Several of the targets were major research universities in Michigan and California, which not only suffered significant physical damage to buildings but also lost years of research findings and records.[81] However, in January 2006, after a 9-year investigation, the FBI indicted 11 people in connection with a 5-year wave of arson and sabotage claimed by the Earth Liberation Front and the Animal Liberation Front. Detailing nearly 20 attacks from 1996 to 2001, causing no deaths but nearly $25 million in damage to lumber companies, a Vail ski resort, meat plants, and electric towers throughout the Pacific Northwest, the "vast ecoterrorism conspiracy" was dealt a very

IN THE NEWS   The Internet: Selected Hate Sites

Stormfront maintains libraries for both text and graphics, foreign language sections, and a large list of links to other Internet sites.

Resistance Radio promotes and sells the music of hate. Its success has unified many Skinhead bands and has given them their first opportunity to target millions of young people.

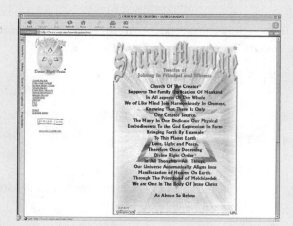

World Church of the Creator and other racist groups attempt to recruit younger and younger followers via the internet.

Source: The New Lexicon of Hate: The Changing Tactics, Language and Symbols of America's Extremists (Los Angeles: Simon Wiesenthal Center, 1999), www.wiesenthal.com. See also Robert W. Taylor, Eric J. Fritsch, John Liederbach, and Thomas Holt, *Digital Crime and Digital Terrorism*, 2nd edition (Upper Saddle River, N.J.: Pearson Prentice Hall, 2011).

severe blow, one that placed a significant dent in the movement.[82] In the last few years, ELF and ALF activities have been limited to a few isolated events involving, again, the firebombing of a UCLA researcher's house in 2006 for research with animals and the arson of four houses in the Seattle region, causing nearly $7 million in damages because the houses were not deemed to be "built green" (2009).[83]

CONCLUSION

Certainly, the face of terrorism in the United States has changed in the past several years. More and more terrorist activities are characterized by random bombings and shootings not aimed at political agendizing or ransom delivery, but done for "effect." That is, they are specific acts of violence aimed at causing significant death, destruction, and widespread pandemonium throughout our communities, leaving the larger society helplessly asking, "Why?" The charge to prevent this type of violence and terrorism has been given to not only federal authorities, but also to local and state police officers. Their ability to use intelligence information relating to terrorist suspects and groups while protecting and maintaining the Constitutional rights of individuals is an important element in making our society safe. The development of fusion centers and participating in a variety of measures that make our communities a difficult place for terrorists to operate can assist police in this mission.

We have learned in this chapter that the world can be a very dangerous place, harboring individuals and groups that would do our country harm. Many of these threats come from the violent actions arising from radical Islamic groups operating abroad (e.g., al-Qaeda, HAMAS, Hezbollah). However, we have also seen new "homegrown" Islamic extremist that participated in terrorist actions both within our country and in foreign lands. Terrorism is not limited to just Islamic radicals. Threats from right-wing hate groups and left-wing anarchists and ecoterrorists must also be considered dangers from within our great country.

CHAPTER REVIEW

1. Define *intelligence*.
2. Describe the Intelligence Cycle as presented in the *National Criminal Intelligence Sharing Plan (NCISP)*.
3. Define a *fusion center* and list its four primary goals.
4. What are the major criticisms aimed at fusion centers and other law enforcement responses to terrorism.
5. List the four primary areas of responsibility within the Department of Homeland Security.
6. Define *terrorism*.
7. Briefly describe the concept of "jihad," and name some of the more radical groups active in the Middle East.
8. Describe the concept of a "homegrown" terrorist and briefly discuss recent trends in radical Islamic terrorism.
9. Define a hate crime.
10. Define an *ecoterrorist*.

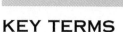

KEY TERMS

al-Qaeda: a radical Islamic, Middle Eastern terrorist organization formally led by the late Osama bin Laden and Ayman al-Zawarahi; it was responsible for the attacks against the United States on September 11, 2001.

all-hazard: able to support operations during an emergency that is either human-made or natural.

critical infrastructure and key resources (CI/KRs): the important facilities, buildings, and installations that provide basic services within a community, such as transportation and telecommunications systems, water and power lines, electronic data systems, key bridges and waterways, emergency facilities, and private sector industries and businesses, that are essential for the defense and security of the United States.

Earth Liberation Front (ELF), Animal Liberation Front (ALF): the two most infamous, single-issue, ecoterrorist groups active in the United States; they are responsible for significant destruction of property caused by arson and vandalism and sometimes resort to more violent means to express their message.

fusion centers: data centers within police agencies that serve as intelligence hubs and clearinghouses for all potentially relevant homeland security and crime information that can be used to assess local terror threats and aid in more traditional anti-crime operations.

HAMAS: the Islamic Resistance Movement of Palestine, representing an outgrowth of the Muslim Brotherhood and Wahhabism, focused on escalating armed conflict and terrorism against Israel.

hate crimes: harms (usually violent crimes) committed against an individual because of his or her perceived race, religion, ethnicity, gender, and/or sexual orientation.

Hezbollah: the "Party of God" terrorist organization primarily based in Lebanon, Syria, and Iran, currently very active in the international arena and responsible for the bombing of the U.S. Marine barracks in Beirut in 1983, killing 241 soldiers.

"homegrown terrorism": instances where U.S. citizens and residents convert to radical Islamic extremism and conduct terrorist acts.

improvised explosive devices (IEDs): Homemade explosive devices and bombs, these "booby-trap" explosives are designed to cause extensive bodily injury or death and are usually located along roads or streets in conflict areas. IEDs are responsible for the majority of the casualties of U.S. troops in Iraq and Afghanistan.

intelligence: data and information that have been evaluated, analyzed, and produced with careful conclusions and recommendations for future decision makers and policymakers.

jihad: a "holy war," a concept perverted by radical Islamists to justify a physical war against the West; a perversion of the concept proscribed in the Holy Koran and *not* representative of mainstream Islam.

narco-terrorism: acts of insurgency by narcotics and drug traffickers aimed at influencing the policies of a specific government or society through violence and intimidation; the violent disruption of legitimate governmental services and security in a specific area.

terrorism: the threat of and/or use of violence to achieve a specific set of political objectives or goals.

ENDNOTES

1 Marilyn Peterson, *Intelligence-Led Policing: The New Intelligence Architecture* (Washington, D.C.: U.S. Department of Justice, BJA, September 2005) NCJ 210681, and K. Riley, G. Terverton, J. Wilson, and L. Davis, *State and Local Intelligence in the War on Terror* (Washington, D.C.: The RAND Corporation, 2005).

2 For a more thorough discussion of the role of intelligence in combating terrorism, see Robert W. Taylor, "Terrorism and Intelligence," *Defense Analysis* 3, no. 2 (1987): pp. 165–175.

3 Peterson, *Intelligence-Led Policing: The New Intelligence Architecture*, p. 3.

4 For a more thorough discussion of the first two schools of thought, refer to R. Godson, ed., *Intelligence Requirements for the 1980s: Analysis and Estimates* (Washington, D.C.: National Strategy Information Center, 1983).

5 Early models of predictive intelligence are discussed in R. Hever, *Quantitative Approaches to Political Intelligence* (Boulder, Colo.: Westview Press, 1978).

6 *National Criminal Intelligence Sharing Plan* (Washington, D.C.: U.S. Department of Justice, 2003, and revised in July 2005).

7 K. Riley, G. Treverton, and L. Davis, *State and Local Intelligence in the War on Terror.*

8 *Fusion Center Guidelines: Developing and Sharing Information and Intelligence in a New Era* (Washington, D.C.: U.S. Department of Justice, 2006).

9 Joseph D' Amico, "Stopping Crime in Real Time," *Police Chief,* September 2006, pp. 20–24.

10 *Fusion Center Guidelines: Developing and Sharing Information and Intelligence in a New Era.*

11 Samuel Walker and Charles M. Katz, *The Police in America,* 5th ed. (Boston: McGraw-Hill, 2005).

12 George L. Kelling and William K. Bratton, "Policing Terrorism," *Civi Bulletin* 43, New York: Manhattan Institute for Policy Research, September 2006, p. 2.

13 See Graeme R. Newman and Ronald V. Clarke, *Policing Terrorism: An Executive's Guide* (Washington, D.C.: U.S. Department of Justice), October, 2008.

14 See Nationwide SAR Initiative (NSI), http://nsi.ncirc.gov/default.aspx (June 2010).

15 *Dallas Morning News*, "City Quits Terrorism Task Force." April 23, 2005, p. 13A.

16 Information received during conversations with various fusion directors at the Fourth National Fusion Center Conference, New Orleans, LA., February 23–25, 2010.

17 For a thorough critique focusing on fusion centers, see Torin Monahan and Neal A. Palmer, "The Emerging Politics of DHS Fusion Centers," *Security Dialogue*, 40:6, December 2009, pp. 617–636.

18 Michael German and Jay Stanley, "What's Wrong with Fusion Centers? Retrieved June 8, 2008 from http://www.aclu.org/pdfs/privacy/fusioncenters_20071212.pdf

19 John Rollins, *Fusion Centers: Issues and Options for Congress* (Washington, D.C.: Congressional Research Services, January 2008).

20 http://change.gov/newsroom/entry/key_members_of_obama_biden_national_security_team_announced/ (May 31, 2010)

21 Bill Gertz, *Breakdown: How America's Intelligence Failures Led to September 11* (Washington, D.C.: Regnery, 2002).

22 Toni Locy, "FBI Too Top-Heavy, Whistleblower Tells Panel," *USA Today,* June 7, 2002, p. 4A.

23 Ibid.

24 Several news agencies have reported on continued problems with the FBI. See Dan Eggen and Griff Witte, "The FBI's Upgrade That Wasn't," *Washington Post,* August 18, 2006; Terry Frieden, "Report Examines FBI's Focus on Terrorism," *CNN,* October 4, 2004; Bill Gertz, "WMD Panel Fires FBI Agent," *Washington Times,* January 13, 2005; and Alfred Cummings and Todd Masse, *FBI Intelligence Reform Since September 11, 2001: Issues and Options for Congress* (Washington, D.C.: CRS Report to Congress, August 4, 2004).

25 Tony Romm, "FBI Computer Upgrade Encounters Serious Hurdle, Delayed Until 2011," *The Hill,* Washington, D.C., (March 19, 2010), p. 1.

26 http://www.nytimes.com/2010/01/16/opinion/16sat2.html

27 Richard Schultz, "Conceptualizing Political Terrorism: A Typology," *Journal of International Affairs* 4, no. 8 (spring/summer 1978), p. 8.

28 Robert W. Taylor and Harry E. Vanden, "Defining Terrorism in El Salvador: La Matanza," *Annals of the American Academy of Political and Social Science* (September 1982), 106–117.

[29] Ibid., p. 109.

[30] Ibid.

[31] For a discussion on the various definitions of terrorism, see Richard Schultz, "Conceptualizing Political Terrorism: A Typology," *Journal of International Affairs* 4, no. 8 (spring 1978); Martha Crenshaw Hutchinson, *Revolutionary Terrorism* (Stanford, Calif.: Hoover Institute Press, 1978); Brian Jenkins, *The Study of Terrorism: Definitional Problems* (Santa Monica, Calif.: The RAND Corporation, 1980); James M. Poland, *Understanding Terrorism: Groups, Strategies, and Responses* (Upper Saddle River, N.J.: Prentice Hall, 1988); Paul Wilkinson, *Political Terrorism* (New York: Wiley Press, 1974); Bruce Hoffman, *Inside Terrorism* (New York: Columbia University Press, 1998); and Jonathan R. White, *Terrorism: An Introduction* (Belmont, Calif.: West/Wadsworth, 2003).

[32] The conceptualization of terrorism is presented in a number of works. See Edward Mickolus, "Statistical Approaches to the Study of Terrorism," in *Terrorism: Interdisciplinary Perspectives,* Yonah Alexander and Maxwell Finger, eds. (New York: McGraw-Hill, 1977), pp. 209–269. For additional reading on this subject, see David Milbank, *International and Transnational Terrorism: Diagnosis and Prognosis* (Washington, D.C.: CIA, 1976), and Richard Schultz, Jr., and Stephen Sloan, *Responding to the Terrorist Threat: Security and Crisis Management* (New York: Pergamon Press, 1980).

[33] Ibid.

[34] For detailed information on the life of Osama bin Laden, see Yossef Bodansky, *Bin Laden: The Man Who Declared War on America* (Rocklin, Calif.: Prima, 1999).

[35] RAND Corporation, RAND Terrorism Incident Data Base. See www.rand.org/ise/projects/terrorism database/. Retrieved June 10, 2010.

[36] Alejandro J. Beutel, "Data on Post-9/11 Terrorism in the United States," *Muslim Public Affairs Council: Policy Memo Backgrounder*, April 1, 2010, pp. 1–16.

[37] See M. J. Stephey, "Daniel Boyd: A Homegrown Terrorist?" *Time Online*, July 30, 2009, retrieved online from www.time.com/time/nationa/article/0,8599,1913602,00.html on April 23, 2010.

[38] See M. Baker, "Daniel Boyd, Six Others in North Carolina, Charged with Terror Conspiracy," *The Huffington Post*, July 27, 2009, retrieved online from www.huffingtonpost.com/2009/07/27/daniel-boyd-six-others-in_n_245792.html on April 23, 2010.

[39] See A. Gary, "Hosam Maher Husein Smadi Arrested for Dallas Bomb Plot," *The Huffington Post*, September 24, 2009, retrieved online from www.huffingtonpost.com/2009/09/24/hosam-maher-husein-smadi-_n_299340.html on April 25, 2010.

[40] See J. Trahan, T. J. Gillman, and S. Goldstein, "Dallas bomb plot suspect told landlord he was moving out," *The Dallas Morning News*, September 26, 2009, retrieved from www.dallasnews.com/sharedcontent/dws/dn/latestnews/stories/092409dnmetbombarrest.1b177db8b.html on April 25, 2010.

[41] Ibid.

[42] Rick "Ozzie" Nelson and Ben Bodurian, "A Growing Terrorist Threat? Assessing 'Home-grown Extremism' in the United States." *Center for International and Strategic Studies,* March 8, 2010, retrieved from www.csis.org/files/publication/100304_nelson_growingterroristthreat_web.pdf on April 22, 2010.

[43] "Najibullah Zazi," *The New York Times,* updated February 22, 2010, retrieved online from http://topics.nytimes.com/topics/reference/timestopics/people/z/najibulla_zazi/index.html on April 18, 2010.

[44] Michael Leiter, Director of National Counterterrorism Center, "*Hearing Before the Senate Homeland Security and Governmental Affairs Committee: Eight Years After 9/11: Confronting the Terrorist Threat to the Homeland,*" September 30, 2009. Transcript online at www.nctc.gov/press_room/speeches/hbshsgac_8years_9-3—29.pdf, retrieved April 22, 2010.

[45] See G. Miller, "Al Qaeda's new tactic is to seize shortcuts," *Chicago Tribune,* March 19, 2010, retrieved online from www.chicagotribune.com/news/nationworld/la-fg-qaeda19-2010mar19,0,3312538.story on April 18, 2010.

[46] See P. Belien, "Jihad against Danish Newspaper," *The Brussels Journal,* October 22, 2005, retrieved online from http://www.brusselsjournal.com/node/382 on April 16, 2010.

[47] Rick "Ozzie" Nelson and Ben Bodurian, "A Growing Terrorist Threat? Assessing 'Home-grown Extremism' in the United States."

[48] Spencer Ackerman, Pakistani Court Indicts "Virginia Five," *The Washington Independent*, March 17, 2010, retrieved online from http://washingtonindependent.com/79466/pakistani-court-indicts-virginia-five on April 10, 2011.

[49] See S. Ackerman, "A Mixed Picture on Domestic Radicalization?" *The Washington Independent,* December 10, 2009, retrieved online from http://washingtonindependent.com/70388/a-mixed-picture-on-domestic-radicalization on April 24, 2010.

[50] See G. Whittell, "Profile: Major Nidal Malik Hassan was trained to treat post-traumatic stress," *The Times,* November 6, 2009, retrieved online from www.thetimes.co.uk/tto/news/world/americas/article2001549.ece on April 20, 2010.

[51] Rick Nelson and Ben Bodurian, "A Growing Terrorist Threat? Assessing 'Home-grown Extremism' in the United States."

[52] See, "Major Hassan's Smooth Ascension," *The New York Times,* January 15, 2010, retrieved online at www.nytimes.com/2010/01/16/opinion/16sat2.html on April 23, 2010. Appeared in print January 16, 2010, p. A-20.

[53] Department of Justice, "Pennsylvania Woman Indicted in Plot to Recruit Violent Jihadist Fighters and to Commit Murder Overseas," Federal Bureau of Investigation Philadelphia Office Press Release, March 9, 2010, retrieved online at http://philadelphia.fbi.gov/dojpressrel/pressrel10/ph030910a.htm on April 24, 2010.

[54] See H. Khan, E. Friedman, and J. Ryan, "'Jihad Jane's' Arrest Raises Fears about Homegrown Terrorists," *ABC News,* March 10, 2010, retrieved online at http://abcnews.go.com/GMA/politics/jihad-jane-arrest-colleen-larose-raises-fears-homegrown/story?id=10056187 on April 22, 2010.

[55] Department of Justice, "Pennsylvania Woman Indicted in Plot to Recruit Violent Jihadist Fighters and to Commit Murder Overseas."

[56] See "Profile: 'Jihad Jane' from Main Street," *BBC News,* last updated March 11, 2010, retrieved online at http://news.bbc.co.uk/2/hi/americas/8561888.stm on April 26, 2010.

[57] Michael Leiter, Director of National Counterterrorism Center, "*Hearing Before the Senate Homeland Security and Governmental Affairs Committee: Eight Years After 9/11: Confronting the Terrorist Threat to the Homeland.*"

[58] Rick Nelson and Ben Bodurian, "A Growing Terrorist Threat? Assessing 'Home-grown Extremism' in the United States."

[59] Jonathon Ferziger, "Israel Eases Import Curbs on Gaza Strip," *Bloomberg Newsweek*, June 13, 2010. p. 1. See: http://www.businessweek.com/news/2010-06-13/israel-eases-import-curbs-on-gaza-strip-ayalon-says-update1-.html

[60] John L. Espisito, The Islamic Threat: Myth or Reality? (Oxford: Oxford University Press, 1999), p. ix.

[61] See A. M. Rosenthal, "As You Sow," *New York Times,* December 22, 1992, p. A21; E. McQuaid, "By Peace or the Sword," *Jerusalem Post,* December 16, 1992; D. Pipes, "Fundamental Questions about Muslims," *Wall Street Journal,* October 30, 1992, p. A11; and A. Permutter, "Wishful Thinking about Islamic Fundamentalism," *Washington Post,* January 19, 1991, p. 16.

[62] See Robert Kupperman and Jeff Kamen, "A New Outbreak of Terror Is Likely," *New York Times,* April 19, 1988, p. 6, and Alan Riding, "Rifts Threaten Plan to Remove Borders," *CJ International* 6, no. 5 (September/October 1990), p. 3.

[63] David W. Balsiger, "Narco-Terrorism 'Shooting Up' America," in *Annual Edition: Violence and Terrorism 1990/91* (Guilford, Conn.: Dushkin, 1990), pp. 164–66.

[64] Ibid.

[65] Nick Allen "Mexican city is 'murder capital of the world'" – *The Telegraph*, October 22, 2009.

[66] See George Grayson, "Los Zetas: the Ruthless Army Spawned by a Mexican Drug Cartel". U.S. Foreign Policy Research Institute. http://www.fpri.org/enotes/200805.grayson.loszetas.html, and Michael Ware, "Los Zetas called Mexico's most dangerous drug cartel". *CNN News*. August 6, 2009 http://www.cnn.com/2009/WORLD/americas/08/06/mexico.drug.cartels/index.html

[67] See Teresa Rodriguez, *The Daughters of Juarez: A True Story of Serial Murder South of the Border* (New York: Atria Books, 2007).

[68] Chris Bowden, "Mexico's Red Days". *GQ* (GQ.com, Conde Nast Digital): 1–6, July 2008. http://www.gq.com/news-politics/big-issues/200807/juarez-mexico-border-murder-drug-war?currentPage=1. Also see Collen Cook, *Mexican Drug Cartels* (Washington, D.C.: Congressional Record Services, 2007).

[69] Kevin Johnson, "Violence drops in U.S. Cities Neighboring Mexico," *USA Today*, December 28, 2009, p. 1.

[70] Conversation between Robert Taylor and Chief Gregory Allen in El Paso, June 17, 2010.

[71] "Families Scoff at Suspect's New Images," *Sunday Oklahoman,* July 2, 1995, p. 24.

[72] Ibid.

[73] Louis A. Radelet and David Carter, *Police and the Community*, 5th ed. (New York: Macmillan, 1994), p. 248.

[74] *The New Lexicon of Hate: The Changing Tactics, Language and Symbols of America's Extremists* (Los Angeles: Simon Wiesenthal Center, 1999).

[75] For more information, see the National Institutes Against Hate Crimes and Terrorism, visit their website: http://www.museumoftolerance.com/site/c.tmL6KfNVLtH/b.5052739/

[76] *Responding to Hate Crimes: A Police Officer's Guide to Investigation and Prevention* (Washington, D.C.: U.S. Department of Justice and International Association of Chiefs of Police, 1999).

[77] Victor Godinez, "Hate Group Wooing Teens by Making a Game Out of Racism," *Dallas Morning News,* March 14, 2002, p. A2.

[78] R. W. Taylor, E. J. Fritsch, and T. J. Caeti, *Juvenile Justice: Policies, Programs, and Practices*, 3rd edition (New York: McGraw-Hill, 2010) pp. 518–520. See also Robert W. Taylor, Eric J. Fritsch, John Liederbach, and Thomas Holt, *Digital Crime and Digital Terrorism*, 2nd edition, (Upper Saddle River, N.J.: Pearson Prentice Hall, 2011).

[79] An interview with leader of the Texas Militia in Dallas (January 2006), reflecting much of the sentiments expressed by Tom Metzger, a leader of the White Aryan Resistance (WAR).

[80] Jonathan R. White, *Terrorism and Homeland Security*, 6th ed. (Belmont, Calif.: Wadsworth Cengage Learning, 2009), p. 233.

[81] Cindy C. Combs, *Terrorism in the Twenty-First Century*, 3rd ed. (Upper Saddle River, N.J.: Prentice Hall, 2003), pp. 164–166.

[82] See Blaine Harden, "11 Indicted in 'Eco-Terrorism' Case," *Washington Post,* January 21, 2006, p. A-3.

[83] See "Terror at UCLA," *Critical Mass* (August 22, 2006) and "Luxury Homes Burn in Apparent Eco-Attack,"*Associated Press* (March 3, 2008).

4

Politics and Police Administration

Power corrupts and absolute power corrupts absolutely.
—Lord Acton

Objectives

- Explain the significance of the U.S. Supreme Court decisions in each of the following cases: *Mapp v. Ohio* (1966), *Gideon v. Wainwright* (1963), *Escobedo v. Illinois* (1964), and *Miranda v. Arizona* (1966).

- Discuss the three distinctly different styles of law enforcement discussed by James Q. Wilson.

- Describe how the type of local government (strong mayor and city manager) impact the way police chiefs are selected.

- Explain the legally defined roles of city councils.

- Discuss the advantages of providing tenure in contracts for police chiefs.

- Describe the differences between a county sheriff and police chief.

- Explain how the state prosecutor impacts police practices.

- Discuss the ways in which the judiciary impacts police practices.

- Describe the two models of citizen oversight.

- Describe the role of public interest groups.

- Discuss the role of chambers of commerce and service clubs.

- Analyze some of the reasons for the conflicts between the media and law enforcement.

- Discuss the political implications of police brutality.

- Analyze the ways in which racial and ethnic profiling can impact on citizen relations with the police.

- Discuss the emerging role and potential political conflict of the local police in illegal immigrant enforcement.

OUTLINE

Introduction

In discussing the relationship between politics and police administration, it is important to distinguish between "Politics" and "politics." **Politics**, when used negatively, refers to attempts to impose external, partisan political influence on the operation of a department.

However, **politics**, used in the positive sense, means governance of a city. Aristotle's original understanding of the word *politics* was "science of the polis," seeking the good of both citizen and city-state.[1]

In order to successfully maneuver through the minefields of politics in any community, a police administrator should possess the following information: (1) how politics at the state level impacts local law enforcement; (2) how the dominant political culture of a community can affect the quality and style of law enforcement services provided; (3) why the politics and organizational structures of police departments and sheriffs' departments are so different; (4) the ways in which judges and prosecutors can impact on enforcement practices; (5) the important roles played by chambers of commerce, churches, and the

media; (6) why some communities have the need for and demand the creation of citizen oversight committees; (7) an accurate assessment of the local political environment in order to be responsive to the local community needs; and (8) how a failure to accurately assess the political environment of a local community can prematurely end the career of a police chief or sheriff.

Federal Influence in Law Enforcement

Some authorities believe that trends occurring from the 1960s to the present have resulted in the partial nationalization of criminal justice. Up to the 1960s, it was safely said that criminal justice was almost completely the responsibility of state and local governments. Federal criminal statutes were limited in their coverage, federal assistance to local law enforcement was generally in the areas of training and the processing of evidence, and the U.S. Supreme Court concerned itself with only the most notorious violations of Constitutional rights by state and local authorities.[2] This trend was reversed in no small measure by a series of opinions, rendered by the Supreme Court under the strong leadership of Chief Justice Earl Warren, that greatly strengthened the rights of accused persons in criminal cases. However, as the Supreme Court has become more conservative in the past two decades, an "erosion" of many of the landmark cases of the Warren era can be observed.

Supreme Court Decisions Affecting Law Enforcement: 1961 to 1966

Significant judicial review of local police actions has been a somewhat recent practice.[3] However, from 1961 to 1966—a period frequently referred to as the "due process revolution"—the Supreme Court took an activist role, becoming quite literally givers of the law rather than interpreters of it. The Warren Court's activist role in the piecemeal extension of the provisions of the Bill of Rights, via the due process clause of the Fourteenth Amendment, to criminal proceedings in the respective states might have been a policy decision.[4] Normally, the Supreme Court writes opinions in about 115 cases during any particular term. During the 1938–1939 term, only five cases appeared under the heading of criminal law; a scant three decades later, during the height of the due process revolution, about one-quarter of each term's decisions related to criminal law.[5] The Supreme Court could scarcely have picked a worse period in which to undertake the unpopular role of policing the police; a burgeoning crime rate far outstripped population increases, and many politicians were campaigning on "law and order" platforms that all too often dissolved into rhetoric on their election. The problem of crime increasingly came to the public's eye through the media. In sum, the high court extended procedural safeguards to defendants in criminal cases precisely when the public's fear of crime was high and there was great social pressure to do something about crime.

Fundamentally, the Supreme Court's role in the due process revolution was a response to a vacuum in which the police themselves had failed to provide the necessary leadership. The era of strong social activism by various special-interest groups was not yet at hand, and neither the state courts nor the legislatures had displayed any broad interest in reforming the criminal law. What institution was better positioned to undertake this responsibility? The Court may even have felt obligated by the inaction of others to do so. Therefore, it became the Warren Court's lot to provide the reforms so genuinely needed but so unpopularly received. The high court did not move into this arena until after it had issued warnings that, to responsive and responsible leaders, would have been a mandate for reform.

Several key decisions were made by a split vote of the Court and drew heavy criticism from law enforcement officers and others as handcuffing police in their struggle with lawlessness. These decisions included:

- *Mapp v. Ohio* (1961), which banned the use of illegally seized evidence in criminal cases in the states by applying the Fourth Amendment guarantee against unreasonable searches and seizures
- *Gideon v. Wainwright* (1963), which affirmed that equal protection under the Fourteenth Amendment requires that legal counsel be appointed for all indigent defendants in all criminal cases
- *Escobedo v. Illinois* (1964), which affirmed that a suspect is entitled to confer with an attorney as soon as the focus of a police investigation of the suspect shifts from investigatory to accusatory
- *Miranda v. Arizona* (1966), which required police officers, before questioning suspects, to inform them of their constitutional right to remain silent, their right to an attorney, and their right to have an attorney appointed if they cannot afford to hire one. Although the suspect may knowingly waive these rights, the police cannot question anyone who, at any point, asks for a lawyer or indicates "in any manner" that he or she does not wish to be questioned.[6]

The impact of these decisions on police work was staggering. In an effort to curb questionable and improper tactics, the Supreme Court essentially barred the use of illegally obtained evidence in a criminal prosecution to prove guilt. This action, known as the *exclusionary rule,* rested primarily on the judgment that deterring police conduct that violates the Constitutional rights of an individual outweighs the importance of securing a conviction of the specific defendant on trial. A need for new procedures in such areas as interrogations, lineups, and seizures of physical evidence was created.

Although the decisions of the due process revolution initially were criticized by many law enforcement officers, over the years that view has changed as new generations of law enforcement officers come along for whom those decisions are simply the correct way to do things. Also, time has seen the exodus of some officers from the police profession who simply could not or would not adapt to a new way of doing business. Finally, there was a growing willingness among law enforcement leaders to acknowledge not only that some of their tactics needed changing but also that *Miranda* and other decisions had accomplished it.

More Recent Supreme Court Decisions

Early appointments to the Supreme Court by President Ronald Reagan and later appointments by President George W. Bush have created a conservative majority who generated decisions more favorable to law enforcement. Beginning in the early 1970s and continuing to today, the Supreme Court has systematically eroded the basic principles set forth in the *Mapp* and *Miranda* decisions.[7]

Exceptions to the exclusionary rule developed in *Mapp v. Ohio* started in 1984. In *Massachusetts v. Sheppard* and *United States v. Leon,* the Court held that evidence obtained by the police acting in "good faith," even if it is ultimately found to be illegally seized because of an error committed by the judge or magistrate, is still admissible in court.[8] In *Leon,* the Court reasoned that the exclusionary rule was designed to deter police misconduct rather than punish the police for the errors of judges. Therefore, the Fourth Amendment's exclusionary rule should not be applied to bar the prosecution from using evidence that had been obtained by police officers acting in reasonable reliance on a search warrant issued by a neutral magistrate, even if that warrant is found to be invalid substantively for lack of probable cause. Critics of the decision suggest that the "good faith" exception will encourage police to provide only the minimum of information in warrant applications and, hence, will undermine the integrity of the warrant process.[9]

Traffic Stops and Arrest

The original decision on automobile stops and searches was developed in 1925 in *Carroll v. United States* (see Figure 4.1).[10] As long as the vehicle was stopped because of reasonable and individualized suspicion (usually a traffic violation), the areas in plain view and the area around the driver were subject to search without a warrant. The mobility of the motor vehicle produced an exigent circumstance to the search warrant requirement. As long as the officer could develop probable cause that the vehicle was transporting contraband or other illegal substances, a warrant was not required. In 1990, the Court expanded the right to stop and search a vehicle without violation or individualized suspicion by allowing sobriety checkpoints and roadblocks. The Court rejected the concept that sobriety checkpoints violated the Fourth Amendment and allowed police agencies to stop vehicles without individualized suspicion.[11]

In 2001, the Supreme Court, in *Atwater v. City of Lago Vista,*[12] ruled that the Fourth Amendment does not forbid warrantless arrests for minor criminal or traffic offenses. The case involved the arrest of a person for a seatbelt violation, an offense punishable by a maximum $50 fine.

This line of reasoning was unanimously upheld by the Supreme Court in 2002, which ruled that, if an officer has reason to suspect a crime, he or she may stop a suspect vehicle without due cause. The case stemmed from a U.S. Border Patrol officer stopping a minivan that turned out to be carrying over 125 pounds of marijuana. The case involved a 1998 traffic stop in Arizona near the Mexican border. The Border Patrol officer observed the minivan on a back road frequently used by drug traffickers. The driver looked nervous and failed to wave at the officer, although children in the van were waving vigorously. According to the officer, the van was registered in a high-crime

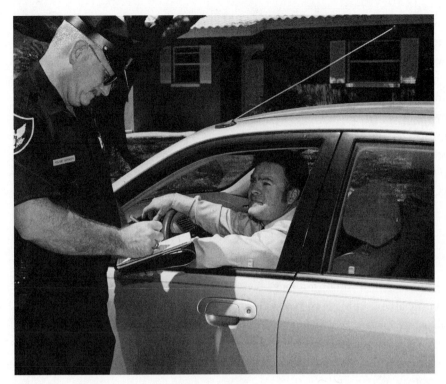

Figure 4.1
The landmark case involving automobile stops and searches was developed in 1925 in Carroll v. United States. (*Source:* © Lisa F. Young/Fotolia)

neighborhood, and minivans are often used in smuggling drugs. A California-based federal appeals court had ruled that the officer did not have enough reason to make the stop and had violated the owner's Constitutional right to be free from unreasonable search and seizure. Chief Justice William Rehnquist wrote for the Court that the appropriateness of a police stop must be judged on the "totality of the circumstances" in each case. This process allows officers to draw on their own experience and specialized training; hence, the appeals court decision was overturned. This case was important to the enforcement of drug and immigration laws. Further, it could also apply to anti-terrorism efforts. As Justice Sandra Day O'Connor indicated, "We live in a perhaps more dangerous age today than when this traffic stop happened."[13]

Self-Incrimination

Nowhere is the erosion of a Warren Court decision more obvious than in the cases impacting the *Miranda v. Arizona* doctrine. During the past 25 years, the Court has systematically loosened the application of the Miranda warning, allowing evidence to be admitted under a variety of exceptions. The most controversial and complex of these cases occurred in 1991. In *Arizona v. Fulminante,* the Court ruled that an error made by the trial court in admitting illegally obtained evidence (in determining that a confession was coerced) does not require an automatic reversal of the conviction if the error is determined to be harmless—that is, if there is no reasonable possibility that a different result would have been reached without the illegally seized evidence.[14] Even though Ful-minante's confession was ruled to be "harmful" and was subsequently reversed, the im-portance of the ruling was the establishment of a more conservative procedure for reversing cases, even when confessions have been coerced and, hence, illegally obtained.

In the foreseeable future, the Supreme Court will likely continue to expand po-lice powers in such areas as search and seizure and interrogation, especially as they re-late to suspected terrorists whose stated goals are to kill as many Americans as possible any place in the world whenever the opportunity presented itself. It is equally likely the Court will produce rulings that will reverse some of the gains made since the due process revolution of the Warren Court regarding misconduct by the police.[15]

The Roles of State and Local Governments in Law Enforcement

From the outset, most Americans had a firm belief that the police should be controlled by local officials organized along municipal lines. For them, a national police, such as the Italian *carabinieri,* was inconceivable, and a state police, such as the German *polizei,* was undesirable.[16] However, the history of state and local relations in the area of law enforcement has often been a rocky and tumultuous one. Fogelson, for exam-ple, has noted,

> By the mid-nineteenth century, it was plain that for most police departments local control meant Democratic control. Hence the Republican leaders, who generally spoke for the upper middle and upper classes, demanded state control, arguing that it would remove the police from partisan politics and improve the quality of law enforcement. Their Democratic opponents countered that state control would merely shift the focus of political interference and plainly violate the principle of self-government. The issue erupted in one city after another, with the Republicans usually getting their way. They imposed state control of the police in New York City in 1857, Detroit in 1865, Cleveland in 1866, New Orleans in 1868, Cincinnati in 1877, Boston in 1885, and Omaha in 1887. They also established metropolitan police departments, with jurisdiction over the central city and adjacent territory, in New York City in 1857, Albany in 1865, and a few other places thereafter.
>
> Under these arrangements the state authorities appointed a board to manage, or at any rate to oversee, the big-city police. But the states did not contribute anything toward the upkeep of the police departments; nor, except in a few cases, did they au-thorize them to operate in the metropolitan area, much less throughout the entire state. Not until the early twentieth century did Pennsylvania, New York, and a few other states form statewide constabularies; and these forces, which patrolled mainly in small towns and rural districts, supplemented rather than supplanted the munici-pal police. Thus despite these changes, the American police remained decentralized to a degree unheard of anywhere in Western Europe. By the late nineteenth century, moreover, state control was well on the wane. The Democrats attacked it at every op-portunity; and in the face of mounting evidence that the state boards had neither re-moved the police from partisan politics nor improved the quality of law enforcement,

the Republicans were hard pressed to defend it. The issue was soon resolved, usually when the Democrats took office. The state authorities not only abolished metropolitan policing in New York and Albany in 1870 but also reestablished local control in Cleveland in 1868, New York in 1870, New Orleans in 1877, Cincinnati in 1880, Detroit in 1891, and Omaha in 1897. By 1900 the big-city police were controlled by local officials and organized along municipal lines everywhere in urban America except for Boston, Baltimore, St. Louis, Kansas City, and a few other places.[17]

The type of direct takeover of local law enforcement by the states described by Fogelson will very likely not occur again, or at least not on the grand scale of the 1800s. However, we may see some isolated cases. For example, several years ago some public officials in Georgia were urging the state to take over the administration of the Atlanta Police Department because of dramatic political upheavals that were affecting the morale and effectiveness of that department. A takeover by the state did not occur, but the political atmosphere was conducive to such a move.

In a positive vein, the impact of the state on the affairs of local law enforcement is continuing via the imposition of pre-employment and training standards, as well as through various funding formulas tied to these standards. The first state to impose minimum standards of training for police officers was California, in 1959. This move was soon followed by the states of New York, Oklahoma, and Oregon. In 1970, the Law Enforcement Assistance Administration (LEAA) did make available discretionary grants to those states that wanted to implement minimum standards programs. Today all 50 states have mandated training for law enforcement officers. It must be noted, however, that much of the impetus for the implementation of minimum standards on a statewide basis comes from the local law enforcement community. Requirements related to the minimum standards for employment for police officers are administered through state organizations, often termed Police Officers Standards and Training Commissions (POSTs), which generally operate under three broad mandates: (1) to establish minimum standards for employment in a state, county, or local law enforcement agency; (2) to articulate curricula of training for police officers; and (3) to conduct and encourage research designed to improve all aspects of law enforcement.[18]

In its assessment of the role of the states in criminal justice planning, in general the National Advisory Commission on Criminal Justice Standards and Goals suggested that the State Planning Agencies (SPAs), which were created by the Omnibus Crime Control and Safe Streets Act of 1968 as the state-level organizations through which federal funds were funneled from the LEAA, bear a special responsibility for the formation of minimum statewide standards.[19] However, with the demise of LEAA in 1982 there has been a reduction in or total dismantling of large state planning agencies.

Local Political Forces

The special dimension of police politics varies from community to community, but law enforcement activities are governed for the most part by the dominant values of the local political culture. James Q. Wilson, in his now classic study of the police in

eight communities, identified three distinctly different styles of law enforcement, all of which were reflective of the political culture of the communities they served: (1) the "watchman" style of law enforcement emphasizes maintenance of order and is found in economically declining cities with traditional political machines; (2) the "legalistic" style of law enforcement is found in cities with heterogeneous populations and reform-oriented, professional governments (law enforcement of both a reactive and proactive nature characterizes this style); and (3) in the homogeneous suburban communities, the "service" style of law enforcement is oriented toward the needs of citizens.[20]

In Wilson's studies, these variations in the community political culture manifested themselves in a number of ways that subsequently affected both the qualitative and the quantitative enforcement action taken by the police. Significant enforcement variations emerged in the areas of vice, juvenile offenses, order maintenance, and traffic enforcement. Numerous variations, linked to the community's political culture, also emerged in the police department's personnel entry standards, promotional policies, extent of specialization, and level of managerial skills. These, in turn, affected the overall operations of the department, which in turn impacted the citizens' perception and confidence in the police department.

There is an unfailing, consistent, and close relationship between the type of law enforcement a community has and its dominant political culture. This is not to suggest, however, that any community's political culture is unalterably fixed. In fact, the reform movements that have been a part of the American political scene throughout much of its history have corresponded with the emergence of new political cultures. Each new dominant political culture in time leaves its own unique mark on the unit of government within its sphere of control.

Strong Mayor

To some extent, the type of local government that a community has impacts the way police chiefs are selected, the freedom they enjoy in the performance of their status, and their **tenure**. For example, with a strong mayor form of government, the mayor is elected to office and serves as the chief executive of the city. The city council constitutes the chief legislative and policymaking body. The mayor nominates a candidate to serve as police chief, and sometimes but not always majority approval is needed from the city council. Once approved, the candidate assumes the position of police chief and serves at the discretion of the mayor.

Ideally, the person the mayor selects as police chief should possess the full range of managerial and administrative skills necessary to operate the police department. However, to a great extent, the kind of person selected to serve as police chief is determined by the mayor's professional qualifications, philosophy about the role of law enforcement, and political commitments. If the mayor is endowed with sound business or public administration skills and has a "good government" philosophy, then the chief of police will very likely be selected on the basis of professional abilities rather than on extraneous political factors. Unfortunately, on too many occasions in the past, this appointment has been a method of repaying political favors. A classical case of the misuse of this appointing authority was illustrated by the Wickersham Commission in 1931:

> A few years ago the mayor of Indianapolis was called upon to introduce the police chief of that city to an assemblage of police chiefs during one of their conferences. In the course of his introductory remarks, the mayor said, "I know that my man is going to be a good chief because he has been my tailor for 20 years. He knows how to make good clothes; he ought to be a good chief."[21]

No big-city mayor would make the same choice today, but the choice will nevertheless be a reflection of the mayor's personal value system and abilities and of the political environment of the community.

In the strong mayor form of local government, the tenure of the chief of police is often linked directly to the mayor, and the nature of the relationship is such that the chief is quite dependent on the mayor for support and guidance on budgetary matters, enforcement practices, and a multitude of other areas essential to the overall success of the police department. If there is mutual respect between the police chief and the mayor, a strong professional and political bond will be formed. If the reverse holds true, however, significant antagonisms may begin to emerge. There are too many situations to enumerate positively or negatively that can affect the working relationship between a mayor and a police chief. The important differences that do emerge are frequently those that evolve out of philosophical and ethical differences rather than questions of legality. These are differences that can occur in any form of government (see Figure 4.2).

City Manager

There is no lack of supporters or detractors for every form of local government found in the United States. The proponents of the city manager form claim that it provides the most conducive atmosphere in which professional law enforcement can operate and minimizes external interference. One of the reasons for this assessment is the balancing mechanisms developed over the years that are typically inherent in the city manager form of government: (1) the city manager is accountable to the elected members of the city council as a body rather than to any individual council member;

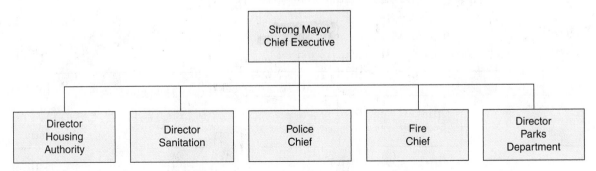

Figure 4.2

The strong mayor form of government. The mayor serves as the chief executive and appoints all department heads. The department heads serve at the pleasure of the mayor.

(2) individual council members are prevented (by law of council rules) from giving administrative, operational, or policy direction to the city manager; (3) the council as a body may not give specific administrative direction to the city manager, who generally has exclusive executive authority over city employees; (4) the city manager, consistent with civil service statutes and subject to employee appeals, has full authority to hire, promote, and discipline city personnel; (5) the city manager has broad authority within state municipal financial statutes to manage the budget and to depart from line item appropriations to meet unanticipated needs; and (6) the council as a body hires the city manager and may dismiss the city manager in its discretion without stating its cause. The city manager model is significant because it has been clearly successful in the American local political milieu and because its separation of the political policy-making body and the independent chief executive is realistically defined.[22]

The city manager, more often than not, is a professional administrator who is recruited for certain skills and training and appointed by the city council. A person with this background tends to make sincere efforts to select a competent individual to serve as police chief because the manager's professional reputation is tied inextricably to the effective management of the city departments.

It is significant that city managers have sought qualified police chiefs and have, in most instances, based their selection on the professional qualifications of the candidate rather than on political or other extraneous considerations that too often have governed appointments to this position in the past.[23] This does not mean the city manager form of government removes the chief from local politics, but it does create more distance and insulation than the one-to-one political relationship commonly found in the strong mayor form of government (see Figure 4.3).

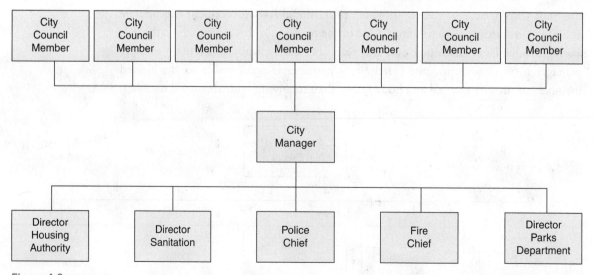

Figure 4.3
The city manager form of government. The city manager is appointed by the council (typically the majority), and the manager serves at the pleasure of the city council. The city manager in turn appoints all department heads, and they serve at the pleasure of the manager.

City Councils

The legally defined roles of a city council are fairly consistent throughout the United States; namely, it acts as the chief legislative and policymaking body. Through its ordinance power, subject to constitutional and statutory provisions, including the city charter, the council carries out its legislative function. When within the council's authority, its enactments have the force of law and are binding on both administration and electorate. In addition to legislative and policymaking functions, the council, in common with most legislative bodies, holds the purse strings and exercises control over appropriations.[24] Thus, the immediate impact of a council's actions on the operation of a law enforcement agency is considerable.

The record of involvement by council members and other elected officials in police operations to the detriment of both the efficiency and the effectiveness of the police establishment is a well-established fact. One observer of this problem has noted,

> Local political leaders frequently promote more abuses of police power than they deter. In seeking favored treatment for a violator of the law or in exerting pressure for police assistance in the sale of tickets to a fund-raising dinner, the politician only encourages the type of behavior he is supposed to prevent. Although such political interference into police work is not as extensive as it once was, it still exists.[25]

James F. Ahern, former chief of the New Haven, Connecticut, Police Department, discusses this issue at length in his book *Police in Trouble*. He describes the extent to which political forces negatively affected the New Haven Police Department and the course of action he took to nullify them:

> There is nothing more degrading or demoralizing to a police department than the knowledge that every favor or promotion within it is controlled by hack politicians and outright criminals. And there is nothing more nearly universal. Five years ago, anyone with the most superficial knowledge of the workings of the New Haven Police Department could point to the political power behind every captain on the force. Every cop who wanted to get ahead had his "hook"—or, as they say in New York, his "rabbi." Everyone owed his success to a politician—from the Town Chairman on down—or to an influential underworld figure. Needless to say, in a situation like this there was no chance whatever of the department functioning in the public interest.
>
> A day after I had taken office, I closed the second-story back door to the Mayor's office and issued a renewal of a long-standing and long-ignored departmental order prohibiting any police officer from seeing the Mayor without the authorization of the chief.
>
> Given the incredible tangle of grimy politics that still existed in the lower levels of government and in the structures of the city's political parties, this action was largely symbolic. But as a gesture it was necessary. It would be immediately evident to everyone in the police department that if I would not permit the Mayor who had appointed me to influence departmental promotions or assignments, I certainly would allow no other politicians to influence them.
>
> Mayor Lee was aware of the connections between politics and police and was himself capable of intervening in the affairs of the police department to advance

cops whom he considered honest and effective who otherwise would have been buried. Riding home with the Mayor in a car one day, I showed him a draft of my order. He frowned slightly, nodded, and then approved.

But this order was only the opening shot in the war to end political interference in the police department. The far more substantive challenge was to make clear in every way possible, to every man in the department, that political influence of any kind was out. There was only one way to handle the problem, and it was somewhat heavy-handed. The men were made responsible for stopping interference themselves. They were warned that if politicians or underworld figures approached me with requests for promotions, transfers, or easy assignments for cops, the officers in question would be barred permanently from those positions.

The immediate reaction among the cops was total incredulity. Political maneuvering had been the basis for advancement in the department for so long that it was doubtful whether they believed there was another way to be promoted. I would not be surprised if they thought that promotions in the department would freeze until I resigned or retired. But they did believe me. And they did convey the message to their hooks. For the time being, political interference in the department all but stopped.[26]

To suggest that the experience of New Haven is typical of most communities would be an inaccurate generalization, but there is little doubt that the council's fiscal control over the police department's budget and its legislative powers make it a political force that is never taken lightly by chiefs of police. As a matter of fact, most police chiefs will go to great lengths to maintain the goodwill and support of their council members.

Politics and the Police Chief

A study conducted in California showed that the average tenure of a police chief in that state was less than 3 years before the chief was fired or resigned.[27] Even though the tenure of police chiefs across the nation has somewhat improved since that time, the national average is still only about 5 years.[28] Of course, the reasons for change are numerous, including movement to another (often larger) police department, resignation, retirement, and, of course, dismissal. Much has been written about the need for some type of protection for police chiefs against the arbitrary and unjustified removal from office by an elected or political officeholder.[29] In some states, such as Illinois, statutory protections have been implemented to protect police chiefs against such actions. Special boards or commissions have been created for the sole purpose of establishing recruitment, selection, and retention policies for chiefs of police. In Illinois, the law prohibits the removal or discharge of a member of the fire or police department (including the chief) without cause; the individual must also be given written charges and an opportunity to be heard in his or her defense. While this is a state mandate, these protections are available only when there is no local ordinance prescribing a different procedure. If such an ordinance exists, the statute requires the municipal appointing authority to file the reasons for the chief's removal but does not require a showing of cause or a hearing.

New Hampshire affords significant protection to police chiefs. It requires written notice of the basis for the proposed termination, a hearing on the charges, and a finding of cause before the dismissal can be effected. Minnesota, on the other hand, provides no mandatory protections for police chiefs but does require they be included in any civil service system adopted by a municipality.

A few other states have attempted to provide police chiefs with at least some job security whenever they have been promoted from within the ranks of the police department. Both Illinois and Ohio allow chiefs who resign or who are removed from their positions to return to the ranks they held within their departments before being appointed chiefs. Most states, however, offer very little protection. Chiefs across the country are therefore forced to look for job protections in local civil service codes, local municipal ordinances, and such individual employment contracts as they are able to negotiate.[30]

However, for the most part, the ability to endure the realities of the position of chief of police requires a unique blend of talent, skill, and knowledge that is often not "guaranteed" in statute or law. The reality is that few protections exist for persons occupying the highest position of a police agency except for those developed in the person themselves. That is to say, the characteristics and qualities of excellent management and leadership imbued in the person are generally the reasons a chief remains in office.

Tenure and Contracts for Police Chiefs

Police chiefs who lack protection from arbitrary and unjustified termination cannot objectively and independently fulfill their responsibilities. For their contracts (an extremely limited number of formal contractual cases exist) to be renewed at the end of the term or their status as an at-will appointee to be continued, compromises of the chief's sense of responsibility may be necessary, especially if his or her decisions run counter to those of city officials. A discussion of the lack of a reappointment agreement for Milwaukee's former Chief Philip Arreola states,

> He wasn't exactly fired, but months before his scheduled reappointment for a second term, word simply filtered out of City Hall that Mayor John O. Norquist no longer saw eye to eye with the chief. It was not a matter of scandal or of incompetence, it was a case of political failure—too many constituencies, all with clearcut agendas, and no way to satisfy all of them at once. . . . It may seem curious for a city to can a respected police chief without any whiff of impropriety or misconduct, but in fact it is the norm these days, not the exception. The sacking of the police chief is part of the routine in urban America.[31]

The advent of community policing as the evolving contemporary policing strategy emphasizes enhanced relations between the police and the public and demands that police chiefs possess new skills and attitudes and become effective visionary leaders. In other words, chiefs must not be reluctant to pioneer innovative programs geared toward community problem-solving policing goals. The inherent risks, however, are obvious, and the failure of these high-profile public projects may jeopardize the chief's position.

Consider where police chiefs come from. Most top police executives today, as in the past, reach their position as police chief in the twilight of their policing careers. Charles Gain, former chief of the Oakland, California, Police Department, argued that police chiefs in this twilight period tend to resist organizational change because they fear the loss of the position for which they have so long waited, and as they are in the final stages of their career, they engage in a "holding action."[32] Gain further commented that, when chiefs make it to the top, they are not going to jeopardize their position by setting new goals and moving ahead.[33]

One researcher cites another example as a demonstration of this bankrupt leadership style. Researchers of the Police Executive Development Project at Pennsylvania State University found that top police executives showed greater devotion to their own job security than for the citizens they served. Their findings also indicated that top police executives showed greater submission to authority than did the general public. This subservient attitude is formed as a result of working in a rigid organizational structure that demands and rewards obedience to authority.[34] The results of the project indicated the average police executive failed to possess initiative, self-reliance, and confidence because of a lifelong habit of submission and social conformity. The study concluded these findings correlate to some extent with the suggestion that police chiefs tend to treat their job as a sinecure and are incapable of innovation at this late stage in their police careers.[35] Without some form of contract protection, it is difficult to expect any police chief to jeopardize his or her job by implementing a vision or a program that has any chance of failure.

Politics and the County Sheriff

There are approximately 3,100 county sheriff's departments in the United States.[36] The county sheriff's office is unique among American law enforcement agencies in terms of both its role and its legal status.[37] However, in discussions about police administration, sheriff's offices are frequently overlooked. Historically, the tasks and roles of sheriff's departments and police departments have been fundamentally different.[38] Sheriff's law enforcement functions have often been relegated to jurisdictions of sparse populations that cannot support municipal police agencies. Sheriffs are typically elected, as opposed to their appointed counterpart police chiefs. In addition, sheriffs routinely have a custodial role in the detention of prisoners not common to municipal police functions. This all changed somewhat after World War II, when populations expanded into rural areas that eventually became the suburbs. This eliminated part of the distinction between sheriffs and chiefs when big-city problems came to these areas.[39]

The 20th century brought a marked decline in the strength of sheriff's departments in many parts of the country. As law enforcement became more abundant, a curious academic neglect of the office of the sheriff resulted in serious breaks of understanding regarding the role of sheriff in the criminal justice system. Literature about policing and law enforcement analyzed the office as a jailer, court bailiff, process server, and county tax collector. Little, if any, emphasis was placed on the office in police literature, and if there was reference to the position, it was generally unfavorable. In 1925, Bruce Smith's book *The State Police* referred to the office as a "dying medieval" throwback. A later book by the same author, *Rural Crime Control,* alluded to county government in general as the "dark continent of American politics." A 1935 book by A. E. Parker and A. Vollmer, *Crime and the State Police,* stated that the sheriff was an outdated law enforcement institution.[40]

Patterns of academic neglect continued after mid-century, even as the nation's police interest was escalating. O. W. Wilson neglected to mention sheriffs in his 1950 book *Police Administration.* R. E. Clift neglected reference to the position in the 1956 edition of *A Guide to Modern Police Thinking* but did make small reference to the office in his third edition in 1970. George Felkenes devoted considerable discussion to the decrease and scope of the office in an inverse relationship with urbanization in his 1973 *The Criminal Justice System: Its Functions and Personnel.* He further observed that sheriffs were banished to only three modes of operation: (1) contract law enforcement for small or rural communities, (2) supervision of metropolitan police agencies along the East Coast only, (3) civil process functions, and (4) custodial functions as prescribed by law.[41] Many other law enforcement journals have noted that the sheriff's law enforcement functions lacked the professional standards of larger police departments.

A strong criticism of the position came from Dana B. Brammer and James E. Hurley, who wrote *A Study of the Office of Sheriff in the United States Southern Region* in 1968.[42] After they alluded to the sheriff as often the most important, if not the sole, law enforcement agency in many unincorporated areas of the South, they added,

> The elected nature of the office has been cause for the most serious indictments of the office. Allegations regarding a sheriff being required to participate in partisan politics in order to hold his office are the most prevalent criticism. Yet in reality, all law enforcement executives are politicians in one form or another. Some may refute this assertion, but only out of misguided notions that politicians are evil or that an administrator cannot be a politician and a professional manager at the same time. Realistically, a politician is nothing more than a person accountable to the public for decisions made in the performance of duty. Certainly a police chief or police commissioner could fall into this category as easily as a sheriff.[43]

The county sheriff's legal status is unique in two ways. First, in 37 states, it is specified by the state constitution. As a result, major changes in the office of sheriff require a constitutional amendment—a lengthy and difficult process.

In terms of size, with some notable exceptions such as the Los Angeles County Sheriff's Department, most sheriff's departments are small. Nearly two-thirds of them employ fewer than 25 sworn officers, and a third employ fewer than 10. About half serve a population of less than 25,000.[44]

Second, unlike most law enforcement executives, sheriffs are elected in all but two states. (In Rhode Island, they are appointed by the governor; in Hawaii, they are appointed by the chief justice of the state supreme court.) As elected officials, sheriffs

Quick
FACTS ▸▸ The Los Angeles County Sheriff's Department

The Los Angeles County Sheriff's Department is among the nation's largest and most diverse law enforcement agencies. Here are just a few interesting facts about the LASD.

- It is the largest sheriff's department and third-largest police agency in the nation.

- It has more than 16,000 employees, including more than 8,400 full-time sworn.

- It staffs and operates the largest jail system in the free world, with more than 20,000 inmates.

- It provides municipal and superior court deputies for the largest county court system in the nation.

- It is the sole police agency for more than 2.5 million of the county's 9.5 million people. This includes nearly half of the county's 88 cities and all of the unincorporated areas, totaling over 75 percent of the county's 4,083 square miles.

- It is the mutual aid coordinator for the region, coordinating the response of federal, state, and local public safety resources during earthquakes, civil unrest, and other catastrophes.

- It patrols areas ranging from densely populated urban communities in South Central, East Los Angeles, and West Hollywood to the beach city of Malibu, to the mountains of the Angeles National Forests, desert communities of the Antelope Valley, and many suburban communities.

- It has specialized units, such as Aero Bureau, Substance Abuse & Narcotics Education (S.A.N.E.), Special Enforcement Bureau (SWAT, K-9, Motors, etc.), Emergency Services Detail (Search & Rescue), Mounted Enforcement Detail, Organized Crime Unit, Arson/Explosives, Joint Regional Intelligence Center (JRIC), and the Terrorism Early Warning (TEW) group.

Source: Parker, Mike, "Big and Complicated: The LA County Sheriff's Department Operates the Largest Jail System in the Free World," *American Police Beat,* May 1996, p. 2, updated August 2007.

are important political figures. In many rural areas, the sheriff is the most powerful political force in the county. As a result, sheriffs are far more independent than appointed law enforcement executives are because, as discussed earlier, police chiefs can be removed by the mayors or city managers who appoint them. However, this is not to suggest that because sheriffs enjoy greater independence than police chiefs they are not subject to powerful political forces within their communities. Indeed, because the office is usually an elected position (in 48 of the 50 states), there is considerable media scrutiny and state accountability. Individuals seeking the position of sheriff must run for public office the same as any other public official. In fact, the office of sheriff is the only local law enforcement position recognized and decreed by many state constitutions, a holdover from the days when local sheriffs were the only law of the land.

The extent to which politics, in the negative sense, enters into the sheriff's race and subsequently into the operations of the sheriff's department varies radically from community to community and even among sheriff's races. For example, in states in which sheriffs—because they are constitutional officers—are not bound by normal purchasing restrictions, some potential for abuse exists. If a candidate running for the office of sheriff has accepted a large donation from a certain business, there would likely be an expectation of reciprocity in return for such "support." This could result in purchases of cars from "loyal" car dealers, food for jail inmates from certain distributors, uniforms from a specific uniform company, and so forth. However, a sheriff who becomes too partisan in his or her purchasing risks disappointing other vendors. As such, a marshaling of support for a different candidate in the next election usually occurs. The "real politics" of such a situation is that, while more purchases will be made from key supporting organizations, the incumbent must "spread around" enough purchasing to appease other vendors.

Then, too, there are potentials in any political environment for dirty campaigns, and sheriff's races are no exception.

Several years ago, an incumbent sheriff who realized he might not be reelected because of strong opposition from a highly qualified opponent contacted one of his vice squad officers to see if he could create a situation that would be embarrassing to his opponent. The vice squad officer made contact with a young and exceptionally attractive prostitute, who also served as his informant. He asked her to approach the man running against the incumbent sheriff at his place of business and try to entice him into joining her in a nearby hotel to have sex. The preselected hotel room had been set up with audiovisual equipment, so that the entire event could be recorded. Once the planned act was consummated and recorded, the videotape would be sent to the candidate's wife, along with copies to his minister and other key people in his life. It was felt that such a tape in the hands of these people would be sufficiently disruptive to the candidate's personal life to make him ineffectual as a campaigner. The prostitute, as instructed, did go to the business of the candidate and attempted to entice him to join her. The candidate, who was a politically astute individual, saw through this transparent farce and told the woman to leave his business. However, as soon as she left, he very discreetly followed her for a couple of blocks and saw her getting into an unmarked sheriff's department vehicle, which was being driven by the vice squad officer, whom he recognized. When the election was held, the incumbent sheriff lost. Since this was only one of many "dirty tricks" attempted by a number of employees of the sheriff's department, the newly elected sheriff immediately "cleaned house" and fired everyone who he could prove (or suspected) was involved in the efforts to embarrass him.

Inside the sheriff's department, politics can also be a decisive factor in the operational effectiveness of the organization. It is no accident that increased enforcement activity by the local sheriff's office usually precedes an election. The activity usually focuses on highly visible suspects or signs of disorder. Characteristic events include the roundup of local prostitutes, the crackdown on street corner vagrants, and the closing of "X-rated" video stores, all of which just happen to ensure considerable positive media attention. The interpretation is obvious—that the incumbent sheriff is "tough" on crime.

One of the most important political processes that impact the internal organization is the absence of local or state civil service boards. In many states, employees of the county sheriff's department serve at the pleasure of the current sheriff. Therefore, if the incumbent sheriff either decides not to run for office or is defeated in the next election, the newly elected sheriff may decide to fire a high percentage of the employees currently working at the sheriff's department. However, if wholesale dismissals do occur, this will result in a lack of continuity in the skill level of employees and affect the quality of service being delivered to the public. It also creates enormous job insecurity and provides a mechanism whereby unqualified persons may be elected to one of the highest positions of law enforcement in the community. Thus, the very nature of the electoral process and the enormous power inherent in the office can foster an environment in which politics prevails.

State Prosecutor

The **prosecutor**, also called the state's attorney or district attorney, is the chief law enforcement officer under the statutes of some states. However, despite this designation, the state prosecutor does not have overall responsibility for the supervision of the police.[45] Even so, the prosecutor's enforcement policies, procedures for review of all arrests before their presentation in court, and overall supervision of the cases prepared by the police do have an observable effect on police practices and enforcement policies. The initial contact of police officers with prosecutors occurs when the former brings a complaint to be charged. This encounter may be critical because it is an important point for making decisions about the disposition of the case and whether the complaint will be dismissed or reduced to a lesser offense. This discretionary power given to the prosecuting attorney has tremendous influence on the ways and the extent to which certain laws are enforced or ignored. Police chiefs who perceive that the prosecutor consistently reduces or fails to vigorously enforce certain types of violations may very likely divert their enforcement efforts and resources elsewhere. Then again, some chiefs may decide to "go public" and try to mobilize community support for enforcing the ignored violations. However, few police chiefs take this course of action because it could result in a serious deterioration in the working relationship with the local prosecutor, a situation most would prefer to avoid.

From the prosecutor's perspective, a cordial relationship with the police is also a desired condition. This is not, however, always possible. For example, the prosecutor cannot ignore suspicions of corruption or other illegal activity by local police officers. When prosecutor-led investigations become public knowledge or lead to indictments, a prosecutor's rapport with the police can be severely strained, requiring years to recultivate. The resulting tension may become high if officers believe that the prosecutor is "sticking it to the police department by dragging the thing out," or by not allowing affected officers to plea bargain to lesser charges, or if the prosecutor is suspected of furthering his or her career at the officers' expense.

The Judiciary

Once the police have made an arrest and brought the arrestee before a judge, from pretrial release onward the case is within the domain of the **judiciary**. In its assessment of the relationships of the judiciary and the police, one government report noted that trial judges have acted as chief administrative officers of the criminal justice system, using their power to dismiss cases as a method of controlling the use of the criminal process. However, except in those rulings involving the admissibility of evidence, this has been done largely on an informal basis and has tended to be haphazard, often reflecting primarily the personal values of the individual trial judge.[46]

In contrast, the function of trial judges in excluding evidence that they determine has been obtained illegally places them very explicitly in the role of controlling police practices. Trial judges have not viewed this role as making them responsible for developing appropriate police practices. However, many trial judges, when asked to explain their decisions, indicate that they have no more responsibility for explaining decisions to police than they have to private litigants.[47]

Occasionally, judges grant motions to suppress evidence to dismiss cases they feel should not be prosecuted because the violation is too minor or for some other reason. The use of a motion to suppress evidence in this manner confuses the standards that are supposed to guide the police and has a disturbing, if not demoralizing, effect on them.[48]

If judges consistently interject their personal biases into the judicial process and make it very clear to the police they will dismiss certain categories of violations, the police may discontinue enforcing that law.

For example, one of the co-authors of this book was a motorcycle officer whose primary functions were traffic law enforcement and accident investigation. It became apparent during the course of investigating traffic accidents that one of the causes of the reoccurring rear-end collisions was because drivers were following too close. However, it was the practice of his agency not to issue traffic citations for following too close unless an accident had occurred. In an effort to be proactive, he decided to start issuing traffic citations to motorists who were clearly following too close but he did so before accidents actually occurred. At the end of his shift, like he routinely did, he submitted his numerous traffic citations for the following too close violations to his supervisor, who wanted to know where the accident reports were. He explained there were no traffic accidents, and that this was his effort to be proactive and prevent rear-end collisions from occurring by enforcing the traffic violations against following too close before the accidents occurred. The sergeant just smiled and accepted the tickets without saying a word. When the court date came to appear before the judge, along with the unhappy citizens who had received the traffic citations, he started to testify about the following too close violations he had witnessed and the rationale for issuing the tickets. When the judge realized the traffic citations were issued without any accidents having occurred, he summarily dismissed all of the cases. The judge never told him to stop writing traffic citations for this particular traffic violation, but suffice it to say, no more traffic citations were written for following too close unless there were rear-end collisions.

Citizen Oversight of the Police

Since the 1960s, civil rights groups have argued that police departments fail to investigate citizen complaints thoroughly or fairly. As an alternative, they have demanded the creation of **citizen oversight** (also called external review or civilian review) of the police. Citizen oversight is defined as a process by which people who are not sworn officers are involved in some way in the review of citizen complaints

against police officers. Citizen oversight rests on the assumption that because of the police subculture, police officers cannot objectively investigate complaints against fellow officers.[49]

Citizen oversight has grown tremendously in the last 30 years. In almost all big cities there is now some form of oversight agency. The U.S. Justice Department recommends an open citizen complaint process as one of its integrity-related "best practices."[50] It recommends that law enforcement "agencies should provide a readily accessible process in which community and agency members can have confidence that complaints against agency actions and procedures will be given prompt and fair attention."[51]

Two Models of Citizen Oversight

Civilian Review Board

Citizen oversight agencies exist in two basic forms. The first is the *civilian review board*—a board of citizens that reviews individual complaints and makes a recommendation to the police chief. There are many variations on review boards. The San Francisco Office of Citizen Complaints (OCC) has its own staff of investigators and conducts the original complaint investigation. The New York City Civilian Complaint Review Board (CCRB) also conducts the original investigation.[52]

Police Auditors

The second form of citizen oversight is the *police auditor*. Police auditors do not investigate individual citizen complaints. Their role is to audit or monitor the operations of the police department. This includes the complaint process, policies, and procedures related to the use of force or traffic stops and other aspects of the agency. For example, the special counsel to the Los Angeles County sheriff's department has investigated employment practices, civil litigation data, the canine unit, foot pursuits, and many other issues since 1993. The San Jose Independent Police Auditor also investigates a wide range of issues.[53] Reviewing policies and procedures and making recommendations for change are known as *policy review*. The San Jose Independent Police Auditor has made over 100 policy recommendations in its first 15 years of operation.[54]

Citizen Oversight: Pros and Cons

Opponents of citizen oversight argue that (1) it intrudes on the professional independence of the police, (2) people who are not police officers are not qualified to review police operations, (3) it is expensive and unnecessarily duplicates the work of internal affairs, and (4) internal affairs units sustain more complaints against police officers than do citizen oversight groups.[55]

Advocates of citizen review, on the other hand, argue that it serves to open up police departments, ending the historic isolation from the public. They cite evidence that the number of citizen complaints is higher in cities with some form of external review, suggesting it enhances public confidence in the complaint process.[56] Hudson's research on the Philadelphia, Pennsylvania police department found that internal affairs sustained a higher percentage of complaints primarily because it generally handled violations of departmental rules, which are inherently easier to sustain than citizen complaints about use of force.[57]

There have been few evaluations of citizen review procedures. Kerstetter found that public confidence in the complaint process did improve with the existence of a citizen review procedure.[58] A Vera Institute study of the New York City Civilian Review Board (CCRB) found that both complainants and police officers thought it was biased against them.[59] The New York CCRB is regularly criticized by the New York Civil Liberties Union, the leading advocate of citizen review.

In short, some forms of citizen review appear to be relatively more effective than others. Effectiveness depends upon several factors, including the agency's definition of its role, its resources, the quality of its staff, and the degree of political support it receives from the community.[60]

Public Interest Organizations

Several years ago the local chapter of the American Civil Liberties Union (ACLU) in Oakland, California, had volunteers systematically call different units of the Oakland police department and ask how to file a citizen complaint. The callers found that few Oakland officers handling their calls gave out correct information. Many, apparently, were simply uninformed about the department's complaint process. Some others may have deliberately not given out the right information. The ACLU report blasting the Oakland police department for this failure was only one in a long series of investigations and reports on police misconduct by that organization.

The ACLU is a private, nonprofit **public interest organization**. Private groups play an important role in police accountability. For the most part, they have been involved in attacking police misconduct. The National Association for the Advancement of Colored People (NAACP) has a long record of fighting police use of excessive force against African Americans. The ACLU was responsible for some of the most important Supreme Court cases involving the police. For example, ACLU briefs were the basis for the Court's decisions in the landmark *Mapp* and *Miranda* cases discussed earlier in this chapter. The ACLU has been the leading advocate of citizen review of the police in New York City, Los Angeles, and many other cities. At the same time, the ACLU has defended the rights of police officers in cases involving, for example, grooming standards and department investigations of alleged police misconduct. The ACLU even published a handbook on *The Rights of Police Officers*.[61]

Chambers of Commerce and Service Clubs

Local chambers of commerce and service clubs typically are supportive of efforts that lead toward efficient and clean government. Although such groups are characterized as being apolitical, they can exercise considerable influence. Their support for improving

the quality of law enforcement in the community is frequently heard in the chambers of city hall and is demonstrated through various community projects intended to assist local law enforcement. Attuned police chiefs realize the benefit to be gained from the support of such groups, encourage personnel to become active members in these clubs, and frequently join one or two themselves. Support from these groups is not surprising when one considers that many are comprised of men and women who are well educated and deeply involved in many aspects of community leadership. Such groups often have mobilized behind a police chief to get much-needed budget increases for salaries, additional personnel, and equipment.

Churches

The religious leaders and congregations of the churches in a community represent one of the most potentially powerful political pressure groups in the community. Their influence can, and frequently does, extend into the voting booth, which assures a high degree of responsiveness from local elected officials. Church leaders and their congregations almost always find an open door and a receptive ear at the office of their local police chief when they present their concerns. The problems that are frequently of greatest concern to such groups are vice-related, such as prostitution, massage parlors, X-rated theaters, and adult bookstores. It is true that individual communities impose different stan-dards and have varying levels of tolerance, but if the church leaders of a community mobilize and call on their police chief to eradicate or reduce what they perceive to be a serious problem, there is a high probability that they will receive some positive response. And if the police chief suggests that the police department cannot cope realistically with the problem because of limited personnel and resources, those church groups will likely begin applying pressure on the city officials to give the police chief the needed resources. Thus, the religious leaders of the community can be powerful allies of the police chief in certain types of enforcement efforts. On the other hand, this pressure group may force the chief to redirect resources away from areas that may have a higher priority.

News Media

It is the responsibility of the police department, and especially its top leadership, to establish and maintain a cordial association with all media representatives.[62] Both the electronic and print news media can be powerful friends or devastating antagonists of a local police department and, to a great extent, this is determined by the attitudes, policies, and working relationships among editors, news directors, and the police chief. When friction does occur between the police and the news media, as it invariably does in every community, it frequently emanates from the events surrounding a major crime or an unusual occurrence.

Often in the case of major crimes or incidents, police departments do not want to release information that will jeopardize the safety of the public or its officers, impair the right of a suspect to a fair and impartial trial, or impede the progress of an investigation. On the other hand, the news media have a different orientation and duty: to inform the public. Although their goals are often compatible, the police and the news media can sometimes disagree irreconcilably.

For example, the investigation of murders committed by Theodore Robert (Ted) Bundy in Tallahassee, Florida several years ago reveal how these differences in philosophy can play out to the detriment of a criminal investigation and cause conflict between the medial and law enforcement. The facts are as follows:

At approximately 2 a.m. on a Sunday morning, Bundy entered an unlocked door to the Chi Omega sorority house, located near the campus of Florida State University. Prior to entering he had armed himself with a tree limb from a pile of firewood that was in close proximity to the sorority house. After entering the sorority house he went to the second floor, which was the floor for the primary dormitory residence of the female students who lived here. In the first room he encountered a lone woman was asleep in her bed. He entered the room and clubbed her with the tree limb, rendering her immediately unconscious. He then strangled her with the pantyhose he had brought to the scene with him. He left her room and went to a second room and proceeded to batter a second sleeping woman with the tree limb. Like the previous victim, he rendered her unconscious and then proceeded to strangle her manually. He also bit off the nipple of her right breast, bit her twice on the left buttocks, and sodomized her with a hairspray bottle. He left her room, went down the hall and entered a third room where he encountered two more sleeping women and proceeded to batter each of them. Neither of them was killed. Still armed with the tree limb, he started walking down the flight of stairs leading to the front door of the sorority house when he was observed by one of the sorority women returning from a date. She had no knowledge at that time that anything had occurred and the presence of a man in the sorority house, even at that time of the morning, was not all that unusual. Bundy then left the premises, but shortly after leaving, one of the injured women started screaming for help and at that point the police and medical personnel were called.

The investigation involved three different law enforcement agencies: the local sheriff's office, the municipal police department, and the campus police. At the end of the first day it was agreed that all 35 criminal investigators who had worked independently of each other on the case would meet at the municipal police department headquarters to discuss facts they had gathered. It was made clear to all those present that highly specific information such as the name of the only eyewitness and the ways in which the victims were killed and assaulted should not be released to the media, because this information would jeopardize the safety of the eyewitness, who said she would be able to identify the man if she ever saw him again. It could also result in the possible destruction of physical evidence by the suspect or perhaps encourage him to flee the area. In spite of this admonition, the following day the local newspaper printed every detail of the crime, including the name of the young woman who had observed the suspect leaving the Chi Omega sorority house. Once she read the headlines, which identified her by name and location, she packed her bags and left for her home state. Her reaction was perfectly understandable considering her concern for her personal safety. The sheriff who was heading this investigation was, to say the least, agitated by the release of this information, which very likely had been provided to the newspaper by one of the investigators at the meeting the day before. He went to the local newspaper to talk to the editor to find out why it was necessary to divulge all of this highly specific information, which endangered the victim's life, and also raising the possibility the suspect might now destroy important physical evidence. The editor's comment was that the public had the right to know all of the facts available on the case and he would continue to publish any information provided from any source as long as it was reliable.

Also, there is little question, from a purely business perspective, that the more sensational and salacious the information printed about the crime, the more papers that would be sold. An old axiom in the media is "if it bleeds it leads" and this is true for both the print and electronic media. Fortunately, Bundy who confessed to murdering 35 young women in three states was eventually arrested, convicted, sentenced to death, and subsequently executed in the electric chair.

Other circumstances for potential tension or conflict in police–news media relationships include "off-the-record" police information appearing in the news media, the occasional claim by a police administrator that he or she was misquoted, and the involvement of press at the scenes of bank robberies, gangland killings, and hostage situations or in the sensitive investigations of kidnapings and drug rings.

From a legal standpoint, the police may release relevant information about a defendant if it is not prejudicial to the defendant's right to a fair trial. Many police departments have policies that protect the defendant's rights, but those policies may obstruct the needs of reporters to gather images and information for the public. For example, with respect to pretrial suspects, the Kentucky State Police policy prohibits personnel from doing the following:

1. Requiring the suspect to pose for photographers
2. Re-enacting the crime
3. Disclosing that the suspect told where weapons, the proceeds of a crime, or other materials were located
4. Referring to the suspect as a "depraved character," "a real no-good," "a sexual monster," or similar terms
5. Revealing that the suspect declined to take certain types of tests or that the suspect did take certain tests—for example, a blood alcohol test to determine the degree, if any, to which the suspect was under the influence of alcohol or other drugs
6. Telling the press the results of any tests to which the suspect submitted
7. Making statements as to the guilt or innocence of a suspect
8. Releasing the identities of prospective witnesses or commenting on the nature of their anticipated testimony or credibility
9. Making statements of a purely speculative nature about any aspect of the case[63]

On the other hand, with the move toward community policing, many officers conduct crime prevention classes, crime block meetings, and media interviews. Some departments have taken a very positive approach to this issue, viewing these interactions as opportunities to communicate with the general public on police affairs.

Despite all potential and actual conflicting interests, the fact is that both the police and the news media have profoundly important duties in a free society. In the course of day-to-day activities, people of considerable conscience in both professions go about performing their jobs in a responsible manner; police–news media clashes are atypical situations. Certainly, if the local news media believe the police are being arbitrary, high-handed, uncooperative, or, worst of all, untruthful, their news stories will reflect that dissatisfaction. Moreover, their coverage may even accentuate negative stories. For example, the dismissal of a felony charge because of insufficient evidence may lead to headlines such as "Shoddy Police Work Lets Burglar Go Free," as opposed to "Attorney Successfully Defends Local Man." Another consequence of a strained relationship with the news media could be minor or no coverage of favorable stories about the police, such as an awards ceremony. Thus, police administrators should exert a great deal of effort in seeing that all personnel understand the role of the press, that the applicable police department policies are current, that those policies are followed, and that open lines of communication with the news media are maintained.

Police Brutality and the Political Fallout

In an era of police reform characterized by significant Supreme Court decisions and sweeping programmatic changes (imbued in the new philosophy of community policing as described in Chapter 2, Policing Today), law enforcement continues to be plagued by the old problems of brutality and scandal. Celebrated cases (e.g., the Rodney King incident, the O. J. Simpson trial, and the Abner Louima case) have revealed only the tip of the iceberg. Police officers across the country have been accused of lying in court, falsifying or withholding of evidence, gross mishandling of case investigations, corruption, racism, physical abuse and violence, and even murder. The phenomenon has not been isolated, with several major cases highlighting police misconduct in rapid succession, which has had powerful political fallout, not only in the community where it occurs but in many cases nationally.[64]

For example, in 1991, in New York City, five officers were indicted on murder charges in the death by suffocation of a 21-year-old Hispanic man suspected of car theft. The officers were accused of having hit, kicked, and choked Federico Pereira while he lay face down and "hog-tied"—his wrists cuffed behind his back while another set of cuffs bound his hands to one ankle. The case led to a sweeping investigation into New York City police brutality and corruption. In a 1993 scandal, a New York state trooper was convicted of falsifying fingerprint evidence to get convictions. In 1995, the O. J. Simpson case highlighted the actions of Detective Mark Fuhrman. Fuhrman testified that he had

Figure 4.4
Abner Louima, police tortured victim.
(© Reuters/CORBIS)

found a bloody glove at Simpson's estate that matched one found 2 miles away near the bodies of Nicole Brown Simpson and Ronald L. Goldman. Such evidence, along with DNA matching of the blood on the glove, directly linked Simpson to the murder. Simpson's lawyers, however, were able to discredit Fuhrman as a liar and a racist who planted evidence, producing a tape-recorded conversation in which Fuhrman spoke of beating African American suspects (commonly referred to by Fuhrman as the "n word") and repeatedly used other racial slurs and epithets.

On August 8, 1997, police in New York City arrested Abner Louima (see Figure 4.4). At the time of his arrest, Louima had no bruises or injuries. Three hours after his arrest, Louima was rushed by ambulance to the hospital in critical condition. Internal affairs investigators confirmed that Louima had been severely beaten by officers during his arrest and subsequent transport to the jail. While in police custody, Louima was taken to a restroom and endured what one investigator described as "torture." Police officers removed Louima's pants and began to sodomize him with a toilet plunger. Medical doctors confirmed that Louima's internal injuries were the result of blunt-force trauma. Two of the five officers indicted for the beating and torture were found guilty and sentenced to prison.[65] Four years later, in July 2001, Louima settled his civil lawsuit against New York City and its main police union. The settlement called for the city to pay Louima $7.125 million and the union, the Patrolmen's Benevolent Association, to pay him $1.625 million. It was the most money that New York City had ever paid to settle a police brutality case and was the first time that a police union had to pay part of the claim. Further, Louima insisted that several policy changes be made to the New York Police Department, including a civilian panel for brutality case oversight, the prosecution of future department officers involved in brutality cases, and an increase in officer training involving ethics and the use of force.[66] The case has had a significant impact on the New York Police Department.

In 2000, an inquiry into the Los Angeles Police Department's Rampart station revealed an extensive and massive corruption scandal in that city. Allegations and the subsequent convictions of 3 officers revealed that over 70 officers had been involved in either committing crimes or covering up criminal activity. The police scandal centered on former members of the Community Resources Against Street Hoodlums (CRASH) anti-gang unit, charged with framing gang members, planting evidence, committing perjury, and even shooting innocent victims. The scandal was declared the worst in the department's history. About 100 criminal cases associated with the Rampart scandal were overturned after investigators found evidence of police abuses. Over 20 officers were relieved of duty, quit the department, were suspended, or were fired during the investigation. In the most notorious of the activities cited, one officer was charged with attempted murder when he shot a handcuffed suspect and left him paralyzed.

Figure 4.5
New York City Mayor Michael Bloomberg met with community leaders and elected officials in the aftermath of the Sean Bell shooting in November 2006.
(Courtesy of AP Photo/Kathy Willens)

In November 2006 members of the NYPD fired 50 shots at a group of unarmed men, killing one of them. Sean Bell, age 23, was leaving his bachelor party at a strip club when he was involved in an altercation with a plainclothes detective who was investigating the club for drug, weapon, and prostitution violations. The officer approached Bell's car, intending to question one of the passengers. Bell's car bumped the officer and then plowed into a minivan carrying additional officers. The car reversed and again struck the van. Officers opened fire on the vehicle after they thought one of the men in Bell's car was reaching for a weapon, shooting 50 rounds before discovering that none of the men were armed. Bell was killed, and two other men were wounded. Thousands of New Yorkers later marched in a series of protests organized by the NAACP and Reverend Al Sharpton, decrying the use of excessive force against Bell, whose wedding was to be held only hours after he was killed. Mayor Michael Bloomberg met with Bell's family after calling the shooting "unacceptable and inexplicable." In the aftermath of the shooting, the officers were placed on leave. The mayor bolstered the budget of a civilian review board designed to investigate claims of police abuse as a result of the shootings (see Figure 4.5).

As a result of these and similar incidents, serious questions concerning the ability of police internal affairs units to control police misconduct and deviance have been raised. Critics of the police argue that civil damage suits are a much more useful deterrent to police brutality than any type of internal disciplinary sanction.[67] Title 42 of the United States

Code, Section 1983, titled *Civil Action for Deprivation of Rights,* specifically provides a mechanism for filing a civil tort action against individual police officers for violation of a suspect's Constitutional rights. Infliction of mental and emotional distress, assault, battery, and excessive use of force, including use of deadly force, are routinely the grounds for a 1983 action against police officers (see Chapter 14, Legal Aspects of Police Administration, for more detail on Title 42 U.S.C., Section 1983). The damages under this section can be punitive and general and cannot be limited by recent state "tort reform" movements. Rodney King brought a $56 million civil suit under this section against all the officers who were involved in the incident and the Los Angeles Police Department, reportedly $1 million for each blow against him. He was eventually awarded $3.5 million for sustained damages. In 2001, over $8.5 million was paid by the City of New York and the New York Police Department Union for just one case—the Abner Louima case. While the courts have ruled that police officers cannot be held individually liable for most actions undertaken on the job, taxpayer concern about the rising cost of lawsuits has revived the popularity of civilian review boards.[68] Such panels are at work in 26 of the nation's 50 largest cities (e.g., Los Angeles County, Philadelphia, New York, Kansas City, and Chicago).[69] Despite the increase in civil litigation and public scrutiny, allegations of brutality and scandal still persist as a major problem in policing.

Racial and Ethnic Profiling

Nothing has fueled the political fire between police and minorities more than the use of race and ethnicity as criteria in police decision making during discretionary traffic and field interrogation stops, often described as "racial and ethnic profiling."[70] Weitzer and Tuch define **racial profiling** as "the use of race as a key factor in police decisions to stop and interrogate citizens."[71] The term has several meanings, most of which are associated with law enforcement officers making the decision to stop an individual because of race or ethnicity. Officers often use the "pretext" or "suspicious vehicle stop" argument to justify their actions as legal (e.g., using a legal pretext, such as an illegal lane change or broken license plate light, to stop the vehicle and then gain a basis to search for illegal drugs). These actions are lawful under *Whren v. United States of America*[72] and were affirmed in *Brown v. City of Oneonta.* The U.S. Court of Appeals for the Second Circuit held that, where law enforcement officials possess a description of a criminal suspect that consists primarily of the suspect's race and gender and where they do not have other evidence of discriminatory intent, they can act on the basis of that description without violating the equal protection clause of the Fourteenth Amendment.[73] This includes the practice of issuing profiles of suspects or offenders in general offenses (e.g., drug traffickers and gang members) as well as more specific offender descriptions. For instance, if a specific crime occurs (e.g., a rape or a murder) and the suspect description by a witness includes race, gender, or ethnicity, it is lawful for the police to stop a citizen on the basis of how closely the individual resembles the characteristics or description within the "profile" (see Figure 4.6).

Figure 4.6
Racial profiling in traffic stops has become an increasingly controversial issue in police procedure.
(Courtesy of Steve Lehman/CORBIS/SABA)

Media Accounts of Profiling on Local and National Politics

In the late 1990s, racial profiling became a major race relations issue in U.S. politics, and the media played a prominent role in bringing it to national attention. As already discussed, the televised beating of Rodney King in Los Angeles as well as the Amadou Diallo shooting in New York raised grave questions about the role of race in law enforcement outcomes. The ACLU sponsored direct investigations of the degree of racial disparity in vehicular stops in several states. For example, in their study of the Philadelphia Narcotics Unit, they found that although blacks make up 42 percent of the population, they comprise 79 percent of all vehicular stops. Working with the ACLU, Lamberth's 1997 study was among the first empirical investigations to substantiate claims of racial profiling among the New Jersey State Police. Similar studies were conducted in Delaware, Maryland, and California, and similar race disparities were observed.[74, 75]

The media's consistent focus on racial profiling helped bring the discussion about the role of race in police outcomes to center stage in local and national politics.

Ultimately, media accounts of gratuitous treatment of minority citizens led many state governments to enact legislation that would ban racial profiling and hold police organizations accountable for systematically targeting minority citizens. In addition to the legislation, in 1999, Attorney General Janet Reno convened the Strengthening Police-Community Relations Conference held in Washington, DC, with the purpose of assisting police organizations in collecting data on this issue. By 2000, more than 4,000 law enforcement agencies across the United States were involved in data collection efforts. As early as 1999, several states—including North Carolina—adopted legislation that

Quick FACTS ▸▸ History of Racial Profiling

The use of racial profiles dates back to the late 1970s when federal agents created drug courier profiles for the purpose of apprehending drug traffickers in American airports. By the mid-1980s, lawsuits were filed in large numbers challenging their use because anyone who fit the profile could be stopped and searched by law enforcement. In *U.S. v. Sokolow* (1989), the U.S. Supreme Court upheld the use of drug courier profiles as an acceptable basis for the temporary detention of potential drug couriers. This practice was later extended to highways and became a widespread policing strategy in the early 1990s after the U.S. Drug Enforcement Agency (DEA) offered drug interdiction training to local and state patrol officers.

Source: Patricia Y. Warren and Donald Tomaskovic-Devey, "Racial Profiling and Searches, Did the Politics of Racial Profiling Change Police Behavior?" *Criminology & Public Policy* 8, no. 2 (2009): 346.

required data collection on every police-initiated stop. In North Carolina, Senate Bill 76 required all state law enforcement agencies to track the race and ethnic backgrounds of motorists stopped to monitor officers who might be targeting minority drivers. Prior to Senate Bill 76, officers recorded the race/ethnicity of motorists who were formally cited for a violation (e.g., citations and written warnings). By 2005, more than 25 states had passed similar legislation.[76]

Police Responses to Allegations of Profiling

As media attention and legislative mandates were adopted across the United States, significant administrative- and officer-level changes were implemented. For instance, the New Jersey Highway Patrol equipped its police vehicles with video cameras to provide evidence of the conduct of officers and citizens during motor vehicle stops. Verniero and Zoubek noted,[77] "Video cameras, coupled with other data-collection systems, will provide the basis for a reliable and trustworthy system to detect problems, to prevent abuses, and to protect officers and citizens alike." In some police jurisdictions, law enforcement reduced its enforcement activities after heightened scrutiny. For example, Mas[78] found that the New Jersey State Patrol significantly reduced its enforcement efforts when it came under scrutiny for arbitrary and unfair policing tactics. A similar weakened enforcement effort was observed in Los Angeles. Even if these observed changes are temporary, the results suggest that social and political scrutiny directed toward police organizations can influence patterns of police enforcement. If drug interdiction strategies encourage pretextual stops in "fishing expeditions" for drugs, then the politicization of racial profiling can be expected to lead to fewer searches, particularly of Black drivers.[79]

In focus groups conducted in 2000 (after racial profiling was delegitimated as a police practice) state troopers vehemently denied they profiled black drivers.[80] They did, however, describe numerous characteristics other than traffic violations that potentially made one car more suspicious than another, which leaves open the possibility of individual officer racial bias in stops and searches. These factors include loud music, bumper stickers connected to drug cultures, Hispanic drivers who the focus groups characterized as unlikely to have valid driver licenses, and cars they felt "were out of place." The use of stereotypes potentially correlated with race or ethnicity is broadly consistent with Kennedy's[81] definition of racial profiling as the use of race as a symbol of criminal activity.[82]

Illegal Immigration: The Police and Local Politics

In recent years local police have become increasingly involved in the identification and arrest of illegal aliens. Such actions are normally the province of federal agents of the Immigration and Customs Enforcement (ICE), a unit of the Department of Homeland Security. A federal program to train local police officers in such duties has existed since 1996. Florida, the first state to join the federal program in the wake of the September 11, 2001 terrorist attacks, tailored its version to help block possible terrorist infiltrators. Interest in the program has taken off recently as the national debate over illegal immigration has heated up. Federal funds have been available to create a program to train local and state police officers in immigration duties.

For example, Alabama decided to join the program because local officials believed ICE's small staff in the state was unable to cope with the swelling numbers of illegal immigrants. The Governor pledged to double the number of state troopers trained to deal with illegal immigrants, saying: "Alabama welcomes those who enter the country legally, but we won't stand idly by when we catch illegal immigrants in our state."

Forty-four of the 650 Alabama state troopers in the state, a figure that includes administrative and field officers, have taken the 5-week training course and are now authorized to enforce federal immigration law. That training involves detecting false identification, understanding the details of federal immigration law as well as the pitfalls of racial profiling and other possible civil rights violations.

The ICE partnership empowers local officers to temporarily detain someone who has violated federal immigration law—something they are typically not allowed to do. That is a valuable tool in states where there are few ICE agents. The trained officers usually do not participate in sweeps or actively search for illegal immigrants; the emphasis is on human smugglers and convicted felons that officers come across during the course of their duties.

However, some police organizations and human-rights groups are concerned that deputizing local officers to handle immigration enforcement might violate civil liberties—and undermine safety.

"A key concern is that state and local enforcement involvement in immigration can have a chilling effect on the relationship with the immigrant community in their jurisdiction," says Gene Voegtlin, legislative counsel for the International Association of Chiefs of Police. That could lead immigrants to become reluctant to report crimes or cooperate with officers investigating incidents. While the association, which has 20,000 members, hasn't taken an official stance on the ICE program, he said it is also concerned that the complexities of immigration law can create liability issues. In addition, many police chiefs and sheriffs have also expressed concerns about the additional number of personnel it would take for these federal immigration laws to be

enforced in their local communities. The landmark study conducted by the Police Executive Research Forum (PERF) in 2008 reported that nearly two-thirds of the sheriffs and police chiefs responding to a national survey expressed this concern.

Some critics argue that federal authorities are specialists and are therefore better suited to handle specific tasks such as immigration enforcement. Lisa Navarrete, a vice president for the National Council of La Raza, the largest Hispanic advocacy group in the United States, says that local police officers who enforce immigration law are bound to engage in racial profiling, in part because they are stopping people they meet during the course of the day instead of pursuing specific investigations based on solid leads. "That can result in harassment of immigrants who are here legally, simply because they are Latino and speak accented English," she said.

Some also worry that the federal government is trying to spread the burden of rounding up illegal immigrants at a time when state and local police departments are already strapped for resources. Virginia Kice, an ICE spokeswoman, stresses that the program is entirely voluntary. "We are not going out and soliciting participation," she says. But, "we are receiving inquiries from all over the country."

The Los Angeles Mayor recently said that the city would not follow the lead of Costa Mesa and involve police officers in identifying illegal immigrants. However, civilian jail personnel in Los Angeles and San Bernardino counties who have undergone ICE training are screening foreign-born inmates to determine whether they can be deported, according to an ICE spokeswoman.[83]

One of the most politically charged events relating to illegal immigration and the police occurred in Arizona in 2010, when the state enacted a sweeping new law against illegal immigrants. The In the News feature below describes the political firestorm that started when this state law was enacted.

IN THE NEWS   Arizona Enacts Stringent Law on Immigration

Governor Jan Brewer of Arizona signed the nation's toughest bill on illegal immigration into law on Friday. Its aim is to identify, prosecute, and deport illegal immigrants.

The move unleashed immediate protests and reignited the divisive battle over immigration reform nationally.

Even before she signed the bill at an afternoon news conference here, President Obama strongly criticized it.

Speaking at a naturalization ceremony for 24 active-duty service members in the Rose Garden, he called for a federal overhaul of immigration laws, which Congressional leaders signaled they were preparing to take up soon, to avoid "irresponsibility by others."

The Arizona law, he added, threatened "to undermine basic notions of fairness that we cherish as Americans, as well as the trust between police and our communities that is so crucial to keeping us safe."

The law, which proponents and critics alike said was the broadest and strictest immigration measure in generations, would make the failure to carry immigration documents a crime and give the police broad power to detain anyone suspected of being in the country illegally. Opponents have called it an open invitation for harassment and discrimination against Hispanics regardless of their citizenship status.

Source: Randal C. Archibold, *The New York Times*, April 23, 2010.

CONCLUSION

Police departments, like all administrative agencies, do not operate independently of external political forces. Federal, state, and local governmental controls and influences are, in most instances, both legal and proper. The extent to which they impact on a law enforcement agency depends in part on both local and national events as well as on the unique political characteristics of each community and the political skills of the chief law enforcement officer.

CHAPTER REVIEW

1. Explain the significance of the U.S. Supreme Court decisions in each of the following cases: *Mapp v. Ohio* (1966), *Gideon v. Wainwright* (1963), *Escobedo v. Illinois* (1964), and *Miranda v. Arizona* (1966).

2. What are the more recent Supreme Court decisions that had a significant impact on law enforcement and what are the facts of these cases?

3. Describe the three distinctive styles of law enforcement presented by James Q. Wilson.

4. What are the major differences between the strong mayor form of government and the city manager form of government as they relate to the appointment of the police chief?

5. Why can police chiefs not objectively and independently fulfill their responsibilities if they lack protection and often resist setting new goals and instituting organizational change?

6. Describe the differences in the status between a county sheriff and a police chief.

7. What are the two models of citizen oversight?

8. What role do public interest organizations play in police accountability?

9. Describe some circumstances in which the police and the media might be in conflict.

10. What were the facts of the Abner Louima and Amadou Diallo cases as they relate to police brutality and political conflict with the community?

11. Briefly discuss the history of racial profiling in the United States.

12. What role should the local police play in enforcing immigration laws in their communities?

KEY TERMS

citizen oversight: a process by which people who are not sworn officers are involved in some way in the review of citizen complaints against police officers.

judiciary: a system of courts of law that administer justice.

politics: in the negative sense, refers to attempts to impose external, partisan political influence on the operation of a police department; in the positive, governance of a city.

prosecutor: a public officer within a jurisdiction representing the citizenry of a state or county who charges and prosecutes an individual for a crime.

public interest organizations: these are organizations such as the American Civil Liberties Union (ACLU) and the National Association for the Advancement of Colored People (NAACP) which play an important role in police accountability, especially as it relates to allegations of police misconduct.

racial profiling: the consideration of race as a key factor in police decisions to stop and interrogate citizens.

tenure: a period, or term, during which a position is held.

ENDNOTES

[1] W. H. Hudnut III, "The Police and the Polis: A Mayor's Perspective," in *Police Leadership in America: Crisis and Opportunity,* ed. William A. Geller (Westport, Conn.: Praeger, 1985), p. 20.

[2] N. G. Holten and M. E. Jones, *The Systems of Criminal Justice* (Boston: Little, Brown, 1978), p. 416.

[3] Treatment of the Supreme Court's influence has been drawn from Thomas Phelps, Charles Swanson, and Kenneth Evans, *Introduction to Criminal Justice* (Santa Monica, Calif.: Goodyear, 1979), pp. 128–131.

[4] In a legal sense, the Supreme Court opted for a piecemeal application when it rejected the "shorthand doctrine" (i.e., making a blanket application of the federal Bill of Rights provisions binding on the states) in its consideration of *Hurtado v. California,* 110 U.S. 516 (1884); therefore, the statement should be read in the context that the activist role was a policy decision.

[5] Fred P. Graham, *The Self-Inflicted Wound* (New York: Macmillan, 1970), p. 37. For a look at the police and due process, see A. T. Quick, "Attitudinal Aspects of Police Compliance with Procedural Due Process," *American Journal of Criminal Law* 6 (1978), pp. 25–56.

[6] T. R. Dye, *Politics in States and Communities* (Englewood Cliffs, N.J.: Prentice Hall, 1973), p. 214.

[7] The concept of the "erosion" of the *Mapp* and *Miranda* decisions is commonly referred to in studies by Thomas Davies as cited in *The Oxford Companion to the Supreme Court of the United States,* ed. Kermit L. Hall (New York: Oxford University Press, 1992), p. 266; G. M. Caplan, *Modern Procedures for Police Interrogation* (Washington, D.C.: Police Executive Research Forum, 1992); and Rolando V. del Carmen, *Criminal Procedure: Law and Practice,* 3rd ed. (Belmont, Calif.: Wadsworth, 1995), pp. 317–36.

[8] See *Massachusetts v. Sheppard,* 468 U.S. 981 (1984), and *United States v. Leon,* 468 U.S. 897 (1984).

[9] Justice William Brennan's dissent in *United States v. Leon.*

[10] *Carroll v. United States,* 267 U.S. 132 (1925).

[11] *Michigan Department of State Police v. Sitz,* 496 U.S. 444 (1990).

[12] See *Atwater v. City of Lago Vista,* 532 U.S. 318 (2001), and S. M. Mamasis, "Fear of the Common Traffic Stop—'Am I Going to Jail?' The Right of Police to Arbitrarily Arrest or Issue Citations for Minor Misdemeanors in *Atwater v. City of Lago Vista.*" *Thurgood Marshall Law Review* 27(2001): 85.

[13] See *United States v. Arvizu,* 232 F. 3d, 1241.

[14] *Arizona v. Fulminante,* 111 S. Ct. 1246 (1991).

[15] "Supreme Court on Police Powers," *Law Enforcement News* 17, nos. 338, 339 (June 15/30, 1991), pp. 1, 9, 10.

[16] Robert M. Fogelson, *Big-City Police* (Cambridge, Mass.: Harvard University Press, 1975), pp. 14–15.

[17] Ibid., p. 14.

[18] Information provided by the National Association of State Directors of Law Enforcement Training.

[19] The National Advisory Commission on Criminal Justice Standards and Goals, *A National Strategy to Reduce Crime* (Washington, D.C.: U.S. Government Printing Office, 1972), p. 149.

[20] James Q. Wilson, *Varieties of Police Behavior* (New York: Atheneum, 1973).

[21] The President's Commission on Law Enforcement and Administration of Justice, *Task Force Report: The Police* (Washington, D.C.: U.S. Government Printing Office, 1967), p. 127.

[22] A. H. Andrews, Jr., "Structuring the Political Independence of the Police Chief," in *Police Leadership in America: Crisis and Opportunity,* ed. William Geller (New York: Praeger, 1985), pp. 9, 10.

[23] V. A. Leonard and H. W. Moore, *Police Organization and Management* (Mineola, N.Y.: Foundation Press, 1971), p. 21.

[24] G. E. Berkeley et al., *Introduction to Criminal Justice* (Boston: Holbrook Press, 1976), p. 216.

[25] Leonard and Moore, *Police Organization and Management,* p. 15.

[26] J. F. Ahern, *Police in Trouble* (New York: Hawthorn Books, 1972), pp. 96–98.

[27] J. J. Norton and G. G. Cowart, "Assaulting the Politics/Administration Dichotomy," *Police Chief* 45, no. 11 (1978): 26.

[28] Interview with staff assistants at the International Association of Chiefs of Police, Washington, D.C., December 8, 1995.

[29] One of the most comprehensive collections of articles and essays focusing on the role of the chief of police is found in Geller, *Police Leadership in America.*

[30] Janet Ferris et al., "Present and Potential Legal Job Protections Available to Heads of Agencies," *Florida Police Chief* 14, no. 5 (1994), pp. 43–45.

[31] Ibid.

[32] J. Ruiz, "The Return of the Ultimate Outsider: A Civilian Administrator as the Top Cop" (unpublished paper, 1997).

[33] Ibid.

[34] Ibid.

[35] Ibid.

[36] See S. Walker, *The Police in America* (New York: McGraw-Hill, 1992), p. 44, and B. A. Reaves, *Sheriff's Departments 1990* (Washington, D.C.: U.S. Department of Justice, Bureau of Justice Statistics), p. 1.

[37] National Sheriff's Association, *County Law Enforcement: Assessment of Capabilities and Needs* (Washington, D.C.: National Sheriff's Association, 1995), p. 1.

[38] Most of the following material has been excerpted from Harry C. Guffardi, "History of the Office of Sheriff," www.hostpc.com/Buffardi/htm

[39] B. L. Garmire, ed., *Local Police Management* (Washington, D.C.: Institute for Training in Municipal Administration, 1982, 2001).

[40] D. R. Struckoff, *The American Sheriff* (Joliet, Ill.: Justice Research Institute, 1994), p. 43.

[41] Ibid., pp. 44–45.

[42] D. B. Brammer and J. E. Hurley, *A Study of the Office of Sheriff in the United States Southern Region* (Oxford, Miss.: University of Mississippi Bureau of Government Research, 1968), pp. 1–2.

[43] R. N. Holden, *Modern Police Management* (Englewood Cliffs, N.J.: Prentice Hall Career and Technology, 1994), p. 13.

[44] Reaves, *Sheriff's Departments 1990,* p. 1.

[45] The President's Commission, *Task Force Report,* p. 30.

[46] Ibid., p. 31.

[47] Ibid.

[48] Ibid.

[49] Samuel Walker and Charles M. Katz, *The Police in America,* 7th ed. (New York: McGraw-Hill Companies, 2008), pp. 486–490.

[50] Ibid.

[51] U.S. Department of Justice, Special Litigation Section: Web site: www.usdoj.gov/crt/split

[52] Samuel Walker, *Police Accountability: The Role of Citizen Oversight* (Belmont: Wadsworth, 2001).

[53] Ibid.

[54] San Jose Independent Police Auditor, *Year End Report,* 2008 (San Jose: City of San Jose, 2009).

[55] Americans for Effective Law Enforcement, *Police Civilian Review Boards AELE Defense Manual, Brief 82-3* (San Francisco: AELE, 1982); Douglas Perez, *Common Sense about Police Review* (Philadelphia: Temple University Press, 1994).

[56] The arguments on both sides are reviewed in Walker, *Police Accountability: The Role of Citizen Oversight,* pp. 54–60.

[57] James R. Hudson, "Organizational Aspects of Internal and External Review of the Police," *Journal of Criminal Law, Criminology, and Police Science* 63 (September 1972), pp. 427–432.

[58] Wayne A. Kerstetter and Kenneth A. Rasinski, "Opening a Window into Police Internal Affairs: Impact of Procedural Justice Reform on Third-Party Attitudes," *Social Justice Research* 7, no. 2 (1994), pp. 107–127.

[59] Michele Sviridoff and James E. McElroy, *Processing Complaints against Police in New York City* (New York: Vera Institute of Justice, 1989).

[60] New York Civil Liberties Union, *A Third Anniversary Overview of the Civilian Complaint Review Board*, July 5, 1993–July 5, 1996 (New York: NYCLU, 1996).

[61] Ibid.

[62] E. M. Davis, "Press Relations Guide for Peace Officers," *Police Chief* 39, no. 3 (1972), p. 67.

[63] See General Order OM-F-4, "Release of Information to the News Media" issued by the Kentucky State Police, January 1, 1990.

[64] Edward Timms, "Scandal Leaving Some Leary of Nation's Law Enforcement," *Dallas Morning News,* September 25, 1995, p. 1.

[65] Adapted from David Kocieniewski, "Injured Man Says Brooklyn Officers Tortured Him in Custody," *New York Times,* August 13, 1997, pp. B1, B3, and "New York Officer to Plead Guilty in Beating," *Dallas Morning News,* May 25, 1999, p. A3.

[66] Alan Feuer and Jim Dwyer, "New York Settles in Brutality Case," *New York Times,* July 13, 2001, p. A1.

[67] Ibid., 21.

[68] Ibid.

[69] Louis A. Radelet and David Carter, *Police and the Community,* 5th ed. (New York: Macmillan, 1994), p. 46.

[70] Special thanks to Brooke Nodeland for her assistance in developing this section on racial and ethnic profiling. See also Robin Engle, Jennifer Calnon, and Thomas Bernard, "Racial Profiling: Shortcomings and Future Directions in Research," *Justice Quarterly* 19, no. 2 (June 2002), pp. 249–273.

[71] Ronald Weitzer and Steven Tuch, "Perceptions of Racial Profiling: Race, Class, and Personal Experience," *Criminology* 40, no. 2 (2002).

[72] See *Whren v. United States,* 517 U.S.806 (1996).

[73] See *Brown v. City of Oneonta,* 221 F. 3d (2d Cir. 2000), cert. denied, 122 S. Ct. 44 (2001), and Elliot B. Spector, "Stopping Suspects Based on Racial and Ethnic Descriptions," *Police Chief,* January 2002, pp. 10–12.

[74] Patricia Y. Warren and Donald Tomaskovic-Devey, "Racial Profiling and Searches, Did the Politics of Racial Profiling Change Police Behavior?" *Criminology & Public Policy* 8, no. 2 (2009), pp. 347–350.

[75] Jeff Dominitz, "How do the Laws of Probability Constrain Legislative and Judicial Efforts to Stop Racial Profiling?" *American Law and Economics Review* 5 (2003), pp. 412–432.

[76] Warren and Tomaskovi-Devey, "Racial Profiling and Searches," p. 349.

[77] Peter Verniero and Paul H. Zoubek, *Interim Report of the State Police Review Team Regarding Allegations of Racial Profiling* (Newark: New Jersey Office of the Attorney General, 1999).

[78] Alexandre Mas, "Pay, Reference Points, and Police Performance," *Quarterly Journal of Economics* 121 (2006), pp. 783–821.

[79] Warren and Tomaskovi-Devey, "Racial Profiling and Searches," p. 350.

[80] William R. Smith et al., *The North Carolina Highway Traffic Study: Final Report to the National Institute of Justice* (Washington, DC: U.S. Department of Justice, 2003).

[81] Randall Kennedy, *Race, Crime, and the Law* (New York: Pantheon, 1997).

[82] Warren and Tomaskovi-Devey, "Racial Profiling and Searches," p. 350.

[83] Miriam Jordan, "The New Immigration Cops," *The Wall Street Journal,* February 2, 2006, p. B1.

part two
The Organization
and the Leader

The five chapters in this section deal with broad aspects of law enforcement agencies, including how to organize them from theoretical and practical perspectives, different approaches to leading departments and what research tells us about these approaches, planning and decision making models, and the legal and "hands-on" aspects of managing officers and other employees.

Chapter 5, "Organizational Theory," is a longer chapter on a difficult and under appreciated subject. All forms of organization make assumptions, one way or another, about officers and other employees and reveal the leader's preferences for one form over another. This chapter provides the basis on which leaders can thoughtfully examine what they implicitly or explicitly believe in with respect to how work is organized and authority distributed.

The lessons from the previous chapter are extended in Chapter 6, "Organizational Design," by showing the practical choices faced by law enforcement administrators when they are designing or modifying their organizations to achieve their missions, e.g., determining to what degree it will be "flat" or "tall," what types of units will be grouped together or separated, and the extent of specialization that will be allowed. Law enforcement agencies share many of the same features in their organizational structure, such as placing line and staff functions in different groupings. Beyond these basic commonalities subtle variations may be seen in organizational structures. Some law enforcement executives may want the Intelligence and Professional Standards units reporting directing to their office so they "can keep their finger on the department's pulse," while others may want to place more distance between their office and these functions so "they can keep their eye on the big picture." Thus, some aspects of organizational structures reflect the idiosyncratic personal preferences of the law enforcement executive and may not be inherently "right" or "wrong."

Chapter 7, "Leadership," is a critical examination of leadership in law enforcement agencies. It examines what leadership is and does, probes the leader-manager dichotomy, enumerates why police leaders fail, and provides comprehensive coverage of leadership theories and research findings on them. The theories discussed span the distance from "Great Man" explanations to the more recent work on transactional, transformational, ethical, charismatic, servant, spiritual, and authentic leaders.

Chapter 8 is titled "Planning and Decision Making;" these two topics are joined because planning can be seen as decision making for the future and these allied topics have some similarities. The chapter covers the importance of these topics, the types of plans, characteristics of effective plans, approaches to planning, including the synoptic or traditional approach, strategic, cost effectiveness, and must-wants analysis, why rationality in decision making is bounded or limited, decision making models, and common decision making errors. Because many law enforcement decisions are made in a crisis environment, this subject is approached using case studies of the sieges at the Branch Davidian Compound and Ruby Ridge.

Personnel and costs associated with them account for at least 80 percent of all expenditures from a police operating budget, which makes mastery of Chapter 9, "Human Resource Management" a necessity. The larger a law enforcement agency is, the more likely it is to have taken on some of the functions performed by the unit of government's central personnel office. A beginning understanding of human resource (HR) management is determining what responsibilities the law enforcement agency has in this area. Many local, state, and federal laws create legal rights for officers and other employees and violations of these can create unnecessary conflict and cause lingering labor relations problems. This chapter examines the applicable federal laws prohibiting discrimination and provides summaries of relevant legal decisions. It is generally thought that the preponderance of personnel problems are created through a faulty selection process; Chapter 9 examines this process in detail. Successive waves of generations hired into policing reveal important differences in their expectations and law enforcement agencies must successfully craft recruiting messages and project working environments conducive to attracting and retaining the Generation Xers and Yers. Other areas covered by this wide-ranging chapter include military call-ups of reservist officers, discipline, performance appraisal, and retirement counseling. Promotional systems and testing also receives significant treatment.

Organizational Theory

Theory and practice are inseparable.
—Douglas McGregor

■ Diagram a basic open systems view of a law enforcement agency.

■ Explain single- and double-loop learning.

■ Describe the entropic process.

■ Critique open systems theory.

■ Define *environmental contingency theory.*

■ Explain the basic thrust of Resource Dependency Theory.

■ Compare networked and virtual organizations.

■ Explain sense making.

■ Summarize chaos theory.

■ Describe the butterfly effect and self-organizing.

OUTLINE

Introduction

Organizational theory, which draws on many disciplines, is a tough subject and it is reasonable to ask why it is important enough to take the time to become familiar with it. Knowledge of organizational theory is important because it: (1) makes organizations more understandable; (2) reveals how authority and decision making are organized and distributed; (3) explains why some police departments are less or more open to change and innovation; (4) makes assumptions, one way or another, about followers; (5) incorporates notions about the environments that the police department faces (e.g., political and legal) and how these can impinge on the department; and (6) provides an essential tool for leaders in deciding how the work will be processed and the structure and relationship of the work units needed to accomplish it.

Formal Organizations

Formal organizations are not a recent innovation.[1] Alexander the Great and Julius Caesar used them to conquer, the pharaohs employed them to build pyramids, the emperors of China constructed great irrigation systems with them, and the first popes created an organization to deliver religion on a worldwide basis.[2] The extent to which contemporary America is an organizational society is such that

> we are born in organizations, educated by organizations, and spend most of our lives working for organizations. We spend much of our time . . . playing and praying in organizations. Most of us will die in an organization and when the time comes for burial, the largest organization of all—the state—must grant official permission.[3]

The basic rationale for the existence of organizations is that they do those things that people are unwilling or unable to do alone. Parsons notes that organizations are distinguished from other human groupings or social units in that, to a much greater degree, they are constructed and reconstructed to achieve specific goals; corporations, armies, hospitals, and police departments are included within this meaning, whereas families and friendship groups are not.[4] Schein defines an organization as the rational coordination of the activities of a number of people for the achievement of some common explicit purpose or goal, through division of labor and function and a hierarchy of authority and responsibility.[5]

Blau and Scott identify four types of formal organizations by asking the question of *cui bono,* or who benefits: (1) **mutual benefit associations**, such as police labor unions, where the primary beneficiary is the membership; (2) **business concerns**, such as Lynn Peavey, which sells crime scene equipment and supplies, where the owner is the prime beneficiary; (3) **service organizations**, such as community mental health centers, where a specific client group is the prime beneficiary; and (4) **commonweal organizations**, such as the Department of Defense and law enforcement agencies, where the beneficiary is the public at large.[6]

Each of these four types of formal organizations has its own central issues.[7] Mutual benefit associations, such as police unions, face the crucial problem of maintaining the internal democratic processes—providing for participation and control by their

IN THE NEWS   Police, City Settle Collective Bargaining Impasse

One of the important things police unions do for its members is to collectively bargain for salaries, health and pension benefits, and other matters. In Toledo, Ohio, city officials and the police union agreed to a contract that ended a collective bargaining impasse, which had caused negotiations to stall out. The new contract erased concessions forced on union members earlier in 2010, replacing them with less-severe cutbacks. Union members will no longer have to pay the full 10 percent employee share pension contribution—that entire cost will now be picked up by the city. Layoffs of officers are prohibited until 2011 and overtime earned between June 2010 and March 2011 will be paid in March on the basis of a 3.5 percent pay increase.

Source: Ignazio Massina and Tom Troy, "Police Union Backs Deal with Toledo," *The Toledo Times*, May 18, 2010.

membership. For businesses, the central issue is maximizing profits in a competitive environment. Service organizations are faced with the conflict between administrative regulations and provision of the services judged by the professional to be most appropriate. In the case of a community mental health center, an illustration is that, following a reduction in funding, a regulation is placed into effect that requires all clients to be treated in group sessions when the psychiatric social worker believes the only effective treatment for a particular client is to be seen individually.

The key issue for law enforcement agencies and other types of commonweal organizations is finding a way to accommodate pressures from two sources: (1) external democratic control and (2) internal control. The public expects to have external democratic control of its police department through its elected and appointed representatives. This external democratic control feature also has the expectation that the internal workings of the police department will be effective and efficient, but not also democratic. This is because democratic control by the members of a police department would inevitably lead to the department being in conflict at various times with the will of the community (e.g., one favoring a hard-line approach to crime control versus the other being in favor of a more moderate approach). Internally, large numbers of officers at the lower levels of the police department do not want to be treated like "cogs in a machine" and desire some voice in how the department operates. Thus, the challenge for police managers is how to maintain an organization that meets society's needs and the needs of the officers who work in it. This requires an understanding of such things as the different ways of organizing and the contrasting assumptions that various organizational forms make about the nature of people. Such knowledge is found within organizational theory.

Traditional Organizational Theory

Traditional theory is associated with organizations described as classical, mechanistic, and closed systems, which assume little influence from outside of the organization. Its underlying assumption is that there is one best way to structure and operate an organization. This body of knowledge evolved over centuries and crystallized between 1900 and the 1950s. The three branches or stems of traditional organizational theory are (1) scientific management, (2) the bureaucratic model, and (3) administrative, or management, theory.

Figure 5.1
Frederick W. Taylor's meticulously combed hair and well-groomed appearance hint at his obsession with details. (Courtesy of the Library of Congress)

Taylor: Scientific Management

The father of **scientific management** is **Frederick W. Taylor** (1856–1915), and the thrust of his thinking was to find the "one best way" to do work (see Figure 5.1). In addition to its status as a theory of work organization, Taylor's scientific management is a theory of motivation in its belief that employees will be guided in their actions by what is in their economic self-interest.

A Pennsylvanian born of Quaker–Puritan parents, Taylor was so discontented with the "evils" of waste and slothfulness that he applied the same careful analysis to finding the best way of playing croquet and of taking a cross-country walk with the least fatigue that was to be the hallmark of his later work in factories.[8] From 1878 to 1890, Taylor worked at the Midvale Steel Company in Philadelphia, rising from the ranks of the laborers to chief engineer in just 6 years.[9] Taylor's experience at Midvale gave him insight into the twin problems of productivity and worker motivation. He saw workers as deliberately restricting productivity by "natural soldiering" and "systematic soldiering."

Natural soldiering came from the natural inclination of employees not to push themselves; **systematic soldiering** came from workers not wanting to produce so much as to see their quotas raised or other workers thrown out of their jobs.[10] To correct these deficiencies, Taylor called for a "complete mental revolution"[11] on the part of both workers and managers, although it is certain that he faulted management more for its failure to design jobs properly and to give workers the proper economic incentives to overcome soldiering than he did workers for not producing.[12]

Taylor's scientific management is only loosely a theory of organization because its focus was largely on work at the bottom part of the organization rather than being a general model. Scientific management's method was to find the most physically and time-efficient way to sequence tasks and then to use rigorous and extensive controls to enforce the standards. Taylor's conversation with "Schmidt" illustrates this:

> Schmidt, you can keep making $1.15 a day like the rest of these workers or you can be a high price man and make $1.85 each and every day. Do you want to be a high price man?"
>
> "Vell yes, I vant to be high price man."
>
> "Good. When this man tells you to load pig iron on the car, you walk, pick up the pig and load it exactly like he tells you. Rest when he tells you to and never give him any backtalk. That's what a high price man does."
>
> "I vant to be a high price man and vill do what this man tells me."[13]

For Taylor, authority was based not on position in a hierarchy but rather on knowledge; **functional supervision** meant that people were responsible for directing certain tasks, despite the fact that this meant the authority of the supervisor might cut across organizational lines.[14] The **exception principle** meant that routine matters should be handled by lower-level managers or by supervisors and that higher-level managers should only receive reports of deviations above or below standard performances.[15] The integration of cost accounting into the planning process became part of some budgeting practices treated in Chapter 12, Financial Management.

Despite the success of scientific management in raising productivity and cutting costs, "Taylorism" was attacked from a variety of quarters. Union leaders saw it as a threat to their movement because it seemed to reduce, if not eliminate, the importance of unions. The management of Bethlehem Steel ultimately abandoned task management, as Taylor liked to refer to his system, because managers were uncomfortable with such an accurate appraisal of their performance[16] and some liberals saw it as an exploitation of workers. Upton Sinclair, one of the muckrakers (See Chapter 1, Evolution of Police Administration) charged that Taylor had given workers a 61 percent increase in wages while getting a 362 percent increase in productivity.[17] Taylor replied to this charge by saying that employees worked no harder, only more efficiently. In hearings before the U.S. House of Representatives in 1912, Taylor's methods were attacked thoroughly, and he died 3 years later a discouraged man. Nonetheless, Henry Ford recast scientific management and used it to increase production and lower costs for the mass-produced Model T Ford (1909–1927).

Scientific management did not disappear with Taylor, however. There remained a core of people devoted to its practice, including Henry L. Gantt (1861–1919); Watlington

---

IN THE NEWS   Traffic Ticket Quotas: The New Scientific Management?

A recurring theme in law enforcement is the issue of traffic ticket quotas. Historically, pressure to "improve ticket productivity," comes from city hall, labeled as "performance standards." Ostensibly, the quotas are established to ensure the safety of pedestrians and the motoring public. As matter of reality, the fines levied are often an important part of small-town budgets. In some states (e.g., Georgia), there is a legal presumption that if an agency writes speeding tickets for which the fines are more than 40 percent of the agency's annual operating budget, the detection devices are being used for something other than public safety. If it is determined that traffic enforcement is being used as a funding mechanism by local units of government, the Georgia State Patrol may assume those duties until the issue is resolved.

Quotas are often resisted by officers, who maintain that no one really knows how many good cases they will see on a monthly basis. They argue that the number and types of offenses vary by geographical area and demographic characteristics; for example, older people commit fewer driving violations than do younger operators. Moreover, officers are also quick to point out that quotas force them to make marginal cases in order to get good evaluations, thereby decreasing public goodwill and support.

In Michigan, Ypsilanti police officer Annette Coppock was reprimanded and charged with misconduct, insubordination, neglect of duty, and unsatisfactory performance in connection with being 18 tickets shy of her agency's 30 per month standard. A union member, Coppock appealed the discipline, which was overturned by an arbitrator who also labeled the quota illegal.

Source: Lee Higgins, "Ticket Quota for Ypsilanti Police Officers is Illegal," AnnArbor.com, February 5, 2010, with restatement.

Task Name	Duration	Start	End	2001				
				12/Sep	19/Sep	26/Sep	03/Oct	1
Order Project Equipment	18.0 d	13/Sep/01	06/Oct/02					
Write Request for Computer, Printer, and Software	2.0 d	13/Sep/01	14/Sep/02					
Obtain Administrative Approval for Equipment Request	3.0 d	15/Sep/01	17/Sep/02					
Order Equipment & Software through Procurement	3.0 d	20/Sep/01	22/Sep/02					
Equipment and Software on Order	8.0 d	23/Sep/01	04/Oct/02					
Receive and Configure Equipment	2.0 d	05/Oct/01	06/Oct/02					
Staff Project	14.0 d	13/Sep/01	30/Sep/02					
Develop Job Descriptions	2.0 d	13/Sep/01	14/Sep/02					
Announce Positions	3.0 d	15/Sep/01	17/Sep/02					
Screen Applicants	3.0 d	20/Sep/01	22/Sep/02					
Interview Finalists	2.0 d	23/Sep/01	24/Sep/02					
Make Hiring Decisions	1.0 d	27/Sep/01	27/Sep/02					
Train Staff	3.0 d	28/Sep/01	30/Sep/02					

Figure 5.2
State police promotional testing project. A portion of a Gantt chart showing the start-up phase of the project.

Emerson (1853–1931), also a promoter of the staff concept; Frank (1868–1924) and Lillian (1878–1972) Gilbreth; and Morris Cooke (1872–1960), who in *Our Cities Awake* (1918) called for the application of scientific management in municipal government. Gantt gained a measure of immortality by developing a basic planning chart, illustrated in Figure 5.2, which remains in wide use today and still bears his name. Developed during the summer of 1917 while Gantt worked at the Frankford Arsenal, the Gantt chart contained the then-revolutionary idea that the key factor in planning production was not quantity but time.[18] Some international interest in scientific management also remained after Taylor's death; in 1918, France's Ministry of War called for the application of scientific management, as did Lenin in an article in *Pravda*.[19] It is, of course, ironic that a communist society should call for the use of a management system based on the principle that economic self-interest guides the behavior of workers.

Although scientific management has long since ceased to be a dominant force, it does not mean that it is all history. In addition to Gantt charts, many of the techniques associated with scientific management remain in use. Time and motion studies have been used to analyze how detectives use their time, identifying wasteful activities such as waiting for a vehicle to become available at the motor pool. Work-flow analysis (depicted in Figure 5.3) remains used in industrial engineering. Other modern successors

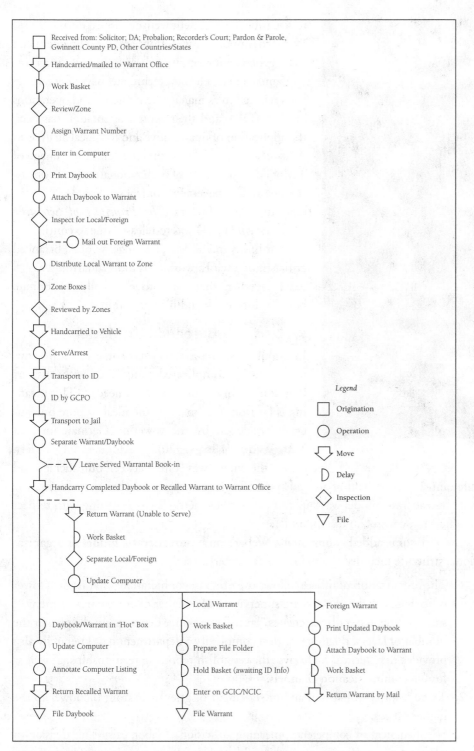

Figure 5.3
Work-flow analysis of criminal warrants in a sheriff's office.

Figure 5.4
Max Weber.
(Courtesy of Library
of Congress)

to scientific management were developed during World War II to support the war effort, and the refinement and more general application of these techniques is a post-1945 movement. The new techniques have alternatively been referred to as management science and operations research (OR), and their central orientation has been the application of quantitative and technical analysis to decision making.[20] Thus, the most enduring image of Taylor is as a promoter of both rationalization in organizations and management control systems.[21]

In 1997, Taylor's *The Principles of Scientific Management* (1911) was re-released due to continuing interest in his methods and Kanigel wrote a balanced criticism of Taylor's work,[22] as did Caldari in 2007.[23] Read together, they serve to essentially rehabilitate both Taylor's work and his reputation.

Weber: The Bureaucratic Model

In popular use, *bureaucracy* has come to mean slow, unnecessarily complicated procedures with answers that don't seem to quite meet our needs.[24] This meaning is far from the image of the ideal or pure bureaucracy developed by the towering German intellect **Max Weber** (1864–1920), the founder of modern sociology (see Figure 5.4). For Weber, the choice was "only between bureaucracy and dilettantism in the field of administration."[25] In this regard, Weber claimed that the pure bureaucratic model was superior to all other methods of organizing with respect to efficiency, control, and stability.[26]

With some added commentary, Weber's pure **bureaucratic model** of organizational structure included the following characteristics:

1. The organization of offices follows the principle of hierarchy; that is, each lower office is under the control and supervision of a higher one. This arrangement of successively higher offices creates "layers" in a police department; the greater the number of layers, the more vertical complexity a department has. Hierarchy also provides the "vertical highways" that establish reporting relationships, as well as formal communication channels.

2. There is a right of appeal and of statement of grievances from the lower to the higher offices.

3. Specified areas of competence, meaning a division of labor, exist. This division of labor or specialization increases the width and horizontal complexity of law enforcement agencies. The greater the amount of specialization in organizations, the more organizations grow vertically to have the ability to coordinate the different units.

4. Official duties are bound by a system of rational rules, such as policies and procedures.

5. Administrative acts, decisions, and rules are recorded in writing, creating an institutional memory.

6. The authority associated with a position is the property of the office or job and not of the occupant of the position.

7. Employees are appointed on the basis of qualifications, and specialized training is necessary.

8. Organizational members do not own it.[27]

Although not all the characteristics of Weber's bureaucratic model can be revealed by an organizational chart, Figure 5.5 does depict two important features: (1) the principle of hierarchy and (2) a division of labor that results in specialization.

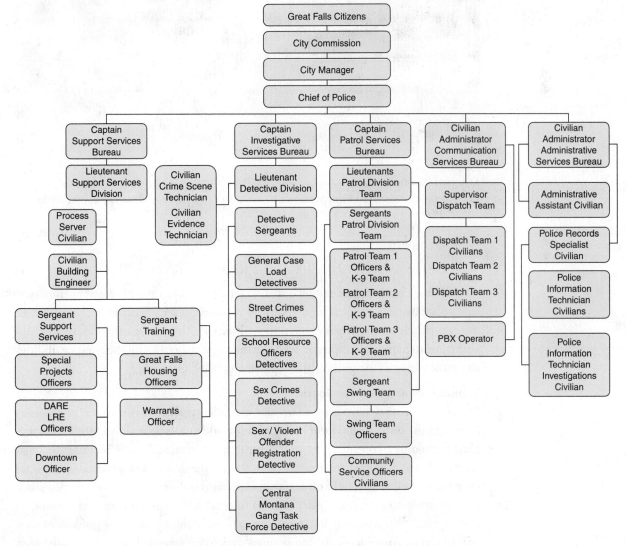

Figure 5.5
Organizational chart for the Great Falls (Montana) Police Department.
Source: Courtesy of the Great Falls, Montana, Police Department.

Figure 5.6
May 1921, Lord John Denton Pinkstone French (1852–1925) inspecting the members of the Royal Irish Constabulary. Inspections help to maintain compliance with standards and to stimulate pride in one's appearance and department.
(Courtesy of Walshe/Topical Press Agency/Getty Images)

Weber's bureaucratic model rested on what he called **rational-legal authority**.[28] In a police context, rational legal authority rests on the legal basis for the existence of the department. Authority is granted to positions within the organization, such as sergeants, lieutenants, and captains, who use that authority to fulfill their responsibilities and to accomplish the goals of the department (see Figure 5.6).

Bureaucracy and Decision Space

Although there may have been a few stray exceptions, police departments for centuries have used the bureaucratic form of organization and continue to do so. While clinging, like the majority of organizations in the world, to the structure of the bureaucratic organizational model, police departments have substantially dropped new processes over it to: (1) attract new generations of officers with expectations different than their predecessors; (2) shift from an almost singular focus on internal administration, such as control, to empowering employees; (3) foster collaboration with constituents; (4) implement new operational philosophies (e.g., community- and intelligence-led policing); (5) employ new models of leadership; (6) operate with greater openness, producing more transparency of administration and operations in the community; (7) increase workforce diversity; (8) use new technologies (e.g. texting, Facebook, and Twitter); and (9) be more nimble in responding to emergent conditions and issues.

Many law enforcement agencies have rapidly moved into **e-government**,[29] facilitating the use of government services on-line. The Springfield (Missouri) Police Department's website allows citizens to obtain crime maps of their neighborhoods, search police reports, request copies of traffic accident and incident reports, locate the residence of sexual offenders, and file a complaint against or extend recognition to officers.

As a result, this "reformatted bureaucracy" falls into the broad category of neoclassical organization theory, meaning taking a fresh perspective on traditional organizational theory. More specifically, the reformatted bureaucratic organization model has also been labeled neoWeberian.[30] The shift from the pure bureaucratic model to the neoWeberian accompanies the rise in the management concept of the **new public management (NPM)**, which began in the 1980s. At its core, NPM called for the use of private sector approaches in public organizations (e.g., creating productivity gains, getting citizens involved, and outsourcing services if it can be done cheaper and as well or better than when using public funds). A 2007 study of 304 California law enforcement agencies in cities identified as immigrant destinations illustrates the neoclassical bureaucratic organizational model.[31]

Illegal immigration provides a backdrop to contrast classical and neoclassical law enforcement agencies. Illegal immigration is a "hot button" issue. American nativists are staunchly anti-immigration on any basis. Others support immigration reform as long as there is no amnesty, while a liberal immigration reform law will have some support as well. Arizona chose to enact a stringent law aimed at identifying, prosecuting, and deporting illegal immigrants (see Figure 5.7), the lone state to have done so.

Elsewhere, if law enforcement agencies were simply classical bureaucratic organizations, they would arrest all violators of immigration laws that come to their attention. However, many law enforcement agencies, often without any direction from city hall have chosen not to cooperate with federal authorities in rounding up illegal immigrants.

These neoclassical agencies recognize that actively seeking out and enforcing federal immigration laws will dry up support and information needed to investigate traditional state and local laws. It is a practical stance; in some cities non-citizens account for half of the foreign born residents.[32]

That a small percentage of illegal immigrants have committed crimes is beyond questioning, as is the fact that they represent a number of nations. From a public policy standpoint in local government, the question is what to do about undocumented immigrants. In the normal course of events, locally elected officials would develop a policy and distribute it to its department heads for implementation. However, the 2007 study found an astonishingly low understanding of undocumented immigrant issues among such officials and a lack or guidance to department heads (e.g., 72 percent of local elected officials did not know if their law enforcement agencies contacted federal authorities when undocumented immigrants were encountered).[33] This results in "**decision space**" for law enforcement agencies, which then have the freedom to forge their own policies (e.g., do we accept the matricula consular identification card issued

Figure 5.7
*President Obama and Arizona Governor Jan Brewer discuss illegal immigration and her request
to mobilize 1,200 National Guard soldiers to protect citizens of her state.*
(Courtesy of Photoshot/Newscom)

by the Mexican government to its citizens? Do we contact federal Immigration and
Customs Enforcement [ICE; see Figure 5.8] when such cards are presented?)[34]

In a pure bureaucratic model under authoritarian leadership, "decision
space" would be filled by "going by the book," strict enforcement. However, the
new strategic law enforcement leadership thinks in terms of the resources available, what should and should not be done in furtherance of a departments' missions, and new processes.[35] Many agencies surveyed had formulated policies
favorable to undocumented immigrants; 81 percent considered bilingualism as a
favorable part of an applicant's background and 87 percent provided additional pay
for language skills.[36] The largest number of agencies accepted the matricula consular identification card, did not inquire about immigration status when it was
presented, and did not contact ICE when, during the course of a contact, immigration status was uncertain or undocumented.[37] However, if a violent crime is involved, law enforcement agencies checked immigration status and/or contacted
ICE nearly 90 percent of the time.[38]

A 2009 national study confirmed that police departments often act without
guidance on undocumented immigrants from elected officials. Fifty-one percent of the
agencies surveyed had no guidance, 9 percent had informal direction, and 4 percent
of the communities chose to create a sanctuary for undocumented immigrants, so long
as they were law abiding.[39]

Figure 5.8
ICE taking a criminal alien into custody during a 2010 roundup that focused on apprehending those with serious criminal histories, outstanding charges, and prior immigration arrest records. Operation Cross Check arrested 596 criminal aliens from 60 different nations in the southeast and Puerto Rico.
(Photo Courtesy of U.S. Immigration and Customs Enforcement [ICE])

In developing their agencies' immigration policies, chiefs are faced with a rough calculation of what is the greater good for their communities and have decided that strict enforcement is likely to alienate relationships with documented and undocumented immigrants, who are often mixed together even among families living together, reducing their willingness to report crimes and to provide assistance to investigators. To some degree these policies reflect that 72 percent of chiefs believed immigration was a federal enforcement responsibility.[40] Unlike pure bureaucracies, neoclassicals are strategic, nimble, and practical-minded.

The Police as Street-Level Bureaucrats
Street-level bureaucrats, such as police officers working in the field, are the face of government, meeting with members of the public and using their discretion on how to implement public policy.[41] In doing so, officers operate out of two modes: (1) "state agents," who believe in following the law and policies and (2) "citizen agents," who will bend or ignore them.[42] Although some officers may operate largely out of one mode or the other, most use both of them. People enter their law enforcement careers with different genders, sexual preferences, educational levels, races, economic backgrounds, and life experiences.[43] By doctrine, police departments expect that through training and supervision, officers will end up handling each similar call in the same manner, as a state agent, which clearly doesn't happen. After the academy and by the

completion of 2 years of service, the sole or predominate orientation toward being a state agent fades under the weight of new experiences, the views of veteran officers, and the policing street culture, which is often antithetical to the values espoused in the academy.[44] In short, officers go from "nobody who breaks the law deserves a break" to "you have to approach things realistically, few situations are exactly the same, sometimes you need to cut somebody some slack."

Several important observations flow from the balancing act officers do with state and citizen agent modes: (1) however official-sounding the law and public policy are, their implementation is to some extent idiosyncratic; (2) the latent power of personal experience on the street is somewhat of an antidote to the expectations of doctrine; and (3) unaccounted for by advocates for the uniform, and therefore equitable, implementation of public policy is the personal circumstances of street officers. For example, some officers who don't have any court cases scheduled, but are forced to make an arrest, will say, "Well, if I have to go to court now, nobody catches a break."

Two dimensions to Weber's work are often not considered. First, he feared that the bureaucratic model's efficiency constituted a threat to individual freedom by its impersonal nature and oppressive routine.[45] Second, Weber deplored the career professional of moderate ambitions who craved security; Weber saw this type of person as lacking spontaneity and inventiveness, the modern-day "petty bureaucrat."[46]

Weber did not invent the bureaucratic model; it had existed for centuries; he only described and didn't like all that he saw.[47] Thus, whereas Weber spawned the formal study of organizations, it scarcely seems fair to lay at his feet any real or fancied inadequacies of the model or its operation. Moreover, although it would be difficult to overstate Weber's contributions, it must be borne in mind that, although some people read him in the original German,[48] his work was not translated into English and was not generally available until 1947, long after the bureaucratic model was well entrenched.

Administrative Theory

Administrative theory, also referred to as management theory and the principles approach, sought to identify generic or universal methods of administration. Its benchmark is the 1937 publication of **Luther Gulick** (1892–1993) and Lyndall Urwick's (1891–1983) edited *Papers on the Science of Administration*. In content, administrative theory is more compatible with the bureaucratic model than with scientific management because it concentrates on broader principles. Administrative theory is distinguished from the bureaucratic model by its "how-to" emphasis. At some risk of oversimplification, the principles both operationalize and reinforce features of the bureaucratic model. Consequently, because of the continuing pervasiveness of the bureaucratic model, the principles either explicitly or implicitly continue to play an important role in organizations, including police departments. Other key contributors to this school are Henri Fayol (1841–1925), James Mooney (1884–1957), and Alan Reiley (1869–1947).

Henri Fayol graduated as an engineer at the age of 19 from France's National School of Mines at St. Etienne and began a 40-year career with the Commentary-Fourchambault Company.[49] His contributions are based on writings that were an outgrowth of his experiences as a manager. Fayol's fame rests chiefly on his *General and Industrial Management* (1916). The first English edition of this appeared in Great Britain in 1923, and although his "Administrative Theory of the State" appeared in *Papers on the Science of Administration (1937),* his main work, *General and Industrial Management,* was not widely available in this country until 1949. Fayol's principles included the following: (1) a division of work or specialization; (2) authority, the right to give orders and expect compliance; whoever issues an order or delegates a task is personally responsible for the task remains with the delegator; (3) discipline, obedience to laws, policies, procedures, and orders to further the accomplishment of the department's mission; (4) unity of command, on any assignment a subordinate shall only be directed by a single supervisor; (5) unity of direction—leaders must establish a direction for the department; unity of command is meaningless without unity of direction; (6) subordination of personal interest to the interest of the department; (7) compensation must be fair and uniform to people with the same jobs, qualifications, and experience; (8) centralization, which allows the active steering of the department in the direction intended; (9) the scalar chain—authority and responsibility must flow in a clear and unbroken line from the top to the bottom of the department through the various ranks, often referred to as the chain of command; (10) order is another manifestation of discipline; the building, equipment, records, and related matters must be properly maintained and accounted for; (11) equity, that quality of leadership and processes that combine kindness and justice; (12) sability of personnel, which allows employees to become familiar with their jobs; (13) initiative at all levels of the organization is a source of productivity; and (14) esprit de corps, harmony, and union of personnel–these constitute a great strength, and efforts should be made to establish them.[50]

Fayol recognized that his scalar principle could produce disastrous consequences if it were followed strictly because it would hamper swift action.[51] He therefore developed Fayol's "gangplank," or horizontal bridge, as a means of addressing this problem. First-line supervisors and middle managers in different units who interact regularly "cut across" the organization on the gangplank, eliminating the time-consuming process of going up one hierarchy and down another. Inside of and between law enforcement agencies e-mail and texting have become modern gangplanks (also see Chapter 10, Organizational and Interpersonal Communication). In 2002, Wren, Bedian, and Breeze concluded that the richness of Fayol's contributions can best be understood be reading the "small, stepping stone" publications that led to his theory.[52]

Mooney and Reiley's *Onward Industry* (1931) was generally consistent with the work of Fayol, as were the subsequent revisions of this publication, which appeared in 1939 and 1947 under the title *The Principles of Organization.*[53] In "Notes on the Theory of Organization," which was included in *Papers on the Science of Administration,* Gulick

Figure 5.9
Gulick's POSDCORB.

Activity	Description
Planning	Identifying the things that need to be done and the methods for doing them to accomplish the goals of the agency.
Organizing	The establishment of a formal structure of authority through which work subdivisions are arranged, defined, and coordinated.
Staffing	Recruiting, screening, hiring, training, and evaluating officers.
Directing	The continuous effort of making decisions, communicating them, and seeing that they are properly implemented.
Coordinating	The all important duty of interrelating the various parts of the work.
Reporting	Keeping those to whom the leader is responsible informed as to what is going on and ensuring subordinates stay informed.
Budgeting	The process of developing a plan stated in financial terms.

coined the most familiar and enduring acronym of administration, **POSDCORB** (see Figure 5.9).[54] Gulick acknowledged that his POSDCORB was adapted from Fayol's principles. Likewise, Urwick drew on the work of another Frenchman, A. V. Graicunas, for his view on the span of control. Urwick asserted that no one should directly supervise five or at the most six subordinates whose work was unrelated.

Critique of Traditional Theory

Scientific management is decried because of its "man as machine" orientation, and ample life is given to that argument by even a casual reading of the conversation between Taylor and the legendary "Schmidt." On balance, although Taylor's emphasis was on task, he was not totally indifferent to the human element, arguing that no system of management can be woodenly applied and all opinions of workers should be considered.[55]

The pure bureaucratic model has no shortage of critics, although their arguments, when read in the context of today's neoWeberian bureaucracies, are largely outdated. Nonetheless, they are covered to provide an understanding of how the bureaucratic model has evolved.

Organizational humanism called for a softening or elimination of many features of the pure bureaucractic model; perhaps foremost of these was Warren Bennis, who leveled the following specific criticisms (1966): (1) bureaucracy does not adequately allow for the personal growth and development of mature personalities; (2) it develops conformity and "group think"; (3) it does not take into account the "informal organization" and emerging and unanticipated problems; (4) its systems of control and authority are hopelessly outdated; (5) it has no adequate judicial process; (6) it does not possess adequate means for resolving differences and conflicts between ranks and, most particularly, between functional groups; (7) communication and innovative ideas are thwarted or distorted due to a tall hierarchy; (8) the full human

High	Low
Centralization	Adaptability
Formality	Job Satisfaction
Stratification	Complexity
Production	
Efficiency	

Figure 5.10
Hage's Summary of the Mixed Characteristics of the Bureaucratic Model.

resources are not utilized due to mistrust, fear of reprisals, and so on; (9) it cannot assimilate the influx of new technology entering the organization; and (10) it modifies the personality structure such that each person becomes and reflects the full, gray, conditioned "organization person."[56]

In 1957, Robert Merton (1910–2003) noted that rigid enforcement of rules can become dysfunctional. Originally intended to promote efficiency and equity in dealing with clients, the intention of the rules can become lost and what is left is a slavish devotion to enforcing them. Merton saw this as creating a "bureaucratic virtuoso," who never forgets a single rule.

Herbert Simon (1916–2001) took issue with administrative theory. In 1945 he noted that if you narrow the span of control to five or six employees, you make the organization "taller," creating more layers and greater vertical complexity, and that decreases efficiency because a matter going up the chain of command is more time-consuming as each layer considers how to handle it.[57]

Less critical than both Bennis and Simon, Hage describes bureaucracy in the mixed terms shown in Figure 5.10.[58] In *Complex Organizations* (1972), Perrow argues that the preoccupation with reforming, humanizing, and decentralizing bureaucracies diverts attention from acknowledging how superior they are to other forms of organization. Goodsell, in *The Case for Bureaucracy* (1985), concludes that denunciations of bureaucracy may be fashionable, but not necessarily solid.[59] He asks the question: "How can we believe that all public bureaucracies, all of the time, are inefficient, dysfunctional, rigid, obstructionist, secretive, oligarchic, conservative, undemocratic, imperialist, oppressive, alienating, and discriminatory?"[60] Gouldner is more blunt, declaring the unending criticisms as being qualitative arguments devoid of any "empirical trimmings."[61]

Human Relations School

The **human relations school** was developed in reaction to the mechanistic orientation of traditional organizational theory, which was viewed as neglecting or ignoring the human element and helped set the stage for organizational humanism. This school rests on the research of Elton Mayo (1880–1949) and Fritz Roethlisberger (1898–1974). Originally started to study worker fatigue, the research (1927–1932) was expanded several times and was carried out near Chicago at the Western Electric Company's Hawthorne Plant.[62] The major contribution of the Hawthorne

Studies is the view that organizations are social systems. Two key studies were conducted: (1) the telephone relay assembly study and (2) the telephone switchboard wiring study.[63]

In the first study, five women assembling telephone relays were put into a room and subjected to varying physical work conditions.[64] Even when the conditions changed unfavorably, production increased. Mayo and his associates were puzzled by these results. Ultimately, they decided that (1) when the experimenters took over many of the supervisory functions, the work environment became less strict and less formal; (2) the women behaved differently from what was expected because they were receiving attention, creating the "**Hawthorne effect**"; and (3) by placing the women together in the relay assembling test room, the researchers had provided the opportunity for them to become a closely knit group.[65] On the basis of these observations, the researchers concluded that an important influence on productivity is the interpersonal relations and spirit of cooperation that had developed among the women and between the women and their supervisors. The influence of these "human relations" was believed to be every bit as important as physical work conditions and financial incentives.[66]

In the telephone switchboard wiring study, 14 men were put on a reasonable piece rate; that is, without physically straining themselves, they could earn more if they produced more. The assumption was that the workers would behave as rational economic actors and produce more, because it was in their own best interest. To insulate these men from the "systematic soldiering" they knew to exist among the plant's employees, the researchers also placed these workers in a special room. The workers' output did not increase, which contradicted scientific management's view that given the opportunity to earn more, workers will be more productive. The values of the informal group appeared to be more powerful than the allure of financial betterment: (1) don't be a "rate buster" and produce too much; (2) if you turn out too little work, you are a "chisler"; (3) don't be a "squealer" to supervisors; and (4) don't be officious; if you are an inspector, don't act like one.[67]

As a result of the Hawthorne Studies, it was concluded that (1) the level of production is set by social norms, not by physiological capacities; (2) often workers react not as individuals but as members of a group; (3) the rewards and sanctions of the group significantly affect the behavior of workers and limit the impact of economic incentive plans; and (4) leadership has an important role in setting and enforcing group norms, and there is a difference between formal and informal leadership.[68]

When workers react as members of an informal group, they become susceptible to the values of that group. Thus, the informal group can be a powerful force in organizations. Illustratively, a number of police unions started as an unorganized, small informal group of dissatisfied officers. Although many factors contribute to the enduring problem of police corruption, such as disillusionment and temptation, an informal group that supports taking payoffs makes it more difficult to identify and prosecute "bad cops." In 1972, the **Knapp Commission**, investigating corruption in the New York City Police Department, distinguished between "meat-eaters" (those who overtly pursued opportunities to profit personally from their police power) and "grass-eaters" (those who simply accepted the payoffs that the happenstances of police work brought their way).[69] The behavior of the grass-eaters can be interpreted within the framework of the power that informal groups have. The Knapp Commission learned that the motive for grass-eaters taking petty graft was to be seen as "one of the boys" and therefore trusted by the meat-eaters.

The foregoing discussion should not be interpreted to mean that informal groups always, or even frequently, engage in troublesome or unethical behavior but rather is an illustration of the potency that such groups have. Astute law enforcement administrators are always alert for opportunities to tap the energy of informal groups to support departmental goals and programs.

Critique of the Human Relations School

Mayo's human relations school has been challenged on a number of grounds:

1. The research methods were not rigorous and such lapses may have tainted the findings.[70]
2. The viewpoint that conflict between management and the worker can be overcome by the "harmony" of human relations attributes too much potency to human relations and ignores the potential that properly handled conflict has for being a source of creativity and innovation.
3. The single-mindedness with which advocates insisted on the importance of human relations was evangelistic.
4. Entirely too much emphasis was placed on the informal side of organization to the neglect of the organization as a whole.[71]

Human relations is also criticized as having a pro-management bias from several perspectives. First, it saw unions as promoting conflict between management and labor, a condition antithetical to the values of human relations. Second, by focusing on workers, the Hawthorne studies provided management with more sophisticated means of manipulating employees. Finally, the end of human relations is indistinguishable from that of scientific management in that both aim for a more efficient organization:

> Scientific management assumed the most efficient organization would also be the most satisfying one, since it would maximize both productivity and workers' pay . . . the Human Relations approach was that the most personally satisfying organization would be the most efficient.[72]

In 2010, job satisfaction in the United States hit a 20-year low.[73] Although the Hawthorne Studies never showed a clear-cut relationship between satisfaction and job performance,[74] the human relations "chant" that satisfied people are more productive has become a widely held and cherished belief. It is a logically appealing and commonsense position whose endless repetition has accorded it the status of "fact." There is, however, no consistent research evidence to support that job satisfactions causes or is correlated with productivity.

A 2008 study reviewed 70 years of research and concluded that uncertainty remains as to whether happier workers are more productive.[75] The study essentially confirms the most scornful dismissal of the human relations school as "contented cows give more milk" theory. In 2009, researchers found that in nonenforcement situations with the public, officers had greater job satisfaction when they perceived higher levels of public support.[76] In a smaller study (2009), the best predictors of job satisfaction among police officers was job autonomy and regular feedback.[77] Job satisfaction can be decreased or increased by the velocity or speed at which a person is able to make progress toward important goals (2010).[78] There is also some evidence (2008) that employer-provided support services, such as child care and exercise opportunities, are a shield to job dissatisfaction and may decrease turnover.[79]

Organizational Humanism

Organizational humanism (OH) shares the human relations school's distaste for traditional organizational theory. OH differs from traditional organizational theory and the human relations school in three fundamental ways: (1) the work intrinsically, in and of itself, should be satisfying and help to motivate workers; (2) organizations must pay attention to the on- and off-the-job needs of workers; and (3) work shouldn't be just something that people endure to make a living.[80] Covered in this section are Maslow's need hierarchy; Argyris's immaturity/maturity changes; McGregor's Theory X–Theory Y; and Herzberg's motivation-hygiene theory. Likert's management systems, a four-step continuum from authoritarian to participative work environments, could also fit here, although it is covered in Chapter 7, Leadership. These organizational humanists must be read in the context of their times; their views were written from 1943 (Maslow, the needs hierarchy) until 1966 (Herzberg, motivation-hygiene theory). Presently, some of their views are archaic; in fairness, they could not foresee the rise of neoclassical organizational theory and the neoWeberian organizational processes. Nonetheless, organizational humanism is an important milestone in helping to move thinking beyond traditional organizational theory and the human relations school and helped to set the stage for new styles of leadership and organizational processes (see Chapter 7, Leadership).

Maslow: The Needs Hierarchy

Abraham Maslow (1908–1970) was a psychologist who developed the **needs hierarchy** to explain individual motivation. The model appeared first in a 1943 article[81] and later received extended coverage in Maslow's *Motivation and Personality* (1954); it is summarized in Figure 5.11.[82]

The needs hierarchy is arranged, like the rungs on a ladder, from the lower-order to the higher-order needs. A person does not move from one level to the next-higher one until the majority of the prior level's needs are met. Once those needs are met, they cease to motivate a person, and the needs at the next level of the hierarchy predominate. For example, one does not attempt to self-actualize until one has feelings of self-confidence, worth, strength, capability, adequacy, and mastery;[83] these feelings are generated only with the meeting of the self-esteem needs. It is important to understanding the needs hierarchy that the character of something does not necessarily determine what need is met but rather to what use it is put; money can be used to buy food and satisfy a basic need, or it can be put in a savings account to satisfy safety needs. Also, any progress up the hierarchy can be reversed; a police officer who is fired or is given a lengthy suspension may be thrust into a financial situation in which the physiological needs will predominate.

Police agencies that are managed professionally attempt to make appropriate use of theoretical constructs. For example, the fourth level of Maslow's needs hierarchy is self-esteem, which includes the need for recognition as evidenced by compliments and commendations. The Ohio State Highway Patrol used this need level to combat vehicle theft by creating the Blue Max Award. Each time a state trooper arrests a suspect in a stolen car, he or she receives a lightning bolt decal to place on the side of his or her patrol car. For five such arrests, a trooper receives a license plate that reads "ACE" with a single lightening bolt next to it. Each additional five arrests results in an additional lightening bolt on the license plate. The trooper with the most arrests at the end of the year receives a citation of merit, a uniform ribbon, and exclusive use of a new patrol car for a year. In 2009, the top trooper recovered 14 vehicles with suspects in them.

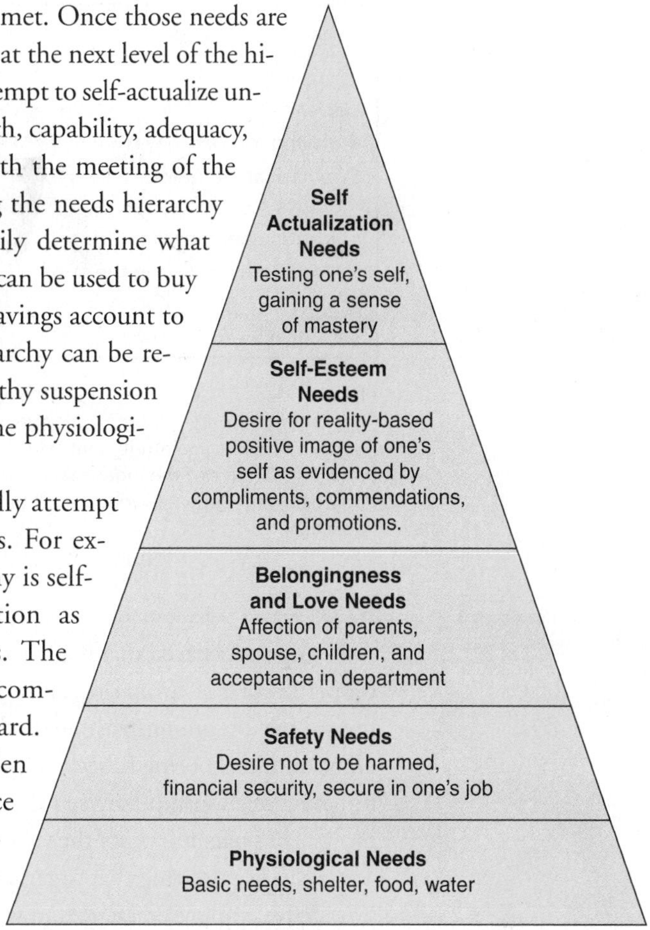

Figure 5.11
Maslow's needs hierarchy.

Argyris: Immaturity-Maturity Theory

Chris Argyris (1923–) is a leading proponent of more open and participative organizations. In *Personality and Organization: The Conflict between System and the Individual* (1957), he states a theory of **immaturity versus maturity**. Argyris believes that, as one moves from infancy toward adulthood in years of age, the healthy individual also advances from immaturity to maturity. The elements of the personality that are changed during this process are summarized in Figure 5.12. Simultaneously, Argyris views formal organizations as having certain properties that are barriers to the development of maturity: (1) specialization reduces worker initiative because employees repeatedly perform unchallenging tasks and (2) the chain of command and narrow span of control make workers submissive, passive, and dependent.[84]

Infancy–Immaturity	Adulthood–Maturity
Passive	Self-initiative
Dependent	Relatively independent
Behaving in a few ways	Capable of behaving many ways
Erratic, shallow, quickly changed interests	Deeper interests
Short time perspective	Much longer time perspective
Subordinate position in the family	Aspirations of equality or superordinate position relative to peers
Lack of self-awareness	Self-awareness and self-control

Figure 5.12
Argyris's Immaturity–Maturity Changes.
Source: "Argyris's immaturity-maturity changes" from *Personality and Organization: The Conflict between System and the Individual* by Chris Argyris, p. 50. Copyright © 1957 by Harper & Row, Publishers, Inc. Copyright renewed 1985 by Chris Argyris. Reprinted by permission of HarperCollins Publishers.

Argryis believed that when the needs of a healthy, mature worker collided with the properties of the formal organization, dysfunctional things could happen, including the worker becoming frustrated, choosing to produce less, developing psychosomatic illnesses, and choosing to seek employment elsewhere.[85] He doubted that it was possible to have a relationship between the individual and the organization that allowed the simultaneous maximizing of the values of both.[86] Argyris modified his theory in 1966 with a mix model, asserting that organizations could reduce some of their unintended, nonproductive employee practices to free up more productive uses of their energy.[87] He also noted that having some unchallenging work was an asset because it allowed recovery time for workers and routine tasks could get done.[88]

McGregor: Theory X–Theory Y

Douglas McGregor (1904–1964) believed that many managerial acts rested on conscious or subconscious assumptions and beliefs about how workers behave.[89] In *The Human Side of Enterprise* (1960), McGregor stated two different sets of assumptions that managers make about people;[90] his **Theory X–Theory Y** reflects two polar opposite characterizations of these assumptions and beliefs (see Figure 5.13).[91]

American police departments have historically been dominated by Theory X assumptions. Even police departments with progressive national images can be experienced as tightly controlling environments by the people who actually work in them:

> The person leading a training session with about 35 managers of a West Coast police department observed that we often react to organizations as though they were living, breathing things. The managers agreed with this and noted the use of such phrases as "the department promoted me this year" and "the department hired me

Theory X	Theory Y
1. The average human has an inherent dislike of work and will avoid it if possible.	1. The expenditure of physical and mental effort in work is as natural as play or rest.
2. Most people must be coerced, controlled, directed, and threatened with punishment to get them to put forth adequate effort toward the achievement of organizational objectives.	2. External control and the threat of punishment are not the only means for bringing about effort toward organizational objectives. People will exercise self-direction and self-control in the service of objectives to which they are committed.
3. The average human prefers to be directed, wishes to avoid responsibility, has relatively little ambition, and wants security above all.	3. Commitment to objectives is a function of the rewards associated with their achievement.
	4. The average human learns, under proper conditions, not only to accept but also to seek responsibility.
	5. The capacity to exercise a relatively high degree of imagination, ingenuity, and creativity in the solution of organizational problems is widely, not narrowly, distributed in organizations.
	6. Organizations only partially utilize the abilities of their employees; unleashing that energy leads to greater organizational achievements and more fulfilled employees.

Figure 5.13
McGregor's Theory X–Theory Y assumptions about workers.

in 2000." They also understood that in fact someone, not the police department, had made those decisions. The managers were then divided into five groups and asked to make a list of what they thought the police department would say about them if it could talk. When the groups reported back, they identified a total of 42 statements, some of which were duplicates of each other. These managers, all of whom were college graduates and many of whom held advanced degrees, indicated the police department would make some positive statements, but would also say "They are idiots," "They don't have any sense," "Watch them or they'll screw up royally."

Theory X assumptions are readily recognized as being those that underpin traditional organizational theory. For example, we can relate a narrow span of control to Theory X's first two propositions. In contrast, Theory Y is formed by a set of views that are supportive of Argyris's mix model; they postulate that the interests of the individual and the organization need not be conflictual but can be integrated for mutual benefit. The principal task of management in a Theory X police department is control. In a Theory Y department, it is supporting subordinates by giving them the resources to do their jobs and creating an environment where they can be self-controlling, mature, contributing, and self-actualizing—within the context of the agency's mission and goals.

Hygiene Factors	Motivators
Supervisory practices	Achievement
Policies and administration	Recognition for accomplishments
Working conditions	Challenging work
Interpersonal relationships with subordinates, peers, and superiors	Increased responsibility
Status	Advancement possibilities
Effect of the job on personal life	Opportunity for personal growth and development
Job security	
Money	

Herzberg: Motivation-Hygiene Theory

Motivation-hygiene theory was developed from research conducted by **Frederick Herzberg** (1923–2000), Bernard Mausner, and Barbara Snyderman on job attitudes at 11 work sites in the Pittsburgh area and reported on in *The Motivation to Work* (1959). The major statement of the theory, which evolved out of this earlier research, is found in Herzberg's *Work and the Nature of Man* (1966).

Herzberg saw two sets of variables operating in the work setting: (1) hygiene factors, which he later came to call maintenance factors, and (2) motivators. Figure 5.14 identifies Herzberg's hygiene factors and motivators. The hygiene factors relate to the work environment; the motivators relate to the work itself. Herzberg borrowed the term *hygiene* from the health-care field and used it to refer to factors that, if not treated properly, could lead to a deterioration in performance, creating an "unhealthy" organization. Hygiene factors that are not treated properly are a source of dissatisfaction. However, even if all of them are provided, a police department does not have motivated officers, just ones who are not dissatisfied. Hygiene factors and motivators operate independently of each other; the police manager can motivate subordinates if they are somewhat dissatisfied with their salaries. However, the greater the level of dissatisfaction, the more difficult it becomes to employ the motivators successfully.

Note that law enforcement leaders have more control over motivators than they do over basic hygiene factors. When leaders exercise control over hygiene factors, they can do a considerable amount of good in reducing dissatisfaction and facilitating the use of the motivators, or they can cause considerable unhappiness:

> The commander in charge of the uniformed division of a 100-officer department suddenly announced that officers were going to be placed on permanent shifts. Surprised and angered by this move, the officers and their wives mobilized to oppose the plan, and after a mass meeting with the commander, the plan was abandoned. The legacy of this incident was a period of barely subdued hostility, distrust, and low morale.

The nature of police work is challenging, and some motivational effect is thus naturally occurring. Police managers can build on this by varying assignments appropriately. Measures that employ various other motivators include an established and active commendation system, the creation of field training officer and master patrol officer designations, an annual police awards banquet, an active staff development program, and a career system with various specialization tracks.

Maslow's needs hierarchy and Herzberg's motivation-hygiene theory can be interrelated; the physiological, safety, and love and belongingness needs of Maslow correspond to Herzberg's hygiene factors; the top two levels of the needs hierarchy—esteem and self-actualization—correlate with Herzberg's motivators.

Critique of Organizational Humanism

In one way or another, OH theories depend to some degree on open and honest communication between organizational members who respect and trust each other. An attractive theme, it gives insufficient weight to the consequences that can occur when authenticity meets power. Illustratively, movie maker Samuel Goldwyn told his staff, "I want you all to tell me what's wrong with our operation even if it means losing your job."[92] An underlying assumption of OH is that people want more rewards than just money from doing their work. Ignored is the reality that some workers, if only a small proportion of them, have a utilitarian involvement with the job. It simply provides the money necessary to live; they save their energies and obtain their rewards from their families, operating their own on-line businesses, or other nonjob-related sources, such as hobbies.

Despite the lack of research and the fact that the few existing studies do not support Maslow, there remains an almost metaphysical attraction to the needs hierarchy,[93] a condition made even more perplexing by noting that Maslow's work on motivation came from a small clinical study of neurotic people.[94] In turn, Maslow points at Theory X–Theory Y and notes that a good deal of what McGregor bases his conclusions on comes from my research ". . . and above all people I know just how shaky that foundation is . . . I am concerned that enthusiastic people will swallow it whole."[95] In contrast to the lack of research on the needs hierarchy, there has been considerable research on Herzberg's motivation-hygiene theory; after reviewing this evidence, Gibson and Teasley concluded the range of findings run from general support . . . to a vigorous condemnation of Herzberg's methodology.[96] The research support for Argyris's immaturity-maturity theory is generally weak. Heavily influenced by Maslow, Argyris's own research only used semi-structured interviews and the theory assumes that workers' needs are uniform.[97] A major test of the theory, which included 800 respondents, did not find sufficient evidence to support it.[98]

Behavioral Systems Theory

The successor to organizational humanism was **behavioral systems theory** (BST), founded by **Kurt Lewin** (1890–1947), a psychologist who fled from Germany in the early 1930s.[99] The theorists in this school saw organizations as being comprised of the behavior of individuals and groups and were interested in making organizations

Figure 5.15
Force-field analysis.

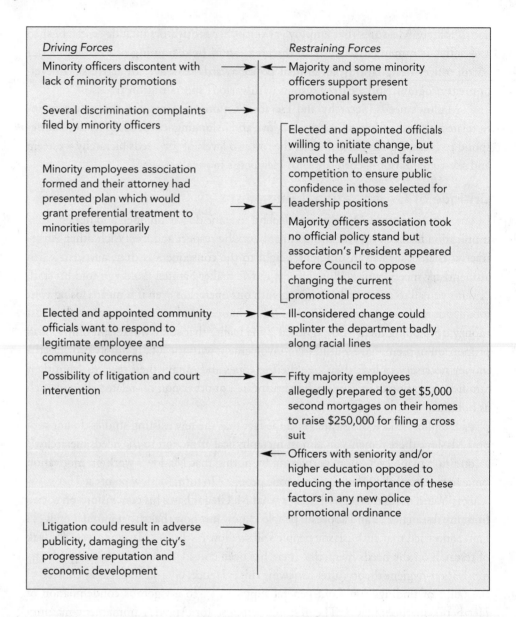

Driving Forces	Restraining Forces
Minority officers discontent with lack of minority promotions	Majority and some minority officers support present promotional system
Several discrimination complaints filed by minority officers	Elected and appointed officials willing to initiate change, but wanted the fullest and fairest competition to ensure public confidence in those selected for leadership positions
Minority employees association formed and their attorney had presented plan which would grant preferential treatment to minorities temporarily	Majority officers association took no official policy stand but association's President appeared before Council to oppose changing the current promotional process
Elected and appointed community officials want to respond to legitimate employee and community concerns	Ill-considered change could splinter the department badly along racial lines
Possibility of litigation and court intervention	Fifty majority employees allegedly prepared to get $5,000 second mortgages on their homes to raise $250,000 for filing a cross suit
	Officers with seniority and/or higher education opposed to reducing the importance of these factors in any new police promotional ordinance
Litigation could result in adverse publicity, damaging the city's progressive reputation and economic development	

more democratic and participative. The work of some organizational humanists is sometimes included in BST.

Lewin was interested in group dynamics—how groups form and how their members relate to each other—and he also developed a decision-making tool, **force-field analysis** (see Figure 5.15). In force-field analysis, driving forces push for a new condition and restraining forces resist the change. If there are exactly opposing driving and restraining forces, the arrows of these opposing forces meet at the vertical zero, or balance, line. In some instances, there might not be an exactly opposite force, in which case an arrow is simply drawn, as in Figure 5.15, to the balance line. After all entries are made and the situation is summarized, the relative power of the driving and restraining forces must be subjectively evaluated. In this regard, the balance line should be regarded as a spring that will be moved in one direction, suggesting the action that needs to be taken or the decision that needs to be made.

In the *Human Group* (1950), George Homans (1910–1989) advanced the idea that groups have both an internal and an external system.[100] The internal system comprises factors that arise within the group itself, such as the feelings that members of a group develop about each other during the life of the group. In contrast, the external system consists of variables in the larger environment in which the group exists. Members of the same patrol shift may form one or more groups and these groups exist within the context of the law enforcement agency employing them. To illustrate, a chief suspends an officer following a high-speed chase in which she had an accident. The groups from her shift see this as unjust and agree not to write any traffic citations during her 3-day suspension.

Much of Warren Bennis's (1925–) effort was in **organizational development (OD)**, a change management process. OD is used to reform the work attitudes and values of employees with respect to the changes the organization wishes to make and often involves surveying and training employees. It is intended to take the chaos and uncertainty out of organizational changes. When police departments plan and implement community or intelligence led policing or servant leadership (see Chapter 7, Leadership) they are engaged in organizational development change (see Chapter 15, Organizational Change).

Critique of Behavioral Systems Theory

Although BST was relatively short-lived, its theorists helped sustain the movement away from mechanistic views of organizations and toward the people in them. Homans's work on internal and external systems served to set the stage for open systems theory.

Organizations as Open Systems

Ludwig von Bertalanffy (1901–1972), a biologist, articulated general systems theory (GST) in 1940, although it lacked prominence until the 1960s. A system is a grouping of separate but interrelated components working together toward the achievement of a common objective (see Figure 5.16). Organizations can be characterized as closed or open systems. In actuality, there are no entirely closed or entirely open organizations; these are terms used only to describe the extent to which an organization approximates one or the other. Closed systems operate under assumptions that they are completely rational, effective, and efficient, and can reasonably predict what is going to happen. In this view, they don't need to be concerned with what's happening in the larger environment because closed systems "know what's best."

Both traditional organizational theory and the early police professionalism movement (see Chapter 1, The Evolution of Police Administration) reinforced a closed

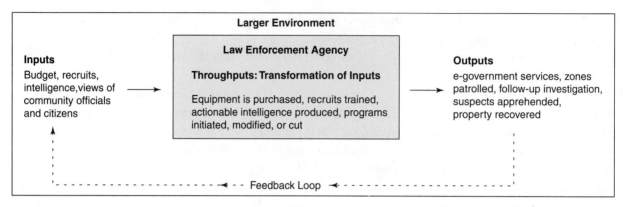

Figure 5.16
A basic open system view of a law enforcement agency with illustrated processes.

system view, which regards whatever is "outside of it" as being inconsequential. In contrast, open systems:

1. Recognize that everything beyond their boundary/structure is part of their environment;[101]

2. Know they have regular on-going relationships with factors in the environment in which they are embedded; this is the quality of being interdependent; numerous factors impinge on law enforcement agencies (see Figure 5.17);

3. Have walls or boundaries that are permeable, allowing things in and out. Too many inputs will overwhelm an open system and threaten its **homeostasis** or balance; from the Greek, *homeostasis* literally means "standing still";

4. Use **coding** to prevent being overwhelmed, which functions like a priority system; important inputs get through quickly: calls from a city manager will usually be received by the chief, but citizens asking to talk to the chief often find themselves redirected and speaking to someone else;

5. Have the tendency to become more complex and specialized; as specialization proceeds, its fragmenting effect on the department is countered by the unifying elements of its **internal subsystems** (see Figure 5.18);

6. Face the prospect of moving toward decline, disorganization, and death—the **entropic process**. Only 13 of the businesses existing at the time of the American Revolution remain as autonomous entities, and during a 20-year period, 46 percent of the companies on the Fortune 500 list of America's largest and most powerful businesses disappeared from that list.[102] Law enforcement agencies have no exemption from the entropic process. In the current financial environment, thousands of agencies have experienced hiring freezes, furloughs, layoffs, and being shut down (see Chapter 12, Financial Management). To fight entropy, departments continuously import more inputs than they can use (e.g. gasoline), and store it to allow operations to continue if supplies are interrupted. "**Buffering**" describes this processing of storing and it allows the department to develop **negative entropy**, or the capacity to resist decline;

7. Must evolve in order to avoid decline, the quality of adaptability;

Illustrative Environmental Factors	Potential Impacts
Police Unions	Oppose increased cost of health and pension benefits; furloughs and layoffs; wage concessions; freezing cost of living increases for their retirees; early release of violent offenders; parole of "Cop Killers"; increases in hiring standards and some disciplinary actions; support specific political candidates; usually gun control; some tax increases; and legislation requires the death penalty for those killing officers in the execution of their duties.
Partners	Multiagency single purpose and standing task forces may create friction about budgetary support, credit for successes, and blame for failures; mutual aide compacts allow agencies to share the use of special resources, aircraft, SWAT teams, and bomb disposal units.
Events	Agency resources may be overrun by natural disasters, protests and riots, catastrophic industrial accidents, terrorist attacks, and searching for children lost in wilderness areas. Events may also be positive, e.g., gifts and grants.
Legal Framework	New court rulings, federal, and state laws may require new expenses and procedures and/or provide agencies with new authority. Some federal laws, e.g., Americans with Disability Act (ADA) and Occupational Health and Safety Act (OSHA) provide protection to officers (See Chapter 9, Human Resources).
Governing Body	May slash budgets, impacting agency operations and keeping high-mileage cars in the fleet; declare city a sanctuary for undocumented immigrants putting the agency between official policy and public demands for strict enforcement; and approve take-home cars.
Special Interest Groups/Stakeholders	May call for special unit to deal with the gay, lesbian, bisexual, and transgendered communites; Washington DC has a GLBT Police Unit for this purpose; advocate for more officers walking beats in business areas; and demand strict enforcement of loitering and noise ordinances.
Technology	Can be used to make agency more transparent, as a recruiting tool, and to provide e-government services.
Other Departments	May see offers to engage in collaborative projects as an attempt by police to "build empire" or use their resources; equipment and supplies selected by purchasing may be seen by rank and file as substandard/inadequate.

Figure 5.17
Illustrative environmental factors potentially impacting on law enforcement agencies.

Subsystems	Illustrative Functions
Managerial	Sets direction for agency, controls, directs, coordinates, evaluates, takes corrective action, empowers employees, sets budget priorities and presents and defends operating budget
Supportive	Acquires resources from larger environment and distributes them; budget and grant preparation, recruits, surplus government property, promotes positive image of agency
Production	Components that transform inputs into outputs, patrol, investigation, crime prevention, DUI checkpoints, E-government services
Maintenance	Building, grounds, equipment, special emphasis on employees, fair compensation and benefits, favorable work environment
Adaptive	Scans environment, identifies problems, opportunities, and challenges; develops response strategies and tactics

Figure 5.18
The internal subsystems of a law enforcement agency.
Source: These subsystems were identified in Danial Katz and Robert L. Kahn, *The Social Psychology of Organizations.* New York: Wiley, 2nd Edition, 1978.

8. Become double-loop learning organizations in order to be adaptive: (1) **single-loop learning** allows organizations to make corrections and carry out their present efforts toward achieving objectives and (2) **double-loop learning** causes organizations to judge whether they are pursuing the right objectives, programs, and policies.[103] Law enforcement practices associated with double-loop learning include after action reports, staff inspections, and program evaluation;

9. Follow the principle of **equafinality**; there are multiple ways to achieve goals; and

10. Can never be more varied than the larger environment.[104] **Isomorphism**, from the Greek meaning equal shape, dictates that the resource-dependent agencies tend to mirror the complexity and demands of their environment and develop policies, programs, and units that are signaled by the environment to be important.

Critique of Open Systems Theory

Some critics wonder if GST, which originated in biology, can unequivocally be used to explain contrived man-made organizations.[105] GST may fail to account for or understate crucial aspects of organizations. Organizations can be systems, but they are not natural systems that are subject to immutable laws.[106] Organizations do not invariably follow the birth, growth, maturity, and death cycle of biological systems. The definition of what is included in system theory is vague, does not account for variations in organizational complexity, and fails to provide guidance about handling conflict between components.

Other Paradigms of Administration

A paradigm is a coherent, internally consistent, and integrated approach to making sense of whatever is being studied. In essence, it is a model. If you are defining a problem in a conventional, habitual, or customary way, you are "thinking inside the box" a condition created by "paradigm paralysis." If trying to solve the problem by thinking "outside of the box," you will have some quirky, unconventional thoughts that may lead you to important innovations, new paradigms. This section covers some theories that are not mainstream, but are interesting ways of looking at organizations.

Environmental Theories

This group of theories relates organizations to the broader environments in which they are embedded: (1) environmental contingency theory, (2) resource dependency, (3) population ecology, and (4) neoinstitutional.

Environmental Contingency Theory

Burns and Stalker (1961, 1968) maintain there is no one best way to structure an organization.[107] Instead, leaders must "read the environment" and decide what type of structure is the best "fit" with the environment being faced. For example, if the environment is stable and the tasks to be performed are routine, than a mechanistic form of organization might be the best choice. Very successful organizations are able to find the best "fit."

Organizations may still survive, with varying degrees of success, with "adequate" or "good" fits, but they are unlikely to excel and may even have to abandon a fit they have chosen. Around 1980, a few police departments tried to "flatten" the seven or eight layers of their hierarchy, which made their structure growth horizontally and shrink in height. These experiments were quickly abandoned because others in the environment (e.g., local, state, and federal agencies), didn't know what unit or person they should contact about any matter. "Fit" is also being used to determine whether a person can be a productive part of an organization or a work team; although ability is a key factor, emotional stability is proving to be even more important.[108]

Resource Dependency Theory

The fullest expression of resource dependency theory (RDT) was produced by Pfeffer and Salancik (1978).[109] The basic thrust of RDT is that all agencies must get the resources they need to operate from the larger environment, creating resource dependency. The control of resource distribution by the larger environment is a source of power over agencies and makes them dependent. Failure to capture resources makes an agency more vulnerable and moves it toward entropy. RDT helps agency leaders identify the standing of other agencies competing for resources and who has power in the environment. RDT views organizational success as organizations maximizing their power. Organizations can do so by forming cooperative ventures with other organizations and by making resource providers view their contributions as crucial.

Population Ecology

RDT and population ecology (PE) share the same views on organization resource dependence and the power of the larger environment. However, they use different levels of analysis; RDT focuses on agencies and PE focuses on the larger environment.[110] PE, which fundamentally had a mid- to late-1970s start, seeks to discover why organizations competing in the same resource pool or ecological niche are more, and others less, successful. Hannan and Freeman's *The Population Ecology of Organizations* (1977) was a major development in this line of thinking.

Neo-institutional Theory

"Old" institutional theory (OIT) is associated with traditional organizational theory. In explaining organizations, it tended to rely on historical justifications for structures and processes, OIT was the legal foundation for the existence of public organizations, holding that the structure of an organization dictated the behavior of its members. Therefore, OIT was relatively uninterested on how organizations impacted on individuals.[111] The old institutional writings were descriptive and value laden, substantially lacking an empirical base. Nonetheless, along with traditional organizational theory, the old institutionalism was part of the progressive era/good government movement that lasted from roughly 1890 into the 1920s (see Chapter 1, The Evolution of Police Administration).

Neo-institutionalism was named by March and Olsen (1984)[112] and its beginning dates from the late 1970s until the mid-1980s. There are a half-dozen or more varieties of neo-institutionalism; the political institutional framework (PIF) is briefly described here.[113] PIF's view is that organizations are not simply acted upon by the larger/external political system (e.g., inevitably pressured into the mandatory adoption of strategies, programs, and policies). Instead, organizations are often themselves potent political forces that can resist pressures and shape part of their external political landscape.[114] PIF recognized that politics is "done" both to, and by, organizations.

Networked and Virtual Organizations

Networked and virtual organizations are goal directed and share many characteristics. Advanced information technology is the glue that allows them to function; geographic proximity may not be an issue; dispersion may provide some advantages; and horizontal communication accounts for most message traffic. As a generalization, **networked organizations** (NOs) have relationships that are planned and stable, whereas **virtual organizations** (VOs) have relationships that often arise spontaneously out of special needs and may be temporary.[115]

Networked organizations (NOs) date from the early 1980s when tall, hierarchical organizations faced a tough economy. They realized there were some things other organizations could do cheaper, faster, and better. The result was a period of corporate downsizing as individual jobs and functions were subcontracted out. The separate members of a networked organization are termed *nodes* and are simultaneously autonomous and collaborative, pooling their resources, and geographically dispersed to one degree or another. The relationships of the nodes are spelled out in contracts. To illustrate, Firm A designs a car; Firm B engineers it; Firm C builds it with parts provided by supplier nodes; and Firm C markets and distributes the vehicle. NOs flatten the organizational hierarchy and broaden the organizational structure horizontally. This requires continuing horizontal communication, which results in personal relationship developing between people in different nodes. These relationships are added value; people go out of the way to help those they know. NOs may use some overarching or meta-management to coordinate functions (e.g., a board of directors). Although NOs can be used for a single project, they tend to be ongoing enterprises with some node members being replaced from time to time to achieve greater efficiency or for other reasons.

Although NOs and VOs are sometimes used synonymously, others describe VOs as being created more spontaneously, not regulated by formal agreements, more informal, and driven by the need to accomplish a single task. Node members, who can withdraw at any point, participate voluntarily and leadership may not be formally designated; the nodes can be self-directed because of their mutuality of needs.

In 2002, a sniper went on a rampage in the Washington, D.C. area; victims were shot with a high-power rifle from a distance, leaving no witnesses and few investigative leads for law enforcement agencies (see Figure 5.19).[116] By the time an arrest was made, there were 14 shootings, 10 deaths, and thousands of local, state, and federal law enforcement officers involved.[117] A total of five different task forces from different involved jurisdictions were in operation and one had three co-equal leaders.[118] The task forces were built "on the fly" and nobody had a chance to step back and critically assess what was being done.[119] Task force leaders said they didn't need more control over the other task forces; they needed more coordination.[120] There was no central hub to coordinate investigative priorities, use of resources, and information sharing.

The sniper cases reflects the following elements, many of which reflect virtual organizational theory: (1) there was a spontaneous need; (2) although some agency and personal relationships pre-existed, other relationships were unplanned; (3) the law enforcement agencies were geographically dispersed; (4) in the absence of a central command and control hub, greater horizontally communication was needed; (5) cooperating agencies could withdraw investigators at any point; (6) the enterprise was driven by a single purpose: apprehension; and (7) it is not clear to what extent any of the task forces operated under memos of understanding (MOUs), and those that did exist lacked written clarity and obscured lines of authority and information-handling procedures.

Figure 5.19
The sniper who terrorized the Washington, D.C. area for 3 weeks in 2002 shot from inside of his car's closed trunk using a Bushmaster .223 rifle with a scope for accuracy and a tripod for stability. Note the cut-out in the body of his car so he could take position and shoot without anyone seeing him.
(Courtesy AP Photo/Mary Altaffer)

Task forces can be established for a single purpose, such as the apprehension of a serial offender, or they can operate continuously, as in the case of the FBI's multi-jurisdictional Joint Terrorism Task Forces (JTTF) that were developed in the wake of 9/11. Mechanism of these types allows for a reasonable time horizon to plan, organize, and implement them under written guidance. The spontaneous sniper case is repeated throughout the country, albeit on a smaller scale. Law enforcement agencies should give some consideration to evaluating the features of networked and virtual organizations, modifying them for off-the-shelf immediate use to meet spontaneous demands.

Sense Making

Sense making in organizations is how we process our experiences and what we do with them. In addition to his other publications, Weicke's *Sense Making in Organizations* (1995) and *Making Sense of Organizations* (2001) mark him as an influential theorist on this topic.

When something happens in a law enforcement executive's "world," the meaning may not be clear. Failure to resolve this uncertainty keeps the executive in an unhealthy state of tension. To resolve it, sense has to be made of the experience. Even if no additional information can be gathered, the event still has to be "processed." The experience is relived, reflected on, interpreted, analyzed, and meaning is assigned to it. From an internal perspective, the meaning just has to be plausible; it doesn't have to rise to the level of objective "truth." Sense making occurs with a single person or in a group. These constructions often become shared and some ultimately achieve the status of organizational lore. This process of sense making is not episodic, but continuous, as experiences pile up. Like digital information, our interpreted experiences can be stored and retrieved.

Accumulated sense making produces **cognitive maps** or "mental understandings." The term may have been coined by Tolman (1948).[121] These maps help us understand our "landscape" and navigate our "world" so we can do such things as: (1) understand the actions of commanding officers, (2) predict what others may do in different situations, (3) know who to take things to for swift handling, (4) decide who is like us, (5) identify potential mentors, and (6) select career paths in the department that match our interest and abilities.

Chaos Theory

Kiel's *Managing Chaos and Complexity in Government* (1994) was an early effort to apply **chaos theory** to the public sector.[122] In organizational theory, chaos is a state of non-equilibrium. It is precipitated by a crisis event(s) during which the everyday predictability and the usual order of things are disrupted, replaced at some level by a mix of factors, such as: (1) widespread uncertainty and fear; (2) the delivery of normal services is not possible; (3) an initial lack of basic information about the event; (4) informational overload caused by inputs from political figures, inquiries from federal agencies or the news media, offers of assistance, and urgent citizen appeals; (5) the realization that plans are inadequate or nonexistent for the event; (6) recognition that available resources and modes of operation are insufficient or ineffective; and (7) the need to resolve unfamiliar problems whose magnitude, complexity, and durability exceed anything we could imagine, a condition referred to as **cosmology**.[123] Under these circumstances maladaptive decisions may increase the level of chaos, producing unintended consequences. **Bifurcation** is the flash-point when chaos overwhelms normal conditions in an agency[124] and compels the use of innovative efforts and alliances to restore stability in the community. The 9/11 attacks and Hurricane Katrina possessed the qualities of cosmology and bifurcation (see Figure 5.20).

Contrary to popular view, chaos theory does more than describe under what conditions events spin out of control and total collapse seems both possible and imminent.[125] Its ultimate value is in how order is restored against seemingly insurmountable adversity. The way off the slippery slope of a chaos event is through self-organization. Police and other agencies don't have to do everything; individuals, neighbors, ad hoc groups, and volunteers from other communities pitch in with helpful acts; they rescue people and pets from debris, open their homes to others, deliver food and water, set up temporary shelters and rudimentary first aid clinics, stand guard, reunite family members, and allow others to use their cell phones. These steps produce the butterfly effect, which ripples across the community, energizing people to help themselves and others. At the organization level, self-organization, or perhaps more precisely, self-reorganization occurs on a continuous basis during a chaos event. Organizations use sense making and, from their understanding of their experiences, use the quality of adaptability, developing new priorities, standards, services, procedures, and alliances. In the wake of a chaos event, organizations evolve into something more complex, with new goals, partnerships, structures, equipment, and communication channels to accommodate what they have learned.

Critique of Other Paradigms of Administration

Environmental contingency theory assumes organizations that are a "misfit" with their operating environment will "shift gears" and move to a "good fit," but fails to provide details on how this occurs and at what velocity. One way to look at a misfit is when the number of risk factors in a community "overpower" the ability of law enforcement agency to provide the desired level of public safety. A 2008 study of 133 local law enforcement agencies in Florida concluded that environmental risk factors (e.g., unemployment rates, renter-occupied rates, population rates for residents ages 15–24 and population rates for age 25 or more) had a significant impact on resource allocation and performance.[126]

Unsurprisingly, agencies with higher per capita earning had lower levels of "risk factors," were less crime prone, and also better resourced.[127] Such agencies were less cost efficient than lower resourced agencies because they had lower demands for service and thus fewer outputs.

Donaldson, an advocate of environmental contingency theory, is highly critical of resource dependency theory, population ecology, and neo-institutionalism. He dismisses them as part of the proliferation of theories by academics seeking momentary fame and diverting attention from studying more "worthy" theories (i.e., contingency theory).[128] Some theorists find Donaldson's criticisms to be too severe and unrelenting.

There are numerous praises of networked and virtual organizations, but they may be overstated with respect to how well NOs and VOs function and their efficiency. The literature is sparse about their failure rates and dysfunctionalities (e.g. the consequences of lingering personality conflicts between node members who have continuous transactions).

Figure 5.20
Hurricane Katrina devastated New Orleans on an unimaginable scale in 2005. Many residents were rescued from their rooftops by boats and others were able to wade to safety through the floodwaters.
(Courtesy of Federal Emergency Management Agency (FEMA)/ Photograph by Win Henderson)

Chaos theory teaches us that crisis events that produce cosmology and bifurcation are not situations to be endured and resolved as much as they important aspects of organizational life whereby a law enforcement agency can adapt to its environment, maintain and renew itself, and ultimately adapt through self organization and emerge stronger.

CONCLUSION

The hierarchical model associated with traditional theory is the dominant structural form for organizations worldwide, largely because it allows for great control or steering of the organization and, properly operated, is highly efficient. Movement away from that structural model is unlikely to change even in the mid-range time horizon. What has changed over the past 50 years is the processes associated with leading people, assumptions about their capabilities, and the view of organizations as open systems. Moreover, other paradigms of administration have given us different sets of lenses for looking at organizations. The hierarchical structure remains, but a new set of clothes has been hung over it.

CHAPTER REVIEW

1. What four types of organizations are associated with answering the question, "Who benefits?"
2. Traditional organization theory has three stems. What are they?
3. The focus of scientific management is to do what?
4. How do functional supervision and the exception principle operate?
5. Weber's bureaucratic model has certain characteristics. What are they?
6. Why are police officers street-level bureaucrats?
7. Can you summarize administrative theory?
8. What does POSDCORB mean?
9. What did the human relations school seek to accomplish?
10. Organizational humanism called for what change?
11. What is Maslow's needs hierarchy?
12. Immaturity-maturity theory says traditional organizations are a barrier to an individual's search for maturity. How does this happen?
13. How do Theory X and Theory Y differ?
14. What is the difference in Herzberg's motivation and hygiene factors?
15. How do you use force-field analysis?
16. Can you diagram a basic open systems view of a law enforcement agency?
17. Single- and double-loop learning accomplish what?
18. What is the entropic process?

19. Can you critique open systems theory?

20. Environmental contingency theory seeks what "fit"?

21. What is resource dependency theory's basic thrust?

22. Can you contrast networked and virtual organizations?

23. What is sense making?

24. Of what value is chaos theory to a law enforcement agency?

25. Can you describe the butterfly effect and self-organizing?

INTERNET ACTIVITIES

Encyclopedia of Organization Theory, *http://faculty.babson.edu/krollag/org_site/encyclop/encyclo.html*

KEY TERMS

administrative theory: also called management theory and the principles approach, sought to find "universal" principles of management that could be used in any setting; also see traditional organizational theory.

Argyris, Chris: developed maturity-immaturity model postulating that traditional organization forms get in the way of workers' development.

behavioral systems theory: sees organizations as made up of the behavior of individuals and groups, wanted to make organizations more democratic and participative. Founded by Lewin.

bifurcation: the "flash-point" when chaos overcomes normal conditions in an agency and forces it in a new directions in terms of priorities and tactics. See cosmology.

buffering: stores inputs (e.g., gasoline) to avoid disruption of services if supply is interrupted; also see negative entropy.

bureaucratic model: organizational form often called classical, mechanistic, and a closed system; comprised of eight characteristics.

business concerns: owners are the primary beneficiaries.

butterfly effect: small, helpful, self-initiated acts have a ripple effect, causing others to become energized and helpful.

chaos theory: an organizational state of nonequilibrium produced by a crisis event that exceeds anything we can imagine. See cosmology and bifurcation.

coding: to prevent overload, an organization codes or prioritizes messages so that important messages get to the right place quickly; citizens with minor problems wanting to talk to the Chief find themselves redirected and talking to some other official.

cognitive maps: accumulated sense making produces "mental understandings" that help us navigate our world. See sense making.

commonweal organizations: the public at large is the beneficiary (e.g., law enforcement agency).

cosmology: chaos event that overwhelms us; beyond the worse conditions we could imagine; problems of magnitude, complexity, and durability on a scope not seen by us before.

decision space: when elected officials do not provide policy guidance, agencies can formulate their own.

double-loop learning: causes organizations to reconsider whether they are pursuing the right objectives, programs, and policies. See single-loop learning.

e-government: provides citizens with on-line access to many governmental services.

entropic process: open systems concept; all organizations face the prospect of moving toward decline, disorganization, and death.

equafinality: there are multiple ways to achieve goals.

exception principle: routine matters should be handled at the lowest possible organizational level that they can be properly addressed, and unusual events, above or below standards, should be brought to the attention of higher-level managers.

force-field analysis: a decision-making tool developed by Lewin. Also see behavioral systems theory.

functional supervision: one person supervises a function, even if it cuts across several organizational units.

Gulick, Luther: coined the most famous acronym of administration: POSDCORB.

Hawthorne effect: people being studied behave differently because they like the attention they get; part of a study by the human relations school at the Hawthorne Electrical Plant.

Herzberg, Frederick: developed motivation-hygiene theory.

homeostasis: when an organization is "in balance."

human relations school: saw traditional organizational theory as ignoring the human element and sought changes; helped set the stage for the emergence of organizational humanism; see Hawthorne effect.

immaturity versus maturity: see Argyris.

internal subsystems: in open systems theory, the internal unifying forces of an agency that prevent fragmentation of the organization and transform inputs into outputs.

isomorphism: resource-dependent agencies tend to mirror the complexities and demands of their environments; when agencies receive signals from important others, they develop responsive policies and programs.

Knapp Commission: studied corruption in the NYCPD, identifying meat- and grass-eaters.

Lewin, Kurt: founder of behavioral systems theory. Also see force-field analysis.

Maslow, Abraham: developed the five-level hierarchy of human needs.

McGregor, Douglas: developed Theory X and Theory Y, two contrasting sets of assumptions about workers.

motivation-hygiene theory: two sets of factors, motivators and hygiene; hygiene factors, if met, don't motivate someone, but unmet they are a source of dissatisfaction. See Herzberg.

mutual benefit association: an association whose primary beneficiary is its members (e.g., a police union).

natural soldiering: the natural inclination of workers not to push themselves.

needs hierarchy: five levels of needs that explain human motivation; see Maslow.

negative entropy: the capacity to resist decline or death, see buffering.

networked organizations: organizations that are heavily dependent on informational technology, often comprised of geographically dispersed units, horizontal communication accounts for most message traffic, their existence is panned and bound together by contract, may be single purpose or continuous in operation. Units are not part of same organization; they are autonomous, but collaborative. See virtual organizations.

new public management (NPM): began in 1980s, called for greater use of business practices to achieve greater efficiency.

open systems theory: a grouping of separate, but interdependent components that work together to achieve common goals.

organizational development (OD): a change management process.

organizational humanism: 1950–1960s movement by theorists that called for the softening or elimination of many of the features of the bureaucratic model; see human relations school.

POSDCORB: planning, organizing, staffing, directing, coordinating, reporting, and budgeting; also see Gulick.

rational-legal authority: authority is granted by the organization to the occupant of a position who uses it to accomplish organizational goals, a Weber-supplied concept.

scientific management: finding the "one best way" to accomplish a task; see F. W. Taylor and traditional organizational theory.

sense making: how people and organizations process their experiences and what they do with them. See cognitive maps.

service organizations: a organization whose specific clientele is the primary beneficiary (e.g. clients of a community health center).

single-loop learning: allows organizations to make corrections and continue operations; see double-loop learning.

street-level bureaucrats: government workers in direct contact with clients who use discretion on how to implement public policy (e.g., police officers and field social workers).

systematic soldiering: keep production rates low so quotas don't increase.

Taylor, F. W.: father of scientific management.

Theory X–Theory Y: see McGregor.

traditional organizational theory: has three stems, bureaucracy, scientific management, and administrative theory; the centerpiece of organizational theory during 1900–1950.

virtual organizations: organizations that arise spontaneously to an urgent need; there is no planning or contract; participation is voluntary and members can withdraw at any time; there is not a command and control structure; they usually disappear when the single purpose that brought them together is accomplished.

Weber, Max: founder of modern sociology whose name is synonymous with bureaucracy.

ENDNOTES

[1] Amitai Etzioni, *Modern Organizations* (Englewood Cliffs, N.J.: Prentice Hall, 1964), p. 1.

[2] Ibid., with some additions.

[3] Ibid.

[4] Talcott Parsons, *Structure and Process in Modern Societies* (Glencoe, Ill.: Free Press, 1960), p. 17.

[5] Edgar H. Schein, *Organizational Psychology* (Englewood Cliffs, N.J.: Prentice Hall, 1965), p. 9.

[6] Peter W. Blau and W. Richard Scott, *Formal Organizations* (Scranton, Pa.: Chandler, 1962), p. 43, with some changes.

[7] The treatment of the central issues of the four types of formal organizations is taken from Blau and Scott, *Formal Organizations*, pp. 43, 55, with some changes.

[8] Daniel A. Wren, *The Evolution of Management Thought* (New York: Ronald Press, 1972), p. 112.

[9] Ibid., p. 114.

[10] Ibid., pp. 114–115.

[11] See the testimony of F. W. Taylor before the Special Committee of the House of Representatives Hearings to Investigate Taylor and Other Systems of Shop Management, January 25, 1912, p. 1387.

[12] Wren, *Evolution of Management Thought,* p. 115.

[13] Frederick W. Taylor, *Principles of Scientific Management* (New York: Harper & Row, 1911), pp. 44–47, with minor restatement.

[14] See Frederick W. Taylor, *Shop Management* (New York: Harper and Brothers, 1911), for a discussion of this concept.

[15] Ibid., p. 126.

[16] Wren, *Evolution of Management Thought,* p. 132. Not only did Bethlehem Steel abandon the system, but it also fired Taylor.

[17] Ibid., p. 131.

[18] L. P. Alford, *Henry Lawrence Gantt* (Easton-Hive Management Series: No. 6, 1972; facsimile reprint of a 1934 edition by Harper and Brothers), pp. 207, 209.

[19] Sudhir Kakar, *Frederick Taylor: A Study in Personality and Innovation* (Cambridge, Mass.: MIT Press, 1973), p. 2.

[20] Fremont E. Kast and James E. Rosenzweig, *Contingency Views of Organization and Management* (Chicago: Science Research Associates, 1973), p. 7.

[21] Mary Jo Hatch with Ann L. Cunliffe, Organization Theory (New York: Oxford University Press, Second Edition, 2006), p. 33.

[22] Robert Kanigel, *The One Best Way: Frederick Winslow Taylor and the Enigma of Efficiency* (New York: Viking Press, 1997).

[23] Katia Caldari, "Alfred Marshall's Critical Analysis of Scientific Management," *European Journal of the History of Economic Thought,* Vol. 14, Issue 1, March 2007, pp. 55–78.

[24] Michael Crozier, *The Bureaucratic Phenomenon* (Chicago: University of Chicago Press, 1964), p. 3.

[25] Max Weber, *The Theory of Social and Economic Organization,* trans. A. M. Henderson and Talcott Parsons (New York: Free Press, 1947), p. 337.

[26] Ibid.

[27] Ibid., pp. 330–332, with limited restatement for clarity.

[28] Ibid., p. 328.

[29] On this point see Paul Henman, *Governing Electronically: E-Government and The Reconfiguration of Public Administration, Policy, and Power* (New York: Palgrave Macmillan, 2010).

[30] For example, see John P. Crank and Andrew Ciacomazzi, "A Sheriff's Office as a Learning Organization," *Police Quarterly,* Vol. 12, Issue 4, December 2009, pp. 351–369 and Phil Johnson, et.al., "The Rise of Post-Bureaucracy," *International Sociology,* Vol. 24, No. 1, January 2009, pp. 37–61.

[31] Paul G. Lewis and S. Karthick Ramakrishnan, "Police Practices in Immigrant Destination Cities," *Urban Affairs Review,* Vol. 42, 2007, pp. 874–900.

[32] Lewis and Ramakrishnan, "Police Practices in Immigrant Destination Cities," p. 889.

[33] Ibid., Table 3, p. 888.

[34] Ibid., pp. 886–887.

[35] Ibid., p. 881.

[36] Ibid., p. 885.

[37] Ibid., pp. 886–887.

[38] Scott Decker, Paul Lewis, Doris Provine, and Monica Varsanyi, "Immigration and Local Policing: Results From a National Survey of Law Enforcement Executives," in *The Role of Local Police: Striking a Balance Between Enforcement and Civil Liberties* (Police Executive Research Forum: Washington, D.C., 2009), p. 177.

[39] Ibid., p. 176.

[40] Ibid., pp. 175–176.

[41] Zachary W. Oberfield, "Shaping the State: The Development of Street-Level Bureaucrats," Midwestern Political Science Association Annual Meeting, Washington, D.C., 2008, p. 1.

[42] Ibid., pp. 3–4.

[43] Ibid., p. 6.

[44] Ibid., pp. 6, 16.

[45] On this point, see Nicos P. Mouzelis, *Organization and Bureaucracy* (Chicago: Aldine, 1967), pp. 20–21 and footnote 29 of that work.

[46] H. H. Gerth and C. Wright Mills, *From Max Weber: Essays in Sociology* (New York: Oxford University Press, 1946), p. 50.

[47] Christopher Hood, "The 'New Public Management' in the 1980s: Variations on a Theme," Accounting, Organization, and Society, Vol. 20, No. 2/3, 1995, p. 94.

[48] Wren, *Evolution of Management Thought,* p. 230.

[49] Henri Fayol, *General and Industrial Management,* trans. Constance Storrs (London: Sir Isaac Pitman, 1949), p. vi.

[50] Ibid., pp. 19–41.

[51] Ibid., p. 34.

[52] Danial A. Wren, Arthur G. Bedian, and John D. Breeze, "The Foundations of Henri Fayol's Administrative Theory," *Management Decision*, Vol. 40, No. 9, 2002, p. 917.

[53] The 1939 edition was coauthored, but the 1947 edition appeared under Mooney's name.

[54] Luther Gulick, "Notes on the Theory of Organization," in *Papers on the Science of Administration,* eds. Luther Gulick and L. Urwick (New York: August M. Kelley, a 1969 reprint of the 1937 edition), p. 13.

[55] Taylor, *Shop Management,* p. 184.

[56] Warren Bennis, "Organizational Developments and the Fate of Bureaucracy," *Industrial Management Review* 7, no. 2 (spring 1966), pp. 41–55.

[57] Herbert A. Simon, *Administrative Behavior* (New York: Free Press, 1945), p. 20. For additional criticism of the principles approach, see Dwight Waldo, *The Administrative State* (New York: Ronald Press, 1948).

[58] J. Hage, "An Axiomatic Theory of Organizations," *Administrative Science Quarterly* 10 (1965–1966), p. 305, Table 4.

[59] Charles Perrow, *Complex Organizations* (Glenview, Ill.: Scott, Foresman, 1972), pp. 6–7.

[60] Ibid., pp. 11–12.

[61] Alvin W. Gouldner, "Metaphysical Pathos and the Theory of Bureaucracy," *American Political Science Review* 49 (June 1955): 501, as quoted by Goodsell, *The Case for Bureaucracy,* p. 12.

[62] As early as 1924, researchers from the National Academy of Sciences had experiments underway; for present purposes, the work at the Hawthorne plant is described following the arrival of Mayo.

[63] The designation of this study as the bank wiring study is also found in the literature; banks were telephone switchboards.

[64] There were actually two relay assembly test room studies, one following the other. The second involved a change in the wage incentive and confirmed the importance of the social group.

[65] Roethlisberger and Dickson, *Management and the Worker,* pp. 58–59, 180–183.

[66] Bertram M. Gross, *The Managing of Organizations,* Vol. 1 (New York: Free Press, 1964), p. 163.

[67] Roethlisberger and Dickson, *Management and the Worker,* p. 522.

[68] Etzioni, *Modern Organizations,* pp. 34–37.

[69] Whitman Knapp, Chairman, "Commission to Investigate Allegations of Police Corruption and the City's Anti-Corruption Procedures," *Commission Report* (New York, 1972), pp. 4, 65; see also Herman Goldstein, *Police Corruption* (Washington, D.C.: Police Foundation, 1975).

[70] Also see H. W. Parsons, "What Caused the Hawthorne Effect?" *Administration and Society* 10 (November 1978), pp. 259–283, and Henry Lansberger, *Hawthorne Revisited* (Ithaca, N.Y.: Cornell University Press, 1958).

[71] These points are drawn, with change, from William H. Knowles, "Human Relations in Industry: Research and Concepts," *California Management Review* 2, no. 2 (fall 1958), pp. 87–105.

[72] Etzioni, *Modern Organizations,* p. 39.

[73] No author, "U.S. Job Satisfaction Rates Hit 20-Year Low," *Quality Progress,* Vol. 43, Issue 2, February 2010, p. 13.

[74] Edward E. Lawler, *Motivation in Work Organizations* (Monterey, Calif.: Brooks/Cole, 1973), p. 62.

[75] John M. Zelenski, Steven A. Murphy, and David A. Jenkins, "The Happy-Productive Worker Thesis Revisited," *Journal of Happiness Studies,* Vol. 9, 2008, p. 521.

[76] Youngyol Yim and Bryan D. Schafer, "Police and Their Perceived Image: How Community Influences Officers' Job Satisfaction," *Police Practice and Research,* Vol. 10, Issue 1, February 2009, pp. 17–29.

[77] Holly A. Miller, Scott Mire, and Bitna Kim, "Predictors of Job Satisfaction Among Police Officers; Does Personality Matter?" *Journal of Criminal Justice,* Vol. 37, Issue 5, September 2009, pp. 419–426.

[78] Daisy Chu-Hsiiang Chang, Russell E. Johnson, and Robert G. Lord, "Moving Beyond Discrepancies: The Importance of Velocity as a Predictor of Satisfaction and Motivation," *Human Performance,* Vol. 23, Issue 1, January/March 2010, pp. 58–80.

[79] Kathryn Wilkins and Magot Shields, "Employer-Provided Support Services and Job Dissatisfaction in Canadian Registered Nurses," *Nursing Research,* Vol. 58, Issue 4, July/August 2009, pp. 255–263.

[80] Michael E. Milakovich and George J. Gordon, *Public Administration in America* (Belmont, CA: Wadsworth/Thomson, 2004), p. 165.

[81] A. H. Maslow, "A Theory of Human Motivation," *Psychological Review* 50 (July 1943), pp. 370–396.

[82] These five elements are identified in A. H. Maslow, *Motivation and Personality* (New York: Harper and Brothers, 1954), pp. 80–92. Maslow later added a sixth category, "metamotivation," but it never received substantial interest. See "A Theory of Metamotivation," *Humanitas* 4 (1969), pp. 301–343.

[83] Ibid., p. 91.

[84] Chris Argyris, *Personality and Organization: The Conflict between System and the Individual* (New York: Harper and Brothers, 1957), pp. 58–66.

[85] Ibid., pp. 76–122.

[86] Chris Argyris, *Integrating the Individual and the Organization* (New York: John Wiley & Sons, 1964), p. 3.

[87] For extended treatment of this subject, see Ibid., pp. 146–191.

[88] Ibid., p. 147.

[89] Douglas McGregor, *The Human Side of Enterprise* (New York: McGraw-Hill, 1960), p. 6. See also Louis A. Allen, "M for Management: Theory Y Updated," *Personnel Journal* 52, no. 12 (1973), pp. 1061–1067.

[90] Ibid., p. 7.

[91] Ibid., pp. 33–57.

[92] Bennis, *Changing Organizations,* p. 77.

[93] Walter Nord, "Beyond the Teaching Machine: The Neglected Area of Operant Conditioning in the Theory and Practice of Management," *Organizational Behavior and Human Performance* 4 (November 1969): 375–401; see also Lyman Porter, "Job Attitudes in Management," *Journal of Applied Psychology* 46 (December 1962): 375–384; and Douglas Hall and Khalil Nougaim, "An Examination of Maslow's Need Hierarchy in an Organizational Setting," *Organizational Behavior and Human Performance* 3 (February 1968), pp. 12–35.

[94] Maslow, *Motivation and Personality,* pp. 79–80. Also see, David L. Rennie, "Two Thoughts on Abraham Maslow," *Journal of Humanistic Psychology,* Vol. 48, Issue, 4, October 2008, pp. 445–448.

[95] Abraham Maslow, *Eupsychian Management: A Journal* (Homewood, IL: Dorsey Press, 1965), pp. 55–56.

[96] Gibson and Teasley, "The Humanistic Model," p. 92.

[97] Ansfried B. Weinert, "Testing Argyris' Theory of Organizational Behavior," *Scandinavian Journal of Management Studies,* Vol. 3, Issue 1, 1986, pp. 26–27.

[98] Ibid., p. 41.

[99] Wren, *Evolution of Management Thought,* p. 324. Lewin lived in this country for the 15 years preceding his death in 1947.

[100] George C. Homans, *The Human Group* (New York: Harcourt Brace, 1950), pp. 81–130.

[101] Clint Fuhs, "Toward an Integral Approach to Organization Theory," unpublished paper, p. 6, by permission. Also see ClintFuhs.com.

[102] Michael T. Hannan and John Freeman, "The Population Ecology of Organizations," *American Sociological Review*, Vol. 82, No. 5, March 1977, p. 960. Some of the disappearances were from mergers and name changes.

[103] Chris Argryris, "Double Loop Learning in Organizations," *Harvard Business Review*, September/October 1977, p. 116. Also see Crank and Giacomazzi, "A Sheriff's Office as a Learning Organization."

[104] Daniel Katz and Robert Kahn, *The Social Psychology of Organization,* 2nd ed. (New York: John Wiley & Sons, 1978), pp. 23–30, with some change.

[105] The thoughts in this paragraph are taken with restatement from Francis Amagoh, "Perspectives on Organizational Change: Systems and Complexity Theories, The Innovative Journal, *The Public Sector Innovative Journal,* Vol. 13, No. 3, 2008, pp. 1–7, an on-line peer-reviewed journal.

[106] Timothy L. Snellnow, Matthew W. Seeger, and Robert R. Ulmer, "Chaos Theory, Informational Needs, and Natural Disasters," *Journal of Applied Communication Research*, Vol. 30, No. 4, November 2002, p. 276.

[107] T. Burns and G. M. Stalker, *The Management of Innovation (*London, Tavistock, 1968).

[108] John R. Hollenback, et. al., "Structural Contingency Theory and Individual Differences," *Journal of Applied Psychology*, Vol. 87, No. 3, 2002, p. 599.

[109] J. Pfeffer and G. Salancik, *The External Control of Organizations* (New York: Harper & Row, 1978).

[110] Hatch with Cunliffe, *Organization Theory,* p. 83.

[111] Guy Peters, *Institutional Theory in Political Science: The New Institutionalism* (New York: Continuum, 2nd Edition, 2005), pp. 6–10.

[112] James G. March and Johan P. Olsen, "The New Institutionalism: Organizational Factors in Political Life," *American Political Science Review*, Vol. 78, No. 3, September 1984, p. 734.

[113] James F. Wolf, "Public Administration's Multiple Institutionalized Framework," *Public Organization Review: A Global Journal,* No. 5, 2005, p. 183.

[114] On this point see Seth Abrutyn, "Toward a General Theory of Institutional Authority," *Sociological Theory,* Vol. 27, Issue 4, December 2009, pp. 449–465.

[115] Hans Jagers, Wendy Jansen, Wichard Steebakkers, "Characteristics of Virtual Organizations," in Pascal Sieber and Joachim Griese, Editors, *Organizational Virtualness* (Bern, Switzerland: Institute of Informational Systems, 1998), p. 65.

[116] Gerard R. Murphy and Chuck Wexler, with Heather J. Davies and Martha Plotkin, "Managing a Multijurisdictional Case," Identifying the Lessons Learned from the Sniper Investigation (Washington, D. C.: Police Executive Research Forum, 2006), p. V.

[117] Ibid., p. 113.

[118] Ibid., pp. 20–21.

[119] Ibid., p. 23.

[120] Ibid., p. 22.

[121] E. C. Tolman, "Cognitive Maps in Rats and Men," *Psychological Review*, Vol. 55, No. 4, 1948, pp. 189–208.

[122] L. Douglas Kiel, *Managing Chaos and Complexity in Government* (San Francisco: Jossey-Bass, 1994).

[123] Snellnow, Seeger, and Ulmer, "Chaos Theory, Informational Needs, and Natural Disasters," p. 271.

[124] Ibid.

[125] Overman, "The New Science of Administration," p. 487.

[126] Jeffrey W. Goltz, "Determinants of Performance of Police Organizations in the State of Florida: An Evidence Based Confirmatory Approach," *International Journal of Public Policy*, Vol. 3. No. 5/6, 2008, Table 2, pp. 423 and 428.

[127] Ibid.

[128] Lex Donaldson, *American Anti-Management Theories of Organization: A Critique of Paradigm Proliferation* (New York: Cambridge University Press, 1995).

Organizational Design

We trained hard . . . but it seemed that every time we were beginning to form up into teams we would be reorganized. . . . I was to learn later in life that we tend to meet any new situation by reorganizing and a wonderful method it can be for creating the illusion of progress while providing confusion, inefficiency and demoralization.
—Petronius, 210 B.C.

Objectives

- Explain the principle of hierarchy as it relates to organizational design.

- Describe the concept of span of management.

- Distinguish between vertical and horizontal differentiation.

- Discuss the differences between tall organizational structures and flat organizational structures.

- List and describe four basic types of police organizational design.

- Discuss the major difference in organizational structure between traditional versus community policing.

- Discuss how policing philosophy (such as community policing and intelligence-led policing [ILP]) can impact organizational design.

- Describe the organizational differences between sheriff's offices and police departments.

- Identify the basic causes for tension between line and staff and suggest strategies to be used as solutions.

- Describe the characteristics of an informal organization.

OUTLINE

Introduction

In Chapter 5, Organizational Theory, we discussed the major theoretical concepts associated with organizations and the ways in which they function. In this chapter, we will see how these theories are applied in police organizations. The topics we will be specifically discussing are (1) the ways in which police administrators can modify or design their organizations in order to fulfill their missions; (2) the principle of hierarchy, which requires each lower level within the organization to be supervised by a higher level; (3) the differences between the span of control and span of management; (4) some of the more common ways in which activities and personnel are grouped within a police department; (5) the impact of community policing and intelligence-led policing philosophies on organizational structure; (6) the organizational differences between municipal departments and sheriff's departments; (7) understanding the importance of line and staff relationships; why there are sometimes problems and how they can be resolved; and (8) the importance of understanding the informal organization and its potential impact on the formal organization.

Organizing: An Overview

Police administrators modify or design the structure of their organization in order to fulfill the mission that has been assigned to the police. An organizational chart reflects the formal structure of task and authority relationships determined to be most suited to accomplishing the police mission. The process of determining this formal structure of task and authority relationships is termed **organizing**. The major concerns in organizing are (1) identifying what jobs need to be done, such as conducting the initial investigation, performing the latent or follow-up investigation, or providing for the custody of physical evidence seized at the scene of a crime; (2) determining how to group the jobs, such as those responsible for patrol, investigation, and the operation of the property room; (3) forming grades of authority, such as officer, detective, corporal, sergeant, lieutenant, and captain; and (4) equalizing responsibility and authority, illustrated by the example that, if a sergeant has the responsibility to supervise a team of detectives, that sergeant must have sufficient authority to discharge that responsibility properly or he or she cannot be held accountable for any results[1] (see Figure 6.1).

Specialization in Police Agencies

Central to this process of organizing is determining the nature and extent of specialization. Some 2,300 years ago, Plato observed that "each thing becomes . . . easier when one man, exempt from other tasks, does one thing."[2] **Specialization**, or the division of labor, is also one of the basic features of traditional organizational theory.[3] As discussed more fully later in this chapter, specialization produces different groups of functional

Figure 6.1
Grades of authority are designated by rank, starting with the police officer and following the chain of command up to Chief of Police.
(© Peter Turnley/CORBIS)

responsibilities, and the jobs allocated to meet those different responsibilities are staffed with people who are believed to be especially qualified to perform those jobs. Thus, specialization is crucial to effectiveness and efficiency in large organizations. However, specialization makes the organizational environment more complex by complicating communication, by increasing the number of units from which cooperation must be obtained, and by creating conflict among differing interests and loyalties. Also, specialization creates greater need for coordination and, therefore, additional hierarchy and can lead to the creation of narrow jobs that confine the incumbents and stifle their willingness or capacity to work energetically in support of the police department's goals. Police departments are not insensitive to the problems of specialization and attempt through various schemes to avoid the alienation of employees. Personnel can be rotated to different jobs, they can be given additional responsibilities that challenge them, they can be involved in organizational problem solving—intelligence-led policing, and the police department can try different forms of organizational structures. Thus, although specialization is an essential feature of large-scale organizations, any benefits derived from it have their actual or potential costs.

One of the first police executives to explore systematically the relationship between specialization and the organizational structure was O. W. Wilson.[4] He noted that most small departments do not need to be concerned with widely developed specialization because their patrol officer is a jack-of-all-trades. Conversely, in large departments, particular tasks (such as traffic enforcement and criminal investigation) are assigned to special units and/or individuals within the organization. Specialization presents a number of advantages for large departments:

Placement of responsibility—The responsibility for the performance of a given task can be placed on specific units or individuals. For instance, a traffic division is responsible for the investigation of all traffic accidents, and a patrol division is responsible for all requests for general police assistance.

Development of expertise—A narrow field of interest, attention, or skill can be the subject of a specialized unit. For instance, many police agencies have highly skilled special weapons and tactics (SWAT) teams that train regularly to respond to critical incidents, such as terrorist activities, hostage situations, or high-risk search warrants (see Figure 6.2). Advanced training in this area yields increased officer safety and a high degree of expertise. Specialization is also helpful during the investigation of narrowly defined, technical crimes, such as computer fraud, arson, and bombings.

Promotion of group esprit de corps—Any group of specially trained individuals sharing similar job tasks and, to some degree, depend on each other for success tends to form a highly cohesive unit with high morale.

Increased efficiency and effectiveness—Specialized units show a higher degree of proficiency in job task responsibility. For instance, a white-collar fraud unit will ordinarily be more successful in investigating complex computer fraud than a general detective division.[5]

Figure 6.2
Specialization occurs when unique tasks require extensive and detailed training, such as helicopter units, search and rescue units, and SWAT operations.
(© Karen Kasmauski/CORBIS)

Specialization appears to be a sure path to operational effectiveness. It allows each employee to acquire expertise in one area, so as to maximize his or her contribution to the overall department. However, as noted earlier, specialization has also been associated with increased friction and conflict within police departments. As units such as traffic, detective, and SWAT teams develop, an increase in job factionalism and competition also develops. The result may be a decrease in a department's overall job performance as individuals within each group show loyalty primarily or only to their unit. This traditional problem can be observed in the relationship between patrol officers and detectives. Patrol officers are sometimes reluctant to give information to detectives because they feel detectives will take credit for their work. Specialization also increases the number of administrative and command relationships, complicating the overall organizational structure. Additionally, each unit requires a competent leader. In some instances, this competent leader must also be a qualified specialist. A thorny problem here is when the specialist does not qualify for the rank usually needed to head a major unit. An example of such a problem is observed in the staffing of an air patrol unit in which the commanding officer may be a lieutenant or a sergeant because that individual is the highest-ranking officer with a pilot's license. In this case, the level of expertise (high) does not coincide with the level of rank (lower), which may cause difficulties when the individual tries to deal with other commanding officers of units who hold the rank of captain or major.

Finally, specialization may hamper the development of a well-rounded police program. As specialization increases, the resources available for general uniformed patrol invariably decrease, often causing a lopsided structure wherein the need for general police services are second to the staffing of specialized programs and units.[6]

The Principle of Hierarchy

This discussion of the principle of hierarchy builds on its coverage in Chapter 5, Organizational Theory. The **principle of hierarchy** requirement that each lower level of organization be supervised by a higher level results not only in the use of multiple spans of control but also in different grades of authority that increase at each successively higher level of the organization. This authority flows downward in the organization as a formal grant of power from the chief of police to those selected for leadership positions. These different grades of authority produce the chain of command.[7] Although there are many similarities from one department to another, the American police service does not have a uniform terminology for grades of authority and job titles.[8] In recent years, some police departments have moved away from using traditional military-style ranks and have adopted, instead, alternative titles as summarized in Figure 6.3. However, in many departments there remains a distinction between rank and title.[9] In these, *rank* denotes one's place in terms of grade of authority or the rank hierarchy, whereas *title* indicates an assignment. Where this distinction is made, a person holding the title of division director, for example, may be a captain, major, or colonel in terms of the rank hierarchy. Interestingly, the trend in today's large police agencies is to flatten the organization (discussed later in this chapter) by reducing the number of executive and command ranks. For instance, several departments have eliminated the rank of "captain" and, hence, placed more responsibility with deputy chiefs and lieutenants. This is particularly true in departments that have adopted a more "community-based" approach to policing.[10] Then too, over the last decade, several large police departments have merged with the surrounding county to

Traditional Ranks	Alternative Titles (Including County Agencies)
Chief of police	Commissioner/Director/Superintendent/Sheriff
Deputy chief	Assistant director/Undersheriff/Chief Deputy Sheriff
Colonel	Division director/Inspector/Commander
Major	Inspector/Commander
Captain	Commander
Lieutenant	Manager
Sergeant	Supervisor
Detective	Investigator/Inspector
Corporal	Senior officer/Master patrol officer
Officer	Public safety officer/Agent/Deputy Sheriff

Figure 6.3
Traditional police ranks vs. alternative titles.

become **city-county consolidated governments**. Policing in these types of governmental structures reflects various ranks and structures. For instance, the county sheriff's rank and title names continue in the Las Vegas, Nevada Metropolitan Police Department, whereas the chief executive of the police in the Louisville, Kentucky Metropolitan Police Department is referred to as the Chief and Director of Police Services. In Kansas City, Missouri, the consolidated police department maintained the more traditional rank and titles of a city department with the Chief of Police at the helm of that agency[11] (refer to Figure 6.3).

Span of Control vs. Span of Management

The term **span of management** instead of "span of control" is used to describe the number of personnel a supervisor can personally manage effectively. The term "span of management" is broader than "span of control" and encompasses factors relating to an individual's capacity to oversee the activities of others directly, such as the police manager's ability, experience, and level of energy.

"Span of management" more suitably describes the process of the number of personnel a supervisor can manage than does the term "span of control." Control is only one aspect of the management process. The term "span of management" encompasses more of the factors relating to the problem of an individual's capacity to oversee the activities of others.

How wide a span of management is depends on many factors. Some state that the ideal number of subordinates reporting to a supervisor is 8 to 12, but the number varies widely depending upon a number of factors[12] (see Figure 6.4).

Although many law enforcement agencies prefer lower spans of management, with multiple layers of hierarchy, as indicated earlier, the growing trend is a move to flatter organizational structures with higher spans of management. This type of structure provides for much better communication within the organization, increased fiscal and personnel responsibility, greater organizational flexibility, and increased delegation by supervisors. Employees also favor flatter structures with higher spans of management because they receive less detailed and micromanaged supervision, and more responsibility, and they feel more trusted by their supervisors. In these types of structures, employees have an environment in which to grow and create and, hence, become more fulfilled in their work.[13]

Organizational Structure and Design

Tansik and Elliot suggest that, when we consider the formal **structure** (or pattern of relationships) of an organization, we typically focus on two areas:

1. The formal relationship and duties of personnel in the organization, which include the organizational chart and job descriptions; and
2. The set of formal rules, policies, procedures, and controls that guide the behavior of organizational members within the framework of the formal relationships and duties.[14]

Factors Enabling an Increased Span of Management

Factor 1: The simplicity of the work
The simpler the task, the less need there is for supervision. The more diversified, complex tasks require more supervision. Traditionally, the patrol function has a larger span of control since the work is similar on each beat, and one supervisor can oversee the work conducted on several beats.

Factor 2: Efficient use of information technology
Readily available information technologies can obtain needed information to do the job as well as receive direction from supervisor increases the span of control. In-car computers, cameras, and individual communication systems enable officers to be in constant touch with supervisors.

Factor 3: The quality, skills, and capabilities of subordinates
Recruiting quality employees having the necessary education, training, and experience to be able to learn and do the assigned work requires providing less supervision by the department. In contrast, hiring the less educated and unskilled subordinates will require extensive coaching by the supervisors to teach these employees the job.

Factor 4: The skills and capabilities of the supervisor
Departments that invest in developing supervisors and managers find that the more knowledgeable and skillful the supervisor—along with the ability to clearly communicate the work—the more people he or she can supervise.

Factor 5: The quality of the department's training program
Subordinates fully knowledgeable of the laws, procedures, and administrative processes require less supervision.

Factor 6: The harmony of the workforce
When the subordinates are of like minds and working toward the same objectives in harmony, fewer incidents require supervision intervention.

Factors Narrowing the Span of Management

Factor 1: Change taking place in the work environment
When the work is forever changing, and new procedures and processes are introduced into the work, the greater the need for narrow supervision.

Factor 2: Dispersed workforce, either by time or geographically
The greater the geographic distances and the difference in time that the force works, the smaller the supervision ratio. This is often observed in the investigative division, which frequently requires more supervisors in relation to the number of investigators.

Factor 3: New and inexperienced workforce
Law enforcement in the next few years is experiencing significant retirement numbers in the supervisory and management ranks. This requires promoting younger persons with lesser experience directing the work of others.

Factor 4: Administrative requirements
The greater the administrative burden on each level of management, the greater the need for a narrow span of control. Jobs free of bureaucratic requirements can focus on the work.

Factor 5: The extent of coordination
When employees' work must be coordinated and the subordinates depend upon each other to accomplish the work, the narrower the supervision requirements. This relationship exists in many of the tactical and technical positions in a police department.

Factor 6: Employees' expectations
The higher the employees' expectations for feedback, career and development coaching, and management interaction, the narrower the requirement for supervision. Many observe that the new workforce entering policing today looks for immediate feedback from management on their progress.

Figure 6.4
Factors impacting the span of management.
Source: Adapted from Troy Lane, "Span of Control for Law Enforcement Agencies," *The Police Chief*, Volume 73, number 10 (October 2006). Retrieved on July 4, 2010:
http://policechiefmagazine.org/magazine/index.cfm?fuseaction=display&article_id=1022&issue_id=102006

Organizational design focuses on two spatial levels of differentiation—vertical and horizontal—depicted in Figure 6.5. **Vertical differentiation** is based on levels of authority, or positions holding formal power within the organization; Figure 6.6 reflects one range of vertical differentiation found in police agencies. Persons with vertical authority have the power to assign work and to exercise control to ensure job performance.[15] In Figure 6.5, the deputy chief has a span of management of three, all of whom are captains and all to whom he or she can give assignments and control.

Horizontal differentiation, on the other hand, is usually based on activity. However, in some cases, horizontal differentiation is based on specific projects or even geographical distribution. For instance, many state police departments are responsible for large geographical areas. Their organizational structure often reflects horizontal differentiation based on location rather than function. Some of the more common ways in which activities of personnel are grouped within a police organization (on a horizontal dimension) are as follows:

Grouping by clientele—The simplest method of grouping within a police department is by clientele. Personnel are assigned by the type of client served, such as juvenile division, senior citizen crime detail, mayor's security unit, gang squad, and human trafficking unit. Each group focuses on the needs of a special clientele, which can be either temporary or permanent. In this manner, officers become

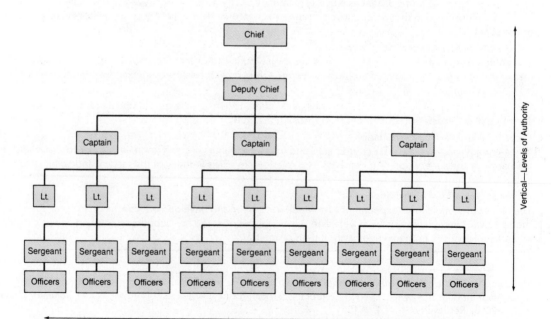

Figure 6.5

Organizational chart showing vertical and horizontal levels of diffentiation. In some departments, especially large ones, a number of other ranks may be present within the chart.

	Staff	
Line	**Auxiliary/Support**	**Administrative**
• Uniformed patrol	Crime laboratory	Personnel
• Investigations	Detention and jail	Training
• Vice and narcotics	Records	Planning and research
• Traffic enforcement	Identification	Fiscal/budgeting
• Juvenile service	Communications	Legal services
	Property maintenance, transportation, and vehicle maintenance	Media relations

Figure 6.6
Line, auxiliary/support, and administrative staff functions.

familiar with the specific enforcement problems and patterns associated with different client populations.

Grouping by style of service—A police department usually has a patrol bureau and a detective bureau. The grouping of uniformed patrol officers on the one hand and of plainclothes investigators on the other illustrates how the former are grouped by the nature of their services (conspicuous, preventive patrol, and preliminary investigations) and how the latter are grouped also by this same principle (follow-up investigations). This form of grouping also takes advantage of specialization of knowledge and skill and permits the pinpointing of responsibility for results.

Grouping by geography—Where activities are widespread over any given area, it may be beneficial to provide local command. Instances of this type of operation are large-city precincts or district-type operations and state police posts that are located throughout a state. An example of this appears in Figure 6.8A and Figure 6.8B. Even in the headquarters building, activities that are related usually share the same floor. Instances of this arrangement are records, communications, and crime analysis in close proximity to each other. This permits supervisors to become familiar with operating problems of related units and to coordinate the various efforts by more direct and immediate control.

Grouping by time—This grouping occurs when the need to perform a certain function or service goes beyond the normal work period of a single shift. Other shifts are needed to continue the effort a period of 24 hours a day. For example, the division of the patrol force into squads, each of which is responsible for patrolling a segment of the city during specific times of the day and night (typically in 10 to 12 hour shifts), is an example of this differentiation process. This form of grouping tends to create problems of coordination and unity of direction because top administrators work normal day hours, whereas many of their officers perform their functions on the evening and midnight shifts. The need to delegate authority becomes critical under these circumstances.

Grouping by process—This involves the placing of all personnel who use a given type of equipment in one function. Examples include a word processing center, crime laboratory personnel placed in a section to handle certain types of scientific equipment, and automotive maintenance units. This type of grouping lends itself to expertise involving a single process and makes the most efficient use of costly equipment.[16]

Top-Down vs. Bottom-Up Approaches

The level of complexity within a police organization is largely determined by the amount of horizontal and vertical differentiation that exists.[17] Size is often, but not necessarily, related to complexity. Some organizations, even relatively small police departments, can be highly differentiated and quite complex in organizational design.

According to Hodge and Anthony,[18] the differentiation process can occur in two basic ways in police agencies. First, the bottom-up, or synthesis, approach focuses on combining tasks into larger and larger sets of tasks. For instance, a police officer's tasks may involve primarily routine patrol but would dramatically increase in complexity when the officer was assigned preliminary investigative duties. Tasks become more complex and therefore require additional training and varied levels of supervision and accountability. The bottom-up approach is shown in Figure 6.7A. Second, the top-down, or analysis, approach looks at the overall work of the organization at the top and splits this into increasingly more specialized tasks as one moves from the top to the bottom of the organization. The top-down approach considers the overall police mission—to protect and to serve the public. At the top level of a police agency, this can be defined into various administrative tasks, such as budgeting, political maneuvering, and leadership, whereas at the street level, such a mission is carried out through activities such as patrol and arrest. This type of approach is shown in Figure 6.7B.

Both approaches are commonly found in police organizations. The top-down analysis is often used in growing organizations because it is easy to visualize the set of tasks to be accomplished and then to break these sets down into specific tasks and subtasks. The bottom-up approach is often used during periods of retrenchment when organizational growth has declined because combining tasks such as those found in patrol and detective bureaus can consolidate jobs or even units.

Then too, policing style or philosophy can often impact top-down or bottom-up approaches. This is exemplified in philosophical changes from community and problem-oriented policing to intelligence-led policing (ILP) over the past decade. Whereas community and problem-oriented policing is a bottom-up philosophy that places street officers at the forefront of problem identification and subsequent solution, Compstat and intelligence-led policing is much more hierarchical and emphasizes the top-down approach. Increasing accountability at supervisory and command levels is an important element of Compstat, often characterized by strong role definitions, tighter lines of control, and smaller spans of management. And in ILP, criminal intelligence flows up the organizational pyramid to executives who set priorities and develop strategies aimed at prevention and enforcement, and then communicate these priorities back down the organizational chain for operational tasking.[19]

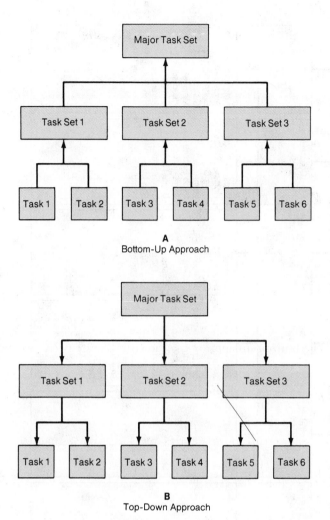

Figure 6.7
The bottom-up and top-down approaches to building structure around differentiation.
Source: Organization Theory: A Strategic Approach, 6/e by Hodge/Anthony/ Gales. Reprinted by permission of Pearson Education Inc., Upper Saddle River, NJ.

Some organizations have narrow spans of management with tall structures and many levels, whereas others reduce the number of levels by widening the span of management at each level. Many narrower spans of control make a police department "taller." Shown in Figure 6.8A, the California Highway Patrol (CHP) appears to have five levels. These levels are commissioner, deputy commissioner, assistant commissioner, field division chief, and area office commander. From a more functional perspective, each area office also has a chain of command consisting of four layers—captain, lieutenant, sergeant, and officer. Thus, when the rank layers in the area offices are considered, the CHP is a tall organization with a number of different levels of authority. Seven to nine levels of rank are fairly typical of large police organizations. Figure 6.8B displays each CHP area office by geographical grouping, as described earlier in this chapter.

The complexity of a police department is increased by the proliferation of levels because they can negatively affect communication up and down the chain of command. For example, during urban riots, police departments found that an initially small

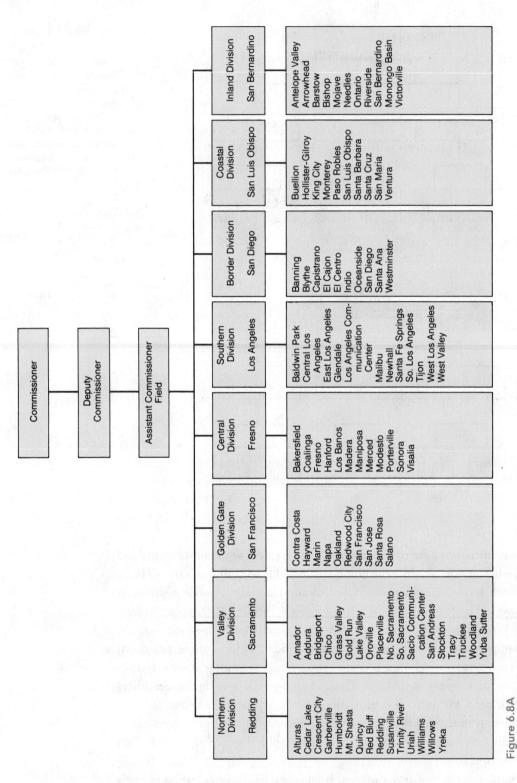

Figure 6.8A

Organizational chart for the California Highway Patrol (Field) with modification, showing five levels of control.

Source: Courtesy of the California Highway Patrol, Sacramento, California.

228

CHP GEOGRAPHICAL ORGANIZATION

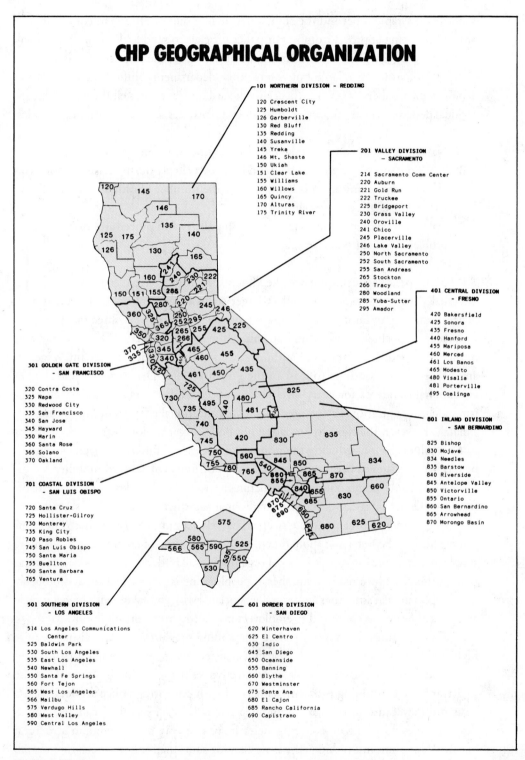

101 NORTHERN DIVISION - REDDING

120 Crescent City
125 Humboldt
126 Garberville
130 Red Bluff
135 Redding
140 Susanville
145 Yreka
146 Mt. Shasta
150 Ukiah
151 Clear Lake
155 Williams
160 Willows
165 Quincy
170 Alturas
175 Trinity River

201 VALLEY DIVISION – SACRAMENTO

214 Sacramento Comm Center
220 Auburn
221 Gold Run
222 Truckee
225 Bridgeport
230 Grass Valley
240 Oroville
241 Chico
245 Placerville
246 Lake Valley
250 North Sacramento
252 South Sacramento
255 San Andreas
265 Stockton
266 Tracy
280 Woodland
285 Yuba-Sutter
295 Amador

401 CENTRAL DIVISION – FRESNO

420 Bakersfield
425 Sonora
435 Fresno
440 Hanford
455 Mariposa
460 Merced
461 Los Banos
465 Modesto
480 Visalia
481 Porterville
495 Coalinga

801 INLAND DIVISION – SAN BERNARDINO

825 Bishop
830 Mojave
834 Needles
835 Barstow
840 Riverside
845 Antelope Valley
850 Victorville
855 Ontario
860 San Bernardino
865 Arrowhead
870 Morongo Basin

301 GOLDEN GATE DIVISION – SAN FRANCISCO

320 Contra Costa
325 Napa
330 Redwood City
335 San Francisco
340 San Jose
345 Hayward
350 Marin
360 Santa Rosa
365 Solano
370 Oakland

701 COASTAL DIVISION – SAN LUIS OBISPO

720 Santa Cruz
725 Hollister-Gilroy
730 Monterey
735 King City
740 Paso Robles
745 San Luis Obispo
750 Santa Maria
755 Buellton
760 Santa Barbara
765 Ventura

501 SOUTHERN DIVISION – LOS ANGELES

514 Los Angeles Communications Center
525 Baldwin Park
530 South Los Angeles
535 East Los Angeles
540 Newhall
550 Santa Fe Springs
560 Fort Tejon
565 West Los Angeles
566 Malibu
575 Verdugo Hills
580 West Valley
590 Central Los Angeles

601 BORDER DIVISION – SAN DIEGO

620 Winterhaven
625 El Centro
630 Indio
645 San Diego
650 Oceanside
655 Banning
660 Blythe
670 Westminster
675 Santa Ana
680 El Cajon
685 Rancho California
690 Capistrano

Figure 6.8B
Geographical organization of area offices for the California Highway Patrol.
Source: Courtesy of the California Highway Patrol, Sacramento, California.

incident grew rapidly beyond the ability of a small group of officers to control it. The process of getting approval from senior police officials to send additional officers took so long that, by the time the officers arrived at the scene, the once-small incident had grown into an uncontrollable riot. Thus, most departments shifted the authority to deploy large numbers of police officers downward, in some cases all the way to the individual police officer at the scene. This example illustrates several important principles:

1. Narrow spans of control make police departments taller.
2. Taller organizations are complex and may react slowly during crisis situations, as effective communication is hampered by the number of different levels present within the chain of command.
3. Successful tall departments must develop policies and procedures that overcome problems created by increased complexity.

Many police agencies, such as the Phoenix, Arizona Police Department, have redesigned their organizations to reflect larger spans of control or management and, hence, flatter organizational structures. Figure 6.9 represents only three major organizational levels—chief, division, and bureau. Although this structure is flatter than that of the CHP, traditional grades of authority, such as commander, lieutenant, sergeant, and officer ranks, continue to exist in the Phoenix Police Department. With higher educational standards for entry-level police officers and efforts toward professionalism, police organizational structures may reflect additional changes of this nature. Ultimately, however, the capacity to flatten out police organizational structures depends to no small degree on reducing the number of traditional ranks, a movement sure to be met with resistance because it means less opportunity for upward mobility.

McFarland[20] points out that flat structures associated with wider spans of control offer numerous advantages over the more traditional tall structures. First, they shorten lines of communication between the bottom and top levels. Communication in both directions is more likely to be faster and more timely. Second, the route of communication is more simple, direct, and clear than it is in tall organizations. Third, distortion in communication is minimized by a reduced number of people being involved. Fourth, and probably most important, flat structures are generally associated with employees with higher morale and job satisfaction as compared to employees in tall, structured organizations.

Flat structures do, however, place demanding pressures on supervisors, require high-caliber managers, and work best in organizations in which employees are held strictly accountable for measurable and objective results. Considering the role of the police and the continuing problems associated with evaluating police services, such a structure may cause inordinate stress on personnel. Top executives can attempt to direct the development of police agencies in such a way as to maintain structural balance. Some amount of hierarchy is needed for coordination, but the extremely tall police organization is neither needed nor particularly functional. In balance, no major city has successfully flattened out both the numbers of organizational layers or units and the traditional rank structure to any significant and continuing degree. Thus, any

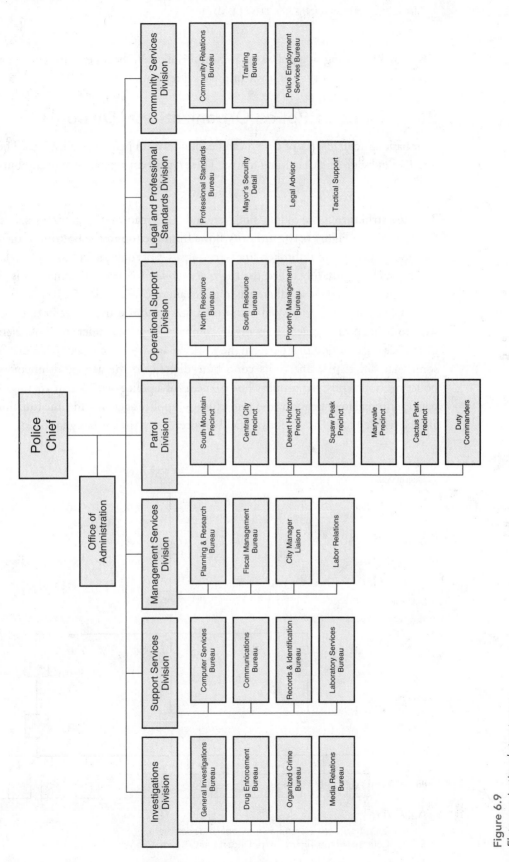

Figure 6.9
Flat organizational structure.
Source: Courtesy of the Phoenix Police Department, Phoenix, Arizona.

substantial flattening of a police organization is likely to be an experiment in organizational design rather than an institutionalized reform.

Basic Types of Police Organizational Design

Four basic structural types of design can be found within police organizations. They are line, line and staff, functional, and matrix. These types exist separately or in combination.

Line Structure

The **line structure** is the oldest, simplest, and clearest form of organizational design. As illustrated in Figure 6.10, authority flows from the top to the bottom of the organization in a clear and unbroken line, creating a set of superior–subordinate relations in a hierarchy commonly called the *chain of command.* A primary emphasis is placed on accountability by close adherence to the chain of command.

The term "line" originated with the military and was used to refer to units that were to be used to engage the enemy in combat. "Line" also refers to those elements of a police organization that perform the work the agency was created to handle. Stated somewhat differently, line units contribute directly to the accomplishment of the police mission. Thus, the primary line elements of a police department are uniformed patrol, criminal investigation, and traffic. Within police agencies, the line function can also be referred to as "operations," "field services," or a similar designation.

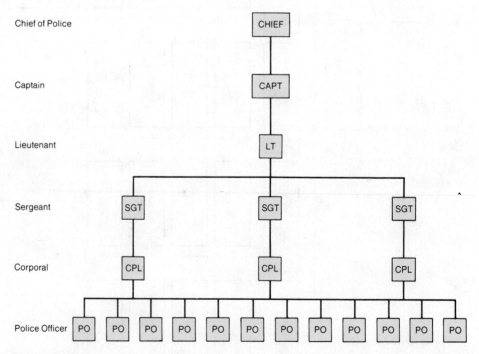

Figure 6.10
Line organizational structure in a small police department.
Source: Courtesy of the Tigard Police Department, Tigard, Oregon.

The pure line police organization does not have any supporting elements that are internal or part of it, such as personnel, media relations, training, or fiscal management. Instead, the line police organization uses its total resources to provide services directly to the public. Typically found only in small towns, the line is the most common type of police organization because of the sheer frequency of small jurisdictions. However, most police officers work in larger departments that retain the basic line elements but to which are added various types of support units. These larger police departments are often referred to as the *line and staff* form of organization.

Line and Staff Structure

As more demands for services are placed on police departments, there is a need to add internal support functions, so that the line functions can continue to provide direct services to the public. The addition of support functions to the line elements produces a distinct organizational form: the **line and staff structure**. The addition of a staff component to the line structure offers a number of advantages because such units are helpful in the following:

1. Providing expert advice to line units in special knowledge areas as demonstrated by the opinions of legal advisers;
2. Relieving line managers from performing tasks they least prefer to do or are least qualified to do, such as training and scientific analysis of physical evidence;
3. Achieving departmentwide conformity in activities that affect the entire organization, such as disciplinary procedures; and
4. Reducing or eliminating special problems, such as corruption, because of the greater expertise they bring to bear on the issue and the greater amount of time they have to devote to the problem.[21]

Staff functions are sometimes further broken down into two types: auxiliary or support and administrative staff services. Under this arrangement, auxiliary or support units, such as communications and crime laboratory services, are charged with the responsibility of giving immediate assistance to the operations of line elements. In contrast, administrative staff units, such as personnel and training, provide services that are of less immediate assistance and are supportive of the entire police department. Figure 6.6 identifies typical line, auxiliary/support, and administrative staff functions. Depending on factors such as the history of the police department and the chief's preferences, there is some variation as to how functions are categorized. Less frequently, legislative enactments may establish the organizational structure, which is another source of variation in how functions are categorized.

Figure 6.11 shows a line and staff structure. In it, the Bureau of Field Services (composed of the patrol districts) is the "heart" or primary line function of the organization and is highlighted to show that purpose. The investigative services bureau is also a line function but smaller than the Bureau of Field Services. The Bureau Administrative Services and upper-echelon offices represent staff functions within the organization. Note in Figure 6.11 that two types of staff report directly to the chief of

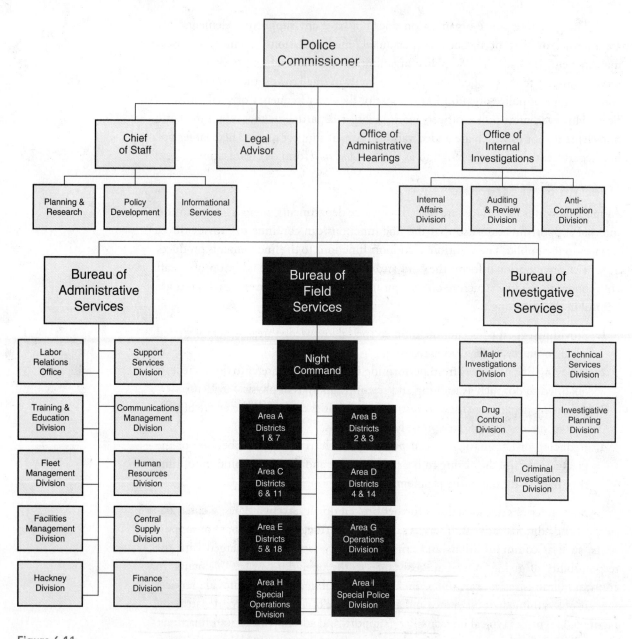

Figure 6.11

Line and staff structure in a police department. Note that line functions are grouped in the middle of the structure of high-lighted as "Bureau of Field Services."

Source: Courtesy of the Boston, Massachusetts, Police Department.

police: the generalist, illustrated by the chief of staff, and the specialist, illustrated by the legal adviser and internal investigations office.

Functional Structure

The **functional structure** is one means by which the line authority structure of an organization can be modified. Hodge and Johnson[22] state that functional structure "is

Quick FACTS ▸▸ Factors Influencing Organizational Design

Organizational structure within police agencies varies widely across the country. While researchers have found it difficult to isolate all the factors that shape police organizations, 14 factors have been identified to influence organizational design in at least three separate studies:

1. Organizational size and environment
2. City governance
3. Region
4. Application and use of technology
5. Crime rates and patterns
6. Organizational age
7. Political culture and environment
8. Population size and density
9. Population heterogeneity
10. Poverty/income
11. Urbanization or ruralization
12. Span of management
13. Time
14. Vertical differentiation

Source: Edward R. Maguire and Craig D. Uchida, "Measurement and Explanation in the Comparative Study of American Police," in *Measurement and Analysis of Crime and Justice,* Criminal Justice 2000, Volume 4, (2000). See also Edward R. Maguire, *Organizational Structures in American Police Agencies: Context, Complexity and Control* (Albany, NY: SUNY Press 2003).

a line and staff structure that has been modified by the delegation of management authority to personnel outside their normal spans of control." Figure 6.12 shows a police department in which the intelligence unit is responsible to three captains whose main responsibility is for other organizational units.

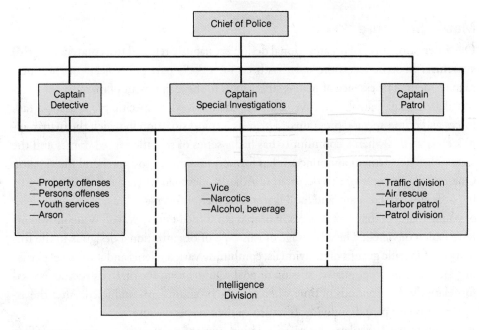

Figure 6.12
Functional structure in a police organization.

Some of these problems can be eliminated by police organizations using functional design. By requiring specific units to be responsible to a variety of other unit commanders, critical information is assured of reaching other line officers. Sharing is promoted, while competing loyalties are diminished. Good examples of functional design can be observed in police departments moving toward geographical responsibility for supervisors on a 24-hour basis. A commander or shift (watch) supervisor (normally a lieutenant) assigned to the day watch may be responsible for solving violent street crimes (e.g., robberies) that occur in a specific area on all three shifts; however, officers on at least two of the shifts (evenings and nights) are not directly assigned to that supervisor. In some departments, the officer might not even know the supervisor from another watch. This often creates a major conflict between supervisors as different deployment strategies or tactics impact all elements of the shift or watch. Dallas and Fort Worth, Texas, as well as San Diego, California are just a few departments that have noted these types of problems stemming from the implementation of geographical responsibility for managers, resulting in a functional design. In some areas, this type of formalized geographically based, or "geo" policing is referred to as **sector policing**. While the name might be different, the approach is still focused on providing a proactive and geographically based structure for police strategies, personnel deployment, and accountability.[23]

Thus, the major disadvantage of the functional design is that it increases organizational complexity. In Figure 6.12, members of the intelligence division receive instructions from several superiors. This can result in conflicting directions, and thus extensive functionalized structures are seldom found in police agencies. Law enforcement executives should explore the use of the functional design but be ever cautious of the confusion that can result if the process is not properly monitored and controlled.

Matrix Structure

One interesting form of organizational design is variously referred to as **matrix (or grid) structure**. In some cases, the style has been inclusively part of "project" or "product" management. The essence of matrix structure is in the assignment of members of functional areas (e.g., patrol, detective, and support services) to specific projects (e.g., task forces and crime-specific programs). The most typical situation in which the matrix approach is used is when a community has had a series of sensationalized crimes and the local police department announces it has formed a task force to apprehend the violator. One notable example of this occurred in Atlanta, Georgia, where a task force comprising over 300 federal, state, and local law enforcement officers searched for the murderer of young males in that city. As a result of that combined effort, Wayne Williams was arrested and convicted. The advantage of this type of organizational design is in the formation of specific groups of individuals, combining varied talents and levels of expertise in order to fulfill a designated mission or goal. Quite often, the matrix structure is used for relatively short periods of time when specific programs are conducted. After the assignment is completed, individuals return to their respective units.

Figure 6.13 displays the matrix design applied to a police organization. This chart reflects the basic line and staff elements found in most police agencies. However,

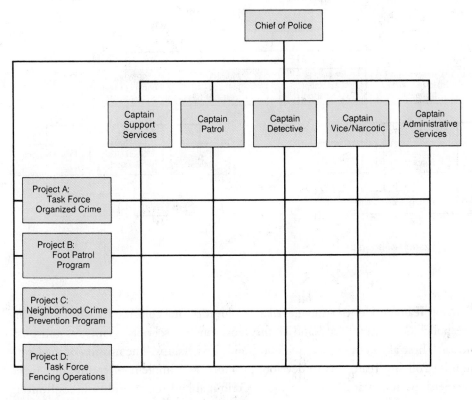

Figure 6.13
Matrix structure in a police organization.

four specific projects have been initiated that require the use of personnel from five different units, which further requires each project to organize along the lines suggested by Figure 6.14.

Although the matrix structure greatly increases organizational complexity, it has been successful only in the short-term delivery of police services.

Organizational Structure Today

The impact of community policing during the late 1990s had a dramatic impact on organizational structure. It was most apparent in agencies that adopted **decentralization** strategies. The purpose behind such strategies was that police departments could more effectively serve their communities through an organizational design focused on individual areas and neighborhoods rather than the entire city. Further, decentralization in organizational structure was seen as being much more flexible and having a fluid design in which to provide essential public and human services.[24]

Electing to compartmentalize the activities of the community policing concept, some departments opted to provide such services solely through one unit or bureau. For instance, the Anaheim Police Department in Anaheim, California, had a single bureau devoted to community policing. Through this one unit, the Community

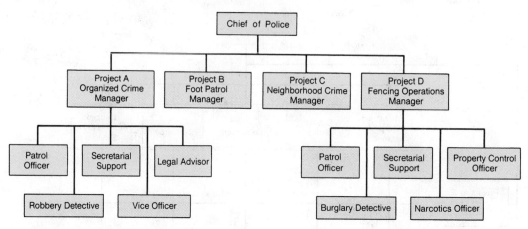

Figure 6.14
The detailed organization of projects.

Policing Team developed strategies that employed a total community effort involving the police department, city and county government, schools, churches, and businesses. These alliances formed neighborhood partnerships. The mission of the Community Policing Team was to develop, promote, and implement community-based partnerships aimed at addressing various criminal and social problems confronting the city of Anaheim.[25] The important note here is that the entire community policing effort was relatively confined to the one unit—the Community Policing Team.

In contrast, other departments (e.g., those in Portland, Oregon; Madison, Wisconsin; Charlotte-Mecklenburg, North Carolina; and Minneapolis, Minnesota) opted to implement the community policing concept holistically; that is, community policing was reflected in all aspects of the organization, and, hence, the organizational structure did not reflect a single unit devoted to community policing but rather an inferred assumption that the community policing philosophy was pervasive throughout the organization. In these cases, the organizational chart was reflective of the philosophical changes imbued in community policing. For instance, under the leadership of then-Chief Lee P. Brown (1990), the Houston Police Department acted as a model for community policing departments (see Figure 6.15). Reflective of these philosophical changes, the organizational chart of the department provided a new and dynamic look. Note that the focus of the department was on service delivery and support rather than the traditional modes of assignment. The police department was viewed more as a community organization than as a control agency. As such, the organization was operated similarly to a service corporation that is fully responsible to an executive board comprising police and community leaders. In this manner, community policing made individual police officers accountable directly to the people of Houston. The chief of police acts more as a chairman of the board or a chief executive officer for a major corporation than as a traditional police manager.

Houston Police Department

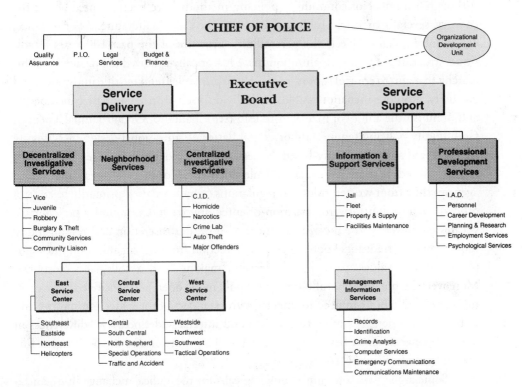

Figure 6.15

Organizational chart of the Houston Police Department reflecting an emphasis on service delivery and support through a community-represented "executive board."

Source: Courtesy of the Houston, Texas, Police Department.

IN THE NEWS · San Jose, California Police Department Targets Excellence

The San Jose Police Department, under the leadership of Chief Rob Davis, has developed a unique group within the Office of the Chief of Police called the Performance Analysis Detail (PAD). The detail consists of a police lieutenant and four sergeants, all certified as law enforcement auditors and efficiency experts. The group's primary mission is to perform statistical and other analysis on the SJPD work functions and processes, yielding operational changes that increase organizational efficiency and reduce costs.

The unit has focused on the SJPD Organizational Design in an effort to consolidate and structure uniform divisions of work. As a result, the San Jose Police Department Organizational Components consists of seven elements as defined below:

Department: "Department" designates the San Jose Police Department, to include all subdivisions and personnel.

Bureau: "Bureau" designates the largest organizational component of the Department.

Division: "Division" designates the largest functional subdivision of a bureau.

Unit: "Units" are subdivisions of a "Division."

Team: "Teams" are groupings of unit members performing the same function.

Section: "Sections" are the functional subdivisions of a unit.

Detail: "Details" are the smallest organizational component and may be formed on a permanent or temporary basis.

Source: Courtesy of the San Jose, California Police Department; http://www.sjpd.org/COP/PAD.html

Traditional Design vs. Structural Change

Although a number of community policing methods have been adopted across the country, several structural problems have been cited in the literature.[26] For instance, community policing rejects the paramilitary structure of the past 100 years. Traditional structures of police organizations have historically followed the principles of hierarchy that aim to control subordinates. These principles tend to stifle innovation and creativity, promote alienation and loss of individual self-worth, emphasize mediocrity, and diminish the ability of managers to lead (see Chapter 5, Organizational Theory). Community policing requires a shorter and flatter organizational design. Services are decentralized and community-based. Necessarily, such a design will be less formalized, less specialized, and less bureaucratic (rule-oriented). Cordner[27] suggests that police agencies shift from written rules and regulations (which are used primarily to control officers) to a straightforward, situation-oriented approach. Community policing advocates empowering the individual officer with greater discretion and responsibility more than does traditional policing; hence, direction from the organization must emphasize shared values, participatory decision making, and a collegial atmosphere. Moreover, the organization of community policing is open and sensitive to the environment, with a built-in need to interact with members of the wider community and to be "results-oriented" rather than closed and internally defined. The differences in organizational structure between traditional policing and community policing are further outlined in Figure 6.16.

Some argue that community policing calls for too radical a change in organizational design—that such changes may be impossible under existing union and civil service constraints. Further, organizations tend to follow Michael's "iron law of oligarchy," which indicates that modern, large-scale organizations tend toward specialization and centralization.[28] However, these organizational traits appear to be in conflict with other community policing structures (see Figure 6.15). Large police departments require a certain amount of specialization to handle diverse tasks efficiently, such as examining various types of physical evidence or handling unique situations, and the amount of hierarchy required to coordinate the various specialized parts produces a tendency toward centralization. This structural conflict causes significant role confusion and ambiguity among officers who are assigned traditional law enforcement duties as well as more contemporary police tasks.

Intelligence-Led Policing (ILP) and Organizational Structure

The Compstat movement during the early 2000s was credited with significantly reducing crime in major cities across the United States, but it had very little impact on the organizational structure or design of police agencies. However, the movement toward intelligence-led policing (ILP) has placed much more emphasis on the "functional structure" of organizations as previously described (see Figure 6.12). Requiring police agencies to be much more proactive and preventative based, the focus is on integrating the intelligence function throughout the organization. ILP requires accurate and timely information, the source of which is often through the development of

Traditional Policing	Community Policing
1. *Bureaucratic and control based*: characterized by detailed standard operating procedures and rigid written policies; high formalization of the organizational pyramid	1. *Nonbureaucratic*: based on the corporate model; more flexible and adaptive than traditional paramilitary structure; focus on building teams within a more collegial environment
2. *Centralized and hierarchical organizational structure*: highly centralized with authority flowing from top to bottom, particularly in operations; characterized by tall organizations with multiple ranks and levels; communication is slow and almost always downward	2. *Decentralization, shorter and flatter organizational structure*: authority and function is derived from community-based demands; characterized by decentralized services with multiple neighborhood storefronts and more service-oriented environments; communication is open and free-flowing between ranks both vertical and horizontal in the organization
3. *Autocratic management style*: Leadership is based on rank with rights associated with the office; emphasis on control-based methodologies in managing people within the organization; loss of individual leadership capabilities within the organization	3. *Democratic and participatory management style*: Leadership is encouraged at all ranks with focus on challenging the status quo, enabling and inspiring others; ennobling shared visions and possibilities, modeling ethical and collaborative behavior, rewarding others, and reflecting on self and individual service
4. *High specialization and task orientation*: police functions performed by smaller units of highly trained and specialized personnel, often characterized by high esprit-de-corps and unique unit identification; personnel loyalty is often observed to the unit versus the larger department (e.g., SWAT-tactical teams, homicide units, motor patrol, gang units)	4. *Generalization*: police officers act as generalists with specialized training in multiple areas; patrol often becomes the primary and emphasized police function with all other units and divisions supporting the patrol function; officers embrace patrol as the primary mechanism for neighborhood and community engagement
5. *Emphasis on random patrol*: the organization employs traditional policing methodologies focused on random-moving patrol vehicles; little use of technology in the patrol function and crime analysis is limited to plotting crime and activities after the fact	5. *Directed patrol based on crime and intelligence analysis*: the patrol function is directed for high impact, preventative-based activities as defined by detailed and real-time crime and intelligence analysis; wide use of technology and highly trained analysts often observed in crime analysis and fusion centers
6. *Large goal oriented*: Preoccupation with crime rates and numbers; arrest orientation with focus on paramilitary structure and function of police to combat crime; individual tasks are quantity oriented	6. *Embraces multiple objectives, problem-solving and individual successes*: Celebration of innovative strategies that have a positive impact on the community; goals and objectives are community/client driven; individual tasks are quality oriented
7. *Crime-fighting officer perspective within reactive organization, emphasis on mediocrity*: focus is primarily on crime detection, investigation, and arrest *after* the fact; orientation for the organization is based on the traditional "crime-fighting and order maintenance" model; organizations focus on arrest, cases cleared and similar measures of success in traditional policing	7. *Preventive-based approach to crime within a proactive organization, emphasis on quality*: focus is on the prevention of crime *before* the activity occurs, with emphasis on broader social issues as well as neighborhood problems; crime prevention through environmental design; success is measured in numbers of interactions with the community and the building of new relations and partnerships
8. *Closed organization orientation*: distinct from environment, resistant to environmental influence and change, internally defined agenda, justification of means over ends; stifling of innovation and creativity; loss of individual worth for group think	8. *Open organization model*: organization attempts to effectively interact with the community, open to change, sensitive to environment; focused on long-term and results-oriented goals; emphasis placed on individual and organizational creativity
9. *"Fear of crime" justifies existence and tactics*: Police are responsible for fighting the "war" on crime; symbols focused on the power of the police and control of the community	9. *Uses evidence-based approaches to justify police functions*: Embraces on-going research to developed cost effective "best practices" in police strategies and tactics; emphasis on knowing contemporary research in policing
10. *High individual and managerial accountability*: Organizational demand on accountability focused on numbers; reaction to increased crime rates result in increased traditional solutions such as more patrol, visible arrests, higher profile policing in specific neighborhoods; CompStat becomes a means to an end	10. *Accountability and police focus is a reflection of community demand*: Police functions and foci are developed with the community at the neighborhood level; the community is actively engaged in measuring police performance through shared meetings; emphasis is on community engagement and partnerships

Figure 6.16
Differences between traditional and community policing.
Source: Adapted by R. W. Taylor (November 2010) from R. W. Taylor, E. J. Fritsch, and T. J. Caeti, "Core Challenges Facing Community Policing" *ACJS Today*, volume XVII, issue 1, May/June 1998 and C. Murphy, *Contemporary Models of Urban Policing: Shaping the Future* (Ontario: Ministry of the Solicitor General, 1991), p. 2.

partnerships and problem-solving methodologies employed with other departments and agencies. ILP also requires energetic and competent analysts to communicate their findings to decision-makers, and much more importantly, that decision-makers then communicate their strategies to lower levels of the organization, again, much more 'top-down' in style.[29] In contrast to community policing, Ratliff asserts that decentralized structures (often stemming from community policing philosophies) reflect a purpose rather than a geographic focus. This tends to produce stovepipes within the organization, separating police specialties from one another, and decreasing communication and information flow between units, a condition critically important for the success of ILP.[30]

The need to employ intelligence activity at almost every level of the organization requires a structure and design that highlights not only effective communication, but also the sharing of information and other resources. The primary methodology, from a structural perspective, to accomplish this task is to organize specialized units (such as organized crime units, gang units, terrorism task forces, narcotics and vice squads, and the like) along geographical hierarchies within the intelligence division—the theme being to highlight intelligence operations within a police department as the central element to planned activities rather than haphazard reactions to crime and potential terrorist strikes. Communication throughout the organization rests primarily on the dissemination of information via technology and planned efforts directed from the highest decision makers in the department. This type of structure necessarily requires the development of a strong fusion center that not only acts as the central hub for intelligence analysis, but also serves as the primary "brain" for dissemination and feedback.

Quite frankly, few police agencies in the United States have attempted to structure around the ILP model. However, many have reverted to more centralized and traditional organizational structures with levels of command and spans of management often observed previous to the community policing movement. This may well be a reflection away from community-based approaches as well as a natural result of the Compstat movement. While the structures may be somewhat flatter, communication within and between organizations continues to be problematic, and the strategies aimed at relatively quick solutions to very complex problems. Even Ratcliffe admits that the criteria for success of ILP is on the immediate detection, reduction, and disruption of criminal and potential terrorist activities, and not on the long-term improvement of social conditions that often encourage crime and disorder. As a result of such difficulties, the continued implementation of ILP should provide a dynamic arena for police organizational structure in the future.

Some Unique Organizational Features of Sheriff's Offices

A detailed discussion of "politics and the county sheriff" was addressed in Chapter 4, Politics and Police Administration. However, in addition to some of the unique political features discussed therein, there are also some organizational differences that typically exist between municipal police departments and sheriff's offices. For example, most police departments do not have a single commanding officer positioned between the police chief and all of the operating and administrative bureaus. However, this is not true of sheriff's offices. Most sheriff's offices have a chief deputy/undersheriff and, with the blessing of the sheriff, this person typically assumes considerable operational command over the entire organization (see Figure 6.17). The position exists because, although the elected sheriff is the chief law enforcement officer of the agency, the sheriff must devote a considerable amount of time addressing the political needs of the sheriff's office within the community to assure that a positive image is created and maintained and public support is maximized. In addition, if the sheriff should decide to run for re-election, he or she must devote considerable time and effort to this endeavor.

In many respects, the role of the chief deputy/undersheriff is very similar to that of the police chief in a municipal police department, in that the person occupying this position assumes direct operational command over the entire organization. However, it is also important to note that, because sheriff's offices typically are responsible for supervising the operation of county jails, the chief deputy/undersheriff should also ideally have a good background in jail administration (see Figure 6.18). This is so because jails consume a substantial portion of the agency's resources for both personnel and operating expenses. Although the position of sheriff, like that of police chief, has traditionally been held by men, this has changed and now women are increasingly being elected as sheriff.

Line and Staff Relationships in Police Agencies

The rapid growth in size of many police agencies has been accompanied by a corresponding rapid growth in specialization and a need for the expansion of staff services to provide support for operating units. This expansion and division of responsibility, which occurs in all police departments except those that are a pure line form of organization, is sometimes fraught with difficulty and dissension. If left uncorrected, these conditions will have a serious negative effect on both the quality and the quantity of service a police agency is able to deliver to its citizens. The following represent some of the major causes of conflict between line and staff.

The Line Point of View

One of the basic causes of organizational difficulties, as line operations view them, is that staff personnel attempt to assume authority over line elements instead of supporting and advising them.[31] Line commanders feel that the chief looks to them for accountability of the operation; therefore, staff personnel should not try to control their operation because they are not ultimately responsible for handling line problems. Another commonly heard complaint is that staff personnel sometimes fail to give sound advice because their ideas are not fully thought out, not tested, or "too academic." This attitude is easy for line commanders to develop because of the belief that staff personnel are not responsible for the ultimate results of their product and therefore propose new ideas too quickly.

HILLSBOROUGH COUNTY SHERIFF'S OFFICE

ORGANIZATIONAL CHART

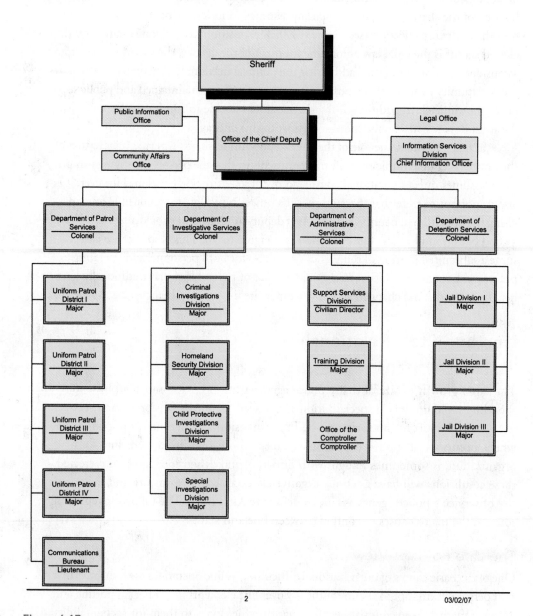

2   03/02/07

Figure 6.17
Hillsborough County Sheriff's Office (organizational chart showing the office of the chief deputy in charge of the entire organization).
Source: Courtesy of the Hillsborough County Sheriff's Office, Tampa, Florida.

Communications problems sometimes emerge between the staff specialist and line commanders. Staff personnel on occasion fail to explain new plans or procedures and do not give line commanders sufficient time to propose changes. For example, a major staff project was installed in a patrol operation after only a very brief period of time had passed from its announcement until the starting date. Some attempts were made to prepare the personnel for the project by the use of general orders and memos, but this was left to line supervisors to do, and they did not have enough information to fully explain the new program. This resulted in confusion. Individual officers were unsure of what they were to do, so they did little. It took several weeks to recognize the problem and several more weeks to explain, train, and guide the personnel to operate under the new plan. After a 3-month delay, the plan began to show results. However, the crime picture for this period was the worst in 4 years. The chief placed the blame at his precinct commanders' doors. They, in turn, blamed staff for poor preparation and lack of coordination.

Line commanders frequently claim that staff personnel take credit for successful operations and point the finger of blame at the line commander when programs fail. In one department, a new report-writing program was installed under staff auspices. This program was designed to improve the statistical

Figure 6.18
Sheriff's departments are often responsible for the county jail, as well as more traditional law enforcement duties.
(© David R. Frazier Photolibrary, Inc./Alamy)

data that the staff group would use in preparing the various departmental reports and to help the patrol commander to evaluate patrol personnel. During the first year of the program, several flaws showed up that prompted staff to write a report that stated the patrol supervisors were not checking the reports carefully, and as a result erroneous information was appearing that made evaluation impossible. A retraining program was instituted, and the defects were ironed out. The personnel assigned to do the training then wrote a report taking full credit for the improvement. The commander of the patrol division took a rather dim view of this self-congratulatory report because he, along with some of his subordinates, worked very closely with the training section in formulating the retraining program.

Operational commanders sometimes express the concern that staff personnel do not see the "big picture" because they have only limited objectives that reflect their own nonoperational specialties. For example, the personnel unit of one police department developed a test for the rank of lieutenant. Most of the sergeants who took the examination did poorly. Many became frustrated and angry because they had built up fine work records and believed that the examination procedure failed to measure their potential ability for the rank of lieutenant accurately. The members of the personnel unit who developed the examination procedure were not sympathetic and suggested that the department just did not have the caliber of personnel who could pass a valid examination. The line commanders claimed that the personnel unit did not know enough about the department's needs, and if they would put more effort into helping instead of "figuring out reasons why we're no good, then we'd be better off."

The Staff Point of View

Staff personnel contend that line commanders do not know how to use staff. Instead of using their analytic skills, staff personnel feel that line commanders simply want to use them as researchers and writers. As an example, in one medium-sized department, the robbery caseload was increasing at an alarming rate. When staff were approached to work on the problem, the chief of detectives told them how he saw the problem, asked them to prepare an order for his signature setting out the changes as he saw them, and refused any staff personnel the opportunity to contact the operating field units to determine what the problems were as they saw them.

Many staff personnel also feel that line officers are shortsighted and resist new ideas. As an example, a department had expanded, and numerous personnel were promoted, but some of the personnel promoted to administrative and executive positions could not function effectively because they had not been properly trained to assume their new roles and responsibilities. The results were inefficiency and personal conflict. The planning and research officer had much earlier wanted to install a training program for career development for the ranks of lieutenant and above, so that there would be a trained group to choose from when needed. The planning and research officer blamed the line commanders for being shortsighted and not cooperating earlier to develop career development programs.

Solutions

The problems of line and staff relationships can be corrected. What is needed is a thorough indoctrination and training program and clear definitions as to the tasks of each.

The line is principally responsible for successful operations of the department, and therefore line employees must be responsible for operational decisions affecting them. Staff, on the other hand, exist to assist the line in reaching objectives by providing advice and information when requested to do so. This does not, however, prohibit staff from volunteering advice they believe is needed.

The use of staff assistance is usually at the option of line commanders, but they must recognize that the chief can decide to use staff services to review any operation and that this decision is binding. As an example, the chief may order a planning and research officer to determine if patrol officers are being properly used. The patrol commander is responsible for making effective use of advice received under such circumstances. If the patrol commander disagrees with staff findings, then an opportunity for reply and review by a higher authority should be available.

Staff exist to help line elements accomplish the objectives of the department. To do this effectively, staff must know what the line elements are doing. Illustratively, the personnel officer who does not know what tasks police officers must perform cannot effectively prepare selection standards for the hiring of personnel. Both staff and line must exert effort to ensure that staff stay in contact with what is going on in line units.

Line personnel are concerned primarily with day-to-day operating objectives within the framework of departmental goals. Staff can perform a valuable task for them by thinking ahead toward future problems and operations before they arise. The possibility of a plane crash in a community that has an airport is a subject that staff, in cooperation with line commanders, can anticipate. Thus, staff can accomplish time-consuming planning and the development of orders and procedures well before they are needed.

Line commanders should know what the various staff functions are and what they can contribute to the improvement of the line units. In some departments, this can be done at meetings by allowing the staff heads to explain what they can do for the line commanders. At the same time, line commanders can make known their expectations about staff support. Such discussions lead to closer coordination and to improved personal relationships that are essential for effectiveness. Staff's ideas will be more readily accepted if they demonstrate an understanding of line operations.

Staff activity deals primarily with change. However, people tend to resist change and ideas that threaten the status quo. Change by itself indicates the possibility that the old way is no longer acceptable. Staff should anticipate and dispel resistance to change by doing the following:

1. Determining to what extent the change proposed will affect the personal relationships of the people involved. Is the change a major one that will affect the social patterns established in the formal and informal organizations discussed later in this chapter? Can the change be broken down into a series of small moves that will have less negative impact than a single, large change?
2. Involving those most affected by the change in the early planning stages. When major changes are involved that will modify the relationships between line commanders and the people who work for them, opposition from commanders can be minimized if they participate from the early planning stages. Although it may not be possible for everyone to participate, the use of representative groups of employees is often effective in helping to facilitate change.
3. Communicating throughout the entire planning stage. The personnel who will be affected by the change will accept it better if: (a) they believe it will benefit them personally—that it will make their work easier, faster, or safer (the change should be tied in as closely as possible with the individual's personal goals and interests—job, family, future); (b) the personnel have an opportunity to offer suggestions, ideas, and comments concerning the change as it affects them—provided these suggestions are sincerely wanted and are given serious consideration; and (c) they are kept informed of the results of the change (see Chapter 15, Organizational Change).

To achieve organizational objectives, a line commander should know how to use staff assistance. The specialized skills of staff people can be used to help achieve these goals more efficiently and economically. By involving staff in the problems of the line, staff personnel can become more effective by learning the line commanders' way of thinking. Line commanders must be able to identify their problems precisely before seeking assistance. They must not vaguely define a problem and then expect the staff unit to do all the work. It is also important for staff to keep other staff informed of decisions that will affect them. As an example, a department was given permission to hire and train 250 new officers, which was double the normal recruit class. The training unit was not advised of this until a week before the class was to start. Subsequently, many problems developed that could have been avoided.

One thing that people working staff functions typically have is necessary time and research skills to delve into operational problems. As an example, when police departments were transitioning from revolvers to semi-automatics, their function would have been to determine which semi-automatic to select; the caliber, the cost, the reliability, and also the type of retraining that would be involved. The same would be true when police departments were transitioning from batons to chemical sprays and to the electronic control devices. Research of these functions takes time, skills, and the disposition to sit at a computer for hours at a time to do the necessary research or make the telephone calls or send e-mails to the agencies that may have already gone through this transition.

The Informal Organization

The **informal organization** does not appear on organizational charts, but it does exist in every organization because people are not simply objects in boxes connected by lines. These people have needs, attitudes, and emotions that rules and regulations are not designed to accommodate. The informal organization is built on friendships and common desires. It, too, may have goals that may or may not coincide with the formal organization's goals. The informal organization has its own communications and behavior patterns, as well as a system of rewards and punishments to assure conformity.[32]

The task of management and supervision is to recognize the existence of the informal organization and to utilize it for the good of the formal organization. Too often, the informal organization is looked upon with disfavor for fear that it will infringe upon the formal organization's authority. As a result, cliques form and develop their own goals and objectives. This usually results in inefficiency, social conflict, and a general breakdown of morale within the formal organization.

It must be remembered that the tools used by management (the process of directing and controlling people and things so the organizational objectives can be accomplished)[33] and supervision (the act of overseeing people)[34] will be most effective and result in cooperation when people feel that they are an integral part of the organization. The task of administration is to make each employee aware of what the formal organizational goals are and how each employee plays an important part in achieving those goals through his or her efforts.

Through the feedback process, the informal organization can be an excellent source of measurement to determine if goals are being met. The feedback process involves both supervisors and managers listening to their employees and asking them questions in regard to operations and procedures. This information is then inserted into the formal organization's communication system to help the chief administrator evaluate how well operational plans are working. Once recognized, it can be an effective means to greater employee participation in both decision making and goal achievement.

The informal organization has several important characteristics:

Naturalness—The informal organization is natural and spontaneous; it does not ordinarily take on the characteristics of a social group as a result of an order or edict from higher authority. Rather, the informal group evolves and develops in response to conditions and needs.

Interactions (or group dynamics)—Group members interact with each other because they want to; they have a natural, spontaneous desire to do so.

Empathy—Members of a social group have a high degree of attraction and sympathy for each other. They like to be with each other. Their social inhibitions are at a minimum and they feel a lack of the type of restraint that results from expected disapproval of one's associates. While some members of a social group are attracted to each other more than others, the general level of mutual attraction is high.

Social distance—Members of a social group do not feel too much social distance. That is, they do not feel that there are status or other types of barriers between themselves and other members. Social distance is the reason that uninhibited interaction often fails to take place in management meetings attended by personnel from several rank levels.

Democratic orientation—The social group has a strongly democratic orientation. The very essence of social group action is the attraction that members have for each other, supplemented by uninhibited communication and self-expression. Naturalness and freedom characterize effective social groups.

Leadership—Leaders tend to emerge naturally from the group. This does not mean, however, that social groups cannot exist where leaders have been designated from the outside. Much depends on the characteristics and behavior of the leader. When an aggregation of people begins to become a social group, some people initiate interaction more than others and they are usually attractive to a large number of people. These are the natural leaders, but they may not necessarily also be designated as hierarchical leaders.

Group pressures—One aspect of the social group is the pressure exerted to get the members to conform to group standards in thought and action. The phenomenon can be used either to thwart the goals of management or to facilitate their achievement.

Cohesiveness and unity—In order to endure, a social group must have a certain amount of cohesiveness. Members must have sufficient desire to belong, to keep the group together and in continued existence. In short, there must be enough attractiveness in group goals and associations to ensure their observance as a means of maintaining the group.[35]

CONCLUSION

This chapter examined the considerable diversity of organizational designs of law enforcement agencies in the United States. Among the factors that will influence the organizational design is the size of the population to be served, the size of the organization, the type of governance in the community (i.e., strong-mayor, city manager, sheriff), and the region of the country where the services are being provided. We have witnessed significant changes in policing philosophies over the last two decades, moving away from traditional policing techniques to more community-based and intelligence-led policing (ILP) strategies. Philosophical approaches to combating crime and preventing terrorism impact organizational design, with more community-based approaches favoring a flatter and more decentralized structure, whereas ILP requires a more centralized, top-down, and geographical based design. We must not forget that organizations are composed of people, and that people often develop strong personal relationships and behaviors within an informal setting. This informal organization can have dramatic impact on the efficiency and effectiveness of the police organization.

CHAPTER REVIEW

1. What is the distinction between rank and title?
2. What six factors will affect the span of management?
3. Distinguish between vertical and horizontal differentiation.
4. What are some of the more common ways in which activities and personnel are grouped within police organizations?
5. Discuss the differences between tall organizational structures and flat organizational structures.
6. List and discuss four basic types of structural designs within police departments.
7. Identify major organizational differences between sheriff's offices and municipal police departments.
8. What are the differences in the organizational structures of traditional policing and community policing?
9. Identify the basic causes of tension between line and staff.
10. Describe the characteristics of the informal organization.

KEY TERMS

city-county consolidated governments: a city and county that have merged into one unified jurisdiction, having the powers and responsibilities of both a municipal corporation (city) and the administrative division of a state (county).

decentralization: the process of distributing the administrative functions or powers of an organization among all levels of the structure.

functional structure: a modified line and staff structure that brings together trained specialists and specialized resources under a single manager to accomplish a core responsibility.

horizontal differentiation: an organizational design that is structured based on activity rather than rank.

informal organization: an unofficial structure within an organization, often based on personal relationships, that has its own goals, communications, and behavior patterns.

line structure: the oldest, simplest, and clearest form of organizational design; authority flows from the top to the bottom of the organization in a clear and unbroken line.

line and staff structure: an organizational structure that retains basic elements from line structure but adds auxiliary and administrative support units.

matrix (or grid) structure: an organizational design that assigns members of functional areas to specific projects, such as a task force.

organizing: the process of determining the formal structure of task and authority relationships best suited to accomplish a mission.

principle of hierarchy: a requirement that each lower level of the organization be supervised by a higher level.

sector policing: an innovative and proactive approach to structuring law enforcement crime-fighting strategies, personnel deployment, allocation of resources, and accountability to a geographical zone or area.

span of management: the number of personnel a supervisor can personally manage effectively.

specialization: a division of labor wherein specific jobs and tasks are allocated to meet different responsibilities with those specially qualified or trained to perform them.

structure: an organizational design that assigns members of functional areas to specific projects, such as a task force.

vertical differentiation: an organizational design based on levels of authority within an organization.

ENDNOTES

1 S. P. Robbins, *The Administration Process* (Englewood Cliffs, N.J.: Prentice Hall, 1976), pp. 17–18.
2 *The Republic of Plato,* trans. A. Bloom (New York: Basic Books, 1968), p. 47.
3 For example, see Luther Gulick and L. Urwick, eds., *Papers on the Science of Administration* (New York: August M. Kelley, a 1969 reprint of the 1937 edition).
4 O. W. Wilson and R. C. Mclaren, *Police Administration,* 3rd ed. (New York: Mcgraw-Hill, 1972), p. 79.
5 Ibid., p. 81.
6 Ibid., p. 83.
7 N. C. Kassoff, *Organizational Concepts* (Washington, D.C.: International Association of Chiefs of Police, 1967), p. 22.
8 Wilson and McLaren, *Police Administration,* p. 56.
9 Ibid.
10 Gary W. Cordner, "Community Policing: Elements and Effects," in Roger G. Dunham and Geoffrey P. Alpert, *Critical Issues in Policing,* 6th edition (Long Grove, IL: Waveland Press, 2010): pp. 432–449.
11 "City and County to Unify," The Kansas City Star (November 11, 2007), p. 1.

[12] Troy Lane, "Span of Control for Law Enforcement Agencies," *Police Chief Magazine,* 73, p. 10, October 2006. Retrieved from http://policechiefmagazine.org/magazine/index.cfm?fuseaction=print_display&article_id=1 (June 25, 2010).

[13] Troy Lane, "Span of Control for Law Enforcement Agencies," *Police Chief Magazine.*

[14] D. A. Tansik and J. F. Elliot, *Managing Police Organizations* (Monterey, Calif.: Duxbury Press, 1981), p. 81.

[15] Ibid.

[16] B. J. Hodge and W. P. Anthony, *Organizational Theory: An Environmental Approach* (Boston: Allyn and Bacon, 1979), p. 240.

[17] Richard Hall, *Organizations: Structure and Process* (Englewood Cliffs, N.J.: Prentice Hall, 1972), p. 143.

[18] This Section is a Synopsis of the "Nature and Process of Differentiation" found in Hodge and Anthony, *Organizational Theory,* p. 249.

[19] Ronald Wells, "Intelligence-Led Policing: A New Paradigm in Law Enforcement" *PATC Bulletin* (Indianapolis, IA: PATC Law Enforcement Training Council, September 2009).

[20] Darlton E. Mcfarland, *Management: Foundations and Practices,* 5th ed. (New York: Macmillan, 1979), p. 316.

[21] Ibid., p. 309.

[22] B. J. Hodge and H. J. Johnson, *Management and Organizational Behavior* (New York: John Wiley & Sons, 1970), p. 163.

[23] W. Michael Phibbs, "Should Sector Policing Be in Your Organization's Future?" *FBI Law Enforcement Bulletin* (April 2010), pp. 1–2, 7.

[24] Richard Kitaeff, "The Great Debate: Centralized vs. Decentralized Marketing Research Function," *Marketing Research: A Magazine of Management and Applications* 6 (Winter 1993), p. 59.

[25] Anaheim Police Department (Anaheim, Calif.), "Community Policing Team Annual Report," 1994.

[26] Several critiques of experimental police methods have been noted in the literature. See Robert W. Taylor and Dennis J. Kenney, "The Problems with Problem Oriented Policing" (paper presented at the Academy of Criminal Justice Sciences Annual Meeting, Nashville, Tennessee, March 1991); Kenneth W. Findley and Robert W. Taylor, "Re-Thinking Neighborhood Policing," *Journal of Contemporary Criminal Justice* 6 (May 1990), pp. 70–78; Jerome Skolnick and D. Bayley, *Community Policing: Issues and Practices around the World* (Washington, D.C.: National Institute of Justice, 1988); Jack Greene and Ralph Taylor, "Community Based Policing and Foot Patrol: Issues of Theory and Evaluation," in *Community Policing: Rhetoric or Reality?* eds. Jack Greene and Stephen Mastrofski (New York: Praeger, 1988), pp. 216–219; Stephen Mastrofski, "Police Agency Accreditation: The Prospects of Reform," *American Journal of Police* (May 15, 1986), pp. 45–81.

[27] Gary W. Cordner, "Written Rules and Regulations: Are They Necessary?" *FBI Law Enforcement Bulletin* 58 (July 1989), pp. 17–21.

[28] See Robert Michaels, *Political Parties* (New York: Dover, 1959).

[29] Jerry H. Ratcliffe, "Intelligence-Led Policing," in R. Worley, L. Mazerolle and S. Rombouts (eds.), *Environmental Criminology and Crime Analysis* (Portland, OR: Willan Publishing, 2008).

[30] Jerry H. Ratcliffe and Ray Guidetti, "State Police Investigative Structure and the Adoption of Intelligence-Led Policing," *Policing: An International Journal of Police Strategies and Management,* Volume 31, p. 1 (2008).

[31] Kassoff, *Organizational Concepts,* pp. 31–38.

[32] Ibid., pp. 22–26.

[33] Nathan F. Ianone and Marvin D. Ianone, *Supervision of Police Personnel,* 6th ed. (Upper Saddle River, N.J.: Prentice Hall, 2001), p. 1.

[34] Ibid.

[35] John M. Pfiffner and Frank P. Sherwood, *Administrative Organization* (Englewood Cliffs, N.J.: Prentice Hall, 1965), pp. 43–44.

7
Leadership

Leadership is not a
spectator sport.
— Kouzes and Posner

Objectives

- Define *leadership*.

- Make four distinctions between leaders and managers.

- Give five reasons why chiefs fail because of their own inadequacies.

- Contrast power and authority.

- Compare socialized and personalized power needs.

- Identify and describe the three components of the leadership skill mix.

- State two Great Man theories.

- Define the Big Five.

- Describe emotional and social intelligence.

- Give definitions of *emotional* and *social intelligence*.

- Distinguish among authoritarian, democratic, and laissez fair leadership.

- Define *organizational citizenship behavior* and *positive organizational behavior*.

- Describe Downs's four leader styles.

- Contrast station house sergeants and street sergeants.

- State three organizational forces from Tannenbaum and Schmidt's contingency theory.

- Identify and describe four of Fiedler's leader behaviors.

- Identify the core of leader member exchange theory (LMX).

- Define the essence of path-goal theory.

- Compare leadership substitutes and neutralizers.

- Contrast transactional theory and transformational theory.

- Identify four traits of charismatic leaders.

- Define *servant*, *spiritual*, *authentic*, and *ethical* leadership.

OUTLINE

Introduction

Knowledge of leadership is important because: (1) officers deserve serious and competent leadership; (2) leadership weakness can reduce unit effectiveness and be a precursor to conduct problems by officers due to a lack of corrective action; (3) leadership failures can result in civil liability problems (see Chapter 14, Legal Aspect of Police Administration); (4) personnel costs, including fringe benefits, may account for 90 or more percent of the police budget (see Chapter 12, Financial Management); (5) leadership style communicates what commanders think about the people they lead; (6) while some people might be "born leaders," everyone else has to learn about it and integrate that knowledge with their behavior in small steps; and (7) leadership mistakes can result in injuries and deaths to those who are led.

Police Leadership

Although effective leadership is desired within police departments and there is an abundance of training programs to help provide it, there is a curious lack of depth in the research on efficacious police leadership processes.[1] Schafer argues that much of what is known is from small cases studies, descriptive accounts, and anecdotal reports from "celebrity chiefs."[2] The police profession is a consumer of leadership theory. The theories relied upon are overwhelmingly developed by academics as general propositions and then researched almost entirely in non-police settings. When the theories are tested in police settings, the studies typically involve small sample sizes and are unreplicated. Evaluations conducted by police departments often consist of a single, cursory analysis lacking rigor and focusing only on the short-term impact.[3]

While many leadership concepts clearly work in law enforcement agencies, might police-generated theories gain faster acceptance, have greater "staying" power, and possibly be as good or better? Like other professions, policing is often "guilty" of chasing the "latest, greatest" approach; presently, transformational leadership leads the pack. An evidence-based approach may be crucial to the long-term development of a body of knowledge about law enforcement leadership. We're not floundering, but there is substantial room for improvement.

Our preoccupation with crime, homeland security, and the need to be seen as "current" by adopting each operational innovation that comes along has diverted attention from developing a passion about leadership excellence. Some of the barriers to such excellence include: (1) insufficient effort and funding are devoted to leadership development at every level of our departments although our chief resource is people (see Chapter 12, Financial Management); (2) the need for a greater number of strong leadership role models; the most potent way to change behavior is by modeling the desired behaviors; (3) the failure to identify potential leaders earlier in their careers; a modest start would be to give them small projects to showcase their abilities, staying out of their way as they grapple with their assignments, and giving them honest critiques; and (4) ineffective police leaders are seldom demoted nor are they thoughtfully retrained; we manage around their shortcomings or transfer them to minor duties for which they are often over ranked, wasting valuable resources and allowing the continuation of a poor role model.[4] It is a practice that is simultaneously humane and costly.

Developing police leadership is not a one-time investment; like the maintenance on police vehicles, it should be conceived of as a continuing expenditure. To help keep our eyes on the ball, the cost of leadership should not be aggregated under training. It must be a separate line in the budget supported by an abundance of individual staff development plans. If leadership is really dispersed in our departments, then it must find its reality in the commitment of dollars.

Implicitly, leadership is often thought of being positive—a good thing, uplifting and guiding toward some important accomplishment. That is the major thrust of this chapter, although the "dark side" of leadership is also covered.

Leader and Manager

There are many definitions of leadership, each reflecting certain perspectives, but all incorporate the notion that the essence of leadership is influencing others. For example, **leadership** can be simply defined as the difference between pushing a string and pulling it or being a "difference maker." More completely, leadership has external and internal components; it is the process of: (1) relating the police department to the larger environment, such as city council, the news media, civic organizations, and the general public and (2) influencing officers to use their energies willingly and appropriately to facilitate the achievement of the department's goals. Perhaps more so than any other local government department head, police chiefs become very public figures and they and their families lose a great deal of privacy.

Leadership occurs in dyads (e.g., a chief and an assistant chief); small face-to-face groups, such as a command staff meeting; at the entire police department level; and externally as a symbol of the department. Some argue that an individual officer can provide leadership to him- or herself by monitoring his or her own behavior, learning from mistakes that are not repeated, and ultimately leading to enhanced performance. This line of thinking seems thin: Leaders need one or more followers. However, in a different way, Anderson's *Every Officer Is a Leader* effectively argues that officers must lead business owners, neighborhood associations, planning and zoning employees, and others to make community policing work.[5] Those that the officers lead are outside of the department and not part of its hierarchical structure (see Figure 7.1).

The terms **leader** and **manager** are used imprecisely.[6] Occasionally, they are erroneously employed to mean the same thing and sometimes synonymously with *leadership* and *managing*. Alimo-Metcalfe and Alimo-Metcalfe argue that many models of leadership are better regarded as management styles; they maintain management is the content of a job and leadership is how it is carried out.[7] Others maintain that a person can be a leader, a manager, both, or neither[8] and the mix can vary over time and situation. Leader and manager can also be examined using three different lenses: (1) placement in hierarchy, (2) organizational theory, and (3) role enactment:

1. Leader and manager are different roles in an organization. We think of leaders as being clustered at the top of an organization and managers as being "farther down" with lesser authority and responsibility (see Figure 7.2). In this view, whether you are a leader or a manager depends on where you stand in the organization's hierarchy.

Figure 7.1
Community policing officers summarizing feedback from neighborhood meeting on flip charts.
(Bruce Montgomery)

Leaders	Managers
1. At or near the top	1. Occupy the middle ground between leaders and first line supervisors
2. Wide responsibility	2. Narrower responsibility
3. Work on a broad stage, both outside and within the organization	3. Primarily directed toward those in their units
4. Have both followers and subordinates	4. Have subordinates
5. Elevate how others do their jobs	5. Makes sure subordinates do their jobs
6. Envision the future, change oriented	6. Oriented toward shorter time frame, create agendas, maintain status quo
7. Think strategically	7. Think tactically

Figure 7.2
Leaders and managers by placement in hierarchy.
Source: By Swanson.

2. Drawing from organizational theory, Weber notes that in the bureaucracy model, each subordinate person and unit is under the command of a higher office. It is from this arrangement that an organizational chart can be drawn. At the top of the pyramid is a lone figure, the police chief. By custom, people refer to the occupant of that office not only as "Chief," but also as "The Leader." Can there be other leaders in a police department? How would we know whether the

commanders of various units on an organizational chart are leaders or managers? Arbitrarily, are those commanding line units "leaders," and staff commanders "managers"? Should job descriptions be scrutinized to see which ones specify "leads" versus "manages"? Other than identifying "The Leader," the bureaucratic model is not very illuminating on this issue.

3. Role enactment is the surest way of determining who is a leader and who is a manager. It is best revealed by how a person with authority over the performance of others behaves. For example, leaders unleash energy and creativity in a police department, by trusting and empowering others to do great things. Leaders know they do not have a lock on good ideas and create the environment in which they can be generated. Unleashing energy scares the hell out of managers; it's unpredictable and therefore "messy," difficult to control, and may turn out bad.

There is some convergence on the perspectives in Figure 7.2. Leaders must have a degree of bias toward the status quo; allowing too much change to occur simultaneously would result in confusion and low morale. Likewise, managers can serve on committees or be assigned responsibility for special studies, contributing to the overall direction of the department.

Of necessity, the challenge of leading and managing the activities of the department must be widely distributed.[9] Police departments, except for very small ones, cannot function without distributed authority. The extension of this reality is that "leaders" and "managers" both need leadership and management skills. Leadership and management skills are not mutually exclusive and are usually not co-equal. It is perhaps inevitable that subconsciously or through introspection, officers recognize the mix of aptitudes they have and gravitate toward assignments that are a good match for their skill set.

Police chiefs have multiple roles, such as preserving the trust and confidence of the public in the department, modeling and communicating values, envisioning the future, determining the operational philosophy, being a change agent and a budget gladiator, allocating resources, resolving conflicts, solving problems, recognizing and celebrating the achievements of officers (see Figure 7.3) and civilian staff, and being a spokesperson. In state police, state patrol, larger county and municipal departments, sheriffs and chiefs have the additional task of leading personnel at district stations/precincts "remotely."[10] These tough roles and other factors lead to an average tenure for police chiefs of about 2.5 to 4.5 years.[11]

Some of this turnover is due to chiefs deciding that leading police departments simply takes too much out of them and their families. The exiting chiefs had to deal with a witch's brew of fiscal constraints, escalating service demands, homeless encampments, political skirmishes, long hours, union conflicts, domestic violence by police officers, achieving diversity, monitoring racial profiling, the escalation in human trafficking, being named in lawsuits, illegal immigrants, drugs, and violent gangs. To this list New Jersey State Police Superintendent Rick Fuentes adds that in the post-9/11 environment there has been a blurring of hometown and homeland security.[12]

Figure 7.3
*Recognition of the achievements of personnel is essential. At this awards
ceremony a deputy sheriff is honored.*
(o44/ZUMA Press/Newscom)

The multiple roles and tough problems also affect recruiting to fill vacant
chiefs jobs; in some areas of the country there are roughly 50 percent fewer candidates seeking them.[13]

Police leaders resign or are terminated for reasons beyond their control. Some of
these dismissals are unfair because of a politically based, almost compulsive, need to
have somebody to blame. Former Los Angeles Police Chief Bill Bratton believes that
if you are going to mobilize support, you must innovate, and that involves taking risks.
In Bratton's view, that means setting goals that can be measured, which is both a
necessity[14] and some chiefs' undoing.

Leaders also fail because of their own inadequacies.[15] They are unwilling to step
in and resolve problems and conflicts, leaving festering wounds. They develop a
personality defect that alienates subordinates; make personal use of property seized as
evidence; have affairs with subordinates; or become aloof and remote, reducing the
communications sent to them, which chokes off their effectiveness. Their drinking
gets out of control; they irritate their subordinates by micromanaging; and their
maladaptive leadership styles lead to short tenures (e.g., "seagull chiefs" who don't give
guidance on the front end swoop in and poop on everyone when a problem arises, and
fly away without providing any solutions).[16]

Leaders also fail because they are toxic. They pit followers against each other, lie
to subordinates, undermine anyone who is seen as a threat, take credit for the ideas and

Police Leadership Makes a Difference

Police leadership doesn't just mean occupying a position; reduced to its simplest, it means being a "difference maker." The example that follows reveals how leaders can focus on one or more programs to make a positive impact.

In 2010, the Baldwinsville, New York, Police Department (BPD) won its tenth award in 10 years from the American Automobile Association's (AAA) Community Traffic Safety Program. The BPD has won two silver, five gold, and three platinum awards. Baldwinsville has not had a pedestrian fatality in the past 30 years.

accomplishments of others, create an image that they are defending the department from outside forces to distract followers, stifle constructive criticism, and make others scapegoats for their own failures.[17] They lack integrity, are incapable of introspection, are blind to their own shortcomings, shrink from hard decisions, and have a reckless disregard of how their actions effect others.[18] In the end, they are found out and lose their jobs, but they leave a legacy that the incoming chief must work hard to overcome (e.g., regaining the trust of the rank-and-file).

Leadership success depends on exhibiting positive leadership behaviors and avoiding a catastrophic error.[19] In the case of "Chief Herbert," a single statement produced a self-inflicted and fatal wound. Herbert led a 38-officer department. A popular chief, he was asked to meet in closed session with the mayor and city council to discuss a raise for the police department. Council members initiated the meeting because they wanted to do something extra for the officers. They proposed a 10 percent increase, to which Herbert, for reasons he couldn't later articulate, replied the officers would be well pleased with 6 percent, which is what they got. One council member felt Herbert had sold out the welfare of officers' families to curry favor with the council. The story was leaked to the newspaper and officers raged at "the betrayal." Officers began making secretive end runs around Herbert to some members of council, giving them inside information on the department. The council gradually sharpened its questioning of Herbert's decisions. As the Fall election drew closer, two candidates for council made "things in the police department" a campaign issue. The rank-and-file waited until the tide was turning against Herbert before giving him a no-confidence vote. Faced with strong internal opposition and dwindling political support, Herbert retired. The moral of the story is that one way or another, the presence or absence of effective police leadership will reveal itself. The following case studies further illustrate this point:

- Police officers, operating a dirty patrol vehicle, approached a motorist they had stopped for a traffic violation. The officers' interaction with the driver was superficially correct, but had a definite underlying tone of arrogance.
- The chief of police of a medium-size city chronically complained to anyone who would listen that his commanders "aren't worth anything" and that he was "carrying the whole department on his back."

- A visitor to a city approached an officer walking a beat and asked where the nearest car rental agency could be found; he replied, "What the hell do I look like, an information booth?" and walked away.
- A woman asked an officer standing on a street corner where the First National Bank Building was. The officer took the woman's arm, escorted her across the street, and said, "Lady, you see that big building on the corner where we were just standing? Well, if it had fallen, we'd have both been killed by First National."
- Based on limited new information, the commander of an investigations bureau reopened the case file on a convicted "no-good" who had already served 14 months for the offense in question. Subsequently, new evidence and a confession resulted in his release and the conviction of another person.

Leadership, Authority, and Power

Weber identified three sources of **authority**: (1) charismatic, resting on the exceptional heroism, exemplary character, or sanctity of a person, such as Medal of Honor recipients, August Vollmer, and the Pope; (2) traditional authority, illustrated by kings and queens; and (3) rational-legal, a grant of authority made by the formal organization to a position, the incumbent of which wields it in fulfilling his or her responsibilities (e.g., a chief of police).[20] French and Raven concluded there were five types of power: (1) legitimate, the belief that someone has the right to make demands on how you do your job, (2) expert, derived from a person's expertise and skill, (3) reward, the ability to compensate others for their compliance, (4) coercive, the expectation that you will be disciplined for your failure to conform to legitimate expectations, and (5) referent, to become liked or respected to such a degree that subordinates willingly follow orders.[21] Whatever the source of a leader's authority, power is a separate concept.

The fact that a formal grant of authority has been made does not mean that the person receiving it is also automatically able to influence others to perform at all, let alone willingly:

> Officer Murphy was among 50 officers to be promoted by the New York City Police Commissioner. Instead of accepting a handshake and his gold detective's shield, Officer Murphy placed it on the dais, and walked out of the ceremony. Officer Murphy took this action to protest the department's investigation of allegations that his unit—the Brooklyn Narcotics Tactical Team—had mistreated prisoners and lied about evidence to shore up shaky arrests. Officer Murphy was not believed to be a target of this investigation. A ranking police official with 40 years of service said he had never seen anything like Murphy's actions before.[22]

This incident illustrates that, while the commissioner had the authority to promote Officer Murphy, he did not have the power to make him accept it. Some power to affect an officer's performance is inherent in positions of formal authority. But to a significant degree, power, as suggested by Barnard, is a grant made by the led to the leader.[23] A police leader whose subordinates refuse to follow orders is not without power; subordinate officers may be given verbal or written reprimands, reassigned, suspended, or terminated.[24] The use of this type of power must be considered carefully; failure to invoke it may contribute to a breakdown in discipline and organizational performance; the clumsy use of it may contribute to morale problems or have other negative side effects, including calling into question the abilities of the leader:

> A uniformed officer riding alone informed the radio dispatcher that he was stopping a motorist who may have been drinking. His sergeant, who had only been promoted and assigned to the squad two weeks previously, heard the transmission and came to the scene as a backup.
>
> When the sergeant, a 9-year veteran, but who had not served in any "street" assignment for the past 6 years, arrived, a Marine corporal had just gotten into a taxicab. The Sergeant talked briefly with the corporal and walked back to the officer. Unseen, the cab eased away. When questioned, the officer told the Sergeant that while the Marine had a few drinks, he was not impaired. The Sergeant accused him of dereliction of duty for not charging a "fellow Marine" with DUI.
>
> The officer received a mild letter of reprimand; the "slap on the wrist" was widely viewed as the platoon commander reluctantly supporting a green sergeant. The squad saw the sergeant as a "water cooler commando" and didn't trust him. Another misstep several months later resulted in the sergeant being transferred to a minor staff position, where he oversaw several functions, but supervised nobody.

Leadership also arises, as demonstrated by the Hawthorne Studies, out of the informal side of an organization. In police departments, officers "give" power to more-seasoned or decorated colleagues, listening carefully to their opinions and suggestions. In some cases, informal leaders take exception to new policies and procedures and have the potential to be disruptive to a unit's harmony. A related problem is when younger officers make sergeant, passing less-test-savvy veteran officers. Dismissing them as "test takers," the more experienced officers may quietly "compete" with the new supervisor to influence the attitudes and actions of the unit. If, however, informal leaders support the police department's goals, they can be a significant additive and even help compensate for mediocre formal leadership.

The Power Motivation of Police Leaders

Power is an indispensable dimension of police departments; it requires that a person have a desire to play a key role in influencing the outcome of activities. Richmond, California, Police Chief Chris Magnus says about power, "I think being a chief is very seductive in terms of power and influence. It's hard not to get caught up in this racket. You sort of lose focus."[25]

As we have seen, power is both a grant from the formal organization to a position, as well as a grant from the led to the leader. Power, however, is not always used for the same purpose; the term "**power motivation**" refers to the reasons, intentions, and objectives that underlie the use of power.[26]

McClelland and his associates studied the motivations of leaders extensively and concluded there were three types of power: (1) a high achievement or a **socialized power**

Police Leaders with Personalized Power Tend to Be	Police Leaders with Socialized Power Tend to Be
• Impulsive and erratic in their use of power	• Inhibited and self-controlled in their use of power
• Rude and overbearing	• Respectful of others' rights
• Exploitative of others	• Concerned with fairness
• Oriented toward strength	• Oriented toward justice
• Committed to the value of efficiency	• Committed to the value of working per se
• Proud	• Egalitarian
• Self-reliant; individualists	• Organization-minded; joiners
• Excited by the certitudes of power	• Ambivalent about power
• Competitive	• Collaborative
• Concerned with exceptionally high goals	• Concerned with realistic goals
• Defensive—protective of own sense of importance	• Non-defensive—willing to seek help
• Inspirational leaders	• Builders of systems and people
• Difficult to replace—leaves behind a group of officers who were dependent on the leader; does little to develop officers	• Replaceable by other managers—leave a system intact and self-sustaining
• Sources of direction, expertise, and control	• Sources of strength for others

Figure 7.4
Personalized and socialized power needs.

motivation—the need to have a positive impact on a police department's administration and operations; (2) a high power or **personalized power needs**—the need to be in control for selfish, self-aggrandizing reasons (see Figure 7.4); and (3) **affiliation needs**—the desire to be liked and accepted. Affiliation needs and aspirations are not true power needs because they reflect a greater preoccupation with being accepted and liked than with having an impact on events. Affiliation needs can mediate some degree of personalized power needs. The contexts for these motivations may also be important; there is limited evidence that in conflict situations, socialized power leaders may make better decisions than those with personalized power needs.[27]

The difference between personalized power and socialized power has practical implications. A police leader with personalized power needs will tend toward being authoritarian, making most decisions and tightly controlling work. An authoritarian chief believes officers will not work without close supervision. This style of leadership ultimately leads to problems because the lack of trust becomes apparent, officers chafe at the tight control, morale suffers, and departmental performance declines, often accompanied by a spike in turnover by officers seeking a better work environment. A study of the department may be called for and the report used as the basis for firing the chief.

In contrast, a chief with socialized power needs can more readily adapt to emerging leadership styles. In Broken Arrow, Oklahoma, the department moved to a participative leadership philosophy, empowering employees. A several-year study of the police department showed that arrests and case clearances were up, citizen complaints were down, and other performance measures were also favorable.[28] Leadership styles are discussed in greater length later in this chapter.

The Leadership Skill Mix

Skill is how knowledge is translated into action. As depicted in Figure 7.5, a police department can be divided into three levels with various mixes of three broad categories of skills associated with them.[29] The ranks indicated at each of the three levels of the organization identified in the figure are illustrative only and will vary depending on departmental size and other factors. Additionally, in the discussion of these skills that follows, it is possible to include only a few of the many examples available.[30]

Human Relations Skills

Human relations skills involve the capacity to interrelate positively with other people and are used at all levels of a police department (see Figure 7.6). Examples include motivation, conflict resolution, and interpersonal communication skills. The single, most important human relations skill is communication; without it, nothing can be set in motion, and programs underway cannot be guided.

As one progresses up the rank hierarchy of a police department, he or she typically becomes responsible for more people but has fewer people reporting directly to him or her. The human relations skills of a police department's top managers remain

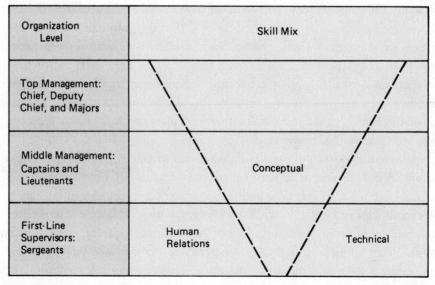

Figure 7.5
The leadership skill mix.

important, however, as they are used to win political support for the agency's programs and to obtain the resources necessary to operate them. In particular, the chief's human relations skills are critical, as this person is the department's key representative to the larger environment. The way in which he or she "comes across" is, to a certain degree, the way in which some significant others—such as the city manager and members of city council—will regard the police department. The question of the fairness of that fact aside, the practical implication is that the chief must be aware of and fulfill the symbolic leadership role.

Figure 7.6
Washington, DC Police Chief Cathy Lanier at a press conference. In part, her reputation as a strong communicator was a factor in her selection.
(Paul J. Richards/AFP/ Getty Images)

Within the department, top management must communicate its goals and policies downward and be willing to receive feedback about them. As mid-level managers, lieutenants and captains play an important linking function, passing downward in implementable forms the communications they receive from top management and passing upward certain communications received from first-line supervisors. Because sergeants ordinarily supervise directly the greatest number of people, they use human relations with great frequency, often focusing on such issues as resolving interpersonal problems, communicating the department's vision, and providing guidance.

Conceptual Skills

Conceptual skills include the ability to understand and to interrelate various parcels of information that seem unrelated, or those for which the meaning or importance is not immediately apparent. Although this skill is used at all levels of the police department, the standards for handling the information become less certain and the level of abstraction necessary to handle the parcels becomes greater as one moves upward. Illustrative is the difference between a sergeant helping a detective evaluate the legal significance of evidence and a chief envisioning a future for the department and how to create and maintain a culture that will support the innovations being considered.

IN THE NEWS   Chief with People Skills Wanted

A Wisconsin police chief who had clearly done some great things for his community stepped down to be a consultant with the city for the next year. This followed complaints not about what he did, but allegations about how he went about it. Among the characterizations made were "rude," "unprofessional," "arrogant," "condescending," and "lack of civility." An outsider, he followed a 30-year chief and started making changes. The chief's attorney described the situation as an attempt by a small number of people to get rid of the chief.

Source: Editorial: "Wanted Police Chief with People Skills," *The Dunn County* (Wisconsin) *News*, February 2, 2010.

Technical Skills

Technical skills vary by level within a police department. Uniformed sergeants assigned to field duties must be able to help develop and maintain the skills of subordinates in such areas as handling domestic violence calls. As one progresses upward toward middle and top management, the range of technical skills narrows and conceptual skills come to predominate. In that upward progression, the character of the technical skills also changes from being operations-oriented to management-oriented and gradually includes new elements, such as budgeting, planning, and the kind of decision making that increasingly requires the use of conceptual skills. To elaborate further, one may not be able to tell by the generic label whether a particular skill is, for example, technical or conceptual. A general understanding of the many aspects of financial management (see Chapter 12, Financial Management) is a conceptual skill, but the actual preparation of the budget is a technical skill required of middle managers and those more senior.

Factors both inside and outside of a police department will impact on the skills that are most important at any particular time. A survey of the 20 best run companies in America revealed that in 2009, the most important leadership skill was execution; in 2010 it shifted to strategic thinking—envisioning the future of the enterprise in a fiscally constrained, uncertain, and highly competitive environment.[31] Top 20 companies consistently invest more and work harder at developing and retaining their leaders.

Theories of Leadership

Theories of leadership attempt to explain the factors associated with the emergence of leadership or the nature of leadership. This chapter examines leadership under the following headings: (1) traditional leadership theory, (2) behavior and leadership styles theory, (3) contingency and situational theory, (4) transactional and transformational theories, (5) comparison of charismatic and transformational leadership, and (6) the "new leadership": servant, spiritual, authentic, and ethical.

Traditional Leadership Theory

There are two branches to traditional leadership theory: (1) great man and (2) the traits approach.

Great Man Theories

"Great man" theories were advanced by Thomas Carlyle (1795–1881) and George Hegel (1770–1831).[32] Carlyle (see Figure 7.7) believed that leaders were unusually gifted individuals who made history. He may not have been entirely wrong—there is preliminary evidence that approximately

Figure 7.7
Thomas Carlyle: unusually gifted people make history.
(Library of Congress Prints and Photographs Division)

30 percent of the variation in leadership styles is accounted for by heredity, the balance being environmental influences, including leadership development opportunities and roles.[33] Reversing the direction of causality, Hegel argued that it was events that produced the "great man." The "born leader" concept is associated with Francis Galton (1822–1911), who espoused that leaders were the product of genetics,[34] transmitted from one generation to the next one.

If Galton is correct—that leaders are born—then police departments are wasting money on leadership development (see Figure 7.8) programs such as Leadership in Police Organizations (LPO) which was adapted from the West Point Military Academy's curriculum.

The Traits Approach

The traits approach is a natural extension of great man theory. **Traits** are relatively stable predispositions to behave in certain ways; examples include being energetic, emotionally stable, and extroverted.[35] Field Marshal Montgomery, one of England's great World War II commanders,[36] believed that leaders were made, not born; however, they had certain traits, such as an infectious optimism, confidence, intellect, and the ability to be a good judge of character.

Beginning around 1910 and continuing through the 1950s, research on traits dominated the thinking about leadership. The research was so substantial that Allport and Odbert (1936),[37] Stogdill (1948),[38] and Goode (1951)[39] attempted to consolidate

FBI
- National Academy (NA): improve administration of agencies, nomination process, by invitation
- National Executive Institute (NEI): agency head of 500 or more sworn
- Law Enforcement Executive Development Seminar (LEEDS): mid-sized agency head
- Regional Command Colleges: 22 nationally, agency head, second in command, fewer than 25 officers

Federal Law Enforcement Training Center (FLETC): Law Enforcement Leadership Institute (LELI): Seminars

Harvard University National Preparedness Leadership Initiative (NPLI): increase leaders who can optimally deal with homeland security preparedness and response activities

International Association of Chiefs of Police, Center for Police Leadership: early proponent of Leadership in Police Organizations (LPO), based on the West Point Leadership Program (WPLP) and adapted for the needs of law enforcement. Core concept: leadership is distributed in a police department and qualities of leadership are expected from all officers. Illustrative users include the Delaware and New Mexico State Police, the Los Angeles and Tulsa Police Departments, and the Minnesota State Patrol and Bureau of Criminal Apprehension.

National Highway Transportation Safety Administration/National Sheriff's Association (NHSTA/NSA) Leadership Program: develop leaders for state of the art highway safety initiatives

University of Louisville, Southern Police Institute, Administrative Officers Course: develop informed, effective, ethically and technically competent police managers

Figure 7.8
Police leadership training program.

Big Five Personality Traits	Specific Traits
Surgency	Extroversion/Outgoing Energy/Activity level Need for power/Assertive
Conscientiousness	Dependability Personal integrity Need for achievement
Agreeableness	Cheerful/Optimistic Nurturing/Sympathetic/Helpful Need for affiliation
Adjustment	Emotional stability Self-esteem Self-control
Intellectance	Curious/Inquisitive Open-minded Learning oriented

Figure 7.9
The correspondence between the "Big Five" and specific traits.
Source: Courtesy of Gary Yukl, *Leadership in Organizations*, Upper Saddle River, NJ: Prentice Hall, 7th Edition, 2010.

hundreds of studies and still ended up with lengthy lists of traits. The earlier traits research suffered from several deficiencies: (1) traits like loyalty, diligence, and perseverance were difficult to define and hard to measure; (2) some traits aren't portable from one setting to another; (3) traits are variable in their importance; and (4) situational factors can diminish the importance of traits or cause others to be needed (e.g., creating a police department for a newly incorporated city).

The traits approach was re-energized beginning in the 1970s as new methodological and statistical techniques were developed and older ones improved. Meta-analysis, first used in 1904 and since greatly enhanced, allows the results from many comparable studies to be analyzed; its use led to the "Big Five" model of traits. The **Big Five** is the result of efforts to find a small number of broad trait categories into which many specific traits can be fitted (see Figure 7.9); it continues to be an important classification system for traits research.[40] In 2010, Erdle and colleagues confirmed the existence of a **Big Two** within the Big Five: (1) stability, consisting of emotional stability, agreeableness, and conscientiousness and (2) plasticity, comprised of extraversion and being open minded.[41]

Zaccaro, after examining research findings, concluded there is mounting evidence that some traits are "precursors" of leadership effectiveness.[42] Emotional intelligence (EI) and social intelligence (SI) appear to be among them. EI and SI have been examined both as single traits and combined. Bar-On used a combined Emotional Social Intelligence (ESI) measure to help the Air Force identify potential recruiters who could be high performers (i.e., consistently get 100 percent of their expected recruits). The use of ESI data resulted in nearly a 300 percent increase in selecting high-performance recruiters.[43]

EI is positively associated with the quality of peer relationships,[44] may account for a lack of progress among intelligent people in psychotherapy,[45] and helps manage stress.

Units with higher levels of EI experience less task and relationship conflict, and when it occurs, it is less intense.[46] A study of EI in Nigerian police officers in 2008 revealed that it was not related to gender, marital status, length of service, or age.[47] In an earlier study, Barbera et. al. (2002) found evidence to the contrary, suggesting the emotional and social intelligence may develop over time.[48] In 2010, Bar-On called for more research into emotional intelligence, particularly with respect to a sense of well-being; happiness; raising and educating well-adjusted, productive, healthy children; and the search for a more meaningful life.[49] Ultimately, researchers may find that the amounts of EI and SI are less important than what combinations of them are related to effective leadership.

Riggio and Reichard (2008) concluded that another way to approach EI and SI was through the skills related to them. They developed a taxonomy—a classification system—for **emotional skills (ES)** and **social skills (SS)**[50] (see Figure 7.10). Riggio and Reichard defined ES as the ability to accurately perceive and appraise your own

Skill	Example	Purpose
EI Skills		
Emotional Expressiveness	Chief communicates nonverbally, e.g., command presence, selection of seat at table, facial expression, posture, or gesture	Communicates place in hierarchy; approval and disapproval to subordinate commanders
Emotional Sensitivity	Chief receives and accurately interprets non-verbal (e.g., body language) expressions of members of command staff	Gains understanding of others needs and emotional states, enhances ability to establish rapport
Emotional Control	Chief controls the display of his/her emotions	Eliminates the immediate display of anger or other strong emotional responses, requires a high degree of self-monitoring. A self-indulgent display of anger may impair relationships and impede goal achievement. A premeditated display may be useful in reinforcing the Chief's priorities, policies, and programs.
SI Skills		
Social Expressiveness	Chief has command of language, evoking powerful images through well-crafted articulation	Increases Chief's effectiveness within the department, at external meetings, and before audiences, enhances performance as mentor and coach
Social Sensitivity	Chief accurately interprets verbal communications from others and monitors social situation	Chief tailors comments and interaction to the conversation or situation at hand, is "smooth"
Social Control	Chief manages how he/she presents him/herself to others; is tactful, but doing so doesn't reduce impact of message; conveys ability to "get things done"	Represents him/herself and department well, creates new opportunities, and responses to criticisms are seen as reasonable, thoughtful

Figure 7.10
Emotional and social skills.
Source: Adapted with restatement into a police framework and some re-organization from Ronald E. Riggio and Rebecca J. Reichard, "The Emotional and Social Intelligences of Effective Leadership," *Journal of Managerial Psychology*, Vol. 23, No. 2, 2008, p. 172, Table 1.

emotions and those of others, to regulate your own emotions, and to do so while adapting and responding to the needs of others.[51] Social skills are closely related to emotional skills and are defined as the ability to express one's self in social situations; the ability to "read" social situations, recognizing different social roles and expected behavior; and interpersonal problem solving.[52]

ES and SS are associated with being: (1) more favorably viewed in social situations, (2) more confident, (3) a better public speaker, (4) more physically attractive, (5) more upwardly mobile in one's career, (6) seen as more effective by followers, and (7) savoir-faire, or seemingly able to know just what to do.[53]

Police officers have also weighed in on leadership traits. While they have some preference for leaders with greater field experience, the characteristics they most prefer in command, middle managers, and first-line supervisors are honesty, dependability, competency, and being broad minded.[54]

Organizational citizenship behavior (OCB) is comprised of subtle things that employees do voluntarily and are not required or expected but contribute to overall organizational effectiveness.[55] Examples include police officers officially at the end of their tour of duty volunteering to back up a unit on a traffic stop or giving words of encouragement or suggestions to another detective who is working a tough, high-profile case. Several studies have found that overall, the Big Five personality traits are positively associated with OCB. Although OCB continues to be researched as a separate topic, by 2008, researchers were increasingly interested in a broader concept, **positive organizational behavior (POB)**. In at least some studies, POB included OCB as a component factor. Presently, POB lacks anything approaching a consensus definition, but it has the potential to do for current leadership interests what the Big Five did for traits research.

Counterproductive work behavior (CWB) also commands research interest. CWB is behavior that has a detrimental effect on relationships with other commanders and officers and/or on the efficiency of operations.[56] Examples include being verbally aggressive or rude to coworkers, emotional outbursts, engaging in anger-producing behavior, refusing to help a coworker, using demeaning language, and maintaining interpersonal conflicts with others.[57] No studies of OCB or CWB are known to have been conducted in a police setting.

Even if chiefs have all of the important traits, their efforts may amount to nothing. "Willow City," with 102 nonunionized officers, hired its first outside chief since the department was founded in 1838. Although the chief had a strong task orientation, his relational skills were also excellent. He had impeccable education and training credentials and, on the basis of having led his former department to accreditation by the Commission on Accreditation of Law Enforcement Agencies (CALEA), Willow City hired him with the understanding he would do likewise with its department. However, the chief only lasted 13 months. His staff dragged their heels on assignments and otherwise thwarted the chief's efforts. Rank-and-file officers were irrational in their opposition to the chief. For example, one officer told another something the chief had allegedly done. The second officer replied that he knew the chief didn't do it, "but would've if he thought he could get away with it." Even when "innocent," the chief was "guilty." The uncooperative staff, rank-and-file carping, and lack of political support became powerful **leadership neutralizers**,[58] negating the chief's efforts. Recognizing he had been rendered ineffectual, the chief resigned; his outstanding background produced nothing because he lacked the most essential trait: being an insider. The assistant chief was promoted to replace him and the department relaxed, although it never became accredited because the process was too deeply associated with the outsider.

Behavior and Leadership Style Theories

Whereas trait theories attempt to explain leadership on the basis of what the leader is, behavioral theories try to do the same thing by concentrating on what the leader does.[59] These behaviors are often described in terms of leadership styles, meaning the continuing patterns of behavior as perceived and experienced by others that they use to characterize the leader. The behavior and leadership style theories were the main focus of researchers during the 1950s and 1960s.

Lewin, Lippitt, and White: Authoritarian, Democratic, and Laissez-Faire

Although the three leadership styles these researchers studied had been previously identified, it was their 1939 study that systematized thinking about them.[60] The **authoritarian/autocratic leader** ("My way or the highway") makes all decisions, closely controls work, and is a micromanager; the **democratic leader** ("Let's talk about it") encourages individual or group participation in matters affecting the organization; and the **laissez-faire leader** (LFL) ("Whatever") takes a passive, "hands-off" posture. Only reluctantly do LFLs use the authority of their position; they do not make necessary decisions and delay taking any kind of action, allowing subordinates substantial autonomy.[61] LFLs provide only episodic leadership and that may be ineffectual. The larger the stakes, the more invisible LFLs become.

Lewin, Lippitt, and White concluded that although the quantity of work was somewhat greater under the autocratic leader, autocracy could generate hostility and aggression. The democratically controlled groups were about as efficient as the autocratically controlled ones, but the continuation of work in the former did not depend on the presence of the leader. Under the laissez-faire leader, less work was produced, the work quality was poorer, and the work was less organized and less satisfying to members of the group.[62] In 2002, a study of leader styles and follower attitudes in a mid-sized New England police agency confirmed the much earlier findings of Lewin, Lippitt, and White.[63]

Likert: Management Systems

In *New Patterns of Management* (1961) and *The Human Organization* (1967), Rensis Likert (1903–1981) echoed and extended Lewin, Lippitt, and White's work by specifying four different management systems (see Figure 7.11) The names of these systems are also used to describe leadership styles and, for that reason, Likert's work is included in this section. Likert believed most people worked in a System 2 organization.

Organizational Variable	System 1	System 2	System 3	System 4
Leadership Processes Used				
Extent to which superiors have confidence and trust in subordinates	Have no confidence and trust in subordinates	Have condescending confidence and trust, such as master has to servant	Substantial but not complete confidence and trust; still wishes to keep control of decisions	Complete confidence and trust in all matters
Extent to which superiors behave so that subordinates feel free to discuss important things about their jobs with their immediate superior	Subordinates do not feel at all free to discuss things about the job with their superior	Subordinates do not feel very free to discuss things about the job with their superior	Subordinates feel rather free to discuss things about the job with their superior	Subordinates feel completely free to discuss things about the job with their superior
Extent to which immediate superior in solving job problems generally tries to get subordinates' ideas and opinions and make constructive use of them	Seldom gets ideas and opinions of subordinates in solving job problems	Sometimes gets ideas and opinions of subordinates in solving job problems	Usually gets ideas and opinions and usually tries to make constructive use of them	Always gets ideas and opinions and always tries to make constructive use of them

Figure 7.11
Likert's management systems.
Source: The Human Organization by Rensis Likert. Copyright © 1967 McGraw-Hill Book Company. Used with permission of McGraw-Hill Book Company.

Swanson and Talarico surveyed 629 officers in 18 different-sized local law enforcement agencies to determine what kind of management system their departments had. Their results provided confirmation for Likert. Some 16.9 percent worked in a System 1 (Exploitive Authoritarian); 42.9 percent in a System 2 (Benevolent Authoritarian); 35.9 percent in a System 3 (Consultative); and a mere 4.6 percent in a System 4 (Participative Group). This unreplicated study is older and new research would be virtually certain to document a shift away from Systems 1 and 2, toward Systems 3 and 4. City councils, mayors, and city managers require better leadership by their chiefs, and the rank-and-file is less likely to tolerate the System 1 and 2 authoritarian approaches.

Authoritarian/autocratic police leaders have mostly gone the way of the dinosaurs. The demise of the authoritarians is due to the world around them changing, becoming more liberal, as well as the perspectives and experiences associated with each new generation of workers entering law enforcement agencies. The characterization of these generations and their attributes vary somewhat in the research literature and are discussed in Chapter 9, Human Resource Management.

Blake and Mouton: The Managerial Grid

Developed by Robert Blake and Jane Mouton,[64] the **Managerial Grid** has received a great deal of attention since its appearance in 1962 in the *Journal of the American Society of Training Directors*. The grid is part of the survey research feedback stem of organizational development and draws on earlier work done at Ohio State University and the University of Michigan.[65]

Depicted in Figure 7.12, the grid has two dimensions: concern for production and concern for people. Each axis, or dimension, is numbered from 1, meaning low concern, to 9, indicating high concern. The way in which a person combines these two dimensions establishes a leadership style in terms of one of the five principal styles identified on the grid. The numbers associated with each of the styles reflect the level of concern for each of the two dimensions of the grid. For example, 9,1 indicates a maximum concern for production or the needs of the organization and a minimum orientation toward the needs of people in the organization.

Some of the leadership styles identified previously can be related readily to the grid. Authoritarian leaders are represented by the 9,1 style; laissez-faire leaders by the 1,1; and democratic leaders by the 5,5. Additionally, the 9,1 and 9,9 styles are consistent, respectively, with the streams of thought summarized in Chapter 5 under the headings of "Traditional Organizational Theory" and "Open Systems Theory."

The leadership style of an individual can be identified by using a questionnaire based on the work of Blake and Mouton. According to the grid, one moves from the

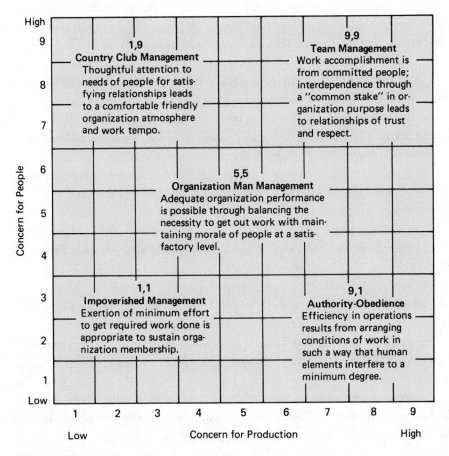

Figure 7.12
The Managerial Grid.

"best" to the "worst" styles as one moves from 9,9 through 5,5; 9,1; 1,9; and 1,1. The most desirable combination of a primary and backup style is the 9,9 with a 5,5 backup.

A difficulty in using the grid questionnaire is that the data produced are no more accurate than the self-perceptions of the person completing the instrument. When consulting with law enforcement agencies, one way to overcome this is to have each commander complete the instrument and then have each of his or her subordinates fill one out on how they experience the commander. Comparing these two sets of data provides useful information. Typically, more weight is given to the subordinate's combined data because they reflect how the leader is "coming across."

Downs: Leadership Styles in Bureaucratic Structures

Downs[66] described four types of leader behavior in bureaucratic structures: (1) climbers, (2) conservers, (3) zealots, and (4) advocates.

Climbers are strongly motivated by power and prestige needs to invent new functions to be performed by their unit, particularly functions not performed elsewhere. If climbers can expand their functions only by moving into areas already controlled by others, they are likely to choose ones in which they expect low resistance. To protect their "turf," climbers tend to economize only when the resultant savings can be used to finance an expansion of their functions.[67] An example of a climber is a newly promoted major commanding the Patrol Division who argues that the Traffic Division should be "folded" into the Patrol Division.

The bias of **conservers** is toward maintaining things as they are. The longer a person is in the same job and the older one becomes, the lower one assesses any chances for advancement and the stronger one becomes attached to job security, all of which are associated with the tendency to become a conserver. Climbers can become conservers when they assess their probability for advancement and expansion to be low. Desiring to make their organizational lives comfortable, conservers dislike and resist change.[68] A captain with 19 years of service and no promotions in the last seven years would tend to be a conserver.

The peculiarities of the behavior of **zealots** stem from two sources: their narrow interest and the missionary-like energy, which they focus almost solely on their special interest. As a consequence, zealots do not attend to all of their duties and often antagonize other administrators by their lack of impartiality and their willingness to trample over all obstacles to further their special interest. Zealots rarely succeed to high-level positions because of their narrowness and are consequently poor administrators. An exception is when their interest comes into favor and they are catapulted into high office.[69] Some Commanders of Special Weapons and Tactics (SWAT) Units fall into this category.

Unlike zealots, **advocates** promote everything under their jurisdiction. To those outside their units, they appear highly partisan, but within their units they are impartial and fair, developing well-rounded programs. Loyal to their organizations, advocates favor innovation. They are also simultaneously more radical and more conservative than climbers. They are more radical in that they are willing to promote programs and views that may antagonize politicians, superiors, and other powerful groups, such as the news media, if doing so helps their departments. They are more conservative because they are willing to oppose changes from which they might benefit but which would not be in the overall interest of their agencies.[70] Advocates may spring up anywhere in a police agency, confident and focused, they are sometimes unaware of how others see them or simply don't care.

Van Maanen: Station House Sergeants and Street Sergeants

In a study of a 1,000-officer police department, Van Maanen[71] identified two contrasting types of police sergeants: "station house" and "street." **Station house sergeants** had been out of the "bag" (uniform) before their promotions to sergeant and preferred to work in an office environment once they won their stripes; this preference was clearly indicated by the nickname of "Edwards, the Olympic Torch who never goes out" given to one such sergeant. Station house sergeants immersed themselves in the management culture of the police department, keeping busy with paperwork, planning, record keeping, press relations, and fine points of law. Their strong orientation to conformity also gave rise to nicknames as suggested by the use of "by-the-book Brubaker."

In contrast, **street sergeants** (see Figure 7.13) were serving in the field when they received their promotions. Consequently, they had a distaste for office procedures and had a strong action orientation, as suggested by such nicknames as "Shooter McGee" and "Walker the Stalker." Moreover, their concern was not with conformity but with "not letting the assholes take over the city."

In addition to the distinct differences already noted, station house sergeants and street sergeants were thought of differently by those whom they supervised: station house sergeants "stood behind their officers," whereas street sergeants "stood beside their officers." Each of these two different styles of working as a sergeant also has its drawbacks and strengths. Station house sergeants might not have been readily available to officers working in the field; however, they could always be located when a signature was needed and were able to secure more favors for officers than street sergeants were. Although immediately available in the field when needed, street sergeants occasionally interfered with the autonomy of their subordinates; unrequested, they responded to calls for

Figure 7.13

A street sergeant on Staten Island, New York. Note his numerous decorations and five "hash marks" on his lower sleeve, each one denoting the completion of 5 years of service.

(© Robert Essel NYC/CORBIS)

service assigned to subordinates and handled them or, otherwise, at least in the eyes of their officers, "interfered."

A consideration of Van Maanen's work leads to some generalizations about the future careers of station house sergeants versus street sergeants. Station house sergeants are learning routines, procedures, and skills that will improve future promotional opportunities. Their promotional opportunities are further enhanced by contacts with senior police commanders who can give them important assignments and who can, if favorably impressed, influence future promotions. In contrast, street sergeants may gain some favorable publicity and awards for their exploits, but they are also more likely to have citizen complaints filed against them, more likely to be investigated by internal affairs, and more likely to be sued. Consequently, very aggressive street sergeants are regarded by their superiors as "good cops" but difficult people to supervise. In short, the action-oriented street sergeant who does not "mellow out" may not go beyond a middle manager's position in a line unit, such as patrol or investigation.

Contingency and Situational Leadership Theories

Contingency leadership and situational leadership are similar; both postulate that there are no approaches that are always right. Contingency theory is somewhat broader, considering both leader capabilities and other factors in any given circumstance; **situational leadership** focuses more on what leaders should do.

Tannenbaum and Schmidt: From Leader Styles to a Contingency Model

In 1958, **Tannenbaum and Schmidt**[1] published "How to Choose a Leadership Pattern," the first situational leadership theory, subsequently revising it in 1973 (see Figure 7.14).[72] They asserted that the societal environment and organizational

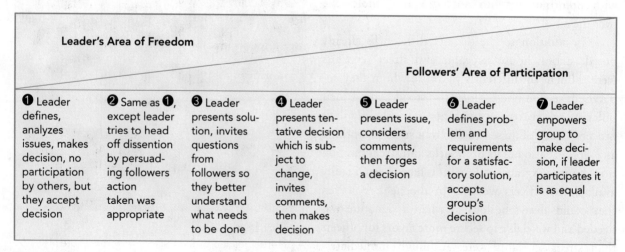

Figure 7.14
The leadership continuum portion of Tannenbaum and Schmidt's contingency theory.
Source: Robert Tannenbaum and Warren H. Schmidt, "How to Choose a Leadership Pattern," *Harvard Business Review,* May/June 1973, p. 167, with minor restatement.

LEADERSHIP   CHAPTER SEVEN   277
LEADERSHIP   CHAPTER SEVEN   277

LEADERSHIP   CHAPTER SEVEN   277

forces interplayed to form situations in which one leadership style would be more effective than other styles and leaders had to find that "good fit." Although we would presently substitute other societal environment examples, Tannenbaum and Schmidt identified: (1) the younger generation's distrust of "establishment" organizations; (2) the civil rights movement with its call for more participation and influence for all people; and (3) a growing desire for workers to have a higher quality of life within the organizations that employ them. The organizational forces, stated here in a police context, are:

1. Forces in the police leader, such as his or her value system, confidence in subordinate officers, leadership inclinations, and need for security in uncertain situations (e.g., "I can afford to be wrong on this one");
2. Forces in subordinate officers, including their knowledge, skills and experience; more can reasonably be expected from a veteran squad than one that is light on experience; and
3. Forces in the department, formal and informal (e.g., a policy not to participate in federal immigration roundups or the practice of not arresting nonpersistent panhandlers).

The most common criticism of Tannenbaum and Schmidt's theory is that while it discusses variables, including the leader, the followers, and the situation, the theory stops short of specifying how the variables are combined and translated into leadership behavior.[73]

Fiedler: Least Preferred Co-Worker (LPC)

Fiedler, a clinical psychologist, was originally interested in the relationship between psychotherapists and patients, later shifting his focus to leader-follower relationships.[74] His *A Theory of Leadership Effectiveness* (1967) attracted wide attention and has been subsequently modified several times. According to Fiedler, group effectiveness is a function of the interaction between the leader's esteem for his least-preferred co-worker (LPC) and three situational variables: (1) the task structure, (2) leader-follower relations, and (3) the power position of the leader.[75] Fiedler's use of "power" should be read to mean "authority" in the sense that Weber uses rational-legal authority; we have substituted "follower" for his "member." Although Fiedler provides scales to determine the level of each of these three variables, only their short definitions are shown here:

1. Task structure refers to the degree a task is or is not clearly spelled out as to goals, methods of handling, and standards of performance. Arresting a motorist for drunk driving has high structure; by policy there are a series of things that officers must do to properly perform the task. In contrast, the police reaction to a terrorist's detonation of a nuclear device in one of our major ports has low task structure. There are no or only very general guidelines; there are many ways to approach the task; and there may be more than one acceptable solution. In the

most extreme situations, the actual outcome of any solution may not be clearly foreseeable.

2. **Leader-follower relations** are characterized by the extent to which commanders enjoy the confidence and goodwill of the officers they lead and relations are cordial. Good relations make many things both possible and easier; poor relations render all things more difficult and if not corrected can become leadership neutralizers.

3. The **leader's position power** is the degree to which the commander has, or is perceived to possess by officers, the authority to reward or punish them for their performance.[76]

The LPC is a single individual with whom the leader presently works or another individual with whom he or she has worked in a different organization; someone who might be described in terms such as difficult, unpleasant, or uncooperative. Underlining LPC theory is the assumption that how leaders regard the person they least like is an indicator of their leadership preference. To determine whether leaders have a task or relationship orientation, they complete the LPC Scale using pairs of descriptors that leaders numerically rate (see Figure 7.15).

The LPC score determines whether a leader is task motivated (low LPC) versus being relationship oriented (high LPC). A third group, the middle-LPC scorers, do not have a distinct preference for task or relationship approaches to leadership and have been somewhat ignored.[77] Low LPCs get their psychological subsistence from completing their assigned tasks and are less concerned about how their drive to complete assignments impacts their followers. Conversely, high LPCs derive their sense of well-being in the workplace by creating and maintaining satisfying interpersonal relationships. Further differences in these two types of leadership approaches are shown in Figure 7.16. Fiedler considered leader behavior fairly stable and difficult to change. The interplay among task structure, leader-follower relations, and the power position of the leader produced situations that were more or less favorable to high and low LPC leadership preferences (see Figure 7.17).

Descriptor	Scale	Descriptor
Unfriendly	1 2 3 4 5 6 7 8	Friendly
Considerate	8 7 6 5 4 3 2 1	Inconsiderate
Insincere	1 2 3 4 5 6 7 8	Sincere
Warm	8 7 6 5 4 3 2 1	Cold
Backbiter	1 2 3 4 5 6 7 8	Loyal

Figure 7.15
A portion of Fiedler LPC Scale.
Source: Fred E. Fiedler and Joseph E. Garcia, *New Approaches to Effective Leadership* (New York: John Wiley & Sons, 1987), extracted from Figure 7.1, p. 71.

Task Motivated (Low LPC)	Relationship Motivated (High LPC)
• Accomplishing tasks is paramount and the source of self-esteem	• Self esteem comes from satisfying relationships with followers
• Highly critical of followers who don't contribute to task completion; may call them "worthless" or "despicable;" blinds them to follower's good characteristics	• Pleaser, reluctant to criticize, overlooks followers deficits and focuses on good attributes
• Courteous and ingratiating when needs cooperation of followers	• Consistently courteous and friendly
• Primary focus is task, but when accomplished may turn to repairing relationships	• Primary focus is people, but may become more directive around assignments they feel competent about
• Follower expertise is important concern	• Follower loyalty is important concern

Figure 7.16
Differences between Fiedler's task and relationship motivated leaders.

Task Structure	Leader-Follower Relations	Leader's Position Power	Situation Favorable to Leader Preference
High	Good	Strong	Low LPC
High	Good	Low	Low LPC
Low	Good	Strong	Low LPC
Low	Good	Low	High LPC
High	Weak	Strong	High LPC
High	Weak	Low	High LPC
Low	Weak	Strong	High LPC
Low	Weak	Low	Low LPC

Figure 7.17
Mix of situational variables and favorableness to high and low LPC preferences.

LPC has been studied extensively; Vecchio's test of the model (1977) concluded that factors other than those specified in the model or different combinations of them were responsible for group performance.[78] Rice (1978) reviewed 25 years of research on it and found general support for the low LPC and high LPC leadership preferences.[79] Peters, Hartke, and Pohlmann (1985) reached the same conclusion.[80] Middle LPCers are less involved with both tasks and relationships and approach their jobs less emotionally than the other two LPC preferences.[81] In 1982, Kennedy found that the middle-LPCers' leadership performance was higher than the other two leadership preferences within the parameters described by Fiedler's model.[82]

House: Path-Goal Theory

Although there was an earlier version of **path-goal theory (PGT)** by Evans in 1970, it is more closely associated with House, who built on Evan's work by formulating a more elaborate version that included situational variables (1971); it has been revised several times.[83] The central thought of PGT is that leaders should remove the obstacles that inhibit, make more difficult, or prevent individual followers from doing a good job.[84] Originally, PGT was not about leadership of groups or work units; it was a dyadic supervisor to an individual subordinate theory.[85]

In 1996, House's early work was reformulated as both an individual and work unit performance theory, stated here in law enforcement terms, that incorporates five notions: (1) the behavior of commanders is acceptable to subordinates to the extent to which it is seen as an immediate source of gratification or as a pathway to future satisfaction; (2) commanders can enhance subordinates' focus on goals to the extent that the commander's behavior increases motivation, builds task relevant skills, provides useful guidance, reduces obstacles to performance and organizational rewards, and provides the resources subordinates need to do their job effectively; (3) commanders can increase subordinates' motivation by providing psychological support and linking their subordinates satisfaction of personal needs to job performance; (4) commanders must be role models. In a 2008 study of 2,130 officers, police leaders modeling ethical behavior was significant in limiting unethical conduct when the modeling occurred in an interpersonal, as opposed to a more distant context;[86] and (5) work unit performance is enhanced by a commander encouraging collaborative support among subordinates, maintaining a good relationship between the work unit and the larger organization in which it is embedded, and demonstrating to the larger department the importance of the work performed by the unit.

In his revised work unit model (1996) House specifies eight types of leadership behavior that is acceptable, satisfying, facilitative, and motivational to subordinates. The essence of PGT is that for leaders to be effective, they must engage in leader behaviors (see Figure 7.18) that compensate for the deficiencies of subordinates, enhances their performance, and is instrumental to their individual and work unit performance and satisfaction.[87] It is unlikely that any single commander will have the ability to engage in the eight leadership behaviors all or even most of the time; effective leaders are likely to select the behaviors with which they are most comfortable, based on their personality and abilities.[88]

Dansereau, Graen, and Haga: Leader-Member Exchange (LMX)

Police officers know that their leaders treat subordinates differently, as do practitioners in other settings. Researchers, until LMX (1975),[89] made two wrong assumptions about leader behavior: (1) its effect on followers was homogenous or "averaged out," affecting their behavior "on average equally" or (2) leaders treated all subordinates in the same manner. The core of LMX is that leaders develop different types of relationships with their subordinates. Exchange relationships can be thought of as the unique quality of the interpersonal relationship between the leader and a follower, which also has practical consequences for the leader, follower, and the department. The "merit" of an officer is contingent on how well he or she fits with the values, attitudes, preferences, and outlook of the leader.

Leader Behavior	Descriptions
Path-Goal Clarifying	Clarifies subordinates' performance goals; the means to be used; the standards by which they will be evaluated; discusses the expectations about job performance which others may hold, e.g., merchants for an officer walking a beat, which should and shouldn't be honored; and judiciously uses rewards and discipline to shape performance.
Achievement Oriented	Achievement motivation is an individual's usually non-conscious desire to measure one's self against some standard of excellence or unique achievement. The ability of the leader to foster an achievement oriented work unit will vary by the individuals assigned to it. Some officers are innately achievement oriented and motivated, "self-starters." Officers with lesser achievement motivation require more effort. In these officers, leaders must identify and arouse the subordinates needs that will lead to a higher achievement motivation.
Work Facilitation	Consists of planning, scheduling, and organizing work; coordinating the work of subordinates; coaching, guiding, counseling, providing feedback, and mentoring them; reducing obstacles to their performance; eliminating bottlenecks to the resources they need; and authorizing them to take actions requiring the leader's prior approval.
Supportive	Supportive behavior provides psychological support to subordinates, especially when the task or incident is distressing, e.g., investigating child abuse and working the murder of another officer; supportive relationships reduce stress and make the leaders-subordinate relationship more satisfying; conversely, when work is satisfying and not dangerous or stressful, supportive behavior has little or no influence on subordinate's behavior.
Interaction Facilitation	Resolving disputes; facilitating communication; giving those in the minority the opportunity to voice their opinion; interaction facilitation may reduce voluntary absenteeism and attrition.
Group Oriented Decision Process	Involves the way in which decisions that affect the group are made; group oriented decision making increases both the quality and acceptance of the decision; leader encourages full participation, inhibits domination by one subordinate or a faction, allows full search for alternatives, facilitates discussion of alternatives, and the group makes the decision.
Representation and Networking	Some work units have a high status and an easier time getting the resources they need from other units. Other units do not enjoy such a favorable situation. Leaders must be able to increase their unit's standing and perceived value to the larger organization and therefore their legitimacy to make claims on resources which will be honored.
Value Based	Value based leaders receive extraordinary commitment from followers, tapping into their cherished beliefs, their identification with the leader, their support of organizational goals, and their self-worth and identities. Value based leaders articulate the vision of a better future; display self-confidence and self-sacrifice in the interest of the vision; take risks to further the vision; communicate high performance expectations for subordinates; and express confidence in their ability to meet those expectations.

Figure 7.18
House's eight leadership behaviors.

An LMX police leader divides officers into two different groups: in-group and out-group, with a small holding category, "try-out" (see Figure 7.19). Through one-on-one encounters, the leader forms opinions about each officer, sometimes in as little as two weeks. Where the leader and an officer are "simpatico," like-minded, congenial, and develop trust and respect in each other, the officer goes to the in-group. Where the "fit" is not good, the officer goes to the out-group. On rare occasions, a leader will move

Figure 7.19
The LMX in-group and out-group model.

an officer from the out-group to the in-group, but this requires potent new evidence, such as clearing a string of burglaries or apprehending a serial killer. Newly hired officers always go to the try-out category. Experienced officers transferred into the unit usually have a reputation of some sort. Still, unless the leader has had prior personal experience with them, they go to "the try-out bin." The new hires and transfers do not know they are in the try-out bin; in time they will come to notice the difference between being an in-group and out-group member. Ultimately they will figure out which group they are in by the way the leader treats them.

In-group members receive more leader attention, have performance appraisals greater than merited, high job satisfaction, faster career progression, a high level of organizational citizenship behavior (OCB), reduced turnover, and more diverse work assignments. Out-group members are given accurate performance appraisals and their characteristics are essentially the "flip side" of the in-groupers.[90]

In 1995, Graen and Uhl-Bien moved away from the in- and out-group model, re-conceptualizing it as a continuum of leader and follower relationships (see Figure 7.20).[91] In it, the purpose of the leaders is to form individual relationships with officers that will help them grow into the Mature Partnership stage to the betterment of leaders, subordinates, and the performance of the organization.

The progress from the Stranger stage to the Mature Partnership stage is not assured. Leadership methods may be ineffective and some officers might simply want to do their job and go home, seeking nothing more than doing an honest day's work for a fair wage. Such officers may see policing not as a profession, just where they work to make a living. Their lack of a richer involvement might signal that their family is the first priority or that they want to put their energy into a family business, hobbies, or recreational pursuits. Thus, some officers are content to remain in the Stranger stage. Regression is possible also; officers in the Acquaintance stage and the Mature Partnership stage may return to an earlier stage if they become discouraged with their career or have catastrophic losses that adversely affect their job performance.

Beyond the three stages identified in Figure 7.20, Graen and Uhl-Bien identify a fourth stage. This involves dropping an overlay of relevant Mature Partnership stage dyads over the task structure of the police department to maximize the use of talent. Developing a research framework to test this fourth stage has proven troublesome and therefore made it resistant to empirical study. Otherwise, the existing research for both the 1975 and 1995 iterations of LMX has generally been favorable. Much of the research on LMX since the 1970s has been on how it correlates with other characteristics, such as OCB, intelligence, gender, and cross-cultural implementation.

Kerr and Jermier: Leadership Substitutes and Neutralizers
In 1978, Kerr and Jermier observed that in some situations, hierarchical leadership didn't seem to make much of a difference in what subordinates did, and under other circumstances, it appeared to be irrelevant. Stopping well short of Miner's 1975 proclamation that the concept of leadership had outlived its usefulness,[92] they asked a startling question: "Are there variables in the work setting that can substitute for, or even neutralize, leader behavior?"[93] Earlier in this chapter the Willow City case study

Characteristic	Stages of Relationship		
	1 **Stranger Stage**	**2** **Acquaintance Stage**	**3** **Mature Partnership Stage**
Phase of Relationship Building	Although roles understood and shaped by rules, leader and follower feel each other out; e.g. "How are we going to relate to each other?" At some point, the leader or the follower must create opening to move the relationship forward on a career interest basis	Some sharing of personal and work information; relationship evolving; "putting meat on the bones of their relationship"	Relationship is at mature stage; mutual roles understood and well accepted
Type of Reciprocity	Formal and limited; leader expects follower to do job and follower does it, but no more	Some formalities of the relationship fade as leader and the follower explore reciprocity; e.g., leader offers new challenge in which follower has an interest	Full reciprocity; relationship has been tested and is dependable
Reciprocity Occurs	Immediately, but only within the job context	Some delay involved as the dynamics of reciprocity with the relationship are figured out; e.g., is immediacy of reciprocity most important or is an equivalent reciprocity received later acceptable?	On-going, comfortable; dynamics have been worked out
Leader-Follower Exchange	Leaders provide only resources needed to do job; followers meet basic job requirements	Followers may have access to additional benefits, e.g., being assigned to patrol a particular area, sent to special training classes.	Highly developed; emotional component becomes more prominent: mutual respect, trust, loyalty, sense of mutual obligation
Mutual Influence	Mostly one-way, leader directing follower's job performance	Still mostly one-way, but some limited mutual influence	Bi-directional; genuine feedback can be provided without damage to relationship

Figure 7.20
Life cycle LMX leadership.

established that leadership can be neutralized. Kerr and Jermier's work gives us a broader understanding of substitutes and neutralizers; it was conducted with reference to two styles of leadership: task oriented and relationship oriented. The model explores how the impact of leadership is contingent upon specific variables in the workplace.

Leadership substitutes are variables or factors that diminish the importance of leadership behavior or take its place entirely. Examples of substitutes include: (1) officers, who accurately perceive that they require little or no personal supervision by virtue of their training, job experience, knowledge, and job commitment—moreover, they may rankle under it. (2) Officers with a professional orientation may be heavily influenced by an external organization, such as the National Tactical Officers Association (NTOA) and the opinions of qualified peers. (3) Sergeants are unlikely to find success trying to motivate officers who find police work intrinsically satisfying. (4) Close-knit peer groups may provide sufficient approval needs to diminish the efficacy of a sergeant using a relationship approach.

Neutralizers are variables that make task and relationship leadership approaches ineffective or impossible. An officer seriously considering leaving the department to work full-time on a graduate degree, attend law school, start a business, or with multiple external job opportunities is outwardly directed, away from the department. Guidance, support, or threats from a supervisor may have little saliency, no real importance, because the officer mentally has "one foot out the door." However, the department does hold one important card: the letter of recommendations leaders may be requested to write. Even going out the door, most officers do not want to "soil their nests." A few officers leaving an agency will tell one or more supervisors what "assholes" they are. Later, when these officers want a letter of recommendation or are seeking reinstatement to the department, they come to regret indulging themselves that way.

Officers who have a misperception of their own abilities and experience and think they don't need any supervision are neutralizers; they are a bad mix of arrogance and faulty perception. The more consistently a leader and followers are separated by location, the greater the likelihood is that without special leader measures, his or her leadership will be seen as less important over time. Thus, chiefs with precincts need to do more than use technology to communicate with dispersed officers; they must also establish a personal presence by visiting those precincts. Other neutralizers include officers who are indifferent to the award system, a perception that leaders occupy a low status in the "food chain"; inflexible work guidelines that create unnecessary work; and leaders who one way or another inflict "wounds" on themselves, which lowers the regard in which their officers hold them.

Researchers have only found mixed support for this theory.[94] However, it still has practical significance in that it identifies factors leaders should consider when they ask themselves "How am I doing?" Perhaps the most important contribution of this theory is that it spawned interest in learning more about the role of trust in organizations. In 2005, Lewicki, Wiethoff, and Tomlinson identified two types of trust in organizations: (1) calculus-based trust (CBT), in which the parties to a relationship must determine the costs of maintaining or severing it, and (2) identification-based trust (IBT), based on a mutual understanding of each other's needs and wants.[95]

Hersey and Blanchard: Situational Leadership Theory

Although many situational variables are important to leadership—such as the demands of time, the leader, the led, superiors, the organization, and job demands—Hersey and Blanchard (1977) emphasize what they regard as the two key variables: (1) the behavior of the leader in relationship to (2) the maturity of followers.[96] Maturity is defined in situational leadership as the capacity to set high but attainable goals, the willingness to take responsibility, and the education and/or experience of the individual or the group.[97] Age may be a factor, but it is not related directly to maturity as used in situational leadership theory.[98] An individual or group is not mature or immature in a total sense but only in relation to the specific task to be performed.[99] This task-relevant maturity involves two factors: job maturity, or the ability and technical knowledge to do the task, and psychological maturity, or feelings of self-confidence and self-respect about oneself as an individual.[100]

Figure 7.21 summarizes the Hersey-Blanchard model, which includes references to task and relationship dimensions in the same manner as the Managerial Grid. Although it is easier said than done, the effective use of Hersey and Blanchard's model depends on police leaders developing or having a diagnostic ability and the flexibility to adapt their leadership styles to given situations.[101] Research on the model has been mixed; Cairns and colleagues (1998) found it intuitively appealing and empirically contradictory.[102] Perhaps, like several other theorists, Hersey and Blanchard's model could be beneficially reformulated, employing emotional intelligence (EI) and social intelligence (SI) concepts.

Vroom, Yetton, and Jago: Normative Decision-Making Theory

Collaborative work between Vroom and Yetton (1973) and Vroom and Jago (1988) resulted in this theory, which is narrow in its focus—decision making—and not a general leadership model. It is "normative," stipulating under what conditions one leadership approach to decision making is more likely to be successful than another. Figure 7.22 summarizes three leadership approaches to decision-making: authoritarian, consultative, and participative. Figure 7.23 identifies eight contingency factors and the corresponding key questions/concerns leaders should consider. Research evidence for the initial model (1973) was adequate, but there were criticisms of it. The reformulation of the model (1988) responded to those criticisms and there was an impressive increase in research evidence supporting it. In one study, effective decisions were made 68 percent of the time using the normative model as compared to 32 percent using other methods.[103] Yukl (2010) concludes that it is "probably the best supported of the contingency theories of leadership."[104]

Maturity/Readiness Level of Followers	Best Leadership Style
M1: Followers are insecure, not willing, and/or not able to take responsibility for task accomplishment	S1: "Telling" style, a high task/low relationship approach; use one-way communication to provide specific instructions and then closely supervise
M2: Followers are willing, but unable to take responsibility for task accomplishment	S2: "Selling" style, a high task/high relationship approach; use two-way communication to explain instructions, ask for clarifying questions, get followers to "buy-in"
M3: Followers are able, but not willing to take responsibility for task accomplishment	S3: "Participating" style, a high relationship/low task approach; mutual exchange of ideas, shared decision making, and a lot of facilitating support from leader
M4: Followers are willing and able to take responsibility for task accomplishment	S4: "Delegating" style, low task/low relationship approach; followers able to perform under loose, general supervision

Figure 7.21
Hersey and Blanchard's situational leadership.

Leader Approach	Description	Decision Maker
Authoritarian	**A1**: Chief uses all information immediately available	Chief
	A2: Chief obtains any necessary information from staff members, may not disclose why the information is needed	Chief
Consultative	**C1**: Chief shares problem/situation/opportunity with relevant staff members individually; decision may or may not reflect input received	Chief
	C2: Chief convenes command staff or other group; gets their input, decision may or may not include any signs of influence from group	Chief
Participative	**Group (G)**: Chief convenes appropriate group; following discussion a consensus decision is made	Group
	Delegation (D): Problem/situation/opportunity is assigned to individual or group with the necessary skills and experience to handle it. Chief gives relevant information, but any decision made will receive Chief's full support	Individual or Group

Figure 7.22
Vroom-Yetton-Jago normative decision-making model.

Contingency Factors	Key Questions/Concerns
Quality of Decision	How important is the quality of this decision, e.g., "just good enough" versus optimum
Leader Information	Does the chief have enough information to make a high quality decision?
Follower Information	Do others have enough information to make a high quality decision?
Structure of the Problem	Clear, action needed well known versus structure unclear, ill-defined, unfamiliar, alternatives need to be identified and evaluated
Goal Congruence	Are followers and organizational goals aligned, a "win-win" situation or in conflict, "win-lose"
Follower Conflict	Are followers divided on what the outcome should be? Failure to build consensus may lead to a lack of commitment/support
Commitment Probability	If an authoritarian decision made, will it matter to followers?
Commitment Required	How important is it to the Chief that follower commitment to the decision be substantial?

Figure 7.23
Contingency factors in the normative decision-making model.

Transactional and Transformational Leaders

Burns (1978) contrasted transactional and transformational leaders, thinking of them as polar opposites.[105] Most leader–follower relationships are transaction based. **Transactional leaders** give something to get something. They motivate followers by appealing to their self-interest; contingent upon a follower doing a good job, the leader will provide favorable evaluations, raises, and desired assignments. Each party to the transaction, or "bargain," is at least implicitly aware of the resources of the other, and the purposes of both are entwined.[106] To function, both parties to a bargain must have certain values, such as reliability, honesty, fairness, and reciprocity.[107] Commanders using a transactional leadership style clearly state their expectations for what subordinates need to do to fulfill their part of the bargain and monitor the performance of followers.

Essentially, **transformational leadership** emphasizes the upper levels of Maslow's needs hierarchy—esteem and self-actualization—to motivate followers[108] (see Chapter 5, Organizational Theory). These two levels of need include such factors as the need to test yourself against challenging work and standards, the quest for self-esteem and confidence, and autonomy in problem solving. Transformational leadership consists of several factors, referred to as the "Four Is" (see Figure 7.24). The use of the Four Is was studied in a Royal Canadian Mounted Police (RCMP) detachment. It concluded that transformational leadership increased commitment, work satisfaction, and motivation. [109]

As conceived of by Burns (1978) and Bass (1985),[110] transformational leaders are inspirational; they motivate followers to "elevate their game," to go beyond their own self-interests for the good of the unit or organization, making more and larger contributions than they had expected to make (see Figure 7.25);[111] in this process, transformational leaders help followers to grow personally and to develop their own capacity for leadership.[112] This help takes the form of individual attention to officers, empowering them, appealing to their ideals and values, and aligning their interests and the goals with the leader, the work unit, and the department. This results in the followers'

---

1. **Idealized Influence (IL):** Transformational leaders serve as role models, generating respect, trust, and admiration. They can be counted on to do the right thing and followers identify with them and emulate them. Chiefs who do not "walk the talk" cannot be transformational because followers quickly discount them.

2. **Inspirational Motivation (IM):** In a genuine manner, Chiefs behave in ways that motivates and inspires those around them. They manage the meaning of events, display optimism and enthusiasm, work hard, and actively demonstrate their own personal commitment to the vision of the future. The ability to communicate ideas nonverbally, verbally, symbolically, and in written form is an essential part of "winning hearts and minds."

3. **Intellectual Stimulation (IS):** Transformational Chiefs supportively probe their followers' progress toward creativity and innovation by questioning their assumptions, line of reasoning, and approach to solving persistent and new problems. This helps followers reframe problems and see new possibilities for their solution. Challenging assignments also stimulates growth. Ideas that are different from the chief's are not just tolerated; they are encouraged.

4. **Individualized Consideration (IC):** The needs of individual followers for growth and accomplishment are attended to by coaching and mentoring, moving them to successively higher levels. Interactions with followers are personalized, e.g., the transformational Chief recalls past conversations about families and work, sees follower as whole person.

Figure 7.24
The Four "Is" of transformational leadership.

Figure 7.25
Frank Limon, appointed Chief of New Haven's (Connecticut) department in 2010. In his former agency, he was a transformational leader of whom departmental members said, "He got us to do things that we weren't used to doing."
(Courtesy *Wednesday Journal* of Oak Park and River Forest, Illinois)

commitment to work "now," a well-articulated vision of the future, and strong organizational citizenship behavior.[113] While accommodating the needs of officers, transformational leaders "send the same message" about their vision and the challenging goals ahead to everyone.[114] "Even when a chief has a vision, implementation is not always easy."[115] In many cases, the chief's vision may clash with that of other entities that do not relate directly with the police department's mission[116] (e.g., indigent and low-income health-care agencies serve local needs, but also attract more homeless from afar, creating more order maintenance needs).

Ideals and values are powerful forces; our Declaration of Independence (1776) rings with them: "All men are created equal . . . with unalienable rights . . . life, liberty, and the pursuit of happiness." Although not the sole contributor to our independence from what was then the most powerful nation in the world, the words resonated and took deep root in the minds of our populace, evoking passion about them. Mohandas Gandhi (1869–1948), the Bapu, or Father of India, led his country to independence from England by advocating noncooperation and mass civil disobedience, tactics used by Dr. Martin Luther King, Jr., in the civil rights movement (see Chapter 1, Evolution of Police Administration). Ironically, both men, who advocated peaceful resistance, were assassinated. However, their lives demonstrate how transformational leaders can use ideals and values to achieve enormous political and social change.

"Charismatic" and "transformational leadership" are used interchangeably by some theorists, largely because the first two of the "Four Is," "idealized influence" and "inspirational motivation" were often combined together in early research as "charismatic leadership."[117] Indeed, some theorists maintain that there can be no transformational leadership without a charismatic leader. However, if the "Four Is" are studied individually, with no combining of the four factors, charismatic leadership becomes *one of the styles* that works with a transformational approach.[118] For example, a leader can be inspirational without being charismatic.[119] Followers can be drawn to the purposes, goals, and vision of an inspirational leader, without being drawn to the person per se as in charismatic leaders,[120] a pivotal and profound difference.

There is ample evidence supporting transactional and transformational leadership. Like transformational leadership, properly executed transactional leadership can result in trusting the leader, organizational citizenship behavior, and commitment; moreover, it may establish the foundation from which transformational leadership can develop.[121] Transformational leadership increases followers' job satisfaction;[122] its individual support of followers may help protect them from depression,[123] builds committed, cohesive work teams,[124] and produces organizational innovations, such as new approaches to doing the work.[125] Women are slightly more likely than men to use transformational leadership.[126]

A study of Texas police chiefs found there were slightly more transactional than transformational leaders.[127] A study of the Four Is in the Royal Canadian Mounted Police (RCMP) found support for them. Officers said that first and foremost aspect of *idealized influence* (IF) was when commanders knew their "true north," leading their personal and professional lives consistent with the values of the RCMP.[128] The RCMP respondents said that *inspirational motivation* (IM) was not complete with respect to the use of community policing because while there was no active resistance to it, "buy-in" by officers wasn't 100 percent. A RCMP commander reported that one of his approaches to *intellectual stimulation* (IS) was to assign unusual cases to a very experienced investigator and then team that person with someone who would learn and grow from being involved. As to *individualized consideration* (IC), another commander stated the most effective tool was simply getting the right person in the right job. The largest study of transformational leadership in a police setting was conducted in England by the Home Office (see Table 7.1). Overall, 70 percent of the 1,066 officers surveyed agreed with 10 statements reflecting a transformational approach. The remaining 30 percent raises interesting questions: (1) How many of that portion might change their opinions?

Table 7.1
BRITISH POLICE OFFICERS (*N* = 1066) PERCEPTIONS OF THEIR LEADERS

Element	Percent Disagree	Percent Agree	Total Percent
Behaves in a way that increases my motivation to achieve	23	77	100
Manages and leads in a way that I find very satisfying	30	70	100
Behaves in way that has a postive effect on my job commitment	25	75	100
Behaves in a manner that has a positive effect on my self-confidence	23	77	100
Behaves in a manner that raises my sense of fulfillment for the job	22	78	100
Reduces my stress level by his/her approach to leadership	37	63	100
Leads and behaves in such a way that it increases my job satisfaction	32	68	100
Manages and behaves in a manner that increases my self-esteem	32	68	100
Has a leadership style that increases my organizational commitment	32	67	100
Acts in a manner that enables me to achieve beyond my expectations	35	65	100

Source: John Dobby, Jane Anscombe, and Rache; Tuffin, Police Leadership: Expectations and Impact (London, England: Home Office, 2004), p. 23. The data was collapsed from a six-point scale.

(2) Over a period of time will the majority experiencing transformational leadership remain stable? and (3) For transformational leadership, as well as other theories, is there a saturation point (e.g., 70 percent) beyond which you simply are not going to get more "converts"? and (4) Is there always some "loyal opposition," albeit it muted?

Comparison of Charismatic and Transformational Leadership

Historically, **charisma** was thought to be a divine gift, bestowed on one who was favored by the "gods." Leaders cannot declare that they are charismatic, nor can they be such if they are not successful (see Figure 7.26). "Charisma" is a label that can only be authentically applied by followers. Charismatic leaders have certain traits: (1) their vision is a significant shift from the present status quo, but still acceptable to followers; (2) they use new, unconventional strategies to implement the vision; (3) they take risks and self-sacrifice to achieve the vision (e.g., possible loss of the chief's position); (4) they are less motivated by self-interest than by concern for followers; (5) they radiate a contagious confidence and enthusiasm; (6) they rely more on emotional appeals to followers than on the use of authority to get performance; and (7) they select a vision that is innovative, relevant to followers, and timely in its implementation.[129] These traits are the "ideal version" of a charismatic leader; however, charisma also has a "dark side" (e.g., Hitler and Stalin). On a smaller scale, Charles Manson gathered a "family" of followers and in 1969 dispatched them to commit gruesome murders, including fatally stabbing actress Sharon Tate, who was nearly 9 months pregnant.

It may not be possible to immediately differentiate whether charisma is positive or good; even charismatics who help their department and followers to substantial

Figure 7.26
*Three of the most successful allied leaders of World War II. England's Prime Minister Churchill (L)
was energetic and inspirational. American General Eisenhower (C) was a strong administrator,
building the allied coalition; although decisive he often relied on persuasion as opposed to
simply giving orders. Field Marshal Montgomery (R) was an effective, but temperamental combat
commander who made harsh criticisms of Eisenhower and other allied leaders after WW II.*
(SSPL/Getty Images)

achievements may also do some damage to other officers along the way. Without dismissing the matter lightly, it is somewhat like breaking a few eggs to make an omelet, except the stakes are much higher: The impact on the lives of officers negatively affected can be catastrophic. Other aspects of charismatic leadership that are problematic include: (1) the desire of officers to be "in good standing" might inhibit useful criticisms from them; (2) widespread approval by officers can breed a dangerous sense of infallibility in chiefs; (3) excessive confidence by charismatic chiefs can lead them into dangerous mistakes; and (4) charismatic behavior inevitably breeds believers, but also determined enemies who prefer to cling to more familiar ways and will opportunistically look for ways to discredit or remove the leader from office.[130]

Charismatic and transformational leadership have been used synonymously, described as overlapping, and sharply differentiated; earlier charismatic leadership theories have been revised, causing some convergence with transformational leadership.[131] Not all charismatic leaders are transformational. While there are some similarities between charismatics and transformationals, there are also some important distinctions: (1) transformationals, by developing followers' abilities and eliminating unnecessary controls, make followers less dependent upon them; (2) transformational leaders are more common, whereas charismatics are rare and their emergence depends upon circumstances being favorable for their leadership approach; (3) charismatics, as described earlier, elicit more diverse and extreme reactions; and (4) charismatics are much more attuned to managing their image.[132]

The "New Leadership" Theories: Servant, Spiritual, Ethical, and Authentic

Because these theories share some common characteristics, and for ease of reference, theorists have labeled them "neo-charismatic" or the "new leadership," independent from when they were actually initially formulated. All of them attempt to explain how leaders: (1) take organizations on an upward trajectory to outstanding accomplishments; (2) engender extraordinary levels of follower motivation, trust, dedication, and loyalty; (3) use symbolic and emotionally appealing behaviors, such as envisioning, empowering, and supporting, to rally followers to their vision; and (4) employ leadership to increase followers' self-esteem, job satisfaction, and performance.[133] They also fall short of being full leadership theories in that the linkage between leader behavior—the resulting follower behavior—and organizational outcomes are neither fully explained or demonstrated.

Servant Leadership

Greenleaf (1904–1990) articulated the core notion of **servant leadership** (1977): The servant leader is servant first . . . making sure that other people's highest priority needs are met.[134] The idea is consistent with many of the teachings of the world's religions. Servant leadership (SL) includes the concepts of nurturing, defending, and empowering followers; helping them to be more complete persons, healthier, wiser, and more willing to accept their responsibilities; listening to their aspirations and frustrations; keeping actions consistent with their own values; and preparing people to lead when their opportunity comes.[135] Law enforcement agencies with servant leadership include

Boone, North Carolina; Haines City, Florida; Carrolton, Texas; and the Stanislaus County Sheriff's Office, California.

A principal difference between transformational leadership and SL is that ultimately, the former focuses on organizational outcomes whereas the latter's "wheelhouse" is followers.[136] Spears (2004) identifies 10 characteristics of SLs:

1. *Listening*—SLers have a deep commitment to listen to others, apprehending both what is said and what is omitted. They are alert to emotional states and nonverbal cues;

2. *Empathy*—Empathy is the ability to vicariously understand and perhaps even experience (e.g., grief) what another person is feeling or a situation. Empathy approximates emotional intelligence (EI) and social intelligence (SI), discussed earlier in this chapter;

3. *Healing*—Many relationships become strained or fractured. Uncomfortable, we avoid the other person involved and worry about what will happen. If we feel misunderstood, disappointed, injured, wounded, or betrayed, moving forward can be a difficult task. The longer we remain in that state, the more we reduce the quality of what our personal and organizational lives can be. The healing brought about by a kind gesture, "closing the distance," a forthright, thoughtful, "air clearing" discussion, forgiveness, or similar action has enormous restorative powers for us and those with whom we are in some sort of a conflict. SLers heal themselves and followers. As a practical matter, many people make a habit of "never letting the sun go down on their anger"; they know lingering anger is destructive. Disciplina was a minor Roman deity; from her identity, we derive *disciplina*, the Latin root word for discipline, meaning to teach and to learn. Properly conducted discipline can also be a healing act, correcting a situation and putting it into the past. The Biblical basis for this is the forgiveness of our sins, which are removed as far as the east is from the west and remembered no more;

4. *Awareness*—This capacity strengthens SLers, helping them to stay in touch with themselves and their values and ethics;

5. *Persuasion*—SLers rely less on authority and more on persuasion and consensus, seeking others to join rather than telling them to perform;

6. *Conceptualization*—Whereas traditional leaders are often captured by the daily "tyranny of events" and focus on short-term operational needs, SLers look beyond day-to-day realities, further into the future, and see new opportunities, delicately balancing both time frames;

7. *Foresight*—Little has been written about the role of foresight in leadership; it is less like tactical and strategic planning and more akin both to awareness and intuitiveness. It allows SLers to draw upon past lessons, factors and situations in the present, and the likely consequences of decisions about the future;

8. *Stewardship*—This characteristic means the responsible care of something entrusted to your care. In SL, the "prime directive" for stewardship is always the commitment to serve others;

9. *Commitment to the growth of people*—SLers are deeply committed to the personal, professional, and spiritual growth of each person in the organization; and

10. *Sense of community*—Our lives are dominated by large-scale organizations (e.g., employers, banks, health care, and school systems). In large part, the movement of families to villages and small towns is an attempt to live life differently, to create a sense of intimate belonging. City dwellers do the same thing without moving, creating their own, typically multiple, "communities" to which they can belong and from which they can derive meaning and psychological sustenance. SLers make organizations viable "communities."[137]

Most of the evidence about SL is from case studies and anecdotal accounts; only now are researchers developing reliable scales to measure its concepts.[138] The sparse evidence on SL correlates with increased organizational citizen behavior, follower trust in the leader and the organization, job satisfaction, and some organizational effectiveness.[139] Some critics of spiritual theory believe that by definition the spiritual leader is so occupied with the needs of followers that legitimate, short-term, organizational needs become secondary in importance. Women, ethnic minorities, and others who have traditionally been held to lesser roles may find the idea of spiritual leadership unappealing.[140] More critically, Eicher-Catt believes it accentuates gender bias.[141] The theory also fails to take into account how SLers behave when the needs of the organization and the followers are in conflict (e.g., the kind of downsizing being seen in police departments during this economic downturn), as well as the possibility that the SLers' emphasis on humility, equality, and empowerment may be seen as weaknesses.[142]

Spiritual Leadership

There is no consensus about **spiritual leadership**. One set of scholars views it within a theological or religious framework, while others approach it as the study of how leaders create an inner motivation in followers to enhance "workplace spirituality."[143] In turn, "workplace spirituality" suffers from the absence of an accepted definition. Confounding matters even further, management gurus author books titled *Jesus, CEO* (1996) and *What Would Buddha Do at Work?* (2002). Within these limitations, this section examines spiritual leadership within the nonreligious, workplace context. Any attempt to use a religious basis for leadership in a public agency would immediately encounter legal challenges. Spiritual leadership has made little or no inroads into law enforcement, perhaps because of the popular perception that it is religion based; overwhelmingly, almost all of what is written about "spiritual" and "policing" is associated with the work of law enforcement chaplains. Nonetheless, it has some instructive components.

In a recent survey, most young adults, 18 to 29 years old, reported they don't pray, don't go to worship services, and don't read the Bible or other sacred texts; 72 percent say they are more spiritual than religious.[144] "Spiritual" is being in the state of close connection or relationship with one's higher values and morality.[145]

These young adults will soon be entering law enforcement or are presently in the early stages of their careers. Many seek to understand the deeper meaning of life, a rich journey that can never be completed, but nonetheless must be taken. Workplace spiritual leadership may be appealing to them.

Spiritual leadership consists of the values, attitudes, and behaviors that are necessary to "intrinsically motivate" oneself and others so they have a sense of "**spiritual survival**."[146] Some followers are motivated by extrinsic factors, which are outside of them. Extrinsic rewards include pay, health benefits, and vacation days. Such officers operate at the bottom levels of Maslow's needs hierarchy. Officers who are extrinsically motivated operate within a simple exchange model. Spiritual leadership taps into the higher-order needs of officers, the intrinsic factors. These include the desire to have work that is interesting, challenging, and socially meaningful, being a key contributor in the officer's work unit, and strong identification with the unit's mission (e.g., drug interdiction).[147] Officers who are described as "self-starters" are intrinsically motivated. The essential components of "spiritual survival" are shown in Figure 7.27.

Both dimensions in Figure 7.28 involve altruistic love and faith/hope. The former includes such attributes as kindness, compassion, gratitude, forgiveness, humility, honesty, loyalty, and trust in others, while faith/hope is associated with optimism, confidence, courage, persistence, resiliency, and serenity.[148]

Research on spiritual leadership is still in an early stage of development. Reave (2005) reviewed over 150 studies, but most were on related topics.[149] Markow and Klenke (2005) found support for the transcendence and membership dimensions.[150] Benefiel (2005) was pointed in her criticism of spiritual leadership theory: The approach to spirituality is shallow, there is a failure to fully develop the theory, and a more robust, fully developed version that can stand up to scrutiny is needed.[151] Nonetheless, Fry (2003), while acknowledging the need for further development, concludes that spiritual leadership is more compact, less confusing, and inclusive of the path-goal, transformational, and charismatic theories.[152]

Dimensions	Components
1. **Transcendence,** a sense of being called to a vocation or profession	A. Interesting and meaningful work that gives officers the opportunity to learn and develop, to develop a sense of competency and mastery; and B. Work that provides a gratifying sense of purpose, making a contribution to something larger than one's self.
2. **Membership,** a sense of belonging	A. Feelings of connectedness, acceptance, and value in the work setting; and B. Living so work and other roles are in harmony with one's essential nature

Figure 7.27
Essential dimensions and components of spiritual survival.

Authentic Leadership

Partially in response to the mismanagement and "ethical meltdowns" of Fortune 500 companies[153] that wreaked so much havoc on the lives of employees and investors, substantial interest in **authentic leadership** (AL) began by the early 2000s. AL is more than being "real" or "genuine"—you can be a "real bastard" and "genuinely insensitive." AL is defined as: (1) being deeply aware of how you think, behave, and are seen by others; (2) being aware of your own and others' values/moral perspectives, knowledge, and strengths; (3) understanding the context in which you and others operate; and (4) being grounded by confidence, hopefulness, optimism, resiliency, and high moral character.[154] While aware of the opinions of others, ALers are not driven by their expectations, and moral character separates them from those who are merely "real" or "genuine." Chief Seabrooks is an advocate of authentic leadership (see Figure 7.28), avowing that "I am about the truth and that does not change."

Figure 7.28
Chief Jacqueline Seabrooks, Inglewood (California) Police Department. She spent 24 years with the Santa Monica Police Department, rising to Captain and also serving as its Acting Chief.
(Courtesy of *The Los Angeles Sentinel*)

Avolio and Gardner (2005) argue that AL is the "root construct" that underlies transformational, charismatic, servant, spiritual, and ethical theories.[155] ALers can incorporate elements of all of these theories into their behavior. For example, an ALer may use a charismatic approach, but may or may not be perceived as such by followers; likewise, when employing a transformational style, little or no emphasis may be placed on the proactive development of followers, although they may have a positive impact by modeling important behaviors.[156]

AL suffers from some of the same deficits that other leadership theories do: (1) there is an absence of a consensus definition; (2) the conceptual distinction between it and other "new" leadership theories is not developed; (3) the claim of being a "root construct" is undemonstrated; (4) how long it will take before the effects of AL can be seen is unknown; (5) whether people can be trained to be authentic is questionable; (6) it fails to explain how authentic leaders should behave when dealing with authentically difficult followers; and (7) it is unknown how many "slips" authentic leaders can make before followers dismiss them as "unauthentic."[157] Until these difficulties are resolved, it is hard to imagine that large-scale studies can be usefully undertaken.[158]

Ethical Leadership

Ethical leadership is the consistent demonstration of moral values through personal actions, in interpersonal relationships, and the communication of those values to followers through two-way communication, reinforcement, and decision making.[159]

Researchers have identified two components to ethical leadership: (1) the **moral person**, a fair and principled decision maker, who is altruistic, cares about people and the broader society and (2) the **moral manager**, who proactively strives to reinforce followers' ethical behavior. Moral managers explicitly make ethics part of their leadership agenda by frequently communicating about it, modeling it, and using discipline to hold followers accountable for ethical lapses.[160] Discipline provides important learning to organizational members, who by the actions taken are able to reliably distinguish between what is acceptable behavior and what is not.[161]

At one level or another, transformational, servant, spiritual, authentic, and ethical leadership are concerned with being a good role model, integrity, and altruism or care for others. While ethical leaders keep their eye on modeling, communicating, and reinforcing moral values, the other "new" leadership styles have different preoccupations: (1) ultimately, transformational leaders are concerned about organizational outcomes or results; (2) servant leaders look to the needs of others; (3) spiritual leaders are interested in their own and their followers' spiritual survival; and (4) authentic leaders are keenly aware of how they think, behave, and are seen by others.

Ethical leadership matters because it influences what followers do. Ethical leaders are attractive role models who followers want to emulate—to be like. This increases ethical reasoning and action, even if the leader is not immediately present, stimulates organizational citizenship behavior, increases job satisfaction and trust in the leader, and reduces counterproductive follower behavior[162] (e.g., abuse of sick leave, being quarrelsome, and failing to complete assignments on a timely basis). Despite the interest in ethical leadership, Yukl notes (2010) that much of the research done has been superficial.[163]

CONCLUSION

Leadership is a slippery concept. It can be the traits exhibited by a leader, the manner or style in which the leader behaves, the way in which subordinates perceive the leader, how the leader affects the behavior and growth of subordinates, and the organizational performance leadership produces and sustains. In almost every situation, one or more leadership approaches are going to work. Many of the theories discussed produce similar affects; this fact is not surprising because researchers attempt to determine if the theories produce a fairly standard set of impacts on subordinates and organizational outcomes (e.g., increased trust and organizational commitment). This chapter describes "pure" or idealized models that rarely have a counterpart in the "real world." Ultimately, leadership is often a hybrid of things leaders do that are within their comfort zone.

CHAPTER REVIEW

1. What is the definition of leadership?
2. Can you make at least four distinctions between leaders and managers?
3. Identify five reasons why chiefs fail because of their own inadequacies.

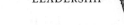

4. Discuss the relationship between authority and power.

5. What are socialized and personalized power needs?

6. Identify and define the three components of the leadership skill mix.

7. Describe two different approaches to "great man" theories of leadership.

8. What are the "Big 5"?

9. Discuss emotional and social intelligence.

10. Define *authoritarian, democratic*, and *laissez-faire leadership*.

11. What is OCB? How does it relate to POB?

12. Identify and define Downs' four styles of leader behavior.

13. What are station house and street sergeants?

14. Discuss three organizational forces from Tannenbaum and Schmidt.

15. Discuss any four of Fiedler's eight leadership behaviors.

16. What is the core of LMX theory?

17. What is the essence of path-goal theory?

18. Contrast leadership substitutes and neutralizers.

19. Compare transactional and transformational leaders.

20. What are four traits of charismatic leaders?

21. Define *servant, spiritual, authentic*, and *ethical leadership*.

22. Define all of the key terms.

INTERNET ACTIVITIES

The Police Executive Research Forum, *www.policeforum.org/perf/pverview.asp*
National Center for Women & Policing, *www.womenandpolicing.org/default.asp*
National Association of Asian American Law Enforcement Commanders,
www.NAAALEC.org
National Organization of Black Law Enforcement Executives, *www.Noblenational.org*

KEY TERMS

advocates: leadership style described by Downs; such leaders promote everything under their control.

affiliation needs: the desire to be accepted and liked.

authentic leadership: (1) being deeply aware of how you think, behave, and are seen by others; (2) awareness of your own and others' values/moral perspectives, knowledge, and strengths; (3) understanding the context in which you operate; and (4) being grounded by confidence, hopefulness, optimism, resiliency, and high moral character.

authoritarian/autocratic: a leadership style; makes all decisions, closely controls work, a micromanager, "my way or the highway."

authority: Weber identified three sources: charismatic, traditional, and rational legal. In police departments it is a formal grant to a position, the incumbent uses it to accomplish organizational goals. Also see power.

Big Five: the traits approach produced long lists of traits; using meta-analysis, five broad trait categories were identified into which the longer lists of traits could be fitted: surency, conscientiousness, agreeableness, adjustment, and intellectance. See Big Two.

Big Two: a refinement of the Big Five: stability and plasticity.

charismatic leadership: Charisma was originally thought to be a gift of abilities from above; failures cannot be charismatic, nor can leaders proclaim themselves to be such. Charismatic leaders have seven traits, including having an innovative vision, inspiring and developing followers, and leading their departments to superior performances.

climbers: leadership style described by Downs; such leaders invent new functions for their units.

conceptual skills: the ability to understand and interrelate various parcels of information that seem unrelated or whose meaning or importance is not immediately apparent.

conservers: leadership style described by Downs; such leaders exhibit bias toward maintaining things under their control.

counterproductive work behavior (CWB): behavior that has a detrimental effect on relationships with coworkers and/or the efficiency of operations.

democratic: a leadership style; encourages individual and group participation, "let's talk about it."

emotional skills (ES): The ability to accurately perceive and appraise your own emotions and those of others, to regulate your own emotions, and to do so while adapting and responding to the needs of others.

ethical leadership: consistent demonstration of moral values though personal actions, in interpersonal communications, and the communication of values to followers. Two components: (1) moral person and (2) moral manager.

"great man" theories: two contrasting views: (1) events that must be responded to produce the great man and (2) great men are "born leaders," exceptionally endowed; one of two branches of traditional leadership theory, the other being the traits approach.

human relations skills: the capacity to interrelate positively with other people.

laissez-faire: a leadership style; takes passive, "hands-off" approach, reluctantly use the authority of one's position, "whatever."

leader: can be contrasted with manager: (1) management is the content of a job, being a leader is how you get it done; (2) one person may be a leader, manager, both, or neither; and (3) a leader is identified by the position he or she occupies in the department's hierarchy. Leaders and managers can be differentiated by the variables identified in Table 7.1. See leadership.

leader member exchange (LMX): theory by Dansereau, Graen, and Haga; those who are like the leader go to the in-group, those unlike the leader go to the out-group, and those about whom the leader is unsure, go to the try-out bin (1975). See life cycle LMX theory (1995).

leadership: (1) relating the police department to the larger/external environment and (2) influencing officers to use their energies willingly and appropriately to achieve the department's goals.

leadership neutralizers: as described by Kerr and Jermier, those who make leadership ineffective or impossible.

leadership substitutes: as described by Kerr and Jermier, those who diminish or take the place of formal leadership.

least preferred coworker (LPC): Fiedler's theory that, underlining LPC is the assumption that how leaders treat their LPC is an indicator of their leadership preference. The relationship of that preference has three situational variables: (1) task structure, (2) leader-follower relations, and (3) the power position of the leader determines group effectiveness.

management systems: as described by Likert, a continuum of four leader styles.

manager: See leader.

Managerial Grid: Blake and Mouton's theory that balances two considerations: (1) concern for people and (2) concern for task to produce five distinct leadership styles.

moral manager: ethical leadership concept, a fair and principled decision maker, who is altruistic, cares about people and the larger society.

moral person: ethical leadership concept, proactively strives to reinforce followers' ethical behavior.

normative decision-making theory: leadership model by Vroom, Yetton, Jago; not a general model of leadership; narrowly focuses on three leadership approaches to decision-making and provides the greatest probability for a good decision, contingent upon follower characteristics.

organizational citizenship behavior (OCB): the extra things followers do that are not required, but contribute to organizational effectiveness. See POB.

path-goal theory (PGT): theory by House, 1996; revised his 1971 theory. The essence of PGT is that for leaders to be effective, they must engage in leader behaviors that compensate for the deficiencies of their subordinates, enhance their performance, and are instrumental to their individual and work unit performance and satisfaction.

personalized power needs: the desire to be in control for selfish, self-aggrandizing reasons.

positive organizational behavior (POB): a broader cluster of organizational behaviors that contribute to its overall success; OCB is included within POB by some researchers. See OCB.

power: when a formal grant of authority is made, some power inherently accompanies it, to maintain standards, correct deficiencies, and discipline as needed. However, even with authority and power, leaders may not be able to compel others to perform. To a significant degree, power is a grant made by the led to the leader. Also see authority.

power motivation: see affiliation, personalized power, and socialized power needs.

servant leadership: as described by Greenleaf, primary orientation is the theory that leaders should first be servants, meeting the legitimate needs of their followers.

situational leadership: leadership model by Hersey and Blanchard; relates the behavior of the leaders to the maturity of followers, identifies the most probable successful leader behaviors for each level of maturity.

skill: how knowledge gets translated into action.

social skills (SS): the ability to express oneself in social situations; the ability to "read" social situations; recognizing different social roles and expected behavior; and interpersonal problem solving; closely related to ES.

socialized power needs: the desire to have a positive impact on the department's operations and administration.

spiritual leadership: leadership divided into two camps: those who are more overtly religious and those who define spirituality in another way. People can be spiritual without being religious, seeking meaning in their lives. Spiritual in this sense means having a closer connection with one's higher values and morality. Spiritual leadership taps into followers' higher-order needs (e.g., challenging work that is socially meaningful). See spiritual survival.

spiritual survival: (1) transcendence, a sense of being called to a profession and (2) membership, a sense of belonging.

station house sergeants: as described by Van Maanen, such sergeants work inside, have a strong conformity orientation, are immersed in the police department's management culture, and make contacts that can help career.

street sergeants: as described by Van Maanen, such sergeants have a distaste for office procedures, are action oriented, are more likely to be investigated and sued, and may not advance beyond middle management.

Tannenbaum and Schmidt: authors who identified a theory of leader styles (1958), revising it to a full situational leadership theory (1973).

technical skills: skills that are essential to doing a job; vary by level within a police organization (e.g., identifying physical evidence versus preparing a budget).

traits approach: relatively stable predispositions to behave in a certain way; since roughly 1910 there has been interest in identifying the traits leaders have. Also see great man theory.

transactional leadership: leadership style that gives something (rewards) to get something (performance by followers). TLers appeal to the self-interest of followers. A basic system of reciprocity. Followers are motivated by lower levels of Maslow's needs hierarchy.

transformational leadership: leadership style that inspires followers to "elevate their game," go beyond self-interests, and make more and larger contributions than they had originally intended. In the process, transformational leaders help them to grow personally and professionally, to develop their own capabilities for leadership. Transformational leaders appeal to followers' ideals and values, aligning them with the organization's.

zealots: leadership style described by Downs; such leaders have narrow interests, focus almost entirely on them.

ENDNOTES

[1] Joseph A. Schafer, "Developing Effective Leadership in Policing: Perils, Pitfalls, and Paths Forward," *Policing: An International Journal of Police Strategies and Management*, Vol. 32, No. 2, 2009, p. 239.

[2] Ibid., p. 239.

[3] Among the exceptions to this is Joseph A. Devine, An Analysis of the West Point Leadership and Command Program's Impact Upon Law Enforcement Leadership, Dissertation in Partial Fulfillment of the Requirements for the Doctor of Education Degree, Seton Hall University, 2007.

[4] Developing Effective Leadership in Policing, pp. 247–250. The authors have extended some of Schafer's cogent points; any distortion or dilution is unintended.

[5] Terry D. Anderson et. al., *Every Officer Is a Leader* (Boca Raton: St. Lucie Press, 2000), p. viii.

[6] J. Gregory Reynolds and Walter H. Warfield, "Discerning the Differences Between Managers and Leaders," *Educational Digest*, Vol. 75, Issue 7, March 2010, pp. 26–29.

[7] Beverly Alimo Metcalfe and John Alimo-Metcalfe, "The Myths and Morality of Leadership in the NHS," *Clinician in Management*, Vol. 12, 2004, p. 49.

[8] John P. Kotter, "What Leaders Really do," *Harvard Business Review*, May/June 1990, pp. 103–111.

[9] See Brigitte Steinheider and Todd Wuestewald, "From the Bottom Up: Sharing Leadership in a Police Agency," Police Practice and Research, Vol. 9, Issue 2, May 2008, pp. 145–163.

[10] On this point see Derrick J. Neufeld, Zeying Wan, and Yulin Fang, "Remote Leadership, Communication Effectiveness and Leader Performance, *Group Decision and Negotiation*, Vol.19, Issue 3, May 2010, pp. 227–246. For more extended information see Suzanne Weisband, *Leadership at a Distance* (New York: Lawrence Erlbaum Associates, 2008).

[11] On the low end, see Fred W. Rainguet and Mary Dodge, "The Problems of Police Chiefs: An Examination of the Issues in Tenure and Turnover," *Police Quarterly*, Vol. 4, No. 3, September 2001, p. 269 and on the high side, Steve Krull, *California Police Chief Demographic Study* (Sacramento: California Police Chiefs Association, 2004), p. 2.

[12] Jim Isenberg, *Police Leadership in a Democracy: Conversations with America's Police Chiefs* (Boca Raton: CRC Press, 2010), p. 28.

[13] Phil Coleman, "New Ideas for Solving the Police Chief Recruitment Crisis" (Sacramento: League of California Cities, October, 2007), p. 1.

[14] Isenberg, *Police Leadership in a Democracy: Conversations with America's Police Chiefs*, p. 42.

[15] Several of these points are taken from Robert Hogan, Gordon J. Curphy, and Joyce Hogan, "What We Know About Leadership," *American Psychologist*, Vol. 49, No. 6, June 1994, pp. 493–504. The police examples were added by the authors.

[16] Kenneth Blanchard, Drea Zigarmi, and Patricia Zigarma, *Leadership and the One-Minute Manager: Increasing Effectiveness Through Situational Leadership* (New York: William Morrow, 1999), p. 38.

[17] Jean Lipman-Blumen, *The Allure of Toxic Leaders* (New York: Oxford University Press, 2005), pp. 19–20.

[18] Ibid., pp. 21–22.

[19] Melissa Horner, "Leadership Theory: Past, Present, and Future," *Team Performance Management*, Vol. 3, No. 4, 1997, p. 276.

[20] Max Weber, *The Theory of Social and Economic Organizations*, translated by A. M. Henderson and Talcott Parsons, (New York: Free Press, 1947), p. 328.

[21] J. R. French and B. Raven, "The Bases of Social Power," in D. Cartwright, editor, *Studies in Social Power* (Ann Arbor: University of Michigan, Institute for Social Research, 1959), pp. 150–167.

[22] Jacques Steinberg, "Police Officer Rejects Promotion," *New York Times*, June 2, 1991. Although an older example, it is a perfect illustration of the point made in the text.

[23] Chester Barnard also wrote on organizations as an open system. See *The Functions of the Executive* (Cambridge, Mass.: Harvard University Press, 15th edition, 1962). *Functions* was originally published in 1938. On many points he must be read in the context of his own time. See Steven M. Dunphy and James Hoopes, "Chester Barnard: Member of the Elite?" *Management Decision*, Vol. 40, No. 10, 2002, pp. 1024–1028.

[24] The flip side of the coin is the question "Under what conditions do organizational members voluntarily elect to leave, stay and protest, or simply stay?" An important book addressing these issues is Albert O. Hirschman, *Exit, Voice, and Loyalty* (Cambridge, Mass.: Harvard University Press, 1970).

[25] Isenberg, *Police Leadership in a Democracy: Conversations with America's Police Chiefs*, p. 119.

[26] The description of power motivation styles is drawn, with restatement into a police context, from Jay Hall and James Hawker, "Interpreting Your Scores from the Power Management Inventory" (The Woodlands, Texas: Teleometrics International, 2000).

[27] See Joe C. Magee and Carrie A. Langer, "How Personalized and Socialized Power Motivation Facilitate Antisocial and Prosocial Decision Making, *Journal of Research in Personality*, Vol. 42, Issue 6, December 2008, pp. 1547–1559.

[28] Todd Wuestewald, "Shared Leadership: Can Empowerment Work in a Police Organization? *The Police Chief*, Vol. 73, No. 1, January 2006. On-line access, p. 5.

[29] The basic model is drawn from Robert Katz, "Skills of an Effective Administrator," *Harvard Business Review*, Vol. 33, No. 1, 1955, pp. 33–42. It continues to draw attention; see Robert L. Katz, "Skills of An Effective Administrator" (Cambridge, Mass.: Harvard Business Review, 2005).

[30] There is no shortage of skill models. For example, see Troy V. Mumford, Michsel A. Campion, and Frederick P. Morgeson, "The Leadership Skills Strataplex: Leadership Skill Requirements Across Organizational Levels, *The Leadership Quarterly*, Vol. 18, 2007, pp. 154–166. The model uses four skills: factors: cognitive, interpersonal, business, and strategic. See p. 156.

[31] No author, "Leadership Trends for 2010," *Business Week Online*, February 17, 2010, p. 1.

[32] Thomas Carlyle, *Heroes, Hero-Worship and the Heroic in History* (New York: A. L. Burt, 1902), and G. W. F. Hegel, *The Philosophy of History* (Indianapolis: Bobbs-Merrill, 1952).

[33] See R. D. Avery et. al., "Developmental and Genetic Determinants of Leadership Role Occupancy Among Women," *Journal of Applied Psychology*, Vol. 92, Issue 3, 2007, pp. 693–706.

[34] Francis Galton, *Hereditary Genius: An Inquiry into Its Laws and Consequences* (New York: D. Appleton, revised with an American preface, 1887).

[35] Gary Yukl, *Leadership in Organizations* (Upper Saddle River, N.J.: Prentice Hall, 2010), p. 190.

[36] Field Marshal Montgomery, *The Path to Leadership* (New York: Putnam, 1961), pp. 10–19. To some extent, Montgomery also holds with Carlyle in that the former asserted that the leader must be able to dominate and master the surrounding events.

[37] W. Allport and H. S. Odbert, "Trait-Names: A Psycholexical Study," *Psychological Monographs*, 1936, 47, No. 211.

[38] Ralph M. Stogdill, *Handbook of Leadership: A Survey of Theory and Research* (New York: Free Press, 1974), p. 81 and "Personality Factors Associated with Leadership: A Survey of the Literature," *Journal of Psychology*, pp. 25–26 (January 1948), pp. 35–71.

[39] Cecil Goode, "Significant Research on Leadership," *Personnel* 25, No. 5, 1951, p. 349.

[40] For example, see Robert J. Allio, "Leadership—The Five Big Ideas," *Strategy and Leadership*, Vol. 37, Issue 2, 2009, p. 412.

[41] Stephen Erdle et. al., "The General Factor of Personality and Its Relation to Self-Esteem," *Personality and Individual Differences*, Vol. 48, 2010, p. 344.

[42] Stephen J. Zaccaro, "Trait-Based Perspectives of Leadership," *American Psychologist*, Vol. 62, No. 1, January 2007, p. 14, on-line access.

[43] Reuven Bar-On, "The Bar-On Model of Emotional-Social Intelligence," in P. Berrocal and N. Extremera, Guest Editors, Special Issue on Emotional Intelligence, *Psicothema*, Vol. 17, 2005, p. 15.

[44] Lynda, Jiwen Song et. al., "The Differential Effects of General Mental Ability and Emotional Intelligence on Academic Performance and Social Interactions," *Intelligence*, Vol. 38, Issue 1, January 2010, pp. 137–143.

[45] Melanie B. Malterer, Samantha Glass, and Joseph Newman, "Psychotherapy and Trait Emotional Intelligence," *Personality and Individual Differences*, Vol. 44, Issue 3, February 2008, pp. 733–743.

[46] Oluremi Ayoko, Victor Callan, and Charmine Hartel, "The Influence of Emotional Intelligence Climate on Conflict and Team Members' Reactions to Conflict," *Small Group Research*, Vol. 39, Issue 2, April 2008, pp. 121–149.

[47] A. Oyesoji Aremu and T. Oluwayemisi, "Assessment of Emotional Intelligence Among Nigerian Police," *Journal of Social Science*, Vol. 16, No. 3, 2008, p. 275.

[48] Kathryn L. Barbera et. al., "Relating Emotional and Social Intelligence to Sex and Age, Nevada State Psychological Association Meeting, Las Vegas, May 17, 2003, p. 3.

[49] Reuven Bar-On, "Emotional Intelligence: An Integral Part of Positive Psychology," *South African Journal of Psychology*, Vol. 40, Issue 1, April 2010, p. 46.

[50] Ibid., p. 170.

[51] John D. Mayer and Peter Salovey, "What is Emotional Intelligence?" in Peter Salovey and D. Sluyter, editors, *Emotional Development and Emotional Intelligence* (New York: Basic Books, 1997), p. 10.

[52] Ronald E. Riggio and Rebecca J. Reichard, "The Emotional and Social Intelligences of Effective Leadership," *Journal of Managerial Psychology*, Vol. 23, No. 2, 2008, p. 171.

[53] Ibid., pp. 172–173, 175–176.

[54] Fatih Tepe, Leadership Characteristics Among Command, Middle, and Line Level Police Department Personnel in the Era of Terrorism, Dissertation Abstracts International, *The Humanities and Social Sciences*, Vol. 69, No. 7, 2002, p. 2564, 2009.

[55] Kuldeep et. al. "Linking the Big Five Personality Domains to Organizational Citizenship Behavior," *International Journal of Psychological Studies*, Vol. 1, No. 2, December 2009, p. 73.

[56] Suzy Fox, Paul E. Spector, and Don Miles, "Counter Productive Work Behavior in Response to Job Stressors and Organizational Justice," *Journal of Vocational Behavior*, Vol. 59, 2001, p. 292.

[57] Ibid., p. 297.

[58] Jennifer M. George and Garth R. Jones, *Organizational Behavior* (Addison-Wesley Publishing Company, 1999), p. 41.

[59] Gary Dessler, *Organization and Management: A Contingency Approach* (Englewood Cliffs, N.J.: Prentice Hall, 1976), p. 158.

[60] See K. Lewin, R. Lippitt, and R. White, "Patterns of Aggressive Behavior in Experimentally Created Social Climates," *Journal of Social Psychology* 10 (May 1939), pp. 271–299; R. Lippitt and R. K. White, "The Social Climate of Children's Groups," in *Child Behavior and Development*, ed. R. G. Baker, K. S. Kounin, and H. F. Wright (New York: McGraw-Hill, 1943), pp. 485–508; Ralph White and Ronald Lippitt, "Leader Behavior and Member Reaction in Three Social Climates," in *Group Dynamics: Research and Theory*, 2nd ed., ed. Dorwin Cartwright and Alvin Zander (New York: Harper & Row, 1960), pp. 552–553; and Ronald Lippitt, "An Experimental Study of the Effect of Democratic and Authoritarian Group Atmospheres," *University of Iowa Studies in Child Welfare* 16 (January 1940), pp. 43–195.

[61] Bernard M. Bass and Ronald E. Riggio, *Transformational Leadership* (Mahwah, N.J.: Lawrence Erlbaum Associates, 2nd ed., 2006), pp. 8–9.

[62] White and Lippitt, "Leader Behavior, pp. 539–545, 552–553.

[63] Stephen A. Morreale, "Perceived Leader Styles in Law Enforcement," Masters Thesis, Nova Southeastern University, 2002, 12 pp. On-line access to abstract.

[64] Robert R. Blake and Jane Mouton, "The Development Revolution in Management Practices," *Journal of the American Society of Training Directors,* Vol. 16, No. 7, 1962, pp. 29–52.

[65] The Ohio State studies date from the mid-1940s and identified the dimensions of consideration and structure; the University of Michigan studies date from the late 1940s and identified employee- and production-centered supervisors.

[66] Anthony Downs, *Inside Bureaucracy* (Boston: Little, Brown, 1967).

[67] Ibid., pp. 92–96.

[68] Ibid., pp. 96–101.

[69] Ibid., pp. 109–110.

[70] Ibid., pp. 107–109.

[71] John Van Maanen, "Making Rank: Becoming an American Police Sergeant," *Urban Life* 13, no. 2–3 (1984), pp. 155–176. The distinction between station and street sergeants is drawn from Van Maanen's work with some restatement and extension of views. The speculation about future career patterns is the work of the present authors.

[72] Robert Tannenbaum and Warren Schmidt, "How to Choose a Leadership Pattern," *Harvard Business Review*, May/June,1973, pp. 162–180.

[73] Victor H. Vroom and Philip W. Yetton, *Leadership and Decision-Making* (Pittsburgh: University of Pittsburgh Press, 1973), p. 18.

[74] John B. Miner, *Organizational Behavior* (New York: Oxford University Press, 2002), pp. 320–321.

[75] Gary Yukl, "Toward a Behavioral Theory of Leadership," *Organizational Behavior and Human Performance*, Vol. 6, Issue 4, July 1971, p. 434.

[76] Fred E. Fiedler and Joseph E. Garcia, *New Approaches to Effective Leadership* (New York: John Wiley & Sons, 1987), pp. 52–61.

[77] Afsaneh Hahavandi and Ali R. Malekzadeh, *Organizational Behavior* (Upper Saddle River, N.J.: Prentice Hall, 1999), pp. 305–306.

[78] Robert P. Vecchio, "An Empirical Examination of the Validity of Fiedler's Model of Leadership Effectiveness," *Organizational Behavior and Human Performance*, Vol. 19, Issue 1, June 1977, p. 203.

[79] R. W. Rice, "Construct Validity of the Least Preferred Coworker Scale," *Psychological Bulletin*, Vol. 85, No. 6, November 1978, pp. 1199–1237.

[80] Lawrence H. Peters, Darrell D. Hartke, and John T. Pohlmann, "Fiedler's Contingency Model," *Psychological Bulletin*, Vol. 95, No. 2, March 1985, pp. 274–285.

[81] *New Approaches to Effective Leadership*, pp. 76–77.

[82] John K. Kennedy, Jr., "Middle LPC Leaders and the Contingency Model of Leadership Effectiveness," *Organizational Behavior and Human Performance*, Vol. 30, Issue 1, August 1982, pp. 1–14.

[83] Yukl, *Leadership in Organizations*, p. 228.

[84] R. J. House, "A Path Goal Theory of Leadership Effectiveness," *Administrative Science Quarterly*, Vol. 16, 1971, pp. 321–329.

[85] Robert J. House, "Path-Goal Theory of Leadership: Lessons, Legacy, and A Reformulated Theory," *The Leadership Quarterly*, Vol. 7, No. 3, Autumn 1996, p. 325.

[86] L. Huberts, M. Kaptein, and K. Lasthuizen, "A Study of the Impact of Three Leadership Styles on Integrity Violations by Police Officers," *Policing*, Vol. 30, Issue 4, November 2007, pp. 587–606. The findings are based on the responses of Netherlands police officers.

[87] "Path-Goal Theory of Leadership: Lessons, Legacy, and Reformulated Theory," p. 348.

[88] Ibid., p. 347.

[89] Although not using the LMX designation, the first articulation of it was Fred Dansereau, George Graen, and William J. Haga, "A Vertical Dyad Linkage Approach to Leadership within Formal Organizations," *Organizational Behavior and Human Performance*, Vol. 13, 1975, pp. 46–78.

[90] The descriptions of these two groups are drawn from Jun Liu and Xiaogu Liu, "A Critical Review of Leadership Research Development," *International Journal of Business and Management*, Vol. 1, No. 4, August 2006, pp. 7–8.

[91] George Graen and M. Uhl-Bien, "Relationship Based Approach to Leadership: Development of a Leader-Member Exchange (LMX) Theory of Leadership Over 25 Years," *Leadership Quarterly*, Vol. 6, pp. 219–247. The concepts were not clearly defined and understanding of them was partially derived by the context in which they were used. Our characterization of the authors' work is our best understanding of what they intended.

[92] J. Miner, "The Uncertain Future of the Leadership Concept," in James Hunt and Lars Larson, Editors, *Leadership Frontiers* (Kent, Ohio: Kent State University Press, 1975).

[93] Steven Kerr and John M. Jermier, "Substitutes of Leadership: Their Meaning and Measurement," *Organizational Behavior and Human Performance*, Vol. 22, No. 3, 1978, pp. 377, 395.

[94] Margaret L. Williams and Philip Podsakoff, "A Preliminary Analysis of the Construct Validity of Kerr and Jermier's Substitutes of Leadership Scales," *Journal of Occupational Psychology*, Vol. 61, No. 4, 1988, pp. 307–333.

[95] R. J. Lewicki, E. C. Wiethoff, and E. Tomlinson, "What is the Role of Trust in Organizational Justice?" in Jerald Greenberg and Jason Colquitt, Editors, *Handbook of Organizational Justice* (Mahwah, N.J.: Lawrence Erlbaum Associates, 2005), pp. 247–270.

[96] Hersey and Blanchard, *Management of Organizational Behavior*, pp. 160–161.

[97] Ibid.

[98] Ibid., p. 163.

[99] Ibid., p. 161.

[100] Ibid., p. 163.

[101] Ibid., p. 159.

[102] Thomas D. Cairns et. al., "Technical Note: A Study of Hersey and Blanchard's Situational Theory," *Journal of Leadership and Organization Development*, Vol. 19, Issue 2, 1998, pp. 113–116.

[103] Bernard M. Bass with Ruth Bass, *The Bass Handbook of Leadership* (New York: Free Press, 2008), p. 493.

[104] Yukl, *Leadership in Organizations*, p. 99.

[105] James McGregor Burns, *Leadership* (New York: Harper & Row, 1978).

[106] Ibid., pp. 4, 19–20.

[107] Yukl, *Leadership in Organizations*, p. 261.

[108] Bass and Bass, *The Bass Handbook of Leadership*, p. 619.

[109] Steven A. Murphy and Edward N. Drodge, "The Four Is of Police Leadership," *International Journal of Police Science and Management*, Vol. 6, Issue 1, March 2004, pp. 1–15.

[110] See B. M. Bass, *Leadership and Performance* (New York: Free Press, 1985).

[111] V. R. Krishan, "Transformational Leadership and Outcomes," *International Journal of Value Based Management*, Vol. 25, No. 5/6, 2005, pp. 19–33.

[112] Bass and Riggio, *Transformational Leadership*, p. 3.

[113] Ronald F. Piccolo and Jason A. Colquitt, "Transformational Leadership and Job Behaviors," *Academy of Management Journal*, Vol. 49, No. 2, 2006, p. 327.

[114] Simon A. Moss and Somon Ngu, *Current Research in Social Psychology*, Vol. 11, No. 6, 2006, p. 71.

[115] Isenberg, *Police Leadership in a Democracy: Conversations with America's Police Chiefs*, p. 115.

[116] Ibid.

[117] Bass and Riggio, *Transformational Leadership*, p. 228.

[118] Ibid., pp. 228–229.

[119] Ibid., p. 229.

[120] Bass and Bass, *The Bass Handbook of Leadership*, p. 580.

[121] J. Lee Whittington et. al., "Transactional Leadership Revisited," *Journal of Applied Social Psychology*, Vol. 39, Issue 8, August 2009, pp. 1860–1886.

[122] Yi-Feng Yang, "An Investigation of Group Interaction Functioning Stimulated by Transformational Leadership on Employee Intrinsic and Extrinsic Job Satisfaction," *Social Behavior and Personality*, Vol. 37, Issue 9, 2009, pp. 1259–1277.

[123] Fehmidah Munir, Karina Nielsen, and Isabella Gomes, "Transformational Leadership and Depressive Symptoms," *Journal of Affective Disorders*, Vol. 120, Issue 1-3, January 2010, pp. 235–239.

[124] Rajinandini Pillai and Ethlyn Williams, "Transformational Leadership, Self-Efficacy, Group Cohesiveness, Commitment, and Performance," *Journal of Organizational Change Management*, Vol. 17, Issue 2, 2004, pp. 144–159.

[125] Rabia Khan, Abaid Ur Rehman, and Afsheen Fatima, "Transformational Leadership and Organizational Commitment," *African Journal of Business Management*, Vol. 3, No. 11, November 2009, p. 683.

[126] Roya Ayman and Karen Korabik, "Why Gender and Culture Matter," *American Psychologist*, Vol. 65, No. 3, April 2010, p. 164.

[127] Mary Sarver, Holly Miller, and Jennifer Schulenberg, "Leadership and Effectiveness: An Examination of the Leadership Styles of Texas Police Chiefs," Paper presented at the 2008 Annual Meeting of the American Society of Criminology, St. Louis. On-line access of abstract.

[128] Steven A. Murphy and Edward N. Drodge, "The Four Is of Police Leadership," *International Journal of Police Science and Management*, Vol. 6, No. 1, 2004, p. 10. The description of all four Is is drawn from this source.

[129] Yukl, *Leadership in Organizations*, p. 262.

[130] Ibid., pp. 272–274.

[131] Ibid., p. 285.

[132] Ibid., pp. 261 and 285–286.

[133] Robert J. House and Ram N. Aditya, "The Social Scientific Study of Leadership: Quo Vadis?" *Journal of Management*, Vol. 23, May/June 1997, pp. 409–473.

[134] Robert K. Greenleaf, *Servant Leadership* (Mahwah, N.J.: The Paulist Press, 1977), p. 13.

[135] Yukl, *Leadership in Organizations*, p. 419.

[136] A. Gregory Stone, Robert Russell, and Kathleen Patterson, "Transformational Leadership: A Difference in Leader Focus," *Leadership and Organization Development*, Vol. 25, Issue 4, 2003, pp. 349–361.

[137] Larry Spears, "Practicing Servant-Leadership," *Lead to Leader Journal*, No. 34, 2004, approximately three pp., on-line access. The authors have restated portions of these 10 points and added commentary. No alteration of the author's position is intended.

[138] Yukl, *Leadership in Organizations*, p. 421.

[139] For example, see John E. Barbuto, Jr., "Scale Development and Construct Clarification of Servant Leadership," *Group and Organization Development*, Vol. 31, No. 3, 2006, pp. 300–326.

[140] Mark McKergow, "Host Leadership," *International Journal of Leadership in Public Services*, Vol. 5, Issue 1, March 2009, p. 20.

[141] Deborah Eicher-Catt, "The Myth of Servant-Leadership: A Feminist Perspective," *Women and Language*, Spring, Vol. 28, Issue 1, 2005, pp. 17–25.

[142] Yukl, *Leadership in Organizations*, p. 421.

[143] Bruce J. Avolio, Fred O. Walumbwa, and Todd J. Wheeler, "Leadership: Current Theories, Research, and Future Directions," *The Annual Review of Psychology*, 2009, p. 438.

[144] Cathy Lynn Grossman, "Survey: 72% of Millennials 'More Spiritual than Religious,'" *USA Today*, April 27, 2010.

[145] Louis W. Fry, "Toward a Theory of Spiritual Leadership," *The Leadership Quarterly*, Vol. 14, 2003, p. 702.

[146] Ibid., pp. 698–700.

[147] Ibid., pp. 699–700.

[148] Yukl, *Leadership in Organizations*, p. 422.

[149] Laura Reave, "Spiritual Values and Practices Related to Leadership Effectiveness," *The Leadership Quarterly*, Vol. 16, Issue 5, October 2005, pp. 655–687.

[150] Frank Markow and Karin Klenke, "The Effects of Personal Meaning and Calling on Organizational Commitment: An Empirical Investigation of Spiritual Leadership," *International Journal of Organizational Analysis*, Vol. 13, Issue 1, 2005, pp. 8–27.

[151] Maragret Benefiel, "The Second Half of the Journey," *The Leadership Quarterly*, Vol. 16, Issue 5, October 2005, p. 727.

[152] Fry, "Toward a Theory of Spiritual Leadership," pp. 715–716.

[153] William L. Gardner et. al., "Can You See the Real Me?" *The Leadership Quarterly*, Vol. 16, 2005, p. 344.

[154] Cecily Cooper, Terri Scandura, and Chester Schriescheim, "Looking Forward But Learning From Our Past: Potential Challenges to Developing Authentic Leadership Theory and Authentic Leaders," *The Leadership Quarterly*, Vol. 16, Issue 3, June 2005, p. 478.

[155] Bruce J. Avolio and William A. Gardner, "Authentic Leadership Development: Getting to the Root of Positive Forms of Leadership," *The Leadership Quarterly*, Vol. 16, Issue 3, June 2005, p. 327.

[156] Ibid., p. 328.

[157] Cooper, Scandura, and Schriescheim, "Looking Forward But Learning From Our Past: Potential Challenges to Developing Authentic Leadership Theory and Authentic Leaders," pp. 481–483.

[158] Yukl, *Leadership in Organizations*, p. 427.

[159] M. E. Brown et. al., "Ethical Leadership," *Organizational Behavior and Human Decision Processes*, Vol. 97, 2005, p. 120.

[160] Michael E. Brown and Linda K. Trevino, "Ethical Leadership: A Review and Future Directions," *The Leadership Quarterly*, Vol. 17, Issue 6, December 2006, p. 599.

[161] Ibid., p. 600.

[162] Ibid., pp. 610–611.

[163] Yukl, *Leadership in Organizations*, p. 416.

8

Planning and Decision Making

Objectives

- Explain some advantages of planning within a police department.

- Discuss the synoptic planning approach. Describe three methods of selecting a preferred course of action.

- Discuss the differences among administrative, procedural, operational, and tactical plans.

- Describe the characteristics of effective plans.

- List the three major decision-making models.

- Discuss Simon's concept of "bounded rationality."

- Explain Lindblom's theory of incremental decision making.

- Describe the decision-making process as presented by William Gore.

- List some of the important recommendations, developed in this chapter, for handling future crisis events.

- Discuss the advantages of group decision making.

- List the steps decision makers should take when confronted with an ethical issue.

- Explain the most common errors in decision making.

The essence of ultimate decision remains impenetrable to the observer, often, indeed, to the decider himself. . . . There will always be the dark and tangled stretches in the decision-making process— mysterious even to those who may be most ultimately involved.
—John F. Kennedy

OUTLINE

Introduction

Planning and decision-making are critical processes for effective police administration because: (1) planning is the first step to the effective operation and good management of a police department; (2) planning is an essential element of decision-making; (3) effective planning can eliminate or reduce potential catastrophe resulting from manmade and natural disasters; (4) decision making can usually be described in three types of theoretical models—rational, incremental, and heuristic—none of which defines *all* of the elements and factors that affect every decision; (5) the decisions individuals make during crisis situations often define their leadership abilities and, in some cases, their career success; (6) police administrators rarely act alone and most decision making within a police department is conducted at the group level; and (7) decision making is rarely perfect, and is often marred by individual and group weaknesses that can be identified and, hence, avoided.

Decision Making: An Overview

Those who are appointed to positions of leadership in police and other law enforcement agencies are generally chosen for their experience, their proven abilities to take charge and guide an agency through the routine day-to-day, as well as through crisis events. Think for a moment about some of the challenges that the last 10 or 12 years have brought to police leadership. The events of 2001 brought about a whole new realm of planning and decision making for law enforcement. Suddenly, municipalities of all sizes were forced to come up with solid plans for responses to terrorist attacks and police executives had to make decisions about special task forces, interagency collaborations, crowd management, and other emergency initiatives that they had never before considered. The new paradigm of the information age has also put decision making and planning at the forefront of leadership considerations in policing. The instant availability of information to both police and the citizens they serve has created more urgency and an increased accountability for decision makers. And now consider the economic realities of the times—police executives are being asked to cut programs, to lay off employees, to operate their departments on shoestring budgets—all while keeping crime rates down and ensuring the safety of their officers. When you consider the concepts of planning and decision making under those circumstances, you begin to really appreciate the important roles that they play in the daily operations of a police agency.

Decision making is a complex process that includes not only procedures for reaching a sound decision on the basis of pertinent knowledge, beliefs, and judgments but also procedures for obtaining the required knowledge, ideas, and preconditions. Moreover, in the case of important decisions, these procedures may involve many minor decisions taken at various stages in the decision-making process. For example, a chief's decision to purchase a new type of squad car for the department usually follows a series of smaller decisions. First, the chief decides that the present fleet is aging and is inadequate for the needs of the officers driving them. Second, a decision is made to evaluate different makes and models of squad cars available on the open market. This decision probably accompanied the decision to address the city council to request additional funding with which to purchase the new vehicles. And finally, the chief must decide if additional equipment will be required to outfit the new fleet. These minor decisions are only part of the overall process in arriving at a major decision. Thus, the decision to take a certain action, if sound, should be based on the judgment that this action probably will have more desirable results than any other action, and this judgment may be based on conclusions as to the probable consequences of alternative decisions.[1]

Decision making also involves the application of our knowledge, our experience, and our mental and moral skills and powers to determine what actions should be taken to deal with a variety of problem situations. Moreover, this decision-making process includes the application of logic for testing conclusions and the use of ethics for testing judgment.[2] For instance, an officer's decision to arrest a violent, drunk husband at a family disturbance is usually based on the officer's past knowledge that, if the current situation is left unattended, the probable result will be a criminal act involving assault, wife or child abuse, or even murder. Ethically, the officer is bound to deter crime and so will take the necessary course of action to prevent the physical harm of any family member.

Decision making is a responsibility that all police officers come to accept routinely. These decisions can be as ordinary as deciding whether to write a motorist a traffic citation or as complex as a split-second decision whether to shoot at someone. The quality and types of decisions made by police managers in their policy formulation and by the street-level officer in invoking arrest action, are based, in part, on the personality characteristics of the individual making the decision, the recruiting and career development practices of the police department, and, equally important, the type of community being served. For example, one merely has to read the works of Wilson[3] and Skolnick[4] to conclude that enforcement decisions that appear to be quite adequate for one community may be totally unacceptable for another and that recruitment practices that would be acceptable to one community would draw objections from another. Thus, police administrators can follow no single model to make the best decisions all the time. However, certain principles, when understood and applied carefully, can result in good decisions much of the time. And although sometimes not understood as such, planning is a basic part of this decision-making process.

Planning

It seems obvious that planning is so important to an organization, and on a surface level, many organizations will pay lip service to their planning processes. But consider for a moment an example from the private sector—that of the BP oil spill in the Gulf of Mexico in 2010. BP had template procedures to address emergency situations, but when an explosion on an oil rig blew out an underwater well, the company took nearly 12 days to formulate its first plan of attack. The templates failed to consider an accident of such magnitude. The result was that a catastrophic amount of oil spilled into the Gulf, infecting coastlines and wildlife around the southeastern United States. Now consider what would happen if police organizations took a similar approach to planning—trying to adapt basic templates to a situation like an active shooter on a college campus. In the case of a crisis like an active shooter, there simply is not the time to make a template fit a given situation. Administrators should have solid ideas about how to address situations from the mundane to the catastrophic as a matter of course, complete with back-up plans, contingency plans, and alternate plans if something goes awry.

Police administrators sometimes do not appreciate the importance of planning because of their pattern of career development. It is ironic that the pattern of career development for typical police managers carries with it seeds that sometimes blossom into a negative view of planning. Having spent substantial portions of their careers in line divisions, such as patrol and investigative services, police managers may see planning as "clerical" or "not real police work." Further, because many agencies have a "planning and research" unit, there is a natural tendency to believe that planning should occur only in that area by individuals assigned to that task. However, planning is an integral element of good management and good decision making.[5] It is one of the most critical ingredients to the success of any organizational undertaking. Management needs to anticipate and shape events; it is weak if it merely responds to them.[6] The police manager whose time is consumed by dealing with crises is symptomatic of a department with no real planning or decision-making process—planning is the most crucial ingredient to the success of any activity within an organization. Police departments are sometimes said to be practicing "management by crisis"; in fact, it is "crisis by management."[7] That is, the lack of attention given by police managers to planning creates an environment in which crises occur with regularity. This is so because management by crisis produces a present-centered orientation in which considerations of the future are minimal. In contrast, planning can be expected to accomplish the following:

1. Improve the analysis of problems
2. Provide better information for decision making
3. Help to clarify goals, objectives, and priorities
4. Result in more effective allocation of resources
5. Improve inter- and intradepartmental cooperation and coordination
6. Improve the performance of programs
7. Give the police department a clear sense of direction
8. Provide the opportunity for greater public support
9. Increase the commitment of personnel

In short, competent planning is a sure sign of good police administration and the first step in accurate decision making.[8]

Definitions of Planning

There are no simple definitions of planning. The word **planning** became common terminology in the vocabulary of criminal justice with the introduction of the Omnibus Crime Control and Safe Streets Act of 1968. However, what appeared to be missing in that document was an examination of what planning actually involved or what it meant in the operation of criminal justice organizations. Hudzik and Cordner[9] have defined planning as "thinking about the future, thinking about what we want the future to be, and thinking about what we need to do now to achieve it." Stated more

Planning Police Responses to Disasters: NOPD's Response to Hurricane Katrina (2005) and the BP Oil Spill (2010)

In the days after Hurricane Katrina made landfall in August 2005, problems in communications and coordination, planning, and execution undermined the ability of the New Orleans Police Department (NOPD) to respond to victims of the storm. Many officers had to be rescued themselves, and the department lost nearly 7 percent of its officers in the days after the storm, because they either quit or were fired. The chief characterized the storm as one that was so incomprehensible that it was nearly impossible to have planned for.

Nearly 5 years later, in April 2010, the Deepwater Horizon offshore rig operated by British Petroleum (BP) exploded, gushing nearly 50,000 barrels of oil per day into the Gulf of Mexico, headed for the sandy beaches and bayou marshes of Alabama, Louisiana, and Florida. Once again, the New Orleans Police Department found itself headfirst in a major catastrophic event of epic proportions. President Obama likened the spill to the terrorists attacks of 9/11—just as the events of September 11, 2001 profoundly shaped our views of the vulnerabilities to attack and significantly changed foreign policy, so too would the BP oil spill impact our planning, policy and decision-making regarding the environment and energy. As the largest city nearest the spill and the closest to the hardest-hit areas of the Mississippi Delta, New Orleans became the center for staging operations and monitoring aimed at protecting the shoreline, safeguarding wildlife, and recovering oil. It also became the site for demonstrations and frustrations resulting in the calamity of lost jobs and environmental destruction.

While communication within New Orleans intermittingly broke down in the handling of protestors in 2010, it was nothing like the perceived atmosphere of absolute lawlessness that marred the Katrina relief efforts. Then too, the command structure remained intact, with officers assigned to squads with specific duties in an effort to coordinate tasks. Setting booms to protect marshlands, organizing work groups, *and* protecting buildings in the French Quarters from rowdy demonstrators resulting from the BP spill supplanted the officer chaos and duplicitous search-and-rescue operations that characterized the NOPD response to Katrina

Unlike Katrina, the police infrastructure as a whole was prepared, as vital communications centers and command-and-control procedures were enacted in 2010 that simply did not exist in 2005. As a result of the catastrophic failure of the NOPD (during Katrina) to maintain even the simplest of communications during the storm, police departments nationwide planned, drilled, and trained all officers on a disaster plan, as well as disaster contingency plans, including operations to thwart protesters and civil unrest. This time the NOPD was ready. Specifically, it had planned over the last 5 years, for the major organizational changes that must be made temporarily to deal with major disasters and problems. These changes include changing priorities in response to specific needs, delaying normal tasks, and shifting and making use of all organizational personnel, as well as absorbing additional, nondepartment personnel (like the thousands of workers that arrived overnight in New Orleans to assist in the cleanup efforts surrounding the oil spill). The NOPD became the "poster child" for police training in disaster management after Katrina.

Five priorities in training police personnel for disaster management and relief have emerged since 2005. The first priority is implementing the new organizational structure required for disaster response. Second, police departments should encourage individual decision making. Third, there should be a clear

(Carolyn Cole/MCT/Newscom)

(Joe Rimkus Jr/Newscom)

understanding of the chain of command, something that was clearly lacking in the case of Hurricane Katrina but remained strong during the BP oil spill in 2010. Fourth, disaster response policies and training should establish centralized command posts. And finally, there should be unambiguous protocols that establish how police operations will be integrated with federal responses.

These protocols were established within the New Orleans Police Department, as part of its commitment to create new and better policies for disaster response after 2005. Clearly, 5 years later, the NOPD planning and training paid off as the department followed clear protocols regarding infrastructure, communications, and command.

Source: Willoughby Anderson, "'This Isn't Representative of Our Department': Lessons from Hurricane Katrina for Police Disaster Response Planning," (Berkeley, CA: Boalt Hall School of Law, University of California at Berkeley, April 2006); *Los Angeles Times*, "Gulf Oil Spill: New Orleans Protestors Rage Against BP" (May 30, 2010); Michelle Krupa, "New Orleans Officials Monitoring Gulf of Mexico Oil Spill, Air Quality in the City, Landrieu Says," The *Times-Picayune* (April 30, 2010).

succinctly, planning involves linking present actions to future conditions. Mottley defines planning as

> a management function concerned with visualizing future situations, making estimates concerning them, identifying the issues, needs and potential danger points, analyzing and evaluating the alternative ways and means for reaching desired goals according to a certain schedule, estimating the necessary funds and resources to do the work, and initiating action in time to prepare what may be needed to cope with changing conditions and contingent events.[10]

There is also the assumption that planning is oriented toward action, which means that thinking is only a part of planning; the real purpose is determining what an organization should do and then doing it. And finally, planning is associated with empirical rationalism: planners gather and analyze data and then reach an objective conclusion.

Synoptic Planning

Synoptic planning, or the rational–comprehensive approach, is the dominant tradition in planning. It is also the point of departure for most other planning approaches, which in general are either modifications of synoptic planning or reactions against it. Figure 8.1 represents the typical synoptic model. It is based on "pure," or "objective," rationality and attempts to ensure optimal achievement of desired goals from a given situation.[11] This model is especially appropriate for police agencies, as it is based on a problem-oriented approach to planning. It relies heavily on the problem identification and analysis phase of the planning process and can assist police administrators in formulating goals and priorities in terms that are focused on specific problems and solutions that often confront law enforcement. For instance, police administrators are more apt to appreciate a planning model centered around problem-oriented goals and priorities (such as the reduction of burglaries in a given residential area) than one centered around more abstract notions (such as the reduction of crime and delinquency).[12] Then, too, police departments are designed for response, and it is easier to

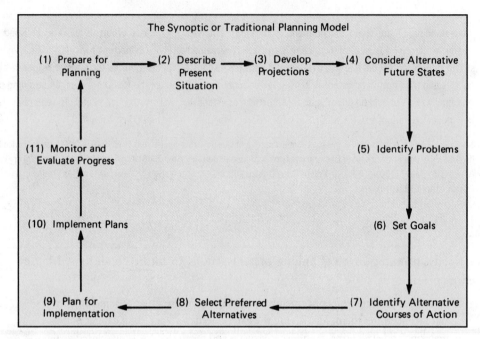

Figure 8.1
Synoptic planning, or the rational–comprehensive approach.
Source: From Robert Cushman, *Criminal Justice Planning for Local Governments* [Washington, D.C.: U.S. Government Printing Office, 1980], p. 26, with minor modification.

mobilize individual officers and gain cooperation between police units if concrete goals and objectives are set in reaction to a given problem.

Synoptic planning consists of 11 steps. Each step is designed to provide the police manager with a logical course of action.[13] The first step in synoptic planning is preparation for planning. It is during this step that the police chief organizes the planning effort with a central theme—what are we trying to accomplish and what type of information is required to understand the problem? Next, the present situation should be described. Weiss[14] states that a primary purpose of planning is in evaluation, or in comparing "what is" with "what should be." The third step in synoptic planning involves developing projections and considering alternative future states. Projections should be written with an attempt to link the current situation with the future, keeping in mind the desirable outcomes. It is important for the police executive to project the current situation into the future to determine possible, probable, and desirable future states while considering the social, legislative, and political trends existing in the community.

Identifying and analyzing problems is the next step in the synoptic model. Police managers should define the nature of the problem—that is, describe the magnitude, cause, duration, and expense of the issue at hand. This provides a clear, conceptual picture of the current conditions in which to develop the means for dealing with the problem. The fifth step of the synoptic model is to set goals. A goal is an achievable end state that can be measured and observed. Making choices about goals is one of the most important aspects of planning.[15] Hudzik and Cordner point out that several kinds of choices must be made concerning goals:

> Several kinds of choices must be made. First, choices must be made about preferred states or goals. An important and sometimes ignored aspect of this choice involves the choice of the criteria for measuring goal attainment. This is often hard, much harder than setting the goal itself. For example, the goal of a juvenile treatment program may be to reduce recidivism among those treated. Yet, in measuring goal attainment several questions arise. First, what constitutes recidivism? Technical or status violation? Arrest for criminal violation? Conviction on a criminal violation, and only for those crimes against which the juvenile program may have been directed? Also, over how long a period will recidivism be monitored? A year? Two years? Five years? Ten years? It is not that those questions cannot be answered, but securing agreement on the appropriate criteria becomes a major difficulty.[16]

The next step in synoptic planning includes identifying alternative courses of action. Alternatives are means by which goals and objectives can be attained. They may be policies, strategies, or specific actions aimed at eliminating a problem. Alternatives do not have to be substitutes for one another or perform the same function. For instance, improving officer-survival skills through training, modifying police vehicles, issuing bulletproof vests, using a computer-assisted dispatch program, and increasing first-line supervision may all be alternatives in promoting officer safety.

It is important that the activities (the means) that a police department engages in actually contribute to the achievement of goals (the ends). If the means are not connected to the ends, then a police agency could expend a great deal of resources in activities that keep personnel busy but do not contribute to fulfilling key objectives or responsibilities.

The seventh step in the synoptic planning process is selecting preferred alternatives. This process is often fraught with complexity and has been researched for decades by scholars in business management, public administration, systems science, and criminal justice in order to assist decision makers in this process. Three basic techniques to select alternatives are (1) strategic analysis, (2) cost-effectiveness analysis, and (3) must–wants analysis.

Strategic Analysis

The first study addressing the selection of preferred courses of action originated at the U.S. Naval War College in 1936 and subsequently was introduced to police management circles.[17] Since that time, the model has been refined into a more systematic and objective treatment.[18] The process is shown in Figure 8.2. To visualize how the technique can be applied and selections made, it will be helpful to use an example currently confronting law enforcement managers—for example, the issue of automating a records division with particular reference to the improvement of officer-generated reports by use of laptop computers.

Given a set of possible alternatives or courses of action, the number of alternatives can be reduced in the following ways. First, make **suitability studies** of all alternatives.

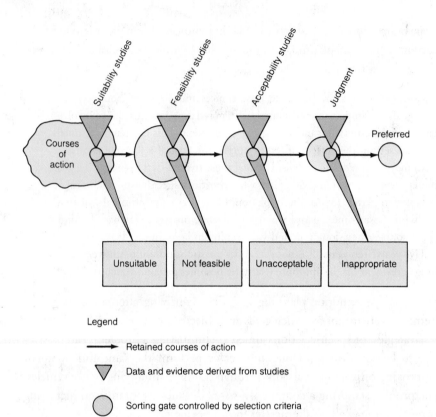

Legend

———▶ Retained courses of action

▽ Data and evidence derived from studies

◯ Sorting gate controlled by selection criteria

Figure 8.2
Strategic analysis: a process for deriving a preferred course of action.
Source: C. M. Mottley, "Strategic Planning," *Management Highlights* 56 [September 1967, p. 271].

That is, each course of action is evaluated in accordance with general policies, rules, and laws. For example, in all jurisdictions it is illegal to maintain an automated records system that contains arrest and conviction data of juveniles to safeguard the juveniles' reputations. A manual records system is deemed more secure because access can be totally controlled.

Second, subject the retained and suitable alternatives to **feasibility studies**. These include the appraisal of the effects of a number of factors weighed separately and together. Continuing with the example, the feasibility of an automated records system would be judged on the basis of meeting (1) the existing standards of operation (e.g., will an automated records system do everything the manual system can do?), (2) the conditions of the operational environment (e.g., is the police department facility large enough to accommodate a computer? Is it air-conditioned? Does it have proper electrical outlets?), (3) the restrictions imposed by the state of the art (e.g., is the desired software compatible with the existing computer system?), and (4) limitations on the resources available (e.g., is the cost for an automated records system beyond police funding approval? Can the records division personnel be retrained, and how much will that cost?).

Third, analyze the retained courses of actions (those judged to be suitable and feasible) in acceptability studies. Four principal factors are combined and enter into this evaluation: (1) the cost of each alternative, (2) the performance, (3) the effect of the alternative on the entire system, and (4) the time involved in implementation and setup. These factors are applied to each alternative to reveal critical limits and trade-offs. Finally, a judgment is rendered that selects the preferred course of action.

Cost-Effectiveness Analysis

This technique is sometimes called cost-benefit or cost-performance analysis. The purpose of this form of selection is that the alternative chosen should maximize the ratio of benefit to cost. The concept is based on economic rationalism: Calculations are made "scientifically" through the collection of data and the use of models in an attempt to maximize benefits and minimize costs. A model is a simplified representation of the real world that abstracts the cause-and-effect relationships essential to each course of action or alternative.[19] Using the example of automating a records division, each course of action would be analyzed in an attempt to compare the cost in dollars of each segment of the system (mainframe, software, laptop computers) with the benefits (increased officer safety, more efficient crime analysis, and subsequent apprehension that diminishes property loss and injury). In the analysis of choice, the role of the model (or models, for it might be inappropriate or absurd to attempt to incorporate all the aspects of a problem into a single formulation) is to estimate for each alternative (or course of action) the costs that would be incurred and the extent to which the objectives would be attained.[20] The model can be as complex as a set of mathematical equations or as simple as a purely verbal description of the situation in which intuition alone is used to predict the outcomes of various alternatives. Figure 8.3 is the structure of cost-effectiveness analysis.

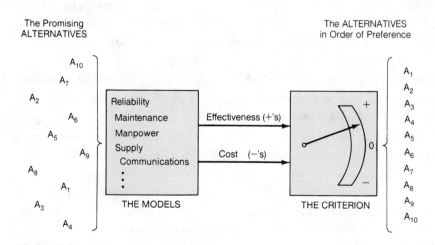

Figure 8.3

The structure of cost-effectiveness analysis.

Source: E. S. Quade, "Systems Analysis Techniques for Planning-Programming-Budgeting," in *Planning, Programming, Budgeting: A Systems Approach to Management,* ed. F. J. Lyden and E. G. Miller [Chicago: Markham, 1972], p. 250.

It is important to note that each alternative is weighed against a criterion: the rule or standard by which to rank the alternatives in order of desirability. This provides a means to analyze cost against effectiveness.[21] Unlike strategic analysis, alternatives are not dismissed from the process but ranked in order of preference.

Must–Wants Analysis

This method of selecting a preferred course of action combines the strengths of both strategic and cost-effectiveness analyses. Must–wants analysis is concerned with both the subjective weights of suitability, feasibility, and acceptability and the objective weights of costs versus benefits.

In this method of selection, a must–wants chart is developed to assist the police administrator. This methodology is particularly well suited for comparing like brands or models of equipment (e.g., in the case of personal weapons, the strengths and weaknesses of 9-mm semiautomatic pistols versus .38-caliber revolvers, or for personal computers, the pros and cons of selecting among Apple, HP, or Dell personal computers). In this example, Figure 8.4 provides a chart for evaluating three popular police patrol vehicles—namely, the Chevrolet Impala, the GMC SU Yukon, and the Ford Police Interceptor.

The must–wants chart is constructed in the following manner:

1. "Musts" are placed at the top of the page. These are conditions that are set by the police chief or selecting committee and that absolutely have to be met in order for an alternative (in this case, a specific police patrol vehicle) to continue to be a viable choice. The failure of any alternative to meet a must condition immediately eliminates it from further consideration. In Figure 8.4, note that alternative B, the GMC Tahoe, did not conform to the must of being a full-size, four-door sedan. Because the 2010 sports utility Tahoe was available only in two-door SUV models, it was eliminated.

2. "Wants" are conditions, performances, characteristics, or features that are desirable but not absolutely necessary. They are listed below the musts, and corresponding data for each want are completed for each alternative that was not discarded at the previous step.

3. Weight (the column marked "wt." in Figure 8.4) reflects the subjective importance of the want as determined by the police chief or selection committee. Weight has a scale of 1 (lowest) to 10 (highest).

4. Score (the column marked "sc." in Figure 8.4) is the evaluation of the actual existence of wants by the chief or committee. A scale of 1 to 10 is also used in this column. The score is set by the evaluator to reflect an assessment of the subjective or actual existence of the want. In this example, the wants under "Excellent ergonomics" are subjective evaluations, while "EPA mileage—city, highway, combined" are objectively determined by an outside source. In general, the scoring of wants should be based on a limited number of factors because too many could distort the choice of an option.

5. The weight and score for each want are multiplied ("wt. × sc." in Figure 8.4) and summed. The sum of each "wt. × sc." column is called the performance total of wants objectives.

Musts	Alternative A: Chevrolet Impala	Alternative B: GMC SU Tahoe	Alternative C: Ford Police Interceptor
Total purchase price not to exceed $24,000	$23,700	$22,900	$23,500
Dual airbags (driver & passenger side)	yes	yes	yes
Power-assisted, four wheel disc, antilock brake system	yes	yes	yes
Heavy-duty, automatic transmission	yes	yes	yes
Full-size, four-door sedan	yes	NO, NO GO	yes
Front & rear heavy-duty suspension	yes		yes
Goodyear police pursuit radial tires	yes		yes

Wants	wt.	Alternative A: Chevrolet Impala	sc.	wt. × sc.	Alternative C: Ford Police Interceptor	sc.	wt. × sc.
Minimum total price	7	$23,700	8	56	$23,500	9	63
High engine displacement	4	350 cu. in.	7	28	281 cu. in.	5	20
High horsepower	7	260 @ 5000 rpm	8	56	210 @ 4500 rpm	7	49
Excellent acceleration (0 to 60 mph)	6	8.02 secs	8	48	9.1 secs	6	36
Good acceleration (0 to 100 mph)	3	21.47 secs	9	27	25.18 secs	6	18
Good top speed	4	139 mph	7	28	135 mph	6	24
Good quarter mile run from stop to finish (seconds/top speed)	5	16.14 sec/88 mph	7	35	16.89 sec/83.83 mph	7	35
Excellent braking—Stopping distance from 60 mph	7	133.1 feet	7	49	133.4 feet	7	49
Excellent turning capability	6	43 feet	7	42	39 feet	9	54
Large fuel capacity	4	23 gallons	7	28	20 gallons	5	20
Heavy frame and body	5	4,249 lbs.	8	40	3,974 lbs.	7	35
Excellent ergonomics:							
Front seating area	9	comfortable/roomy	9	81	slightly cramped	7	63
Interior headroom	8	39.2—very good	8	64	38.4—good	6	48
Rear seating area	5	easy entry & exit	8	40	tight and "bouncy"	7	35
Clarity of instrumentation	4	good	7	28	fair	6	24
Communications accessibility	4	good	8	32	good	8	32
High EPA mileage							
City	10	17 mpg-very good	8	80	17 mpg-very good	8	80
Highway	8	26 mpg-excellent	9	72	23 mpg-good	7	56
Combined	9	20 mpg-excellent	9	81	19 mpg-very good	8	72
Performance totals of wants objectives:				**915**			**813**

Figure 8.4

Must–wants chart for selecting a police patrol vehicle. The "results" in the illustration of must–wants analysis are hypothetical and should not be used as a basis of action.
Source: 2007 Model Year Patrol Vehicle Testing, prepared by Michigan State Police [Washington, D.C.: National Institute of Justice, Office of Justice Programs, November 2006].

6. The second part of the must–wants chart, shown in Figure 8.5, is called the "possible adverse consequences worksheet." On this worksheet, statements concerning possible detriments or negative outcomes are listed for each alternative. The probability and seriousness of each comment are subjectively

Alternative A: Chevrolet Impala	Probability	Seriousness	P×S
Relatively large turning circle (difficult to perform u-turns)	8	7	56
100,000-mile bumper-to-bumper warranty is extra, $1,800	9	8	72
Chevrolet does not have a CNG option for fuel	6	5	30
Dealership is downtown, will be more difficult for precincts to access	9	8	72
Totals:			230

Alternative C: Police Interceptor	Probability	Seriousness	P×S
Relatively small gas tank, will require more frequent refueling	5	3	15
Smaller vehicle with smaller inside and trunk volume	6	8	48
Department master mechanics are all GM trained, service & parts agreement with GM	8	6	48
Overall EPA mileage is lower in all categories, reducing cost savings	9	7	63
Totals:			174

Figure 8.5

Possible adverse consequences worksheet—police patrol vehicles.

scored. The probability of an adverse consequence happening is scored on a scale from 1 (very unlikely) to 10 (certain to happen). Seriousness is scored on the same type of scale, with 1 representing "extremely unserious" and 10 denoting "very serious." The final scores are summed and used in the last choice, the selection step.

7. Some advocates of using the must–wants chart recommend that the totals of the possible adverse consequences worksheet be considered only advisory, whereas others recommend that the performance totals for each alternative be mathematically reduced by the value of the possible adverse consequences score. If the latter approach is used, the alternative with the highest total points should be chosen. In Figure 8.6, alternative A, the 2010 Chevrolet Impala, would be selected as the primary police patrol vehicle for the agency, with a total point score of 685.

Despite the "rational" and "objective" appearance of the must–wants analysis approach, there are a number of subjective scores, weights, and probabilities in the chart. The "bottom line" values in Figure 8.6 (685 and 639) were calculated on subjective measures. The real value in must–wants analysis is in the methodology. The chief must not become a captive of the device and follow the results mechanistically. He or she should use a must–wants chart to consider and weigh the intangibles that are not easily quantifiable among the alternatives. The value of must–wants analysis is not in the end product but rather in the sharpening of differences or similarities between alternatives or courses of action.

	Alternative A: Chevrolet Impala	Alternative C: Ford Police Inceptor
Must-have objectives:	All met	All met
Wants performance total:	915	813
Possible adverse consequences total:	(230)	(174)
	685	**639**

Figure 8.6

The final step in must–wants analysis—selecting an alternative. The alternative with the highest point value should be chosen. The facts and figures presented are for illustrative purposes only and should not be the basis for action.

As with must–wants charts, the other two approaches (strategic and cost-effectiveness analyses) are methods of selecting a preferred alternative or choosing a desired course of action. In the final analysis, the judgment of the police chief plays a key and indisputable role, one that cannot be taken lightly; the chief cannot afford to be ill informed about the alternative courses to be made.

The next two steps in synoptic planning include planning and carrying out implementation. Once a preferred course of action is selected, the police chief is required to execute plans that fulfill the goals or objectives of the process. Implementation often requires a great deal of tact and skill to alleviate complexities and anxieties related to change. It may be more important "how" an alternative is introduced into a police department than "what" it actually is.

The final step of the synoptic planning model is evaluation: Were the objectives achieved? Were the problems resolved? The answer to these questions should be obtained through a system that monitors the implementation process.

Evaluation requires comparing what actually happened with what was planned for—and this may not be a simple undertaking.[22] Feedback must be obtained concerning the results of the planning cycle, the efficiency of the implementation process, and the effectiveness of new procedures, projects, or programs. This is an important step of synoptic planning—trying to figure out what, if anything, happened as a result of implementing a selected alternative. It is for this reason that baseline data are so critical (step 2—describe the present situation). Hudzik and Cordner[23] point out that evaluation completes the cycle of rational planning. The issue of identifying problems must be considered again. Does the original problem still exist, or was it solved? Is there a new problem?

Summary of the Synoptic Planning Approach

Considerable attention has been given to synoptic planning because it is the most widely used approach in police management. Most other approaches have been derived from the model just described. Synoptic planning basically comprises four activities: preparing to plan, making a choice between alternatives, implementing the plan, and evaluating the plan. Although the steps can be reduced or named differently, the 11-step synoptic approach is a refinement of this cyclical process. As shown, this process has proven to be very successful in many police departments and is especially well suited for implementing new technology within the organization (see Figure 8.7).

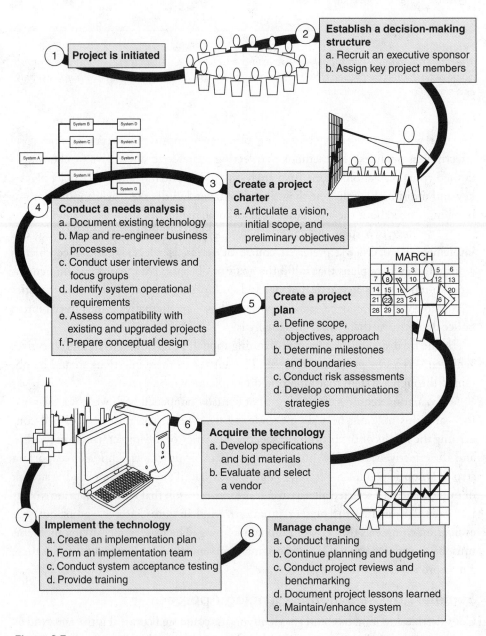

Figure 8.7
Law Enforcement Information Technology Projects: A Roadmap to Guide. The U.S. Department of Justice offers a guide to technology compiled by the Office of Community Policing. This excerpt is a visualization of initiating and implementing new information technology systems.
Source: "Law Enforcement Tech Guide," www.cops.usdoj.gov

Types of Plans

From an applications perspective, the planning process yields an end product—a plan. These can be categorized by use and are delineated into four groups:[24]

1. **Administrative or management plans** include formulation of the department's mission statement, goals, and policies; the structuring of functions, authority, and responsibilities; the allocation of resources; personnel management; and other concerns that they are prevalent throughout the agency.

2. **Procedural plans**, in line with many but certainly not all management plans, are ordinarily included as part of a police department's written directive system, a copy of which is assigned to every officer and is updated periodically. Procedural plans are the guidelines for the action to be taken under specific circumstances and detail such matters as how evidence is to be sent or transported to the crime laboratory, the conditions under which male officers may search arrested females and the limits thereto, and how to stop and approach traffic violators.

3. **Operational plans** are often called work plans and describe specific actions to be taken by line units (patrol officers, precinct groups, and/or division teams). Work plans are usually short and terse, giving both direction and time constraints in accomplishing a given task. In community policing ventures, the work plan usually focuses on a defined community need in a specific neighborhood.

4. **Tactical plans** involve planning for emergencies of a specific nature at known locations. Some tactical plans are developed in anticipation of such emergencies as the taking of hostages at a prison or a jailbreak and are subject to modification or being discarded altogether in peculiar and totally unanticipated circumstances. Other tactical plans are developed for specific situations as they arise, such as how to relate to a demonstration in the park or a march on city hall. Although well-operated police agencies invest considerable effort in developing tactical plans that may seldom or never be used, their very existence stimulates confidence among field officers and lessens the likelihood of injury to officers, the public, and violators.

Effective Plans

Regardless of how plans are classified, the bottom line is that organizations with a formal and continuous planning process outperform those without one. This discrepancy in performance increases as the larger environment becomes more turbulent and as the pace and magnitude of change increase.[25] This is the type of environment that police administrators have faced in recent years, as we alluded to in the introduction to this chapter. As discussed in Chapter 12, Financial Management, the current depression began in 2007. In 2009, the stock market experienced a major correction, creating further fiscal pressures. Considering these and other circumstances, police administrators not only must have a planning process but also must be able to recognize the characteristics of effective plans:

1. The plans must be sufficiently specific, so that the behavior required is understood.
2. The benefits derived from the achievement of the goals associated with the plan must offset the efforts of developing and implementing the plan, and the level of achievement should not be so modest that it is easily reached.
3. Involvement in plan formulation must be as widespread as is reasonably possible.
4. Plans should contain a degree of flexibility to allow for the unforeseen.
5. There must be coordination in the development and implementation of plans with other units of government whenever there appears even only a minimal need for such action.
6. Plans must be coordinated in their development and implementation within the police department to ensure consistency.
7. As appropriate, the means for comparing the results planned for versus the results actually produced must be specified before implementation. For tactical plans, this often takes the form of an analysis, referred to as an after-action report.

Keep in mind that no matter the type of planning process an agency uses, there are some common elements that are shared between the different options. The first of these elements is that of needs and risk assessments. The needs assessment is the appraisal of whether a problem or a need for planning exists. For instance, is the city near a fault line, or on a river that floods, or is a major political rally or sports event planned in the city. A risk assessment simply means that an organization identifies the possibility of a threat, such as a specific type of crime, a terrorist attack, a natural disaster, or a pandemic illness. Next, alternative courses of action are considered. This is where methodologies like the cost-effective analysis discussed under synoptic planning section will come into play. Finally, there is, naturally, the selection of the action plan best suited to the situation and the agency. The selection of the action plan should be bolstered by support from within the organization, the community, the consumer, the entity responsible for granting budget approval, and other agencies that might have an interest in the plan.[26]

Decision Making

As stated previously, planning is a primary and integral part of decision making. Planning involves coming to understand the present situation (problem) and widening the range of choices (alternatives or courses of action) available to the police chief (decision maker). Therefore, planning is aimed at providing information (a plan), whereas decision making is aimed at using this information to resolve problems or make choices.[27]

Decision-Making Models

The literature dealing with decision making specifically in the police management field is not very extensive, and most of it is devoted to methods of applying the decision-making process. Whereas in theory it should be easy to divide decision-making

▸▸ Tactical Planning for Major Sports Events

Many police administration students take for granted that police chiefs plan for crisis events or natural disasters. However, few people consider the tactical planning that goes into recreational events, such as parades or sports events. The 1990 riots in Detroit following the Pistons' National Basketball Association Championship victory, which killed seven and injured hundreds, as well as outbreaks of violence in 2000 and 2009 after the Los Angeles Lakers won the title led Los Angeles law enforcement officials to implement extensive planning for the 2010 Championship, for which the Lakers were again a heavy favorite. Officials brought together representatives from all various agencies, including the Sheriff's Office, Fire Department, transportation agencies, and city government to ensure that post-game celebrations did not get out of hand. Together, the groups arrived at a plan that involved a heavy police presence, the set-up of perimeters around the basketball stadium, deployment of tactical units to discourage the congregation of rowdy crowds, and strategic stationing of fire-rescue in case emergency situations did arise. Ultimately, when the Lakers beat the Boston Celtics, there were some instances of violence among revelers. There were several reports of fires, a handful of injuries, and about a dozen arrests. However, police officials should be proud that such a major event yielded few serious incidents. The relatively peaceful aftermath of the 2010 NBA Championship can be attributed to careful planning, coordination, and inter-agency cooperation in advance of the event.

(Christopher A. Record/KRT/Newscom)

Source: "Los Angeles police plan strong presence outside NBA Finals venue to prevent repeat of riots," Daisy Nguyen, Associated Press, June 16, 2010.

processes into discrete, conceptual paradigms, in reality it is extremely difficult to separate one approach from another.

However, three models derived from decision-making theory appear to be basic in most of the literature. They are (1) the **rational model**, (2) the **incremental model**, and (3) the **heuristic model**. These are the foundations for most decision-making theory, but in the past decade, alternative models have gained quite a bit of popularity and are popping up in police leadership training across the country. Alternative models include more intuitive types of decision making. For example, the recognition-prime decision (RPD) model is based on recognizing situations and knowing how to handle them.[28] Other types of alternative decision-making models come from notions popularized by best-selling books such as Malcolm Gladwell's *Blink*.[29]

The Rational Model

The traditional theory of management assumes that people are motivated predominantly by "economic incentives" and will, therefore, work harder given the opportunity to make more money. The "economic actor" concept also prevails in early decision-making theory. In Chapter 5, Organizational Theory, the scientific management approach developed by Taylor was presented. Within this concept, the economic person is presumed to act in a **rational** manner when faced with a decision-making situation. The assumptions for this rational behavior are (1) that a person has complete knowledge of all alternatives available to him or her, (2) that a person has the ability to order preferences according to his or her own hierarchy of values, and (3) that a person has the ability to choose the best alternative for him or her. Money is usually used as a measure of value for the decision maker. It is considered only natural that a person will want to work harder if that person can maximize the return of money by so doing. But these assumptions are difficult for a person to achieve in real life. Just by looking at the first assumption—that a person has knowledge of all available alternatives and their consequences in any given decision situation—we can see how impossible it would be to fulfill these requirements in most circumstances.

There is some evidence to suggest that administrative rationality differs from the "economic actor" concept of rationality because it takes into account an additional spectrum of facts relative to emotions, politics, power group dynamics, personality, and mental health. In other words, the data of social science are facts just as much as the carbon content of steel, but they are difficult and, in many cases, impossible to quantify with a high degree of accuracy.[30]

Police administrators bring to administrative decision making their own personal value system, which they inject into the substance of decision making while clothing their decision with a formal logic of the "good of the organization." They clothe the decision with the official mantle of the department's logic and respectability while their eyes remain fixed on more personal goals. But this does not lead to chaos because there is frequently a large element of commonality in personal value systems as related to organizational goals.[31] For example, the police executive who develops and directs a specialized unit to solve a series of murders will be accomplishing a law enforcement goal: to apprehend criminals. Although the executive's personal motives are to gain the public success of his or her unit, the personal objectives are in line with the organizational goals. Thus, conflict does not arise unless the personal values begin to compete with the department's mission.

In Chapter 5, Organizational Theory, the work of Gulick and Urwick was discussed as a description of administrative behavior focusing on the work of the chief executive. Part of their theory includes the act of making rational choices by following prescribed elements of work (PODSCORB). Their contribution set the stage for the rational model of decision making by suggesting that executives follow orderly and rational steps before making decisions. Subsequently, Simon[32] responded to these assumptions in his article "The Proverbs of Administration," in which he outlined several requirements for a scientifically based theory of administration. Simon's article was then included in his *Administrative Behavior* (1947).[33]

Simon explains that rational choices are made on a "principle of efficiency." His model of rationality contends that there are three essential steps in decision making: (1) list all of the alternative strategies, (2) determine and calculate all of the consequences of each strategy, and (3) evaluate all of these consequences in a comparative fashion.[34] Whereas Simon is given credit for the development of this approach, its comprehensive expansion can be observed in the literature of several other theorists. Drucker's concept of the "Effective Executive," Iannone's "style" in *Supervision of Police Personnel*, and Sharkansky's decision-making model in *Public Administration* all exhibit an expansion of Simon's original work.[35] The rational model, often referred to as the rational–comprehensive model, sets forth a series of formalized steps toward "effective" decision making. These steps can be generally observed and listed as follows:

1. Identify and define the problem.
2. Ascertain all information regarding the problem.
3. List all possible alternatives and means to solving the problem.
4. Analyze the alternatives and assess the facts.
5. Select the appropriate alternatives and find the answer.

It is important to observe the elaboration on Simon's original method. The decision-making model assumes an ideal condition whereby the decision maker is aware of all available information related to the problem and has an unlimited amount of time in which to explore and narrow down proposed alternatives by a "rational" and comparative process. Unfortunately, actual practice rarely allows for the ideal.

Highly criticized for being too idealistic and irrelevant to the administrative functions of a police organization, the rational decision-making model has been subjected to harsh criticisms. Many of these criticisms have been noted as limitations by proponents of the method. For instance, Sharkansky[36] provided a detailed discussion of "roadblocks" to the fulfillment of the rational–comprehensive model in practical administration. He documented constraints of all available data and emphasized contingencies in the human ability to make decisions. Additionally, Simon elaborated on the concept of a "rational man." Noting that human beings are "bounded" by a triangle of limitations, he stated,

> On one side, the individual is limited by those skills, habits, and reflexes which are no longer in the realm of the conscious . . . on a second side, the individual is limited by his values and those conceptions of purpose which influence him in making decisions . . . and on a third side, the individual is limited by the extent of his knowledge that is relevant to his job.[37]

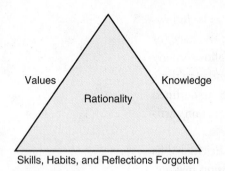

Figure 8.8
Simon's concept of bounded rationality.

It is apparent that Simon understood not only the decision-making process but also the human factors associated in the term "rationality." A prerequisite to effective decision making is an acute awareness of the social, environmental, and organizational demands placed on the administrator. Simon[38] accurately stresses that one's ability to make rational decisions is bounded by the limitation of one's knowledge of the total organization. From this critical observation, Simon formulates a modified rational–comprehensive idea entitled "bounded rationality."[39] The emphasis, of course, is on human beings' inherent limitations to make decisions (refer to Figure 8.8).

The Incremental Model

Another important approach concerning the modification of rational decision making is the "incremental" and "muddling through" theories explored by Lindblom.[40] Based on his study of government institutions in the United States, Lindblom states that the decision-making process is so fragmented and so complex, incorporating the interaction of various institutions, political entities, pressure groups, and individual biases, that rationality can have only a marginal effect. That is, the police administrator faces a set of limiting political factors (such as the mayor's wish to be re-elected) that prevent the decision-making process from being truly rational. For elected sheriffs, the political agendas can be so strong that purely rational decision making is inhibited.

Lindblom asserts that decision making is serial—that it is limited by time and resources as it gropes along a path where means and ends are not distinct, where goals and objectives are ambiguous, and where rationality serves no purpose. Contending that police managers and administrators "play things safe" and opt to move very slowly (incrementally) in decision making, Lindblom[41] proposes that managers "muddle through" problems rather than analytically choosing decisions. In Lindblom's view, decision making that occurs through a series of incremental steps provides the police administrator (and hence the public) with a number of safeguards against error:

> In the first place, past sequences of policy (decision) steps have given him knowledge about the probable consequence of further similar steps. Second, he need not attempt big jumps toward his goals that would require predictions beyond his or anyone else's knowledge, because he never expects his policy (decision) to be a final resolution of a problem. His decision is only one step. . . . Third, he is in effect able to test his previous predictions as he moves on to each further step. Lastly, he often can remedy a past error fairly quickly—more quickly than if policy (decision) proceeded through more distinct steps widely spaced in time.[42]

Lindblom's ideas have support—if not in theory, at least in practice—as many police managers find them to be "a description of reality."[43]

The Heuristic Model

In another opposing concept to rationality and logic, Gore[44] identifies the crucial element of humanism in decision making. He presents a **heuristic model** appropriately referred to as "the gut-level approach" when considering the police organization. The seasoned patrol officer frequently refers to an unknown quality or phenomenon known as "moxie" or the ability to be "streetwise." This unknown dimension is captured in Gore's decision-making method for police administrators. In an antithesis to the rational model, Gore identifies a process by which a decision is the product of the maker's personality. Gore views the heuristic process as "a groping toward agreements seldom arrived at through logic . . . the very essence of those factors validating a decision are internal to the personality of the individual instead of external to it."[45] Whereas the rational method is concrete, formalized by structure and calculations, the heuristic concept is nebulous, characterized by "gut feelings reaching backward into the memory and forward into the future."[46]

For Gore, decision making is basically an emotional, nonrational, highly personalized, and subjective process. Therefore, the facts validating a decision are internal to the personality of the individual instead of external to it. The key word in this statement is "validating"; it is intended to convey a sense of personal psychological approval or acceptance. The optimum situation is to select the decision alternative that creates the least anxiety about or disruption to the individual's basic needs, wants, and desires. In effect, every "objective" decision should be modified to meet the emotional needs of the various members of the police department who will be affected by the decision. The passage from which this statement was taken provides additional insight into Gore's heuristic decision-making scheme:[47]

> Whereas the rational system of action evolves through the identification of causes and effects and the discovery of ways of implementing them, the heuristic process is a groping toward agreement seldom arrived at through logic. The very essence of the heuristic process is that factors validating a decision are internal to the personality of the individual instead of external to it. Whereas the rational system of action deals with the linkages between a collective and its objectives and between a collective and its environment, the heuristic process is orientated toward the relationship between that private core of values embedded in the center of the personality and its public counterpart, ideology. The dynamics of personality are not those of logic but rather those of emotion.[48]

In other words, although logic and reason may be the basic intellectual tools needed to analyze a given problem or to structure a series of solutions to a given situation, logic and reason may not prove to be completely effective in establishing intraorganizational agreement in connection with any given decision.[49]

Applauded for its contribution to the decision-making process, Gore's approach is also highly criticized as being too simplistic and nonscientific. Souryal[50] writes that "Gore's analysis is too unreliable. . . . It could complicate an existing situation, promote spontaneity, discredit the role of training and delay the advent of professionalism" in police organizations. This is an unfair assessment of the method. Gore views heuristic applications as adjuncts or alternatives to rational models. Further, some type of credibility must be assessed to that vague, unknown, and nonmeasurable entity we call experience, talent, or the "sixth sense." It was these elements that Simon had so much trouble with in calculating his "bound and limited" argument regarding the

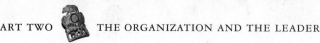

rational model. In any event, Gore's contributions remain as an opposite to decision making based solely on figures, formulas, and mathematical designs.

Alternative Decision-Making Models

Another attempt to outline various approaches to the decision-making process is Allison's[51] account of the 1962 Cuban missile crisis. He contends that the rational decision-making model, although most widely used, is seriously flawed. Allison presents two additional models (the organizational process model and the government politics model) to explain the decision making during crisis events that police and other government agencies often face. The organizational process model is based on the premise that few government decisions are exclusively the province of a single organization. In other words, police agencies are dependent on information and advice from other government units (such as the mayor's office, the FBI, and the district attorney's office) to make major decisions that affect public policy. The government politics model purports that major government policies are rarely made by a single rational actor, such as the chief of police. Rather, policymaking and general decision making are the outcome of a process of bargaining among individuals and groups to support those interests. Implicit in both of the models is that the decision maker requires direction from his or her internal staff as well as support from other government agencies in the making of important decisions. This is especially true during crisis situations.[52]

Operational modeling. Other alternative models to decision making have evolved from the systems approach to management as described in Chapter 5, Organizational Theory. These techniques are vastly influenced by large, complex systems of variables. The application, collection, and analysis of data from decision making within the organization are called **operations research**.[53] In response to a need for a management science that addressed complex problems involving many variables, such as government planning, military spending, natural resource conservation, and national defense budgeting, operations research employs the use of mathematical inquiry, probability theory, and gaming theory to "calculate the probable consequences of alternative choices" in decision making.[54] As a result, techniques such as Program Evaluation and Review Technique (PERT) and Planning, Programming, and Budgeting Systems (PPBS) were developed for use in managerial planning, forecasting, and decision making.[55] By their very nature, these techniques must structure the system for analysis by quantifying system elements. This process of abstraction often simplifies the problem and takes it out of the real world. Hence, the solution of the problem may not be a good fit for the actual situation.

PERT is a managerial attempt to convert the disorganized resources of people, machines, and money into a useful and effective enterprise by which alternatives to problem solving can be assessed. This process is conducted by a cost-effectiveness analysis or an estimation for each alternative of the costs that would be incurred and the extent to which the objectives would be attained, which is similar to those discussed in the synoptic model.

Another model, the decision tree, is illustrated in Figure 8.9. In this model, the probabilities for various outcomes are calculated for each branch of the tree. In the

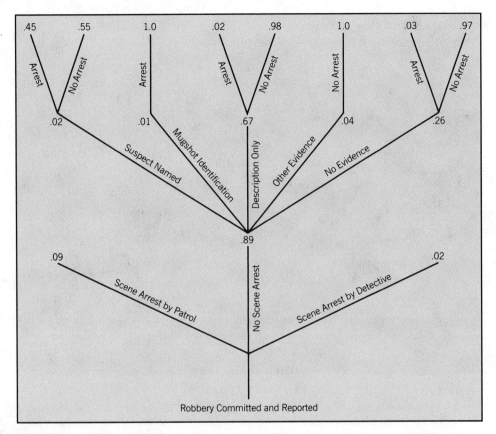

Figure 8.9
Decision tree of hypothetical probabilities of various outcomes in a robbery investigation.

example used in the figure, the first branch of the trunk has three possible outcomes: (1) arrest at the scene by a patrol officer, (2) no arrest at the scene, and (3) arrest at the scene by a detective. Note in the figure that the probabilities for those three events total 1.0, which is the mathematical value for certainty; all possible outcomes for that branch of the example are accounted for. The next-higher branch of the example decision tree deals with the various types of evidence obtained from investigation, and the final branches deal with the probability of arrest associated with the gathering of each type of evidence. Decision trees are very useful in analyzing situations and for reference when series of decisions that flow from one event are involved. For example, decision trees would be useful to the commander of a detective bureau in formulating policy and guidelines on when to continue or inactivate an investigation based on the types of evidence that were involved in order to make the best use of investigative resources. In this regard, decision trees can be seen as a tool of operations research. If an administrator is facing a decision for which there are no actual data, a decision tree can still be useful in analyzing the situation, and the "probabilities" can be the administrator's own subjective estimations based on past experience. Decision tree models are commonly used in **e-learning software** programs that provide simulation training scenarios to

Figure 8.10
Officers have a wide variety of software programs and games that represent real life simulations for decision making. Many of these programs can be found on the Internet and represent the latest in police training technology.
(LETN)

police officers and executives. The program changes and alternatives appear as the student makes various decisions that alter the precise path incorporated into the gaming simulation. These types of simulation software programs represent the latest technology in police training relating to officer and executive-level decision making (see Figure 8.10).

These approaches are highly sophisticated elaborations of the rational model using quantitative techniques. The weakness of the methods is in their practicality to real-world situations in which time and resources are not directly structured to gather intelligence about every problem and possible alternative. Further, these models assume that human biases will not enter the decision-making process. The most critical aspect of the approaches appears to be in their overriding insistence that decision making is not a human activity but the product of some scientific, computerized, and unimpressionable robot that digests quantitative information.

Wildavsky[56] has continually warned that the application of decision making to costs, benefits, resources, and budgets frequently results in the adoption of meaningless data, and places unwarranted stimuli into the process.

Naturalistic methods. Recognition-primed decision making (RPD) is a model based on a more naturalistic view of decision making. While the previously discussed models focus on different courses of action, and the selection of one course of action over others, RPD distinguishes itself by focusing more on the assessment of the situation, its dynamics, and the experience of the decision maker. Much like incrementalism and heuristic models, RPD asserts that formal models of decision making are not possible in real-life situations, where decision makers are under time constraints and face poorly defined tasks, dynamic conditions, and ill-structured goals. RPD contains elements of the incremental and heuristic models and considers how a police official's experience affects his or her decisions. In RPD, police officials are primed to act in a situation and do not wait for a complete analysis of the facts before acting. Instead, elements of the situation are recognized as typical and action is taken based on previous experience. RPD relies heavily on the concept of satisficing, in which a solution is not so much optimal as it is sufficient, given the circumstances.[57] In other words, decision makers utilizing RPD identify an option that will suffice in a given situation based on past experiences with similar situations, then try to elaborate and improve on that option. Of course, the RPD model brings to mind questions about how decision makers react when they encounter situations that are absolutely not typical. In these cases, the RPD model states that the decision maker must identify anomalies in the situation and obtain as much information about the anomaly as possible in order to make a decision. The RPD model does not allow for much creativity or ingenuity in a situation, and it certainly allows for previous mistakes to be repeated. However, research indicates that RPD is the dominant form of decision making used in command and control organizations.[58]

Thin-slicing. Malcolm Gladwell, in his 2005 book *Blink*, described a model of decision making called "thin-slicing." The **thin-slicing theory** states that, in situations where snap decisions are required, whether by a police administrator, a line officer, or anyone else in a decision-making capacity, instantaneous decisions can often be the best, particularly when paired with training and expertise.[59] Thin-slicing is clearly an offshoot of the heuristic model, as Gladwell maintains those decisions that are made in an instant can be equally good, or even better, than those made deliberately and with a lot of information. However, thin-slicing is more rational than traditional heuristic models. Unconscious decision making, which Gladwell describes as "a kind of giant computer that quickly and quietly processes a lot of the data we need in order to keep functioning as human beings,"[60] allows decision makers to thin-slice, a rational exercise in which we find patterns in situations and behavior based on very narrow slices of experience. According to Gladwell, our unconscious allows us to sift through situations that confront us, to the point that we throw out all irrelevant information and focus on the parts of the issue that are most relevant.

However, there is a dark side to rapid decision making, and Gladwell spends a good deal of time incorporating this into his theory. Often, unconscious attitudes and prejudices sneak into the decision-making process, leading thin-slicing astray. Under extreme pressure, researchers have found that decision makers tend to fall back on stereotypes and prejudices. The best way to counter this type of bias, according to Gladwell, is to train decision makers to slow down, even slightly, and find ways to mitigate the effects of stereotypes and biases by changing the environment where decisions might occur. This may at first glance seem paradoxical, and some might argue that Gladwell's concept of thin-slicing is at odds with itself because the theory asks that the decision maker go with his or her first reaction, but set rules ahead of time for the way that he or she might think. Gladwell acknowledges this but asserts that those with enough training and expertise are more able to extract the most meaningful amounts of information from the smallest, thinnest slice of an experience and are able to control the environment in which rapid cognition takes place.[61]

Decision Making During Crisis Events

Police agencies, like all government organizations and private entities, are not immune to the necessity of effective decision making during crisis events. In this chapter, we have examined decision making in law enforcement from the traditional aspects of planning, organizational needs, theoretical models, and administrative roles. However, two major events, both nearly 20 years old, remain banner incidents for the exploration of police decision making despite their age. The raid of the Branch Davidian Compound in Waco, Texas, in 1993 and the FBI siege of the Weaver family at Ruby Ridge, Idaho, in 1992 remain prime examples of the need for an examination of police executive decision making during protracted crisis events. These types of events span hours, days, and even months to end and must *not* be confused with active shooter situations requiring immediate action and discussed later in this chapter. The purpose of this analysis is to bring applications of the various decision-making models to reality. It is not intended to be taken as a critical editorial but rather as an educational essay designed to identify the commonalities of the incidents and bring potential reason to action. It should not be taken lightly that each incident began with a sense of duty, good faith, honor, and courage yet ended in tragic losses of careers, agency reputations, and human life.

The Branch Davidians, Waco, Texas (1993)

During the early 1990s, a young, charismatic religious leader began to develop a group of followers known as the Branch Davidians. The group settled slightly northeast of Waco, Texas, and began building a well-fortified compound in which to protect themselves from the outside world and the impending "Last Judgment Day." Their spiritual leader, David Koresh (commonly referred to by followers as "the Lamb of God"), was a high school dropout with a perceived mystical ability to teach from the apocalyptic Book of Revelation in the New Testament.

Police investigations of the Branch Davidians did not begin until late in 1992, when Alcohol, Tobacco and Firearms (ATF) agents were contacted by a postal driver who reported seeing hand grenades in a partially opened package delivered to the Waco compound. As a result of the investigation, an arrest warrant for Koresh was issued, along with a search warrant to seek out additional illegal weapons and explosives at the Waco compound.

In the early morning hours of February 28, 1993, tactical teams totaling approximately 75 people stormed the Waco compound. The agents were met with a fusillade of heavy gunfire. In the resulting exchange, four ATF agents and six Branch Davidians were killed. The incident prompted a 51-day standoff between federal agents and the Branch

Davidians. Immediately following the initial confrontation between ATF and the compound occupants, the FBI assumed control of the operation. While negotiations during the ordeal were targeted initially at a peaceful resolution, the FBI began preparations to re-enter the compound by force, using armored vehicles to break through heavily fortified walls and distribute a debilitating dose of CS tear gas. The gas was supposed to be nonlethal, would not permanently harm adults or children, and would not cause fire during the delivery stage. As time lingered and negotiations lulled, Attorney General Janet Reno gave orders to commence with the assault. At 6:00 A.M. on April 19, 1993, several M-60 military tanks, reconfigured with tear gas delivery booms, began breaking through the compound walls (see Figure 8.11). Within hours of the operation, fire broke out. Fanned by 35-mile-per-hour winds, the fire raged, and the compound was rapidly incinerated. Seventy-two bodies were found among the remains, including several children.

Unfortunately, the political flames of Waco have not been extinguished. In 1999, the Texas Rangers and lawyers for the Waco survivors revealed a blatant cover-up by the FBI. For 6 years, the FBI insisted that the Branch Davidians burned their own compound and denied to Congress that its agents fired any flammable tear gas canisters in the attack on April 19, 1993. Renewed investigations revealed that not only did the FBI mislead Congress, but top decision makers may have overtly lied, finally admitting that the FBI did, indeed, fire at least two pyrotechnic M651 grenades at the Branch Davidian bunker. Even more troubling was the revelation that the U.S. military provided federal law enforcement agents with more than $1 million worth of support (supplying tanks, helicopters, aerial reconnaissance, munitions, and support personnel) during the standoff at Waco. At least 10 military advisers or observers attached to the U.S. Army's elite Delta Force were present at various times throughout the incident. The entire action came dangerously close to violating the Posse Comitatus Act, prohibiting the use of federal soldiers to act as police officers or in a law enforcement capacity within the borders of the United States. Further, Attorney General Reno admitted that her decision to allow the FBI to rush the Davidian compound was heavily based on tales of Koresh abusing children. Later, a Justice Department "clarification" said that there was no evidence of child abuse. According to Reno, the FBI convinced her that Koresh was a suicidal madman bent on destroying himself and others within the compound; however, she was never shown a letter by Koresh, dated just days before the attack, that promised that he would come out peacefully after completing his writing. The resulting publicity and trials caused serious questioning of the FBI's tactics, operations, and decision making.

The Weaver Family, Ruby Ridge, Idaho (1992)

In March 1992, federal prosecutors indicted Randy Weaver, a known white separatist, on a charge of selling two sawed-off shotguns to an undercover federal informant. The job of arresting Weaver, who had fled to his secluded and fortified retreat at Ruby Ridge, Idaho, was assigned to the U.S. Marshal Service. On August 12, 1992, marshals began their surveillance of the Weavers' cabin and surrounding terrain under the code name "Operation Northern Exposure."

THE LAST ASSAULT

At 5:55 A.M. on April 19, an FBI hostage negotiator called the Branch Davidians to tell them that agents were about to inject tear gas. A cult member threw out the phone. Six hours later almost everyone inside was dead.

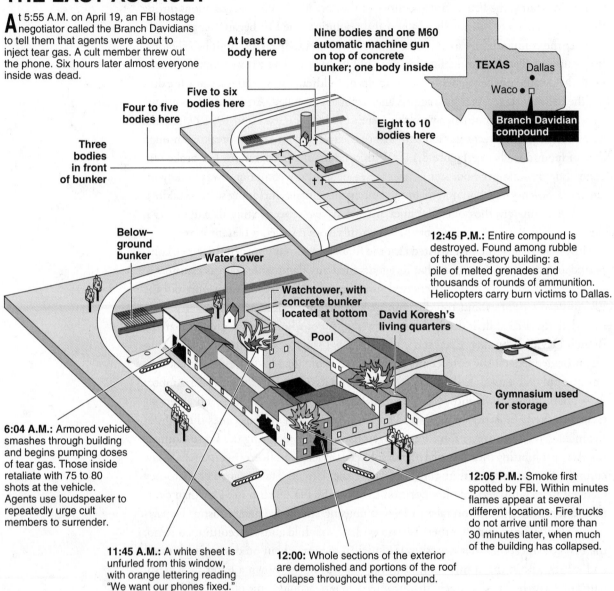

At least one body here

Nine bodies and one M60 automatic machine gun on top of concrete bunker; one body inside

Five to six bodies here

Four to five bodies here

Three bodies in front of bunker

Eight to 10 bodies here

TEXAS   **Dallas**

Waco

Branch Davidian compound

Below-ground bunker

Water tower

Watchtower, with concrete bunker located at bottom

Pool

David Koresh's living quarters

12:45 P.M.: Entire compound is destroyed. Found among rubble of the three-story building: a pile of melted grenades and thousands of rounds of ammunition. Helicopters carry burn victims to Dallas.

Gymnasium used for storage

6:04 A.M.: Armored vehicle smashes through building and begins pumping doses of tear gas. Those inside retaliate with 75 to 80 shots at the vehicle. Agents use loudspeaker to repeatedly urge cult members to surrender.

12:05 P.M.: Smoke first spotted by FBI. Within minutes flames appear at several different locations. Fire trucks do not arrive until more than 30 minutes later, when much of the building has collapsed.

11:45 A.M.: A white sheet is unfurled from this window, with orange lettering reading "We want our phones fixed."

12:00: Whole sections of the exterior are demolished and portions of the roof collapse throughout the compound.

Figure 8.11

The siege of the Branch Davidians near Waco, Texas, resulted in a serious questioning of police (FBI) tactics, operations, and decision making.

Source: *Newsweek*, May 3, 1993, illustration by Dixon Rohr. © 1993, Newsweek, Inc. All rights reserved. Reprinted by permission.

Nine days later, on August 21, Randy Weaver; his 14-year-old son, Sam Weaver; and a family friend, Kevin Harris, followed their dog into the woods adjacent to the cabin. Deputy U.S. marshals surveilling the cabin were discovered, and gunfire was exchanged between the two groups. Sam Weaver and one U.S. marshal were fatally wounded. Confusion and speculation about who fired first and whose bullets killed the two victims continued to plague the investigation. In any event, information soon reached Washington, D.C., that federal agents were under attack at Ruby Ridge and that assistance was badly needed. The FBI deployed its Hostage Rescue Team (HRT) to the location, beginning an 11-day standoff between the FBI and the Weaver family.

Under normal circumstances, the HRT snipers followed specific rules of engagement that dictated the use of deadly force only under the threat of "grievous bodily harm." Although the reasoning behind changing this operational policy at Ruby Ridge and who was responsible for it are unclear, FBI snipers were told that they "could and should fire at any armed adult male" in the cabin. Hence, on August 22, one day after the initial confrontation and the deaths of Sam Weaver and a U.S. marshal, FBI snipers fired on cabin occupants to protect a surveillance helicopter. The resulting shots struck Kevin Harris and Vicki Weaver (Randy Weaver's wife), who was standing just inside the cabin, holding her infant child. Although Mrs. Weaver died of her wounds, FBI personnel did not learn of her death until Randy Weaver surrendered 9 days later.

The actions of the FBI were debated in Congress, and a special Senate judiciary subcommittee was formed to investigate the incident. Both Randy Weaver and Kevin Harris were acquitted of murdering the U.S. marshal in the initial confrontation.

Analysis of Decisions Made During Protracted Crisis Events

At first glance, these incidents represent a series of individual decisions that seriously depart from the major theoretical models presented by Simon, Lindblom, and Gore. However, on closer inspection, each decision maker may have started out with firm plans to adhere to the step-by-step, purely rational model prescribed by Simon but was swayed by the emotionality and national attention of the event as it unfolded. Similar to the incremental model, each event followed its own course, without direction or clear goal, disjointed and separated from a logical, straightforward path. Surely, decision makers relied on their "gut-level" feeling at the time.

The decision-making models developed by Simon, Gore, and Lindblom are not the only credible efforts to help students understand the decision-making process. Indeed, their models may be more appropriate for noncrisis, routine administrative ventures.

Irving Janis and Leon Mann have outlined a decision-making model, based on psychological conflict, that emphasizes the decision-making process under stress.[62] In contrast to the intellectual (rational) process presented by Simon, Janis and Mann indicate that decision making involves "hot" emotional influences, similar to Gore's theory. The need to make a decision is inherently stressful. When a decision maker is faced with an emotionally consequential, no-win choice, how he or she copes with the problem depends on two major factors: hope and time. This process causes great stress, as the factors of hope and time are rarely within the control and purview of the decision maker. This can be uniquely observed in protracted, high-stress incidents involving the police, such as those observed in Waco and Ruby Ridge.

When the decision maker has control of time and has hope that conciliation is possible, that person's efforts are more likely to follow the desired pattern of the "vigilant decision maker."[63] The vigilant model closely resembles the rational–comprehensive model developed by Simon. The vigilant decision maker (1) thoroughly canvasses a wide range of alternatives; (2) surveys a full range of objectives to be fulfilled and the values implicated by choice; (3) carefully weighs the costs and risks of negative consequences as well as the positive consequences that could come from each alternative; (4) intensively searches for new information relevant to further evaluation of the alternatives; (5) correctly assimilates and takes account of new information or expert judgment to which he or she is exposed, even when the information or judgment does not support the course of action initially preferred; (6) re-examines the positive and negative consequences of all known alternatives, including those originally regarded as unacceptable, before making a final choice; and (7) makes detailed provisions for implementing or executing the chosen course of action, with special attention to contingency plans that might be required if various known risks materialize.[64]

While Janis is better known among students of politics, policy, and management for his earlier work on "groupthink,"[65] his development with Leon Mann of the concept of the vigilant decision maker has provided a practical model for measuring administrative responsibility. Most notable is the excellent essay by Jack H. Nagel in applying the decision-making theories of Janis and Mann to the 1985 MOVE incident in Philadelphia.[66] In his highly critical work, Nagel identifies several decision-making paradoxes that, unfortunately, are not uncommon in similar incidents (e.g., the SLA [Symbionese Liberation Army] shoot-out in Los Angeles in 1968, the AIM [American Indian Movement] siege of Wounded Knee in 1977, the FBI shootings at Ruby Ridge, and the ATF raid on Branch Davidians in Waco).

These paradoxes are identified and elaborated on by Taylor and Prichard.[67] All the incidents have commonality. They were all police precipitated—that is, each incident grew from the police advancing on the homes of well-armed, openly defiant, and hostile groups of individuals. Each incident grew from earlier encounters with the police, often highly charged, emotional encounters involving everything from civil and slander suits against the police for harassment to police–group shootings. In all of the incidents, the police intelligence concerning the actual location of the assault and/or the number of suspects and their armaments were in gross error. To complicate the issue, the primary decision maker was not at the scene. In both the Waco and Ruby Ridge incidents, critical decisions were made in Washington, D.C., several thousand miles away. Then, too, the incidents were characterized by an overreliance on technology. Decision makers believed that tear gas would not ignite and burn but rather force hostages and suspects from their barricaded positions. The illusion of invulnerability also impacted each incident—who would believe that suspects would not surrender to a large, powerful, tactically trained, well-armed group of federal agents? This certainly was the case in the ATF raid on the Branch Davidians in Waco. The overreliance on intellectual rationality failed as police decision makers underestimated the power and control of a charismatic leader in a relatively small, religiously inspired group. Further, the belief that police Special Weapons and Tactics (SWAT) agents could act as an effective, highly specialized military unit performing a "surgical strike" on a bunker belonged more in the movies than in reality. Police officers and agents are simply not experienced, trained, or equipped to handle such encounters. Contrary to popular belief, highly trained police tactical units are rarely successful because they must rely on meticulous timing, superlative intelligence, surprise, and the ability to use deadly force effectively. None of these conditions existed in the protracted events of Waco and Ruby Ridge.

Finally, in each incident, the decision maker lost hope for a peaceful outcome. When such a condition occurs, the decision maker enters the downward spiral of "defensive avoidance."[68] The pattern is characterized by procrastination and delay, followed by passing the buck and other ways of denying personal responsibility, followed by bolstering and gaining superficial support from others. The distorted view produced by bolstering results in a spreading of responsibility and an exaggerated value of the chosen course of action. More often than not, the chosen course is a "do something" reaction. As Janis and Mann state, the process of defensive avoidance "satisfies a powerful emotional need—to avoid anticipatory fear, shame, and guilt."[69] Delay followed by haste can result in wishful thinking, oversimplification of the problem, and the selection of the force option. Confusion, catastrophe, and denial soon follow.

Handling Crisis Events in the Future

Several new directions for handling such crisis events in the future can be developed from the lessons of the past. These recommendations have been adopted as policy for the FBI Critical Incident Response Group, created in 1994 as a response to the Waco and Ruby Ridge encounters. Recommendations for protracted conflict can be summarized as follows:

1. Jack H. Nagel strongly argues that policies to deal with such events must be institutionalized.[70] That is, they must be concrete, written directives that reflect the overall philosophy of the department or agency. These policies must not be changed arbitrarily during a crisis event or for a specific operational strategy. Further, policies must identify key players and decision makers during such events. Who is the primary decision maker? Who is in charge of operational management? Who is in charge of coordination, communication, logistics, and so on? These are critical positions that must be identified in writing, well before an incident occurs.

2. Police agencies must adopt a philosophy that clearly articulates the importance of the safety and security of human life during such incidents. The force option through the use of SWAT team assault, selective sniper fire, and tear gas distribution must be last resorts. The primary philosophy must emphasize a patient, no-force negotiation strategy rather than a tactical solution for outcome. This is not a new concept. Frank Bolz and others have pressed for this type of departmental philosophy for the past 25 years.[71]

3. Police agencies must consider withdrawal as a strategy. Certainly, in most of these cases, the police could have arrested the primary leaders of these groups outside

the confinement of a barricaded compound. The use of more modern surveillance equipment using forward-looking infrared (FLIR) and wall-penetrating radar technology could do much to increase the accuracy of intelligence and the development of an arrest plan before a barricaded standoff occurs.

4. Police executives must reconsider the role and use of SWAT teams. Their role must be limited to containment and use during routine search warrant executions. They should not be used as a skilled military group capable of executing high-risk operations requiring precision and exceptional teamwork. Police executives must fight the "testosterone syndrome" of SWAT team commanders who argue that their training and expertise prepare SWAT teams for such missions. They simply do not. The comparison between police SWAT teams and military strike force

Quick FACTS ▸▸ SWAT Teams: Militarization of the American Police

The first Special Weapons and Tactics (SWAT) team was created by the Los Angeles Police Department under the direction of then-Chief Daryl Gates in 1966 as civil unrest marred cities across America. These teams of highly specialized officers focused on police responses to riots, demonstrations, barricaded persons, and hostage situations as these situations mushroomed in agencies across the nation. The growth of SWAT teams found further justification during the 1980's 'war on drugs' with the passage of the Military Cooperation with Law Enforcement Officials Act, which allows the military to provide intelligence, material, transport services and training, as well as to participate in drug interdiction efforts in almost every way short of direct search, seizure, and arrest. The police could now be deployed as highly trained units rather than individuals, use high-tech sophisticated equipment and weaponry, and dress significantly different in camouflage BDUs (battle dress uniforms) than their police patrol counterparts. SWAT teams were often trained by elite military groups, and their use was expanded to the service of high-risk search warrants.

By the late 1990s, the first alarm about the militarization of the police began to arise. In a well-noted study, Kraska and Kappeler surveyed 548 police departments serving jurisdiction of 50,000 people or more. In 1982, about 59 percent of the police departments surveyed had a SWAT team, by 1990, the figure had increased to 78 percent, and by 1995, it reached 89 percent.

Today, in the wake of 9/11 and the impact of threat of terrorism, every major police department in the United States has a SWAT team, and many smaller jurisdictions have joined together to make multi-jurisdictional units. Every state police department also has a SWAT team, along with several federal agencies including the FBI Hostage Rescue Team, which employs a SWAT unit in each of its 56 field offices. The National Tactical Officers Association (NTOA) estimates that there are nearly 1,500 SWAT teams in police agencies across the United States, conducting between 50,000 to 75,000 call-outs per year, as compared to 3,000 times a year in the 1980s.

Controversy has erupted as some legislative bodies have attempted to reign in these paramilitary police units. Unfortunately, botched raids and operations have come along with the success of some units. Critics point out that the sheer number of SWAT teams is staggering and that they are often duplicitous in effort; they are also very expensive in terms of manpower, equipment, and training especially for smaller municipalities. In 2009, the Maryland legislature passed a bill making it the first state to require police agencies with a SWAT team to file annual reports detailing their activities and the results of their call-outs and/or raids. The controversy continues as other states have started to impose stricter training standards and other statewide protocols for SWAT teams within their jurisdictions.

Sources: Peter B. Kraska and Victor E. Kappeler, "Militarizing the American Police: The Rise and Normalization of Paramilitary Police Units," *Social Problems*, Volume 44:1 (February 1997).

Dianne C. Weber, "Warrior Cops: The Ominous Growth of Paramilitarism in American Police Departments." (Washington, D.C.: The CATO Institute, 1999). See http://www.cato.org/pub_display.php?pub_id=1489 (retrieved July 4, 2010).

Radley Balko, "Overkill: The Rise of Paramilitary Police Raids in America (Washington, D.C.: The Cato Institute, July 17, 2006). See http://www.cato.org/pub_display.php?pub_id=6476 (retrieved July 4, 2010).

Drug War Chronicles, "Reining in SWAT – Towards Effective Oversight of Paramilitary Police Units" (May 28, 2010).

teams (such as the Navy SEALS or Army Delta Force) must be broken. The rules of engagement for each unit are unique, as are the desired goals and outcomes.

5. Training for protracted conflicts must include the top-level decision makers as well as operational commanders and chiefs. Attorney generals, governors, city managers, mayors, councilpersons, and top police executives must be trained in coping with such conditions. Significant attention must be paid to the development of a policy that emphasizes the no-force negotiation option. Further, decision makers should be trained to recognize the characteristics of "defensive avoidance" and "**groupthink**" (discussed later in this chapter) before courses of action are taken.[72] Mock scenarios and role playing should accompany the training.

6. During crisis events, outside and neutral referees or observers should assist in the situation. These individuals should be well versed in the no-force negotiation option and should act as "coaches" for the negotiation team. These individuals should have no ownership or responsibility in the situation and should be paid a small fee for their time only. These are not high-level consultants but rather well-trained, neutral observers with whom operational managers and top-level decision makers can review potential tactics and strategies. Outside observers must be protected from any type of potential ensuing liability through the agency involved. Their main purpose is to act as a "reality check and review" for actions to be taken by the police.

Decision making during these types of protracted events, when the suspects appear to be anything but rational, is always a very difficult task. It is also a very human endeavor, and, as such, mistakes will inevitably occur. Remember that the purpose of studying these cases is not to criticize the agencies involved (hindsight is always 20–20) but rather to offer students and police executives alternatives to past experiences and tactics. No one decision-making model guarantees success. However, we owe it to the brave men and women who died in these past incidents to ensure that future decision makers always attempt to maximize the two most important factors in the negotiation strategy: hope and time. This can be accomplished by eliminating the force options of direct assault, selective sniper fire, and tear gas dispersal.

"Active Shooter" Situations

Just as the process for making decisions during protracted crisis changed with two highlighted events nearly 20 years ago (Ruby Ridge and Waco), so has the police response to "active shooter" scenarios changed with the terrible events of the Columbine massacre on April 20, 1999. In the Columbine School shooting, Eric Harris and Dillon Klebold murdered 13 people on the school campus before they committed suicide, bringing the total to 15 people dead. The first responding patrol officers told horrific stories of arriving at the scene and hearing shots fired and victims screaming for over 10 minutes, yet having no training or advanced weaponry to enter the school and stop the killing. This event, more than any other, changed police responses to similar events noted as "active shooter" situations.

There are similarities in the nearly 100 school shootings (in the United States and Canada since 1966) that make them significantly different than those of the protracted crisis discussed earlier:

- Most of the victims are school-age children, some as young as 6 years old, who were shot *randomly*.
- The shootings have little, if any, logical reason or purpose other than causing massive carnage and human death.
- The suspects are for the most part, also students, or at least student age (11 to 22 years), working alone.
- The vast majority of the suspects are white males with a history of school issues, including social conflict, disenfranchisement, and/or mental problems.
- The suspect's actions were planned and well-thought-out, and in some cases even rehearsed, with suspects bringing guns to the school before their planned event. The suspects even made threats that they wanted to hurt people, but were not taken seriously.
- The suspects had easy access to firearms and were often well-armed with multiple weapons and ammunition.
- In most cases, the suspect(s) commits suicide or is killed by the police.[73]

The need to act quickly in these types of scenarios often precludes the use of SWAT teams that must be called out with some delay. Further, the presence of an active shooter at the scene also requires that responding patrol officers take action to save lives and human destruction rather than cordon off the area and wait. Police have devised a new technique often referred to as **Quick Action Deployment—QUAD** or "Active Shooter Response" that provides officers with a tactical philosophy and solution to use in such situations.[74] Most active shooter situations are over within 5 to 7 minutes, while some may last for as long as 30 minutes. Under the active shooter philosophy, the first responding officers to the scene must take action immediately. The one and only mission is to locate and stop the active shooter(s).

With a minimum of four well-armed officers, a modified diamond formation (consisting of one point officer, two utility officers [one on the right and one on the left], and a rear guard) is developed and the team enters the building. Again, the purpose is not to rescue wounded persons, but rather to find the active shooter and stop the carnage.

This immediate response to active shooter incidents is not without controversy. Some argue that the response is risky, especially to officers, because there is a serious lack of accurate intelligence information relating to how many suspects exist and the nature of their armament. For instance, what would happen to police officers with minimal training and armament who approach a group of well-armed terrorists that have entered a school (similar to the Beslan[75] incident in Russia in 2004)? Responding officers might fall, providing additional weaponry to the suspect(s) and heightening the emotionality of the entire incident. Then too, will responding officers actually know who the suspect "student" is amongst a room of other students? They will be entering a school without exact knowledge of the floor plan of the building as well as very limited, if any, suspect(s) description. Acting on this type of scant information can potentially lead to the police accidently shooting victims. The resulting liability could be devastating. Despite these issues, many police departments in the United States have opted to train their officers on QUAD response to active shooters.

The concept that it is much better for experienced officers to immediately assess the situation and then respond in a coordinated effort to neutralize the situation brings our discussion of decision making back to those heuristic elements noted by Gore[76] and "thin-slicing" from Gladwell; that is, the ability of individuals to discern relevant facts from a very narrow perspective of experience and actual knowledge and then act accordingly.[77] The idea is simple—most people make spontaneous decisions that are just as good, or even better, than well thought-out and planned ones.

Quick FACTS ▸▸ New Tactical Responses to School Shootings

School shootings continue to be tragic events in American history. Police responses to such incidents have changed, with more recent endeavors focused on taking immediate action to locate and stop the active shooter, and save lives. Quick Action Deployment (QUAD) and Advanced Law Enforcement Rapid Response Training (ALERRT) are two training techniques that have garnered wide appeal to law enforcement. Both methodologies employ "real-life" simulations with a focus on active shooter response and survival stress reaction.

For more information on QUAD Training, see http://www.nasta.ws/quad.htm

For more information on ALERRT Training, see http://www.alerrt.com/

(Paul Harris/ZUMA Press/Newscom)

Up to this point, we have concentrated mainly on individual decision making. However, police administrators rarely act alone. They are surrounded by deputy chiefs, bureau commanders, and division captains who provide input into the working structure of a police department. Group actions in the decision-making process are critical to the success of a specific decision and therefore require exploration.

Group Decision Making

Research on group decision making reveals that this approach has both advantages and disadvantages over individual decision making. If the potential for group decision making can be exploited and its deficiencies avoided, it follows that group decision making can attain a level of proficiency that is not ordinarily achieved. The requirement for achieving this level of group performance seems to hinge on developing a style of leadership that maximizes the group's assets and minimizes its liabilities. Because members possess the essential ingredients for the solution, the deficiencies that appear in group decisions reside in the processes by which group decisions are made. These processes can determine whether the group functions effectively or ineffectively. With training, a leader can supply these functions and serve as the group's central nervous system, thus permitting the group to emerge as a highly efficient entity.[78]

Group Assets

The following advantages are found in group decision making.

Greater Total Knowledge and Information

There is more information in a group than in any of its members; thus, problems that require the use of knowledge (both internal and external to the police agency) should give groups an advantage over individuals. If one member of the group (e.g., the police chief) knows much more than anyone else, the limited, unique knowledge of lesser-informed individuals can fill in some gaps in knowledge.

Greater Number of Approaches to Making a Decision

Most police executives tend to get into ruts in their thinking, especially when similar obstacles stand in the way of achieving a goal and a solution must be found. Some chiefs are handicapped in that they tend to persist in their approach and thus fail to consider another approach that might solve the problem in a more efficient manner. Individuals in a group have the same failing, but the approach in which they are persisting may be different. For example, one police administrator may insist that the best way to cope with the increasing number of robberies of local convenience stores in a community is to place the businesses under surveillance by specially trained police officers who are equipped with sufficient firepower to either arrest or shoot the robbers if necessary. Another police administrator might insist that the best way to reduce the number of robberies is through the implementation of crime prevention programs designed to use procedures that would make the businesses in question either less attractive or less vulnerable to robberies (e.g., keep the amount of cash available to a minimum, remove large signs from the front of the store windows that block the view of passing patrol cars and other motorists). It is sometimes difficult to determine which approach or approaches would be most effective in achieving the desired goal. But undue persistence or allegiance to one method tends to reduce a decision group's willingness to be innovative.

Participation in Problem Solving Increases Acceptance

Many problems require solutions that depend on the support of others to be effective. Insofar as group problem solving permits participation and influence, it follows that more individuals accept solutions when a group solves the problem than when one person solves it. When the chief solves a problem alone, he or she still has the task of persuading others. It follows, therefore, that, when groups solve such problems, a greater number of persons accept and feel responsible for making the solution work. A solution that is well accepted can be more effective than a better solution that lacks acceptance. For example, the decision to establish a crime prevention program in a ghetto neighborhood must have support from the level of chief to individual beat officer. Although other measures to reduce crime (such as increasing the number of patrol officers or stricter enforcement of juvenile gang activity) might have a more substantial impact, it is important to remember that most of the program participants must support the effort.

Better Comprehension of the Decision

Decisions made by an individual but that are to be carried out by others must be communicated from the decision maker to the decision executors. Thus, individual problem solving often requires an additional state: that of relaying the decision reached. Failures in this communication process detract from the merit of the decision and can even cause its failure or create a problem of greater magnitude than the initial problem that was solved. Many police organizational problems can be traced to inadequate communication of decisions made by superiors and transmitted to officers who have the task of implementing the decision. The chances for communication failures are reduced greatly when the individuals who must work together in executing a decision have participated in making it. They not only understand the solution because they saw it develop but also are aware of several other alternatives that were considered and the reasons why they were discarded. The common assumption that decisions supplied by superiors are reached arbitrarily, therefore, disappears. A full knowledge of goals, obstacles, alternatives, and factual information tends to open new lines of communication, and this communication in turn is maximized when the total problem-solving process is shared (see Figure 8.12).

This maxim is especially important concerning law enforcement because officers assigned to regular beats often provide the administrator with additional information or new dimensions to the problem. Additionally, almost any new program aimed at reducing crime in a specific area (neighborhood crime prevention or neighborhood watches) must necessarily include the patrol officer for implementation and success.

Figure 8.12
Open communication and increased participation increases effective group decision making.
(© Michael Newman/PhotoEdit)

Group Liabilities

Notwithstanding the benefits of group decision making, a number of liabilities are worth mentioning as a precautionary measure.

Social Pressure

Social pressure is a major force for increasing conformity. The desire to be a good group member and to be accepted may become more important than whether the objective quality of a decision is the most sound. Problems requiring solutions based on facts, independent of personal feelings and wishes, can suffer in group decision-making situations.

It has been shown that minority opinions in leaderless groups have little influence on the decisions made, even when these opinions are the correct ones. Reaching agreement in a group often is confused with finding the right answer, and it is for this reason that the dimensions of a decision's acceptance and its objective quality must be distinguished.

Individual Domination

In most leaderless groups, a dominant individual emerges and captures a disproportionate amount of the influence in determining the final outcome. Such individuals can achieve this end through a greater degree of participation, persuasive ability, or stubborn persistence (wearing down the opposition). None of these factors is related to problem-solving ability, so that the best problem solver in the group may not have the influence to upgrade the quality of a solution (which the individual would have had if left to solve the problem alone). The mere fact of appointing a leader causes this person to dominate a discussion. Thus, regardless of the individual's problem-solving ability, a leader tends to exert a major influence on the outcome of a discussion. In police circles, the influence of the chief's opinion is undeniable. All too often, the chief dominates the group process so much that participation is squelched. The chief needs to be aware of his or her influence and make a cognitive effort to listen rather than dominate.

Conflicting Secondary Goals: Winning the Argument

When groups are confronted with a problem, the initial goal is to obtain a solution. However, the appearance of several alternatives causes individuals to have preferences, and, once these emerge, the desire to support a particular position is created. Converting those with neutral viewpoints and refuting those with opposing viewpoints now enter the problem-solving process. More and more, the goal becomes having one's own solution chosen rather than finding the best solution. This new goal is unrelated to the quality of the solution and, therefore, can result in lowering the quality of the solution.

Groupthink

The theory of groupthink was first introduced by Irving Janis in 1972.[79] Groupthink is an interesting psychological phenomenon that most often occurs in cohesive groups that are isolated from other political and decision-making bodies. This condition often occurs within police leadership circles, especially during crisis events. The political pressure and stress to make a decision, coupled with the presence of a strong leader, escalate the condition. Groupthink is most often characterized by a serious lack of methodical procedure that forces a misperception of the problem and a hurried search for answers. During groupthink, there is considerable focus on a shared rationalization that bolsters the least objectionable alternative as a decision, a suppression of unfavorable outcomes, and an illusion of unanimity and invulnerability. Indeed, Janis and Mann warn that the decision-making process may be so intense that more effort is expended on striving for concurrence than on finding an appropriate decision.[80] During such conditions, the leader should attempt to remain impartial, listening to ideas and alternatives. He or she must invite dissent and encourage individual advisers to express their reservations about suggested decisions. The leader should challenge the group's actions and play the devil's advocate, asking what might go wrong and what the possible adverse consequences might be to the proposed actions. Finally, outside experts or critical evaluators should be asked to review agreed-on actions or plans. The leader must accept criticism of his or her own judgments as well as those proposed by the group. Janis and Mann are quick to point out that groupthink occurs not only during crisis times but also during rather mundane policymaking meetings.[81] It is incumbent that the leader, as well as individual members of the group, be on guard for the signs and characteristics of groupthink. The best defense to such a condition is continual, open debate and discussion. This requires a highly democratic and participatory leadership style (refer to Chapter 7, Leadership). In addition, this practice needs to be reinforced by the development of a methodological procedure that encourages dissent and, of course, the acceptance of criticism by all parties involved.

Factors That Can Serve as Assets or Liabilities

Depending on the skill of the discussion leader, some elements of group decision making can be assets or liabilities.

Disagreement

Discussion may lead to disagreement and hard feelings among members, or it may lead to a resolution of conflict and, hence, to an innovative solution. The first of these outcomes of disagreement is a liability, especially with regard to the acceptance of solutions; the second is an asset, particularly where innovation is desired. A chief can treat disagreement as undesirable and thereby reduce both the probability of hard feelings and innovative thought. The skillful police administrator creates a climate for disagreement without risking hard feelings because properly managed disagreement can be a source of creativity and innovation. The chief's perception of disagreement is a critical factor in using disagreements. Other factors are the chief's permissiveness, willingness to delay reaching a solution, techniques for processing information and opinions, and techniques for separating idea elicitation from idea evaluation.

Conflicting vs. Mutual Interests

Disagreement in discussions can take many forms. Often, participants disagree with one another with regard to the solution, but when the issues are explored, it is discovered the solutions are in conflict because they are designed to solve different problems. Before there can be agreement on a solution, there must be agreement on the problem. Even before this, there should be agreement on the goal and on the various obstacles that prevent the goal from being reached. This is where the synoptic planning model can be an invaluable tool. Once distinctions are made among goals, obstacles, and solutions (which represent ways of overcoming obstacles), the opportunities for cooperative problem solving and reduced conflict are increased.

Often, there is also disagreement regarding whether the objective of a solution is to be of the highest quality or merely acceptable. Frequently, a stated problem reveals a group of related but separate problems, each requiring a separate solution, so that a search for a single overall solution is impossible. Communications are often inadequate because the discussion is not synchronized, and each person is engaged in discussing a different aspect of the problem. Organizing the discussion to explore systematically these different aspects of the problem increases the quality of solutions. The leadership function of guiding such discussions is quite distinct from the function of evaluating or contributing ideas.

When the discussion leader helps separate different aspects of the problem-solving process and delays the inclination of the group to come to a quick but not-well-thought-out solution, both the quality of the solution and the acceptance of it improve. When the leader hinders the isolation of these processes, there is a risk of deterioration in the group process. The leader's skill thus determines whether a discussion drifts toward conflicting interests or whether mutual interests are located. Cooperative problem solving can occur only after the mutual interests have been established, and it is interesting how often they can be found when a discussion leader makes this a primary task.

Risk Taking

Groups are more willing than individuals to reach decisions that involve risk. Taking risks is a factor in the acceptance of change, but change may represent either a gain or a loss. The best protection against the latter outcome seems to be primarily a matter of the quality of a decision. In a group situation, this depends on the leader's skill in using the factors that represent group assets and avoiding those that make for liabilities.

Time Requirements

In general, more time is required for a group to reach a decision than for an individual to reach one. Insofar as some problems require quick decisions, individual decisions are favored. In other situations, acceptance and quality are requirements, but excessive time without sufficient returns also presents a loss. On the other hand, discussion can resolve conflicts, whereas reaching consensus has limited value. The practice of hastening a meeting can prevent full discussion, but failure to move a discussion forward can lead to boredom and fatigue, and group members may agree to anything merely to put an end to the meeting. The effective use of discussion time (a delicate balance between permissiveness and control on the part of the leader), therefore, is needed to make the time factor an asset rather than a liability. Unskilled leaders either tend to be too concerned with reaching a solution and, therefore, terminate a discussion before the group's agreement is obtained or tend to be too concerned with getting input, allowing the discussion to digress and become repetitive.

Who Changes

In reaching consensus or agreement, some members of a group must change. In group situations, who changes can be an asset or a liability. If persons with the most constructive views are induced to change, the end product suffers, whereas if persons with the least constructive points of view change, the end product is upgraded. A leader can upgrade the quality of a decision because the leadership position permits the individual to protect the person with the minority view and increase the individual's opportunity to influence the majority position. This protection is a constructive factor because a minority viewpoint influences only when facts favor it.

In many problem-solving discussions, the untrained leader plays a dominant role in influencing the outcome, and when the person is more resistant to changing personal views than are the other participants, the quality of the outcome tends to be lowered. This negative influence of leaders was demonstrated by experiments in which untrained leaders were asked to obtain a second solution to a problem after they had obtained their first one. It was found that the second solution tended to be superior to the first. Because the dominant individual had influenced the first solution and had won the point, it was not necessary for this person to dominate the subsequent discussion that led to the second solution. Acceptance of a solution also increases as the leader sees disagreement as producing ideas rather than as a source of difficulty or trouble. Leaders who see some of their participants as troublemakers obtain fewer innovative solutions and gain less acceptance of decisions than do leaders who see disagreeing members as persons with ideas.

Brainstorming

Brainstorming is a type of group decision making developed initially in advertising to help trigger creativity. The idea behind brainstorming is to establish a group environment in which individuals can present any idea that seems to apply even remotely to the subject being considered with the understanding that criticism will be withheld unless it can somehow improve on the original idea.[82] The practitioners of brainstorming have been able to determine some specific procedures that improve the effectiveness of brainstorming sessions. Whiting points out the following:

1. The sessions should last 40 minutes to an hour, although brief, 10- to 15-minute sessions may be effective if time is limited.
2. Generally, the problem to be discussed should not be revealed before the session.
3. The problem should be stated clearly and not too broadly.
4. A small conference table that allows people to communicate easily should be used.[83]

This approach can be useful in dealing with many public policy or administrative problems. When the major problem is one of discovering new ways of dealing with a situation, brainstorming may prove useful. One of the most difficult aspects of brainstorming, however, is creating a situation in which it can occur. Most of the "rules of the game" are based on an implicit level of trust between individuals, which sometimes does not exist in a politically volatile organization. This kind of trust must be developed for the procedure to be successful; thus, people tend to become freer and better able to use the process as they have repeated experiences with it.[84]

Ethics and Decision Making

Making ethical decisions requires training and sensitivity to ethical issues. Ethical behavior is difficult to define, and while ethics aren't wholly based on feelings, religion, law, or science, individuals may take those things into account when defining their standards of behavior. In fact, simply put, **ethics** are standards of behavior that dictate how humans are supposed to act within the roles that they find themselves in, whether that role is as a parent, friend, police administrator, supervisor, police officer, or private citizen. Ethics differ among individuals, depending on their personal values, cultural influences, or what they feel is the level of personal behavior that they should aspire to. Police administrators must identify ethical issues in decision making and develop strategies to confront ethical dilemmas. However, this process does not differ from the decision-making process used by any other individual.[85]

There are various ways to deal with ethical issues. One strategy for administrators is the following, developed by the Santa Clara University Markkula Center for Applied Ethics.[86] The first step in this framework is to recognize an ethical issue. Decision makers should ask themselves if there is something wrong personally, interpersonally, or socially and determine if the conflict, the situation, or the decision might be damaging to people or to the community. Then they should consider whether the issue goes beyond legal or institutional concerns and what it means to people who have dignity, rights, and hopes for a better life.

The next step in the framework is to get the facts, by determining what facts are relevant to the specific issue and what facts are unknown. Next, decision makers should decide what individuals and groups have an important stake in the outcome and should consider whether all stakeholders have been consulted or what they would say if they were consulted.

Decision makers should always evaluate alternative actions from various ethical perspectives when faced with an ethical dilemma. For instance, the utilitarian approach to ethics looks at which action is the one that will produce the greatest balance of benefits over harms. In this case, the decision maker asks which option will produce the most good and do the least harm. In approaching the decision using the rights approach, in which the ethical action is the one that respects the rights of all affected by the decision, one asks if everyone's rights and dignity will be respected, even if not everyone gets what he or she wants. The fairness approach, which defines an ethical action as one that treats people equally, or at least proportionately and fairly, requires that the decision maker ask which option is most fair to all stakeholders. The common good approach requires that an individual consider which option would help everyone involved participate more fully in society, and the virtue approach requires the decision maker to consider whether or not the action is one that embodies the habits and values of people at their best.

After decision makers carefully evaluate their options from one or more perspective, the framework requires that they make their decision based on which option they feel is the best or the right thing to do and then test it. After acting, it is important for decision makers to examine how it turned out for all concerned and to evaluate whether they would make the same decision if they had to do it all over again. Ethical decisions are not always the most cost-effective or popular ones, and they often cause some personal discomfort in the short term. However, by carefully evaluating the best course of action, a police administrator can avoid situations that may, over the long term, cause a great deal of personal stress, as well as remorse. Considering that ethical blunders in police administration tend to generate a great deal of negative publicity, taking the ethical route may also save police administrators from public shame or disgrace.

Common Errors in Decision Making

Analysis of the decision-making process indicates that certain types of errors occur at a higher frequency than others. Nigro and Nigro[87] have indicated that these errors are (1) cognitive nearsightedness, (2) the assumption that the future will repeat the past, (3) oversimplification, (4) overreliance on one's own experience, (5) preconceived notions, (6) unwillingness to experiment, and (7) reluctance to decide.[88]

Cognitive Nearsightedness

The human tendency is to make decisions that satisfy immediate needs and to brush aside doubts of their long-range wisdom. The hope is that the decision will prove a good one for the future also, but this actually is counting on being lucky. The odds for such good fortune to occur consistently across all decisions are poor.

Attempting to find a "quick fix" may create infinitely greater difficulties in the future. An example of this phenomenon is observed in barricaded hostage situations, in which the chief wants to assault the location immediately with a SWAT team. In crisis situations such as this, time has always proven to be an ally of the police.[89] Unfortunately, the complicated environment in which police officials function sometimes creates pressure to act on relatively narrow considerations of the moment. Also related to cognitive nearsightedness is the "narrow view," or the consideration of only one aspect of a problem while neglecting all other aspects of that problem, as occurred in the Branch Davidian and Ruby Ridge incidents.

Assumption That the Future Will Repeat Itself

In making decisions, police officials must try to forecast future conditions and events. Human behavior controls many events; in relatively stable periods of history, the assumption can safely be made that employees, client groups, and the public in general will behave much as they have in the past. The present period is, however, far from stable; many precedents have been shattered, and police officers, along with other public employees, can sometimes behave in surprising ways. Very rarely do dramatic changes occur without some warning signals. Early trends frequently can serve as valuable indicators of future behavior, but the police administrator must make the effort to be aware of these trends and develop strategies to cope with them.

Oversimplification

People tend to deal with the symptom of a problem rather than with its true cause because the cause may be too difficult to understand. It is also easier for those participating in the decision-making process to understand a simpler solution: it is more readily explained to others and therefore more likely to be adopted. Although a less-involved solution may actually be the better one, the point is that the decision maker looking for an acceptable answer may take the first simple one, no matter how inferior it may be to other, somewhat more complicated alternatives.

Overreliance on One's Own Experience

In general, law enforcement practitioners place great weight on their own previous experience and personal judgment. Although an experienced police executive should be able to make better decisions than a completely inexperienced one, a person's own experience may still not be the best guide. Frequently, another police executive with just as much experience has a completely different solution and is just as certain that his or her solution to a problem is the most satisfactory one. In fact, past success in certain kinds of situations may be attributable to chance rather than to the particular action taken. Thus, there is frequently much to be gained by counseling with others whose own experience can add an important and uniquely different dimension to the decision-making process.

Preconceived Notions

In many cases, decisions allegedly based on facts actually reflect the preconceived ideas of the police executive. This appears to be dishonest, and it is dishonest if the facts are altered to justify the decision. However, in many cases, individuals are capable of seeing only the facts that support their biases. Administrative decisions might be better if they were based on social science findings, but such findings are often ignored if they contradict the ideas of the police chief.[90] In administrative policymaking, conclusions are often supported by a structure of logic that rests dangerously on a mixed foundation of facts and assumptions.[91] Decision makers may appear as if they are proceeding in an orderly way from consideration of the facts to conclusions derived logically from them, when, in fact, sometimes the conclusion comes first and then the facts are found to justify them.

Unwillingness to Experiment

The best way in which to determine the workability of a proposal is to test it first on a limited scale. However, pressure for immediate, large-scale action often convinces the police chief that there is no time to proceed cautiously with pilot projects, no matter how sound the case for a slow approach. Sometimes police executives are reluctant to request funding and other needed support for the small-scale implementation of new programs for fear that such caution may raise doubts about the soundness of the programs. In all fairness to the cautious police administrator, sometimes this assessment has merit.

Reluctance to Decide

Even when in possession of adequate facts, some chiefs try to avoid making a decision (see Figure 8.13). Barnard speaks of the natural reluctance of some people to decide:

> The making of a decision, as everyone knows from personal experience, is a burdensome task. Offsetting the exhilaration that may result from a correct and successful decision is the depression that comes from failure or error of decision and in the frustration which ensues from uncertainty.[92]

Improving Decision Making

Recognizing some of these common errors in decision making can be a springboard for strengthening the ability to make good, ethical decisions in the future. Often, police executives fall into the trap of focusing on the outcome of a bad decision. Obviously, in the classic examples of Ruby Ridge and the Camp Davidians, the majority of us know *what* happened but are unable to fully articulate *why* it happened. We know about the number of people killed, but don't necessarily focus on the process that led the decision makers to take the actions that they did. By looking at mistakes on a personal level, as well as looking at mistakes made by contemporaries, police executives have an opportunity to capitalize on what didn't work so well in the past. Michael J. Mauboussin discusses this process at length and encourages all decision makers to take three steps toward better decision making: preparing, recognizing, and applying past mistakes to determine future courses

Figure 8.13
During future crisis situations, police executives will be forced to make decisions influencing a wide range of organizational, community, and political issues.
(© Richard Wong/Alamy)

of action.[93] Preparation is simply the process of gathering information about past mistakes and understanding why they happened. For example, in Ruby Ridge, it could be said that there was an over-reliance on the "gut-instinct" decision process. Once a police executive recognizes that this is a common mistake in crisis events, he or she can place that mistake in the context of his or her current situation. The goal here, according to Mauboussin is *"to recognize the kind of problem you face, how you risk making a mistake, and which tools you need to choose wisely."*[94] Finally, Maubossin suggests applying what you have learned about past mistakes in decision making to diminish the opportunity for a repeat. Police executives should put together a mental toolbox of sorts to cope with situations as they come up. Filing away and flagging errors in decision making as they come up is an excellent way to avoid making the same mistake, no matter what the circumstances.

CONCLUSION

Planning and decision making are simple concepts with exceptionally complex implications in policing. In this chapter, we discussed how planning is one of the precursors to the decision-making process. There are a number of approaches to planning that are useful to police organizations, with synoptic being among the most popular.

Decision making is a process rife with the potential for pitfalls, but is one of the starkest realities for the police executive. Decisions made by police administrators can affect the safety and well-being of officers and citizens alike. With this in mind, we discussed how different models of decision making might be applicable in policing, and how an individual person's own values can affect the decisions that they make.

Nowhere is the decision-making process more evident than in protracted crisis situations. Even though the decisions made in the Branch Davidian crisis in 1993 and at Ruby Ridge in 1992 are nearly 20 years in the past, we still recognize these events as turning points in American law enforcement, and both are classic examples of well-intentioned decision makers erring with unforgiving consequences. As is evidenced from these two case studies, protracted crisis events require special planning and consideration, as opposed to situations requiring immediate action, such as those posed by an active shooter in a school scenario. These are highly volatile situations often requiring officers to think and act on the "thinnest" of information. It is also necessary to look at common errors in decision making to avoid making the same mistake, particularly given the changing dynamics in the world around us. Economic crises, terrorist threats, and any number of other potential issues will continue to affect police executives and the way they make decisions in the years to come, and understanding how sound planning and decision making abilities can mitigate the effects of these problems is critical to the long-term success of any law enforcement agency in this country.

CHAPTER REVIEW

1. Explain some advantages of planning within a police department.
2. Discuss the synoptic planning approach and describe the three methods of selecting a preferred course of action within the process.
3. Discuss the synoptic planning approach and describe the three methods of selecting a preferred course of action within the process.
4. Discuss the characteristics of effective plans.
5. List the three major decision-making models.
6. Discuss Simon's concept of "bounded rationality."
7. Explain Lindblom's theory of incremental decision making.
8. Describe the decision-making process as presented by William Gore.
9. List some of the important recommendations, developed in this chapter, for handling future protracted crisis events. Compare these recommendations to responses for active shooter scenarios.
10. Discuss the advantages of group decision making.
11. List the steps decision makers should take when confronted with an ethical issue.
12. What are the most common errors in decision making.

KEY TERMS

e-learning software: computer-based training software designed to incorporate case studies and simulation in the learning experience.

ethics: rules and standards governing conduct.

feasibility studies: the determination of whether an action is possible, given current standards of operation, conditions, and restrictions.

groupthink: decision making by a group, characterized by a lack of both creativity and individual responsibility.

heuristic model: a simplified, gut-level method of decision making that emphasizes internal personality attributes of the decision maker.

operations research: the application, collection, and analysis of data from decision making within an organization.

planning: a process that links present actions to future conditions.

Quick Action Deployment—QUAD: A relatively new police methodology designed for arriving officers to take immediate action in active shooter situations; locate and stop the shooter.

rational model: the traditional model of decision making based on logic or reason.

recognition-primed decision making (RPD): method of decision making that focuses on the assessment of the situation, its dynamics, and the experience of the decision maker

suitability studies: the process that determines the appropriateness of an action in accordance with general policies, rules, and laws.

SWAT: special weapons and tactics police teams often used by the police during critical incidents such as barricaded felons, hostage situations, and felony search warrants.

synoptic planning: a process that comprises four activities: preparing to plan, making a choice between alternatives, implementing a plan, and evaluating the plan.

thin-slicing theory: the concept that instantaneous or quick decisions made by well-trained and experienced administrators may often be better than those made more deliberately and with significantly more information and time.

ENDNOTES

[1] G. S. Fulcher, *Common Sense Decision-Making* (Evanston, Ill.: Northwestern University Press, 1965), p. 4.

[2] Ibid., pp. 4–5.

[3] J. Q. Wilson, *Varieties of Police Behavior* (Cambridge, Mass.: Harvard University Press, 1978). In this study, Wilson considers how the uniformed officers of eight communities deal with such offenses as assault, theft, drunkenness, vice, traffic violations, and disorderly conduct. He also analyzes the problems facing the police administrator both in deciding what patrol officers ought to do and then in getting the officer to do it, how patrol officers in various cities differ in performing their functions, and under what circumstances such differences are based on explicit community decisions.

[4] J. H. Skolnick, *Justice without Trial* (New York: John Wiley & Sons, 1966). This book is based on the author's actual participation as a detective plus comparative community and case material. He discusses key issues, such as the organization of the police in America; the effects of police bureaucracy on criminal justice, narcotics, and vice investigation; the informer payoff and its consequences; and the relation between the police and black citizens. His findings are analyzed in light of organizational and legal controls over the police and their effect on the decision-making processes with law enforcement.

[5] Israel Stollman, "The Values of the City Planner," in *The Practice of Local Government Planning,* ed. Frank S. So et al. (Washington, D.C.: International City Management Association, 1979), p. 13.

[6] Ibid.

[7] Robert C. Cushman, *Criminal Justice Planning for Local Governments* (Washington, D.C.: U.S. Government Printing Office, 1980), p. 8; five of the elements identified are provided by Cushman, and the others have been added.

[8] Ibid.

[9] John Hudzik and Gary Cordner, *Planning in Criminal Justice Organizations and Systems* (New York: Macmillan, 1983), p. 1.

[10] Charles M. Mottley, "Strategy in Planning," in *Planning, Programming, Budgeting: A System Approach to Management,* 2nd ed., ed. J. F. Lyden and E. S. Miller (Chicago: Markham, 1972), p. 127.

[11] The term "pure," or "objective rationality," is taken from the alternative planning models identified by Tony Eddison, *Local Government: Management and Corporate Planning* (New York: Harper & Row, 1973), pp. 19–23.

[12] Cushman, *Criminal Justice Planning,* p. 4.

[13] The synoptic model is thoroughly discussed in Cushman, *Criminal Justice Planning.* Some of the following information relating to the model is paraphrased from that work.

[14] Carol Weiss, *Evaluation Research: Methods of Assessing Program Effectiveness* (Englewood Cliffs, N.J.: Prentice Hall, 1972), p. 7.

[15] P. Davidoff and T. A. Reiner, "A Choice Theory of Planning," *Journal of the American Institute of Planners* (May 1982), pp. 103–115.

[16] Hudzik and Cordner, *Planning in Criminal Justice,* p. 14.

[17] U.S. Naval War College, *Sound Military Decisions* (Newport, R.I.: U.S. Naval War College, 1942).

[18] The following discussion of strategic analysis is taken from Charles M. Mottley, "Strategic Planning," *Management Highlights,* Release 56, Office of Management Research, U.S. Department of the Interior, September 1967, pp. 103–119.

[19] E. S. Quade, "System Analysis Techniques for Planning-Programming-Budgeting," in Lyden and Miller, ed., *Planning, Programming, Budgeting,* p. 249.

[20] Ibid.

[21] Ibid.

[22] Hudzik and Cordner, *Planning in Criminal Justice,* p. 196.

[23] Ibid.

[24] A number of sources identify plans according to their use; see O. W. Wilson, *Police Planning,* 2nd ed. (Springfield, Ill.: Charles C Thomas, 1962), pp. 4–7, and Vernon L. Hoy, "Research and Planning," in *Local Government Police Management,* ed. Bernard L. Garmire (Washington, D.C.: International City Management Association, 1977), pp. 374–375.

[25] Stanley S. Thune and Robert J. House, "Where Long-Range Planning Pays Off," *Business Horizons* 13 (August 1970), pp. 81–90.

[26] P. J. Ortmeier and Edwin Meese, III. *Leadership, Ethics and Policing: Challenges for the 21st Century* (Upper Saddle River, N.J.: Prentice Hall, 2010). pp. 190–195.

[27] Hudzik and Cordner, *Planning in Criminal Justice,* p. 195.

[28] Gary A. Klein, *Sources of Power: How People Make Decisions* (Cambridge, MA: MIT Press, 1998).

[29] Malcom Gladwell, *Blink: The Power of Thinking without Thinking* (New York: Little, Brown, 2005)

[30] J. M. Pfiffner, "Administrative Rationality," *Public Administration Review* 20, no. 3 (summer 1960), p. 126.

[31] Ibid., p. 128.

[32] Herbert A. Simon, "The Proverbs of Administration," *Public Administration Review* (winter 1946): 53–67.

[33] Herbert A. Simon, *Administrative Behavior* (New York: Macmillan, 1961), p. 39.

[34] Ibid., p. 40.

[35] For a complete discussion of the rational–comprehensive model, see Peter F. Drucker, *The Effective Executive* (New York: Harper & Row, 1967); N. F. Iannone, *Supervision of Police Personnel* (Englewood Cliffs, N.J.: Prentice Hall, 1970); and Ira Sharkansky, *Public Administration* (Chicago: Markham, 1972).

[36] See Sharkansky, *Public Administration,* p. 44, and Sam S. Souryal, *Police Administration and Management* (St. Paul, Minn.: West, 1977), p. 315.

[37] Simon, *Administrative Behavior,* p. 40.

[38] Ibid.

[39] See Paul M. Whisenand and R. Fred Ferguson, *The Managing of Police Organizations,* 2nd ed. (Englewood Cliffs, N.J.: Prentice Hall, 1978), pp. 202–2033, for a discussion of Simon's "bounded-rationality" concepts.

[40] Charles F. Lindblom, *The Policy-Making Process* (Englewood Cliffs, N.J.: Prentice Hall, 1968).

[41] Ibid., p. 209.

[42] Charles F. Lindblom, "The Science of Muddling Through," *Public Administration Review* 19 (spring 1959), p. 86.

[43] Jack Kuykendall and Peter Unsinger, *Community Police Administration* (Chicago: Nelson-Hall, 1975), p. 132.

[44] William J. Gore, *Administration Decision-Making: A Heuristic Model* (New York: John Wiley & Sons, 1964).

[45] Ibid., p. 12.

[46] Souryal, *Police Administration,* p. 318.

[47] L. G. Gawthrop, *Bureaucratic Behavior in the Executive Branch* (New York: Free Press, 1969), pp. 98–99.

[48] Gore, *Administrative Decision-Making,* p. 12.

[49] Gawthrop, *Bureaucratic Behavior,* p. 99.

[50] Souryal, *Police Administration,* p. 319.

[51] Graham T. Allison, *Essence of Decision: Exploring the Cuban Missile Crisis* (Boston: Little, Brown, 1971).

[52] Some of this discussion was excerpted from an excellent review of Allison's book by Robert B. Denhardt, *Theories of Public Organization* (Monterey, Calif.: Brooks/Cole, 1984), pp. 81–85.

[53] John Ott, "The Challenging Game of Operations Research," in *Emerging Concepts of Management,* eds. Max S. Wortmann and Fred Luthans (London: Macmillan, 1970), p. 287.

[54] Ibid.

[55] Peter P. Schoderbeck "PERT—Its Promises and Performances," in Wortmann and Luthans, *Emerging Concepts,* p. 291; E. S. Quade, "Systems Analysis Techniques for Planning-Programming-Budgeting," in *RAND Report* (Santa Monica, Calif.: RAND Corporation, 1966), p. 7.

[56] Aaron Wildavsky, *Speaking Truth to Power: The Art and Craft of Police Analysis* (Boston: Little, Brown, 1979), p. 84.

[57] C. Zsambock, and G. Klein, *Naturalistic Decision Making* (Mahweh, N.J.: Erlbaum, 1997), p. 286.

[58] Ibid., p. 219.

[59] Malcom Gladwell, *Blink: The Power of Thinking without Thinking* (New York: Little, Brown, 2005), pp. 10–14.

[60] Ibid., p. 11.

[61] Ibid., p. 253.

[62] Irving L. Janis and Leon Mann, *Decision Making: A Psychological Analysis of Conflict, Choice, and Commitment* (New York: Free Press, 1977).

[63] Ibid., chap. 1.

[64] Ibid., pp. 11–15.

[65] Irving L. Janis, *Victims of Groupthink* (Boston: Houghton Mifflin, 1972).

[66] John H. Nagel, "Psychological Obstacles to Administrative Responsibility: Lessons of the MOVE Disaster," *Journal of Policy Analysis and Management* 10, no. 1 (1991), p. 3.

[67] Robert W. Taylor and Leigh A. Prichard, "Decision-Making in Crisis: Police Responses to Protracted Critical Incidents" (paper delivered at the Academy of Criminal Justice Sciences Annual Meeting, Las Vegas, Nev., March 13, 1996).

[68] The concept of "defensive avoidance" was first developed by Janis and Mann in *Decision Making.* However, Nagel uniquely applied the concept to reality in his article "Psychological Obstacles to Administrative Responsibility."

[69] Janis and Mann, *Decision Making,* p. 85.

[70] Nagel, "Psychological Obstacles," p. 21.

[71] The concept of a negotiated solution to crisis events has been developed over the past 25 years. See Frank A. Bolz and Edward Hershey, *Hostage Cop* (New York: Rawson, Wade, 1979); Ronald C. Crelinsten and Denis Szabo, *Hostage-Taking* (Lexington, Mass.: Lexington Books, 1979); Murray S. Miron and Arnold P. Goldstein, *Handbook for Hostage Negotiations: Tactical Procedures, Negotiating Techniques and Responses to*

Non-Negotiable Hostage Situations (New York: Harper & Row, 1979); and Robert W. Taylor, "Hostage and Crisis Negotiation Procedures" in *Police Civil Liability*, ed. Leonard Territo (New York: Hanrow Press, 1984).

[72] See Nagel, "Psychological Obstacles"; Janis and Mann, *Decision Making*; and Taylor and Prichard, "Decision-Making in Crisis."

[73] See Bryan Vossekuil, Robert Fein, Marissa Reddy, Randy Borum, and William Modzelski, *The Final Report and Findings for the Safe School Initiative: Implication for the Prevention of School Attacks in the United States* (Washington, D.C.: U.S. Secret Service, 2002), Glenn Muschert, "Research in School Shootings," *Sociology Compass*, Volume 1: Number 1 (2007), pp. 60–80, and Chicago Tribune, "School Shootings Through the Years," (February 15, 2008), accessed at: http://www.chicagotribune.com/news/local/chi-080215schoolshootings-photogallery,0,1575678.photogallery

[74] David R. Wood, QUAD: Quick Action DepLoyment: Law Enforcement's Preferred Response to "Active Shooter" *Situations, Law and Order*, Volume 49, Number 9 (September, 2010). See also: http://www.nasta.ws/quad.htm

[75] The Beslan School Massacre took place over three days in Beslan, Russia wherein several dozen armed Chechen rebels took nearly 1,100 people hostage (777 were school children) on September 1, 2004. After a series of failed negotiations, the Russian security forces stormed the building with heavy armament and rockets. The building exploded in fire, resulting in the death of 334 hostages, with 186 being children.

[76] Gore, *Administrative Decision-Making*.

[77] Malcom Gladwell, *Blink*.

[78] N. R. F. Maier, "Assets and Liabilities in Group Problem Solving: The Need for Integrated Function," *Psychology Review* 74, no. 4 (1967), pp. 239–248. Much of the information in this chapter dealing with the discussion of group decision making was obtained from this source.

[79] See Irving L. Janis, *Victims of Groupthink* (Boston: Houghton Mifflin, 1972).

[80] Janis and Mann, *Decision Making*, pp. 398–400.

[81] Ibid.

[82] W. Gortner, *Administration in the Public Sector* (New York: John Wiley & Sons, 1977), p. 124.

[83] C. S. Whiting, "Operational Techniques of Creative Thinking," *Advanced Management Journal* 20 (1955), pp. 24–30.

[84] John Schafer, "Making Ethical Decisions: A Practical Mode," *FBI Law Enforcement Bulletin,* May 2002.

[85] For more information about the framework for ethical decision making, visit www.scu.edu/ethics

[86] Markkula Center for Applied Ethics, Santa Clara University, "A Framework for Thinking Ethically." See http://www.scu.edu/ethics/practicing/decision/framework.html (September 2, 2007).

[87] Much of the information in this chapter dealing with the discussion of common errors in decision making was obtained from F. A. Nigro and L. G. Nigro, *Modern Public Administration* (New York: Harper & Row, 1977), pp. 226–232.

[88] D. Katz and R. L. Kahn, *The Social Psychology of Organizations* (New York: John Wiley and Sons, 1966), p. 285.

[89] Robert W. Taylor, "Hostage and Crisis Negotiation Procedures: Assessing Police Liability," *TRIAL Magazine* 19, no. 4 (1983), pp. 64–71.

[90] See, for example, A. Leighton, *Human Relations in a Changing World* (Princeton, N.J.: Princeton University Press, 1949), p. 152.

[91] Ibid.

[92] C. Barnard, *The Functions of the Executive* (Cambridge, Mass.: Harvard University Press, 1938), p. 189.

[93] Michael J. Mauboussin. *Think Twice: Harnessing the Power of Counterintuition* (Boston, Mass: Harvard Business Press, 2009), pp. 137–143.

[94] Mauboussin, *Think Twice*. p. xvi.

9

Human Resource Management

Individually we are one drop; together we are an ocean.
—R. Satoro

Objectives

- List 10 functions a police human resource unit might perform.

- Identify the main objective of the Equal Pay Act.

- Describe how the Age Discrimination in Employment Act is applied to law enforcement agencies.

- Explain the four major theories of discrimination.

- Name two categories of sexual discrimination.

- Summarize the protection afforded by the Pregnancy Discrimination Act.

- Define *disability* and *reasonable accommodation*.

- Discuss the law enforcement exemption of the Genetic Information Nondiscrimination Act.

- Contrast exempt and nonexempt employees.

- List the four reasons for which leave may be taken under the Family Medical Leave Act.

- Summarize how the economy affects recruiting applicants.

- Define *validity* and *reliability*.

- Explain why law enforcement agencies might rely on outside providers for their entrance and promotional tests.

9

- Identify the four obligations under Uniformed Services Employment and Reemployment Rights Act that law enforcement officers called to active military duty have.

- Summarize the three goals of an Early Identification and Intervention System.

- Explain the meaning of *discipline and progressive discipline.*

- Explain how a discipline matrix works.

- List six purposes of performance appraisals.

- Name the five different purposes promotional testing can serve.

- Describe the assessment center process.

- Explain rank order, all-qualified, and banded promotional rosters.

- Discuss the problem of identity loss that some officers experience in retirement.

OUTLINE

Introduction

There are some compelling reasons to have a strong working knowledge of human resource management: (1) at least 80 percent of a law enforcement agency's annual operating budget is spent on personnel and personnel support costs; (2) an agency competes in the same labor market with businesses and other police organizations; it should strive to become the law enforcement employer of choice; (3) some number of personnel problems can be traced back to faulty human resource management practices; (4) serious mistakes by weak selection processes and inadequate training are inevitably revealed by the actions of officers; (5) high turnover costs not only result in repetitive selection and training costs, but drive down the experience level of patrol officers—a threat to the quality of service delivery; (6) achieving and maintaining a diverse work force is a strong element in working effectively with the different populations in our communities; (7) there is a maze of local, state, and federal laws and regulations pertaining to public sector employees; failure to understand and follow them will bring adverse attention to an agency and can result in litigation by employees; (8) a department embroiled in job discrimination litigation puts the community at a significant disadvantage when trying to recruit potential employers to relocate there; for some potential employers it will be sufficient to scratch your city or county off of their list; (9) valid and reliable promotional practices will identify leaders (see Chapter 7, Leadership) who can involve officers and help maintain a high level of agency performance; and (10) a community needs and deserves the best possible law enforcement agency, whose effectiveness and image ultimately rests on the people that represent it.

Functions of a Police Human Resource Unit

In small jurisdictions, human resource (HR)/personnel services will primarily be provided by the city's or county's central personnel office. As law enforcement agencies progressively become larger, they assume a larger portion of the HR responsibilities. Larger departments may have a HR division, but in many agencies HR management is a function within their Administrative or Personnel and Training Divisions.

Depending on the size of a law enforcement agency and the division of responsibilities with the central personnel office, a police HR unit may have oversight of the following areas:

1. Complying with Peace Officers Standards and Training Commission (POST) requirements and guidelines;
2. Maintaining currency with federal job discrimination laws;
3. Developing agency HR policies, subject to executive approval;
4. Recruiting and selecting sworn and civilian personnel;
5. Monitoring turnover, retention, and diversity;
6. Providing or contracting for psychological services (e.g., entry screening and critical incident counseling);
7. Delivering or arranging for academy, in-service, and advanced training;
8. Conducting special studies (e.g. staffing, benefits, and compensation surveys);
9. Administering benefits programs (e.g. health and life insurance, workers compensation);
10. Preparing payroll;
11. Directing labor relations;
12. Coordinating random drug screening;
13. Administering promotional testing;
14. Managing intern programs;
15. Advising commanders on personnel matters;
16. Coordinating the employee evaluation process;
17. Organizing promotions and awards ceremonies;
18. Coordinating off-duty work;
19. Directing Professional Standards/Internal Affairs efforts;
20. Acting as personnel records custodian;
21. Preparing content for the agency's website;
22. Conducting job exit interviews to identify factors associated with turnover; and
23. Serving as liaison to the central personnel office.[1]

Key Federal Laws Prohibiting Job Discrimination

In addition to the protections afforded by state laws, local ordinance, and civil service or merit commissions, there are several prominent federal laws prohibiting job discrimination. An overview of them is provided for general familiarity and not as a substitute for legal counsel. Some of these statutory laws are further referred to in a more specific context in subsequent sections of this chapter.

These laws discussed in this section are administered by the Department of Justice's **Equal Employment Opportunity Commission (EEOC)** and the **U.S. Department of Labor**. Despite the differences in the laws, the remedies available to plaintiffs are often similar or the same.

Job Discrimination Laws Administered by the Equal Employment Opportunity Commission

The Equal Pay and the Lilly Ledbetter Fair Pay Acts

The Fair Standards Labor Act (FLSA, 1938) was amended in 1963 by the **Equal Pay Act (EPA)**, which prohibits discrimination in wages based on gender. Still, it was not until 1970 that a federal court ruled in *Schultz v. Wheaton Glass Company* that for EPA purposes, the job of a woman did not need to be identical to a man's, only substantially similar. Although there has been progress, the EPA has never fully achieved its intended objective. In 2010, women, on average, still made only 77 cents for every dollar earned by men.[2]

In 2009, the **Lilly Ledbetter Fair Pay Act (LLFPA)** was signed into law, overturning the Supreme Court's decision in *Ledbetter v. Goodyear Tire & Rubber Co.,* which held a discrimination charge under EPA had to be filed within 180 days of the date of the original compensation decision leading to the charge or within 300 days in jurisdictions that have a state or local law prohibiting the same kind of compensation discrimination. The LLFPA carried a retroactive effective date of May 28, 2007 and vindicated EEOC's position that each discriminatory paycheck was a new violation.

LLFPA quickly provided a victory to Mary Lou Mikula, who was hired as a grants coordinator for the Allegheny (PA) County Police Department.[3] After being hired, Ms. Mikula began inquiring about an adjustment in pay because she was doing work equal to a similarly situated male, but making $7,000 less annually. Ultimately, she litigated and the suit was dismissed because it was not filed in a timely manner. She refiled the suit under LLFPA and the federal 3rd Circuit Court of Appeals reinstated it, remanding the litigation for further proceedings (2009).

Age Discrimination in Employment Act (ADEA)

The **Age Discrimination in Employment Act, ADEA** (1967) only forbids age discrimination against people who are age 40 or older.[4] Some states have laws protecting younger workers from such discrimination. ADEA forbids age discrimination in any aspect of employment, including hiring, job assignments, promotions, layoffs, training, fringe benefits, and any other term or condition of employment. Harassment of older workers, such as continuing offensive remarks about their age, may rise to the level of creating a hostile working environment and may also be actionable.

In *Smith v. City of Jackson* (2005), the U.S. Supreme Court reviewed a case filed by Jackson (Mississippi) police officers who were 40 years of age and older, which sued under a theory of disparate impact, alleging that their employer's new adopted pay plan was more favorable to younger officers and fell more harshly by comparison on older officers.[5]

Factually, officers with less than 5 years tenure received higher raises than those with more service. The defendant, City of Jackson, argued it had a legitimate, nondiscriminatory reason for the plan, desiring to raise starting salaries to the regional average. The Supreme Court affirmed the lower court's summary judgment in favor of the defendant, concluding that while there were other ways to achieve the city's goal, the method selected was not unreasonable.

Nassau County (New York) reached a voluntary settlement with the EEOC in 2008 on an age discrimination suit. Although protected by the ADEA, four Nassau County Police Department Marine Bureau officers with excellent records and no negative performance evaluations were transferred to precinct jobs that were less desirable and were replaced by younger officers. The plaintiff officers argued that the personnel actions were motivated by an attempt to get them to retire. The settlement included $450,000 in damages for the plaintiffs and other injunctive relief.[6]

ADEA has a law enforcement exemption provision; local units of government can refuse to hire a person for a sworn position if the applicant is over their maximum age for hiring and the refusal to hire was part of a bona fide hiring or retirement plan and not a subterfuge to evade ADEA's purposes.[7] This position was also reached in 2010 in *Kannady v. City of Kiowa*. It was undisputed that the City of Kiowa refused to hire the plaintiff because he was 45 years old and thus not eligible to participate in the state-operated Oklahoma Police Pension and Retirement System, which had a 45-year-old cutoff for membership since 1989. In response, Kannady filed an ADEA suit. The trial court dismissed the suit and upon appeal, the federal 10th Circuit Court of Appeals affirmed the District Court's decision.

Title VII (1972) of the Civil Rights Act of 1964

Title VII prohibits discrimination in hiring, pay, promotion, firing, wages, job assignments, fringe benefits, and other terms and conditions of employment because of race, color, sex, national origin, or religion.[8] These five categories are referred to as **protected classes**. The law covers federal, state, and local governments, private employers with 15 or more employees, labor unions, and employment agencies.

Remedies for relief available to plaintiffs include: (1) injunctive relief, a court order prohibiting future discrimination; (2) hiring, promotion, or reinstatement; (3) backpay with interest; (4) if discriminatorily denied a job or terminated and there is no current vacancy, frontpay will be ordered until a position is available. Frontpay may also be an appropriate remedy when employer-employee hostility would make a continuing employment relationship difficult; (5) compensatory damages, to make the victim financially whole for past losses and emotional distress; (6) attorney fees; and (7) punitive damages, against nongovernmental entities, where the discrimination was undertaken with malice or reckless indifference.[9]

EEOC's enforcement of the law is based on four theories of discrimination. These theories apply both to Title VII violations and to the other job discrimination laws that EEOC administers:

1. *Disparate treatment*—An applicant or officer may rightly believe that he or she has been dealt with unfairly in an employment decision. To rise to the level of a disparate treatment claim, the person must have been intentionally treated differently because of his or her membership in a protected class; the discrimination must be more than slight to be actionable.[10]

African American police officers in Houston filed a Title VII suit alleging racial discrimination. The officers complained they could not serve in four divisions that prohibited officers from wearing beards. The department's position was that those divisions would be most likely to respond to chemical, biological, radiological, or nuclear attack and the bearded African American officers could not safely wear respirators. In *Stewart et al. v. City of Houston Police Department,* the District Court granted summary judgment to the defendant, the Houston Police Department, and the dismissal was afffirmed by the Appellate Court (2010).[11]

In *Endres v. Indiana State Police* (2003), a Baptist officer refused assignment as a full-time gaming commission agent at a casino because gambling violated his religious belief that games of chance were sinful.[12] The plaintiff requested other duties and was denied. The suit was dismissed; juggling unpopular enforcement duties and the preferences of officers would be a daunting task to managers and create operational hardships.

Religious discrimination may also be litigated on Constitutional, as opposed to Title VII, grounds. An Orthodox Jewish Las Vegas detective, Steve Riback, sued his department for religious discrimination because it would not allow him to grow a short beard or wear a yarmulke skullcap, even though he was on desk duty and not in contact with the public (see Figure 9.1). In 2009, the First Amendment case was settled with the plaintiff receiving $350,000, the right to grow a beard, and permission to wear a baseball cap in lieu of a yarmulke.[13] Newark Sunni Muslim police officers also successfully litigated a First Amendment claim, allowing them to grow beards in fulfillment of their religious practices (1999).[14] In its decision, the court noted the

Figure 9.1
Detective Steve Riback (left) discusses his religious discrimination suit against the Las Vegas Metropolitan Police Department with two members of the American Civil Liberties Union (ACLU).
(John Gurzinski)

department had already made an exception for African American officers prone to develop infections from shaving.

2. ***Adverse impact***—Prior to 1965, the Duke Power Company hired only African Americans into the lowest-paying job classifications, while Whites were hired into better-paying positions. The two races worked in segregated departments and promotions were made within those racially divided departments. Following the enactment of the Civil Rights Act of 1964, Duke Power changed its employment practices.

In 1965, new applicants and employees seeking transfer to traditional White classifications were required to have a high school education and pass two aptitude tests. The tests excluded 94 percent of the minorities, but only 42 percent of the majority group. At that time in Duke Power's home state of North Carolina, only 12 percent of African Americans had a high school education. Willie Griggs, an African American employee of Duke Power, filed a class action suit under the new Civil Rights Act.

In *Griggs v. Duke Power Company* (1971), the Supreme Court found for plaintiff, Griggs. The tests and the high school education requirement continued past discriminatory practice and both requirements were not job related. Griggs established the principle that the absence of discriminatory intent is unimportant and it is the consequences that matters. Although Duke Power's requirements were seemingly innocuous, their impact fell more harshly on African Americans, excluding them from better-paying positions, creating an adverse impact. An adverse impact is an employment practice that, although lacking any discriminatory intent and on its face appearing to be neutral, an employer is prohibited from using because it has an unjustified impact on members of a protected class.

In 1978, the EEOC developed **Uniform Guidelines for Employee Selection Procedures**. The purpose of the Guidelines was to create a single set of principles designed to help covered employers comply with federal laws prohibiting employment practices that discriminated on the basis of race, color, sex, religion, and national origin. As defined by EEOC, "selection procedure" means any measure, or combination of measures or procedures used as a basis for any employment decision. The term includes the full range of evaluation techniques from traditional paper and pencil tests, performance tests, training programs, probationary periods, and physical, educational, and work experience requirements through informal or casual interviews and unscored application forms.

Using the example of a written promotional test, a rough, rule-of-thumb method of assessing adverse impact is the "**4/5ths rule**."[15] If the passing rate on the test for any race, sex, or ethnic group is less than 4/5ths, or 80 percent, of the passing rate for the group with the highest passing rate, an adverse impact exists (see Figure 9.2). In such a case the employer must defend its practices or under EEOC guidelines adopt a selection process that is equally valid and reliable, reasonably meets the employer's legitimate business needs, and is less discriminatory. The replacement selection process might be a different written test or it could be an entirely different process, such as an oral board.

Test Data	White Candidates	African American Candidates	Totals
Took Test	400	100	500
Passed	120	10	130
Failed	280	90	370
Passing Rate	30%	10%	26%

Figure 9.2

Example of the 4/5ths rule applied to a police promotional written test.[a]
[a]Adverse impact calculation: 10% (lowest passing rate) ÷ 30% (highest passing rate) = 33.3%, substantially less than 80%, indicating an adverse impact. To avoid adverse impact in this example, the African American passing rate would have to be a minimum of 24%.

Law enforcement agencies are sensitive to the problems of adverse impact. However, as noted above, under EEOC guidelines all adverse impact is not illegal, although defending such practices imposes a substantial burden. That is a fight, even if winnable, in which most employers don't want to engage . It is likely to be costly, time-consuming, reduce prospects for increasing diversity, and tarnishes the image of the employer. The flip side is that abandoning the results of a test with adverse impact may result in a suit by officers who passed the test.

In *Ricci v. DeStefano* (2009), the Supreme Court ruled that New Haven, Connecticut couldn't simply dismiss the results of promotional tests for Fire Lieutenant and Captain that produced adverse impacts because it feared Title VII liability. The data for an adverse impact was clear—under the 4/5ths rule, the minority passing rate was 34 percent, only 59 percent of the passing rates for majority officers. The Court concluded that before being used the tests had been subject to "painstaking analysis," New Haven had turned a "blind eye" toward its validity evidence, and another process that met the employer's needs was not available at that time.

A case with a fact situation striking similarity to Ricci is *Joe Oakley v. City of Memphis*. The 40 plaintiffs in Oakley included a racially and gender mixed group of candidates that litigated over a promotional test to police major that Memphis discarded amid concerns about Title VII litigation despite strong possibilities for its defense. Both the trial and appeals court found for the defendant city of Memphis and plaintiffs appealed to the Supreme Court. In the wake of its decision in *Ricci*, the Supreme Court remanded Oakley for further consideration. Upon reconsideration, the plaintiffs prevailed. Note should be taken that both the original trial and appeals court decisions were based upon the prevailing decisions prior to Ricci.

3. *Harassment*—Although technically harassment is a form of disparate treatment, EEOC recognizes it as a separate theory of discrimination.[16]

Harassment is a discriminatory, unwelcome action toward an individual on the basis of race, color, sex (including pregnancy), national origin, age, religion, disability, or genetic information. Unwelcome actions that may rise to the level of harassment include speech, touching, and other conduct that create an intimidating "hostile work environment" that employees reasonably should not have to endure. Mild teasing and occasional off-hand comments will fall short of being recognized as creating a hostile environment; the conduct involved must be more severe or pervasive, but need not be totally intolerable.[17] Gender harassment can occur without it being specifically sexual harassment[18] (e.g., "You're pigheaded like all other women").

A single significant act may constitute harassment. In *Chris Sanford v. Department of Veterans Affairs* (2009), the Associate Director grabbed the plaintiff's arm, turned him around, pushed him into a desk, and screamed at him.[19] The incident was sufficiently severe as to allow a claim of harassment to be made. However, the more usual situation is a pattern of continuing conduct. Harassers can be supervisors, coworkers, and non-employees; the more severe the harassing actions, the less need there is to show a pattern.

Sexual harassment is perhaps the most immediately recognizable form of harassment. The victim and harasser may be of the same gender; a victim may also be someone other than the person being harassed who finds the conduct offensive. There does not have to be an economic injury to the victim before a claim can be filed.[20] Although victims of sexual harassment can be men, they are most often women; in rare occasions they may be very young. A 14-year old girl working in a Wichita, Kansas fast-food restaurant settled a claim in 2002 against her manager.[21]

Traditionally, **sexual harassment** has been categorized as: (1) **quid pro quo**, from Latin, meaning an exchange or literally "something for something." It is constituted by unwelcome sexual advances, requests for sexual favors, and other verbal or physical conduct of a sexual nature when: (A) submission to such conduct is either explicitly or implicitly a term or condition of an individual's employment or (B) submission or rejection of such conduct by an individual is used as the basis for employment decisions affecting that individual[22] and (2) **hostile environment**, which is created when the prohibited and unwelcome behavior has the purpose or effect of unreasonably interfering with an individual's work performance or by creating an intimidating, hostile, or offensive working environment.[23]

Examples of conduct that contribute to a hostile work environment include crude language; displaying sexually suggestive cartoons, calendars, posters, photographs, sex toys, or pornographic material; unnecessary touching; off-color, lewd, and obscene jokes; sexually suggestive gestures and body language; references to sexual activity and questions about another's sexual life; social invitations to discuss a promotion, raise, performance appraisal, or other terms and conditions of employment; and demeaning or offensive language, such as "babe," or "work spouse."[24] In determining whether such unwelcome conduct may have established a hostile environment, a variety of factors are considered, such as frequency, severity, and whether the conduct is intimidating or humiliating.

In Virginia, a female deputy successfully alleged sexual harassment. Although the sheriff avowed there would be no toleration of sexual harassment, he was self-described as a "touchy-feely person." Periodically the sheriff had contact with the plaintiff, making inappropriate or suggestive remarks and touching her in sexually aggressive ways. Subsequently, he insisted on hugging her when they encountered each other at work and would grab her buttocks. At one point he required her to sit on his lap and forced a kiss on her lips, admonishing her that if she wanted a transfer or promotion, she had to choose him over her boyfriend. These and other episodes made the plaintiff dread going to work. She resigned, filed suit, and prevailed at trial; on appeal the judgment of the trial court was affirmed (2010).[25]

Employers have a substantial responsibility in curbing all forms of prohibited harassment. Figure 9.3 illustrates common elements in a sexual harassment policy. Such policies often include the names, telephone numbers, and physical and e-mail addresses of those outside of the department to whom sexual harassment can be reported. Not shown in Figure 9.3 are the specific procedures related to the policy.

4. *Retaliation*—Unlawful retaliation can take one of two forms: (1) retaliation for participation and (2) retaliation for opposition.

Under retaliation for participation, employers are prohibited from retaliating against a job applicant or an employee because he or she made a charge, testified, assisted, or participated in any manner in an investigation, proceeding, or hearing involving a covered job discrimination claim; for the employee's expression or conduct to be protected from retaliation, it must make reference to a protected class or type of prohibited job discrimination.[26]

Under retaliation for opposition, employers cannot discriminate against an applicant or employee who opposed covered job discrimination practices or said so in response to the

---

Policy

All Departmental employees have a right to work in an environment free from unsolicited and unwelcome conduct of a sexual nature. Sexual harassment is against the law and is prohibited conduct that will not be tolerated in the department. Violations will be swiftly investigated and appropriate action taken at the earliest possible point. It may be necessary to transfer the accused to another position pending resolution.

In addition to being legally wrong, sexual harassment is also misconduct that undermines the integrity of the employment relationship. All employees have a responsibility to prevent the development of a department climate that allows, supports, promotes, condones, tolerates, or ignores sexual harassment and are required to report violations orally or written at the earliest possible opportunity.

Reports of misconduct may be made with any of the following: (1) any departmental supervisor, including outside of the normal chain of command; (2) the Internal Affairs Unit; (3) the city's Human Resource Department or EEO Officer; (4) any Assistant City Manager or the City Manager; (5) the State Civil Rights Commission; and (6) the federal Equal Employment Opportunity Commission.

All supervisors are responsible for preventing sexual harassment by: (1) monitoring the workplace on a daily basis; (2) ensuring that employees understand their rights and requirements to comply with the law and this policy; (3) taking immediate corrective action when misconduct is observed even if the involved employee is outside the normal chain of command; and (4) reporting allegations and observed misconduct in writing to the Office of the Chief of Police within 24 hours of occurrence. Reports shall be hand carried by the initiating supervisor to the Office of the Chief of Police in a sealed envelope bearing no outer details to protect privacy.

Figure 9.3
Sexual harassment policy statement.
Source: Drawn, with restatement for brevity, from the policies of the Denver, Colorado; Santa Cruz, California; and Peoria, Illinois Police Departments.

employer's questions. Protection is afforded so long as the opposition is based on a reasonable and good faith belief that the practice opposed is illegal. In the event the practice opposed is not prohibited, the employee is still protected. However, if such opposition is unreasonable, in bad faith, deliberately false, or malicious there is no protection.[27]

In 2008, a consent decree was entered into by the City of Colorado Springs and plaintiff Lance Lazoff in a retaliation case.[28] Both Mr. Lazoff and his wife were police officers. She filed an ADA complaint, which he actively supported. Subsequently, he was denied promotion to Sergeant 16 times. The consent decree remedies included back pay and retroactive seniority.

The Pregnancy Discrimination Act (PDA)

Pregnancy, childbirth, and related medical complications were not originally conceived of as discrimination issues. Still, some agencies developed policies to prevent such discrimination and the courts allowed litigation under the 1964 Civil Rights Act. To formalize what had previously been an ad hoc process and to promote uniformity of rights, the **Pregnancy Discrimination Act (PDA)** of 1978 was enacted. In some circumstances the Americans with Disabilities Act (ADA), and the Family Medical Leave Act (FMLA) protections may also be envoked. The PDA is the primary law prohibiting discrimination against pregnant women and is applicable to businesses with 15 or more employees and all public employers.

Broadly, the act makes it illegal to discriminate in employment practices against a woman because of pregnancy, childbirth, or medical conditions arising from such.[29] Hiring a pregnant woman is not required, but such an applicant must be treated equal to all other candidates. Women applying for pregnancy leave cannot be required to give more than the 30 days notice mandated by the FMLA. Poor performance and attendance problems by pregnant women need not be tolerated by an employer, but such employees cannot be held to a higher standard than any other employee. A woman cannot be forced from her job even if it exposes her to dangerous conditions although the employer should provide her with written notice of the hazards.

In 2006, six Suffolk County (New York) Police Department (SCPD) female officers sued their employer for denying women officers limited duty, desk-type jobs during their pregnancies. Until 2000, the SCPD provided access to such positions and then changed its policy to limit the use of such positions to officers injured on-duty. The SCPD also failed to provide bullet-proof vests and gun belts that would fit pregnant women. The result was that women could not work for much of their pregnancies and were unpaid after exhausting their annual leave. The trial court found for the women in *Lochren et al. v. Suffolk County* and awarded damages. The plaintiffs requested more substantial damages and sought relief in the Appeals Court, which remanded the case for further proceedings only on the financial issues (2009).[30]

The Americans with Disabilities Act (ADA) 1990

The **Americans with Disabilities Act (ADA)** was enacted in 1990 to guarantee equal opportunity to jobs for qualified individuals with disabilities and to provide covered individuals with other protections as well. The ADA Amendment Acts of 2008

| IN THE NEWS | The Pregnant Police Officer: Are Existing Policies Sufficient? |

Findings from a major review of research studies lead to the question of whether existing law enforcement policies related to pregnant officers are sufficiently comprehensive and informative.

Few departments have policies regarding firearms training by pregnant officers. Although nonlead rounds are used by some law enforcement agencies, others employ them. Lead toxicity is harmful to the fetus and exposure during pregnancy is associated with serious complications, including spontaneous abortion and hypertension. Noise toxicity is also related to acute disorders, including miscarriages. Lead and noise combined have a higher toxicity with significant consequences (e.g., heart lesions).

Gun-cleaning solvents may not be safe and pregnant officers should not clean firearms. Heavy physical activity during the last trimester may injure the baby or the mother. Pregnant officers should not be tasered during training due to a risk of miscarriage. Chemicals at clandestine labs, haz-mat spills, and traffic accidents are also health risks, as are contact with potentially infectious subjects and violent assaults. Shift work and night duty are associated with preterm births.

Source: Fabrice Czarnecki, M.D., "The Pregnant Officer," *Clinics in Occupational and Environmental Medicine,* Vol. 3, Issue 4, August 2003, pp. 641–648 and Karen J. Kruger, Fabrice Czarnecki, and Gary W. McLhinney, "Pregnancy and Policing: Are They Compatible?" Paper presented at the 2008 International Association of Chiefs of Police Annual Meeting, San Diego.

provided broader protections to job seekers with disabilities and put in place less-restrictive interpretations of the law than those held by the courts. The law covers private employers, state and local governments, employment agencies, and labor organizations and is enforced by the U.S. Equal Employment Opportunity Commission.

Other protections provided by ADA include guidelines as to how working police officers should deal with people with disabilities (e.g., those who are deaf). In 2009, the New York City Police Department entered into a settlement with the U.S. Department of Justice to implement practices that would enhance effective communication when its officers are in contact with deaf persons.[31] ADA further requires easy access and use by covered individuals to a wide range of facilities, including banks, theaters, recreational opportunities, transportation, hotel/lodging, child care centers, voting centers, restaurants, and assistance at self-serve gasoline stations.

ADA legislation has had a significant impact on the hiring and other human resource practices of law enforcement agencies. It makes it unlawful to discriminate in all employment practices with respect to covered individuals, including recruitment, hiring, pay, firing, promotion, job assignments, training, leave, lay-offs, and benefits. The law does not require that preferences be given to covered individuals.

In the employment context, a **qualified individual with a disability** is a job applicant or employee who meets legitimate skill, experience, education, or other requirements of an employment position that he or she seeks or holds.[32] The person must be able to perform the essential or core job functions versus the marginal requirements, with or without a **reasonable accommodation** for his or her disability by the employer; job requirements that screen out people with disabilities are legal only to the extent that they are job related and consistent with business necessity.[33] Examples of reasonable accommodations by employers include modifying equipment and facilities, redesigning jobs, modifying work schedules, and approving transfers to other vacant jobs that can be performed.[34] There are federal and some state tax credits for businesses to offset the cost of providing reasonable accommodations.

Accommodations cannot impose an "undue hardship" on employers, such as substantial expense. This is evaluated in terms of the employer's own circumstances. Accommodations will vary according to individual needs (e.g., an applicant may need a sign language interpreter during an interview, blind employees may need someone to read job instructions to them, and diabetics may need periodic breaks to eat properly and monitor their blood sugar and insulin levels).[35] Employers are not required to lower production or quality standards as an accommodation, nor must they provide one unless a request is made.[36]

With respect to an individual, a **disability** is: (1) a physical or mental impairment that *substantially* limits one or more major life activities, (2) a record of such an impairment, or (3) a perception that a person has such an impairment.[37] Major life activities include, but are not limited to by federal law, caring for one's self, performing manual tasks, seeing, hearing, eating, sleeping, walking, standing, lifting, bending, speaking, breathing, learning, reading, concentrating, thinking, communicating, and working.[38] Major bodily functions are also covered, including digestive, bowel, bladder, respiratory, circulatory, and reproductive functions.[39] Determining "substantial limitation" is a "common sense judgment"; the limitation need not totally prevent a major life activity nor rise to the level of a significant or severe restriction.[40] Although individuals may take "mitigating measures" to reduce or eliminate their impairment (e.g., insulin or use of a prosthetic limb), in ADA's view, the test of impairment is whether the person would have a substantial limitation of a major life activity without it.

Perception of a disability played a central role in a West Virginia incident. Claude Green, Jr. had a heart attack while driving. Billy Snead, a passenger in the vehicle, was giving CPR to Green when Welch Police Chief Bowman arrived at the scene. It was alleged that Chief Bowman knew or believed Green was gay, pulled Snead away from giving CPR, falsely warning him that Green was HIV positive, and 10 minutes later repeated the warning to arriving EMS workers, who nonetheless performed CPR. Green died a short time later at the hospital after attempts to revive him failed.[41] Chief Bowman labeled the allegations a "bold-faced lie."[42] *The Estate of Claude Green, Jr. v. Robert Bowman* was settled out of court, the terms of which cannot be discussed.[43]

Genetic Information Nondiscrimination Act (GINA)

Passed in 2008, the **Genetic Information Nondiscrimination Act (GINA)** covers employers with 15 or more workers, labor unions, training programs, and employment agencies. It effectively extends the reach of Title VII of the Civil Rights Act of 1964. The law defines "genetic information" broadly; it includes information about an individual's genetic tests and the genetic tests and medical histories of "family members" (i.e., their diseases, disorders, and conditions). *Family members* means to the fourth degree (i.e., great-great-great grandparents). In addition to other provisions, GINA strictly limits the disclosure of genetic information and requires its storage in special medical files. The law provides for compensatory damages for violations, which make plaintiffs whole, restoring them, and punitive damages, which are intended to punish violators and deter future offenses.

Title I forbids the use of genetic information by health insurers. Excluded from the definition of genetic information are cholesterol and liver-function tests, the sex of a person, or his/her age. Blood tests are permitted to the extent they are not designed to detect genotypes, mutations, or chromosomal changes.

Title II regulates the use of genetic information in the work setting. Employers cannot: (1) use genetic information when making employment decisions about applicants and the terms and conditions of employment for employees (e.g., a law enforcement agency cannot refuse employment to applicants because they have a family history of cancer); (2) classify, segregate, or limit employees based on genetic information; (3) retaliate against someone who asserts opposition to actions or practices forbidden by GINA; or (4) request, require, purchase, or disclose genetic information about employees. For example, employers may not use a health risk questionnaire requesting family medical history unless an "exception" applies.

The law recognizes six narrow exceptions to acquiring genetic information: (1) the "water cooler" situation, when an employer overhears someone talking about a family member's illness; (2) accidental discovery acquisition through a newspaper obituary or other publically available source (e.g., reading that an employee's mother died of heart failure); (3) voluntary participation in an employer's wellness program where the employee gives written consent; (4) when the information is required as part of a Family Medical Leave Act or similar state or local law provision to establish the medical necessity for which an employee is asking for leave (the Family Medical Leave Act is discussed in the next section of this chapter); (5) genetic testing that monitors the biological effects of toxic substances in the workplace, where program participation is voluntary or required by law; and (6) law enforcement agencies may request genetic information from employees to determine if they have contaminated forensic evidence and to identify human remains.

As a recent law, which took effect on November 21, 2009, with broad terms it is likely that there will be a substantial amount of litigation as employers and plaintiffs seek to establish exactly how the law should be applied.

Job Discrimination Laws Administered by the Department of Labor

The Fair Labor Standards Act (FLSA)

The goal of the original **Fair Labor Standards Act (FLSA)** (1938) was to create jobs in a struggling economy in the belief that business employers would rather pay normal or "straight time" to new employees than pay overtime to existing workers— 1.5 times their normal hourly rate—when they worked more than 40 hours a week.[44] In 1974, Congress amended the FLSA to make it applicable to public sector employees; two years later in *National League of Cities v. Usery*,[45] the Supreme Court held the amendment to be unconstitutional. Subsequently, the Supreme Court reversed itself on this issue in *Garcia v. San Antonio Metropolitan Transit Authority* (1985),[46] ruling that Congress did have the authority to apply FLSA to state and local governments.

The purpose of the FLSA is to establish national minimum wage, work hours, overtime pay, child labor, and required record-keeping standards. Of concern here are the work hours and overtime provisions pertaining to law enforcement agencies:

1. FLSA does not require holiday, vacation, or sick leave days; shift differential pay, hazardous duty compensation, overtime pay for working holidays, specific work schedules, fringe benefits, meal breaks, a written notice of the reason a person is fired, or any type of severance pay or package.[47] It also does not speak to job-sharing arrangements. Such things may be provided by a police department as part of its HR program or by written agreement with the officers' union.

2. Nothing in the FLSA prevents employers from paying more than the national minimum wage. This wage varies by state; in 2010, Washington had the highest hourly rate at $8.55 and Minnesota the lowest, $6.15. The most common hourly rate was $7.25.

3. Employees are grouped into two categories for purposes of overtime pay: (1) **nonexempt**—the group that is entitled to overtime pay and (2) **exempt**—the group that is not. To be exempt under the executive standard, employees must: (1) make more than $23,600 annually, (2) be paid by a fixed salary as opposed to an hourly rate, and (3) regularly supervise two or more employees, be in a position that is primarily managerial in nature, and be able to hire, fire, assign, and promote employees or have their opinions on such matters given "particular weight."[48] If they have been properly classified, exempt employees have no rights under FLSA.[49] Sheriffs and their personal staffs are exempt under FLSA, but deputies are not.

4. Employers with less than five law enforcement officers working during a 7-day week have a complete FLSA exemption from paying overtime for such weeks.[50] The law does not differentiate between full and part-time officers when counting the number of officers working.

5. Many employers must pay overtime when the number of hours worked exceeds 40 hours during a week; for such employers a "work week" may start on any day and consists of 7 consecutive 24-hour periods that total 168 hours. Law enforcement employers have wider latitude before the overtime compensation requirement is triggered, as shown in Figure 9.4. In contrast to a "work week," police employers can use a "work period" that ranges in length from 7 to not more than 28 consecutive days. "Work period" and paydays do not have to coincide.

6. Overtime compensation must be paid at least as 1.5 times the employee's normal hourly rate. In lieu of overtime pay, law enforcement employers can award compensatory time on the same basis; "comp time" acts as a bank of additional vacation or days off time. Officers can accrue up to 480 hours of comp time. Any hours worked beyond that accrual point must be compensated with pay. Officers may apply to take "comp time" off at any point, but agencies may consider their own operational needs and are not required to approve it as requested. However, agencies must allow officers to take comp time within a "reasonable period" following a denied request.

Work Period Days	Maximum Hours	Work Period Days	Maximum Hours
28	171	17	104
27	165	16	98
26	159	15	92
25	153	14	86
24	147	13	79
23	141	12	73
22	134	11	67
21	128	10	61
20	122	9	55
19	116	8	49
18	110	7	43

Figure 9.4
Thresholds triggering overtime compensation requirements for law enforcement officers. Source: 29 Code of Federal Regulations, Section 553.230, current to June 25, 2010.

Recent FLSA case law emanating from law enforcement officers has not been substantial in recent years. Police officers were not entitled to compensation when putting on and taking off their uniforms and accompanying gear in *Bamonte, Cota, Perine et. al. v. City of Mesa* (2010).[51] Although the officers were permitted, as a convenience, to change at the police station, there was no requirement to do so. The court contrasted the officers' situation with those working in a chemical plant who are mandated by the employer to change into and out of protective clothing on-site and who cannot safely perform their essential duties without doing so.

Adams et al. v. United States (2006) concluded that police officers commuting to and from work in an agency provided a "take-home car" are not entitled to be compensated under FLSA unless they perform some substantial police functions (e.g., working a wreck, intervening in a violent assault, or apprehending an offender).[52] In *Cleveland et al. v. City of Elmendorf, Texas* (2004), the court decided that small law enforcement agencies employing fewer than five officers need not count the unpaid service of reserve officers in determining whether they are FLSA exempt.[53] Compensation for K-9 officers caring for their dogs off-duty has been litigated under a variety of fact situations. As held in *Bull v. Customs and Border Protection Service* (2007) and other K-9 cases, the courts have generally been favorable to FLSA claims by such officers.

In general, when officers are on standby duty in anticipation of being recalled to work, they are not entitled to FLSA overtime compensation if they are able to conduct personal business and have freedom of movement. The more restrictive the conditions a law enforcement agency places on its standby officers, the closer it moves toward having to pay FLSA overtime compensation (e.g., state police troopers being required to remain in state patrol barracks when on standby).

The Family Medical Leave Act

Enacted in 1993, the **Family Medical Leave Act's (FMLA)** intention is to help employees balance their career and family needs. States are allowed to enact more generous terms, but cannot adopt more restrictive measures. Illustratively, in 2009, Wisconsin extended some state-level FMLA benefits to same-sex partners, a measure being considered by the federal government in mid-2010.[54]

"Covered employers" must grant "eligible workers" a total of 12 work weeks of unpaid leave during any 12-month period for one or more of the following reasons:

1. the birth and care of the newborn child of the employee;
2. placement with the employee of an adoptive or foster care son or daughter;
3. care of an immediate family member, spouse, child, or parent, with a serious health condition; and
4. medical work when the employee is unable to work because of a serious health condition.

A "covered employer" is a business with at least 50 employees and all public sector organizations. An "eligible worker" is a person who has worked for the employer 12 continuous months and at least 1,250 hours immediately prior to the request for FMLA leave. Employers may require a medical certification of the condition of a covered family member or that of an employee. The employer may seek a second medical opinion about such certification. Employees seeking FMLA leave must give the employer 30 days notice except for "unforeseeable circumstances," in which case the employee must explain and provide answers to any questions about why the request was unforeseeable. The use of sick or vacation days may be permitted in conjunction with a request for FMLA leave; the use of those days does not count as part of the 12-week FLMA leave period.

The FMLA was amended in 2009 and added two additional circumstances in which FMLA leave may be requested:

5. because of a "qualified exigency" arising out of the fact that the spouse, child, or parent of a police officer is on active duty in the armed forces or has been notified of an impending call to active duty and
6. to care for a covered military service member's serious illness or injury if the eligible police officer is the child, spouse, parent, or next of kin of the service member.

In *Goelzer v. Sheboygan County, Wisconsin* (2010), Dorothy Goelzer was dismissed from her 20-year clerical position with the county 2 months before she was to began a 2-month FMLA leave. Her employer contended that the dismissal was based on the desire to replace her with someone with a larger skill set, although she was replaced initially by a college intern. During the previous 4 years she used a considerable amount of FMLA leave, but received good evaluations. However, in one evaluation her supervisor commented on her use of sick leave and the "challenges" that presented to the office. Her initial FMLA suit was dismissed by the District Court, but that finding was reversed by the Appeals Court and remanded for further proceedings.[55] In contrast, Judith Gunzburger filed a FMLA violation suit against the Broward County (Florida) Sheriff's Office.[56] She failed to report to work for nearly 3 months although her medical certification stated that she did not have a serious medical condition and she failed to provide any evidence to the contrary. The trial court dismissed the suit (2009) and the appeal court upheld the finding (2010).

In *Knussman v. State of Maryland* (1999), the principle was established that under FMLA, a man cannot be denied FMLA leave on the basis of gender to be the primary caretaker for a seriously ill family member.[57] The plaintiff was a 22-year veteran of the Maryland State Police whose wife was bedridden with several medical conditions following childbirth.

The Police Personnel Selection Process

Figure 9.5 summarizes police applicant processing, selection, and training. The flow of this chapter substantially parallels this figure.

Applicants and Recruiting

Minimum standards for the employment of law enforcement officers are established by each state's **Police/Peace Officer Standards and Training Commission (POST)**. Employers may establish further or higher standards. Recruiting is the process of attracting a pool of candidates from which well-qualified applicants can be selected. The attractiveness of any pool of applicants can vary from one time to another. The economy has an impact on the number and quality of applicants for law enforcement positions; in a good economy the applicant pool is shallow, and in a down cycle there are more quality applicants.[58] As the U.S. economy soured, the New York City Police Department received 54 percent more applications in 2008 than in the previous year and the FBI was sorting through 227,000 applications in 2009 for 3,000 openings.[59] In a down economy, police employers must excel at recruiting.

A 2006 study of 850 California academy recruits explored their views about the recruiting process and revealed:[60]

1. The top two reasons for joining a law enforcement agency were a desire to serve and a sense of adventure and excitement, although most recruits were also influenced by health and retirement benefits.
2. The length of time it took to process their applications (54 percent) and the lack of personal contact and updates during the process (34 percent) were negative experiences.
3. The professional reputation of a potential employer (i.e., well-respected) was a major attractor (86 percent).
4. The most productive recruitment strategies were websites with information and on-line application forms followed by contacts with officers who were friends or family members or other employee referrals.

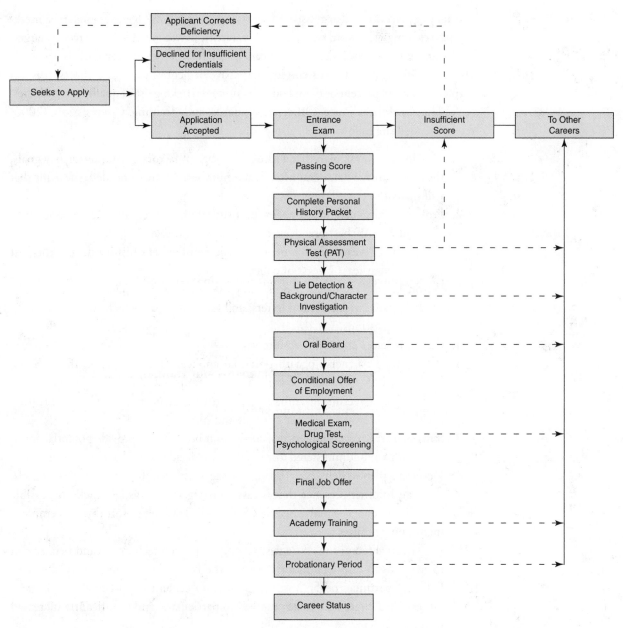

Figure 9.5
Applicant screening model.

5. Recruits had long-term interest in law enforcement; 20 percent were interested in a police career in elementary school and 50 percent by the time they graduated from high school.

A 2003 study surveyed 205 North Carolina state and local law enforcement agencies.[61] Respondents classified their recruiting techniques as passive (35 percent), neutral (34 percent), and aggressive (31 percent). Overall, the agencies' preferred methods of recruiting were word of mouth (95 percent), newspaper ads (83 percent), targeting community college students (72 percent), and the Internet (63 percent). With nearly 70 percent of the departments employing passive or neutral recruiting efforts, it is not surprising that 68 percent of them had no waiting or backlog list of qualified candidates.

The California Peace Officers Standards and Training Commission (2006) recommended the following recruiting practices:[62]

1. Develop an overall plan that addresses a range of factors, including agency goals, the community's demographics, future number of officers needed, the skills that will be required, and diversity.
2. Profile the ideal candidate, review past successes, failures, and future opportunities, and identify best practices; one agency found that its most successful candidates were 27-year-olds, who had a stable employment history during the past 2 years, and at least 2 years of college.
3. Personalize the recruiting process; stay in contact with applicants, update them on their status with calls and letters, and let them know which staff members to call with questions.
4. Carefully select and train recruiters.
5. Build strong partnership with potential applicant pipelines (e.g., the military, educational institutions, and student associations).
6. Make officers recruiting ambassadors, provide them with excellent recruiting packets, and reward them for referrals and hires.
7. Streamline the recruiting process, cutting out bottlenecks; provide potential applicants with a self-administered form so they can decide if they have any disqualifiers.
8. Develop a plan to deliver recruiting messages using multiple means or channels.
9. Have an Internet presence that is easy to navigate with as few clicks as possible to accommodate the many people who use the Internet to sort through employment opportunities.
10. Use effective recruiting strategies, relying on proven techniques and being open to new possibilities. Thinking "outside the box," the Sacramento (California) Police Department began hosting a Law Enforcement Expo/Female Health and Fitness Challenge, with males allowed to participate, and significantly increased its hiring of females.

Recruiting strategies and the expenditure of any recruiting funds should be carefully considered in light of human resource objectives, and the results carefully scrutinized. A 2009 study of the recruiting practices of the Los Angeles Police Department (LAPD) found results that may vary elsewhere, but illustrate the point that successful recruiting requires careful thought. The site of a recruiting event yields differential results; as compared to recruiting on military bases, the LAPD produced three times the number of applicants at community colleges.[63] Recruiting at events that focused on employment (see Figure 9.6) produced more applicants

Figure 9.6
A San Francisco Police Department recruiter talks with job seekers at an employment fair.
(Justin Sullivan/Getty Images)

than those at cultural celebrations and athletic events; events that charged an entry fee and advertised in advance were also productive.[64] Women are more likely than men to attend events.[65]

The cost of reaching applicants varies by the methods used and also may yield applicants with different characteristics. It costs the LAPD $29 to attract each applicant from its e-government recruiting site and $1,012 from radio advertising.[66] Asian and Pacific Islanders report significantly more exposure to the Internet than do other racial and ethnic groups; African Americans report more exposure to events and direct mail than do other groups.[67] The LAPD advertises on only one television station, an Asian language channel, where it broadcasts ads in Korean, Chinese, and Tagalog; it is a cost-effective effort at $147 per applicant.[68] The cost of recruiting efforts must also be evaluated in the context of keeping a law enforcement agency's "brand" before the public in a positive light.

By 2007, the EEOC began focusing more attention on recruiting efforts to determine to what degree they were unbiased or discriminatory. Recruiting messages cannot express a preference for any race, sex, color, ethnic group, or religion. Although most police departments depend, to a degree, on word-of-mouth recruiting by its officers, in a nondiverse department it might constitute a barrier to equal employment opportunity and limit diversity. Likewise, homogenous recruiting occurs when law enforcement agencies fail to use minority newspapers or Internet job sites such as Asian Nation, which might also be a barrier to equal opportunity.

The professionalization of policing has long been linked to college education for police officers. Only 1 percent of agencies require a college degree, 9 percent a 2-year degree, and another 8 percent, some college education; the high school degree is the basic educational credential for 81 percent of all agencies.[69] These requirements do not, however, reflect the actual numbers of police officers working in agencies who have some college to graduate degrees.

The Entrance Examination

EEOC's Uniform Guidelines for Employee Selection requires that tests be valid and reliable. **Validity** means that a test actually measures what it is intended to measure and conclusions and decisions based on test scores are appropriate and meaningful. The starting point to establish the validity of any test is a detailed job analysis.

A job description falls substantially short of being a job analysis because it is just a broad description of duties and responsibilities. Job analysis techniques can be used to identify: (1) the important types of knowledge to test for on a written examination and the number of questions to be written for each knowledge area; (2) the skills to be measured in a single job simulation exercise, such as requiring an applicant to play the role of an officer who has been stopped by an elderly citizen who is hard of hearing, a little confused, and asking for directions. The importance of each skill needed for a job varies and each skill identified by the job analysis should have its own statistical weight. A series of job simulations may constitute an assessment center. Additionally, the job analysis can identify: (3) the knowledge and skills to be tested by an oral board; and (4) the physical tasks police officers must perform in carrying out their duties. Validity gives tests the quality of being job related.

Reliability means that if the same test was given again or in a parallel form to the same group of people, they would score substantially the same. Reliability speaks to getting consistent, rather than random, results.

Larger municipalities and counties can develop their own entry tests. However, because establishing test validity and reliability can be time-consuming and technically challenging, many police entry-level tests are purchased or rented from test providers. Such providers include Peace Officers Standards and Training Commissions, Police Chief and Sheriff Associations, the International Personnel Management Association (IPMA), and private companies. Typical entry-level areas tested include reading comprehension, basic mathematical calculations, grammar, spelling, reasoning, memory, vocabulary, and clarity of expression (see Figure 9.7).

Passing scores on entry-level tests for all jobs in local government have traditionally been set at 70 by local civil service/merit boards. The courts have been disinclined to alter that standard when it has been challenged. Jurisdictions allow a failed candidate to retake the test after the passage of time (e.g. 3 months). To avoid potential liability, test administrators make sure that all applicants take the test under the exact same conditions (e.g., everyone starts and stops at the same time, no one is allowed to use a cell phone, and lighting is adequate throughout the room). In large longitudinal studies published in 2009 and 2010, respectively, the passing rate on

Vocabulary: Select the word that has the closest meaning to the word in bold print.
1. The suspect's employer **corroborated** her alibi.
   a. doubted
   b. verified
   c. contradicted
   d. denied

Clarity: Compare the two statements. Pick the one that is most clearly stated.
   a. The hairs were gathered in a clear envelope by the evidence technician.
   b. The hairs were gathered by the evidence technician in a clear envelope.

Figure 9.7
Examples of vocabulary and clarity of expression questions on an entry-level examination.

entry-level examinations for LAPD applicants was 84 percent versus 83 percent in Rochester, New York.[70]

Although entry-level tests are most often written or a job simulation exercise, assessment centers are also used. The key advantages to the written test are low cost, ease of administration, and rapid scoring. Entry-level tests cannot cover what applicants are expected to learn in the academy or on the job, only the things the knowledge and/or skills they are expected to bring to the job.

The Physical Assessment Test

The physical demands of police work are considerable at times. Illustratively, officers must have a level of strength and cardiovascular fitness to sustain themselves in a fight with a resisting subject or in pursuit of a subject fleeing on foot.[71] Physical fitness, condition, assessment, readiness, and agility tests are all intended to gauge to the extent to which applicants can do so (see Figure 9.8). Physical assessment tests (PATs) are developed from a job analysis physical task inventory. The important tasks are translated into physical requirements by a qualified person, such as an exercise physiologist, and a battery of tests is developed to measure those attributes (e.g., bench pressing weights or doing push-ups to determine upper-body strength, as well as timed runs to gauge cardiovascular condition and endurance).

Many agencies rely on the standards and testing protocols of outside providers for PATS for the same reasons they use their entrance examinations. PATs are usually assessed on a fail/pass basis, with applicants being excluded from further participation at any point in which they cannot pass a subtest of the PAT. Figure 9.9 summarizes a PAT test battery.

The EEOC prohibits requiring a medical examination before an applicant is offered a job contingent on passing it. Police departments have opted for two strategies to avoid liability if candidate injures him/herself or dies in association with the PAT: (1) applicants are advised of all activities and potential dangers and must sign a waiver to participate or (2) the candidate must provide a "medical certification," stating that a physician has examined the candidate and that he or she can participate. EEOC

Figure 9.8
Police applicants participating in a physical assessment test.
(Courtesy FitForce)

Vertical Jump	Bench Press	Bench Press*	Sit Ups	Agility Run	300 Meter Run	Push Ups	1.5 Mile Run
11.0–20.5″	90–205 lbs.	57–93%	25–42	17.8–22.0 seconds	56–92 seconds	12–34	14:05–19:48

Figure 9.9
PAT test battery.
*Percent of current body weight.
(Courtesy FitForce)

allows the medical certification because it is not a full medical examination and no specific medical data are provided with the certification. A study of the Rochester, New York, Police Department covering 2000 to 2008 found that 61 percent of those tested passed the physical agility test.[72]

Women have successfully challenged some PATs on the basis that they produce a discriminatory adverse impact. *United States v. City of Erie* (Pennsylvania, 2005) illustrates this problem. A police lieutenant was assigned to develop a new PAT, although he had none of the needed specialized education, training, or experience. Nonetheless, he developed a series of tests with cut-off scores. During its use, from 1996 to 2002, 71 percent of the men taking it passed, but only 13 percent of the female applicants. There was no job analysis or validity evidence and the court held the test to be neither job related nor consistent with the employer's business needs.[73]

The Lie Detection/Truth Verification Examination and Background/Character Investigation

The **Employee Polygraph Protection Act** (**EPPA**, 1988) is administered by the federal Department of Labor and restricts the use of the *polygraph* and other mechanism of lie detection with respect to employees. Included within this meaning is the **computer voice stress analyzer** (**CVSA**, see Figure 9.10), which is used by a number of police departments, including West Palm Beach, Florida; Toledo, Ohio; and Salt Lake City, Utah.

The EPPA provides certain exceptions, including screening security services employees (e.g., guards for banks and armored cars), national defense and security, certain portions of the pharmaceutical industry, some business-conducted investigations involving theft and fraud, and law enforcement agencies.[74] A national study found that even when combining the use of polygraphs and CVSAs, only 29 percent of the law enforcement agencies responding to the survey used them in the selection process.[75]

Studies of the accuracy of the polygraph and the CVSA vary considerably; to some degree this is due to the research design, whether the subjects were students playing a role versus "real-world" applications, and the training and experience of examiners. A National Academy of Sciences analysis labeled the evidence supporting the polygraph weak and lacking scientific rigor.[76] Still, other studies place its accuracy between 64 and 98 percent; the reports of CVSA accuracy are similar to those of the polygraph.[77]

Figure 9.10
The computer voice stress analyzer (CVSA).
(Courtesy CVSA1.com)

In several federal court circuits there has been somewhat of a relaxation of the practice of automatically barring lie detection results, although the clear majority view is that the scientific evidence is not sufficiently substantial.[78] Some state courts admit lie detection evidence if the parties to a proceeding stipulate to its admission prior to the test being administered; New Mexico allows its admission in state courts as scientific evidence.[79]

Consistent with the EPPA, a lie detector is used with police applicants to verify the information on their detailed personal history questionnaire. In addition to that, all applicants are asked an additional set of questions that are standard in each jurisdiction, but vary somewhat across law enforcement agencies. Examples of these include whether they have ever used a different name or social security number, received an unfavorable work evaluation, been paid for work "under the table" or "off the books," used illegal drugs while working, falsified a time sheet, shoplifted or switched price tags, been involved in a fight, carried a weapon illegally, driven without a license or insurance, or been involved with a group that advocates violence, hate, racial prejudice, terror, or subversive activities. Thus, the lie detector examination both verifies personal history information and may suggest particular things requiring special attention by the background/character investigator.

During lie detection examinations, applicants may be disqualified for deception, using countermeasures, or admitting actions that disqualify them (e.g., thefts and acts of family violence). Except for these reasons or closely allied ones, eliminating a candidate solely on the basis of a lie detection examination is not a good practice. Two large studies placed the passing rate for polygraph examinations at 63 and 70 percent.[80]

In *Mullen v. County of Suffolk* (2007), a polygraph examiner determined that a police officer applicant to the Ocean Beach (New York) Police Department was deceptive in responding to questions about his drug involvement.[81] The applicant was disqualified from further consideration and appealed that decision. The court ordered the polygraph evidence reviewed. The record was independently evaluated by the Vermont State Police, which concurred with the initial findings, and the plaintiff's suit was dismissed.

The background/character investigation is a specialized type of investigation and one best learned through training and the guidance of more experienced personnel. Like other types of investigations, it requires strong attention to detail and executing all required steps. The first step is to review the applicant's personal history questionnaire and the findings of the lie detector examination. Combined, these documents will key the investigator to contradictions, inconsistency in details, admissions made that need to be discussed with the candidate, and other matters.

Prior to the initial meeting with the applicant, the investigator should prepare a series of questions to probe areas of concern and have information release forms ready for the applicant to sign (e.g., education, military, and credit). Any documents that the applicants are required to present should be copied and the originals returned to the applicant. The copies should be dated and countersigned by the applicant and the assigned investigator so it is clear where the documents came from and who received them. Documents that agencies commonly request from applicants include a current color photograph signed on the back, birth certificate/naturalization order, divorce decree, name change, social security card, restraining orders, selective service card (if subject to the draft), DD 214 record of military service, passport, driver's license, and POST training record if presently or previously serving as a peace officer in another state.

Even when presented with apparently genuine documents, verification is essential. An applicant submitted his documents, including an original DD 214. In the initial meeting with the applicant, the investigator asked about the 3-month employment gap between his honorable discharge from the Coast Guard and his application to the law enforcement agency. The man related he and his wife had taken an extended vacation to "see the country." Nonetheless, the investigator had the man sign a military records release form. Once received, the record showed the applicant had been separated from the Coast Guard twice. The first DD 214 was accurate in all respects. However, there had been no extended vacation. Several weeks after being discharged the applicant reenlisted and several weeks later was drunk, beat his wife badly, and assaulted the military authorities who came to his on-base quarters to handle a domestic disturbance complaint. The applicant told the investigator that he gambled his DD 214 would be accepted at face value or that the record of his second enlistment and dishonorable discharge would never be discovered.

Other aspects of the background investigation include checking references and interviewing family, friends, roommates, coworkers, landlords, neighbors, spouse and/or a former spouse, and such others as the investigator feels necessary. Prior to writing the final report on the candidate it might be necessary to have a second interview to resolve any lingering questions. A study found that 8 percent of the applicants making it to the background stage are eliminated.[82]

The Oral Board

Oral board panelists cannot ask whatever suits them and then simply subjectively evaluate applicants; in the past such shoddy practices were so rampant that Doerner characterized police oral interviews as a fallible practice that had outlasted their usefulness,[83] and Gaines and Lewis concluded they were the largest source of errors in making decisions about people.[84] The use of oral boards has improved substantially over the past several decades, although there are still some jurisdictions whose use of oral boards lags behind best and legal practices:

> A law enforcement executive hired a consultant to assist with the agency's effort to become accredited. The promotional process consisted of an oral board scored by three departmental supervisors. When asked why the question "How do you feel about emigrants?" was used by the board, the executive said it was because people came to that county and his department had to deal with them. The consultant pointed out that "emigrants" meant people who left the county and that even if the language was corrected to "immigrants," the questions would still not be job related. The scoring sheet used by the board was simply a piece of paper labeled "The Scale" with numbers listed from 1 to 10 with no definitions or indication which were the high and low ends; members of the board were selected by "seeing who was in the building" and they were not trained. Dissatisfied with the consultant's findings the executive fired him, concluding "I just don't think you're going to be able to help us."

Perhaps the typical configuration of an applicant oral board is three members, one of whom may represent the central personnel officer or community and two who are supervisors in the law enforcement agency to which the candidate has applied. To satisfy legal requirements, the questions asked must be job related and not be impermissible. "Tell us about your writing skills; how good do you think they are?" or "Would you describe a time when you got really angry?" would be established as job related by any competent job analysis. In contrast, "When is your baby due?" or "What provisions will you make for child care?" may lead to a charge that the Pregnancy Protection Act and Title VII were violated if the person is not hired and otherwise qualified.[85]

The length of an oral board varies across agencies, but generally falls in the 20 to 45 minute range. The members must be adequately trained in using a well-developed scoring system and the questions must have been validated. Although shorter training times are common, 8 hours of it, including the opportunity to evaluate multiple mock applicants, should provide the skills needed by panel members and a good level of defensibility if the adequacy of training is challenged.

As questions are asked at an oral board, each member makes his or her own notes. When the candidate leaves the room, each member reviews his or her own notes and translates them into a numerical score. As a protocol, all scores on a skill, such as oral communication, must be within one point. When there are discrepancies greater than that, the panel discusses the applicant's behavior until the discrepancy is resolved.

A portion of a scoring sheet for oral communication is shown in Figure 9.11. A training manual provided to each panel member gives substantial guidance as to the exact types of behavior that place an applicant in each score level.

Conditional Job Offer

The **conditional job offer (CJO)** is a letter from the employing agency to the applicant offering a job contingent upon there being a funded position available and the applicant passing the medical, drug, and psychological screening. A CJO is usually extended only to the best qualified/most competitive candidates. An agency may not

---

To what extent did the applicant:

_____1. Speak in a clear voice.

_____2. Use voice volume appropriate to the situation.

_____3. Complete all sentences began.

_____4. Use correct grammar.

_____5. Avoiding distracting hand and/or other nonverbal body gestures.

_____6. Actively listen to the instructions to him/her at the beginning of the panel.

Figure 9.11
A portion of an oral board scoring sheet for oral communication.

know exactly how many positions it has available because the new budget has not been finalized, and resignations, retirements, and terminations may be more or fewer than projected, thus the need to condition the offer on a position being available.

The Medical Examination, Drug Test, and Psychological Screening

The purpose of this phase is to ensure that applicants can medically and psychologically perform the essential functions of a law enforcement officer. Some state POSTs have validated standards for medical, drug, and psychological screening. The exact sequence of these three tests varies and, except in large jurisdictions, are out-sourced. In addition to the usual components of a health examination, an audio test is conducted to verify that candidates meet hearing standards. Vision is tested for acuity, narrowing, and color deficiency. Vision acuity must be correctable to a reasonable standard, such as 20/30. Drug screening is based on urine samples, although a handful of agencies use hair analysis, which can reveal drug use over a longer period of time.[86] The physical assessment test may be a surrogate for the medical examination; a study found that 95 percent of those who passed the PAT also passed the medical examination.[87]

Psychological tests used in police selection vary, although the Minnesota Multiphasic Personality Inventory-2 (MMPI-2, revised 2001) has perhaps been the most common.[88] The Inwald Personality Inventory (IPI, 1992) has gained supporters over the past two decades and is designed specifically for use in law enforcement agencies. A study found that combining the results from the MMI-2, IPI, and Costa and McCrae's Neo Personal Inventory-Revised (Neo PI-R, 1995) contributed significantly to predicting recruit academy success.[89] In 2003, the MMPI-2 Restructured Form (RF) became available and is making inroads into policing. In 2010, San Diego issued a request for proposal (RFP) to provide applicant psychological screening to its police department, stipulating that the MPPI-2 RF must be one of two instruments used. Psychological tests are often followed by a one-hour interview with a licensed clinical psychologist or a psychiatrist.

The Formal Offer of Employment

At this point, there is a completed file for each applicant documenting the results of the selection process. The appointing authority decides on those to whom a formal offer of employment will be made. In larger law enforcement agencies, the names on the formal offer list will have been compiled by a staff member for the chief or sheriff. As the size of the agency decreases, the probability increases that the chief executive of the agency has a larger hand in deciding who will be offered a position.

The Recruit Academy

Based on a single major analysis, 12 percent of those taking the entrance exam make it to the academy; there is no significant difference between the success rates of men and women getting there; those with at least some college enter the academy at a marginally higher rate than those with a high school degree, as do applicants in their thirties compared to younger candidates; and among ethnic/racial groups, the ability to get into the academy ranged from 16 to 22 percent, with African Americans lagging other groups.[90] More men (88 percent) complete academy training than women (81 percent).[91]

The length and content of the recruit academy/basic course is established by each state's Peace Officers Standards and Training Commission (POST) (see Figure 9.12); agencies can require training beyond the minimum established. The basic course in Texas is 618 hours, whereas the Austin Police Department operates a 1,280 hour academy. The national average for POST mandated entry training is 588 hours.[92]

Nationally, there are 626 academies providing entry-level training, employing 12,200 full-time instructors and about twice that number in part-time faculty.[93] Recruit academies must be certified by their state's POST. They can be operated by mid-sized to larger departments that allow smaller agencies to use a few seats at a nominal fee, by vocational/technical schools, community colleges, and by university police departments as a service to agencies in their region. If a state has a central police training facility, it may do some basic training, although the main effort of this type of facility is typically focused on advanced/specialized courses. POSTs also require the completion of annual training to remain certified as a peace officer, with the national average being 24 hours.[94]

Figure 9.12
Emergency Vehicle Operation Course (EVOC) training is a standard part of POST mandated academy training. The Louisiana State Police EVOC course has an exterior circumference of two miles, an urban grid, a simulated interstate, and dirt/gravel roads.
(© Weberfoto/Dreamstime.com)

A study of 250 police academies concluded they failed to provide adequate training to investigate child sexual abuse;[95] the same criticism could also be made of preparation for other types of offenses (e.g., of white collar and organized crime, homeland security threats, human trafficking, and kidnapping). Almost any academy subject could benefit from additional training hours, but some useful topics simply cannot be squeezed into the overall time available. The academy's objective is to produce an adequate or better beginning generalist; within the resources available, often every additional hour added to one subject must be taken from some other subject area.

Police cadets socialize and drink more with their fellow recruits as compared with their previous circle of friends.[96] Scarfo found a significant relationship between education and police academy scores; however, neither a criminal justice degree nor military experience was related to academy performance.[97] In a comparison between a traditional academy and one oriented toward community policing, more educated officers and women did better in the latter although overall recruits from both types of academies performed similarly.[98]

In 2010, the New York City Police Department began a $1.5 billion revision to its facilities and teaching approach; the first phase, at a cost of $656 million, will be completed in 2013.[99] Ultimately, the new facility will look like a small city, including five-story buildings, a tactical village with moveable walls so cadets cannot memorize the course, and a firearms range. Outdoors, trainees will be put through trench collapse and other scenarios. The facilities provide the setting to make a shift from predominately classroom-based instruction to more hands-on scenario training.

Probationary to Career Status

The probationary period is the last step in the entry-level selection process and the opportunity to observe the recruit under actual work conditions. In many jurisdictions probationary periods can be extended, although most often that flexibility is not needed. The length of police probationary periods and when they start varies (see Figure 9.13), although one year following graduation from the police academy may be typical. Nationally, 4 percent of probationary officers are rejected.[100]

Law Enforcement Agency	Length
Anchorage, Alaska	One year from the end of field training period, but not longer than 18 months from the date of hire. Established by collective bargaining agreement ending December 31, 2013
Iowa City, Iowa	9 months from academy graduation date
Milwaukee, Wisconsin	16 months
Pasadena, California	18 months from the date of being sworn in
Wauchula, Florida	6 months, beginning with the first day assigned to a Field Training Officer

Figure 9.13
Illustrative probationary period lengths.

Following completion of the recruit academy, a probationary police officer is placed in a field training program to prepare officers to function on their own. The national average length for POST-mandated field training programs is 147 hours[101] although many jurisdictions have longer ones.

Officers in training (OITs) ride with a **field training officer (FTO)** whose primary responsibility is to demonstrate skills from a checklist and then develop the OIT's proficiency to perform them by certain points in the program (e.g., perform 25 traffic stops correctly by the end of week 4). FTOs are experienced officers; in some states they must complete a POST-required certification course to ensure they are qualified for their duties.

The Mesa, Arizona Police Department (MPD) has a nationally recognized 19-week FTO program.[102] OITs are rotated through the department's patrol districts and must be supervised by at least three different FTOs. Daily Observation Reports (DORs) are completed by FTOs and become the basis for the Sergeant's Weekly Report (SWR) on each OIT under his or her supervision. OITs may acquire the needed proficiencies before the end of the 19-week program. If so, they are allowed to ride solo, although the supervising sergeant continues to fill out SWRs. In the MPD and elsewhere, those successfully completing the OIT program will be recommended for career status.

Work Generations and the New Recruiting

Recruits entering law enforcement have been shaped by forces such as their genetic predispositions and life experiences. After their academy training, the "locker room wisdom" passed on to them, and they become socialized into the norms of the agency. In short, police work changes people. This section explores several generations of recruits who have entered law enforcement. While it is true that law enforcement agencies still change people and that, to a degree, each generation has changed policing, the more recent generations must be recruited with new messages attuned to their skills and values and more generous benefits.

The Silent Generation

Born between 1925 and 1945, the **Silent Generation** is generally loyal, security conscious, and conforming.[103] They were born during the Great Depression and the end of World War II; as adults, many of the men served in the military and, like the women they married, they believe in the American way of life. The silent generation is substantially retired. Recruiting members of this generation to jobs in police departments and supervising them did not present unusual challenges because of their experiences and values.

The Baby Boomers

Baby boomers have turned grey. In 2006, 62 percent of them were still in the workforce, but approaching the end of their careers.[104] Born during 1946 to 1964, after millions of men returned home from the war, boomers grew up during a period of widespread social change. Early boomers personally experienced the unfolding of rock and roll, military service during the Vietnam War, civil rights demonstrations, the proliferation of drug use, assassinations, and all of the other manifestations of the turbulent 1960s (see Chapter 1, Evolution of Police Administration). With some college or more, boomers are better-educated and more liberal than their parents. As teenagers and young adults they challenged conventional values, with the slogan "Never trust anyone over 30." Still, they were influenced by the strong work ethic of their parents. Ultimately goal and achievement oriented, the boomers are work focused and sacrificed, including some neglect of their families, to get ahead in their careers. Women had more career opportunities. Divorces were sometimes followed by second marriages to "start another family and get it right." Overall, 27 percent of baby boomers never married.[105]

Police departments did not hire boomers who admitted, or were discovered during the character/background investigation, to having used drugs. This eliminated some otherwise outstanding candidates, some of whom experimented with drugs while in the military. Eventually, departments softened their stance on drug use, although use of "hard" drugs was still an automatic disqualifier. Boomers were at the forefront as college education became more common in policing. Some supervisors routinely gave "college boys" lower performance appraisals than their less-educated counterparts. Sergeants were annoyed by the boomers' "disturbing tendency" to ask why things had to be done a certain way. To accommodate officers attending college, some received special work schedules, further irritating their routine-oriented supervisors. Authoritarian middle-managers were aggravated by the periodic written suggestions boomers submitted to improve operations, regarding them as a lack of respect for "proven methods." Eventually, the boomers proved their worth, even to skeptics, rising through the ranks to senior leadership positions with new styles of leadership. There are 30 million more boomers than the number of the next generation of workers, the "Xers."[106] The retirement of boomers will be a signification attrition of experience and institutional memory in police departments.

Generation X

Presently, **Generation X** makes up the largest number of officers employed by police agencies and they are moving into leadership positions.[107] Birthed from 1965 to 1980, Xers are more ethnically diverse than boomers, grew up in families where both parents worked, and were the first generation of "latch-key" children.[108] More than one-half have divorced parents and one-third were physically or sexually abused, often by a step-parent.[109] Drive-by shootings, abortions, AIDS, school violence, and missing children were also part of their lives. Technologically, Xers tend to be computer fluent.

Early Xers grew to adulthood in a mixed economy; as toddlers their nation's economy was sound, but turned sour during the 1970s with stagflation. Stagflation, or a stagnant economy, is produced by a combination of a high unemployment and high inflation. It resulted in interest rates hitting 21.5 percent in 1980. As a result of stagflation, there was a noticeable migration of Xers back to their parents' homes to make ends meet.[110] The economic instability left Xers with concerns about their financial circumstances and retirement, and with good reason: They are the first generation predicted to have a lower standard of living than that of their parents.[111] Xers marry later, delay having children, and expect their spouses to work; the women place a great emphasis on the family life many of them missed and are less inclined to sacrifice their families for career gain as the boomers did.[112] Rejecting the political platforms of the major parties, most Xers are independents (43 percent), followed by Democrats (30 percent) and Republicans (27 percent).[113] The three leading causes of death for Xers are automobile accidents, homicide, and suicide.[114]

Xers have been branded in various ways, including crybabies, grunge, and the lost generation. They have also been described in positive ways, including clear sighted, practical, intelligent, curious, good strategists and negotiators, seeing the whole person—not just the good or bad qualities, comfortable with diversity, and voracious learners.[115] There is some truth to these various characterizations because Xers are less homogeneous than boomers.

A Census Bureau study identified Xers' core values as equality, honesty, and respect in dealing with others, hard work, family values, and a sense of public service, which leads them to be high in volunteerism for social causes such as homelessness and social harmony.[116]

In the work setting, Xers have been restless; they welcome change and move from one employer to improve their financial circumstances and to be where they can make lasting contributions. At some point Xers will run out of the number of times they can shift from one job to another and many settle down into something more like a conventional career as opposed to a succession of jobs with different employers. Managed properly they will go the extra mile and beyond to get things done well, but will resist being micro-managed; given job autonomy, they are determined to succeed.[117]

Many police departments adapted their recruiting messages to attract Gen Xers, including: (1) ensuring that the recruiting messages and their cultures are aligned to avoid turnover with repeated recruitment, screening, selection, and training costs; (2) communicating that policing is a noble, exciting public service career; (3) emphasizing there are many career paths in law enforcement that will require life-long learning in order to be effective, giving them a sense of possibilities about their futures;[118] (4) highlighting that their sense of self-reliance is a substantial asset for them and their department; (5) illustrating how the Xers' skills at multitasking can be used; (6) underscoring that they will often be working without direct supervision, giving them desired flexibility and freedom in carrying out their job responsibilities;[119] and (7) giving them examples of how suggestions made by departmental members have improved operations.

As Xers entered law enforcement, some of their sergeants quickly noticed two characteristics that required attention: (1) their propensity to innovate occasionally made them somewhat resistant to supervision; sergeants lamented "I can tell them what to do until I'm blue in the face and they still do some part of the job their own damned way" and (2) their strong self-reliance and individuality led some patrol division Xers to emphasize a single or small number of duties, such as DUI enforcement, neglecting their broader responsibilities.

Generation Y

Born during 1981 to 1994 and largely the children of baby boomers, **Generation Y** babies are entering our law enforcement agencies. The "Yers" have also been called the Millenniums, dot.com babies, and "thumbers" because of the speed with which they can text message (see Figure 9.14). Less favorably, they have been tagged as Kids in Parents Pockets or "KIPPers," a slap at certain Yers prolonged dependence on their family of origin. Some of this dependency is created by overly supportive parents who get in the way of their children's journey to living as independent adults.

Raised in an era of gaming and rising modes of instant communication, social network sites (SNSs) have become a staple for Yers, including MySpace (2003), FaceBook (2004), and Twitter (2006); they cruise Craigslist ads and subscribe to Internet dating services like Match.com (1995) and eHarmony (2005). Some SNSs target Yers, such as BrazenCareerist and MyYearBook, giving them forums to discuss their careers and workplace issues.

They are more optimistic than Xers, seek a better balance between work and the rest of their lives, have high expectations for their employers, enjoy diversity and challenges, prefer teamwork over individual efforts, feel a need to volunteer and fundraise, desire honest feedback about their job performance, and are unafraid to question authority. There is a trend toward traditional family values and Yers are spiritual about love, although not necessarily religious.[120]

Figure 9.14
Generation Y "thumbers."
(Iconica/Jetta Productions/Getty Images)

Generation Z

Generation Z, the "Zedders," fall in the birth range of 1995 to 2010. Although their profile is still emerging, their fascination with virtual realities may lead to impoverished social and interpersonal skills. Beyond Zedders is the **Alpha Generation**, which will be the best-educated of all of the generations and the most technologically sophisticated. Alphas are in their infancy with a birth cohort of 2011 to 2025.

The New Recruiting

The combination of Xers and Yers entering law enforcement has resulted in a better understanding that part of the process of recruiting officers might also be about recruiting their families, leading to the development of elaborate family information packages and videos about all aspects of a community, including job opportunities for spouses and departmental partnerships with children's day-care centers.

In addition to the usual benefits, such as life and disability insurance and deferred compensation plans, police recruiting tools have been elevated.[121] Although the practices of individual jurisdictions vary, officer incentives have become more varied[122] and may include relocation reimbursement; signing bonuses of $5,000 to $10,000; a stipend of $6,000 for graduation from the recruit academy and another $4,000 for completing the probationary period; allowing the use of GI Bill benefits while attending the academy; 45 or more college credits for academy completion; interest-free home loans up to $75,000 and forgiveness of home loans of up to $28,000 on the basis of 5 percent for each year of service;[123] increased vacation time; and enhanced longevity pay and retirement systems. In some cities, officers retire with 20 years of service, based on 70 percent of the average of their three highest-paying years or 80 percent at 25 years. Some of these incentives have "taken a hit" in this fiscally constrained environment; Los Angeles and Dallas are among the large cities trimming such incentives.

Job flexibility and job sharing are used in law enforcement, but only to a small extent. Flexibility scheduling means that police departments present officers a choice of schedules within those established by the department; in contrast, job sharing means two or more officers share a single job.[124] Since 1999, the Orange County, California Sheriff's Department has offered job sharing to its 4,000 members; the Huntington Beach, California Police Department made it available to its 224 employees in 2001, and the Medina, Washington Police Department allows 2 of its 12 members to job share. Job sharing reduces stress and absenteeism, increases job satisfaction, and allows valuable employees enough "wiggle room" to remain on the job.[125] For managing dwindling budgets and as a regular tool, job sharing may be attractive to personnel winding down their careers, as a prelude to their actual retirement. Used as a "decompression" period, job sharing would be beneficial in making the transition from work to retirement.

Military Call-ups and Reinstatement

With substantial military commitments in Iraq and Afghanistan, the activation/call-up of National Guard and Reserve units, including police officer members, has been ongoing (see Figure 9.15). Even personnel classified as Individual Ready Reserve (IRR), who do not participate in National Guard or Reserve activities, have been called to duty, usually because of the need for reservists with special skills, such as helicopter pilots.[126]

How many law enforcement agencies have experienced personnel call-ups is somewhat of a question; two national studies came up with different answers: 21 percent and 44 percent.[127] In a 40-officer department, the loss of four officers represents a 10 percent drop in staffing, creating operational difficulties and generating overtime costs. Even in departments where call-ups have been minimal, the loss of a single key person can create an impact: In Youngstown, Ohio the SWAT Team's only qualified sniper was activated.[128] Some agencies have officers who have been deployed several times on tours of up to 16 months.

Administered by the U.S. Department of Labor, the purpose of the **Uniformed Services Employment and Reemployment Rights Act** (USERRA, 1994) is to

Figure 9.15
Officers graduating from the police academy. Some will be called to active military duty as a skilled individual or as a member of a reserve unit.
(© Mediaonela/Dreamstime.com)

encourage noncareer participation in the uniformed military service by eliminating barriers to such service, minimizing the disruption of the lives of those called to active duty, and prohibiting discrimination against them. The Palm Beach County (Florida) Police Benevolent Association filed a grievance when a deputy on military leave was allowed to take a promotional test elsewhere, asserting that the collective bargaining agreement made no allowance for such a test. The arbitrator found for the Sheriff's Office; the provisions of USERRA supersede collective bargaining agreements.[129]

Under USERRA, a police officer called to active duty must give advance notice of his pending absence to the department unless it is precluded by military necessity or otherwise impossible or unreasonable. The cumulative period of absence with that department cannot be longer than 5 years, and service separation cannot be under dishonorable or other punitive conditions. The officer must report back to duty on a timely basis or file a timely application for reemployment unless impossible or unreasonable.[130] Figure 9.16 summarizes the reporting back to duty timelines.

When called to active duty, officers can keep their individual and family health insurance for up to 24 months, although they may be required by their department to pay up to 102 percent of the full premium. USERRA also provides guidelines for seniority, pension, and other rights of returning officers who are returning from active duty call-up. The "escalator principle" requires reemployment at the position officers would have attained, but for their military service. If the officer is not qualified for the escalator position, the employer must provide the nearest approximation to it, and if that is not possible, to the pre-military service position.

Assuming the example of a state trooper called to active duty who misses a promotional examination, her employer is required to give her a make-up exam and promote her with back-dated seniority to the point she reasonably would have been

Length of Service	Reporting Requirement
Less than 31 days	After the end of the last calendar day of duty, time to return home safely, 8 hours of rest, and then report for the next regularly scheduled work period
31 to 180 days	Make application for reemployment within 14 days of separation; if impossible or unreasonable through no fault of the employee, as soon as possible
181 days or more	Apply for reemployment within 90 days of separation
Service-connected illness or disability	Reporting and reemployment application deadlines are extended up to 2 years while hospitalized or convalescing

Figure 9.16
USERRA reporting obligations following military service.

expected to be advanced in rank.[131] A federal court approved a jury award of double-pay, $300,000 for emotional distress, and promotion without testing for a New York City Fire Department promotional candidate who was denied an opportunity for a make-up exam when the absence was due to his military service.[132]

The call-up of officers also raises some POST certification issues that should be included in an agency's policy on military activation. As an illustration, in Michigan, officers are not considered to have discontinued their law enforcement employment for license purposes, unless they voluntarily extended their active duty commitment. Upon return to their agencies officers must provide a copy of their DD 214s (Certificate of Release or Discharge from Active Duty) or a DD 220 if the active duty lasts less than 90 days. If separated dishonorably, an investigation must be conducted to determine if the circumstances still allow POST licensing.

Activated officers may also be entitled to other rights under some state statutes and other federal laws (e.g., the federal **Servicemembers Civil Relief Act [SCRA**, 2003]). Some of SCRA's protections require that debts or leasing agreements entered into must pre-date the call to duty and the relief applying to them may be limited to the period during which the officer is on active duty or a short period thereafter. Key SCRA protections include: (1) service members and their family members cannot be evicted from leased housing costing less than $2,932 monthly; (2) interest charged on debts cannot be greater than 6 percent; (3) if the officer receives permanent change of station orders, a housing lease can be terminated, if present at the new location for 90 days or more; (4) car leases can be terminated if the officer is called to duty for 180 days, or after entering the service, the officer executes a lease and is deployed outside of the continental United States for 180 days or more; (5) up to $250,000 of life insurance cannot be cancelled for nonpayment while on active duty; and (6) protections begin with the date of activation and may apply until as much as 180 days after return to civilian life.

Paul Sutton, a former police lieutenant, sued the City of Chesapeake, Virginia, claiming that contrary to USERRA he was denied reemployment after completing call-up service in the Coast Guard. Sutton had been employed with the police department from 1974 until he was activated in 2000. In 2007, he was denied reemployment and continued to serve on active duty until 2009, when he retired from the Coast Guard and litigated.

The federal court noted that Sutton had retired from the police department before going on active duty, cashing out his vacation and sick time, and that he began drawing a police pension. Sutton argued that his retirement should not be a barrier to reemployment. The court dismissed the suit, reasoning that to find for Sutton would be an expansion of rights beyond those contemplated by USERRA and his absence from the police department was greater than the law's 5-year limitation.

Despite some difficulties created by a call-up of officers, law enforcement agencies are proud of their service. Such officers exhibit a strong commitment to our nation and often return with sharpened or new skills that are relevant to the police setting. However, inevitably someone will attempt to take advantage of a situation. A police officer claimed he was being called to active duty. However, the officer went to another city in the state and took a high-paying job in business. The employing agency continued to deposit money into the officer's bank account, reaching $8,700 before the scheme was discovered. Convicted of fraud, the officer lost his job and served a jail sentence of 90 days.[133]

Early Identification and Intervention Systems (EIIS)

In reaction to public concerns about police abuse of force and the number of complaints being generated by some officers, early-warning systems (EWSs) began appearing in the late 1980s. The police departments of New York City, Oakland, Kansas City, Miami, and Miami Dade were early leaders in this movement.[134] It is axiomatic among law enforcement executives that 10 percent of the officers cause 90 percent of the problems. Research somewhat supports this belief: An 8-year study of the San Francisco Police Department showed that of its 2,200 officers, just 100 were associated with 25 percent of the use of force reports.[135]

EWS were subsequently "rebadged" as **Early Identification and Intervention Systems (EIIS)**. In some agencies, EWS had developed a negative image with rank-and-file members because the term "problem officer" was closely associated with the program. In contrast, EIIS is framed as being a support system for officers and includes them in decision making.

Well-operated EEISs have assumed even greater importance since the passage of the federal Violent Crime Control and Law Enforcement Act (1994). The Act authorizes the Attorney General to file lawsuits to reform police departments engaging in a pattern or practice of violating citizens' federal rights. Suits may also be brought by the Attorney General under the Omnibus Crime Control and Safe Streets Act (1968) and Title VII (1972) for discrimination by law enforcement agencies on the basis of race, color, sex, or national origin if they receive federal funds.[136]

EIISs have three goals: (1) to guide officers to more successful performances; (2) to reduce the number of incidents involving officers that create liability exposure; and (3) to enhance the accountability of supervisors for the actions of their subordinates.[137] An EIIS can be a fully automated management tool that reviews the performance of all sworn personnel daily. While manual EIISs may work well in smaller departments, in larger agencies the system must be automated to be effective.

The police human resource unit supports commanders and supervisors by coordinating the delivery of some interventions determined to be useful (e.g., stress counseling).[138]

An EIIS is a nonpunitive intervention, intended to provide supervisory guidance, training, or other means to change the trajectory of officers' performances before discipline is necessary. The Phoenix, Arizona Police Department's (PPD) EIIS system is transparent. Officers can access their EIIS status on-line at any time and see where they stand in relation to the threshold standards that would trigger an EIIS identification, allowing them to be self-monitoring.[139]

Whenever a Phoenix officer is "tagged" by the EIIS, a case manager is automatically notified electronically. Case managers review each file to make sure the identification is not a "false positive," an error. Once contacted, the actual supervisor of the officer involved has 21 days to complete the intervention review.[140] Officers are part of the intervention review process, helping to design the responses that are most helpful to them.

Ten years ago, only 27 percent of the agencies responding to a national survey reported using EIISs, although that number is thought to be much higher now.[141] The number of variables tracked in an EIIS largely depends on whether it is a manual or automated system. Common variables include use of force reports, the ratio of use of force reports to arrests, the number of force incidents in which its use is questionable, citizen complaints, the numbers of resist arrests, the frequency of high-speed pursuits, assignment history, and disciplinary record. The PPD EIIS system has "threshold values" that when reached result in an officer being "tagged" by the computer (e.g., two sustained citizen complaints in a 3-month period or three in a year).[142]

EIISs have produced dramatic results in curbing citizen complaints and related performance indicators—the New Orleans Police Department reported a 62 percent drop in a single year.[143] Significant results from using EEIS have also been reported in other countries; in Victoria, Australia, a 71 percent reduction over a 12-month period was achieved.[144]

Discipline

If law enforcement executives are to be held accountable for the performance of their agencies, they must have ways to control them. This system of controls is well-understood and includes staff inspections to make sure policies are being followed; line inspection at roll call to verify officers are adhering to grooming, uniform, and other standards; financial audits; periodic evaluation of programs and units; and stringent selection procedures.

Discipline is part of the control system and, in some agencies, the wooden application of sanctions for violations of standards of conduct has made discipline synonymous with punishment—far from its actual meaning and intention. **Discipline** is related to three Latin words: (1) *disciplina,* or instruction to a disciple; (2) *discipulus,* or pupil; and (3) *discere,* or to learn, to acquire knowledge. Although discipline is often thought of as punishment, its core meaning is instruction.

Standards of Conduct and Progressive Discipline

The standards of conduct for police officers are set forth in their oath of office; their agency's policies, rules, and regulations; local ordinances; state statutes; federal laws; and consent decrees (e.g., prohibition against racial profiling). In addition to departmental discipline, an officer's POST license may be in jeopardy in some fact situations (e.g., acts of **moral turpitude**, conduct that is contrary to honesty, justice, or good morals). Law enforcement agencies use a system of **progressive discipline**, invoking progressively more serious penalties for transgressions. A progressive discipline system may include many of the following steps:

1. Verbal counseling;
2. Oral reprimand;

3. Written reprimand;
4. Monetary fine;
5. Transfer/reassignment;
6. Suspension without pay;
7. Loss of promotional opportunity;
8. Demotion; and
9. Termination.[145]

In some situations, progressive discipline is not possible and termination is the only reasonable course of action (e.g., an officer steals money from the informant fund or drugs from the evidence room). In some jurisdictions, monetary (e.g., New Jersey), fines may be used in lieu of a suspension when the absence of an officer is detrimental to public health, welfare, or safety; when the fine is restitution; or when the officer agrees to the fine.[146]

Administration of Discipline

Of necessity, the chief executive of a law enforcement agency must delegate the authority for discipline to individuals in the chain of command and to the professional standards/internal affairs (PS/IA) unit. Many agencies have clearly specified rules about what misconduct may be handled by the first-line supervisor, within a division, at the bureau level, or those that must be referred to PS/IA. In addition to unit commanders being required to refer more serious misconduct to PS/IA, such action may also be called for when officers from different divisions are involved. Criminal acts by officers employed by smaller law enforcement agencies are often investigated by an external agency, such as a nearby larger department or the state police. Larger agencies will usually refer such acts to their own investigative unit.

Entities outside of the department may also be involved in the disciplinary process. In some jurisdictions, civilian review boards (CRBs) evaluate law enforcement agencies' completed internal affairs investigations and the chief's disciplinary decisions and offer their own recommendation as to the appropriate sanctions. CRB members are usually appointed by the relevant local official, such as a mayor. CRBs can be relatively "toothless," with only the power to make recommendations. Alternatively, CRBs can receive complaints directly from the public, have an investigative staff and subpoena power, and are able to make disciplinary decisions on the cases that fall within the scope of their authority. Independent monitors may be appointed by the mayor or other official or as part of a consent decree; they have no investigative power and their function is to scrutinize and report on the disciplinary process (e.g., why does it take so long to complete internal affairs investigations?). District attorneys do not want to prosecute police officers accused on a criminal act because they want to maintain a close working relationship with law enforcement agencies. In such cases a special prosecutor may be temporarily hired for this purpose.

In addition to oral and written reprimands and suspensions, officers may lose privileges, such as: (1) eligibility to work extra-duty assignments and grant provided overtime (e.g., driving while intoxicated checkpoints and patrol; (2) use of a take-home car; and (3) serving on specialty teams, such as scuba, search and rescue, canine, hostage negotiation, and SWAT.

All disciplinary actions are subject to review through the chain of command and may be appealed by the officer. Under collective bargaining agreements, disciplined officers may be able to grieve the action taken, potentially requiring a binding decision by a neutral arbitrator. A study analyzed 100 police cases selected at random from the Labor Arbitration Reports and compared them to another randomly selected 100 cases from nonlaw enforcement public agencies.[147] Law enforcement executives' disciplinary recommendations were sustained at a higher rate, suggesting better handling by them. An alternative explanation is that officers are held to a higher standard. A 5-year study of arbitrator discipline decisions involving the Houston Police Department revealed the sanctions being sought were reduced by a net amount of nearly 50 percent.[148]

Because most misconduct is relatively minor (e.g., violation of grooming standards or late to roll call), first-line supervisors play a primary role in the disciplinary process. This dictates that supervisors have substantial training in policies, forms, officers rights, and counseling techniques. On incidents referred to PS/IA, the first-line supervisor is no longer a key figure.

In cases of serious misconduct, the unit commander may immediately suspend officers pending the outcome of an investigation because: (1) they are unfit for duty; (2) they would constitute a hazard to themselves or others if allowed to remain on the job; (3) the action is necessary to protect health, safety, order, or effective direction of services; or (4) they have been charged with crime. Where immediate action is required in these situations, some law enforcement agencies allow the first-line supervisor to place the officer on "temporary relief from duty," pending review by higher authority. Officers so relieved must ordinarily be advised of their duty status within 24 hours by the higher authority.

Officers may also be placed on administrative leave, with full pay and benefits, pending the completion of an investigation. In an unusual situation during 2010, an Arizona police chief was placed on administered leave as part of an on-going inquiry into his leadership, including inconsistency in handling disciplinary actions.[149]

A barrier to PS/IA investigations continues to be the "blue wall," or code of silence. Although 83 percent of officers responding to a national survey rejected the notion that a code of silence is necessary for good policing, 25 percent reported whistle-blowing was not worth it and 67 percent indicated that those who report misconduct by their peers would get the "cold shoulder."[150] Fifty-two percent of the respondents said that it was not unusual to turn a blind eye toward improper conduct by other officers and 61 percent disagreed with the statement that police officers always report serious criminal violations involving abuse of authority by fellow officers.[151]

One study concluded that officers with at least some college were not better behaved than those with a high school degree.[152] In contrast, a larger Florida analysis indicated that high school graduates made up about 50 percent of all law enforcement officers in the state, but accounted for 75 percent of all disciplinary actions.[153] Among those who lost their POST certification, high school graduates were disproportionally represented also: 76 percent versus 12 percent for those with a bachelor's or higher degree.[154] An analysis of discipline in the New York City Police Department found no evidence of race, gender, or national origin bias.[155] In an unnamed large-city police agency, minorities were over-represented in documented complaints, specifically those initiated by fellow officers and supervisors.[156] In a year, use of force complaints nationally may average about 6.6 per 100 officers and one sustained complaint for every 200 officers (see Figure 9.17).[157]

The Discipline Matrix

The perceived or actual unfairness of discipline is a long-standing problem in law enforcement agencies. In traditional disciplinary systems this condition has been exacerbated because: (1) fact situations may appear the same or similar on the surface, but the variance in individual circumstances leads to lesser or greater sanctions, which have gone unexplained and (2) variance in the disciplinary measures taken by supervisors was seen as part of the essential discretion they needed to deal with misconduct. As a matter of informal practice in many traditional discipline departments, a probationary officer late to roll call is not likely to "catch a break" while a veteran officer with "credits" in the agency will with many supervisors.

A **discipline matrix** is a formal schedule for disciplinary actions, specifying both the presumptive or presumed sanction to be imposed for misconduct and any reduction or increase in the presumptive sanction for mitigating or aggravating factors (see Figure 9.18).[158] Its primary purpose is to develop consistency in discipline, eliminating disparities and ensuring those who commit similar acts of misconduct will be sanctioned *equally*, as adjusted for *fairness* based on their mitigating and aggravated circumstances.[159] Discipline matrixes incorporate the concept of progressive discipline.

A matrix system identifies categories of conduct or perhaps more accurately, misconduct; a typical figure seems to be six (see Figure 9.19). Listed under each category are numerous examples of what policies, procedures, rules, or regulations fall within it. Sanctions to be imposed are associated with each category (see Figure 9.20) and may run from Level 1 (least serious, oral or written reprimand) to Level 8 (90 days suspension or termination).

Disposition	Percentage*
Not Sustained, insufficient evidence to support allegation	34
Unfounded, complainant factually wrong or did not occur	25
Exonerated, the incident occurred but the officer's action was lawful and proper	23
Sustained, sufficient evidence to discipline officer	8
Other disposition (e.g., complaint withdrawn)	9

Figure 9.17
National disposition of use of force complaints.
*Does not add to 100 percent due to rounding.
Source: Matthew J. Hickman, *Citizen Complaints About Police Use of Force* [Washington, D.C.: Bureau of Justice Statistics, June 2006], p. 5.

Mitigating	Aggravating
1. Demonstrated willingness to acknowledge wrong-doing and accept personal responsibility	1. Endangerment, injury, or harm to others
2. Mental state, the extent to which the employee acted intentionally or willfully with the knowledge the behavior amounted to misconduct or a violation of law; acted with reckless disregard of factors a reasonable person would have considered; or acted in a negligent manner	2. Creation of a financial/legal risk to the agency
3. If a minor offense, its severity and the absence or presence of collateral negative impacts	3. Leaders may be held to a higher standard and their misconduct subject to more than the presumptive sanction
4. The circumstances/fact situation	4. Damage/loss of property, harm to the agency's relationship with other departments and the public, impairment of operations
5. Positive departmental history as determined from letters of commendation, awards, and other sources	5. Dishonesty; conduct involving prejudice, impermissible action toward protected classes or criminal conviction for the act involved
6. Work history, including performance evaluations and service on departmental committees	6. Mental state
7. No disciplinary history or in relationship to years of service, a minimal disciplinary history	7. Prior disciplinary history (e.g., how recent, frequent, severe, and any pattern of similar misconduct); character of work history
	8. Three or more misconduct actions occurring contemporaneously

Figure 9.18
Illustrations of mitigating and aggravating circumstances.
Source: These points are drawn with restatement and consolidation from the Denver Police Department, *Discipline Handbook*, October 1, 2008, pp. 23–26 and the Lansing (Michigan) Police Department, *Discipline Matrix and Rules of Conduct by Class of Offense*, 2008, p. 3.

In actual use multiple tables are used in a matrix system; for purposes of illustration Figure 9.20 combines them, showing their interaction. If two or more charges against an officer arise from a single incident, a decision is made as to which one is the primary.

Matrix systems have been opposed by officers and unions when they have not been included in their development. In a few jurisdictions there have been complaints by officers that supervisors have not been held to the same degree of accountability. Other critics wonder about the fairness of rank being an aggravation factor. When all is said and done, matrix systems are a leap forward and traditional discipline agencies should take a close look at them.

Category	Definition
A	Conduct that has a minimal negative impact on the operations or professional image of the department.
B	Conduct that has more than a minimal negative impact on the operations or professional image of the department.
C	Conduct that has a pronounced negative impact on the operations or professional image of the department or that negatively impacts relationships with other officers, agencies, or the public.
D	Conduct that is substantially contrary to the values of the department or that substantially interferes with its mission, operations, or professional image, or that involves a demonstrable serious risk to officers or public safety.
E	Conduct that involves the serious abuse or misuse of authority, unethical behavior, or an act that results in an actual serious and adverse impact on officers or public safety, or to the professionalism of the department.
F	Any violation of law, rule, or policy which foreseeably results in death or serious bodily injury; or constitutes a willful and wanton disregard of department values; or involves any act which demonstrates a serious lack of the integrity, ethics or character related to an officer's fitness to hold the position of police officer; or involves egregious misconduct substantially contrary to the standards of conduct reasonably expected of one whose sworn duty is to uphold the law; or involves any conduct which constitutes the failure to adhere to any contractual condition of employment or requirement of certification mandated by law.

Figure 9.19
Categories of conduct in a discipline matrix.
Source: Denver Police Department, *Discipline Handbook*, October 1, 2008, pp. 16–17.

Category A: Conduct that has a minimal negative impact on the operations or professional image of the department.

Policy Involved	1st Violation in Three Years	2nd Violation in Three Years	3rd Violation in Three Years
Giving testimonials, seeking publicity	Discipline level 1	Discipline level 2	Discipline level 3
Use of tobacco in police facilities	Discipline level 1	Discipline level 2	Discipline level 3
Appearance in court	Discipline level 1	Discipline level 2	Discipline level 3
Testifying in civil cases	Discipline level 1	Discipline level 2	Discipline level 3
Sanctions Table			
Mitigation	Not applicable	Oral reprimand	Written reprimand to 1 fined day
Presumptive	Oral reprimand	Written reprimand	2 fined days
Aggravated	Written reprimand	1–3 fined days	4–6 fined days

Figure 9.20
Illustration of relationship between a conduct category, policies, level of discipline, and sanctions.
Source: Drawn from the Denver Police Department Discipline Handbook: Conduct Principles and Disciplinary Guidelines, Appendix F, pp. 1–2, October 1, 2008.

Legal Aspects of Discipline

Disciplining police officers also has a legal component to it; illustratively, to prevent disciplinary abuses, many states have enacted police officer bill of rights legislation; content related to discipline is also commonly included in collective bargaining agreements; and except for narrow restrictions in some areas, officers retain all of their Constitutional rights. These and related topics are covered in Chapter 14, Legal Aspects of Police Administration.

Performance Appraisal

Performance appraisals are sworn by and at. Supporters claim they are essential and detractors label them as "annual rituals," a "global scourge,"[160] and are based on the erroneous assumption that the supervisors completing them have sufficient relevant information to complete them accurately and do so without any bias or prejudice.

Assuming that the performance of individuals does not vary greatly, it is reasonably expected that their ratings would remain relatively stable. A study of 6,000 business employees reporting simultaneously to two different bosses revealed ratings ranging from "very weak" to "outstanding." Sixty-two percent of those receiving "outstanding" evaluations from the first boss got lower scores from their other boss.[161]

A majority of 393 constables, sergeants, and staff sergeants surveyed across 15 Canadian cities reported that their performance appraisal system was "deficient."[162] Officers did not receive regular feedback during the rating period, had little or no input into the evaluation, the supervisors were not sufficiently trained in evaluation, and personality often triumphed over actual performance criteria.

The truth is that getting a performance appraisal system to have real meaning requires a substantial organizational commitment, a stream of informal feedback, good supervisory record keeping, employee participation, validated forms, and rater training. In broad terms, the purpose of ratings is to: (1) reinforce organizational values, (2) have a basis for impartial personnel decisions, (3) reinforce performance expectations, (4) stimulate performance, (5) identify the officers' training needs, and (6) extend recognition to those who perform their duties well. The results of performance appraisals are used to determine or influence:

1. pay raises;
2. eligibility for promotion;
3. shift bids/duty assignments;
4. career development decisions (e.g., attendance at the FBI National Academy);
5. eligibility for reinstatement;
6. layoffs/reduction in force decisions; and
7. terminations.

Officers satisfactorily completing their probationary periods are awarded career status and cannot be terminated except for serious misconduct. During financial emergencies, career-status officers can be furloughed indefinitely. Career-status officers are commonly rated once annually by their immediate supervisors. However, special circumstances may cause an evaluation to be written on an other than annual basis: (1) officer resignations and terminations and (2) transfers to another unit and promotions may trigger a probationary requirement for monthly or quarterly evaluations for a year.

In preparing a standard evaluation form, a supervisor considers notes he or she has made about the officer and the factors identified on the form such as adherence to safety procedures, relationships with coworkers and supervisors, report quality, commendations, complaints, attendance, and training.

Informally, some supervisors initially fill out the appraisal in pencil and at a preliminary meeting give the officer an opportunity to provide input that may alter the ratings. A similar practice is to give the officers to be rated a copy of the appraisal form and ask them to evaluate themselves. Before the actual rating conference the supervisor's and officers' preliminary ratings are compared and discussed. By policy in many law enforcement agencies, officers headed toward an unsatisfactory rating must be advised of their deficiencies at least 90 days before the end of the rating period so they have an opportunity to improve.

Signing a performance appraisal is akin to signing a traffic ticket; the signature means that you have received a copy of it, not that you necessarily agree with it. Officers seldom formally appeal a performance appraisal; although they may ask that a statement prepared by them be attached to it for the record.

Promotions

Promotional tests can serve several objectives: (1) determining which candidates' names should be placed on the promotional roster; (2) reinforcing organizational change (e.g., when the Savannah, Georgia Police Department adopted community-oriented policing, all sworn personnel had to complete a 40-hour course in that philosophy. The next written promotional tests drew questions from the course material, communicating the message "you need to be on-board with COP if you plan to get promoted)"; (3) refreshing familiarity with critically important policies, such as use of force and high-speed pursuits, by asking questions about them; (4) increasing the level of important knowledge in the organization through candidates studying the resource material for written tests; and (5) improving the candidates' understanding of their skill levels by their behaviors being tested in assessment centers, which roughly equate to a series of job simulations, and receiving feedback about their performance.

A dilemma for many law enforcement executives is the disparity between the limited number of promotional openings they have versus the pool of well-qualified candidates. Even so, that pool might be more substantial were it not for the fact that some officers choose not to participate in promotional testing. Seventy percent of nonparticipating women and 51 percent of men do not want to be moved from their current assignment or shift.[163] They know that a transfer usually accompanies a promotion; by doctrine, a new supervisor should not lead those with whom they have worked as equals. Other reasons for nonparticipation include child-care/family responsibilities, not wanting supervisory responsibilities, and loss of overtime pay; overall, one in five potential candidates is simply not interested.[164]

Although infrequent, officers do cheat on promotional exams and supervisors sometimes help them to do so. An officer hired someone to take the Hudson County (New Jersey) Sheriff's Office's Sergeant's exam for him; both men were sentenced to prison terms on a variety of charges.[165] In Providence (Rhode Island), a chief directly or indirectly provided four favored candidates with an advance copy of the materials for a written exam, giving them more time to study, and also dictated who would score first, second, and third in the interview phase.[166]

With respect to the rules and testing processes used to identify those eligible for promotion, law enforcement officers want: (1) clear and unambiguous guidelines, (2) the rules to be evenly applied to all candidates, (3) confidence in the integrity of the testing process, (4) a reasonable amount of material to study for a written test, and (5) prompt feedback on the results.[167]

The rules and practices that comprise the promotional system can be specified in departmental policy, civil service/merit rules, local ordinances, the city or county charter, or state statutes. Broadly, the promotional policy specifies who is eligible, what the steps in the promotional process are, how the final scores are calculated, and how officers passing the process will be selected from the eligibility roster. Policies must use carefully crafted language to avoid potential problems. A well-written promotional policy might specify that to be eligible for promotion to sergeant, "An officer shall have completed at least 36 months of continuous service with this agency on the date immediately preceding the administration of the written examination." In contrast, another policy might simply provide "Three years of police service must be completed to be eligible." Does that mean with the present agency? Could some of it be with another department? Do breaks in service affect eligibility? Assume an officer works for a department 32 months, then he resigns to work in at an insurance company. Eight months later he is rehired by his former agency. After completing 4 months of service, is the officer eligible for promotion?

Promotional tests are subject to the same EEOC validity and reliability requirements as are entrance examinations and physical assessment tests. Despite these requirements, some agencies attempt to prepare their own written promotional tests. There are reasons they should be reluctant to do so: (1) most frequently they will not have conducted a validity study, (2) the perception or actuality of the test "getting out" is substantial, (3) the skills to write good test items may not exist in the department, (4) a command officer teaching part-time in a criminal justice program is usually selected. Some agency officers taking the promotional exam will have taken classes from him and have a perceived or real advantage. Additionally, (5) if the test results are challenged under Title VII, the prospects for successfully defending them are dim. If other types of promotional tests are prepared internally (e.g., an oral board or an assessment center), they face the same hurdles as do written examinations.

Regardless of what form a promotional test takes, the reading level of the materials must be closely monitored. On average, high school graduates read at a tenth-grade level; only 35 percent of them achieve a "proficient" or higher level of performance.[168] Most law enforcement agencies require a high school diploma as an entry-level education requirement. In those departments, if the promotional materials are written at more than a tenth-grade level, a court may find the test is not job related. A related matter is a review of the job analysis study before each promotional cycle begins. Roughly, if an agency has no major shifts in operational philosophy, does not significantly reallocate tasks or have other major transitions, a job analysis study might remain in use for 5 years. However, a committee should carefully review the study annually, record comments about its currency, and certify in writing that in the group's judgment, it can be relied upon for the next promotional cycle. A more conservative approach is to conduct the annual reviews and do a new job analysis study every 3 years.

Written Promotional Tests

Written promotional tests from test providers come in three basic models:[169]

1. *Off-the-Shelf/Stock*—Test providers have validity data from a large number of departments from across the country that can be "transported" or used with virtually all other law enforcement agencies. The provider gives clients a list of the five to eight books from which the questions are drawn. The clients buy enough copies to establish a lending library for candidates. Some candidates buy their own books and small study teams pool their money to do the same thing. The test questions are generic and can be used with the "Anywhere U.S.A." police department. Off-the-shelf/stock tests rent for about $15 per copy, with price breaks for larger orders. Additional sources of profit for providers include: (a) a transportability study at a cost of roughly $1,500; (b) the sale or rental of candidate study guides, around $7.50 each; and (c) scoring services.

2. *Custom-Developed*—The provider may have validity data from a large-scale study on which the test is based or can validate the test for use in a single agency. When the knowledge areas and the number of questions to come from each area are known, the test developer sits down with a liaison committee from the agency and they decide from which sources the test questions will come. This allows questions to come from sources unique to the agency, such as the policy manual and training materials.

   Custom test developers also write scenario questions that incorporate local information (see Figure 9.21). Too many scenario questions on a test require more time to complete the test. An overly long test creates the danger that test fatigue will occur and applicants will not be able to perform at a level that reflects their actual knowledge. As a rule of thumb, 15 to 20 scenario questions is probably a reasonable limit for a 100-item test.

   Custom developers also charge a transportability study fee or, if a job analysis for one agency is done, a fee for that. If a sergeants test is going to be developed, all sergeants will be asked to complete the job analysis questionnaire. Job analysis fees vary widely depending on the number of job incumbents in the target position, but

Thirty-year-old Wilbur is 6'5" tall. He weighs 295 pounds. Wilbur is a mean drunk. He has a history of fighting in bars. Tonight, Wilbur is drunk in Charlie's Tavern on Hancock Avenue. Patrons there have seen Wilbur pick a fight. Wilbur is in the restroom. Milford comes in and sits at the bar. He is a timid man. Milford is 31 years old and 5'4". He weighs 140 pounds. Wilbur returns to the bar. He sees Milford. He reaches for the front of Milford's shirt. Then he pulls back his fist. He screams "I'm going to hit you hard! You'll be 6 months older when you quit rolling!" Milford passes out. He falls to the floor. Wilbur's actions violate which of the following offenses?
a. Menacing
b. Battery
c. Terrorist threats
d. Assault

Figure 9.21
Scenario question using local information.

the fees range from several thousand dollars to considerably more. Custom test questions cost $35 to $60 each, with a minimum number, such as 75 or 100, plus a base fee of $250 to several hundred dollars more. Like off-the-shelf/stock providers, custom test providers provide other services for additional fees.

3. *Semi-Custom Tests*—These exams include stock questions plus some custom-written items. Providers may require that if a client selects this option, he or she must agree to use a minimum number of custom questions, such as 10 or 25, plus the base fee and charges for other services.

Study guides should be provided to all candidates taking a written test. It is also essential that law enforcement agencies conduct seminars on how to study and take multiple-choice exams. All sessions of seminars should be video recorded and placed on the department's intranet for four primary purposes: (1) candidates can review their own session to refresh their recollection, (2) those unable to attend can have access to the same information, (3) different questions will arise if there are multiple training sessions; everyone should have access to the same information, and (4) if controversies or litigation exist, the videos might be useful in defending the agency's practices. Although some argue that a video record may be used to bolster a plaintiff's case, they may also guide the agency to making a pre-trial settlement, which avoids costly litigation and leads to mistake-free seminars.

The contents of a study guide often have the following elements: (1) information about the test; (2) study tips; (3) strategies for taking multiple choice tests; (4) creating a good study environment; (5) sample questions; and (6) the list of source materials from which the test is drawn.

Less frequently, two other elements can be included in a study guide: (1) a copy of the test plan (see Figure 9.22) and (2) copies of all source material. While many test providers simply supply a list of books, a test plan is narrower and more specific. If one purpose of written testing is to increase the level of knowledge in

2010 Columbus Georgia Police Department Lieutenant Written Test Plan

Knowledge Number	Knowledge Area	Approx. Number of Questions	Source Materials
K1	Basic legal standards (including state statutes; arrest, search and seizure laws; court procedures; warrants; rules of evidence; legal terms and definitions; legal rights of accused; civil liability)	10	• Swanson, CR, Chamelin, NC, Territo, L, and Taylor, R (2006). Criminal Investigation. Boston: McGraw Hill. Pages 22–44. • Bill of Rights. • Columbus Consolidated Government Code. Selected portions of Chapter 14. • Georgia State Statutes. Title 16. Selected Portions including: 5–20; 5–21; 5–23; 5–23.1; 5–24; 5–40; 5–41; 5–42; 10–2; 10–93; 10–94; 11–30; 11–31; 11–33.
K2	Correct and safe use of equipment	9	• CPD Policies and Procedures. 3–3: Firearms; 3–4: Discharging of Firearms; 3–11: Responsibility and Accountability of Police Equipment; 3–12: Permanently Assigned Vehicles; 3–14: Vehicle Operations; 3–15: Operations of Motor Vehicles While Responding to Requests for Police Services.
K3	Investigative concepts, principles, methods, procedures, and practices (including crime scene search, physical evidence, and modus operandi of criminals)	19	• Swanson, CR, Chamelin, NC, Territo, L, and Taylor R (2006). Criminal Investigation. Boston: McGraw Hill. Pages 46–91. • CPD Policies and Procedures. 5–2: Criminal Process; 6–5: Property and Evidence Procedures; 7–1: Criminal Investigation; 7–2: Collection and Preservation of Evidence.
K4	Interview and interrogation concepts, principles, and practices	4	• CPD Policies and Procedures. 2–6: Inter-department Investigations; 5–2: Criminal Process; 7–1: Criminal Investigation.
K5	Columbus Police Department policies and procedures	11	• CPD Policies and Procedures. 1–7: Disciplinary Action; 3–1: Non-Deadly Force/Less Lethal Munitions; 3–2: Deadly Force; 3–7: Required Court Attendance; 3–10: Off-Duty Employment; 3–16: Motor Vehicle Pursuit; 3–17: Hot Pursuit, Extradition, and Fugitive Warrant; 3–25: Guidelines for the Release of Information; 4–4: Performance Evaluations; 4–8: Drug and Alcohol Testing Policy.
K6	Leadership and Motivation concepts, practices, and principles	18	• Iannone, NF, and Iannone, MP (2009). Supervision of Police Personnel. Upper Saddle River, NJ: Prentice-Hall. Pages 28–52; 141–149.
K7	Interpersonal and organizational communication concepts, principles, and practices	10	• Swanson, CR, Territo, L, and Taylor, RW (2008). Police Administration. Upper Saddle River, NJ: Prentice-Hall. Pages 349–379.
K8	Counseling and discipline concepts, principles, and practices (including administrative principles and practices)	19	• More, HW and Miller, LS (2007). Effective Police Supervision. Matthew Bender & Company, Inc. Pages 261–285; 289–318.

Figure 9.22

Portion of a test plan.

Notes:

1. Questions may be drawn from any source cited regardless of the alignment of knowledge areas and sources shown above.

2. The number of questions drawn from each knowledge area is based on the 2010 job analysis conducted by the Carl Vinson Institute of Government. The number of questions on the actual written promotional test may vary somewhat from the exact number of questions shown in this test plan. Any such variation, if necessary, would be minor.

3. For the purposes of developing a test plan, the following K areas were merged due to similar source material: Investigative concepts (merged with Crime Scene Search, Physical Evidence, and Modus Operandi of Criminals); Leadership (merged with Motivation); Counseling and Discipline (merged with Administrative principles and practices).

4. Total number of questions is 100.

the agency, narrowing the amount of material to be studied encourages it by making preparation less formidable. Including all source material eliminates the need for the agency to establish a lending library and places everything candidates need to know in a single volume. In addition to permission costs to reprint all copyrighted material, which can range from $300 to as much as $800, printing each all-inclusive study guide of 350 to 425 pages ranges from $16 to $22. Besides its fairness to all candidates, the use of an all-inclusive study guide cuts down on complainants and grievances. Those who perform poorly on the written test often make the comment "It's my own fault, I had everything I needed handed to me." Study guides do not inflate written test scores, which typically range in the low 30s to the lower-mid-90s.

Promotional practices are not normally addressed in a collective bargaining agreement except for the study time allowed before testing; most providers recommend 60 to 90 days, and unions push for a 30- to 45-day period to get their members promoted quicker. Sixty days is actually ample study time if an all-inclusive study guide is provided, but 90 days provides a humane safety buffer for candidates who need operations, get married, go on vacation, have deaths in the family, become a primary caregiver under FMLA, or other related events.

Oral Boards and Assessment Centers

Promotional oral boards are conducted in the same manner as entry-level oral boards, although the questions are different, and therefore require no further elaboration. An *assessment center* is both a process and the place where the process is conducted. Such places might be a hotel, a technical school or community college, a civic center, or National Guard installation.[170] Police facilities are not a good choice for testing; to candidates they reek of the possibility of command influence and lack a factually neutral feeling.

Assessment centers were first used to select German Army officers during World War I; during World War II, the British War Officer Selection Boards (WOSBs) employed them to find competent officers. The United States Office of Strategic Services (OSS), the forerunner of the Central Intelligence Agency, utilized them to screen for agents who could be infiltrated into enemy territory to gather intelligence. The first large-scale test of assessment centers in this country was carried out by AT&T.[171] By the mid-1980s, American law enforcement agencies began using assessment centers.

Assessment centers are an attractive alternative to written tests because they produce less or no adverse impact. As compared to both written tests and oral boards, assessment centers are more difficult to administer, use a great amount of officers' time, and are more costly. A 2006 sergeants assessment center for the Dallas Police Department processed 208 candidates at an average cost of $764.[172]

An **assessment center** consists of several exercises or job simulations designed to elicit from candidates the behaviors found to be important to job success by the job analysis. At least one of the exercises must require candidates to interact with someone

Perception: Being able to identify the key elements of a situation, the importance of these elements, and their relationship to one another.

Oral Communication: Clear, unambiguous, composed, and effective expression of one's self through oral means and gestures. Included are active listening, appropriate eye contact, and the use and interpretation of nonverbal communication, such as hands, facial, and body movements/positioning.

Written Communication: Preparing written documents that are well-organized, flow logically, have clear meaning, and use correct grammar and spelling.

Decisiveness: Willingness to take action, make a decision, commit to a course of action, and accept responsibility for those actions.

Judgment: Making sound and logical decisions based on factual information.

Planning and Organizing: Effectively and efficiently establishing a direction and sequence of prioritized actions for self/others to complete a task/accomplish a goal.

Leadership: Getting ideas accepted and the direction, guidance, and control of the activities of others, interrelating individual/departmental needs, monitoring performance, delegation, control, and follow-up.

Figure 9.23
Short definitions of various dimensions.

else. Behaviors are also referred to as dimensions or competencies.[173] Examples of dimensions are shown in Figure 9.23. Several exercises are required so that candidates have multiple opportunities to have their behavior assessed by panels staffed by different teams of assessors.

Assessors must at least hold the rank for which a candidate is competing. Customarily, other law enforcement agencies allow their supervisors to serve as assessors for other departments with the tacit understanding that the favor will be returned. Assessor panels should reflect diversity. Departments should not use their supervisors in their own assessment centers because charges of favoritism, bias, and prejudice will discredit the process. Assessors are paid no fee, although their travel, hotel, and meal costs are covered by the department hosting them.

Some law enforcement agencies do not host assessors well and have them evaluate too many candidates each day, which can lead to rating errors. Good hosting etiquette includes having per diem checks ready for the candidates on the first day of their training, arranging transportation to the agency's bank to cash them, the hotel room charge being directly billed to the department's account, bringing in varied and quality lunch meals, allowing assessors in departmental cars to fill up at the police motor pool, and arranging special tours of the city. Depending on the length of exercises, which influences the time needed to properly assess the candidates, assessors can reasonably see 8 to 12 candidates a day.

Figure 9.24 provides examples of assessment center exercises; it assumes that the candidate is seeking promotion to the rank of sergeant. In each example, the candidate has just been promoted to sergeant and this is "day one" in that rank. The types of exercises illustrated could be used for any rank. The length of time each exercise takes depends on its complexity; the times indicated are approximations.

Type	Brief Description
Press Conference (PC)	The candidate must brief "members of news media" on an incident. Assessors may play the role of news media members or others may do it. Length: 5 minutes.
Role Play (RP): Citizen Meeting	The sergeant meets with agitated citizen who wants to complain about one of the sergeant's subordinates. A role play can be conducted with any subject matter. Variations include meeting with an officer who is a declining performer and selecting members of a robbery investigation task force from a pool of candidates. Length: 20 minutes.
In-Basket (IB)	The candidate replaces a sergeant who was killed in an accident while on vacation, had a heart attack and took a medical retirement, or is otherwise gone. His in-basket has been filled up pending the selection of a replacement. The new sergeant must go through a stack of papers and make dispositions and write necessary memos. Length: 45 minutes to 3 hours.
The Written Problem Analysis (WPA)	The sergeant's boss has delegated a problem to be solved (e.g., abuse of sick leave). A packet of information about the problem is on the sergeant's desk. A memo must be written to the boss explaining the situation and making a recommendation. Length: 45 minutes to 2 hours.
Leaderless Group Discussion (LGD)	The candidate and four other sergeants have been assigned to discuss a problem (e.g., a large subdivision has been hit with four to seven car burglaries in four of the last 10 days). A leader for the group has not been designated. Each candidate has the same packet of information. The group must come up with a consensus strategy to attack this problem. The LGD is hard to score and is unpopular with officers because it doesn't square with actual practice where someone is always in charge. Put differently, it lacks "face validity" to candidates. The use of LGDs appears to have been on the wane in industry and policing. Length: 45 to 60 minutes.
Video-Based	A DVD is made showing an officer making traffic stops and performing other duties. The sergeant is asked to identify the policy violations committed. This format may also be used with other scenarios. Length: 7 to 12 minutes.

Figure 9.24
Examples of assessment center exercises.

A minimum of two, but usually three, trained raters observe each exercise, making their own notes during the exercise, and making their individual ratings after the candidate leaves the room (see Figure 9.25). The individual ratings are then discussed by the assessor panel and the final score for that exercise formed in the same manner as described for entry-level oral boards. Each candidate's overall score is formed by combining the scores from each of the exercises (see Figure 9.26).

The number of exercises used in an assessment center is not a fixed requirement. Some assessment centers use six or so short exercises of perhaps 5 to 8 minutes each, while others might have three or four exercises that each last 15 or 20 minutes. Short exercises require little or no time for candidates to prepare. Often they are simply given a single sheet of paper with a few lines of information immediately before they begin the exercise.

The longer exercises require that candidates have more time to prepare. A typical cycle is 30 minutes of candidate preparation time followed by 15 or 20 minutes before the assessor panel. For purposes of illustration, a candidate may assume the role of a just-promoted sergeant. On his "first day" as a sergeant, he arrives at work, finding that his major has left a stack of papers for him to review. At the end of 30 minutes, he is to go to his "lieutenant's office" to discuss what he has learned (i.e., an assessment center staff member will come get him from the preparation station and take him to the

Rating	Definition of Behavior	Extent to Which Behavior Falls Short/ Exceeds Normally Expected Standards
1	*Unable to perform.* Completely unacceptable. Improvement required in every aspect of the dimension.	Completely unacceptable
2	*Needs much improvement.* Definite improvement needed in nearly all aspects of the dimension.	Clearly below acceptable
3	*Needs some improvement.* Approaches, but falls short, of acceptable on this dimension. Some aspects of standards met, but improvement needed.	Marginally unacceptable
4	*Satisfactory, Adequate.* Performs consistently at acceptable level on this dimension.	Acceptable
5	*Effective.* Consistently better than acceptable performance on this dimension, characteristically above acceptable standards.	Above acceptable
6	*Outstanding.* Demonstrates high degree of proficiency on this dimension. Far exceeds normally expected standards consistently.	Outstanding

Figure 9.25
Example of an assessment center rating scale.
Source: By Swanson.

Candidate Name: Joe Jones

Candidate Identifier: Badge 181

Dimensions/ Exercises	Role Play 1	In-Basket	Press Conference	Role Play 2**	Average	Dimension Weight***	Total
Perception	6,5,6	5,5,5	4,5,5	6,5,5	5.16	8.23	42.46
Oral Communication	5,6,5	NM*	5,5,5	6,6,5	5.33	7.93	42.26
Written Communication	NM*	4,4,5	NM*	5,5,4	4.50	6.71	30.19
Decisiveness	5,6,5	5,5,5	3,4,4	4,5,5	4.66	7.33	34.15
Judgment	4,5,5	5,5,4	3,3,4	5,5,5	4.41	8.15	35.94
Planning & Organizing	5,5,5	5,6,5	3,4,4	6,6,5	4.91	6.82	33.48
Leadership	5,5,6	NM*	4,3,3	5,5,5	4.55	8.41	38.26
						Overall score:	256.7

Figure 9.26
Sergeants assessment center score summary sheet.
*Not Measured.
** After Role Play 2 candidates returned to their office with the requirement to write a summary memo to their major.
***Statistical importance of dimension to doing the job of a captain as derived from the job analysis study.
Source: By Swanson.

assessor panel). The staff member knocks on the "lieutenant's" door and announces, "Your new sergeant is here to see you." One of the three assessors assumes the role of the lieutenant and greets him, directing him to sit at a desk. The lieutenant then asks a standard series of questions. The "meeting" ends when time expires or, when asked, the sergeant says he has nothing left to add. The length of time spent in the exercise room is not an assessed factor, only what the candidate accomplished.

The sergeant's preparation ("prep") station is set up like an office and includes staple removers, pads of papers, sticky notes, a dictionary, other accouterments, and sometimes a telephone and/or computer. The telephone can be used to simulate the lieutenant calling him to add information or a requirement for their meeting. This call must be made at the same point in each candidate's preparation time. Many assessment centers allow candidates to bring their policy manual for reference and place a count-down timer on their desk so they know how much preparation time they have left. The staff member administering the exercise also keeps time, but is not in the room while the candidate prepares. In lieu of a telephone call, the staff member may knock on the door and announce "Here is a another piece of paper the lieutenant wants you to look over for the meeting. Like the telephone call, the paper must be delivered at the same time for each candidate (e.g., 6 minutes into the exercise).

Most commonly, the only feedback candidates get about their assessment center performance is a letter telling them how they scored on each dimension in the assessment center and where their overall score places them on the eligibility list. The "Cadillac" of feedback begins with each interactive exercise (e.g., a new "sergeant" meeting with an "officer" who is a declining performer), being video recorded. After candidates have received their feedback letter, they may sign up for a feedback session. Supervisors from other law enforcement agencies are trained in providing feedback. Each feedback session lasts 30 to 60 minutes, during which time the candidate can review everything in his or her file. The videos from the interactive exercises are shown to the candidates; this vividly illustrates the scores given to the candidates and they can see the specific skills they need to improve upon. This approach uses feedback as a staff development opportunity.

Selection from the Promotional Roster

In selecting those to be promoted from a promotional roster, law enforcement executives are usually restricted in their choices by civil service/merit rules or other measures (e.g., the city charter or state law). A common promotional roster method is to list all candidates in the **rank order** of their final scores. A rule of three can be used, meaning that for a single promotional vacancy, any one of the top three candidates can be selected. A variation is to use a rule of 5 or 10. When someone is promoted under the rule of three, the fourth-ranked candidate becomes part of the top three. This has the same effect on rules of 5 or 10.

Various jurisdictions provide that an otherwise eligible person cannot be passed over more than twice during the life of a promotional roster, although this rule does not appear to be common. Absent such a provision a person ranked first on a promotional list may "die on it" if others are chosen for nondiscriminatory reasons.[174] Depending on the applicable provisions of a promotional system, a candidate passed over for promotion may or may not be entitled to a reason, although the latter seems to be more usual.

An unknown number of agencies use an **all-qualified** promotional roster, allowing the executive to pick anyone on the list, which is alphabetized and the appointing authority does not know what the test scores were. From a risk management perspective, this virtually eliminates adverse impact in promotional decisions. However, the premise of a valid and reliable test is that higher scores are reasonably expected to be associated with higher performance of important job attributes. Stated somewhat differently, the primary purpose of testing is to make useful distinctions between people. All qualified lists simply separate the unqualified from the qualified and toss out the finer distinctions that undergird the notion of merit.

Banded promotional rosters are widely used. Their essence is placing candidates with similar scores into groups, called bands. The most common method of doing so is through any of several statistical processes. There are two types of bands:

1. *Fixed bands*—All officers in the top band must be promoted before anyone in the next-highest-ranked band can be offered a promotion. There are two exceptions to this: (a) some systems provided that if no candidates in the top band accept a promotional offer, then someone from the next-highest band may be selected. For example, the last state police trooper in the top band might decline a promotion because it would mean moving her family to the far end of the state. There may also be a provision that if two promotional opportunities are declined, the candidate's name is struck from further consideration from the life of the list, and (b) court orders to correct past discrimination may exist, functionally requiring either that lower-scoring minorities are "lifted into the top band" or otherwise selected off of the promotional list.

2. *Sliding bands*—The width of the band is adjusted when all members holding the top score are exhausted. If the range of the scores in the top band is 88–93, then when all those with 93 are promoted, the bottom of the range is adjusted by including all of those who scored an 87. The promotion of those with the top score first is not required; however, doing so acknowledges the merit principle incorporates.

Banded systems have been criticized on the grounds that they invite bias, favoritism, and politics into promotional decisions. These fears loom larger when the chief executive and command staff do not enjoy the trust of the rank and file. Where collective bargaining is allowed, philosophical differences almost naturally exist about promotional decision-making. The unions want their members treated equally and those responsible for making the decisions want some discretionary authority. A properly conceived banded system dispenses with at least the intensity of some of these fears by a written policy that clearly identifies the factors that will be used when making selections from within a band.

Using a strict rank order list to make promotions from is fraught with danger. In Bridgeport Guardians v. City of Bridgeport,[175] 68 percent of whites taking the test passed versus 30 percent of African Americans, creating an adverse impact. Despite this impact, Bridgeport insisted on relying on a rank order list and litigation ensued. The court essentially saw this reliance as a pretext for discrimination and ordered the use of a banding system, which reduced, but did not totally eliminate, the adverse impact and reasonably met the employer's needs.

As was the case with new hires, the final step in the selection process for supervisors is the probationary period or "**working test**." Most of those promoted will successfully complete the probationary period for two reasons: (1) while promotional tests do not totally eliminate "false positives" (those who test well, but cannot do the job), they reduce the frequency with which that happens and (2) law enforcement agencies are reluctant to revert probationers to their previously held rank.

Retirement Counseling

Retirement is a not central thought for newly hired officers. They are focused on beginning their careers and getting on the streets "doing police work." Unless a law enforcement agency provides retirement counseling, these eventually-grey officers will arrive at retirement unprepared. Although many departments provide the counseling, the quality of it is not documented.

Officers may benefit in the long run from their agency offering retirement counseling with the content geared to the different stages of their career. In the earliest stage the content might emphasize the value of participating in a supplemental retirement account, the difference between a disability in the line of duty pension versus one that is not service connected, and in states where applicable, that a pension earned while married is divisible property. Later-stage counseling might include such subjects as the different plans for survivor benefits, tax exposure for withdrawals from supplemental retirement accounts, cost-of-living-adjustments (COLAs), and Social Security benefits.

Police unions and associations appear to have done a good job in keeping their members informed about matters affecting their retirement, particularly by providing up-to-date information on their websites. As the federal Pension Protection Act (PPA) of 2006 made its way through Congress, their websites carefully followed its progress. Parenthetically, for state and local police officers, the PPA eliminated the 10 percent penalty for early withdrawals from certain types of tax-sheltered savings plans and allows up to $3,000 in annual tax credits when health insurance costs are deducted directly from qualified plans.

Retirement creates challenges for police officers and can be stressful.[176] The Chief of the Lake Oswego, Oregon Police Department died unexpectedly from an apparent heart attack the night before his retirement ceremony.[177] Although the relationship between the chief's imminent retirement ceremony and heart attack is not certain, the proximity of the two events suggests it may have been more than mere coincidence.

A common retirement problem is the loss of professional identity. Many people, when asked who they are, respond with both their names and what their job is. Retirement punches a hole in that identity, leaving officers unable to define themselves as anything other than what they were. Lacking plans to retire to something, some former officers become bored, drink more heavily, develop health problems, become despondent, and commit suicide.[178]

Important relationships may be disturbed as stressed retirees struggle with redefining themselves; they are more often at home, aimless, restless, and sometimes agitated.[179] A lack of long-term financial planning (e.g., the failure to create a supplemental pension or other streams of income such as rental property), may create financial pressures as retirees come to grips with the fact that their pension does not go as far as they thought it would.

The general consensus is that people fare better in retirement when, instead of just retiring from, they are retiring to something (e.g., a new job, devoting time to hobbies, travel, a family business, or learning a new skill like making jewelry). In addition to other benefits, retirement counseling can implant the notion to simultaneously celebrate the end of one career while embracing the opportunity to reinvent oneself.

CONCLUSION

People are a primary asset for law enforcement agencies. Police executives should strive to make their department the premier employer in their field. Recruiting incentives should be geared to the values of the labor pool from which agencies draw their applicants. Important federal job discrimination laws shape virtually every aspect of employment practices and knowledge of them is an important requirement for everyone in leadership positions. Military call-ups strain some agencies, presenting operational challenges. Public accountability requires the use of an EIIS or some similar system and is an important part of the management control system. Failure to maintain such control may result in federal litigation against wayward departments. A sound discipline system is essential to maintaining accountability in the eyes of the public, should be based on progressive discipline, and be consistent and equitable.

Performance appraisals are used to make, or influence, a number of personnel decisions. Organizations must ensure they are meaningful and not just an annual ritual. Promotional testing can serve multiple objectives and law enforcement executives should be alert to these possibilities. Retirement counseling cannot simply be a 20-hour seminar conducted on the eve of officers' retirement dates. Such counseling must be on-going, providing officers with the information and tools to make good decisions about their futures.

CHAPTER REVIEW

1. What are 10 functions of a police human resource unit?

2. The Equal Pay Act was intended to achieve what objective?

3. The Age Discrimination in Employment Act has a law enforcement exemption. What is it?

4. EEOC recognized four major theories of discrimination. What are they?

5. Sexual discrimination has two categories. How are they defined?

6. The Pregnancy Discrimination Act provides what protections to women?

7. How are *disability* and *reasonable accommodation* defined?

8. The Genetic Information Nondiscrimination Act has a law enforcement exemption. For what does it provide?

9. Exempt and nonexempt employees are categories under the Fair Labor Standards Act (FLSA) that differ in what regard?

10. Family Medical Leave Act leave may be granted on what four reasons?

11. How does the economy affect recruiting applicants?

12. Validity and reliability defined tell us what?

13. Why do some law enforcement agencies rely on outside providers for their examinations?

14. How are lie detectors used in applicant screening and what is the main criticism of them?

15. How do oral boards operate?

16. What is a conditional job offer?

17. How does a state's Peace Officer Standards and Training Commission (POST) affect academy and field training?

18. Can you name four characteristics of Generation X and Generation Y?

19. Why is the "new recruiting" necessary?

20. Under USERRA, law enforcement officers called to active military duty have four obligations to their employer. What are they?

21. What are three goals of an Early Identification and Intervention System?

22. *Discipline* means what?

23. Can you describe *progressive discipline*?

24. Of what benefit is a discipline matrix?

25. What are the six purposes of performance appraisals?

26. Promotional testing can serve what five purposes?

27. Officers cite three common reasons for not participating in the promotional process. What are they?

28. Test providers offer three different models of written promotional examinations. Can you identify and briefly describe them?

29. How does an assessment center operate?

30. What are rank-order, all-qualified, and banded promotional systems?

31. What impact might identity loss have on police retirees?

INTERNET ACTIVITIES

Background Investigation Manual, *www.post.ca.gov/selection/bim/bi-manual.asp*
Denver Police Department Discipline Handbook, *www.denvergov.org/portals/338/documents*

KEY TERMS

adverse impact: an employment practice, which although lacking any discriminatory intent and on its face appearing to be neutral, an employer is prohibited from using because it has an unjustified impact on members of a protected class.

Age Discrimination in Employment Act (ADEA): (1967), forbids age discrimination in any aspect of employment for those 40 or older.

all-qualified list: promotional roster method in which anyone on the list can be selected in any order.

Alpha generation: born 2011–2025, projected to be best-educated and most technologically sophisticated.

Americans with Disability Act (ADA): (1990), provides equal opportunity to jobs for qualified persons with a disability as well as other protections. Job requirements that screen out people with disabilities are legal only to the extent they are job related and consistent with business necessity.

assessment center: consists of several exercises or job simulations designed to elicit from candidates the behaviors found to be important to job success by the job analysis.

baby boomers: born 1946–1964, many still employed by law enforcement agencies, reaching the end of their careers; grew up in era of widespread social change.

banded list: promotional roster method in which candidates with similar scores are grouped together.

computer voice stress analyzer (CVSA) : a lie detection mechanism.

conditional job offer (CJO): an employment offer made contingent on passing a medical screening.

disability: under ADA: (1) physical or mental impairment that substantially limits one or more major life activities; (2) a record of such impairment; and (3) a perception of such impairment.

discipline: the core meaning is to teach or instruct.

discipline matrix: a formal schedule for disciplinary actions, specifying both the presumptive or presumed sanction to be imposed for misconduct and any reduction or increase in the presumptive sanction for mitigating or aggravating factors.

disparate treatment: an EEOC theory of discrimination; a member of a protected class is intentionally discriminated against in an employment decision.

early identification and intervention systems: (EIIS), also called early warning systems or locally by some more unique term. Intended to: (1) guide officers to more successful performances; (2) reduce the number of incidents that create liability exposure; and (3) increase the accountability of supervisors for the actions of their subordinates.

Employee Polygraph Protection Act (EPPA): limits the use of lie detectors by employers, provides a law enforcement exception.

Equal Employment Opportunity Commission (EEOC): a unit within the U.S. Department of Justice (USDOJ) that administers several key job discrimination laws. EEOC recognizes four theories of discrimination.

Exempt Employee: not entitled to overtime pay under FLSA.

Equal Pay Act (EPA): (1963), prohibits wage discrimination based on gender.

Fair Labor Standards Act (FLSA): (1938, private sector, 1985 public sector), establishes national minimum wage, work hours, overtime pay, child labor, and recordkeeping requirements.

Family Medical Leave Act (FMLA): (1993), provisions to help employees balance their career and family needs. Mandates unpaid leave by covered employees for eligible workers for up to 12 weeks during any 12-month period for four specific reasons.

field training officer (FTO): guides the field training of a recent basic/academy graduate; see officer in training.

4/5ths rule: a rule of thumb used to determine whether adverse impact has occurred, not a legal standard.

Generation X: born 1965–1980, the largest generation working in law enforcement presently; grew up in mixed economy; first-generation latch key children; tend to be computer fluent. Many departments adapted their recruiting practices to attract Gen Xers.

Generation Y: born 1981–1994, largely the children of baby boomers, recently entering law enforcement agencies. Tend toward traditional family values; spiritual, but not necessarily religious.

Generation Z: born 1995–2010, the "Zedders," little known about them; fascination with virtual realities may lead to impoverished social and interpersonal skills.

Genetic Information Nondiscrimination Act (GINA): (2008), limits the use of genetic information, provides a law enforcement exemption.

harassment: a discriminatory, unwelcome action toward an individual on the basis of race, color, sex (including pregnancy), national origin, age, religion, disability, or genetic information. Sexual harassment is perhaps the most well-known type of harassment.

hostile environment: created when the prohibited and unwelcome behavior has the purpose or effect of unreasonably interfering with the individual's work performance or by creating an intimidating, hostile, or offensive working environment.

Lilly Ledbetter Fair Pay Act (LLFPA): (2009), law that states that each discriminatory paycheck is a new violation.

moral turpitude: conduct contrary to honesty, justice, or good morals.

non-exempt employees: entitled to overtime pay under FLSA.

officer in training (OIT): a recent academy graduate under the supervision of a field training officer.

Peace Officers Standards and Training Commission: (POST), a state level organization that sets standards for police employment, basic and annual training, special certifications (e.g., use of radar, license revocations and other matters).

Pregnancy Discrimination Act: PDA (1978), the Act makes it unlawful to discriminate against women in employment practices because of pregnancy, childbirth, or medical conditions rising from such.

progressive discipline: slowly increasing the severity of sanctions unless a higher level is immediately required (e.g., termination).

protected class: a Title VII (1972) designation, race, color, sex, national origin, or religion.

qualified individual with a disability: job applicant or employee who meets the employer's legitimate requirements for the position sought or held and is able to perform the essential/core functions with or without a reasonable accommodation by the employer.

quid pro quo: "something for something," a category of sexual harassment.

rank-order list: promotional roster method in which candidates are listed in their rank order. Selections are usually made from the list using a rule of 3, 5 or 10.

reasonable accommodation: employers may tell applicants what the selection process consists of and whether they will need a reasonable accommodation by the employer. Examples of selection accommodations include large-print examinations and scheduling a wheelchaired applicants' interview on the first floor rather than the second floor where there is no elevator. After a conditional job offer is extended, employers may ask whether a reasonable accommodation is needed for any aspect of the job (e.g., modifying the equipment the person will use).

reliability: if the same test or a parallel form is given to the same group, substantially the same results will occur; results are not random.

retaliation: one of four EEOC theories of discrimination; two types: (1) retaliation for participation and (2) retaliation for opposition.

Servicemembers Civil Relief Act (SCRA): (2003), provides protections to service members, including those called to active duty; key provisions apply to leasing arrangements, the amount of interest that debtors can charge, and life insurance.

sexual harassment: a specific type of harassment, two categories: (1) quid pro quo and (2) hostile environment; violates Title VII.

silent generation: born 1925–1945, loyal, security conscious, and conforming are key attributes. Almost entirely retired from law enforcement.

Title VII: 1972, law that amends the Civil Rights Act of 1964; prohibits job discrimination in employment based on race, color, sex, national origin, or religion.

Uniform Guidelines for Employee Selection Procedures: "Uniform Guidelines," 1978, developed by EEOC to create a single set of selection principles designed to help covered employers comply with federal laws prohibiting employment decisions that discriminated against members of protected classes.

Uniformed Services Employment and Reemployment Rights Act (USERRA): (1994), encourages noncareer participation in the uniformed military service by eliminating barriers to such service, minimizing the disruption of the lives of those called to service and prohibiting discrimination against them.

U. S. Department of Labor: administers some job discrimination laws in addition to other responsibilities.

validity: quality of a test that means it actually measures what it is intended to measure.

working test: the probationary period for a position.

ENDNOTES

[1] These functions were taken on June 22, 2010 from 31 different police websites across the country that described their HR responsibilities.

[2] No Author, ACLU Marks 47th Anniversary of Equal Pay Act With Call to Pass Paycheck Fairness Act. June 9, 2010. WWW.ACLU.org

[3] Amy Onder, *HR Magazine*, "Ledbetter Law Leads to Equal Pay Victory," December 2009, pp. 1–2. On-line access, June 23, 2010. WWW.Shrm.org/Publications/HR Magazine

[4] The statements in this paragraph are drawn from U.S. Equal Employment Opportunity Commission, Age Discrimination, 2 pp. On-line access June 23, 2010, WWW.EEOC.gov/laws

[5] 544 U.S. 288 (2005).

[6] Equal Employment Opportunity Commission, Nassau County Police Department to Pay $450,00 for Age Bias, p. 1, October 23, 2008, on-line access, WWW.EEOC.Gov

[7] See 29 United States Code, Section 623 (j)(1)(A).

[8] No author, *EEOC Training Institute Resources Guide: Employer Responsibilities*, on-line access June 28, 2010, p. B-2.

[9] Ibid., p. B-2 to B-4.

[10] Ibid., p. B-2 and B-5.

[11] *Stewart et al. v. City of Houston Police Department*, No. 09-20680, U.S. Court of Appeals for the Fifth Circuit (2010).

[12] Benjamin P. Endres, Jr. and the United States of America v. Indiana State Police, No. 02-1247, United State Court of Appeals for the 7th Circuit 349 F.ed 922, U.S. App Lexis 23570 (2003).

[13] Carri Geer Thevenot, "Las Vegas Police Settle Officer's Lawsuit Over Religious Clothing," *Las Vegas Review-Journal*, January 23, 2009.

[14] *Fraternal Order of Police v. City of Newark*, 170 F.3d 359 (3d Cir, 1999).

[15] 41 Code of Federal Regulations (CFR) 60-3.4(D), 1978.

[16] Laurie Wardell and Michael K. Fridkin, *Title VII and Section 1981* (Chicago: Chicago Lawyers' Committee for Civil Rights Under the Law, October, 2009), p. 15.

[17] *Jackson v. County of Racine*, 474 F.3d 493 (7th Cir. 2007).

[18] *Hall v. Gus Construction Co.*, 842 F.2d 1010, 46FEP, Cases 57 (8th Circuit), 1988.

[19] *Chris Sanford v. Department of Veterans Affairs*, EEOC Appeal No. 0120082632 (2009).

[20] U.S. Equal Employment Opportunity Commission, Facts About Sexual Harassment, accessed on-line June 30, 2010, www.eeoc.gov/publications

[21] U.S. Equal Employment Opportunity Commission, Fourteen-Year-Old Reports Sexual Harassment and Assault at Kansas Fast Food Restaurant, WWW.eeoc.gov/youth/case3.html, accessed June 30, 2010.

[22] 29 Code of Federal Regulations, Section 1604.11(a)(1) and (2), 2003.

[23] Ibid., Section 1604.11(a)(3).

[24] On some of these points see *Robinson v. Jackson Shipyards*, 760 F.Supp 1486, Cases 971 (M.D. FLa), 1991.

[25] *King v. Macmillan*, U.S. Court of Appeals for the 4th Circuit, 594 F.3d 301 (2010).

[26] Wardell and Fridkin, Title VII and Section 1981, p. 24.

[27] Ibid.

[28] Civil Action No. 07-cv-02560-LTB-CBS, *The United States of America and Lance Lazoff v. City of Colorado Springs, Colorado,* in the United States District Court of Colorado (2008).

[29] No author, Laws Enforced by the EEOC (U.S. Equal Employment Opportunity Commission: Washington, D.C., 2010), p. 1.

[30] *Lochren et al. v. County of Suffolk,* No. 08-2723-cv, United States Court of Appeals, 2nd Circuit (2009).

[31] Settlement Agreement Between the United States of America and the New York City Police Department, November 18, 2009.

[32] No Author, *Questions and Answers: The Americans with Disabilities Act and Hiring Police Officers*, p. 1, on-line access, June 23, 2010. WWW.ADA.Gov

[33] Ibid.

[34] U.S. Equal Employment Opportunity Commission, *Facts About the Americans with Disabilities Act*, p. 1, on-line access, June 23, 2010. WWW.EEOC.Gov

[35] Ibid.

[36] Ibid.

[37] Americans with Disabilities Act (1990) as Amended (2008), Section 12103((1).

[38] Ibid., Section 12103((2).

[39] U.S. Equal Employment Opportunity Commission, *Questions and Answers on the Notice of Proposed Rulemaking for the ADA Amendments Act of 2008* (ADAAA); p. 3. On-line access, June 23, 2010. WWW.EEOC.Gov

[40] Ibid.

[41] No Author, *ACLU Sues West Virginia Police Chief Who Blocked Life-Saving Measures for Gay Heart Attack Victim Assumed to Be HIV Positive.* WWW.ACLU.Org, March 2, 2006.

[42] The Associate Press, W.Va. Police Chief Denied Gay Man CPR, March 3, 2006. WWW.MSNBC.Com/id/11651307/

[43] The case was filed by the Charleston, W.VA. ACLU Office. It does not appear in any legal index. A July 1, 2010 call to the ACLU on Charleston confirmed the basic facts in this case, but no other information could be provided.

[44] Michael E. Brooks, "The Fair Standards Labor Act and Police Compensation, *FBI Law Enforcement Bulletin*, Vol. 73, No. 6, June 2004, p. 1 and Ted H. Bartlestone, "Issues to Consider in Defending Overtime Claims Under the Fair Labor Standards Act," *Journal of the Missouri Bar*, November/December, 2009, p. 290.

[45] 426 U.S. 833 (1976).

[46] 469 U.S. 528 (1985).

[47] U.S. Department of Labor, "Handy Reference Guide to the Fair Labor Standards Act," July 2007, p. 1.

[48] Ibid., p. 2.

[49] Ibid., p. 4.

[50] FLSA, Section 213(b)(20).

[51] *Fred Bamonte, Javier Cota, Ricardo Perine and other similarly situated employees v. City of Mesa (AZ),* 598 F. 3rd 1217 (2010).

[52] *Stephen S. Adams, et al. v. United States,* 471 F. 3d 1321 (2006).

[53] *David A. Cleveland, Mark S. Vojodich, Andres W. Aston, Brian Benavides v. City of Elmendorf, Texas,* 388 F.3d 522 (2004).

[54] Robert Pear, "Gay Workers to Get Access to Federal Family Leave," *The Charlotte Observer*, June 22, 2010.

[55] 604 F.3d 987 (7th Cir., 2010).

[56] 210 U.S. App. Lexis 3987 (2010).

[57] *Knussman v. State of Maryland,* No. B-95-1255 (D. MD. February 2, 1999).

[58] MaCherie Placide, "In Search of the Best," Paper presented at the Annual Meeting of the Midwest Political Science Association, Chicago, April 3–6, 2008 addresses the quality of recruits and recruiting difficulties.

[59] Kevin Johnson, "Police Agencies Buried in Resumes," *USA Today*, March 12, 2009.

[60] No author, *Recruitment and Retention Practices* (Peace Officers Standards and Training Commission: Sacramento, April 2006), drawn with restatement from p. viii. and 25–26.

[61] Douglas L. Yearwood, *Recruitment and Retention Study Series* (North Carolina Criminal Justice Analysis Center: Raleigh, North Carolina, April 2003), p. i.

[62] *Recruitment and Retention Practices*, pp. xi and 25–26. Also see no author, *POST Recruitment Strategic Planning Guide* (Peace Officers Standards and Training Commission: Sacramento, 2009).

[63] Nelson Lim et. al., *To Protect and Serve: Enhancing the Efficiency of LAPD Recruiting* (Santa Monica, CA: The Rand Corporation, 2009), p. xviii.

[64] Ibid., p. xvii.

[65] Ibid., p. 39.

[66] Ibid., p. 40.

[67] Ibid., p. 39.

[68] Ibid., pp. 42 and 40.

[69] Matthew Hickman and Brian Reaves, *Local Police Departments, 2003* (Washington, D.C.: Bureau of Justice Statistics, May 2006), p. 9.

[70] Lim et. al., *To Protect and Serve: Enhancing the Efficiency of LAPD Recruiting,* p. 60 and Michelle Comeau and John Klofas, *The Police Recruiting Process: Rochester: N.Y.,* p. 5.

[71] See W. Payne and J. Harvey, "A Framework for the Design and Development of Physical Employment Tests and Standards," Vol. 53, Issue 7, July 2010, pp, 858–871.

[72] Comeau and Klofas, *The Police Recruiting Process: Rochester: N.Y.,* p. 7.

[73] United States v. City of Erie, 411 F.Supp.2d 524 (2005).

[74] 29 Code of Federal Regulations (CFR) 801.10, current to July 2, 2010.

[75] Hickman and Reaves, *Local Police Departments*, p. 8.

[76] No author, *Polygraph Testing May Be Flawed for Security Screening*, National Academy of Sciences, October 8, 2002, p. 1.

[77] Charles Swanson, Neil Chamelin, Leonard Territo, and Robert Taylor, *Criminal Investigation* (New York: McGraw-Hill, 2006), pp. 218–219.

[78] *United States, Petitioner v. Edward G. Scheffer* 523 U.S. 303 (1998). Also see Christopher Domin, "Mitigating Evidence? The Admissibility of Polygraph Results in the Penalty Phase," *University of California, Davis, Law Review*, Vol. 43, No. 4, April 2010, pp. 1461–1490 and Leonard Saxe and Gershon Ben-Shakhar, "Admissibility of Polygraph Tests: The Application of Scientific Standards Post-Daubert," *Psychology, Public Policy, and Law*, Vol. 5, Issue 1, March 1999.

[79] Ibid.

[80] Lim et. al., *To Protect and Serve: Enhancing the Efficiency of LAPD Recruiting*, p. 61.

[81] *Thomas J. Mullen v. County of Suffolk, Supreme Court of the State of New York*, D16143(2007).

[82] Lim et. al., *To Protect and Serve: Enhancing the Efficiency of LAPD Recruiting*, p. 60.

[83] William G. Doerner, "The Utility of the Oral Board in Selecting Police Academy Admissions," *Policing: An International Journal of Police Strategies and Management*, Vol. 20, Issue 4, 1997, pp. 777–785.

[84] Larry Gaines and Bruce Lewis, "Reliability and Validity of the Oral Board in Police Promotions," *Journal of Criminal Justice*, Vol. 10, Issue 5, 1982, pp. 403–420.

[85] This section draws on the 38 years of experience of Charles Swanson in designing oral boards, job simulations, and assessment, as well as training panel members from over 26 states.

[86] T. Mieczkowski, "Drug Testing The Police: Some Results of Urinalysis and Hair Analysis in a Major U.S. Metropolitan Police Force," *Journal of Forensic Medicine*, Vol. 3, June 2004, pp. 115–122.

[87] Comeau and Klofas, *The Police Recruiting Process: Rochester: N.Y.*, p. 8.

[88] Martin Sellbom, Gary L. Fischler, and Yossef S. Ben-Porath, "Identifying the MMPI-2 Predictors of Police Integrity and Misconduct," *Criminal Justice and Behavior*, Vol. 34, No. 8, August 2007, pp. 985–1004.

[89] John T. Chinall and Paul Detrick, "The Neo PI-R, Inwald Personality Inventory and the MMPI-2 in the Prediction of Police Academy Performance: A Case for Incremental Validity," *American Journal of Criminal Justice*, Vol. 27, No. 2, March 2003, pp. 233–248.

[90] Lim et. al., *To Protect and Serve: Enhancing the Efficiency of LAPD Recruiting*, pp. 61, 69–70.

[91] Matthew Hickman, *State and Local Law Enforcement Training Academies-2002* (Washington, D.C.: Bureau of Justice Statistics, 2005), p. iii.

[92] Hickman and Reaves, *Local Police Departments*, p. 9.

[93] Ibid.

[94] Hickman and Reaves, *Local Police Departments*, p. 9.

[95] Lawrence W. Daly, "Police Officers Do Not Receive Adequate Training to Prepare Them to Handle Child Sexual Abuse Investigations," *Issues in Child Abuse Accusations*, Vol. 15, Issue 1, Winter 2005, p. 1.

[96] Patricia Obst and Jeremy Davey, "Does the Police Academy Change Your Life?" *International Journal of Police Science and Management*, Vol. 5, Issue 1, 2003, p. 31.

[97] Stephen J. Scarfo, "Validity Study Relationship Between Police Academy Performance and Cadet Level of Education and Cognitive Ability," *Applied H.R.M. Research*, Vol. 7, No. 1, 2002, p. 39.

[98] Allison Chappell, "Police Academy Training: Comparing Across Curricula," *Policing: An International Journal of Police Strategies and Management*, Vol. 31, No. 1, 2008, p. 52.

[99] Nadine Post, "Police Academy to Set Stage for Scenario-Based Training," *ENR: Engineering News-Record*, Vol. 264, Issue 6, February 22, 2010.

[100] Hickman and Reaves, Local Police Departments, 2003, p. 8 and James Hannah, "Military Call-Ups Strain Police Forces in Ohio and Elsewhere," *The Enquirer* (Cincinnati, Ohio) February 20, 2003.

[101] Ibid., p. 9.

[102] For more details, including forms, see WWW.Mesaaz.gov/police/FTO

[103] Francis L. McCafferty, "The Challenge of Selecting Tomorrow's Police Officers from Generations X and Y," *The Journal of the American Academy of Psychiatry and Law*, Vol. 31, No. 1, 2003, p. 81. This note is only for the qualities of the silent generation. As a separate matter, McCafferty uses a 1930–1948 birth range for this group. Our own reading of sources led us to use a 1925–1945 range.

[104] Population Division, U.S. Census Bureau, "Selected Characteristics of Baby Bomers," (Washington, D.C., U.S. Census Bureau, 2009), from unnumbered PowerPoint presentation.

[105] Ibid.

[106] Commission on Peace Officers Standards and Training (POST), Recruitment & Retention (Sacramento, California: POST, 2006), p. viii.

107 Eric P. Werth, "Adult Learning: Similarities in Training Methods and Recruits Learning Characteristics," *The Police Chief*, Vol. LXXVI, No. 11, November 2009, p. 1, on-line access.

108 "The Challenge of Selecting Tomorrow's Police Officers from Generations X and Y," p. 80.

109 Ibid., p. 80.

110 Melinda Crowley, Generation X Speaks Out on Civic Engagement and the Decennial Census: An Ethnographic Approach (Washington, D.C.: U.S. Census Bureau, June 17, 2003), p. 2.

111 "The Challenge of Selecting Tomorrow's Police Officers from Generations X and Y," p. 80.

112 Ibid., p. 80. Also see Marisa Dinatale and Stephanie Boraas, "The Labor Force Experience of Women from Generation X," *Monthly Labor Review*, Vol. 125, No. 3, March 2002, pp. 3–15.

113 Elwood Carlson, 20th-Century Generations, *Population Bulletin*, Vol. 64, No. 1, 2009, computed from Table 4, p. 11.

114 "The Challenge of Selecting Tomorrow's Police Officers from Generations X and Y," p. 80.

115 Ibid., p. 82.

116 Generation X Speaks Out on Civic Engagement and the Decennial Census: An Ethnographic Approach, pp. 10–16.

117 "The Challenge of Selecting Tomorrow's Police Officers from Generations X and Y," p. 82.

118 Tamara Erickson, "Don't Treat Them Like Baby Boomers," *Business Week*, Issue 4097, August 25, 2008, p. 1, on-line access.

119 Neil Simons, "Leveraging Generational Work Styles to Meet Business Objectives," *Information Management*, Vol. 44, Issue 1, Jan/Feb 2010, p. 29.

120 "The Challenge of Selecting Tomorrow's Police Officers from Generations X and Y," p. 81.

121 See Christopher D. Licher, Devon Reister, and Christopher Mason, *Vermont Statewide Law Enforcement Study* (Chicago: I/O Solutions, Inc., 2006).

122 See *Major Cities Chiefs and the Federal Bureau of Investigation, National Executive Institute, Retention: Understanding the Generations, Recruitment, and Selection*, Employee Leadership Development, 2007.

123 Liz Martinez, Real Life Recruiting, Officer.com, on-line access, August 2006, pp. 2–3.

124 Lisa Perrine, "Job Sharing: A Viable Option for Law Enforcement?" *The FBI Law Enforcement Bulletin*, Vol. 78, No. 3, March 2009, pp. 14–15.

125 Lisa Perrine, "Is Job Sharing a Viable Option for Law Enforcement?" (Sacramento: California Commission on Police Standards and Training), 2007 Paper for Command College 41, p. 5.

126 Donna Leinwand, "IRR Call-Up Puts Lives in Disarray," *USAToday*, August 5, 2004, Also see Leonard Territo, "Military Combat Veterans: What They Mean to Your Department," The Florida Police Chief, August 2008, pp. 26–31. This comprehensive article also discusses the psychological issues facing returning Veterans and the necessity for re-entry psychological evaluation of returning police officers.

127 Hickman and Reaves, *Local Police Departments*, 2003, p. 4.

128 Hannah, "Military Call-Ups Strain Police Forces in Ohio and Elsewhere."

129 Palm Beach County Sheriff's Office and PBC PBA, AAA Case No. 32-390-100713-04, 121 LA (BNA) 1624 (Smith, 2005; Reported 2006).

130 38 United States Code, Sections 4301 to 4335, December 19, 2005.

131 20 Code of Federal Regulations (CFR) 1002.193(6), current to July 1, 2010.

132 *Fink v. City of New York*, 129 F.Supp.2d 511 (E.D. N.Y. 200 (1).

133 Missy Diaz, "Former Fla. Officer Gets 90 Days for Faking Military Call-Up," PoliceOne.Com, August 26, 2007. WWW.PoliceOne.com

134 Samuel Walker, *Early Intervention Systems for Law Enforcement Agencies: A Planning and Management Guide* (Washington, D.C.: Office of Community Oriented Policing Services, 2003), p. 48.

135 Susan Sward and Elizabeth Fernandez, "The Use of Force/Counting Without Consequence/Police System of Tracking is Outdate, Often Ignored, SFGate.com, February 6, 2006. SFGate is the on-line version of the *San Francisco Chronicle*. The study covered 1996–2004.

136 No Author, *Conduct of Law Enforcement Agencies, Civil Rights Division, U.S. Department of Justice*, current to July 7, 2010. WWW.Justice.Gov

137 No Author, *Early Intervention and Personal Assessment FAQs, Phoenix (AZ) Police Department*, December 10, 2007, p.1. WWW.Phoenix.gov/Police/PAS.1.html

138 Ibid., p. 2.

139 Ibid.

[140] Ibid.

[141] Samuel Walker, *Early Warning Systems: Responding to the Problem Officer*, Washington, D.C. Office of Justice Programs, July 2001, p. 2.

[142] *Early Intervention and Personal Assessment FAQs*, Phoenix (AZ) Police Department, p. 5.

[143] Walker, *Early Warning Systems: Responding to the Problem Officer*, p. 3.

[144] Stuart MacIntyre, Tim Prenzler, and Jackie Chapman, "Early Intervention to Reduce Complaints," *International Journal of Police Science and Management*, Vol. 10, Issue, 2, Summer 2008, pp. 238–250.

[145] No Author, *Internal Affairs Policy and Procedures*, N.J. Office of the Attorney General, November 2000, p. 11–20.

[146] Ibid.

[147] Helen LaVan, "Public Sector Employee Discipline: Comparing Police to Other Public Sector Employees," *Employee Responsibilities and Rights Journal*, Vol. 19, No. 1, March 2007, pp. 17–30.

[148] Mark Iris, "Police Discipline in Houston: The Arbitration Experience," *Police Quarterly*, Vol. 15, No. 2, June 2002, pp. 132–151.

[149] Lisa Halverstadt, *The Arizona Republic*, July 9, 2010.

[150] David Weisburd et. al., *Police Attitudes Toward Abuse of Authority: Findings From A National Study* (Washington, D.C.: Bureau of Justice Statistics, 2000), p. 5.

[151] Ibid.

[152] Jennifer Manis, Carol A. Archbold, and Kimberly D. Hassell, "Exploring the Impact of Police Officer Education Level on Allegations of Police Misconduct," *International Journal of Police Science and Management*, Vol. 10, Issue 4, Winter 2008, pp. 509–523.

[153] No Author, "For Florida Police, Higher Education Means Lower Risk of Disciplinary Action," *Law Enforcement News*, October 31, 2002, pp. 1 and 10.

[154] Ibid.

[155] James J. Fyfe et. al., "Gender, Race, and Discipline in the New York City Police Department," paper presented at the Annual Meeting of the American Society of Criminology, Washington, D.C., 1998.

[156] Jeff Rojek and Scott H. Decker, "Examining Racial Disparity in the Police Discipline Process," *Police Quarterly*, Vol. 12, Issue 4, December 2009, pp. 388–407.

[157] The data is for 2002. Matthew J. Hickman, Citizen Complaints About Police Use of Force (Washington, D.C.: Bureau of Justice Statistics, June 2006) p. 1.

[158] With modification, from Samuel Walker, Conference Report, "The Disciplinary Matrix: An Effective Police Accountability Tool?" January 2003, University of Nebraska at Omaha.

[159] Ibid., with modification.

[160] Bernd Debusmann, "Performance Reviews-A Global Scourge," June 1, 2010. On- line access http://blogs.Reuters.com/great-debate, p. 1.

[161] Ibid., p. 2.

[162] Larry M. Coutts and Frank W. Schneider, "Police Officer Performance Appraisal Systems: How Good Are They?" Policing: An International Journal of Police Strategies and Management, Vol. 27, Issue 1, 2004, pp. 67–81. Also see David Lilly and Sameer Hinduja, "Police Officer Performance Appraisal and Overall Satisfaction," *Journal of Criminal Justice*, Vol. 35, Issue 2, March/April 2007, pp. 137–150.

[163] Thomas Whetstone and Deborah G. Wilson, "Dilemmas Confronting Female Police Officer Promotional Candidates," p. 69, in Jim Ruiz and Don Hummer, *Handbook of Police Administration* (Boca Raton, FL: CRC Press, 2008).

[164] Ibid.

[165] No Author, Former Police Officer Convicted in Hudson County Promotional Exam Cheating Case, N.J. Office of the Attorney General, March 6, 2006 press release.

[166] Gregory Smith, "Ex-Chief Who Helped Officers May Face Pension Cut," *The Providence (R.I.) Journal*, June 12, 2007.

[167] These points are repeatedly mentioned by agency personnel to Charles Swanson.

[168] Mark Schneider, "National Assessment of Educational Progress," February 22, 2007. http://NCES.ed.gov

[169] Ibid.

[170] For the most current standards see No Author, Guidelines and Ethical Consideration for Assessment Center Operations, *International Journal of Selection and Assessment,* Vol. 17, No. 3, September 2009, pp. 243–252.

[171] This history is recited in numerous publications; for example, see Kris Hogarty and Max Bromley, "Evaluating the Use of an Assessment Center Process for Entry Level Police Officer Selections in a Medium Sized Agency," *Journal of Police and Criminal Psychology*, Vol. 11, No. 1, March 1996, p. 27.

[172] George C. Thornton and Michael J. Potemra, "Utility of Assessment Center Promotion of Police Sergeants," *Public Personnel Management*, Vol. 39, No. 1, Summer 2010, p. 57.

[173] On the relationship of dimensions and exercises, see Filip Lievens, Stephen Dilchert, Deniz S. Ones, "The Importance of Exercise and Dimension Factors in Assessment Centers," *Human Performance*, Vol. 22, Issue 5, November 2009, pp. 375–390.

[174] For example, see *Oliver v. Scottsdale*, 969 F.Supp.564 (D.Ariz. 1996).

[175] 933 F.2d 1140 (2nd Cir. 1991).

[176] On this point see Jim Ruiz and Erin Morrow, "Retiring the Old Centurion: Life After a Career in Policing: An Exploratory Study," *International Journal of Public Administration*, Vol. 28, Issue 13/14, December 2005, pp. 1151–1186.

[177] Rick Bella, *The Oregonian*, OregonLive.com, Lake Oswego Police Chief Dan Duncan Dies," May 20, 2010.

[178] Michelle Perin, "Police Suicide," *Law Enforcement Technology*, Vol. 34, Issue 9, September 2009, pp. 8, 10, 12, 14, and 16.

[179] Organizational culture and workload remain as key stressors; see P. A. Collins and A. Gibbs, "Stress in Police Officers: A Study of the Origins, Prevalence, and Severity of Stress-Related Symptoms with a County Police Force," *Occupational Medicine*, Vol. 53, No. 4, 2003, p. 256. The findings are based on a sample of 1,206 officers.

part three
The Management
of Police Organizations

This section *addresses* three core areas of managing law enforcement agencies: communication *within the organization*, the relationship with a unionized workforce, and the financial resources entrusted to the agency.

In an earlier chapter, it was asserted that communication *was* a crucial skill because nothing can be set in motion and programs underway cannot be guided without it. Chapter 10, "Organizational and Interpersonal Communication," confirms this assertion from another viewpoint: a lack of communication is the primary complaint people have about their immediate supervisors. Chapter 10 examines the communication process in detail, how organizations communicate, how to communicate effectively, and gender, cultural, and generational differences in communicating.

Chapter 11, "Labor Relations," examines police collective bargaining from *an historical perspective*, from its inception through the present, describing the process and its multiple impacts, e.g. on the community and the law enforcement agency. The advent of collective bargaining created a new power center with which law enforcement executives had to contend: the union. Arguably, this has made leadership more difficult *as* the collective bargaining agreement regulates many aspects of *managing* the work force.

Chapter 12 is titled "Financial Management"; this topic is dismissed by some as "drudgery" and "the province of bean counters." However, those who fail to gain an understanding and appreciation of this *critically important* subject will seldom rise beyond mid-management because they cannot meaningfully apprehend that the budget is what translates policies and programs into action. Moreover, as demonstrated in *this* chapter, those who appropriate budgets are *demanding accountability: Do the programs we are funding making any difference?* The budget is the single most important policy statement any unit of government makes in any year, expressing its priorities in financial terms.

10

Organizational and Interpersonal Communication

The difference between the right word and the almost right word is the difference between lightning and lightning bug.
—*Mark Twain*

Objectives

- Discuss the steps that make up the communication process.

- Describe sender-caused barriers, receiver-caused barriers, and other barriers in communications.

- Identify five types of downward communications in an organization.

- List the order of effective communication from most effective to the least effective.

- Analyze the ways in which the use of electronic technology has impacted on police organizations.

- Describe the four phases of group interaction.

- Analyze the major differences between the ways female and male officers communicate, especially during conflict resolution.

- Discuss the two main issues in communication between law enforcement and citizens from other cultures.

- Identify the major communication characteristics of Generation X officers and Generation Y officers (Millennial).

OUTLINE

Introduction

Research in recent years has indicated that communication is the number one problem in management and that lack of communication is the employees' primary complaint about their immediate supervisors.[1] There are many components to the communication process and it is essential for police administrators to understand not only what they are but also why they are so important. These include (1) what it takes for a police administrator to be an effective communicator, (2) an understanding of the communication process, (3) the ability to examine the numerous barriers in the communication process, (4) an awareness of the multidirectional flow of information in the organization, (5) the importance of interpersonal communication and how police managers can become more effective communicators, (6) differences in the ways that males and females communicate, (7) important variations in cross-cultural communication, and (8) the differences in communication styles and needs of those officers who are classified as Generation X and Generation Y (Millenials).

The Communication Process

An explanation of communication begins with the basic problem that it cannot be examined as an isolated event. Communication is a process, so it must be understood as the totality of several independent and dynamic elements. An aggregate **communication** can be defined as the process by which senders and receivers interact in both professional and social contexts.

Steps in the Communication Process

To understand the steps in the communication process, assume that a midnight shift lieutenant informs a midnight shift patrol sergeant that there has been a dramatic increase in the number of burglaries in the sergeant's patrol sector during the past month and then suggests it might be the result of inattention on the part of the sergeant and the sergeant's subordinates. The following are the steps that are occurring in this communication process:

Sender—The sender (in this case, the lieutenant) is attempting to send a spoken message to the sergeant. The perceived authority and credibility of the sender are important factors in influencing how much attention the message will receive. Because of the authority and rank of the lieutenant, it is very likely the patrol sergeant will not ignore the message.

Message—The heart of the communication event is the message—a purpose or an idea to be conveyed. Many factors influence how a message is received. Among them are clarity, the alertness of the receiver, the complexity and length of the message, and how the information is organized. The patrol lieutenant's message will most likely get across if the lieutenant says directly, "I need to talk to you about last month's dramatic increase in burglaries in your patrol sector."

Channel (medium)—Several communication channels, or media, are usually available for sending messages in organizations. Typically, messages are spoken (as in this case), written (increasingly electronically), or a combination. When a message is spoken, it is typically accompanied by nonverbal signs, such as a frown, smile, or hand gesture.

Receiver—A communication is complete only when another party receives the message and understands it properly. Perceptual distortions of various types act as filters that can prevent a message from being received as intended by the sender.

Feedback—Messages sent back from the receiver to the sender are referred to as **feedback**. Without feedback, it is difficult to know whether a message has been received and understood. The feedback step also includes the receiver's reactions. If the receiver—in this case, the patrol sergeant—takes appropriate action as intended by the lieutenant, then the message has been received satisfactorily. Effective

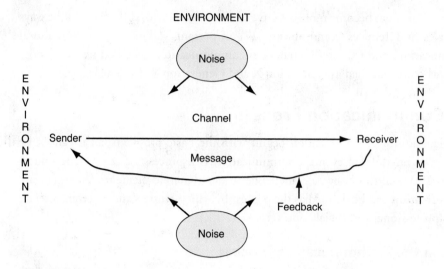

Figure 10.1
A basic model of the communication process.
Source: Dubrin, Andrew J., *Human Relations: Interpersonal, Job-Oriented Skills,* 8th edition,
© 2004. Reproduced by permission of Pearson Education, Inc., Upper Saddle River, New Jersey.

interpersonal communication involves an exchange of messages between two people.
The two communicators take turns being receivers and senders.

Environment—A full understanding of communication requires knowledge of the
environment in which messages are transmitted and received. The organizational
culture (attitudes and atmosphere) is a key environmental factor that influences
communication. It is easier to transmit controversial messages when trust and
respect are high than when they are low.

Noise—Distractions, such as noise, have a pervasive influence on the components of
the communication process. However, within this context, **noise** can also mean
anything that disrupts communication, including the attitudes and emotions of the
receiver, such as stress, fear, negative attitudes, and low motivation[1] (see Figure 10.1).

Communication Barriers

Barriers to communication, or communication breakdowns, can occur at any place in
the system. Barriers can be the result of improper techniques on the part of either the
sender or the receiver.

The sender hinders communications when the following conditions occur:

- The sender is not clear about what is to be accomplished with the message.
- The sender assumes incorrectly the receiver has the knowledge necessary to
  understand the message and its intent and does not adapt the message to the
  intended receiver. For example, experienced criminal justice instructors who
  teach at the community college and university level understand that when
  they have a class comprised primarily of pre-service students, as opposed to

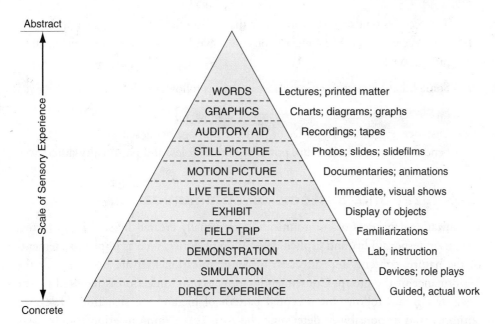

Figure 10.2
Scale of sensory perception.

in-service police practitioners, the way in which the material is presented, if done correctly, is quite different even when the same textbook is being used. They will also tell you that among the more challenging classes to teach are those comprised of an almost equal number of pre-service and police in-service students.

- The sender uses a communication medium not suited for the message. For example, some messages are better transmitted face-to-face, others in writing, while others most effectively transmitted with the use of visual aids. Still others are best taught with direct, hands-on experience. Figure 10.2 displays a scale of sensory perceptions that can be useful as a guide in determining which medium of communication is most effective for a particular message.
- The sender does not develop a mechanism for receiving feedback to determine if the message was understood correctly.
- The sender does not interpret feedback correctly or fails to clarify the message on the basis of feedback from the receiver.
- The sender uses language that causes the receiver to stop listening, reading, or receiving.
- The sender analyzes the audience improperly.
- The sender's background, experiences, and attitudes are different from those of the receiver, and the sender does not take this into account.

The receiver hinders communication when the following occur:

- The receiver is a poor listener, observer, or reader and therefore misinterprets the meaning of the message.
- The receiver jumps to conclusions.
- The receiver hears or sees only certain parts of the message.

- The receiver tends to reject messages that contradict beliefs and assumptions.
- The receiver has other concerns or emotional barriers, such as being mentally preoccupied.

Some other barriers to communication are as follows:

- Noise, temperature, and other physical distractions
- Distance or an inability to see or hear the message being sent
- Sender–receiver relationship, power structure, roles, and personality differences

Organizational Systems of Communication

Organizational systems of communication are usually created by setting up formal systems of responsibility and explicit delegations of duties, such as implicit statements of the nature, content, and direction of communication that are necessary for the performance of the group. Consequently, formal communication is required by the organization and follows the accepted pattern of hierarchical structure. Delegated authority and responsibility determine the path that communication should take, whether upward or downward. Messages that travel through the formal channels of any organization can follow routine patterns; they may be expected at a given time or presented in a standard form and receive a regularized degree of consideration.[2]

Most police managers prefer a formal system, regardless of how cumbersome it may be, because they can control it and because it tends to create a record for future reference. However, motivational factors of the individual and organizations affect the flow of communication. Employees typically communicate with those who help them achieve their aims and avoid communicating with those who do not assist or who may retard their accomplishing those goals. They direct their communications toward those who make them feel more secure and gratify their needs and away from those who threaten or make them feel anxious or generally provide unrewarding experiences. In addition, employees communicate in a manner that allows them to increase their status, belong to a more prestigious group, attain more power to influence decisions, or expand their control. The moving transaction identified as organizational communication can occur at several levels and can result in understanding, agreement, good feeling, and appropriate behavior; the converse may also be true.[3]

Downward Communication

Classical management theories place primary emphasis on control, chain of command, and downward flow of information. **Downward communication** is used by management for sending orders, directives, goals, policies, procedures, memorandums, and so forth to employees at lower levels of the organization. Five types of such communication within an organization can be identified:[4]

1. *Job instruction*—communication relating to the performance of a certain task
2. *Job rationale*—communication relating a certain task to organizational tasks

3. *Procedures and practices*—communication about organization policies, proce-dures, rules, and regulations

4. *Feedback*—communication appraisal of how an individual performs the as-signed task

5. *Indoctrination*—communication designed to motivate the employee.[5]

Other reasons for communicating downward implicit in this listing are opportunities for management to spell out objectives, change attitudes and mold opinions, prevent misunderstandings from lack of information, and prepare employees for change.[6] A study conducted by the Opinion Research Corporation some years ago revealed that large amounts of information generated at the top of an organization did not filter down to the working levels. Studies of the flow of communications within complex organizations repeatedly demonstrate that each level of management can act as a bar-rier to downward communication.[7] In perhaps the best-controlled experimental research in downward communication, Dahle[8] proved the efficacy of using oral and written media together. His findings indicate the following order of effectiveness (from most effective to least effective):

1. Oral and written communication combined
2. Oral communication only
3. Written communication only
4. The bulletin board
5. The organizational grapevine

The research conducted thus far seems to indicate that most downward channels in organizations are only minimally effective. Findings indicate further that attempts at disseminating information downward in an organization should not depend exclu-sively on a single channel.

Upward Communication

Even though police administrators might appreciate the need for effective upward communication, they often do not translate this need into action.[9] It becomes appar-ent at once that to swim upstream is a much harder task than to float downstream. But currents of resistance, inherent in the temperament and habits of supervisors and em-ployees in the complexity and structure of modern police agencies, are persistent and strong. Let us examine some of these deterrents to **upward communication**.

Barriers Involving Police Organizations

The physical distance between superior and subordinate impedes upward communi-cation in several ways. Communication becomes difficult and infrequent when supe-riors are isolated so as to be seldom seen or spoken to. In large police organizations, executives can be located in headquarters or operating centers that are not easily reached by subordinates. In other police agencies, executive offices might be placed re-motely, or executives might hold themselves needlessly inaccessible.

Barriers Involving Superiors

The attitudes of superiors and their listening behaviors play a vital role in encouraging or discouraging communication upward. If, in listening to a subordinate, a supervisor seems anxious to end the interview, impatient with the subordinate, or annoyed or distressed by the subject being discussed, a major barrier to future communication can be created.

There is always the danger that a supervisor may assume the posture that "no news is good news" when, in fact, a lack of complaints or criticism might be a symptom that upward communication is operating at a dangerously low level.

Supervisors may also assume, often incorrectly, they know what subordinates think or feel and believe that listening to complaints from subordinates, especially complaints about departmental policies or even specific supervisors, is an indication of disloyalty. This attitude tends to discourage employees with justifiable complaints from approaching their superiors.

One of the strongest deterrents to upward communication is a failure of management to take action on undesirable conditions previously brought to their attention. The result is that subordinates lose faith both in the sincerity of management and in the value of communication.

Barriers Involving Subordinates

Communication can flow more freely downward than upward because a superior is free to call in a subordinate and talk about a problem at will. The subordinate does not have the same freedom to intrude on the superior's time and is discouraged from circumventing the chain of command and going over a superior's head or from asking for an appeal from decisions made by superiors. Thus, neither the system available nor the rewards offered to the subordinate for upward communication equal those for downward messages.

Horizontal Communication

When an organization's formal communication channels are not open, the informal horizontal channels are almost sure to thrive as a substitute.[10] If there is a disadvantage in **horizontal communication**, it is that it is much easier and more natural to achieve than vertical communication and, therefore, it often replaces vertical channels rather than supplementing them. Actually, the horizontal channels that replace weak or nonexistent vertical channels are usually of an informal nature. There are, of course, formal horizontal channels that are procedurally necessary and should be built into the system. Formal horizontal channels must be set up between various bureaus and divisions for the purposes of planning, interwork task coordination, and general system maintenance functions, such as problem solving, information sharing, and conflict resolution.

We can begin by acknowledging that horizontal communication is essential if the subsystems within a police organization are to function in an effective and coordinated manner. Horizontal communication among peers may also furnish the emotional and social bond that builds esprit de corps or a feeling of teamwork. Psychologically, people seem to need this type of communication, and police managers would do well to provide for this need and thus allow peers to solve some of their own work problems together.

Suppose, for example, that patrol sergeant A is having great difficulty communicating certain mutually beneficial information to detective sergeant B because the police department requires strict adherence to the chain of command in transmitting information. As indicated in Figure 10.3A, sergeant A would have to go up through the various hierarchical complexities of the patrol division and back down through the detective division to communicate with sergeant B. The time being wasted and the level-to-level message distortion occurring in the classically managed organization was recognized by Fayol[11] in 1916. Fayol proposed the creation of a horizontal bridge (see Figure 10.3B) that would allow more direct communications between individuals within an organization. The major limiting factor to the use of Fayol's bridge is a loss of network control and the subsequent weakening of authority and random scattering of messages throughout the system. Such random communication channels can lead to diagonal lines of communication, such as direct communication between sergeant A in the patrol division and sergeant B in the detective division. Diagonal lines of communication are not in and of themselves bad; however, they are very difficult to control from the management point of view.[12]

Despite the need for formal horizontal communication in an organization, there may be a tendency among peers not to formally communicate task-related information horizontally. For instance, rivalry for recognition and promotion can cause competing subordinates to be reluctant to share information. Subordinates may also find it difficult to communicate with highly specialized people at the same level as themselves in other divisions.

In the main, then, formal horizontal communication channels are vital as a supplement to the vertical channels in an organization. Conversely, the informal horizontal channels, although socially necessary, can be detrimental to the vertical channels. Informal horizontal channels not only can carry false or distorted information but also may sometimes tend to replace the vertical channels.[13]

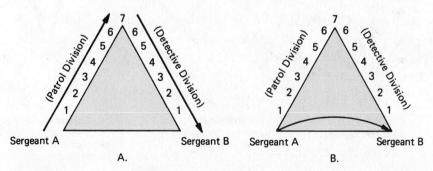

Figure 10.3

Horizontal lines of communication: (A) message path from sergeant A to sergeant B following the usual structured channels; (B) message path from sergeant A to sergeant B following Fayol's bridge.

The Grapevine

The best-known system for transmitting informal communication is the **grapevine**, so called because it meanders back and forth like a grapevine across organizational lines. The grapevine's most effective characteristics are that it is fast, it can be highly selective and discriminating, it operates mostly at the place of work, and it supplements and relates to formal communication. These characteristics can be divided into desirable or undesirable attributes.

The grapevine can be considered desirable because it gives management insight into employees' attitudes, provides a safety valve for employees' emotions, and helps spread useful information. Dysfunctional traits include its tendencies to spread rumors and untruths, its lack of responsibility to any group or person, and its uncontrollability. Attributes of the grapevine—its speed and influence—may work either to the good or to the detriment of the organization. The actual operation of the grapevine can be visualized in four ways (see Figure 10.4):[14]

1. *The single strand*—A tells B, who tells C, who tells D, and so on.
2. *The gossip chain*—A seeks and tells everyone, thus becoming the organizational Paul Revere.
3. *The probability chain*—A communicates randomly to D and F, then with the laws of probabilities, D and F tell others in the same manner.
4. *The cluster chain*—A tells three selected others; perhaps one of them tells two others and one of these tells one other person.

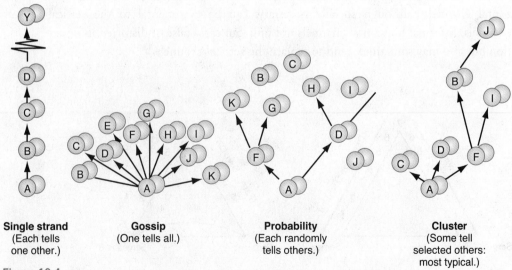

Single strand
(Each tells
one other.)

Gossip
(One tells all.)

Probability
(Each randomly
tells others.)

Cluster
(Some tell
selected others:
most typical.)

Figure 10.4
Grapevine patterns.
Source: John W. Newstrom and Keith Davis, *Organizational Behavior: Human Behavior at Work*, 9th ed., p. 445.
© 1993 McGraw Hill Companies. Reproduced with permission from The McGraw Hill Companies.

The grapevine is a permanent factor to be reckoned with in the daily activities of management, and no competent manager would try to abolish it. Rather, the astute manager should analyze it and consciously try to influence it.[15]

Organizational Electronic Communication

In recent years, the nature of organizational communication has changed dramatically, mainly because of breakthroughs in electronic communication technology, and the future promises even more changes. Decades ago, electric typewriters and photocopying machines were considered cutting-edge technology. The photocopier, for example, made it possible for a police manager to have a typed report distributed to large numbers of personnel in an extremely short period of time. Personal computers accelerated the process. E-mail networks, the Internet, and corporate intranets have carried communication technology even further and it is imperative that police managers continue to avail themselves of the latest communications technology as it develops.

However, police managers should also be aware that sometimes unintended problems result from the introduction of new technology. These unforeseen problems actually increase communication with some unfortunate consequences. The tips discussed in the Quick Facts box, if adhered to, will do much to eliminate some of the unfortunate consequence that can result from violations of commonsense etiquette in the communication process when using e-mail in business correspondence.

It is also becoming more common, especially in law enforcement agencies spread over a wide geographical area, to have teleconferences in which police managers stay at their own location but are seen on closed-circuit television or computer monitors as they "meet." A police manager at one location can keyboard a letter or memorandum

---

Quick FACTS ▶▶ 10 Tips for Successful E-mail Business Correspondence

- Maintain professionalism in e-mail correspondence, as in any other business correspondence; business etiquette does not change when a message is digitized.
- Respond to e-mail promptly, even if only to acknowledge initial receipt and that a more detailed response will follow.
- Check e-mail frequently, but do not allow it to interrupt other scheduled tasks.
- Read and reread e-mails for quality, tone, grammar, spelling, and punctuation before sending them. Do not rely solely on spell check to catch errors.
- Remember that e-mail is not private correspondence and can easily become public without intent or consent. It is a permanent record of written communication.

- Do not use business e-mail for jokes or frivolous messages.
- Deal with personal or sensitive issues in person, not through an impersonal electronic medium.
- Use business e-mail as a means to get information to a number of people in an expeditious fashion and to quickly involve others, but do not send e-mails to persons who do not need to receive it.
- Use caution when responding to e-mails. How something is said in e-mail language is just as important as what is said. No matter how emotional the issue or the contents of the e-mail received and the resultant need to verbalize emotions, do not vent and send.
- Treat an e-mail inbox similar to a paper one: review the document, act on it, and move on.

Source: James D. Sewell, "Handling the Stress of the Electronic World," *FBI Law Enforcement Bulletin*, August 2003, p. 14.

to his or her subordinates, point and click with a mouse, and have it delivered to hundreds or, in the case of very large police agencies, thousands of employees in a matter of seconds. In addition, highly detailed information can be retrieved with ease from large electronic databanks.

Cellular telephones and texting have made it even easier for police managers to communicate with one another and their subordinates. Personal computing devices, such as netbooks and enhanced cell phones, are revolutionizing how people within the police organization communicate with one another. Wi-Fi technology is further extending the impact of these devices.

However, as already suggested, these rapid technological advances are not without their side effects and psychologists are beginning to associate some problems with these communication advances. For one thing, police managers may unwittingly drop out of the organizational grapevine and miss out on very important informal communication that takes place. Moreover, the use of electronic communication at the expense of face-to-face meetings and conversations makes it more difficult to build a strong culture, develop solid working relationships, and create a mutually supportive atmosphere of trust and cooperativeness. Finally, electronic communication is opening up new avenues for dysfunctional employee behavior, such as the passing of lewd or offensive materials to others.[16]

Electronic Communication Interaction Between Citizens and the Police

There has been a dramatic increase in the electronic interactions between police departments and their citizens and, in many cases, to the benefit of all. One of many examples can be found in the communication between the Chicago Police Department and its citizens. The following case study examines the results of e-mail feedback for the Chicago Police Department's Citizen Information Collection for Automated Mapping (ICAM).

In response to rising crime rates, community policing emerged in the 1990s as a method by which law enforcement and citizens cooperatively identify and solve community problems. In 1993, the Chicago Police Department (CPD) launched its community policing program, Chicago's Alternative Policing Strategy (CAPS). To implement the CAPS program, the city divided Chicago's 25 districts into 279 "beats" (smaller geographically based policing areas). For each shift in each beat throughout Chicago, police officers were assigned to focus on community policing. Organized interaction occurred at local beat meetings, where residents identified community problems and worked with police officers to identify solutions to these problems. Police officers worked with community members to discover community priorities and utilize community intelligence to solve crimes.

In 1994, the department developed a crime-mapping program, Information Collection for Automated Mapping (ICAM), as a beat-level crime information tool. This application gave officers and residents working through CAPS continuously updated information on crime activity and crime trends at any administrative and geographic unit of analysis. However, as CAPS gained momentum and more residents were engaged in the process, police officers working through CAPS were spending large amounts of the time responding to resident requests for accurate data on crime.

In response, the CPD developed Citizen ICAM, which is a Web-based technology that provides citizens with location specific information about crime from the same data source the police use. Citizens are able to interact directly online with the CPD's crime database to conduct statistical queries on crime at the intersection, school, address, and beat levels. The website also offers an e-mail feedback opportunity. The main goal of Citizen ICAM was to provide citizens with a clearer picture of the crime occurring in their neighborhoods, thereby making beat meetings, officer activity, and other problem-solving efforts more efficient.

The development of the Citizen ICAM application represents a significant departure from the prior policy in which police representatives acted as crime data intermediaries. The availability of crime data from the same database for both citizens and police represents an increase in the level of content sophistication because greater control over access to information was given to the citizen. Combined with the new feedback link on the ICAM website, this created a new commitment by police to enhance cyber-interactivity between citizens and police. The following two brief examples illustrate how the cyber interactivity process unfolded and how it affected the police organization.[17]

In the first example, a bus passenger used ICAM feedback to report an accident between a bus and a car in which the bus driver did not appear to have reported the incident properly. The report was detailed and included the bus number, intersection of the accident, description of the damaged car, bus line, and other relevant information. The Citizen ICAM officer responded immediately to the citizen with a tracking number and an explanation of a referral to the accident investigation unit (AIU). In turn, the citizen responded by thanking the officer for the prompt e-mail reply. The AIU conducted an investigation within 2 days and forwarded the results of the investigation to the Technology Section, which then responded to the citizen about the outcome of the investigation. Citizen ICAM also forwarded the citizen report and the investigation reference number to the Chicago Transit Authority, the operator of the bus service.

In the second example, a citizen used the feedback function to identify problems with a specific drug user loitering at an apartment building and causing disturbances. The two-page e-mail detailed instances of encounters with the drug user and a physical description. Further, the citizen pledged her support of police activities, stated that she is active in the community policing, and offered suggestions for improvement of patrol. Within 2 days, an original response was sent to the citizen, informing her that a referral was made to her local district. Less than 2 weeks later, the commander of the referral district sent the Technology Section correspondence stating that an arrest had been made in connection with the original e-mail from the citizen. The citizen was informed of the arrest via e-mail.

South Dakota's Public Safety Department isn't the only agency using on-line communication tools to get information to the public. Law enforcement agencies across the United States are experimenting with Twitter, YouTube, and Facebook.

In Baltimore, in April, "we did a drug raid and we posted it on Twitter in real time," says police spokesman Anthony Guglielmi. Police started using Facebook and Twitter in March, and a YouTube site in April, he says.

In Boynton Beach, Florida., the police department began its Twitter experiment at 3:16 p.m. on January 5, with this brief text message: "Alabama father who sent child porn to Boynton detective arrested," recalls department spokesman Stephanie Slater. The department now has 545 people following its Twitter posts, she says.

In Dalton, Georgia, 291 people were following police Twitter messages. After a bomb threat that led to the evacuation of a school and much of downtown, Bruce Frazier, the department's public information officer, says he sought a better way to update the public from the scene of the crimes, accidents and other emergencies.

The new trend in communicating is driven, in part, by the availability of the technology, says Brian Mennecke, an associate professor at Iowa State University. Plus, he says, "it's just cool right now."

Source: Jeff Martin, "Police Go Online to Connect With Public," *USA TODAY*, May 1, 2009.

These are just a couple of examples of the cyber interactivity that takes place as a result of the ICAM feedback; such electronic communication interaction between citizens and the police is now fairly common. Both have benefitted significantly from it.[18]

Interpersonal Communication

The information available about how to communicate persuasively and effectively is extensive.[19] In this section we will focus primarily on creating the high-impact communication that contributes to effective leadership. Both formal and informal leaders must be persuasive and dynamic communicators. Effective **interpersonal communication** skills often help informal leaders be selected for formal leadership positions.

Suggestions for becoming effective communicators can be divided into the following two categories: (1) speaking and writing, and (2) nonverbal communication. We will also discuss certain basic principles of persuasion.

Speaking and Writing

Many people are already familiar with the basics of effective spoken and written communication, yet the basics, such as writing and speaking clearly, maintaining eye contact, and not mumbling, are only starting points. Most effective leaders have extra energy in their communication style. The same excitement is reflected in both their speaking and their writing styles. Kouzes and Posner underscore the importance of colorful language in communicating a vision (one of the leader's most important functions) in these words:

> Language is among the most powerful methods for expressing a vision. Successful leaders use metaphors and figures of speech; they give examples, tell stories, and relate anecdotes; they draw word pictures; and they offer quotations and recite slogans.[20]

Group members and other constituents generally have more exposure to the spoken words of leaders, yet clearly the increased use of e-mail, printed memos, and the written word exerts considerable influence. The following are some suggestions for dynamic and persuasive oral and written communication.

Be Credible

Attempts at persuasion, including inspirational speaking and writing, begin with the credibility of the message sender. It has long been recognized that credibility is a powerful element in the persuasive process. If the speaker is perceived as highly credible, the attempt at persuasive communication is more likely to be successful.[21] The perception of credibility is influenced by many factors. Being trustworthy heavily influences being perceived as credible. A leader with a reputation for lying will have a difficult time convincing people of the merits of a new initiative. Being perceived as intelligent and knowledgeable is another major factor contributing to credibility.

Gear the Message to the Listener

An axiom of persuasive communication is that a speaker must adapt the message to the listener's interests and motivation. A review of the evidence concludes that the average intelligence and experience level of the group is a key contingency factor in designing a persuasive message. People with high intelligence tend to be more influenced by messages based on strong, logical arguments. Also, bright people are more likely to reject messages based on flawed logic.[22]

Persuade Group Members on the Benefits of Change

Sometimes a leader is constrained by the willingness of agency group members to conform to the leader's suggestions and initiatives for change. As a consequence, the leader must explain to agency members how they can benefit from what is being proposed.

For example, let us assume the head of a law enforcement agency has decided to radically modify the agency's policy on high-speed pursuits (a topic discussed in much greater detail in Chapter 14, Legal Aspects of Police Administration). In the past, the agency has had a very liberal policy that allowed officers considerable latitude to pursue fleeing motorists irrespective of the violation, but the agency head is now seriously considering restricting the policy, so that officers will only be permitted to pursue known dangerous felons.

Selling agency members is quite often done more effectively when the persuader takes the time to build consensus rather than to change the policy through administrative fiat. Instead of trying simply to order a change without any discussion, it might be more effective to win over key personnel within a reasonable time frame. Persuasion guru (note the appeal to credibility) Jay Conger writes that successful persuasion often requires ongoing effort and suggests this pattern be followed:

- At the first meeting of key personnel, make every effort possible to ask them to consider the initiative carefully.
- At the second meeting, after they have had the opportunity to think about this modification, see if it is necessary to make adjustments in the policy.

- At the final meeting, it is imperative to have all the key members come to a consensus. If a consensus cannot be obtained but a final decision has been made to modify the policy, it is important that key personnel understand the importance of not undermining the policy. It should also be made very clear that such action will not be tolerated.[23]

Use Heavy-Impact and Emotion-Provoking Words

Certain words used in the proper context give power and force to speech. Used comfortably, naturally, and sincerely, these words project the image of a self-confident person with leadership ability or potential.

Closely related to heavy-impact language are emotion-provoking words. An expert persuasive tactic is to sprinkle one's speech with emotion-provoking—and therefore inspiring—words. Emotion-provoking words bring forth powerful images. For example, agency personnel must be made to understand that the existing policy on high-speed pursuits increases the likelihood of "death" and/or "injury" to them, as well as to "innocent" third parties, the fleeing motorist and, in some cases, "innocent" passengers in the fleeing vehicles. It will also result in "lawsuits" against the officer and the agency and, in some rare cases has actually resulted in their being "criminally charged," "convicted," and sent to "prison."

Back Up Conclusions with Data

A message either spoken or written will be more persuasive if it is supported with solid data. Published sources provide convincing data for arguments. Supporting data for many arguments can be found in professional journals, in government studies, in scholarly research, in books, on the Internet, on TV, and in newspapers. Specific examples and statistics can be extracted from those various documents to support the previously discussed significant changes in the agency's high-speed pursuit policy. For example, the National Law Enforcement Officers Memorial Fund has reported that the second-leading cause of deaths of law enforcement officers between 2000 and 2009 were auto accidents (the leading cause was officers being shot in the line of duty).[24] These figures do not include the many thousands of police officers who have been seriously injured and disabled as a result of automobile accidents, many of which occurred during high-speed pursuits for what turned out to be, in most cases, minor traffic violations or misdemeanors.

Minimize Language Errors and Vocalized Pauses

Using colorful, powerful words enhances the perception of self-confidence. The use of words and phrases that dilute the impact of a speech, such as "you know," "you know what I mean," and "uhhhhhhh," should be minimized. Such "junk words" (also known as parasitic words) and vocalized pauses convey the impression of low self-confidence—especially in a professional setting—and detract from a sharp communication image. The word "like" has emerged, especially among young people, as one of the most popular parasitic words. For example, "the test was like so hard"; "the weather was like so bad"; and "I am like so tired."

An effective way to decrease the use of these extraneous words is to tape record or video record one's own side of a conversation and then play it back. Many people are not aware that they use extraneous words until they hear recordings of their speech.

It is always important to write and speak with precision to convey the impression of being articulate and well informed, thus enhancing one's stature.

Write Crisp, Clear Memos and Reports, Including a Front-Loaded Message

According to Mercer, high achievers write more effective reports than do their less-highly achieving counterparts. Mercer examined the business writing (memos, letters, and reports) of both high achievers and low achievers. He observed that the high achievers' writing was distinctive in that it had more active verbs than passive verbs, more subheadings and subtitles, and shorter paragraphs.[25]

Writing, in addition to speaking, is more persuasive when key ideas are placed at the beginning of a conversation, an e-mail message, a paragraph, or a sentence. Front-loaded messages are particularly important for leaders because people expect leaders to be forceful communicators.

Use a Power-Oriented Linguistic Style

A major part of being persuasive involves choosing the right linguistic style, which is a person's characteristic speaking pattern. According to communications specialist Deborah Tannen, linguistic style involves such aspects as amount of directness, pacing and pausing, word choice, and the use of such communication devices as jokes, figures of speech, anecdotes, questions, and apologies.[26] Linguistic style is complex because it includes the culturally learned signals by which people communicate what they mean, along with how they interpret what others say and how they evaluate others. The complexity of linguistic style makes it difficult to offer specific prescriptions for using one that is power-oriented. However, there are several components of a linguistic style that will, in many situations, give power and authority to the message sender. Some of these, as observed by Tannen and other language specialists are the following:

- Downplay uncertainty. If you are not confident of your opinion or prediction, make a positive statement anyway, such as saying, "I know this new restrictive high-speed pursuit policy will reduce deaths, injuries, and litigation."
- Keep an open mind and accept verbal opposition to ideas, especially at staff meetings, rather than becoming upset and defensive.
- Emphasize direct rather than indirect talk, such as by saying "I need your report by noon tomorrow" rather than "I'm wondering if your report will be available by noon tomorrow."
- Speak up without qualifying or giving other indices of uncertainty. It is better to give dates for the completion of a project rather than to say, "Soon," or "It shouldn't be a problem." Instead, make a statement like "I will have my portion of the strategic plan shortly before Thanksgiving. I need to collect input from my team and sift through the information."

- Know exactly what is needed. The chances of selling an idea increase to the extent that it is clarified in the mind of the presenter. The clearer and more committed the person is at the outset of the session, the stronger he or she will be as a persuader and the more powerful the language becomes.
- Strive to be bold when making statements. As a rule of thumb, be bold about ideas but tentative about people. If the head of the agency says something like "I believe that our new high-speed pursuit policy will significantly reduce injuries and deaths to our officers and citizens, as well as result in a reduction in liability to our agency," then it is an idea that is being attacked and not one's predecessor who may have been reluctant to implement a more conservative high-speed pursuit policy.[27]

Despite these suggestions for having a power-oriented linguistic style, Tannen cautions there is no one best way to communicate. How one projects power and authority is often dependent on the people involved, the organizational culture, the relative rank of the speakers, and the other situational factors. The power-oriented linguistic style should be interpreted as a general guideline.

Nonverbal Communication

Effective leaders are masterful nonverbal as well as verbal communicators. Nonverbal communication is important because leadership involves emotion, which words alone cannot communicate convincingly. A major component of the emotional impact of a message is communicated nonverbally—perhaps up to 90 percent.[28] The classic study behind this observation has been misinterpreted to mean that 90 percent of communication is nonverbal. If this were true, facts, figures, and logic would make a minor contribution to communication, and acting skill would be much more important for getting across one's point of view. This, however, is not the case.

A self-confident leader not only speaks and writes with assurance but also projects confidence through body position, gestures, and manner of speech. Not everybody interprets the same body language and other nonverbal signals in the same way, but some aspects of nonverbal behavior project a self-confident, leadership image in many situations. For example:

- Using an erect posture when walking, standing, or sitting. Slouching and slumping are almost universally interpreted as an indicator of low self-confidence.
- Standing up straight during a confrontation. Cowering is interpreted as a sign of low self-confidence and poor leadership qualities.
- Speaking at a moderate pace, with a loud, confident tone. People lacking in self-confidence tend to speak too rapidly or very slowly.
- Smiling frequently in a relaxed, natural-appearing manner
- Maintaining eye contact with those around you
- Gesturing in a relaxed, nonmechanical way, including pointing toward others in a way that welcomes rather than accuses, such as using a gesture to indicate "You're right" or "It's your turn to comment"[29]

A general approach to using nonverbal behavior that projects confidence is to have a goal of appearing self-confident and powerful. This type of autosuggestion makes many of the behaviors seem automatic. For example, if you say to yourself, "I am going to display leadership qualities in this meeting," you will have taken an important step toward appearing confident.

External image also plays an important role in communicating messages to others. People have more respect and grant more privileges to those they perceive as being well dressed and neatly groomed. Appearance includes more than the choice of clothing. Self-confidence is projected by such items as the following:

- Freshly polished shoes
- Impeccable fingernails
- Clean jewelry in mint condition
- Well-maintained hair
- Good-looking teeth

A subtle mode of nonverbal communication is the use of time. Guarding time as a precious resource will help project an image of self-confidence and leadership. A statement such as "I can devote 15 minutes to your problem this Thursday at 4 P.M." connotes confidence and control. (However, under certain circumstances, too many of these statements might make a person appear unapproachable and inconsiderate.) Other ways of projecting power through the use of time include such behaviors as being prompt for meetings and starting and stopping meetings on time.

Group vs. Interpersonal Communication

For our purposes, interpersonal communication can be defined as the sharing of information between two persons. **Group communication** involves interaction among three or more individuals in a face-to-face situation. The three people have a common need that is satisfied by the exchange of information.[30]

Size of the Group

The term *group* has been defined as a number of persons gathered or classified together.[31] The definition of group communication does not set limits on the ultimate size of the group. However, practical considerations inherent in the definition do define a maximum number of people who would be able to interact effectively. Individuals attending a professional sporting event may have a commonality of interest, but they may not have an opportunity to become involved in a face-to-face situation where they can exchange information that satisfies a common need. If we compare the Super Bowl, with an attendance of 100,000 people, to a group of five fans planning a tailgate party before the game, it is easy to see that the size of the group can be a factor in determining the ability of individuals to communicate with each other.

Numerous scholars have examined the dynamics of group communications.[32] Various research has determined that the range between 3 and 20 is a natural size for purposes of defining group interactions.[33] Once the size of the group exceeds 20 people, the ability of individual members to influence each other diminishes. The nature of the gathering takes on more of the characteristics of a mass meeting or conference, in which one person may influence the group but the ability of individual members within the group to influence each other is limited. The size of the group has a direct bearing on the type of communication involved. Therefore, we will limit our discussion of communication to groups that do not exceed 20 individuals. Once the size of the group involved in the communication process has been determined, group interaction must be addressed.

Group Interaction

It is generally accepted by leading scholars that there are four phases in group interaction: (1) orientation, (2) conflict, (3) emergence, and (4) reinforcement.[34]

In the *orientation* phase, group members attempt to get to know each other and discover the problems that face the group. This may occur as strangers meet in a group for the first time, or it may happen with people who know each other and attend periodic meetings, such as roll call before the beginning of patrol shifts. In the latter situation, group members already know each other, and the orientation is aimed at common problems facing the group. These problems could range from new shift hours to planning a social gathering after the shift.

The second phase, *conflict,* involves disagreement among the members of the group. This phase is characterized by an atmosphere of polarization and controversy. Using the previous two examples, patrol officers may be sharply divided concerning the benefits of the new shift hours or have strong feelings regarding the location of the social gathering.

During the *emergence* phase of group interaction, there is more emphasis on positive statements. This phase allows dissenting members to save face by moving toward the majority's position. Officers who oppose the new shift hours may begin to find other benefits not previously discussed. Similarly, the location for the social gathering may be a third alternative that is acceptable to all members.

The final phase is *reinforcement.* In this phase, group members comment on the positive aspects of the group and its problem-solving ability.

The preceding discussion focused on the dynamics that normally occur in a problem-solving group; however, this interaction is usually present in most groups.[35] A police officer may determine what phase a group is in by listening to the types of comments being made by members of the group, then use that information to express personal views in the most effective manner. Group interaction is an important aspect of any organization. Law enforcement officers need to understand these group dynamics in order to carry out their duties effectively. Once a group has been established, certain communication networks begin to emerge.

Cross-Gender Communication

Generally, an examination of the differences in the ways men and women communicate would be confined to scholarly books in the area of linguistics or perhaps to books in the popular market that examine male/female relationships. However, it is essential

Figure 10.5
It is important for male officers and male superiors to understand that men and women in our society often communicate quite differently and may solve problems in dramatically different ways. In this photo, a male field training officer is interacting with a female officer.
(Courtesy of Bob Daemmrich/Bob Daemmrich Photography, Inc.)

that police supervisors who must evaluate the actions of their subordinates understand that men and women in our society often communicate quite differently and may solve problems in dramatically different ways. A failure to understand these differences can result in erroneous evaluations of police officers' actions and even result in unfair criticism by fellow officers and superiors (see Figure 10.5). The following scenario used to illustrate this point was witnessed by one of the authors.

> A young woman pulled up to the gas pumps at a filling station to fill up her car. While at the pumps, a young man pulled up behind her in his vehicle. She did not see him pull up. He walked up to her from behind, turned her around, and slapped her across the face. An off-duty police officer in plainclothes and in his personal car was filling up his car at an adjoining pump and witnessed the assault. He immediately identified himself as a police officer and advised the man he was under arrest. The officer requested that the filling station attendant call for a patrol unit. Prior to the arrival of the patrol unit, the assailant was placed in the front seat of the off-duty police officer's car unhandcuffed. Two uniformed officers arrived in separate police cars. One was a male, and the other was a female. The off-duty officer explained to the uniformed officers what he had witnessed and requested their assistance in filling out the necessary paperwork and transporting the assailant to the county jail. However, as the officers were conversing, the assailant, who was still agitated, was loudly expressing his anger at his female companion, who had apparently been out with another man the evening before.

The female officer walked over to the assailant and in a very conciliatory way attempted to calm him down, which did not work. After a couple of minutes, the male officer became agitated with the prisoner still "running his mouth." He walked over to the assailant and, in very close physical proximity, said very angrily, "If you don't shut your damn mouth, your ass is really going to be in trouble." At that point, the man became quiet.

Now let us assume this scenario was being witnessed by a traditionally trained male supervisor. He might believe the female officer should have been less conciliatory and more assertive and that her failure to be more assertive could have been interpreted as a sign of weakness by the arrested man, thereby encouraging him to become more belligerent. The supervisor might have assessed the male officer's approach as being more effective because he did, in fact, get the individual to quiet down and there were no further difficulties. However, let us assume, on the other hand, as sometimes happens, the individual being arrested was sufficiently agitated that, when the agitated male officer spoke to him, he in turn responded angrily and decided he would rather fight than go peaceably to jail. (Such scenarios are certainly not uncommon in police work.) If this had occurred, the outcome could have been quite different, and someone could have been injured or perhaps even killed.

The fact of the matter is the female officer was behaving in a way that women in our society are generally taught to behave when attempting to resolve a conflict—namely, in a nonconfrontational, conciliatory, nonphysical manner. In fact, this technique is recommended and employed in conflict resolution in many facets of police work.

Insights into the differences between the ways males and females communicate are important for police supervisors. If such insights are not present, the actions of female officers might be unfairly judged. Worse yet, if a female officer is criticized, she may believe that, in order to be accepted by her peers and her supervisor, she has to be overly aggressive, more confrontational, and more physical. This is not to suggest that assertiveness is not a positive quality for police officers to possess. However, like anything else, too much can lead to unfortunate consequences.

Communication with Other Cultures

Communication with other cultures is an area in law enforcement that is still evolving.[36] The United States is a melting pot (or, as some have characterized it, a salad) for other races and cultures. With the increase of Southeast Asian refugees and the rapidly increasing Hispanic population, the problem of communicating with persons who do not speak English as a primary language is critical within the law enforcement community.[37]

For example, Hispanics constitute the fastest-growing minority group in the United States. Population experts predict this group will outnumber African Americans by the end of the first quarter of the 21st century.

Development of "Survival Spanish for Police Officers" began in mid 1986 at Sam Houston State University in Texas in a cooperative effort between the police academy and

Figure 10.6

A Hispanic female and an African American female are discussing career opportunities in law enforcement with an African American female officer. Such officers not only can provide excellent role models for young minority females considering careers in law enforcement, but, because of their own status and gender, have considerable credibility.
(© Robert Maass/CORBIS)

a faculty member of the university's Spanish department. The cross-cultural training grew from a minor part of the language component when it became apparent that cultural barriers were just as important as the language barrier and had to be addressed in more detail.

Even with the awareness that minority populations continue to expand in the United States, the ability to communicate with them will continue to be a problem for most law enforcement agencies. Various departments are attempting to solve this problem in a number of ways. Some departments are hiring bilingual officers and offering additional compensation for their services, others maintain lists of qualified interpreters, and many others are including cultural awareness programs in their roll-call training (see Figure 10.6).

Methods of Responding in Language Differences

An officer who arrives at the scene of a crime and is confronted by a non-English-speaking citizen must attempt to gather information from that person. In some cases, this information must not only be gathered quickly but also be accurate. The citizen might be the victim of a crime or a witness who can provide a description of the suspect. One of the most obvious places to turn for assistance is family or neighbors who are bilingual. By using these individuals as on-the-scene interpreters, the officer can obtain the initial information quickly. The officer should ensure that not only the name of the witness, but also the name and address of the translator, are recorded. Follow-up investigations normally utilize the services of trained translators. In some cities, the courts, prosecutors, and police agencies maintain lists of interpreters to call on if the need arises. For example, in the main Los Angeles County Courthouse, interpreters are available for 78 languages.

However, there are inherent problems with using family or neighbors as interpreters. They may have difficulty with the English language, and some terms may be outside their knowledge or vocabulary. In addition, they may be biased and want to help the victim or witness, to the detriment of others. Because of these issues, departments should try to utilize bilingual officers. These are officers who are able to speak and write in both English and another language. In many cases, these officers not only speak a second language but are members of that ethnic group and are familiar with the history, traditions, and customs of the culture.

Many departments offer additional compensation to bilingual officers. Those officers respond to situations where their language skill is needed and provide an independent neutral interpretation without bias.

IN THE NEWS   Bilingual Law Enforcement Officers Bridge Cultural Divides

Law enforcement officials in Tampa, Florida, face the challenges of dealing with a community where up to 18,000 households are characterized as having no resident over the age of 13 with a basic understanding of English. Up to 80 percent of those households are Spanish-speaking. Bilingual officers and sheriff's deputies in Hillsborough County are crucial to addressing language and cultural issues that come up during routine patrols and calls for service. As a result, both the police department and the sheriff's office have been working to recruit bilingual officers who speak Spanish.

Officer Jeff Sanchez, center, is one of the Tampa Police Department's bilingual officers, who in combination with other officers are fluent in languages.
(Photo by Tampa [Florida] Tribune photographer Victor Junco)

Source: "The Power of Words: Tampa's Bilingual Law Enforcement Officers Bridge Cultural Divides," *Tampa Tribune,* October 21, 2004, p. 1.

Many departments provide both roll-call training and inservice courses that focuses on the cultures of minorities within their jurisdiction. This is another method by which officers can learn basic phrases of a different language. Some agencies will reimburse officers if they take and pass conversational language courses that enable them to interact with minority groups.

Other Multicultural Issues

The term **culture** can be applied to various population categories. However; it is normally associated with race and ethnicity. It is this diversity that both enriches and obstructs a law enforcement officer's involvement and interaction with other persons, groups, and cultures.

Officers should remember that most minorities have developed a sharp sense for detecting condescension, manipulation, and insincerity. There is no substitute for compassion as the foundation, and sincerity as its expression, in carrying out law enforcement services equally and fairly.

The first contact minorities have with law enforcement officers will either confirm or dispel suspicion as to how they will be treated. Proper pronunciation of a person's surname is an excellent place to begin contact with him or her. Surnames have histories and meanings that allow for conversation beyond the introduction. In working with immigrant, refugee, or native populations, it is helpful to learn a few words of greeting from those cultures. This willingness to go beyond what is comfortable and usual conveys the officer's intent to communicate.

Listening is fundamental to human relationships. The principles and manner of listening, however, differ among cultures. Asians and Pacific Islanders, for example, deflect direct eye contact in conversation as a sign of patient listening and deference. These groups therefore consider staring to be impolite and confrontational. Many Western cultures, on the other hand, value direct eye contact as a sign of sympathy or respect. Looking elsewhere is seen as disinterest or evasiveness. Misunderstanding in the communication process can occur if some allowance is not made for these differences. Multicultural issues must be understood by all law enforcement officers. Understanding that "different" does not mean "criminal" will assist officers attempting to communicate in an environment that continues to become more and more diverse.

Consider the following hypothetical scenario.

A cab driver from Nigeria runs a red light. An officer pulls him over in the next block, stopping the patrol car at least three car lengths behind the cab. Before the police officer can exit the patrol car, the cabbie gets out of his vehicle and approaches the officer. Talking rapidly in a high-pitched voice and making wild gestures, the cab driver appears to be out of control, or so the officer believes.[38]

As the officer steps from his car, he yells for the cab driver to stop, but the cabbie continues to walk toward the officer. When he is about 2 feet away, the officer orders the cabbie to step back and keep his hands to his sides. But the cab driver continues to babble and advance toward the officer. He does not make eye contact and appears to be talking to the ground.

Finally, the officer commands the cab driver to place his hands on the patrol vehicle and spread his feet. What began as a routine stop for a traffic violation culminates in charges of disorderly conduct and resisting arrest.

This scene typifies many of the encounters that take place daily in the United States between law enforcement personnel and people of other cultures. A simple traffic violation escalates out of control and becomes more than a matter of communication and common sense. It represents two icebergs—different cultures—colliding with devastating results.

To understand the final outcome, we need to examine the breakdown in nonverbal communication. First, most Americans know to remain seated in their vehicles when stopped by the police. But the cab driver exited his cab because he wanted to show respect and humility by not troubling the officer to leave his patrol car. The suspect used his own cultural rule of thumb (common sense), which conveyed a completely different message to the officer, who viewed it as a challenge to his authority.

The cab driver then ignored the command to "step back." Most likely, this did not make any sense to him because, in his eyes, he was not even close to the officer. The social distance for conversation in Nigeria is much closer than in the United States. For Nigerians, it may be less than 15 inches, whereas 2 feet represents a comfortable conversation zone for Americans.

Another nonverbal communication behavior is eye contact. Anglo Americans expect eye contact during conversation; the lack of it usually signifies deception, rudeness, defiance, or an attempt to end the conversation. In Nigeria, however, people often show respect and humility by averting their eyes. While the officer saw the cabbie defiantly "babbling to the ground," the Nigerian believed he was sending a message of respect and humility.

Most likely, the cab driver was not even aware of his exaggerated gestures, high-pitched tone of voice, or rapid speech. But the officer believed him to be "out of control," "unstable," and probably "dangerous." Had the cab driver been an Anglo American, the officer's reading of the cabbie's nonverbal behavior would have been correct.

One of the primary results of a breakdown in communications is a sense of being out of control, yet in law enforcement, control and action are tantamount. Unfortunately, the need for control combined with the need to act often makes a situation worse. "Don't just stand there. Do something!" is a very Anglo American admonition.

With the cab driver, the officer took control using his cultural common sense when it might have been more useful to look at what was actually taking place. Of course, in ambiguous and stressful situations, people seldom take time to truly examine the motivating behaviors in terms of culture. Rather, they view what is happening in terms of their own experiences, which is ethnocentric—and usually wrong.

Law enforcement professionals need to develop cultural empathy. They need to put themselves in other people's cultural shoes to understand what motivates their behavior. By understanding internal cultures, they usually can explain why situations develop the way they do. And if they know their own internal cultures, they also know the reasons behind their reactions and realize why they may feel out of control.

Here's another scenario.

During face-to-face negotiations with police at a local youth center, the leader of a gang of Mexican American adolescents suddenly begins to make long, impassioned speeches, punctuated with gestures and threats. Other members of the group then join in by shouting words of encouragement and agreement.

A police negotiator tries to settle the group and get the negotiations back on track. This only leads to more shouting from the Chicano gang members. They then accuse the police of bad faith, deception, and an unwillingness to "really negotiate."

Believing that the negotiations are breaking down, the police negotiator begins to leave, but not before telling the leader, "We can't negotiate until you get your act together where we can deal with one spokesperson in a rational discussion about the issues and relevant facts."

At this point, a Spanish-speaking officer interrupts. He tells the police negotiator, "Negotiations aren't breaking down. They've just begun."

Among members of certain ethnic groups, inflammatory words or accelerated speech are often used for effect, not intent. Such words and gestures are a means of getting attention and communicating feelings.

For example, during an argument, it would not be uncommon for a Mexican American to shout to his friend, "I'm going to kill you if you do that again." In the Anglo culture, this clearly demonstrates a threat to do harm. But in the context of the Hispanic culture, this simply conveys anger. Therefore, the Spanish word *matar* (to kill) is often used to show feelings, not intent.

In the gang scenario, the angry words merely indicated sincere emotional involvement by the gang members, not threats. But to the police negotiator, it appeared as if the gang was angry, irrational, and out of control. In reality, the emotional outburst showed that the gang members wanted to begin the negotiation process. To them, until an exchange of sincere emotional words occurred, no negotiations could take place.

Each culture presents arguments differently. For example, Anglo Americans tend to assume there is a short distance between an emotional, verbal expression of disagreement and a full-blown conflict. African Americans think otherwise.[39,40] For African Americans, stating a position with feeling shows sincerity. However, White Americans might interpret this as an indication of uncontrollable anger or instability and, even worse, an impending confrontation. For most African Americans, threatening movements, not angry words, indicate the start of a fight. In fact, some would argue that fights do not begin when people are talking or arguing but rather when they stop talking.

Anglo Americans expect an argument to be stated in a factual–inductive manner. For them, facts presented initially in a fairly unemotional way lead to a conclusion. The greater number of relevant facts at the onset, the more persuasive the argument.[41]

African Americans, on the other hand, tend to be more affective–intuitive. They begin with the emotional position, followed by a variety of facts somewhat poetically connected to support their conclusions. African Americans often view the mainstream presentation as insincere and impersonal, while White Americans see the Black presentation as irrational and too personal. Many times, arguments are lost because of differences in style, not substance. Deciding who's right and who is wrong depends on the cultural style of communication and thinking used.

Differences in argumentative styles add tension to any disagreement. As the Chicano gang leader presented his affective–intuitive argument, other gang members joined in with comments of encouragement, agreement, and support. To the police-negotiator, the gang members appeared to be united in a clique and on the verge of a confrontation.

Sometimes Anglo Americans react by withdrawing into a superfactual–inductive mode in an effort to calm things down. Unfortunately, the emphasis on facts, logical presentation, and lack of emotion often comes off as cold, condescending, and patronizing, which further shows a disinterest in the views of others.

Law enforcement officers should remember that racial and cultural perceptions affect attitudes and motivate behavior. In close-knit ethnic communities, avoiding shame is very important. Then, too, loss of individual dignity and respect often comes with loss of economic means and wealth. In the community policing model described in Chapter 2, Policing Today, police officers are being asked to confront a myriad of social and criminal problems (e.g., juvenile runaways, neighborhood disputes, vagrants, gangs, and homeless people). They often find themselves acting the role of mediator or facilitator between conflicting or competing groups. Their goal is to bring about compromise and share other potential resources in the community.

In complex urban societies, there is no assumption of indirect responsibility. If a matter must be resolved by intervention, then the police must appear neutral and service-oriented for the greater good. Resolution is determined by a decision of right or wrong based on the facts or merits of the case. Compromise and respect for individual dignity, racial pride, and cultural heritage must characterize the communication process of the police.

Because of naive assumptions, the criminal justice community seldom views cross-cultural awareness and training as vital, yet as society and the law enforcement workforce become more diverse, the ability to manage cultural diversity becomes essential. Those agencies that do not proactively develop cultural knowledge and skills fail to serve the needs of their communities. More importantly, however, they lose the opportunity to increase the effectiveness of their officers.

Unfortunately, cross-cultural training in law enforcement often occurs after an incident involving cross-cultural conflict. If provided, this training can be characterized as a quick fix, a once-in-a-lifetime happening, when in reality it should be an ongoing process of developing awareness, knowledge, and skills.

At the very least, officers should know what terms are the least offensive when referring to ethnic or racial groups in their communities. For example, most Asians prefer not to be called Orientals. It is more appropriate to refer to their nationality of origin, such as Korean American, assuming the officer is positive about their nationality of origin.

Likewise, very few Spanish speakers would refer to themselves as Hispanics. Instead, the term "Chicano" is usually used by Mexican Americans, while the term

"Latino" is preferred by those from Central America. Some would rather be identified by their nationality of origin, such as Guatemalan or Salvadoran.

Many American Indians resent the term "Native American" because it was invented by the U.S. government. They would prefer being called American Indian or being known by their tribal ancestry, such as Crow, Menominee, or Winnebago.

The terms "Black American" and "African American" can usually be used interchangeably. However, "African American" is more commonly used among younger people.

Law enforcement executives need to weave cross-cultural awareness into all aspects of law enforcement training and realize it is not enough to bring in a "gender expert" after someone files sexual harassment charges or a "race expert" after a racial incident occurs. Three-hour workshops on a specific topic do not solve problems. Cross-cultural issues are interrelated; they cannot be disconnected.

Developing a Culturally Aware Workforce

What can the law enforcement community do to ensure a more culturally aware workforce? To begin, law enforcement professionals must know their own culture. All personnel need to appreciate the impact of their individual cultures on their values and behaviors. Sometimes, the best way to gain this knowledge is by intensively interacting with those who are culturally different. However, law enforcement professionals must always bear in mind that culture, by definition, is a generalization. Cultural rules or patterns never apply to everyone in every situation.

The next step is to learn about the different cultures found within the agency and in the community. However, no one should rely on culturally specific "guidebooks" or simplistic "dos and don'ts" lists. While such approaches to cultural awareness are tempting, they do not provide sufficient insight and are often counterproductive.

First, no guidebook can be absolutely accurate, and many cover important issues in abstract or generic terms. For example, several nations constitute Southeast Asia. Therefore, when promoting cultural awareness, law enforcement agencies should concentrate on the nationality that is predominant within their respective communities—that is, Vietnamese, Laotian, Cambodian, and so on. At the same time, these agencies should keep in mind that cultures are complex and changing. Managing cultural diversity also means being able to adjust to the transformations that might be occurring within the ethnic community.

Quick
FACTS ▸▸ Cultural Diversity Training in Police Academies Is the Norm

Ninety-eight percent of police training academies included cultural diversity as a core component of their curriculum in 2006, the last year for which data were available. A median of 11 hours of instruction in cultural diversity was reported.

Source: Brian A. Reaves, *State and Local Law Enforcement Training Academies, 2006* (Washington, DC: Bureau of Justice Statistics, 2006), p. 6.

Second, relying on a guidebook approach can be disastrous if it does not provide the answers needed to questions arising during a crisis situation. It is much more useful to have a broad framework from which to operate when analyzing and interpreting any situation. Such a framework should focus on internal, not just external, culture. Knowing values, beliefs, behaviors, and thought patterns can only assist law enforcement professionals when dealing with members of ethnic communities.

Law enforcement professionals should also understand the dynamics of cross-cultural communication, adjustment, and conflict. When communication breaks down, frustration sets in. When this happens, law enforcement reacts. This presents a potentially dangerous situation for officers because of the emphasis placed on always being in control. Understanding the process of cross-cultural interaction gives a sense of control and allows for the development of coping strategies.

Finally, law enforcement professionals should develop cross-cultural communicative, analytic, and interpretive skills. Merely having a casual familiarity about the history and religion of a particular culture or ethnic group will not in and of itself allow police officers to communicate effectively or understand someone from that group. Although the ability to communicate effectively is often best learned through experience, police officers can also gain valuable insights into the various facets of these groups by inviting respected leaders from these groups to participate in police academy training or specifically designed in-service training course. All related training should be designed to provide insights into important characteristics of these groups. These can also be accomplished by reading authoritative books about these groups or by listening to lectures from experts in the field. All of these combined will assist law enforcement officers in analyzing and understanding the ways in which people of different cultures or ethnic groups communicate and resolve conflict.

IN THE NEWS | Hartford, Connecticut, Police Department Implements Cultural Sensitivity Training

Cultural sensitivity training was ordered for all Hartford, Connecticut, police supervisors following a complaint from an officer who claimed his lieutenant had issued him racially charged instructions during a roll call. The 2-hour training block put together by the department and one of Hartford's community organizations had already been given to community service officers, their supervisors, and the incoming recruit class when Chief Patrick J. Harnett received a written complaint from Officer John Szewczyk, Jr., stating that his supervisor, Lieutenant Stephen Miele, had told him to go after people who do not belong downtown. Officers had been told to be more aggressive in an attempt to stanch an increase in downtown burglaries. When Szewczyk asked Miele exactly what he meant, the officer said he was told, "If they aren't white and they aren't wearing a suit I'd better have them in the back of my car and find something to arrest them for." An internal investigation found insufficient evidence to sustain the allegation of biased policing; however, Miele was demoted to sergeant for having retaliated against Szewczyk and another officer who sought an explanation of his orders. In addition to diversity training, Harnett promised a revision of the agency's general orders clarifying language on racial profiling and officers' encounters with residents.

Source: "Hartford Takes Another Crack at Cultural Sensitivity Training," *Law Enforcement News,* Fall 2004, pp. 1, 10.

Communicating Across Generations

It is generally accepted by those who do research in the area of communications that the biggest divide in the communication process does not always result because of gender or cultural differences but rather sometimes from differences in the way the various generations communicate. In Chapter 9, Human Resource Management, certain important characteristics were discussed about the various generations; however, this chapter focuses primarily on the communication characteristics of the two generations that make up most of the employees in police departments today—namely, Generation X (those born between 1965 to 1980) and Generation Y or Millennials, born between 1981 and 1994.

Some Generalizations

There are certain characteristics each of these two groups have in their communication style and it is important for each group to be aware of the differences so miscommunications are less likely to occur. The following represent what can best be described as some broad but useful generalizations about the communication styles of these two groups.

Generation X

The generation of officers falling into this category have grown up with sophisticated communications technology and are most certainly different from previous generations. Their way of thinking has been characterized as having an information age mindset. Some of the characteristics of this mindset include:

- *Computers are not technology*—Officers falling into this category have never known life without computers and the Internet. To them the computer is an assumed part of life.
- *The Internet is considered better than TV*—In recent years, the number of hours spent watching TV by this group has declined, being supplanted by time spent online. Among the reason for the changes are interactivity and the increased use of the Internet for socializing.
- *Doing is more important than knowing*—Knowledge is no longer perceived to be the ultimate goal, particularly in light of the fact that the half-life in information is so short. Results and actions are considered more important than the accumulation of facts.
- *Learning more closely resembles Nintendo than logic*—Nintendo symbolizes a trial-and-error approach to solving problems; losing is the fastest way to mastering a game because losing represents learning. This contrasts with the problem-solving approaches of previous generations, who employ a more logical, rule-based approach.
- *Multitasking is a way of life*—Generation X officers appear to be quite comfortable when simultaneously engaged in multiple activities, such as listening to music, texting, and talking on the phone. **Multitasking** may also be a response to information overload.
- *Typing is preferred to handwriting*—Generation X officers prefer typing to handwriting and many admit their handwriting is atrocious. Penmanship has been superseded by keyboard skills.

- *Staying connected is essential*—Generation X officers stay in touch both on and off duty via multiple devices, as they move throughout the day. Cell phones, smart phones, personal digital assistants (PDAs), netbooks, Blackberries, tablets and pads, and computers ensure they remain connected anyplace and anytime. As the network becomes more ubiquitous, increasing numbers of Generation Xers participate in real-time dialogues from anywhere using a variety of devices.
- *There is zero tolerance for delays*—Having grown up in a culture that places a strong demand on immediacy, Generation Xers have little tolerance for delays. They expect services to be available 24/7 in a variety of modes (cell phone, texting, social media (Facebook, etc.), Twitter, e-mail, camera phone, SKYPE, and in person) and that responses will be quick.[42] This generation is equally comfortable giving feedback to others.
- *They are comfortable in multicultural settings*—This group tends to work well in **multicultural settings** and takes a pragmatic approach to accomplishing tasks.[43]
- *They have a need for effective mentoring*—A mentoring program is essential. They seem to like feedback on their performance and appreciate the opportunity to create new ways to accomplish tasks. It is important to inform Generation Xers of the agency's expectations and how their progress will be measured. They work best when they are informed of the desired outcome and given specific instructions on how to achieve it.[44]

Generation Y

Many officers from Generation Y, also called Millennials, are just beginning to enter law enforcement. This is a generation that has been raised in one of the most child-centric times in our history. Perhaps because they were showered with attention and felt high expectation from their parents, they display a great deal of self confidence, to the point that they have sometimes been characterized as having an attitude of entitlement. They are certainly the most technically literate generation ever because they have spent their entire lives working with the Internet, computer, cell phones, Blackberries, PDAs, netbooks, digital readers, etc.

Like Generation X officers, they are good multitaskers, having juggled sports, school, and social interests as children, and can be expected to work hard. Millennials seem to expect structure in the workplace. They acknowledge and respect positions and titles and want a relationship with their superiors.

Because Generation Yers are new to the professional workplace, no matter how smart and confident they are, they are definitely in need of mentoring. Also, they will respond well to the personal attention. Because they appreciate structure and stability, mentoring Millennials should be more formal, with set meetings and a more authoritative attitude on the mentor's part.

They prefer lots of challenges but also need the structure to back it up. This means breaking down goals into steps, as well as offering any necessary resources and information they will need to meet the challenge. Consideration should be given to

mentoring Millennials in groups because they work well in team situations. In this kind of a setting they can act as each other's resources or peer mentors.[45]

Generational Differences in Formal and Informal Styles of Communication

A particular problem area is that involving forms of address. For example, informal talk or an over familiarization with superiors from Generation Y (Millennials) may be offensive and seem somewhat disrespectful to Generation X officers. In many instances, the younger officers who engage in this informal conversation do not mean to be disrespectful, but just have a more informal and casual style of communicating with friends and co-workers.

One thing is certain: Some things are important to nearly all employees, regardless of age. Simple gestures like listening, acknowledging what others have said, and acting on their suggestions when appropriate are all signs of respect. People tend to appreciate being addressed with a "hello" or a "good-bye," or being greeted by name. Saying something like "yo, dawg" (meaning a friend and not a member of the canine variety) is probably not going to be appreciated by all generations.

The best solution is to try to be considerate of the views of members of other generations. If someone from another generation says something problematic, or their manner or tone is causing a problem, efforts should be made to discuss it openly to resolve the situation.[46]

Generational Lingo

A Millennial employee may use a term such as "phat" (excellent or great) and mean it as a compliment. However an older co-worker may hear it as "fat" and take it as an insult. This is not meant to be an insult. However, unless it is understood, intergenerational communication can jeopardize workplace morale and productivity when employees of different generations miscommunicate.[47]

Creeping Computerese

Technology is not just changing the ways we communicate but is also changing the words or phrases we use when we communicate. For example, items of computerese, which many see as acceptable in e-mail or instant messaging, are starting to find their way into nonelectronic communication as well. Computerese, such as *btw* (by the way) or *imo* (in my opinion), is somewhat acceptable to many generations when inserted in an e-mail but, as of yet, may not be acceptable to older generations, especially when included in more formal written memos. Computer emoticons (i.e., animated smiley faces used in e-mail) to indicate humor, for example, are more likely to be acceptable to younger generations.[48]

What Is Said Is Not Always What Is Heard

Regardless of the generational category an employee falls into, it is important to understand that what is said needs to be completely understood by each generation. It is advisable to anticipate intergenerational miscommunications as much as possible and tailor all messages to be as clear as possible to all generations.[49]

Learning how to communicate across the generations can eliminate many of the misunderstandings. If a Generation X manager says, "We need to get this report written," another Generation X employee would correctly interpret this as a nicely stated command. On the other hand, if that same Generation X manager made the same statement to a Millennial, the Millennial could well hear this comment as an observation and not an order. Thus, this kind of cross-generational communication is not always clear. It is important to understand that what a person in one generation hears may not be what the person of another generation means to say or to communicate.

CONCLUSION

There is considerable evidence to support the premise that for administrators to be truly effective they must understand the dynamics involved in both organizational as well as interpersonal communication. It is consistently true that those administrators who are the most effective are those who have the most highly developed and refined communication skills.

CHAPTER REVIEW

1. Discuss the elements that make up the communication process.
2. Describe sender-caused barriers, receiver-caused barriers, and other barriers in communications.
3. List and describe the five types of organizational downward communication.
4. What is the order of effective communication from most effective to least effective?
5. What have psychologists said about the potential problems associated with an administrator's dependence upon technology in the communication process?
6. What suggestions were made for dynamic and persuasive oral and written communication?
7. What are the major differences between the way that female and male officers communicate, especially during conflict resolution?
8. What are the two main issues in communication between law enforcement and citizens from other cultures, and how should law enforcement agencies address these challenges?
9. What are the major characteristics of the ways in which Generation X officers communicate?
10. What are the major characteristics of the ways in which Generation Y (Millennial) officers communicate?

KEY TERMS

communication: the process by which senders and receivers interact in both professional and social contexts.

culture: the beliefs and behaviors characteristic to a particular ethnic, racial, or other population.

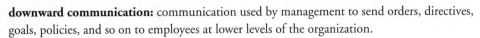

downward communication: communication used by management to send orders, directives, goals, policies, and so on to employees at lower levels of the organization.

feedback: messages sent from the receiver to the sender in a communication.

grapevine: a system of informal information that meanders across organizational lines.

group communication: interaction among three or more individuals in a face-to-face situation where all parties have a common need that is satisfied by the exchange of information.

horizontal communication: communication among peers.

interpersonal communication: the process of message transmitting between two people to create a sustained shared meaning.

mentoring: individuals selected to train, as well as provide role models to individuals new to a particular position.

multicultural settings: the organizational environment in which there are individuals from numerous cultures, and racial and religious backgrounds.

multitasking: engaging in multiple activities such as listening to music, working on the computer, and talking on the phone.

noise: anything that disrupts communication, including the attitudes, the emotions of the receiver, such as stress, fear, negative attitudes, and low motivation.

upward communication: communication used by lower-level employees.

ENDNOTES

[1] A. J. DuBrin, *Human Relations: Interpersonal Job-Oriented Skills,* 8th ed. (Upper Saddle River, N.J.: Prentice Hall, 2004), pp. 42–46.

[2] P. V. Lewis, *Organizational Communication: The Essence of Effective Management* (Columbus, Ohio: Grid, 1975), p. 36.

[3] Ibid., pp. 36–37.

[4] Ibid., pp. 37–38.

[5] D. Katz and R. L. Kahn, *The Social Psychology of Organizations* (New York: John Wiley & Sons, 1966), p. 239, as cited in Lewis, *Organizational Communication,* p. 38.

[6] Lewis, *Organizational Communication,* p. 38.

[7] R. L. Smith, G. M. Richetto, and J. P. Zima, "Organizational Behavior: An Approach to Human Communication," in *Readings in Interpersonal and Organizational Communication,* 3rd ed., ed. R. C. Huseman, C. M. Logue, and D. L. Freshley (Boston: Holbrook Press, 1977), p. 11.

[8] T. L. Dahle, "An Objective and Comparative Study of Five Methods of Transmitting Information to Business and Industrial Employees" (Ph.D. diss., Purdue University, 1954), as cited in Smith et al. "Organizational Behavior," p. 12.

[9] E. Planty and W. Machaver, "Upward Communications: A Project in Executive Development," *Personnel* 28 (January 1952), pp. 304–319.

[10] R. K. Allen, *Organizational Management through Communication* (New York: Harper & Row, 1977), pp. 77–79.

[11] H. Fayol, *General and Industrial Administration* (New York: Pitman, 1949), p. 34.

[12] Allen, *Organizational Management,* p. 78.

[13] Ibid., pp. 78–79.

[14] K. Davis, "Management Communication and the Grapevine," *Harvard Business Review* (September–October 1953), pp. 43–49, as cited by Lewis, *Organizational Communication,* p. 41.

[15] Lewis, *Organizational Communication,* pp. 41–42.

468   PART THREE   THE MANAGEMENT OF POLICE ORGANIZATIONS

[16] Ricky W. Griffin, *Fundamentals of Management* (Boston: Houghton Mifflin Company, 2008), pp. 363–367.

[17] Eric W. Welch and Shelley Fulla, "Virtual Interactivity Between Government and Citizens: The Chicago Police Department's Citizen ICAM Application Demonstration Case," *Political Communication* 22, no. 2 (2005), pp. 226–227.

[18] Ibid., pp. 229–230.

[19] Andrew J. Dubrin, *Leadership* (New York: Houghton Mifflin, 2004), pp. 364–371, 373, 374.

[20] James M. Kouzes and Barry Z. Posner, *The Leadership Challenge: How to Get Extraordinary Things Done in Organizations* (San Francisco: Jossey-Bass, 1987), p. 118.

[21] Roberta H. Krapels and Vanessa D. Arnold, "Speaker Credibility in Persuasive Work Situations," *Business Education Forum* (December 1997), pp. 24–25.

[22] Stephen P. Robbins and Phillip L. Hunsaker, *Training in Interpersonal Skills: Tips for Managing People at Work* (Upper Saddle River, N.J.: Prentice Hall, 1996), p. 115.

[23] Refer to Jay A. Conger, *Winning 'Em Over: The New Model for Management in the Age of Persuasion* (New York: Simon & Schuster, 2001).

[24] From 2000 through 2009 469 deaths. "Causes of Law Enforcement Deaths," From the National Law Enforcement Officers Memorial Fund website, available from http://www.nleomf.org/facts/officer-fatalities-data/causes.html

[25] Michael W. Mercer, "How to Make a Fantastic Impression," *HR Magazine,* March 1993, p. 49.

[26] Deborah Tannen, "The Power of Talk: Who Gets Heard and Why?" *Harvard Business Review* (September–October 1995), pp. 138–148.

[27] Ibid, "How You Speak Shows Where You Rank," *Fortune,* February 2, 1998, p. 156; "Frame Your Persuasive Appeal," *Executive Strategies,* September 1998, p. 7; "Weed Out Wimpy Words: Speak Up without Backpedaling, Qualifying," *Working Smart,* March 2000, p. 2.

[28] Albert Mehrabian and M. Wiener, "Decoding Inconsistent Communications," *Journal of Personality and Social Psychology* 6 (1947), pp. 109–114.

[29] Several of these suggestions are from *Body Language for Business Success* (New York: National Institute for Business Management, 1989), pp. 2–29 and "Attention All Monotonous Speakers," *Working Smart,* March 1998, p. 1.

[30] Harvey Wallace, Cliff Roberson, and Craig Steckler, *Written and Interpersonal Communication Methods for Law Enforcement* (Upper Saddle River, N.J.: Prentice Hall, 2001), pp. 39, 40. Reprinted by permission of Pearson Education, Inc., Upper Saddle River, N.J.

[31] *Webster's New World Dictionary* (New York: Warner Books, 1990), p. 262.

[32] See Michael Burgoon, Judee K. Heston, and James McCroskey, *Small Group Communication: A Functional Approach* (New York: Holt, Rinehart & Winston, 1974), pp. 2–3, 12, 39.

[33] See Robert Ardrey, *The Social Contract* (New York: Atheneum, 1970), p. 368, where the author theorizes that the range for a natural group is 11 or 12, and Marvin E. Shaw, *Group Dynamics* (New York: McGraw-Hill, 1971), which places the maximum number of persons at 20.

[34] B. Aubrey Fisher, "Decision Emergence: Phase in Group Decision-Making," *Speech Monographs* 37 (1970), pp. 53–66.

[35] Field, "The Abilene Paradox," p. 89.

[36] Harvey Wallace, Cliff Roberson, and Craig Steckler, *Written and Interpersonal Communication Methods for Law Enforcement* (Upper Saddle River, N.J.: Prentice Hall, 2001), pp. 39, 40. (This discussion of communications with other cultures was adapted with permission from this source.)

[37] Spanish is not the only language that officers will encounter. For a discussion of law enforcement agencies' experiences with Chinese, see C. Fredric Anderson and Henriettee Liu Levy, "A Guide to Chinese Names," *FBI Law Enforcement Bulletin,* March 1992, p. 10.

[38] This section is adapted from Brian K. Ogawa, *Focus on the Future: A Prosecutor's Guide for Victim Assistance* (Washington, D.C.: National Victim Center, 1994).

[39] G. Weaver, "Law Enforcement in a Culturally Diverse Society," *FBI Law Enforcement Bulletin,* September 1992, pp. 3–7. (This discussion of cross-cultural diversity in communication was taken with modification from this source.)

[40] Thomas Kochman, *Black and White Styles in Conflict* (Chicago: University of Chicago Press, 1981).

[41] Edmund Glenn, D. Witmeyer, and K. Stevenson, "Cultural Styles of Persuasion," *International Journal of Intercultural Communication* 1 (1977), pp. 52–66.

[42] Diana Oblinger, "Boomers & Gen-Xers, and Millennials: Understanding the New Students," *Educause Review* (July/August, 2003), p. 40.

[43] Diane Thielfoldt and Devon Cheef, "Generation X and the Millennials: What You Need to Know About Mentoring the New Generations," *Law Practice Today* (2010).

[44] Ibid.

[45] Ibid.

[46] Linda A. Panszczyk, *HR How-to: Intergenerational Issues* (Chicago, IL: CCH KnowledgePoint, 2004) p. 168.

[47] Ibid., pp. 168–170.

[48] Ibid., p. 170.

[49] Ibid., pp. 170–171.

11

Labor Relations

"You, a lowly policeman, is going to tell me how to run my department! . . . Get out!" and you had to go; he hated me. . . .
—Rank-and-file organization leader John Cassese on an early meeting with New York City Police Commissioner Kennedy

Objectives

- Identify and briefly discuss the seven major events that led to public sector collective bargaining.

- Discuss the impact of police unions on the community.

- Explain the general structure of laws governing collective bargaining for law enforcement officers.

- Analyze how a bargaining relationship is established.

- Describe how a union begins an organization drive.

- Identify who generally serves on management and union teams during negotiations.

- Describe the four potential major types of job actions a police union can take and the appropriate administrative actions that can be taken in response by police administrators.

OUTLINE

Introduction

No single force in the past 50 years has had a greater impact on the administration of police agencies than collective bargaining by officers. Police unions represent a major force with which police managers must reckon. It is important for the police administrator to possess the following information in order to enhance their effectiveness in dealing with police unions: (1) the historical aspects of the creation of police unions in the United States, (2) the impact police unions have had on their communities and on their respective agencies, (3) the general structure of laws governing collective bargaining for law enforcement officers, (4) how a bargaining relationship is formed, (5) the various job actions that police unions will sometimes take when they are dissatisfied with the negotiation process or other political issues arising in the community, and (6) the most efficient ways for police administrators to handle job actions.

Unionization of the Police: A Historical Perspective

From 1959 through the 1970s, a number of events combined to foster public-sector collective bargaining. These significant forces were (1) the needs of labor organizations, (2) the reduction of legal barriers, (3) police frustration with the perceived lack of support for their "war on crime," (4) personnel practices in police agencies, (5) salaries and benefits, (6) violence directed at the police, and (7) the success of other groups.[1]

The Needs of Labor Organizations

The attention of labor organizations was devoted almost entirely to the private sector until the 1960s. However, as the opportunity to gain new members became increasingly constrained because of the extensive organization of industrial workers, unions cast about for new markets, and statistics such as these impressed them: "Government employment accounts for more than 22 million jobs—17 percent of total U.S. employment," in 2009.[2] That figure is up from 13 million employees on government payrolls in the 1970s.[3] Thus, as with any organization that achieves its primary objective, labor groups redefined their sphere of interest to include public employees. Concurrently, there were stirrings among public employees to use collective action to improve their lot.

The Reduction of Legal Barriers

Although workers in the private sector had been given the right to bargain collectively under the federal National Labor Relations Act of 1935, it was another quarter-century before the first state enacted even modest bargaining rights for public employees.

Quick
FACTS ▸▸ The Boston Police Strike of 1919 and Its Aftermath

The first campaign to organize the police started shortly after World War I, when the American Federation of Labor (AFL) reversed a long-standing policy and issued charters to police unions in Boston, Washington, D.C., and about 30 other cities. August Vollmer and many other police chiefs promptly condemned this move. Following the logic of the military analogy, they insisted that policemen had no more right to join a union than soldiers and sailors and no more right to affiliate with the AFL than the National Association of Manufacturers. This argument was lost on thousands of policemen who were caught up in a nationwide inflation that had just about doubled the cost of living since the outbreak of World War I and were unable to make ends meet, and the rank and file were fed up with the indifference of the authorities. Capitalizing on this resentment, the fledgling unions signed up about six out of seven policemen in Washington, three out of four in Boston, and a similar proportion in a dozen or so other cities.

Their success was short-lived. Commissioner E.U. Curtis refused to recognize the Boston police union, forbade the rank and file to join it, and filed charges against several union officials, and Commissioner Louis Brownlow ordered the Washington police to quit the union or face dismissal. The Washington union secured a temporary injunction that stayed Brownlow's order. But when Commissioner Curtis (ignoring a settlement worked out by a citizen's committee that called on the union to give up its charter and was endorsed by the union officials) suspended more than a dozen policemen, roughly three-quarters of the force went out on strike. The strike—or to be more accurate, the newspaper accounts of it, which exaggerated the accompanying surge of crime and violence—generated a furor not only in Massachusetts but throughout the nation. On orders from Governor Calvin Coolidge, the Commonwealth dismissed the strikers and destroyed the union, an action hailed by President Woodrow Wilson, who claimed that policemen had the same obligation as soldiers branded the walkout "a crime against civilization." Shortly thereafter, the Congress, which had opposed the Washington union from its inception, upheld Brownlow's ultimatum, and by 1920 the organizing effort was defunct.

Source: Robert M. Fogleson, *Big-City Police* (Cambridge, MA: Harvard University Press, 1977), pp. 193–195.

Beginning with the granting of public-sector collective bargaining rights in Wisconsin in 1959, many of the legal barriers that had been erected in the wake of the Boston police strike of 1919 began to tumble.

Other states that also extended such rights to at least some classes of employees at an early date included California (1961) and Connecticut, Delaware, Massachusetts, Michigan, Oregon, Washington, and Wyoming, all in 1965. Many other states followed this lead, particularly from 1967 to 1974.[4] President John F. Kennedy granted limited collective bargaining rights to federal workers in 1962 by Executive Order 10988. The courts, too, were active in removing barriers; for example, in *Atkins v. City of Charlotte* (1969), the U.S. District Court struck down a portion of a North Carolina statute prohibiting being or becoming a union member as an infringement on the First Amendment right to free association.[5] While *Atkins* involved firefighters, the federal courts reached similar conclusions involving Atlanta police officers in *Melton v. City of Atlanta* (1971)[6] and a Colorado deputy sheriff in *Lontine v. VanCleave* (1973).[7]

Police Frustration with the Perceived Lack of Support for Their War on Crime

Historically, the police have felt isolated in their effort to control crime. This stems from two factors: perceived public hostility and the impact of the due process revolution.

The police perceive there is a great deal more public hostility than actually exists. Illustrative of this is a survey of one big-city department, which found that over 70 percent of the officers had an acute sense of citizen hostility or contempt.[8] In contrast, a survey conducted by the National Opinion Research Center revealed that 77 percent of the respondents felt the police were doing a "very good" or "pretty good" job of protecting people in their neighborhoods, and a Gallup poll showed that 70 percent of the public had a great deal of respect for the police.[9] These data notwithstanding, the police saw the public as hostile, and the most persuasive "evidence" of this emerged in the attempts to create civilian review boards, which carried several latent messages to police officers. First, it created anger with its implied allegation that the police could not, or would not, keep their own house in order. Second, it fostered the notion that politicians were ready to "throw the police to wolves" and thus were part of "them."

Particularly among street-level officers, the reaction of the police to the whirlwind of Supreme Court decisions, discussed in Chapter 4, Politics and Police Administration, was one of dismay at being "handcuffed" in attempts to control crime. It tended to alienate the police from the Supreme Court and to contribute to a general feeling that social institutions that should support the police effort in combating crime were, instead, at odds with that effort.

Personnel Practices in Police Agencies

Past practices become precedent, precedent becomes tradition, and tradition in turn becomes the mighty anchor of many organizations. By the late 1960s, the tendency to question the appropriateness of certain traditions was pervasive. Police rank-and-file members were no exception. This tendency was heightened by the increased educational achievement of police officers. Although management's general performance was often judged to be suspect, traditional personnel practices were the greatest concern, as these directly affected the individual officer.

Among the practices that were most distasteful to rank-and-file members were: the requirement to attend, unpaid, a 30-minute roll call immediately before the 8-hour tour of duty; uncompensated court attendance during off-duty time; short-notice changes in shift assignments; having to return to the station from home for minor matters, such as signing reports without pay or compensatory time for such periods; favoritism in both work assignments and selection for attendance at prestigious police training schools; and arbitrary disciplinary procedures. Gradually, the gap between officers and management widened. Officers began turning to employee organizations to rectify collectively the shortcomings of their circumstances. Subsequently, the solidarity of police officers was to prove a great benefit to employee organizations.

Salaries and Benefits

As did other government workers in the 1960s, police officers felt their salaries, fringe benefits, and working conditions were not adequate. In 1961, mining production workers were averaging $111 a week in earnings, lithographers $114, tire and inner-tube producers $127, and telephone line construction workers $133,[10] whereas the pay of police officers averaged far less. Even by 1965, the salary range for patrol officers in the larger cities—those with more than 100,000 in population—was only between $5,763, and $6,919.[11] The rank-and-file members believed increasingly that, if what was fairly theirs would not be given willingly, they would fight for it. In New York City, the Patrolmen's Benevolent Association (PBA) was believed to have been instrumental, from 1958 to 1969, in increasing entry-level salaries from $5,800 to $11,000 per year; obtaining longevity pay, shift differential pay, and improved retirement benefits; and increasing the death benefit from $400 to $16,500.[12] In 1968, the Boston PBA, in negotiating its first contract—which required mediation—obtained increased benefits for its members, such as an annual increase of $1,010; time and a half for all overtime, including court appearances; and 12 paid holidays.[13] However, in recent years, police unions have been called upon not only to fight for pay raises for their members but also to oppose threatened pay cuts (see Figure 11.1).

Violence Directed at the Police

In 1964, there were 9.9 assaults per 100 officers; in 1969, this figure rose to 16.9. Before 1968, the killing of police officers by preplanned ambushes was unheard of; in that year, there were seven such incidents.[14] The escalating violence had considerable psychological impact on the police, who saw themselves as symbolic targets of activists attacking institutional authority. Rank-and-file members began pressing for body armor, special training, the placement of special weapons in police cars, and sharply increased death benefits.

Figure 11.1
San Diego police officers stand in support of their union representative during a city council meeting recently in San Diego. San Francisco police officers are wondering how they will meet their financial commitments if they are forced to take a 6.5 percent pay cut to help the city out of its financial crisis.
(Courtesy of Denis Poroy/AP Wide World Photos)

The Success of Other Groups

During the 1960s the police witnessed mass demonstrations on college campuses that used many of the tactics associated with the Civil Rights movement. Among the campus demonstrations that were highly publicized were the University of Chicago (1965), Columbia University (1968), and San Francisco State College (1969). By 1970, campus demonstrations reached the point that, within 10 days of President Richard Nixon's announcement to invade enemy sanctuaries in Cambodia, a total of 448 campuses were either shut down or otherwise affected by campus unrest.[15]

The Impact of Police Unions on the Community

There is little question that the presence of a police union in a community has an impact both upon the police department as well as the community it serves. There are essentially four areas that need to be examined in order to fully understand and appreciate the impact of police unions, both within their respective agencies as well as in the community. These include the impact on discipline and accountability, the impact on the police subculture, the impact on city or county finances, and the impact on politics.

Impact on Discipline and Accountability

The impact of police unions on discipline and accountability is arguably the issue that causes the greatest concern among community activists, public officials, and many police executives. The impact is felt in several different ways.[16]

For example, police unions play a role in reinforcing the norms of police subculture. One of the most important aspects of this involves the **code of silence**, which results in the refusal of officers to testify against other officers who are accused of misconduct. The code has been widely cited as perhaps the most familiar obstacle to the effective investigation of alleged allegations of misconduct against officers.[17] Missing from these discussions, however, is any analysis of the extent to which the police union sustains the code of silence by (1) providing tangible support for accused officers in the form of experienced legal representation, (2) providing moral support for accused officers through organized group solidarity, and (3) negotiating a contract that inhibits thorough investigations of misconduct. As an example, there are specific provisions in many collective bargaining agreements that inhibit investigations. Police union contract provisions typically specify detailed procedures for the investigation of alleged misconduct, including the time, place, and manner of interviews or interrogations. Many, if not most of these provisions represent legitimate due process protections for employees. These include the right to notice of charges, the right to legal representation, the right to a hearing, and the right to an appeal, among others.[18]

About 14 states also have state Police Officers Bills of Rights (POBR), which contain provisions similar to those in police union contracts. In their content analysis of these statutes, there are a few provisions that inhibit accountability. For example, the Maryland POBR prohibits questioning of officers by investigators who are not sworn officers. Such a prohibition precludes the investigation of complaints by an independent citizen oversight agency.[19]

Police unions have had a major impact on the development of citizen oversight agencies, whether in the form of civilian review board or police auditors, or some other arrangement. Most famously, pressure by the local police unions was responsible for the demise of the two major civilian review boards in the 1960s, in New York City and Philadelphia.[20]

Impact on the Police Subculture

Another important area of policing is the so-called police subculture. The Christopher Commission report on the Los Angeles Police Department, for example, contains a chapter with "LAPD Culture" in the title. The report does not, however, contain any substantive discussion of that culture or the role of the local union in maintaining it.[21] The related issues of the police subculture and of organizational cultures within police departments have not as yet received sufficient scholarly attention.[22] The 2006 Community Oriented Policing (COPS) report, for example, argues that "failing to understand and respect the culture of the agency" is one of the major factors explaining the failure of police chiefs to be effective and retain their jobs. This conclusion represents a recognition of the importance of the police culture and the fact that local police cultures vary, but like other references to this phenomenon, it is based on anecdotal evidence. [23]

There has been very little research on the concept of the police subculture, and apart from Herbert's recent work, most of the discussions are based on dated and unexamined assumptions.[24] However, we can formulate three tentative hypotheses regarding the relationship of police unions to the police subculture: (1) following Herbert's discussion, the police subculture is a multi-dimensional phenomenon, of which the police union is only one aspect or influence; (2) there are great differences in the informal cultures among police departments, and the relative influence of the police union varies from department to department; and (3) the differences in local police subcultures have some significant and measurable difference in all aspects of policing, including overall management practices, accountability and discipline, police officer interactions with citizens, and local politics.

The idea of a distinct police subculture originated in the 1950s and early 1960s, emphasizing group solidarity, hostility to the public, secrecy and toleration of misconduct, and even violence against citizens.[25] Much has changed for the better in policing since publication of the works that defined the police subculture. At that time, African Americans and Hispanics were grossly under-represented among sworn officers, and women were not employed on a basis equal to men. In the last 40 years, the composition of the rank and file has changed dramatically as a result of both equal employment opportunity considerations and a significant rise in educational levels of officers.[26] One index of the growing diversity of the rank and file is the prevalence of nonunion employee associations based on race, ethnicity, and gender.

As a result, the entire concept of a distinct police subculture needs consideration. Herbert has described a complex, multi-dimensional view of the police subculture that is far more sophisticated than the original concept.[27] There is evidence of very different attitudes on the part of African American officers compared with Whites, particularly on the issue of the use of force.[28] In some departments, African American associations have been publicly critical of positions taken by both management and police unions that tend to be dominated by White males. A significant body of research, however, has found no meaningful differences on the street behavior among White, African American, Hispanic, or female officers. The exception to this rule is that female officers appear to be far less involved in serious misconduct, repeated misconduct, and as recipients of citizen complaints.[29] (See Chapter 10, Organizational and Interpersonal Communication for the possible reasons for gender differences.)

Impact on City or County Finances

Police unions have been generally successful in negotiating good salary and fringe benefit packages for their members. The resulting contract provisions undoubtedly have some significant impact on the finances of cities and counties. The nature of this impact is not known, however. It is believed that police (and sometimes firefighters) negotiations set the standard for negotiations by other municipal employees, although this proposition has not been researched. It is not known to what extent negotiated police salaries and benefits force cities and counties to reduce expenditures for other services such as streets, parks, and libraries.[30]

On the positive side, it is generally accepted that the advent of police unionism in the late 1960s and early 1970s resulted in significant improvements in police salaries and fringe benefits. This in turn has helped to improve the relative attractiveness of law enforcement as a career. It should be noted that the President's Crime Commission in 1967 reported both lagging salaries and benefits and an inability of some agencies to attract qualified recruits.[31] It might also be noted that 20 years later, a report on police education found that the educational levels of police recruits had risen dramatically in the two previous decades.[32]

Impact on Politics

Police unions are well-organized, may have substantial financial resources, and possess political clout. Police unions regularly endorse political candidates for office, support or oppose proposed ordinances or referenda, and influence city or county budgets. The political context of actions by police unions is discussed in greater detail later in this chapter.

IN THE NEWS   Police Unions Are a Political Force in Local Elections

The Omaha police union's decision to target a mayoral candidate for defeat has raised the ire of some, while others defend the union's right to get involved in politics.

The union has "crossed the line" in its attacks on Republican Jim Vokal, said Paul Landow, former chief of staff for Democratic Mayor Mike Fahey and now political science professor at the University of Nebraska at Omaha.

Aaron Hanson, a spokesman for the police union said, "Police officers, like anybody else, are entitled to their First Amendment rights to take exceptions to elected officials and people trying to seek public office."

The debate over the union's role in the mayoral race grew stronger last week after the union unleashed another ad against Vokal.

The ad targets Vokal for voting for a union contract that contributed to the city's pension fund woes. Vokal has made the pension issue a big part of his campaign, saying he is the only candidate willing to "stand up to the unions" in contract negotiations.

Police unions are almost always major players in urban elections and want to help choose the person who will be in charge of contract negotiations, said Peter Berg, a labor professor at the Michigan State University.

Candidates also know that union endorsements would allow them the opportunity to tap into the pool of volunteers that unions can provide for knocking on doors or phoning potential voters.

Additionally, unions can deliver a solid bloc of votes that can be crucial in a tight election.

Source: Robynn Tysver, "OMAHA PRIMARY ELECTION Police union's political role sparks debate," *Omaha World-Herald*, Monday March 30, 2009.

The General Structure of Laws Governing Collective Bargaining for Law Enforcement Officers

Without question, the broadest grant of rights to law enforcement officers exists in **collective bargaining** agreements. Under collective bargaining agreements, the wages and benefits of law enforcement officers are guaranteed for the duration of the agreement. Most significantly, officers who dispute a decision of their employer concerning working conditions usually have the right to appeal that decision through a grievance procedure that culminates with a final and binding decision by a neutral third party.

Under the terms of the federal National Labor Relations Act, state governmental bodies and their political subdivisions, such as cities and counties, are excluded from the definition of "employer" and are not brought within the scope of that federal law. As a result, laws regulating collective bargaining for state, county, and city law enforcement officers have developed on a state-by-state basis and, occasionally, on a local basis. Most states which allow public sector collective bargaining have created a Public Employees Relations Commission (PERC) to administor the enabling law.

Although public employee collective bargaining laws in each state are different, the general thrust of the laws can be summarized by three simplified models: the binding arbitration model, the meet and confer model, and the bargaining not required model.[33]

Binding Arbitration Model

In states following the **binding arbitration model**, public employees are granted the right to select exclusive representatives for the purposes of bargaining with their employers. In such states, the public employer and the labor organization are required to bargain in good faith until impasse, then to submit any unresolved disputes to a process known as "interest arbitration," in which a neutral third party selected by the parties makes a final and binding resolution of those issues.

In binding arbitration, the neutral third party decides what the terms and conditions of the new collective bargaining agreement will be, usually using standards established by state statute. For example, Michigan's collective bargaining law contains standard language governing the right of law enforcement labor organizations to binding arbitration, a right that is always accompanied by a ban on the right of law enforcement officers to strike:

> It is the public policy of this state that in public police and fire departments, where the right of employees to strike is by law prohibited, it is requisite to the high morale of such employees and the efficient operation of such departments to afford an alternate, expeditious, effective and binding procedure for the resolution of disputes, and to that end the provisions of this act, providing for compulsory arbitration, shall be literally constructed.[34]

There are three general types of binding arbitration laws, reflecting differences in the latitude given arbitrators to render decisions. Under the first type, known as an "issue-by-issue" law, an arbitrator has the obligation to render a decision on each issue independently and to craft an award on each issue that best accomplishes the purposes of the arbitration statute. Under the second type of law, known as "final offer, issue-by-issue," each party submits a final offer on each issue. The arbitrator then renders a decision on each issue independently, but must award the final offer made by one of the parties, and is not free to craft a compromise position that has not been specifically proposed by either party. The third type of law, known as "total package" arbitration, requires the arbitrator to select the most reasonable of the total packages submitted by each party, even if selected elements of that party's total package might not have been awarded by the arbitrator on an issue-by-issue basis. All states with binding arbitration require an arbitrator to analyze a set of criteria established by statute, usually including factors such as the wages and benefits paid in comparable jurisdictions, the cost of living, and an employer's ability to pay.[35]

Employers have challenged binding arbitration laws under a variety of theories, including arguments that binding arbitration is an unconstitutional delegation of legislative authority and that binding arbitration inappropriately interferes with a city or county's home rule status. Almost uniformly, such challenges have not been successful, with courts upholding binding arbitration as a rational means to bring about the resolution of bargaining disputes involving law enforcement officers.[36]

Meet and Confer Model

Labor leaders commonly refer to the meet and confer model as "collective begging" because it confers little or no bargaining rights on employees. There are variations in meet and confer models, but most commonly they permit the governmental employer and the employees representative to meet and discuss "permissible" topics, such as wages, benefits, and working conditions. Some topics, such as pensions, may be specifically excluded from discussion. The governmental employer has the final decision on any topics discussed and there is no neutral impasse resolution mechanism.

Meet and confer laws may be established by state statue or local enactments. They may describe how officers select their representatives, the obligation to freely exchange information, meet for reasonable periods of time, bargain in good faith, and that agreements be in writing and approved by a majority of the officers being represented and the governing body. Under the least labor friendly meet and confer laws, neither the governmental employer nor the employees are required to meet. Such meetings are often only an opportunity, not a requirement.

Bargaining Not Required Model

The third model for police-sector collective bargaining laws, the **bargaining not required model**, is found in states that do not statutorily require or, in some cases, allow collective bargaining for law enforcement officers. In some of these states, bargaining laws have been enacted by the state legislature, only to be declared unconstitutional later by the courts (Indiana, for example, has such a history) or even have the bargaining rights rescinded by a state's governor (see Figure 11.2). In the majority of

IN THE NEWS   Bargaining Rights Rescinded

The International Union of Police Associations, which represented 1,400 state troopers and other law enforcement personnel in Indiana, dissolved its local branch in the state as a result of an executive order by Governor Mitch Daniels to end collective bargaining rights for state employees. Governor Daniels signed the executive order on January 11, 2005, the same day that Governor Matt Blunt of Missouri signed a similar executive order. The Indiana governor canceled union contracts covering nearly 25,000 employees, stating that the unions stood in the way of his efforts to overhaul the state government. Union officials across the country believe this may be a trend at both the national and state levels, citing the precedence of the U.S. Department of Homeland Security in slashing collective bargaining rights for 75,000 union member employees.

Source: (Joe Torres, "Bargaining Rights Eliminated" *American Police Beat*, March 2005, 34.)

Figure 11.2
Incoming Missouri Governor Mike Blunt decided to eliminate collective bargaining on his first day of office.
(AP Photo/News Tribune, Julie Smith)

such states, a statewide collective bargaining statute covering law enforcement officers has never been enacted. In some states where collective bargaining has not been granted on a statewide basis, certain cities and counties within the state have voluntarily chosen to bargain with their law enforcement officers.[37]

Table 11.1 summarizes the current status of collective bargaining laws governing law enforcement officers and lists which of the three general models is followed

Table 11.1

COLLECTIVE BARGAINING LAWS GOVERNING LAW ENFORCEMENT OFFICERS

State	Binding Arbitration Model	Meet and Confer Model	Bargaining Not Required Model
Alabama			X
Alaska	X		
Arizona			X
Arkansas			X
California	X		
Colorado			X
Connecticut	X		
Delaware	X		
District of Columbia	X		
Florida		X	
Georgia			X
Hawaii	X		
Idaho			X
Illinois	X		
Indiana		X	
Iowa	X		
Kansas	X		
Kentucky		X	
Louisiana			X
Maine	X		
Maryland		X	
Massachusetts	X		
Michigan	X		
Minnesota	X		
Mississippi			X
Missouri		X	
Montana	X		
Nebraska		X	
Nevada	X		

Table 11.1 (*Continued*)
COLLECTIVE BARGAINING LAWS GOVERNING LAW ENFORCEMENT OFFICERS

State	Binding Arbitration Model	Meet and Confer Model	Bargaining Not Required Model
New Hampshire	X		
New Jersey	X		
New Mexico		X	
New York	X		
North Carolina			X
North Dakota		X	
Ohio	X		
Oklahoma	X		
Oregon	X		
Pennsylvania	X		
Rhode Island	X		
South Carolina		X	
South Dakota		X	
Tennessee			X
Texas			X
Utah			X
Vermont	X		
Virginia			X
Washington	X		
West Virginia			X
Wisconsin	X		
Wyoming			X

Source: Will Aitchison, *The Rights of Law Enforcement Officers*, 6th ed. (Portland, OR: Law Enforcement Relations Information System, 2009), p. 12.

in each state.[38] As can be seen, the distribution of states with collective bargaining and those without such laws is quite geographically distinct. States without bargaining laws are centered in the South and the Southwest. States with bargaining laws are found in the Northeast, in the Midwest, and on the West Coast.

Unfair Labor Practices

States with collective bargaining almost always have statutes that list a number of labor practices deemed to be "unfair." The usual list of unfair labor practices includes the following:

- A refusal to bargain in good faith over subjects that are mandatory for bargaining[39]
- Interference, restraint, or coercion of employees because employees have exercised their collective bargaining rights
- The "domination" of a labor organization by an employer
- The failure to furnish information relevant to the collective bargaining process
- Inappropriate "interference" by an employer with the internal activities of a labor organization
- Discrimination against employees who have exercised their collective bargaining rights[40]

The usual form of challenging any of these practices is through the filing of an "unfair labor practice" or "prohibited practice" complaint with the state agency responsible for administering the collective bargaining laws. Most states have a relatively quick statute of limitations—some as short as 6 weeks—for the filing of such complaints.[41]

Mandatory Subjects for Bargaining

Where a law enforcement employer is obligated to bargain collectively, the bargaining topics over which bargaining may be conducted are generally classified under one of three categories—mandatory, permissive, or illegal topics of bargaining.[42] Mandatory subjects of bargaining—usually those described as topics pertaining to wages, hours, and terms and conditions of employment—must be bargained if raised by either side.[43] Permissive subjects of bargaining—usually falling under the general heading of "management rights"—are those over which bargaining may occur but is not compelled.[44] Illegal subjects of bargaining are those over which the employer is forbidden by law from bargaining.[45] The distinction among the categories of bargaining subjects is particularly important when interest arbitration is the last step in the bargaining process, because only mandatory subjects of bargaining may generally be referred to interest arbitration.[46]

Where the obligation to bargain exists, it has importance, not only when negotiations for an actual contract are being conducted, but also during the term of the contract and after the contract expires. The obligation to bargain is continual, a characteristic that can significantly limit an employer's flexibility in making certain decisions. If a matter is a mandatory subject for bargaining, an employer cannot make changes in past practices affecting the matter without first negotiating with the labor organization representing its officers.[47] This restriction applies whenever a labor organization has been certified as the bargaining representative for employees. The continuing duty to bargain can even invalidate an employer's efforts to change its past practices through enacting a charter amendment.[48]

Two cases from the state of Washington provide a good example of this so-called continuing duty to bargain. In one case, the collective bargaining agreement covering a city police department had expired when the employer decided to change from a fixed-shift system, in which shifts were selected by seniority, to a system in which shifts rotated every few months. In the second case, the employer made changes in the method of allocating standby assignments. Even though a contract was in effect at the time of the changes, the contract did not address the method of standby assignment allocation. In both cases, the employers were held to have committed unfair labor practices by making the changes without first negotiating with their respective unions. The Washington State **Public Employment Relations Commission** held that, absent a clear waiver of the union's right to bargain, the continuing duty to bargain prohibited the implementation of any changes in such mandatorily negotiable hours of work issues.[49]

A labor organization can waive the right to bargain over changes in past practices in one of two ways: by "inaction" and by "contract." A waiver by inaction occurs when the labor organization has knowledge that the employer intends to make a change in past practice (or has actually made such a change) but does not demand to bargain over the change in a timely manner.[50] Even a 6-week delay in demanding the right to bargain has been held to waive bargaining rights.[51] In order to have a labor organization's demand to bargain held untimely, the employer generally must establish that it provided actual and timely notice of its intended action.[52]

A waiver by contract exists when the labor organization has contractually given the right to the employer to make changes in mandatory subjects of bargaining. To be effective, "contract waivers" must be specific and clearly articulated. For example, a management rights clause that generally gives the employer the right to establish hours of work would likely not be specific enough to allow the employer the unilateral right to change work shifts, or to change from fixed to rotating shifts.

For bargaining rights to exist mid-contract, the labor organization must establish that the past practice the employer is intending to change has been consistent and longstanding.[53] The labor organization must also establish that there has been an actual change in past practices in order to demand bargaining during the term of the contract. For example, in one case, the police association in New York City was attempting to bargain over a department directive that banned "hog-tying" of suspects. The court ruled the directive was not negotiable because the labor association failed to prove the existence of a past practice that allowed hog-tying, resting its decision on testimony that hog-tying was not taught during training and on the word of the supervisor of the patrol force that, in 41 years of service, he had never seen hog-tying used in the department.[54] In addition, an employer's right to make changes in mandatory subjects of bargaining can also be limited by a collective bargaining agreement. Contractual clauses typically labeled "maintenance of benefits" or "existing conditions" forbid an employer from changing wages, hours, or working conditions. The contract covering Buffalo, New York police officers contains an example of such a clause:

> All conditions or provisions beneficial to employees now in effect which are not specifically provided for in this Agreement or which have not been replaced by

provisions of this Agreement shall remain in effect for the duration of this Agreement, unless mutually agreed otherwise between the Employer and the Association.[55]

Maintenance of benefits clauses enhance a labor organization's ability to prevent changes in past practices. When under the general continuing duty to bargain, a labor organization has the ability to demand only that an employer bargain to impasse over changes in past practices that are mandatory negotiable; a maintenance of benefits clause allows a labor organization simply to refuse to agree to the change, even if the employer is willing to bargain over the issue. This distinction is particularly important in states where the bargaining process does not culminate with binding arbitration but, instead, allows an employer to unilaterally implement its last best offer on a bargaining issue.

When a topic is mandatory for bargaining, the employer must negotiate about the topic with the labor organization, not with individual union members. For example, because discipline is mandatorily negotiable, an employer would violate its bargaining obligation if it entered into a "last chance" agreement with a troubled employee unless the employee's labor organization also was a party to the agreement.[56] This ban on one-on-one contracts with individual union members is a strong one and has invalidated a wide variety of employer agreements with individual union members, including the payment of a signing bonus,[57] a contract with the newly hired officers that they will repay the costs of their training if they quit to go to work for another law enforcement employer,[58] and an agreement with a probationary employee to extend the probationary period.[59]

Establishing the Bargaining Relationship

The Process

Assuming the existence of a legal provision for collective negotiations, the process of establishing a bargaining relationship is straightforward, although fraught with the opportunity for disputes. The mere fact that most members of a police department belong to a single organization does not mean it automatically has the right to represent its members for the purpose of collective bargaining.[60] Those eligible to be represented may, in fact, select an organization to which they already belong for this purpose, or they may select another one. This choice must be made, however, in ways that conform to the legislation providing the collective bargaining if the employee organization hopes to gain certification by the PERC.

The union begins an organizing drive, working to get 30 percent of the class or classes of employees it seeks to represent to sign authorization cards, of which Figure 11.3 is typical. Once this goal is reached, the union notifies the police department. An election is held, and the union must get 50 percent plus one officer to prevail. If management believes the union has obtained a majority legitimately and that it is appropriate for the class or classes of officers to be grouped together as proposed by the union, it will recognize the union as the bargaining agent of the officers it has sought to represent. Once recognized by the employer, the union will petition the PERC or

INTEREST CARD
INTERNATIONAL UNION OF POLICE ASSOCIATIONS, AFL-CIO

DATE _____

I, the undersigned, hereby authorize the International Union of Police Associations, AFL-CIO,
to represent me for the purpose of collective bargaining with my employer.

_____
(Name of employer; and/or its successor)

and to seek an election for that purpose.
(PLEASE PRINT CLEARLY)   RANK _____

NAME _____   _____
                                          Social Security Number

ADDRESS _____
         Number and Street

        _____
         City   State   Zip Code

HOME PHONE _____   WORK PHONE _____

SIGNATURE _____   WITNESS _____

Figure 11.3
A typical authorization card.
Source: Reprinted with permission from the International Union of Police Associations.

another body responsible for administering the legislation for certification. In such cases, the PERC does not check the authorization cards but only the appropriateness of the grouping of the officers. If the grouping is deemed appropriate by the PERC or a similar administrative body, then the employee organization is certified as the bargaining representative.

If the employee organization is not recognized by management, it can petition the PERC for an election; the petition must be accompanied by signed and dated representation cards from 30 percent of the group of employees the union seeks to represent. A secret vote is then held at the direction of the PERC, with the ballot including the union or unions that are contesting the right to represent the officers, along with the choice of no union. The union that receives a majority of the votes from among the officers who are eligible to be represented by the employee organization and who actually cast ballots is then certified. Alternately, a majority of those casting ballots might vote for no union. In the event that no majority is achieved, a runoff election is necessary.

The Opportunity for Conflict

In establishing the bargaining relationship, there is ample opportunity for disputes to develop. Management may undertake a campaign to convince officers they are better off without the union at the same time that the union is mounting its organizing drive. The employee organization may wish access to bulletin boards, meeting space, and mailing lists to publicize the advantages of unionizing to the officers, all of which management may not wish to provide. The decision as to what is an appropriate grouping of officers for the purposes of collective bargaining, technically referred to as "unit determination," is profoundly significant and one about which management and the union may have sharp differences.

Questions such as the following may arise: Are lieutenants part of management and therefore not eligible for representation by the union for purposes of collective bargaining? Should civilian radio dispatchers be part of the same bargaining unit as uniformed officers? Should detectives be in a bargaining unit by themselves? These decisions are important because they can affect the operation of the police department and can determine, to some degree, the dynamics of the employee organization. They can impact the scope of bargaining and affect the stability of the bargaining relationship, or they can even be decisive in the outcome of a representation election.[61]

Both the union and management are pragmatic when it comes to defining the appropriate bargaining unit. In general, both might prefer a broad unit, the union, because the numbers will give it strength, while management resists the proliferation of bargaining units because each one that is recognized officially must be bargained with separately. Here, too, despite a similar orientation, disputes can arise. The union may know that it has the support of only one category of employees (e.g., detectives) and seeks to represent them as a single bargaining unit. Management may feel that particular union is too militant and, consequently, favors, as a part of a hidden agenda, the inclusion of detectives in a wider unit as a means of promoting the election of a more moderate union that is also seeking to represent employees. What constitutes an appropriate unit may be defined by state law. The most common method of unit determination, however, is for the PERC or a similar administrative body to make decisions on a case-by-case basis, applying certain criteria stipulated in the legislation.[62] Among the criteria often identified are the desires of the employees, the "community of interests" shared by the employees, the need to avoid creating too many bargaining units, the effects on efficiency of operations, and the history of labor relations in the police department.

Negotiations

Selection of the Management and Union Teams

Figure 11.4 depicts a typical configuration of the management and union bargaining teams. The union's chief negotiator will usually not be a member of the bargaining unit; rather, he or she will be a specialist brought in to represent it.

This ensures a certain level of expertise, wider experience, an appropriate degree of objectivity, and an autonomy that comes from knowing, once the bargaining is over, he or she will not be working daily for the people sitting across the table. It is not

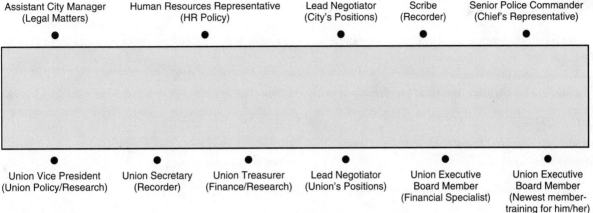

Figure 11.4
The management and union bargaining teams. Although the composition of management's and the union's bargaining teams varies somewhat from one jurisdiction to another and even within jurisdictions over time, the configuration shown here approximates the "typical" municipal situation. Occasionally, a member of the city council also sits in as an observer.
Source: Courtesy of Chuck Foy, past president of the Arizona Conference of Police and Sheriffs Local 7077 and past president of the Peoria [Arizona] Police Officers Association.

automatic that the union president will be a member of the bargaining team, although customarily a union officer is, and often it is the president. Accompanying the union's chief negotiator and president will be two or three team members who have conducted in-depth research on matters relating to the bargaining issues and who will have various types of data, facts, and documents—such as wage and benefit surveys, trends in the consumer price index, and copies of recent contracts for similarly sized jurisdictions—with them. Although there will be only several union research team members at the table, they will have had assistance in gathering their information from others in the union. Unless the union's chief negotiator is an attorney, there will seldom be an attorney sitting at the table with the union's team.

The chief negotiator for management may be the director of labor relations or the human resources director of the unit of government involved or may be a professional labor relations specialist. Some jurisdictions prefer the latter because, if there are acrimonious occurrences, once the bargaining is over the director of labor relations can step back into the picture and assume a relationship with the union that is unscarred by any incidents. The chief of police should not appear at the table personally, but a key member of the command staff who has his or her confidence should. The appearance of the chief at the table makes the task of leadership more difficult; to appear there on equal footing with the union's bargaining team on one day and then to step back atop the organizational hierarchy on the next requires greater adjustments by both the chief and the union members than the creation of any benefits associated with his or her presence are worth.

The way in which issues are presented, and the flexibility that both sides have, will impact strongly on how the bargaining sessions will go. Perhaps equally important are the decisions made as to who will represent each side at the table, and in

IN THE NEWS   Police Union Leaders go to Harvard

Where can you get advice from a real-deal king-maker, learn about the causes and effects of illegal immigration, and see a Red Sox/Yankees game, all in the same weekend?

If you run a big-city police association you may already know the answer—the annual Police Union Leadership Seminar at Harvard University. Sixty-five big-city association leaders from most of the 50 largest cities in the United States and Canada attended the intensive 3-day seminar.

Known as the "Big 50," the seminar was developed to help union leaders of major cities improve their leadership, management, and negotiation skills.

Newly elected and experienced association presidents have appreciated the opportunity to update their knowledge about a wide range of issues including health-care benefits, pensions, developing a strategic media plan, and the impact of illegal immigration on law enforcement.

Source: Leadership Seminar at Harvard Law, *American Police Beat,* June 2008, pp. 1 and 64.

what role. The proper training of all involved in the negotiation process is absolutely essential.

The one thing that is to be avoided are zealots, those with "axes to grind." Firebrands are also poor choices, as are those with a sarcastic, acrid, or abrasive personality. The purpose of bargaining is to produce a bilateral written agreement to which both parties will bind themselves during its lifetime. This is not only a profoundly important task but also one that is sufficiently difficult without including people on either side who have an agenda other than negotiating in good faith or whose personalities create yet another obstacle. For these reasons, management must exercise careful consideration in deciding who will represent the police department at the table and, if necessary, influence the selection of the city's other representatives.

Preparing for Negotiations

Management can ill afford to simply wait until the employee organization prepares its demands and presents them; effective action requires considerable effort on management's part before it receives the union's proposal. Management's negotiating team must be selected, agreement with the union obtained on the site where the negotiations will take place; the bargaining schedule established in conjunction with the union; and various types of data and information gathered, tabulated, and analyzed. Although final preparations for negotiating will begin several months before the first bargaining sessions, the preparation process is a continuous one; management should begin preparing for the next negotiations as soon as these are completed. The demands not obtained by the union in the past year may be brought up again in this year's bargaining sessions, and management should be prepared for this.

Various types of records should be kept and summaries made of such factors as the union membership; the types and outcomes of grievances; the costs of settling grievances; the numbers, kinds, and consequences of any contract violations by the employee organization; the subject matters brought before the union–management committee during the life of the expiring contract and the disposition of them; and the themes reflected in the union's newsletter. Additionally, just as the employee organization's bargaining team is doing, the management team must be familiarizing itself with changes in the consumer price index and the provisions of recent contracts in similarly situated jurisdictions and conducting its own wage and benefit survey or cooperating with the union on one.

From all of these sources, and others, it is essential that management do three things. First, it must develop fairly specific anticipations as to what the union will be seeking and the relative importance of each demand to the union. Second, it must develop its position with respect to the anticipated preliminary demands it believes the union will present. Third, it must develop the objectives it seeks to achieve during the forthcoming process of bilateral determination. If it is not already an institutionalized practice, arrangements should be made to have the union submit its demands in writing prior to the first scheduled round of negotiations. These demands may be submitted either in the form of a proposed contract or as a "shopping list," which simply lists the demands being made. The presentation of the demands in writing before the first bargaining session allows for a more productive use of the time allotted for the first negotiating session.

If management has done a good job, there will be relatively few surprises when the proposed contract is submitted. Surprises do not indicate that management's preparation was wasted; the knowledge gained through the process of anticipating the union's demands adds to the negotiating team's depth of understanding and overall confidence, key ingredients of bargaining table success. It is difficult to know precisely when management's bargaining team is prepared, but the employee organization will easily detect and capitalize on a lack of preparation.

The Negotiating Sessions

The publicity and attending atmosphere preceding the negotiating sessions focus considerable attention on them and can be barometers of or may influence how the sessions unfold. However, prebargaining publicity is also part of attempts to influence public opinion, to impress the public or rank-and-file members with the city's or union's resolve, and to create a façade behind which both sides can maneuver for advantage. Thus, one should not be too encouraged or discouraged about the content of such publicity; it should be considered and evaluated but not relied on solely as an informational source.

The number of bargaining sessions can run from one to several dozen, lasting from 30 minutes to 10 or more hours, although half-day sessions are more common, depending on how close or far apart the union and management are when they begin to meet face to face. Traditionally, any means of making verbatim transcripts, such as the use of a stenographer or tape recorder, have generally been excluded from the bargaining sessions, as it was believed they tended to impede the progress of negotiations because people would begin speaking for the record.

In a related vein, the enactment of Florida's "sunshine law" opened up many previously closed government meetings to the general public, including bargaining sessions, and stirred up some controversy. Advocates of the legislation argued it opened up government to the people, making it both more responsive and responsible. With respect to its application to collective negotiations, critics of the law maintained the real bargaining would be done secretly, the scheduled public bargaining sessions would be merely a ritualistic acting out of what had been agreed on privately, and real negotiating would be difficult because both sides would tend to "play to the audience." This last point is underscored by one negotiator's wry observation that bargaining under the sunshine law was like "a Roman circus with kibitzers."[63]

At the first meeting, friendly conversation might be passed across the table, or there may be merely strained greetings before the formal session begins. Much like the prenegotiations publicity, this may or may not reflect how the session will go. Friendly conversation might suggest that rapid and amicable bargaining will follow but instead no mutually acceptable positions will be reached because the friendly conversation has veiled only thinly the hostility or aggressiveness of one or both sides, which quickly comes to the fore. On the other hand, strained greetings might reflect the heavy responsibility each party to the negotiations feels, and quick progress may follow.

In the initial session, the chief negotiator for each party will make an opening statement; management's representative will often go first, touching on general themes, such as the need for patience and the obligation to bargain in good faith. The union's negotiator generally will follow this up by voicing support for such sentiments and will outline what the union seeks to achieve under the terms of the new contract. Ground rules for the bargaining may then be reviewed, modified as mutually agreed on, or developed. The attention then will shift to the terms of the contract that the union is proposing, and the contract will be examined thoroughly in a "walk-through," during which time management will seek to learn what the union means by particular wording. This is a time-consuming process but of great importance because both parties need to have a common understanding of what it is they are attempting to commit each other to, or there will be frequent unresolved conflicts and many complex and expensive grievances filed during the lifetime of the contract. For purposes of illustration, the union may have proposed that "vehicles will be properly maintained to protect the health and safety of officers." Discussion of this proposal may reveal their expectations are much more specific:

1. This is to apply to all vehicles, including marked, semimarked, and unmarked.
2. Each patrol vehicle, whether marked, semimarked, or unmarked, will be replaced at 60,000 miles.
3. All vehicles will be equipped with radial tires.
4. Plexiglas protective shields will be installed between the front and rear seats.
5. Shotguns or rifles in locking mounts accessible from the front seat will be provided in all marked and semimarked cars.
6. First-aid kits of a particular type will be placed in all vehicles.
7. Comprehensive blood body fluid pathogen protection kits will be provided.

Another illustration is reflected in Table 11.2; assuming the union is seeking a 2-year contract and wants a 20 percent raise during the lifetime of the contract, there

---

Table 11.2

ALTERNATIVE WAYS TO COSTING OUT A 20% RAISE OVER A 2-YEAR CONTRACT

1. 10% increase each year of contract
   Year 1 cost: 10% of 980,000   = $ 98,000
   Year 2 cost: 10% of year 1 wages, $1,078,000   =   107,800
   plus continuation of year 1   =   98,000
                                                            $303,800

2. 15% increase in year 1; 5% in year 2
   Year 1 cost: 15% of $980,000   = $147,000
   Year 2 cost: 5% of year 1 payroll of $1,127,000   =   56,350
   plus continuation of year 1   =   147,000
                                                            $350,350

3. 20% in year 1; nothing in year 2
   Year 1 cost: 20% of $980,000   = $196,000
   Year 2: no new increase but continuation of year 1 raise = $196,000
                                                            $392,000

---

are several ways the cost of that raise might be spread. Management must find out what the union is bargaining for in very specific terms and then cost it out, so the administration knows the budgetary implications of its commitments and counterproposals beforehand.[64] The walk-through may take several sessions to complete; during this time, little bargaining is being done, as management is basically attempting to obtain clarity about what the union's expectations are.

For bargaining purposes, the union will have categorized each clause in the proposed contract as being (1) "expendable," meaning under certain circumstances it will be withdrawn as a symbol of good faith; (2) a "trade-off," indicating it will be dropped as total or partial payment for obtaining some other benefit; (3) "negotiable," meaning the benefit needs to be obtained in one form or another; and (4) "non-negotiable," meaning the benefit is wanted exactly as proposed.[65] Management will study the information gained from the walk-through for several days, and then both parties will return to the table. Management then will respond to the union's proposal by indicating which clauses it has (1) "accepted," (2) "accepted with minor modification," (3) "rejected," and (4) wishes to make its own proposals and counterproposals to. Management cannot simply reject a clause out of hand; to do so would not constitute bargaining in good faith. Instead, it must give a reason for the rejection that is reasonable, such as an actual inability to pay.

Having been told formally of management's position on the contract proposed, the bargaining begins, concentrating on the items upon which agreement can be reached immediately or fairly rapidly. Such an approach helps foster a spirit of mutualism that can be useful in dealing with the issues about which there are substantial differences. As bargaining enters the final stages, the issues that must be dealt with usually become fewer but also more difficult in terms of securing agreement.

At such points, "side trips" may threaten to make the sessions unproductive. These side trips might involve wild accusations, old recriminations, character assassinations, or discussion of a specific clause in philosophical or intellectual terms as a means of not dealing with the concrete realities that may be threatening and anxiety provoking for one or both parties. At these times, a caucus or even a slightly longer space of time than ordinary until the next session may give enough time for tempers to calm or for more perspective to be gained. At other times, the police union may feel the need to "up the stakes" by engaging in picketing as a form of political pressure.

Ultimately, unless a total impasse is reached, agreement will be obtained on the terms of a new contract. The union's membership will vote on the contract as a whole. If approved by the membership, the contract then goes before the necessary government officials and bodies, such as the legislative unit that appropriates the funds, for its approval.

Grievances

Why Grievances Are Inevitable

There is a notion that, once the bargaining is completed and an agreement signed, the most difficult part of labor relations has been passed through and easy times are ahead. Such a notion is natural. Bargaining is high drama, with a great deal of attention focused on it by the news media and the community. The production of an agreement acceptable to both the union and management is, in fact, a significant achievement. Beyond it, however, is the day-to-day administration of the contract during its lifetime. Because the contract outlines the duties and rights of each party in its dealings with the other, it is ironically the basis not only for accord but also for conflict:

> It would, of course, be ideal for all concerned, including the public, if in the negotiation of the agreement both parties were able to draft a comprehensive document capable of foreseeing and forestalling all potential disputes which might arise during its life. Unfortunately, such crystal-ball vision is usually lacking, particularly when the parties are pressured to obtain agreement in a period of negotiation tensions and time deadlines. It is not humanly possible in a new collective bargaining relationship to draft such a perfect document.
>
> Therefore it is inevitable that questions will arise concerning the interpretation and application of the document drafted in the haste and pressure of contract negotiations. What is the meaning of a particular clause of the agreement? How does it apply, if at all, to a set of facts which occurred after the agreement was signed? These questions are not at all uncommon in any contractual relationship.[66]

The Definition of a Grievance

Whereas in common usage a **grievance** is a complaint or an expression of dissatisfaction by an employee with respect to some aspect of employment, what can be grieved formally is usually defined within the contract itself. Grievances may be limited to

matters discussed specifically in the contract, that are primarily contract-related, or that pertain to the job, as is seen in these clauses from three different agreements:

1. A grievance is defined as a complaint arising out of the interpretation, application, or compliance with the provisions of this agreement.

2. For the purpose of this agreement the term "grievance" shall mean the difference of dispute between any police officer and the city, or a superior officer in the chain of command, with respect to the interpretation, application, claim or breach, of violation of any of the provisions of this agreement, or with respect to any equipment furnished by the city.

3. A grievance, for our purposes, shall be defined as any controversy, complaint, misunderstanding, or dispute arising between an employee or employees and the City, or between the Brotherhood and the City.

The Grievance Procedure

The grievance procedure is a formal process that has been the subject of bilateral negotiations and is detailed in the contract. It involves seeking redress of the grievances through progressively higher levels of authority and most often culminates in binding arbitration by a tripartite panel or a single neutral. A typical sequence of steps includes the following:

Grievances shall be presented in the following manner and every effort shall be made by the parties to secure prompt disposition of grievances:

Step 1. The member shall first present his/her grievance to his/her immediate supervisor within five (5) days of the occurrence which gave rise to the grievance. Such contact shall be on an informal and oral basis, and the supervisor shall respond orally to the grievance within five (5) working days.

Step 2. Any grievance which cannot be satisfactorily settled in Step 1 shall be reduced to writing by the member and shall next be taken up by his/her division commander. Said grievance shall be presented to the division commander within five (5) working days from receipt of the answer in Step 1. The division commander shall, within five (5) working days, render his/her decision on the grievance in writing.

Step 3. Any grievance not satisfactorily settled in Step 2 shall be forwarded, in writing, within five (5) working days, to the Chief of Police, who shall render his/her written decision on the grievance within five (5) working days.

Step 4. If the grievant is not satisfied with the response of the Chief of Police, he/she will forward his written grievance within five (5) working days to the City Manager, who will have ten (10) working days to reply, in writing.

Step 5. If the grievance has not been settled to the satisfaction of the grievant in Step 4, the matter will be subject to arbitration. An arbiter will be selected, without undue delay, according to the rules of the American Arbitration Association. The arbiter will hold an arbitration hearing. When the hearing has ended, the arbiter will be asked to submit his/her award, in writing, within fifteen (15) days. His/her decision shall be final and binding on both parties.[67]

Because the union must share equally the cost of arbitration with management, the decision to take a grievance to the last step is customarily the prerogative of the union rather than the individual officer who is grieved.

Enumerated in the agreement are not only the steps of the grievance procedure but also such matters as the manner of selecting the tripartite panel or the single neutral, along with their duties and powers. If the panel is used, management and the union each appoints one member, and those two appoint the third; where the two cannot agree on the neutral, the contract may provide for the referral of the choice of a chairperson to a designated agency,[68] such as the Federal Mediation and Conciliation Service, or a state agency. Where a single arbitrator is used, a variety of techniques are employed in selection, ranging from agreement on the person by the union and management on a case-by-case basis, to the appointment of a permanent arbitrator during the lifetime of the contract, to having an outside agency submit a list of qualified arbitrators from which management and the union take turns eliminating names until only one remains or they agree to accept any of some number remaining, such as three.

The arbitration hearing is quasi-judicial, with more relaxed rules of evidence than are found in either criminal or civil proceedings. The burden of proof is on the grieving party, except in discipline cases, where it is always on the employer. The parties may be represented by legal counsel at the hearing, and the format will generally include obtaining agreement on what the issue is, an opening statement by each side (with the grieving party going first), examination and cross-examination of witnesses, and closing arguments in the reverse of the order in which the opening statements were made.

Arbitration Issues and Decision Making

Despite the many types of matters that can be and are grieved, the largest single category of cases, about 90 percent of the total, brought to an arbitration hearing are those involving discipline against an officer. Some arbitration decision making is not difficult because one side, perhaps the union, chooses to take a losing case to arbitration, because of its symbolic importance, and the need to appear supportive of union members. This rationale can also be applied on management as well in order to show support for managers.

If an employee is found to have done what he or she has been accused of, the arbitrator may then consider certain factors that might mitigate the severity of the penalty, including the officer's years of service to the department; the provocation, if any, that led to the alleged offense; the officer's disciplinary history, including the number, types, and recency of other violations; the consistency with which the applicable rule is enforced; and the penalties applied for similar offenses by other officers.[69]

One study of arbitrated police grievances reveals that the officer involved in the grievance was assigned to uniformed patrol 84 percent of the time, another police officer was involved in the incident slightly more than half the time (56 percent of the cases), the grieving officer's supervisor supported him or her 14 percent of the time, and in exactly three-quarters of the cases the involved officer had a clean disciplinary record.[70] Given that police unions must be selective in terms of the cases they take to arbitration, the results are not too surprising: the union won 77 percent of the grievances.

A key advantage of arbitration is the speed with which issues are heard and a decision is made, as compared with seeking resolution of the dispute in court. The deadline for issuance of the award may be established by statute; the parties; a government authority, such as the PERC; the arbitrator, if he or she is acting as an independent; or the body appointing the arbitrator.[71] The AAA requires arbitrators to render their decisions in writing within 30 days of (1) the conclusion of the hearing; (2) the receipt of the hearing transcript, if one has been made; or (3) the receipt of posthearing briefs.[72] In general, except in such instances as fraud or bias by the arbitrator, the hearing officer's decision, where binding arbitration is provided for, will not be reviewed by the courts.

Job Actions

Job action is a label used to describe several types of activities in which employees may engage to express their dissatisfaction with a particular person, event, or condition or to attempt to influence the outcome of a matter pending before decision makers, such as a contract bargaining impasse. Job actions carry the signal "we are here, organized, and significant, and the legitimacy of our position must be recognized." Four types of job actions are recognizable: the vote of confidence, work slowdowns, work speedups, and work stoppages.

The Vote of Confidence

The vote of confidence, which typically produces a finding of no confidence, has been used somewhat sparingly in law enforcement. Such a vote is how rank-and-file members signal their collective displeasure with the chief administrator of their agency. Although such votes have no legal standing, they may have a high impact because of the resulting publicity.

Work Slowdowns

Although officers continue to work during a slowdown, they do so at a leisurely pace, causing productivity to fall. As productivity drops, the unit of government employing the officers comes under pressure to restore normal work production. This pressure may be from within the unit of government itself. For example, a department may urge officers to write more tickets, so more revenue is not lost. Or citizens may complain to politicians and appointed leaders to "get this thing settled," so the police will answer calls more rapidly and complete the reports citizens need for insurance purposes. In

Chief Says No-Confidence Votes Are Routine

In Illinois, the Peoria Police Benevolent Association has taken a vote of "no confidence" in its police chief, but so far there is very little in the way of details as to why.

"This vote was demanded by the rank and file in order to express concerns over issues within the department and with the administration," Association officials said in a news release. The main point of contention between the chief and the union is a proposal by Chief Setttttingsgaard to move to staggered shifts. The plan was touted as a way to put more officers out on the street, but officers have complained the proposal would tweak the hours of the three primary shifts—first, second, and third—something the union says would cost the city more money and disrupt the officers' lives.

Another source of conflict is the idea of appointing supervisors to new assignments without opening up the bid process to other qualifying supervisors with more seniority, meaning those with more time on the job would lose the ability to bid for shifts and days off.

Chief Settingsgaard told the *Peoria Journal Star* he wasn't surprised to hear the union voted it had no confidence in him because of the ongoing contract disagreements between them.

"This no-confidence vote has been bandied about several times since I've been here," he told the *Star* in a recent interview.

Source: American Police Beat, November 2008.

New York City, police officers protesting stalled contract negotiations staged a ticket-issuing slowdown that resulted in a loss of $2.3 million in just 2 months. This action also produced strong conflict within the rank and file among officers who did and did not support the slowdown. In order to counter New York City Police Department pressure to stop the ticket slowdown, the Patrolmen's Benevolent Association—which represents the city's 29,000 officers—picketed outside traffic courts, denouncing what it called the administration's traffic ticket quota policy.[73]

The adoption of new technologies in a police department, intended to speed up police responses, also offers the opportunity to create a work slowdown. For example, several years ago before department-issued cell phones were regularly provided to police officers, 150 police officers in Alexandria, Virginia turned in their department-issued pagers to protest a pay scale that lagged behind those of neighboring jurisdictions. The pagers were used to call in off-duty officers in specialized units, such as homicide and hostage negotiations, when needed. Detective Eric Ratliff, president of Local 5, International Union of Police Associations, said "I won't sugar-coat it. The response time of specialized units . . . will be slower. What this does is take us back to the early '80s, before we had pagers, which is basically where our pay is."[74] In East Hartford, Connecticut, the police union contract approved by the city council included a provision to pay officers required to carry pagers an extra $1,500 annually, avoiding the wholesale return of pagers that Alexandria experienced.[75]

Work Speedups

As the term suggests, work speedups are an acceleration of activity, resulting in the overproduction of one or more types of police services. The purpose is to create public pressure on elected and appointed government leaders to achieve a union-desired goal. The purpose of a work speedup may be to protest a low pay increase proposed by the employer, to force the employer to make more or particular concessions at the bargaining table, or to pressure the employer to abandon a policy change that adversely affects union members. Examples of speedups include "ticket blizzards" and sudden strict enforcements of usually ignored minor violations, such as jaywalking, littering, or smoking in prohibited areas. The intent with this type of job action is to so anger the public that citizens will direct their hostility toward public officials—via angry e-mails, phone calls, letters, etc.—who are likely to be in a position to solve or at least ameliorate the problem so the issue causing their dissatisfaction can be resolved politically in their favor.

Work Stoppages

Work stoppages are the biggest hammer in any union's toolbox. The ultimate work stoppage is the strike, which is the withholding of *all* of labor's services (see Figure 11.5). This tactic is most often used by labor in an attempt to force management back to the bargaining table when negotiations have reached an impasse. However, strikes by public employees are now rare. In 1969, public employee strikes peaked at 412.[76] Today, there are fewer than 50 a year. The reasons for the sharp decline in strikes include the extension of collective bargaining rights to many public employees, state laws prohibiting strikes, the fines that may be levied against striking unions and employees, and the fact that striking employees may be fired. President Ronald Reagan's wholesale dismissal of the air traffic controllers remains a potent lesson for unionists. Additionally, the climate starting in the 1990s and continuing today has not been favorable to unionism. This is so because of the growing conservatism in this country

Figure 11.5
Police officers walk a picket line.
(AP Photo)

and the view that the unions are adept at getting what they want at "our expense" are also factors that make both private and public unions less likely to strike.[77] In states where public-sector bargaining is not allowed, tough laws affecting strikers have made public employees think long and hard before striking. Even in those states, many public employers know what they have to do in order to reap the benefits of a well-trained and seasoned workforce, and they do so to prevent the labor unrest that would impede economic development. Companies are not likely to relocate to cities that cannot govern effectively. Without these relocations, a city's budget becomes increasingly tight because tax revenue is flat or falling; residents and business are hit with increased and new taxes, and they begin to leave to find more hospitable locations in which to live and work.

Briefer work stoppages may affect only specialized assignments or involve a large number of police officers, but not all of them. Epidemics of the **blue flu** can last only a few days. Work stoppages of this type are an important police labor tactic. While, like strikes, these briefer collective actions may be intended to force management back to the table, they are also used occasionally to punctuate the extreme displeasure of officers with a policy (e.g., one unreasonably restricting moonlighting by officers) or with particular actions by officials inside and outside the department (e.g., the decision of a district attorney to prosecute a police officer on what is seen as a public image-enhancing but "thin" case). These briefer job actions sometimes follow a vote of no confidence.

IN THE NEWS   Chief Navarre: Blue Flu Is a Violation of Policy

Toledo Police Chief Mike Navarre spoke out Tuesday about what he is calling an "organized and illegal effort" on the part of police officers, which could result in reprimands, suspensions or even dismissals.

Navarre says more than 70 officers failed to show up for duty Tuesday. That amounted to 50 percent of the night shift. This could cause problems, Navarre said, because "... there's a safety concern."

This situation came a day after concession talks with the city of Toledo Police Patrolman's Association (TPPA) failed to find a solution to the question of who will cover pensions and health-care costs.

The union wants to negotiate a deal regarding an officer pension pickup of less than 10 percent and an overtime payment deferral. They said the city refused.

The city demands a full 10 percent pension pickup with the officers picking up 20 percent of health-care costs.

The TPPA is displeased.

"You're taking over $600 a month out of an officer's paycheck," said Dan Wagner, head of the TPPA.

Navarre is calling what the officers are doing a violation of policy, though the union said it discouraged the action. He said he instructed internal affairs to investigate.

"Once that investigation is completed and we're able to identify individuals involved, we will take the appropriate disciplinary action," Navarre said.

The chief thanked the officers who showed up and told them, for their own safety, not to make many traffic stops or misdemeanor warrant arrests. He then called Lucas County Sheriff James Telb to put deputies on standby in case police calls got out of hand.

He says it's a plan that will work if it happens again.

The union may have plans of its own.

"We're looking into a legal opinion to see whether or not we can strike," Wagner said.

Source: Lisa Rantala, "Chief Navarre: Blue Flu is a Violation of Policy," WTOL TV, Toledo, Ohio, 6 April 2010.

In Boston, three members of the department's sexual assault unit—a specialized unit—refused to be on call overnight for emergencies, protesting the fact that the officers were not paid well for such assignments.[78] Los Angeles officers staged their third blue flu when 45 percent of the daily workforce called in sick for 2 days in a row, just as the tourist season was beginning. This protest was made because officers had been working 21 months without a contract or pay raise and wanted to move the bargaining process forward.[79] In East St. Louis, police officers, angry that firefighters made more money, called in sick for one day—during which county and state police officers stepped in to patrol the streets. As a result, the city agreed to grant salary increases.[80] Ninety-five of 130 disgruntled Cook County, Illinois deputies assigned to court security duties called in sick. Officials estimate that, in the juvenile court alone, some 700 cases had to be postponed. Other police departments that have experienced blue flu epidemics recently include New Orleans, Louisiana; Pontiac, Michigan; Sacramento County, California; and Santa Ana, California.

Police Unions: The Political Context

Although union job actions frequently center on economic factors, unions also take stances on other issues. In the 1990s, in Washington, D.C., Ron Robertson, president of the local Fraternal Order of Police, asked the federal government to take over the police department because the public and officers were in a "killing field."[81] Two days prior to Robertson's request, an officer working alone was shot four times and killed as he sat in his patrol car at a traffic light outside a nightclub. The city's inability to staff two officers to a car had been a continuing union concern.

While contract negotiations were ongoing between the state and the State Police Association of Massachusetts (SPAM), the association opted at the last minute not to air an ad that blamed (now former governor) Governor Weld for the death of a state trooper gunned down by a convicted murderer who had been released early by the parole board. In the midst of the state–SPAM negotiations, Governor Weld reappointed one of the members of the parole board. This member had voted for the murderer's early release, prompting the preparation of the ad. Despite the fact that the ad was not aired, a controversy ensued. Weld aides asserted the union's tactics were designed to make the governor capitulate to the union's demands, and one of the governor's political allies, a state senator, called the ad "the lowest." The union responded by stating the state senator was "intruding into the collective bargaining process and acting beyond his realm."[82]

When Riverside County, California deputies beat two suspected undocumented Mexican immigrants after a well-documented high-speed chase seen on the evening news, the AFL-CIO took strong exception. AFL-CIO Executive President Linda Chavez-Thompson said, "the movement will not tolerate this kind of brutality, nor will we excuse officers because the situation [was] volatile. . . . This is not a question of immigration rights, but of basic civil and human rights."[83]

The Lautenberg Amendment to the federal "Brady Bill" gun control legislation retroactively denies anyone convicted of a domestic violence misdemeanor from having a gun. When applied to police officers and federal agents, this controversial law ends their careers. Women's rights groups have supported the law because it denies a firearm to "cops who batter." Police unions have been angered by the retroactive application of the law, claiming it is unfair to take away an officer's livelihood with no advance notice. The Grand Lodge of the Fraternal Order of Police filed a lawsuit challenging the constitutionality of the law, a move supported by a number of unions, including the Detroit Police Officers Association.

Police unions also use high-visibility, high-impact tactics to further their objectives. Fraternal Order of Police Lodge 89 in Prince George's County, Maryland, spent $7,000 to erect billboards assailing what they saw as County Executive Wayne Curry's inaction on rising crime and an understaffed police department. Other police unions have used radio stations to broadcast 30- to 60-second messages designed to "bring heat" on politicians by mobilizing the public to their side. The Florida PBA (FPBA) has a plan that delivers 100 uniformed police officers every day to the state legislature while legislators are in session to lobby for bills the FPBA supports. Some police unions also have in-state toll-free numbers that can be automatically connected to the offices of key legislators, so members can lobby for their bills. When a sheriff spoke against the FPBA before a legislative committee, the FPBA campaigned against him in the next election; the incumbent was defeated, a strong showing of political muscle by the union.

Administrative Reaction to Job Actions

Anticipatory Strategies

There are no simple answers for what police administrators should do in the face of a job action. A short period of ignoring a work slowdown may see its natural dissipation, or it may become more widespread and escalate. Disciplinary action can effectively end a job action, or it might simply aggravate the situation further, causing the job action to intensify and become more protracted. In choosing a course of action, one must read the environment, assess the situation, review alternatives, decide on a course of action, implement it, monitor the impact, and make adjustments as necessary. In short, it is a decision-making process, albeit a delicate one.

The best way to handle job actions is for both management and the union to take the position that they have mutual responsibilities to avoid job actions. This may not, however, be uniformly possible; a union leadership that is seen to be too cooperative with management might, for example, be discredited by rank-and-file members, and a sick-out may occur. Negotiations that do not meet expectations of militant union members, however unrealistic, may produce a walkout. In general, the following can be expected to reduce the possibility of a job action:[84]

- The appropriate city officials (both appointed and elected), union leaders, and management must be trained in the tenets and practices of collective bargaining, particularly as they relate to mutual trust and the obligation to bargain in good faith.

- Formal and informal communications networks should be used freely within city government, the police agency, and the union for the transmission of messages between them. The timely sharing of accurate information is essential to good labor relations in that it reduces the opportunity for misinformation or non-information to create distance and build barriers.
- On a periodic basis, key managers from the police department, along with the staff and its labor relations unit, should meet with union leaders and the representatives, including elected officials, of the city who are responsible for the implementation of its labor relations program. This strengthens existing communications networks, it allows new networks to open, and it is a continuing affirmation of the mutualism that is central to the process of collective bargaining.
- Well before any job actions occur, management must develop and publicize the existence of a contingency plan that contemplates as many of the problems as reasonably can be foreseen with respect to each type of job action. For example, in planning for a strike, one must consider such things as how the rights and property of nonstrikers will be protected.[85] What security measures are to be invoked for government buildings and property? What are the minimum levels of personnel and supplies required? What special communications arrangements are necessary? Does the city's insurance cover potential liabilities to employees and property? What legal options exist, who has authority to invoke them, and under what circumstances? What coordination arrangements are needed with other police departments and government agencies? What effect will various strike policies have on labor relations after the strike? How will nonstriking officers and the public react to various strike policies? Can a striking employee injured on the picket line be placed on sick leave? Do striking employees accrue leave and retirement credit for the time they are out?
- In attempting to determine the possibility of various job actions, management must assess the philosophy, capabilities, strengths, weaknesses, and propensities of the union—its officers, negotiators, legal counsel, and members. That, along with an estimate of the financial resources of the union, will be useful in anticipating the actions in which it is likely to engage and toward which planning can be directed. Although the hallmark of good planning is that it provides for future states of affairs, management is most likely to underestimate the union's capabilities, and the planning bias should therefore be toward an overstatement of what is possible.

During the Job Action

Police managers must appreciate the long-range implications of any job action—a strike, for example. The striking officers are engaging, as is the employer, in a power struggle that has an economic impact on both parties. The union is not attempting to divest itself of its employer, and for both legal and practical reasons, the employer cannot unilaterally rid itself of its relationship with the union; at some point in the very near future, it is most likely that they will resume their former relationship.[86]

Considering this, managers must be temperate in their private and public remarks regarding striking officers; emotionally laden statements and cynical characterizations regarding strikers may provide a degree of fleeting satisfaction, but at some cost to the rapidity with which antagonisms can be set aside and the organization restored to its normal functioning. The union leadership and the rank-and-file membership have the same obligation; in the face of either management or the union not fulfilling its obligation, it becomes even more important that the other side be restrained in its remarks, or the ensuing trail of recriminations and biting comments will lead only to hostility and a degeneration of goodwill, both of which will have negative effects on future relations.

Managers should strive to maintain a fair and balanced posture on the subject of the strike, and their dominant focus should be on ending it. In addition, the following points should be noted:

- No reaction to a strike or another job action should be taken without first anticipating the consequences of a reaction from the union and the officers involved. For example, the decision to seek an injunction ordering the officers to terminate the action and return to work could result in the officers disobeying the order and forcing a confrontation with the court issuing the order. A public statement that all officers involved in the action will be fired places the chief in the difficult position after the conflict is terminated of either firing participating officers or losing face with his or her employees.
- All management responses to a strike should be directed toward terminating it only, not toward an ulterior purpose, such as trying to "bust" the union. There have been job actions in which the employer's sole objective was to destroy the union, an objective that frequently results in aggravated hostility between the employer and the union, between the chief and the officers participating in the action, and among the officers themselves. The long-range effect of this approach is to injure the morale of the police department, affecting the quality of police services and ultimately the level of service to the public.[87]

The degree of support that nonstriking employees, the media, the public, and elected and appointed officials will give management in the event of a strike is a product not only of the soundness of management's position but also of how effective management is in communicating. For a department whose workforce is depleted by a walkout, personnel are a scarce resource, and not to invest in communications efforts is a natural temptation tinged heavily by the reality of other needs that must also be considered. To be borne in mind, however, is the perspective that the effective use of some personnel in communications efforts may shorten the strike.

It is essential during a strike that communications be rapid, accurate, consistent, and broadly based. Nonstriking employees can be kept informed by the use of the daily bulletin, briefings, or other devices. Letters can be sent to the homes of striking officers, informing them of the applicable penalties for their actions, the status of negotiations, and management's present position with respect to these issues. Facsimile letters for this and other actions should already have been prepared as part of the development of the contingency plan.

Personal appearances by police managers before neighborhood groups, professional associations, civic clubs, and similar bodies can be useful in maintaining calmness in the community, in providing one means of informing the public of special precautionary measures they can take to protect themselves, and in galvanizing public opinion for management's position. Care must be taken to ensure that in this effort the needs of lower-socioeconomic groups are not overlooked. Special attention must be given to how they will be informed and how their needs will be listened to.

In the Aftermath

At some point, either the strike will collapse or an agreement will be reached, or both sides will agree to return to the bargaining table on the return of personnel to the job. Often, a tense atmosphere will prevail for some time. Nonstrikers will resent any threats made and any damage to their personal property. Those who walked out will view those who continued to work as not having helped maintain the solidarity necessary for effective job actions. Union members dissatisfied with what the strike did or did not produce may engage in the petty harassments of nonstrikers, display thinly veiled contempt for management, or surreptitiously cause damage to city property. Management's posture during the strike can in part reduce the tensions inherent in the poststrike adjustment period, but it cannot eliminate the need for responsible action by the union or overcome the intransigence of a subversely militant union.

As soon as an agreement ending the strike is reached, a joint statement with the union should be released, announcing the settlement and highlighting its key features, and letters should be sent to the homes of all officers, urging them to put aside the matter and return to the business of public service with renewed commitment. All personnel in the department should take particular care not to discriminate between those who struck and those who did not.

Other items of business that must be handled after a strike relate to whether strikers are to be disciplined, although the union will typically insist on amnesty for all striking officers as a precondition to returning to the job; in addition, it must be determined what disciplinary measures are to be taken against those who destroyed private or public property during the course of the strike; what measures are to be taken against those who undertook various actions against officers who did not walk out; and the securing of a union commitment not to act in any way against nonstrikers and to actively discourage such actions by union members.

There has been some experimentation with reconciliation meetings of parties to promote goodwill. Experience has demonstrated that, in most cases, the wounds are so fresh and the feelings so intense that it simply creates the opportunity for an incident. In one notable instance, a reconciliation party resulted in each of the groups remaining separated for 2 hours. Finally when each group reached the buffet table, a fight broke out between the strikers and nonstrikers.[88]

CONCLUSION

In the past 50 years, collective bargaining by police unions has had a profound impact on how police departments operate as well as the relationship between management and rank and file members. Their impact has been found on organizational discipline, accountability, city and county finances, as well as local, state, and federal politics.

CHAPTER REVIEW

1. Identify and briefly discuss the seven major factors combined that led to public sector collective bargaining.

2. What are the four areas that need to be examined in order to fully understand the impact of unions on a community. How do they impact the community?

3. Although public employee collective bargaining laws vary by state, the general thrust of the laws can be summarized by three simplified models. What are these three models?

4. Explain the process of a union organization drive.

5. Who generally serves on union and management teams during negotiations?

6. What is the typical sequence of steps involved in the grievance process?

7. List and describe the four major forms of job action.

8. Describe five anticipatory strategies police administrators can employ to reduce the possibility of job actions.

KEY TERMS

bargaining not required model: the model for police-sector collective bargaining law in which collective bargaining is not statutorily required by the state.

binding arbitration: a judgment made by a neutral third party to settle a dispute between labor and management, in which both parties agree in advance to abide by the result.

blue flu: a job action in which officers organize mass absences on the pretext of sickness for the purpose of protest against their employer.

code of silence: refusal of officers to testify against other officers who are accused of misconduct.

collective bargaining: negotiation between an employer and a labor union, usually regarding issues such as wages, benefits, hours, and working conditions.

grievance: an official expression of dissatisfaction brought by an employee or an employee organization as the initial step toward resolution through a formal procedure.

job action: a label used to describe several types of activities in which employees may engage to express their dissatisfaction with a particular person, event, or condition or to attempt to influence the outcome of a matter pending before decision makers, such as a contract bargaining impasse.

meet and confer model: referred to by some as "collective begging" because the laws or agreements establishing it confer little or no rights on employees. In the meet and confer model least friendly to employees, neither the employer nor the employees are required to meet. Such meetings are an opportunity, not a requirement.

Public Employment Relations Commission: an administrative body, often on a state level, responsible for administering legislation related to union bargaining.

ENDNOTES

[1] These themes are identified and treated in detail in Hervey A. Juris and Peter Feuille, *Police Unionism* (Lexington, Mass.: Lexington Books, 1973).

[2] Donald J. Boyd, *State/Local Employment Up Slightly Since the Start of Recession, But Cuts Are Now Underway* (Albany, NY: The Nelson A. Rockefeller Institute of Government, August 20, 2009).

[3] C. M. Rehmus, "Labor Relations in the Public Sector," Third World Congress, International Industrial Relations Association, in *Labor Relations Law in the Public Sector*, ed. Russell A. Smith, Harry T. Edwards, and R. Theodore Clark, Jr. (Indianapolis: Bobbs-Merrill, 1974), p. 7.

[4] Public Service Research Council, *Public Sector Bargaining and Strikes* (Vienna, Va.: Public Service Research Council, 1976), pp. 6–9.

[5] 296 F. Supp. 1068, 1969.

[6] 324 F. Supp. 315, N.D. Ga., 1971.

[7] 483 F. 2d 966, 10th Circuit, 1973.

[8] President's Commission on Law Enforcement and Administration of Justice, *Task Force Report: The Police* (Washington, D.C.: U.S. Government Printing Office, 1967), p. 144.

[9] Ibid., p. 145.

[10] From various tables, U.S. Department of Labor, *Employment and Earnings* 8, no. 4 (October 1961).

[11] Bureau of the Census, *Statistical Abstract of the United States, 1975* (Washington, D.C.: U.S. Government Printing Office, 1975), p. 162.

[12] John H. Burpo, *The Police Labor Movement* (Springfield, Ill.: Charles C Thomas, 1971), p. 34.

[13] Albert, *A Time for Reform*, p. 29. Several studies have reported that market forces other than unions explain better the rise in public employees' salaries than does union activity.

[14] The data were extracted from the Federal Bureau of Investigation's *Uniform Crime Reports* (Washington, D.C.: U.S. Government Printing Office, 1965, 1970).

[15] William W. Scranton, *Report of the President's Commission on Campus Unrest* (Washington, D.C.: U.S. Government Printing Office, 1970, p. 18).

[16] Samuel Walker, "The Neglect of Police Unions: Exploring One of the Most Important Areas of American Policing," *Police Practice and Research* 9, no. 2 (May 2008), pp. 102–107. (This discussion has been adapted from this source.)

[17] Christopher Commission, *Report of the Independent Commission to Investigate the Los Angeles Police Department* (Los Angeles, CA: City of Los Angeles, 1991), p. 120, available from http://www.parc.info; Human Rights Watch, *Shielded from Justice* (New York: Human Rights Watch, 1998); Mollen Commission, *Report* (New York: Mollen Commission, 1994), p.53, available from http://www.parc.info; J.H. Skolnick and J.J. Fyfe, *Above the Law* (New York: Free Press, 1993), pp. 108–112.

[18] H. A. Juris and P. Feuille, *Police Unionism* (Lexington: Lexington Books, 1973), pp. 142–145.

[19] K. Keenan and S. Walker, "An Impediment of Police Accountability? An Analysis of Statutory Law Enforcement Officers' Bill of Rights," *Boston University Public Interest Law Journal* 14 (2005), pp. 189–243.

[20] S. Walker, *Police Accountability: The Role of the Citizens Oversight* (Belmont, CA: Wadsworth, 2001).

[21] Christopher Commission, *Report of the Independent Commission,* 1991, pp. 97–106.

[22] B. Armacost, "Organizational Culture and Police Misconduct," *George Washington Law Review* 72, (2004), pp. 515–547.

23 S. Greenberg, "Police Chief Selection and Survival: Looming Crisis in America's Major Police Departments," in *Police Labor-Management Relations* (Vol. 1, pp. 47–57*)* (Washington, D.C.: Office of Community Oriented Policing Services, Department of Justice, 2006), p. 51.

24 S. Herbert, "Police Subculture reconsidered," *Criminology* 36, no. 2 (1998), pp. 343–368.

25 J. H. Skolnick, *Justice Without Trial* (New York: MacMillan, 1994); W. Westley, *Violence and Police* (Cambridge, MA: MIT Press, 1970).

26 S. Walker, "Racial Minority and Female Employment in Policing: The Implications of 'Glacial' Change," *Crime and Delinquency* 31, no. 4 (1985), pp. 555–572.

27 S. Herbert, "Police Subculture Reconsidered," *Criminology* 36, no. 2 (1998), pp. 343–368.

28 D. Weisburd, et al., *Police Attitudes Toward Abuse of Authority: Findings from a National Study* (NCJ 181312) (Washington, DC: Department of Justice, 2000), available from http://www.njcrs.gov

29 National Academy of Sciences, *Fairness and Effectiveness in Policing: The Evidence* (Washington, D.C.: National Academy Press, 2004), chap. 4; S. Walker and C. M. Katz, *The Police in America: An Introduction,* 6th ed. (New York: McGraw-Hall, 2008); S. Walker, et. al., *The Color of Justice: Race, Ethnicity, and Crime in* America, 4th ed. (Belmont, CA: Wadsworth, 2007), chap 4.

30 Juris and Feuille, *Police Unionism*, pp. 53–55.

31 President's Commission on Law Enforcement and Administration of Justice, *Task Force Report: The Police* (Washington, D.C.: Government Printing Office, 1967), pp. 163–178.

32 D. L. Carter, *The State of Police Education* (Washington, D.C.: Police Executive Research Forum, 1989).

33 Will Aitchison, *The Rights of Law Enforcement Officers*, 5th ed. (Portland Ore: Labor Relations Information Systems, 2004), pp. 8–11, 18–21. (This discussion and accompanying references were adapted from this source with permission.)

34 See §423.231 et seq., Michigan Comp. Laws Annotated (West, 1994).

35 *Hillsdale PBA v. Borough of Hillsdale*, 644 A. 2d 564 (N.J. 1994).

36 *Municipality of Anchorage v. Anchorage Police Department Employee's Association*, 839 P.2d 1080 (Alaska 1992); *City and County of San Francisco*, 43 Cal. Rptr.2d 421 (Cal.App. 1995); *City of Detroit v. Detroit Police Officers' Association*, 294 N.W.2d 68 (Mich. 1980); *City of Richfield v. Local 1215, Intern. Ass'n of Fire Fighters*, 276 N.W.2d 42 (Minn. 1979); *Medford Firefighters' Association v. City of Medford*, 595 P.2d 1268 (Or.App. 1979). But see *County of Riverside v. Superior Court*, 30 Cal.4th 278 (Cal. 2003) (binding arbitration violates unique provision of California state constitution); *Salt Lake City v. Inter. Assn. of Fire Fighters*, 563 P.2d 768 (Utah 1977) (overturns binding arbitration as unconstitutional delegation of legislative authority).

37 This "local option" has been adopted by such cities as Phoenix, Arizona; Boise, Idaho; Denver, Colorado; and San Antonio, Texas. In states that follow the meet and confer model, there usually exists a local option to allow interest arbitration as the last step in the bargaining process. For example, even though for years California followed the meet and confer model, cities in California such as Oakland and San Jose had local laws providing for interest arbitration.

38 This table is taken from *Interest Arbitration*, 2nd ed. (Portland, Ore: Labor Relations Information System, 1988).

39 E.g., *Village of Dixmoor*, 16 PERI ¶2038 (Ill. SLRB Gen. Counsel 2000).

40 E.g., *California Correctional Peace Officers Association v. State California*, 25 PERC ¶32,015 (Cal. PERB ALJ 2000).

41 *Borough v. Pennsylvania Labor Relations Board*, 794 A.2d 402 (Pa.Cmwlth. 2002).

42 A good early discussion of bargaining topics can be found in Clark, *The Scope of the Duty to Bargain in Public Employment, in Labor Relations Law in the Public Sector* 81 (A. Knapp ed. 1977).

43 *Portland Firefighters Association v. City of Portland*, 751 P.2d 770 (Or. 1988).

44 If an employer chooses to agree to include a permissive subject of bargaining in a collective bargaining agreement, and finds the provision to its distaste, it may simply refuse to include the provision in a subsequent agreement. *Paterson Police Local v. City of Paterson*, 432 A.2d 847 (N.J. 1981).

45 *City of Portland*, 8 PECBR 8115 (Or. 1985).

46 *City of Buffalo*, 13 NPER NY-13036 (N.Y. PERB 1990).

47 *County of Perry*, 19 NPER IL-124 (Ill. LRB2003).

48 *Plains Township Police Bargaining Unit v. Plains Township*, 33 PPER ¶33,019 (Pa. LRB ALJ 2001).

49 *City of Bremerton*, PEB ¶45,352 (Wash.) (CCH, 1987).

[50] *City of Iowa City*, 17 NPER IA-26005 (Iowa PERB ALJ 1995) delay of 90 days in filing unfair labor practice charge); *County of Nassau*, 35 NYPER ¶4583 (NY PERB ALJ 2002); *City of Reading*, 17 NPER PA-26132 (Pa. LRB ALJ 1995)); *City of Philadelphia*, 13 NPER PA-22042 (Pa. LRB Hearing Examiner 1991) (six-week delay between filing of unfair labor practice charge and violation of duty to bargain did not render the charge untimely).

[51] *Throop Borough*, 16 NPER PA-25012 (Pa. LRB ALJ 1993).

[52] *Law Enforcement Labor Services, Inc. v. City of Luverne*, 463 N.W.2d 546 (Minn.App.1990).

[53] *Peekskill Police Association*, 35 NYPER ¶3016 (N.Y. PERB 2002).

[54] *Caruso v. Board of Collective Bargaining of the City of New York*, 555 N.Y.S.2d 133 (A.D. 1990).

[55] Quoted in *Model Law Enforcement Contract, 1993 Edition* (Portland, Ore.: Labor Relations Information System, 1993).

[56] *Washington State Patrol*, 3 (8) Public Safety Labor News 7 (Wash. PERC 1995).

[57] *City of Grosse Pointe Park*, 14 MPER ¶32051 (Mich. ERC 2001).

[58] *City of Mt. Vernon*, 23 GERR 667 (New York)(BNA 1986).

[59] *Howard County*, 1 (9) Public Safety Labor News 5 (Fishgold, 1993).

[60] William J. Bopp, *Police Personnel Administration* (Boston: Holbrook HSS, 1974), p. 345.

[61] See Richard S. Rubin et al., "Public Sector Unit Determination Administrative Procedures and Case Law," Midwest Center for Public Sector Labor Relations, Indiana University Department of Labor Contract J-9-P-6–0215, May 31, 1978.

[62] In this regard, see Stephen L. Hayford, William A. Durkee, and Charles W. Hickman, "Bargaining Unit Determination Procedures in the Public Sector: A Comparative Evaluation," *Employee Relations Law Journal*, 5, no. 1 (summer 1979), p. 86.

[63] Donald Slesnick, "What Is the Effect of a Sunshine Law on Collective Bargaining: A Union View," *Journal of Law and Education* 5 (October 1976), p. 489.

[64] On costing out contracts, see Marvin Friedman, *The Use of Economic Data in Collective Bargaining* (Washington, D.C.: U.S. Government Printing Office, 1978).

[65] Charles W. Maddox, *Collective Bargaining in Law Enforcement* (Springfield, Ill.: Charles C Thomas, 1975), p. 54.

[66] Arnold Zack, *Understanding Grievance Arbitration in the Public Sector* (Washington, D.C.: U.S. Government Printing Office, 1974), p. 1.

[67] Maddox, *Collective Bargaining*, p. 109.

[68] Zack, *Understanding Grievance Arbitration*, p. 4.

[69] Maurice S. Trotta, *Arbitration of Labor–Management Disputes* (New York: Amacon, 1974), p. 237, with changes.

[70] See Helen Lavan and Cameron Carley, "Analysis of Arbitrated Employee Grievance Cases in Police Departments," *Journal of Collective Negotiations in the Public Sector* 14, no. 3 (1985), pp. 250–251.

[71] Zack, *Understanding Grievance Arbitration*, p. 32.

[72] Ibid.

[73] Michael Cooper, "Police Picket Traffic Courts, as Pact Protests Go On," *New York Times*, January 27, 1997, p. B3.

[74] Peter Finn, "Police Officers Send Pointed Message: More Than 150 Pagers Turned in to Protest Alexandria Pay Scale," *Washington Post*, January 24, 1997, p. B6.

[75] Stephanie Reitz, "Council Approves Police Contract in East Hartford," *Hartford Courant*, March 19, 1997, p. B1.

[76] Jack Rabin, Thomas Vocino, W. Bartley Hildreth, and Gerald J. Miller, eds., *Handbook of Public Sector Labor Relations* (New York: Marcel Dekker, 1994), p. 6.

[77] On these and related points, see Robert P. Engvall, "Public Sector Unionization in 1995 or It Appears the Lion King Has Eaten Robin Hood," *Journal of Collective Negotiations in the Public Sector* 24, no. 3 (1995), pp. 255–269.

[78] Indira A. R. Lakshmanan, "3 Allegedly Protest On-Call Police Duty," *Boston Globe*, July 10, 1995.

[79] Daniel B. Wood, "Police Strike Hits L.A. as Tourist Season Opens," *Christian Science Monitor*, June 3, 1994, p. 2.

[80] Kim Bell, " 'Blue Flu' Strikes in St. Louis," *St. Louis Post-Dispatch*, May 30, 1993, p. D1.

[81] *Detroit Free Press*, February 8, 1997.

[82] Don Aucoin, *Boston Globe*, September 27, 1997.

[83] http://204.127.237.106/newsonline/96apr22/beatings.html

[84] On September 29, 1976, Richard M. Ayres presented a paper, "Police Strikes: Are We Treating the Symptom Rather Than the Problem?" at the 83rd International Association of Chiefs of Police meeting, Miami Beach, Florida. Although it is not quoted here, some of his themes may be identifiable, and his contribution in that regard is acknowledged.

[85] This list of questions with modifications and additions is drawn from Charles C. Mulcahy, "Meeting the County Employees Strike," in *Collective Bargaining in the Public Sector*, pp. 426–430. See also Carmen D. Saso, *Coping with Public Employee Strikes* (Chicago: Public Personnel Association, 1970).

[86] Harold W. Davey, *Contemporary Collective Bargaining* (Englewood Cliffs, N.J.: Prentice Hall, 1972), p. 195.

[87] John H. Burpo, *Labor Relations Guidelines for the Police Executive* (Chicago: Traffic Institute, Northwestern University, 1976), p. 14, with modifications and additions.

[88] Lee T. Paterson and John Liebert, *Management Strike Handbook* (Chicago: International Personnel Management Association, 1974), p. 42.

12

Financial Management

*Not least among the
qualifications of
administrators is their
ability as a tactician and
gladiator in the budget
process.*
—Frederick C. Mosher

Objectives

- Give three definitions of *budget*.

- Explain what a fiscal year is and give examples of two different fiscal years.

- Contrast operating and capital budgets.

- Describe the steps in the budget cycle.

- Describe financial and performance audits. Why are performance audits more varied in their approach from financial audits.

- Identify the focus of a line item budget and a program budget.

- Define *performance budget* and explain why performance budgets have substantially abandoned cost measures.

- Discuss hybrid budgets and why they exist.

- Identify three major ways in which a police budget can be supplemented.

OUTLINE

Introduction

This chapter is important to the development of police leaders for the following reasons: (1) budgeting does not occur simply in a police context, it occurs within a larger framework of state laws and regulations, city or county charters, guidance from city/county chief executives and finance officers, legislative bodies, local ordinances, and regulations, and the social, political, and economic environments; complete police administrators must understand the larger context and their own departmental budgeting practices to be effective; (2) essentially, three things fuel law enforcement agencies: funding, people, and information; continuous learning about all three is essential; (3) an administrator's role in the budget process increases as he or she climbs the rank ladder; learning now prepares one for the future; (4) the budget process is closely watched by more senior appointed and elected officials, police associations and unions, auditors, and the news media; to a large degree the measure of police administrators is how well they prepare, present, and execute their department's budget; and (5) a reputation as a good financial manager is a major asset when fighting cutbacks or seeking appropriations for new programs.

The Economy and Police Budgets

This recession began in December 2007 and is the longest since the 1930s.[1] Falling property values causes tax revenues to decline, unemployment figures are not favorable, consumer spending is restricted, and mortgage foreclosures, loan defaults, and personal bankruptcies are significant. Recovery forecasts vary, but improvement is likely to be sluggish. In the current environment, many public agencies are in fiscal stress. In 2010 and 2011, state governments faced a collective budget shortfall of $375 million,[2] resulting in state police and patrol agencies cutting staff; closing district offices; delaying, reducing, or charging for forensic services to local law enforcement agencies;[3] and no longer patrolling sections of interstate highways passing through municipalities, creating an additional demand for services on cash-starved local police departments.[4] All of this illustrates again the point of Chapter 1, "Historical Development of Policing," that policing is affected by the currents of the society in which it is embedded.

Municipalities are also confronted with many of the financial challenges facing the states. Cities are currently faced with fiscal shortfalls that may reach $83 billion by 2012.[5] As a result, cities are renegotiating their debts and cancelling capital infrastructure projects, including school construction, repair of aging water and sewer lines, improvements to ports, redevelopment of business districts, and improvements to police communication systems.

Law enforcement agencies are freezing new hires, cancelling recruit training classes,[6] forcing officers to take unpaid days off, reducing their salaries as much as 22 percent,[7] closing precincts,[8] delaying the purchase of replacement vehicles, selling helicopters,[9] closing police stations to the public,[10] slashing popular community-oriented police staffing,[11] eliminating mounted patrol, motorcycle, and marine patrol units,[12] and laying off officers and slashing overtime funding. The financial management skills of law enforcement executives are being severely tested by the circumstances of our economy. Even their best efforts may not be sufficient: Hundreds of small towns have abolished their police departments[13] often these small towns contract with the state police or a sheriff's office for minimal law enforcement services.

For many police departments, the fat has been trimmed and the cuts are now into muscle and bone, affecting service delivery, such as increased response time, in ways that citizens can feel. Slashed budgets are particularly vulnerable to deficit spending because there are so many "budget busters" that cannot be foreseen—for example, natural disasters,[14] such as hurricanes (see Figure 12.1), tornadoes, earthquakes, floods, floods, mudslides, and fires, rioting following a city winning a championship, prolonged searches for missing persons, protracted union strikes, complex investigations involving serial offenders, unforeseeable surges in the price of gasoline, terrorist

IN THE NEWS Investigations Sit Idle as LAPD Detectives Hit Overtime Caps

In dire financial circumstances, the LAPD has, with rare exceptions, put an end to paying detectives overtime. This delays important investigative work, such as interviewing witnesses. Contrary to past practices, fewer detectives are now sent to the crime scene, including killings when the first 48 hours of investigative effort can make a crucial difference. Detectives are now required to take time off for overtime in lieu of overtime pay, creating a further drain on staffing.

Source: LOS ANGELES TIMES, April 12, 2010, with restatement.

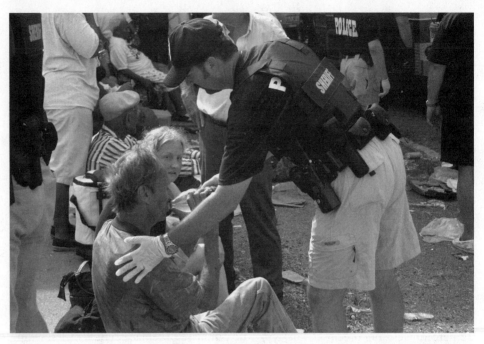

Figure 12.1
New Orleans, Louisiana, two days after Hurricane Katrina struck (2005). A sheriff's deputy helps an elderly man, too weak to lift his bottle of water, take a drink.
(Photo by Win Henderson/Federal Emergency Management Agency [FEMA])

Quick
FACTS ▸▸ Budgeting and Accounting

Some police personnel are dismissive about budgeting, claiming it's "accountant's work." The claim reveals a lack of information about how the two concepts are related. Budgeting is prospective, future oriented; accounting is retrospective, past oriented.

Source: Robert D. Lee, Ronald W. Johnson, and Philip G. Joyce. *Public Budgeting Systems* (Boston: Jones and Bartlett, 8th Edition, 2008), p. 17.

---

attacks, demonstrations, and the cost of using private labs to process key evidence in significant cases. In many of these examples, cutting staffing and reducing overtime funds in the police budget are not compatible strategies because the need to respond to special circumstances quickly overspends the overtime budget. In very small departments, the budget may be "busted" by lesser events, such as having to replace a copier machine or buying a new patrol car because of an accident.

Police executives are not going to be criticized about financial management when unforeseeable "budget busters" occur. However, when mistakes are made on basic matters, budget appropriators are typically unsympathetic. A state police commissioner failed to request $4 million to train the new troopers the state legislature had authorized hiring. To express its displeasure, the state legislature froze trooper hiring for one year.

Politics and Financial Management

Anything done by government involves the expenditure of public funds.[15] Even the expenditure of grant money from a private foundation to a law enforcement agency requires the use of public funds to audit it. Budgeting is inherently a political process because elected members of city councils, county commissions, and state legislatures express their preferences when they vote on appropriations. The appropriators' personal views and those of their constituents, the news media, police unions, polls, special interest groups, lobbyists, and other sources shape these decisions. Politics do not stop when a budget is adopted; in some circumstances the politics can actually intensify (see Figure 12.2).

Like the Boston Tea Party of 1773, opposition to President Obama's health plan sparked furious opposition from groups dubbed "Tea Partiers." The Tea Party has no affiliation with any political party and has no national leader.[16] Anti-tax and -big government, the Tea Partiers have not abandoned their opposition to the enacted health plan and are making their views known on local government spending issues. While the Tea Partiers' impact on local budgeting is not yet known, it is a force for police chiefs to watch carefully.

Figure 12.2
NYPD officers investigating the scene of a shooting (2010). Mayor Bloomberg blames the spike in murders on budget cuts that put fewer officers on the streets.
(Bryan Pace/*New York Daily News*)

State and Local Influences on Financial Management

Cities and counties are under the authority of their respective state governments, which have considerable authority over them, including their financial management. Local governments cannot be created, nor can they levy taxes or deliver services without the prior approval of the state. Following the economic crash of 1929, thousands of local governments went bankrupt because they could not meet their financial obligations. As a result, many states passed laws that regulate local finance in such areas as revenue sources, tax collection, level of permissible indebtedness, budgeting procedures, and audits. Typically, states prohibit cities and counties from borrowing to fund annual operating budgets; historically such borrowing signaled bankruptcy was on the near horizon.[17] States also require detailed financial reports from local governments, which are carefully studied for signs of fiscal weakness.

In addition to whatever requirements the state establishes, local financial management is guided by a maze of other guidelines, including the city or county charter, ordinances, executive orders, regulations, and customary practices. The form of local government, discussed earlier in Chapter 4, Politics and Police Administration, shapes who the dominant figures are in finance. In a strong mayor system, the mayor is the key player, whereas in the weak mayor form, the council is the predominant force. In a mayor–city manager system, the manager holds great power. These generalizations are affected by other factors, such as how much influence a long-serving finance director has accrued and the degree to which a council is more or less proactive in the budget process.

Key Budget Terms

Every year, the most important statement governments make is the approval of their budgets because it reveals in financial terms what their priorities are. There are different ways to define a **budget**. For example, it is a plan expressed in dollars, it is the use of financial resources to meet human needs, and it is a contract between those who appropriate the money and those who execute the budget.[18]

A budget year is called a **fiscal year (FY)**, and it may coincide with the calendar year. Often, FYs run from July 1 of one year until June 30 of the next year. A budget, which begins on July 1, 2012 and ends on June 30, 2013, is called a FY '13 budget. Some local units of government have changed their fiscal year to October 1 of one year

Quick
FACTS ▸▸ Budget Definition

"Budget" comes from the French *bougette,* meaning a leather bag. Originally, it referred to the bag in which the Chancellor of the | Exchequer carried budget documents to the English Parliament. Later, it came to mean the documents themselves.

Source: A. E. Buck, *The Budgets in Governments Today* (New York: Macmillan, 1945), p. 5.

until September 30 of the next year to coincide with the federal budget year. About half of the states and some local units of government use a **biennial budget**, which covers a 2-year period.

Budgets can also be defined as operating and capital.[19] An **operating budget** usually covers a 12-month period and is for such things as salaries, fringe benefits, uniforms, crime scene supplies, ammunition, training, and telephone service. It is a recurrent budget. A **capital budget**, or a single **capital improvement project (CIP)**, is for large-scale expenditures that may be "one-time" in nature and take place over several years, such as acquiring land and building a new police station. In contrast to operating budgets, CIPs are typically nonrecurrent.

The city/county's finance/financial services department (F/FSD) provides guidelines covering what types of expenditures should be in the operating versus the capital budget, and these guidelines vary from one jurisdiction to another. For example, in one city any equipment that costs $500 or less per unit (e.g., one shotgun) is in the operating budget, while in another municipality if the unit cost is $250 or more and it has a useful life of more than one year, it is in the capital budget. Operating and capital budgets are normally considered at separate times by the legislative bodies that appropriate the funds.

The Budget Cycle

At its heart, the **budget cycle** is a stream of four sequential steps that are repeated at about the same time every year in a jurisdiction: (1) preparation and submission of the budget by all of a city or county's departments, which includes getting input from stakeholders, such as citizens and advisory boards; (2) review and approval by the legislative body, which may involve controversies; (3) execution, doing the things for which public funds have been appropriated; and (4) the audit and evaluation.[20] Many of these activities are going on simultaneously because the current fiscal year and the next budget cycle overlap or are "scrambled" together.[21] For example, while a sheriff's, or police department is executing this year's budget, last year's budget is being audited and the next year's budget is being prepared.

Quick **FACTS** ▸▸ Citizen Centric Reports (CCRs)

Citizens in the United States have long had multiple opportunities to provide input on budget priorities and appropriations. Such opportunities are now being enhanced by a new technique, which may take the name of "citizen guide" or some similar title. In plain language and usually limited to four pages, citizen guides answer four questions: (1) What are we chartered (required) to do? (2) How are we doing?—a summary of service delivery outcomes; (3) What does it cost?—the cost data are linked to the service delivery outcomes; and (4) What's new?—covers challenges and the economic outlook. Citizen guides are widely distributed in print and are typically available on the city or country's website.

Well before a police department starts preparing its budget, the F/FSD has been at work preparing the revenue forecast for the city and other data, including the budget preparation manual. These manuals focus on the technical aspects of putting the budget together and include definitions, forms, and the **budget calendar** (see Figure 12.3). The city or county manager then sends the budget manual to the

Action	Responsibility	Deadlines
Budget kickoff: Budget manual and city manager's transmittal letter (the "budget call") distributed to all departments, often done in a meeting with additional comments[a]	City manager	October 1, 2012
Department heads issue their budget message to immediately subordinate unit commanders (e.g., deputy chiefs or majors in charge of bureaus or divisions)	Police chief	October 15, 2012
City holds budget preparation workshops; police representatives—may be mix of civilians and sworn personnel—involved in preparing police budget attend	F/FSD holds workshop	October 22–23, 2012
Recommended budgets for all police bureaus or divisions developed with justification and submitted to police budget office	Bureau/division commanders	February 1, 2013
Recommended bureau or division budgets reviewed with the respective commanders	Police budget office with bureau or division commanders; chief may participate	February 18–22, 2013
Bureau or division budgets consolidated into overall department budget	Police budget office	March 1, 2013
Overall police budget reviewed by chief	Chief, bureau or division commanders, police budget office	March 4–15, 2013
Police department budget approved for submission to city manager or F/FSD	Chief	March 18, 2013
City manager meets separately with department heads to review their budget requests	City manager, police chief, other department heads	April 1–12, 2013
Department budgets revised per city manager's guidance	Chief, police budget office	April 15–May 10, 2013
City manager forwards recommended budget to city council	City manager	May 16, 2013
City council as a whole or through its finance/ways and means committee reviews departmental budgets	City council	May 17–31, 2013
City manager and departments present their respective budgets separately to city council and respond to questions	City manager, department heads, city council	June 3–14, 2013
City council holds public hearings on city budget[b]	City council	June 17–21, 2013
City council approves budget and it becomes effective	City council	July 1, 2013

Figure 12.3
A police department's FY '13 budget calendar.
[a]Budget calendars vary widely in local government. This figure omits the handling of capital improvement projects (CIPs) and advanced financial topics, such as the submission of departmental earnings estimates, setting the tax millage rate, and forums for getting citizen input on priorities and programs.
[b]The number of public hearings required may be set in the city/county charter, by local ordinance, or by state law.

department heads with specific guidelines on services to be emphasized and specific fiscal guidance as to the amount the budget may increase or must decrease, the availability of funds to give employees raises, limits on new positions and programs, and other fiscal data. Often, the budget message from the city or county manager, the budget preparation manual, and past budgets are available online, along with the software needed to prepare the budget. Budget workshops can be held by the F/FSD to explain the process and help promote uniformity in the budget process across departments.

Before sending out the budget preparation manual, city and county managers usually meet with their mayor and council or commission informally or formally to get their views on budget priorities to avoid major conflict later in the budget process. Many jurisdictions conduct strategic planning and budget workshops at various points in the budget process to get citizen and city council or county commission input early in the process, especially with respect to goals, priorities, and target budget figures. These measures do not guarantee there won't be conflict later, but they do reduce some potential for it. Occasionally, differences arise in budgeting over seemingly minor programs (see Quick Facts: Geese Police Restored in Budget).

Step One: Budget Preparation in the Police Department

In small police departments, those with roughly 10 or fewer officers, the chief's role in budget preparation is minimal.[22] Most frequently, strong mayors or city managers will have several conversations with the chief and formulate the budget themselves. In larger departments with seven or eight layers of hierarchy, the budget process is more formal. A chief's budget is shaped by the guidance given by a city or county manager and, in that context, is a top-down process. However, to know what the actual needs are, the lowest-ranking supervisors in the department, usually sergeants, may be involved in identifying needs and, in that regard, the budget is a bottom-up process. The budget is built by combining the budget requests from smaller units to form the budgets of bureaus or divisions. The single most important element in a police budget is people and their support costs, such as salaries, medical insurance, life insurance, and pension benefits, as well as overtime and training. In many departments, personnel and personnel support costs may consume 80 or more percent of the budget, limiting what can be done with the overall budget.

 Quick FACTS ▸▸ Geese Police Restored in Budget

The Eatontown, New Jersey city finance staff cut the budget $12,000 by eliminating the "Geese Police," a dog that chased the geese from Wampum Memorial Park. The city council's president expressed anger at the cut. One council member said the program was very effective, it maximized the use of the park, and the budget should be amended to fund the Geese Police.

Source: Sherry Conohan, Atlanticville [Long Branch, New Jersey], March 5, 2004.

In a tight budget year, some chiefs cut back on training dollars. This might make the budget work, but it is a poor strategy. Any chief who submitted a budget without dollars in it for preventive maintenance of the police fleet would be criticized; yet, training is the preventive maintenance on people. It keeps personnel fresh and at the cutting edge, prevents litigation or can be a defense to it, and is a principal means of importing new ideas and techniques into the police department.

As to delaying the purchase of replacement vehicles, officers operating vehicles with 100,000 and more miles are using cars that are dangerously worn out, no matter how well they have been maintained.

When the chief meets with bureau or division commanders to review their budget requests, it is an opportunity to reward the "faithful" and to informally discipline those who are seen as "not toeing the party line" and are therefore "disloyal." In lean budget years, however, it is harder to reward the faithful and easier to harm a wayward subordinate's interests.

Chiefs are also concerned with budget strategy and making the best case for funding. If solid justifications cannot be made for programs, they should not be included in the request lest it set budget analysts in the F/FSD on a quest to find more programs to cut. As a matter of strategy, chiefs typically include some "fat" in the budget, so that they can withstand a certain degree of reductions. The fat is not wasteful spending; it represents new positions or programs the department would like to have and would make good use of but whose loss would not endanger the delivery of important services.

In transmitting the budget to the city manager, the chief's cover letter will highlight accomplishments from the current budget and will call attention to the importance of new initiatives and the ills likely to arise if the request is cut. No matter what is happening in terms of the amount of crime, chiefs have an explanation that favors a budget increase. If crime is up, more personnel and programs are needed to reduce it; if things are going well, new funding will help keep crime in check.

Step Two: Budget Review and Approval

At some point, the city manager will meet with the police chief to review the department's request. Prior to that meeting, the F/FSD will have reviewed the budget and had discussions about it with the city manager. How the meeting with the city manager goes depends on many factors, including the chief's reputation as a fiscal manager, the priorities and direction given by the city council, and the confidence the public has in the chief and the police department. Even recent events can affect the outcome. For example, the chief may have a street crime unit whose tactics include using decoys who are similar to the types of victims being targeted by predatory criminals (e.g., indigents, the elderly, and lone females). If in the past week an offender was killed attempting to rob a decoy, the newspapers and public sentiment may run toward disbanding this "killer" unit. Ultimately, the city manager and chief come to an understanding about the department's request. That understanding is reflected in the budget the city manager recommends to council.

At budget hearings before their city councils, chiefs must tread a narrow path. If they attempt to restore cuts made by the city manager, they risk alienating the city manager. Conversely, if the cuts have gone too deep, chiefs as a matter of public safety may feel obliged to appeal for the funds to be restored (see Figure 12.4). Safer than initiating the appeal on their own, experienced chiefs may plant key questions with friendly members of council so that the discussion can be had without them openly spearheading the discussion. City managers know this game and can tolerate it, versus having their chiefs openly defy them. Generally, even council members who favor increasing the police budget may be reluctant to do so if it means voting for a tax increase.

Following several years of severe major budget cuts, one chief wrote a "budget impact" statement, explaining in detail to the city council that the effect of mandated cuts would be the loss of 110 positions and several programs.[23] This statement became a means of building budget support and mediating criticisms of slow service by the police department. One immediate result was that, through public donations, the mounted patrol continued to operate, albeit at about half its previous number of officers.

When making their budget "pitch" to the city council, chiefs should be able to anticipate questions. For example, if the U.S. Department of Justice has just released

Figure 12.4
2010, Baltimore Police Commissioner Bealefeld tells Mayor Rawlings-Blake that it would take 10 years for the police department to recover from the proposed budget cuts.
(*The Baltimore* [Maryland] *Sun/Amy Davis*)

Figure 12.5
Immigration reform demonstrators on the Mall in Washington, D.C., (2010).
(Nicholas Kamm/AFP/Getty Images)

a study on racial profiling, the chief is going to have to field the question "Are we involved in racial profiling?" or if there is a large Hispanic population, "What provisions have you made for immigration reform demonstrations?" (see Figure 12.5). In the final analysis, in some years chiefs, no matter how good a presentation they made, simply have to be political realists and gracefully take their "budgetary lumps."

Table 12.1 shows the operating budget approval process for a police department's patrol division for FY 2010. The first column, "Org," refers to the organizational unit (01474), which refers to the patrol division; each division in the police department has a different "Org" number. "OBJ" is the number of the object of expenditure for each line; the object of expenditure for "6003" is "Payroll-Regular." The columns labeled "FY 2006 Actual" to "FY 2009 Actual" give council members a quick 4-year summary of patrol's budget trend. "FY 2010 Mayor Proposed" is the budget recommendation of the mayor to the town council, which, as the legislative body, has the final authority on budgets. The town council agreed with the mayor on eight lines in the patrol budget, but came to different conclusions on two others. The budget format used in Table 12.1 is a "line item," discussed in more detail in a later section of this chapter.

Step Three: Budget Execution

This section deals with three key aspects of **budget execution**: (1) budget execution objectives, (2) budget execution adjustments, and (3) budget execution control.

Table 12.1
BUDGET APPROVAL PROCESS

ORG	OBJ	Department/ Description	FY 2006 Actual	FY 2007 Actual	FY 2008 Actual	FY 2009 Budget	FY 2010 Mayor Proposed	FY 2010 Town Council Approved	Percent Change
		Police Patrol							
01474	6003	Payroll — Regular	4,283,889	4,428,791	4,612,450	4,497,410	4,510,787	4,510,787	0.30%
01474	6008	Special Officers/ Events	67,297	90,414	149,508	60,480	122,823	112,823	86.55%
01474	6009	Payroll — Supplementary	202,006	226,554	188,437	240,000	140,000	140,000	−41.67%
01474	6020	Payroll — Overtime	137,398	204,775	127,687	84,000	125,000	125,000	48.81%
01474	6021	Court Time & Travel	—	—	—	1,960	—	—	−100.00%
01474	6022	Shift Differential	113,690	125,089	117,547	124,460	124,460	124,460	0.00%
01474	6024	Callback	659,794	551,044	441,546	425,000	393,000	383,000	−9.88%
01474	6058	Uniform Maintenance	64,991	69,774	72,282	64,800	69,600	69,600	7.41%
01474	6156	Prisoner Meals	5,358	6,557	2,665	2,500	2,500	2,500	0.00%
01474	6302	Equipment Service	19,533	20,198	10,360	19,600	19,600	19,600	0.00%
			5,553,956	5,723,198	5,722,482	5,520,210	5,507,770	5,487,770	−0.23%

Budget Execution Objectives

Budget execution is the action phase of budgeting, the phase in which plans contained in the police budget are put into operation.[24] During this phase police chiefs:

1. must rigorously pursue achieving the goals of the agency;
2. document service gaps, the distance between the types and amounts of service delivery planned for versus actual demand;
3. provide timely information on expenditures, program accomplishments, and milestones for any CIP projects to senior appointed and elected officials, as well as the legislative body, such as city council, which appropriated the budget;

4. publicize police department successes; and

5. maintain budget execution control, a responsibility which is shared with the F/FSD and discussed in a subsequent section.

Budget Execution Adjustments

It is said that people plan and fate laughs; like other types of plans, budgets must be monitored and adjusted as needed. Common methods of adjusting the budget include (1) reallocating funds from one category to another, subject to any approval that is needed, (2) seeking a budget amendment to provide supplemental funds some months into the execution phase when it is clear that anticipated demands for police services are outstripping resources, (3) freezing expenditures when the city's or county's revenue collection may be slower than anticipated, and (4) cutting the budget due to significant shortfalls in revenue collection.[25] Police chiefs can seek budget adjustments by the first two methods; a chief in anticipation of pending fiscal stress might freeze expenditures. However, freezing expenditures and cutting budgets is ordinarily a decision made by a strong mayor or city manager in consultation with city council.

Budget Execution Controls

Even if the budget is not changed during its execution, budget controls are crucial to public accountability for the use of resources entrusted to the unit of government involved. Means of control are specified by state law and regulations, city/county charters and ordinances, and the policies and procedures established by the F/FSD, and the police chief.

Budget controls serve several purposes: (1) ensuring that laws, regulations, and accepted accounting procedures are followed, (2) making sure the funds are expended for the purposes authorized by the appropriators, (3) protecting resources from mismanagement or fraud,[26] (4) eliminating waste to preserve public funds, (5) preventing deficit spending, (6) identifying problems so responsibility can be fixed and remedial action taken, and (7) identifying gaps in control procedures that must be rectified.

The single most important aspect of both external and internal controls is separating the responsibility for various functions, which promotes the benefits of specialization and limits the ability of a few people to misuse or corrupt the system. Thus, for example, the purchasing department obtains competitive bids for equipment, but a different office, accounts payable, actually writes the checks, the police department verifies the delivery of the equipment, and a separate inventory control office accounts for the placement and use of the equipment. [27]

External Controls. External control is the control exercised on a police department's budget from outside of the police department. Each city or county's F/FSD is the primary external control agent for the police and other departments. The control methods here are illustrations; the full range of controls is much richer.

One universal method of external control is the allotment system. The F/FSD breaks each department's budget into portions, called **allotments**, which are amounts of money made available to the departments for specific periods of time, such as for a month or a 3-month period, called a quarterly allotment. Allotments allow the F/FSD to time the availability of funding in the police department to the actual need for their expenditure. Therefore, allotments may vary in their amount from one month or quarter to another. This allows governments to invest funds not immediately needed. Freezing expenditures and cutting the budget are also external budget control measures.

In jurisdictions and particularly where there has been fraud or abuse in agencies, the F/FSD may conduct a "pre-audit" of transactions before purchases can be made. The F/DSD periodically generates financial reports, such as Table 12.2, which they send to all departments. These budget status reports play a significant role in monitoring expenditures. The final element in external control is audit and evaluation, discussed later in this chapter, as it is also the fourth and last component of the budget cycle.

Internal Controls. A police department's internal control encompasses both its own accounting controls and policies and procedures intended to safeguard access to, and use of, organizational assets, to verify financial transactions (such as cash payments from the informant fund), to encourage operational efficiency, and to foster adherence to fiscal policies. All together, the fundamental purpose of internal controls is to prevent mistakes before they happen and to rectify them when they occur.

Table 12.2
A PORTION OF A POLICE DEPARTMENT'S BUDGET STATUS REPORT, DECEMBER 31, 2010

Line Item	Approved	To Date Expended	Encumbered*	Balance	% Expended
Salaries	$1,710,788.00	$848,161.05	$0.00	$862,626.95	49.58%
Training	$15,000.00	$5,374.47	$6,098.00	$9,625.53	35.83%
Professional services	$6,000.00	$2,000.00	$0.00	$4,000.00	33.33%
Travel	$8,500.00	$3,500.57	$1,500.25	$4,999.43	41.18%
Dues and subscriptions	$3,100.00	$1,800.00	$0.00	$1,300.00	58.06%
Utilities	$35,000.00	$17,213.81	$0.00	$17,786.19	49.18%
Office supplies	$22,000.00	$7,688.93	$634.39	$14,311.07	34.95%
Printing	$8,300.00	$4,187.23	$0.00	$4,112.77	50.45%
Uniforms	$38,000.00	$18,725.13	$0.00	$19,274.87	49.28%
Totals	**$1,846,688.00**	**$908,651.19**	**$8,232.64**	**$938,036.81**	49.20%

*Before a contract is signed or a purchase order issued, the F/FSD first determines if the funds are available in the budget. If they are, the amount involved is encumbered, meaning that it is held in reserve for payment upon delivery of the services or goods and is not part of the available balance in the budget.

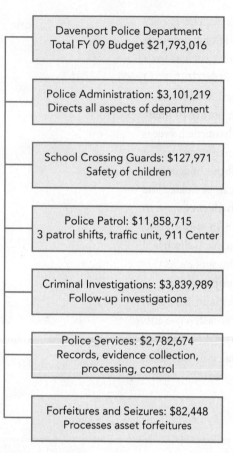

Figure 12.6
Major cost centers in the Davenport, Iowa, Police Department's FY '09 budget.

Examples of internal controls include breaking the overall budget for the police department into smaller, more easily managed amounts based on units or activities, often referred to as cost centers (see Figure 12.6). Expenditures must be authorized in advance by appropriate documentation and authorizations.

Internal controls are crucial not only in the budget context but for the operation of the police agency as well. Operational controls include policies on the use of tasers, impact weapons, pursuits, and use of deadly force.

Step Four: The Audit and Evaluation

Stated simply, an **audit** is a check on something; Governments audit themselves on an on-going basis throughout the FY. Historically, annual audits were of a department's budget, expenditures, and financial management practices—a financial audit (**FA**). In most states the annual FA is submitted to the Office of State Auditor, where it is reviewed and any needed follow-up action taken. Financial auditors systematically collect and examine records and reports, conduct interviews, and otherwise rely on competent evidence to determine whether:

1. Required financial records and reports were made in a timely and complete form;
2. Public funds were subject to any waste, fraud, or abuse;
3. Unauthorized charges to the budget or reimbursements from the budget were made;
4. Computations are accurate;
5. Unauthorized transfers from one budget category to another were made;
6. Procurement requirements were followed; and
7. Expenditures were at or less than the approved budget.

Although there was some earlier movement, another type of annual audit began stirring in the late 1970s, determining how good of a job an agency was doing—a **performance audit (PA)**. Today, in many jurisdictions, an "audit" often encompasses both financial and performance components. Because financial audits have a lengthy history, the standards for them are well established and they have a fixed focus to them.[28] The U.S. Government Accountability Office's (GAO) guidelines for both FAs and PAs are contained in its *Generally Accepted Government Auditing Standards* (GAGAS, 2007). GAGAS, often referred to as the "yellow book," notes that the focus of a PA is variable, according to the purpose stated for its execution. PAs may focus on some aspect of a police department's performance (e.g., compliance with legal mandates, program effectiveness and results, or a prospective analysis, such as the future value of a street crime decoy unit).[29]

The essence of all audits is that an independent party who has no stake in the outcome of the audit does the checking. To ensure the independence of auditors, some jurisdictions elect them, in others the legislative body, such as a city council or county commission, may appoint the auditor or a firm specializing in auditing governments will be retained.

Before an audit report is submitted in any unit of government, it is discussed with the chief of police and any errors of fact, representation, interpretation, or conclusion are corrected. If there is still content for which the auditor and the chief have differing opinions, the chief may write a **letter of exception**, setting forth the reasons why he or she believes that the audit report is wrong or manifestly unfair. After the city council reviews the audit report, the chief may be directed to appear before the council to answer questions, or the council may simply task the city manager or finance director to make sure the police department takes any needed corrective action. No one enjoys criticisms because they identify weaknesses, yet a wise chief knows that correcting deficiencies is a pathway to enhanced performance and makes any needed changes without rancor.

Budget Formats

At the turn of the 20th century, there was nothing resembling the budget cycle previously described in this chapter. The power center in budgeting was the legislative body and its respective committees. Budgeting was a chaotic process because there was no central point, such as a budget office, where budget requests from departments were reviewed or revised. Moreover, committees, rather than a legislative body as a whole, often had the authority to appropriate funds for departments. Lump sum budgets were requested by the departments without any supporting details and sent directly to the legislature. There was no uniform system of accounts because each department used its own method, and either audits were not done or decades went by between them.[30]

It is not surprising that legislative bodies had little interest in giving up their central role in budgeting. When President Taft submitted an executive budget for FY 1914, Congress received it coldly and practically ignored it.[31] However, strong reform forces were at work. In 1899, the Model Municipal Corporation Act, which proposed an executive budget under a mayor, received significant national attention. Executive budgets were also called for by New York Bureau of Municipal

---

IN THE NEWS | Police Chief: Some Inaccuracies in Hoboken Audit

The Hoboken (New Jersey) Police Chief contested parts of a recent audit of the department, which took the position that lost productivity was due to a 35-hour work week and that a staff reduction of 30 to 35 positions was warranted. Chief Falco asserted there has never been a 35-hour work week in the history of the department and the audit should not have relied on "out of date" data from the 2000 Census. The Public Safety Director concurred with these points.

Source: WWW.NJ.Com/HobokenNow, February 23, 2010.

Research's *Making a Municipal Budget* (1907) and the National Municipal League's model 1916 city charter. Between roughly 1915 and 1925,[32] the executive budget and standard budget cycles and formats gained considerable use in local government. These appeared in the federal government with the passage of the 1921 Budget and Accounting Act.

These events are important because they (1) explain why substantial emphasis was placed on the control orientation in the early stages of budget reform and (2) underscore that budget control remains at the heart of budget execution, regardless of the type of budget format used. The sections that follow address five types of budget formats: (1) line item, (2) program, (3) performance, (4) PPBS and zero-based, and (5) hybrid.

The Line Item Budget

The **line item**, or object of expenditure, is the oldest and simplest budget format; it remains widely used today, although it is most closely associated with the period from 1915 to just after World War II. The line item is the basic system on which all other budget formats ultimately rest because of its excellence as a control device. It gets its name from its nature: Every amount that is requested, recommended, appropriated, and expended is associated with a particular item or class of items appears as a separate line in the budget (refer to Table 12.1). Table 12.3 summarizes the advantages and disadvantages of the line item budget format.

In police departments large enough for functional specialization, there is an overall line item budget, and that budget is broken down into smaller line item budgets for the various organizational entities (cost centers; refer to Figure 12.6), such as patrol, investigation, and

Table 12.3
ADVANTAGES AND DISADVANTAGES OF A LINE ITEM BUDGET

Advantages	Disadvantages
• Focus is on controlling expenditures	• Perpetuates the status quo: once items become a line in the budget, they tend to stay there, creating inertia.
• Simplest format	
• Expenditures organized around categories or object of expenditures (e.g., "SWAT Training," "Paper for Copy Machines," or "Gasoline")	• No specific, measurable goals, without which police agencies have nothing to drive toward and measure their accomplishments/performance.
• Easy to prepare, present, and understand	• No program structure (e.g., "DUI Enforcement" or "Abatement of Drugs in Nightclubs"). Although some police line item budgets have headings called programs, they are often just a line item budget broken down into major units, such as the patrol division.
• Every item or class of items for which expenditures made is controlled	
• Control systems prevents overspending budget	
• "Behind" all other budget formats there is a line item budget for control	• Budget changes tend to be incremental, small changes up or down in various categories.
	• Inhibits reviews of what the valuable activities in the police department are versus the need to downsize, recombine, or eliminate some units that exist simply by the weight of tradition.
	• Long-range planning is neglected.

crime prevention. These smaller budgets further facilitate control and serve as the basis of allocations within the police department. Cost centers can be used with any budget format.

Workload indicators for past years and the forthcoming budget year may also be included as part of a line item budget, although such are not present in a classical, or "pure" line item budget format. Typically such things as numbers of (1) arrests by various categories, (2) calls for service, (3) traffic and parking citations, (4) accident investigations, and (5) criminal investigations, along with other indicators, such as miles patrolled.

The Program Budget

The roots of the **program budget** spring from work by the (New York) Bureau of Municipal Research, which called for a new budget format (1907)—the program budget. Although the term *program budget* was not initially used, its elements were clearly defined: "For each department, the budget shall be separated to show the kinds of services to be provided."[33] The next year New York City adopted a program budget. Both Dupont and General Motors used program budgeting during the 1920s and it was used by the federal government beginning in 1942. Program budgets were "center stage" from the 1940s until the 1960s, although they continue to be widely used.

For present purposes, a police program budget is a planning tool that links the expenditures for each program to the achievement of goals. Table 12.5 summarizes the advantages and disadvantages of a program budget.[34] Its basic components include: (1) a program structure, (2) the attachment of goals to each program, and (3) a line item budget for control. Table 12.4 is a portion of a program budget. It shows the name of the program (Field Operations), its definition (Program Outcomes), and the program objectives (e.g., 85% of citizens in the Southern District will rate the district as safe). Other parts of this budget not shown include the staffing table with the number of personnel by rank (149), and the line item budget detailing planned expenditures of $24,086,254. Each subordinate unit in Field Operations would have parallel information. Table 12.5 summarizes the advantages and disadvantages of a program budget.

The Performance Budget

Within several years, the (New York) Bureau of Municipal Research quickly improved on its program budget by advocating that each program should now be accompanied by cost data, such as the cost for sweeping each mile of road. The 1912 Taft Commission on Economy and Efficiency called for a budget with cost data for the type of work being done. The weight of these two recommendations led to the adoption of what is now called a **performance budget** in New York City (1913). This format was so complicated and unwieldy that New York City soon dropped it.

In the 1930s, during the Depression, some cities (e.g., San Diego) made brief use of performance budgeting, although generally there was little experimentation with it until the 1950s. Faced with a large debt from World War II, the federal government sought to achieve greater spending efficiency. In 1949, the Commission on the Organization of the Executive Branch (the "Hoover Commission") endorsed a performance budget for the federal government, which quickly began using it. By

> **Table 12.4**
> **THE CONCORD (CALIFORNIA) POLICE DEPARTMENT'S FY '09 PROGRAM STRUCTURE FOR FIELD OPERATIONS**
>
> 70-Police
> 7300-Field Operations   Performance Based Budget Summary
> Manager: Stuart Roloson   For Council 2008–09
>
> **PROGRAM OUTCOME**
>
> To provide effective and efficient police services to the City of Concord 24 hours a day including: Protection of life and property; maintenance of order; investigation of criminal events; prevention of crime; orderly flow and parking of vehicles in the City; field evidence collection; support services for all emergency communications between department and community; and delivery of a myriad of assigned municipal services.
>
> **Program Objectives**
>
> 1A Operate the Southern District so that 85% of those citizens and business owners surveyed rate the district as safe.
> 1B Operate the Northern District so that 85% of those citizens and business owners surveyed rate the district as safe.
> 1C Operate the Valley District so that 85% of those citizens and business owners surveyed rate the district as safe.
> 1D Provide police services for the protection of life and property by handling of citizen demands.
> 1F Provide flexible teams of officers (SET team) that are a resource to other work units to address community problems.
> 1G Ensure safety of pedestrians, bicycle and vehicular traffic by providing patrol and radar enforcement to achieve a 0% increase per year in accidents; Parking Enforcement & Vehicle Abatement.
> 1I Provide Community Services Desk services so that 40% of the total number of incidents requiring a police report are handled by taking telephone reports or using other alternatives to dispatching a police officer.
> 1Z Administrative support for program's objectives and resources.
>
> *Source:* Courtesy Office of the City Manager, Concord, California.

the 1990s, performance budget had regained favor in the federal government. Forty-seven of 50 states have performance budget requirements; roughly one-third of cities above 25,000 in population and counties use some form of performance measurement system, which may not include a full performance budget.[35]

Over the past 60 years, performance budgeting has continued to evolve and is a mainstay of budgetary practice. Even the terminology for it has shifted, with the terms **performance-based budget (PBB)** or **results-based budgeting (RBB)** currently being in favor. The "pure form" of a PBB is a results-oriented tool designed to relate the amount of various types of work done to the amount of money spent to produce work. In theory, a performance budget characteristically has the following:

1. A program structure
2. A budget for each program
3. A line item component for fiscal control
4. A system of performance measures/indicators and cost measures (e.g., the cost for answering each call for police service or investigating each burglary).

Table 12.5
ADVANTAGES AND DISADVANTAGES OF A PROGRAM BUDGET

Advantages	Disadvantages
• Focus is on achieving broad police goals	• Labor intensive to develop
• Links programs, expenditures, and goals (e.g., 85% of citizens in the Southern District feel safe)	• Some police goals are hard to measure.
• Budget justification is more concrete and thus easier for police chiefs	• Ineffectual program may be difficult to reduce or cut due to political champions of it.
• Appropriators can easily shift resources from one program to another	• Lacks a full system of performance indicators, such as number of hazardous moving traffic citations issued and percent of cases investigated resulting in arrest warrant issuance.
• Excellent management tool for police chiefs	• Doesn't reveal priority of each program.
• Because of goal orientation, easier to explain to public and garner their support	

Table 12.6
FY 2010 PERFORMANCE MEASURES FOR VIOLENT CRIMES INVESTIGATION IN THE SCOTTSDALE (ARIZONA) POLICE DEPARTMENT

Violent Crimes Investigations

PERFORMANCE MEASURES

Program/Service Outputs: (goods, services, units produced)

	Actual 06/07	Actual 07/08	Projected 08/09	Estimated 09/10
# of medical examiner (death) cases investigated	324	335	350	365
# of robbery cases investigated	153	130	160	160

Program/Service Outcomes: (based on program objectives)

	Actual 06/07	Actual 07/08	Projected 08/09	Estimated 09/10
Achieve a 100% clearance rate for homicides exceeding the 56.4% West Region UCR rate	100%	100%	100%	100%
Achieve a 43% or higher clearance rate for robberies exceeding the 24.2% West Region UCR rate.	33%	42%	43%	43%

As currently practiced, PBB has substantially shifted away from using cost measures; cost accounting requires a high level of expertise and is expensive. Any PBB cost measures are typically minimal or may not even be present. Today's police PBB will have performance measures/indicators, which may be modest or more fully developed, depending on the practices in a jurisdiction. Table 12.6 shows the performance measures portion of the Scottsdale (Arizona) Police Department's (SPD)

FY 2010 budget. Its service outcomes specify that SPD clearance rates for homicide and robbery must be higher than the clearance rates for the same crimes as reported in the Uniform Crime Reports Western Region, which has 13 states. This practice is called **benchmarking**. Other police agencies using benchmarking compare themselves on UCR data to all other cities in their state that are in the same population range or similar sized departments which are recognized as being excellent. The average crime rates for comparison cities may be used or a department can use the data on selected crimes. The outcome measure may specify that a police department must be in the upper third or half as compared to the other cities. Table 12.7 summarizes the advantages and disadvantages of PBB.

The Planning, Programming Budgeting System (PPBS), and Zero-Based Budgeting (ZBB)

During the 1960s, the federal government used the **Planning, Programming Budgeting System (PPBS)**. PPBS's dominant feature was planning and required extensive use of cost effectiveness data. The process was cumbersome and unpopular with the federal agencies using it; PPBS made almost no headway in state and local government and by the very early 1970s it disappeared.

Another short-lived budget format was **Zero-Based Budgeting (ZBB)**, developed at Texas Instruments in the early 1970s and introduced into the federal government in 1977 by President Carter. Pure ZBB requires that every governmental program or activity must justify its entire existence each new operating budget year. In ZBB, each program or activity requested in a budget is organized into a decision

---

Table 12.7
ADVANTAGES AND DISADVANTAGES OF A PERFORMANCE-BASED BUDGET

Advantages	Disadvantages
• Focus is on results (i.e., measuring results through the use of performance measurement indicators (PMIs))	• May measure what is easy rather than what is important.
• As presently practiced, the virtual absence of cost measures eliminates expensive cost accounting techniques.	• Expensive if extensive use of cost measures is used.
• Provides comprehensive data to decision makers, strengthens oversight by appropriators.	• Can tell whether current programs are being done right, but not whether the right things are being done.
• Results of PMIs assist chiefs in allocating resources, a plus in strategic planning and management.	• How do you determine if the results are "good enough"? Benchmarking? Decisions by appropriators, citizens, special interest groups?
• PMIs can be useful in program evaluation.	• Additional resources dedicated to successful programs do not guarantee even better results.
• Chiefs can use on-going PMI measurement data to guide and control current programs, identify deviations, and "keep things are on track."	• May be time consuming to distinguish between poorly performing police programs that are under resourced and those that must be abandoned.
• Like Citizen Centric Reports, PBB makes government more transparent, enhancing government openness, which is associated with greater citizen satisfaction.	• Some PMIs may imply quotas and provoke public controversy.

package (DP) and includes three alternative funding levels: eliminated or reduced, current, and enhanced. New service DPs can also be submitted. Police chiefs prioritized the DPs and appropriators determined what DPs would be funded at what level, but tended to honor a chief's priorities. The massive paperwork required doomed ZBB as a budgeting process and it also faded, although here and there a less comprehensive use of DPs can be found as part of program or performance budgeting. Examples of jurisdictions labeling their budget ZBB include the state of Idaho; Renton, Washington; and Scottsdale, Arizona.

The Hybrid Budget

Budget formats can be described with a great deal more purity than actually exists in many real-world applications. The reason for this is that each jurisdiction, and by extension its police department, uses a system that makes sense to it. History, unique city charter provisions, state laws and local ordinance, past practices, the preferences of key people in the budgeting process, and other variables contribute to the reality that many budgeting systems incorporate features from one or more formats. The test of a budget format is how it's constructed, not what it's labeled. Many budgets are **hybrid budgets**, incorporating features of several different types of budget formats.

Supplementing the Police Budget: Tactics and Strategies

There are a number of strategies for supplementing a budget, including asset forfeiture, grants, and police foundations and donation programs.

Asset Forfeiture

In 11th-century England, horses, carts, and other property involved in a fatal accident were deemed *deodand* (literally, to be given to God) and forfeited to the king for "pious use." The practice was abandoned by an act of Parliament in 1846 due to the seizure of trains involved in fatal accidents.[36] Presently, property can be subject to forfeiture in the United States if it is (1) contraband, (2) the proceeds of criminal activity, (3) used to facilitate criminal activity, or (4) connected to criminal enterprise.[37] Asset forfeitures regularly help some police agencies bridge gaps in their budget.[38]

A maze of federal and state laws regulate forfeitures. Forfeitures may follow a criminal conviction or be by civil forfeiture, which is independent of criminal proceedings.[39] The standard of proof in a criminal case—beyond the exclusion of a reasonable doubt—is higher than preponderance of proof in civil cases— preponderance of evidence—so most forfeitures are civil. Ninety percent of civil forfeitures are not accompanied by criminal prosecutions, often because of insufficient evidence to support them.[40]

Forfeiture laws have been used to seize planes, mansions, tracts of land, bank accounts, drug houses and cheap hotels with criminal tenants, and the cars of men

soliciting prostitutes, street racers, persons driving on a revoked or suspended license, and repeat drunk drivers.[41] Cash forfeited is transferred to an asset forfeiture fund; personal property and real property, land, and all the permanent attachments thereto are sold at auction and placed in the forfeiture fund, after the sale costs are deducted.[42] Forfeitures can be complicated by liens or other factors.

Not all assets forfeited help police departments. State forfeiture laws can be characterized as "generous" or "restricted." Nevada allows all forfeitures to be used by the police agency initiating the case, whereas in Missouri all forfeit proceeds go into an educational fund.[43] Some states use formulas to divide up forfeitures, with law enforcement agencies getting anywhere from 25 to 90 percent.[44] Formulas can also include distribution to prosecutors' offices. To avoid restrictive state laws, some agencies turn their completed criminal cases over to the federal government, which pursues asset forfeiture. Under such "adoptive forfeitures," the department may receive as much as 80 percent of the value of the assets through "equitable sharing." Nationally, during 2005 to 2008, local police agencies seized in excess of $1.6 billion; in Texas, public safety departments confiscated $125 million in a single year.[45] While sounding impressive, the seizure figures are only a small portion of the $12 billion in drug money that flows south to Mexico from the United States annually.[46]

Forfeitures have been controversial because in civil actions the standard of proof is low and the police, in some cases, focus their investigation on assets instead of people, leading to charges of policing for profit. In some jurisdictions, police drug raids are timed to coincide when dealers were low on product and flush with cash. Some law enforcement agencies appear to be unusually aggressive. In Texas during 2009, the Tenaha Police Department (TPD) came under sharp criticism for its practices (see Figure 12.7).[47] Allegations are that some motorists have been told to forfeit their jewelry, cash, cell phones, and other belonging or face felony charges for money laundering or other serious crimes. Court records show that from 2006 to 2008, nearly 200 TPD cases involved seizure of some kind of assets, of which about 50 involved drug possession. In 147 cases, no contraband was found, nor were any charges filed. Racial profiling has been implied by one attorney, who contacted 40 motorists directly and discovered 39 were African Americans. A federal class action suit has been filed to stop the practices alleged and several members of the Texas legislature may introduce a bill requiring tighter legal controls on asset forfeiture.

Grants

The largest amount of grant funds flowing to the police has always been through the federal government. Although a number of federal agencies, such as the Department of Homeland Security and the National Highway Traffic Safety Administration, provide grants for law enforcement agencies, the U.S. Department of Justice provides a wider array of grant opportunities in support of community-oriented policing, reduction of gun and gang crimes, DUI abatement, enhancement of crime

Figure 12.7
City of Tenaha, Texas, which serves a community of 1,000. In 2009, Tenaha seized nearly $1.2 million in cash, mostly from out-of-town motorists.
(*San Antonio Express News/ZUMA Press*)

analysis, acquisition of new technologies, reduction of violence against women (including stalking and human trafficking), enforcement of protective orders, and date and domestic violence.

Some large corporation foundations have an interest in the police; the Met Life Foundation makes grants nationally to support innovative partnerships between community groups and the police to promote neighborhood safety and neighborhood revitalization. Other foundations have an interest in funding projects with a single state or community. One of the most spectacular awards to a law enforcement agency by a community foundation was made by the Caruth Foundation in 2008. The Dallas Police Department (DPD) received $9.5 million to train a new generation of leaders for the 21st century, leading to the creation of the Caruth Police Institute (CPI). An endowment for perpetual support was created with $6 million and the remaining $3.5 million was dedicated to startup costs. In 2010, CPI graduated the first class— 23 DPD Lieutenants, who completed a 6-week course taught by leading national experts. The graduates reported that the course taught them to think differently and to set higher goals. Even the smallest foundations, which may restrict applicant eligibility to one county, make police awards. Illustratively, the Harrison County (Indiana) Community Foundation funds small police projects, often for the acquisition of a single piece of equipment.

Police Foundations and Donations

Nonprofit police foundations have proliferated over the past 20 years, literally dotting the landscape from Los Angeles to New York City. Their prominence is such that the International Association of Chiefs of Police (IACP) has a Police Foundations Section. Police foundations are a conduit from the public and businesses that wish to promote excellence in their police departments through the donation of money, goods, and services.[48] The goal is to provide resources unavailable to departments through the budget process. Most police foundations serve multiple purposes, such as promoting wellness, recognizing valorous officers, and making purchases of equipment and newer technology, such as license plate scanners. CompStat may have never been or its development delayed without a $15,000 check from the New York City Police Foundation, which was ready 2 days after the request was initiated.[49] Police foundations in smaller jurisdictions have a narrower focus and may be limited to a single purpose. The Jackson, Mississippi Police Foundation funds for one-time purchases such as noise decibel readers to enforce the noise pollution ordinance; the foundation also engages in advocacy for the Jackson Police Department (JPD), orchestrating an agreement with a local hospital to perform police physicals, saving the JPD $100,000.[50]

    Donations to law enforcement agencies are widely varied. Two examples of good corporate citizenship illustrate this point. When four police officers were killed in Lakewood in 2009, all of the Papa John's Pizza restaurants in the state of Washington gave 100 percent of two days' receipts to the families of the slain officers.[51] Police departments also rally to help their own when tragedy strikes (see In the News: Fund Established for Injured Officer). In 2010, QualComm and Leap Wireless International gave 200 cell phones and 2 years of service to the San Diego Police Department. Among the units facing a loss of cell phones were child abuse, sex crimes, narcotics, and auto theft.[52] Individually, actor David Spade donated $100,000 to the Phoenix, Arizona Police Department to help purchase new firearms. Another sign of hard times are police websites, like that for Oshkosh, Wisconsin, which prominently feature a donations section advising readers how to help the department by making donations.

IN THE NEWS   Community Assists Injured Reserve Deputy

A reserve deputy responding to a drug overdose call crashed at 3:00 a.m. en route to the scene, suffering a skull fracture and broken bones. He remains unconscious since being admitted to the hospital. When 30-year-old Adam Schrader did not arrive at the scene, an Indiana State Police Trooper searched the area and found him. Already, donations are being made to assist the family. The Friends of Police and Fire Fund and The Whitely County Sheriff's Reserve have both donated $1,000. Additional donations can be made at the Sheriff's Office.

Source: Chris Meyers, Donations Made to Help Officer's Recovery, *The Post and Mail* (Columbia City, Indiana), March 26, 2010, www.ThePostandMail.com

CONCLUSION

A long running recesssion has produced substantial shortfalls in local, state, and federal governmental revenues, forcing severe budgetary cuts.

In many situations these cuts have gone well beyond "fat cutting" and are into muscle and bone, affecting operational capabilities. Law enforcement agencies have not been exempted from these cuts. They have responded by such measures as selling their heliocopters, marine patrol boats, horses used for mounted patrol, delayed the acquisition of new equipment, and laid off thousands of officers. Still, these measures have been insufficient and governments are searching for new ways to further trim their budgets.

The curtailing of public employee collective bargaining rights in Wisconsin, also being considered in other states, clearly signals we are in a new fiscal environment, the dimensions of which cannot presently be chartered. Now, perhaps more than ever before, knowledge of financial management is among the premium skills of law enforcement leaders.

CHAPTER REVIEW

1. Give three definitions of *budget*.
2. What is a fiscal year and give examples of two different fiscal years.
3. Contrast operating and capital budgets.
4. Define the steps in the budget cycle and briefly describe them.
5. Describe financial and performance audits. Why are performance audits more varied in their approach?
6. Identify the focus of a line item budget and a program budget.
7. What is a performance budget and why have performance budgets substantially abandoned cost measures?
8. What are hybrid budgets and why do they exist?
9. Identify three major ways in which a police budget can be supplemented.

KEY TERMS

allotments: small amounts into which a budget is broken and given to the police department monthly or quarterly, instead of giving all of it at once to the police department.

audit: an independent verification by someone who has no stake in the outcome; audits can be financial or programmatic.

benchmarking: the practice of comparing one's organizational performance to those that are recognized leaders in the field or otherwise relevant competitors.

biennial budget: a 2-year police budget.

budget: a government's priorities expressed in financial terms, a plan stated in financial terms, the use of resources to meet human needs, a contract between the appropriators and those who execute the budget.

budget calendar: a schedule of events for the preparation and approval of a budget.

budget cycle: a four-step, sequential process repeated annually in government.

budget execution: the action phase of budgeting, budget implementation.

capital budget: groups together multiple large-scale, nonrecurring projects such as the construction of a new police station and has a multi-year time horizon, often 5 years.

capital improvement project (CIP): a single capital improvement project, a component of a capital budget.

fiscal year (FY): the 12-month period usually covered by a budget; also see biennial and capital budgets as exceptions.

hybrid budget: budget formats that incorporate features from one or more other budget formats versus being purely one type of format.

letter of exception: a letter written by a chief of police to whatever office authorized the audit contesting one or more findings by the auditor.

line item budget: budget whose focus is on controlling expenditures; each object of expenditure has a separate line in the budget.

operating budget: a recurrent budget for salaries, fringe benefits, uniforms, training, telephone service and kindred expenses.

performance audit (PA): a study to see how well an organization is achieving its objectives.

performance budget (PB): also referred to as a performance based budget (PBB) on results-based budgeting (RBB). In theory, a PB has four characteristics.

Planning, Programming Budget System (PPBS): a budgeting innovation used in the federal government from the mid-1960s to the early 1970s; little use of it in state and local government.

program budget: budget whose focus is on achieving goals; is organized around programs/activities, has line item budget for control.

results-based budget (RBB): see performance budget.

Zero-Based Budget (ZBB): in pure form, every program in a budget starts from "zero" and must be justified each year. Three alternative service levels are prepared for each program. As currently practiced, departments "have" 75 or 80 percent of their prior year's budget and use ZBB from there.

ENDNOTES

[1] Elizabeth McNichol and Nicholas Johnson, "Recession Continues to Batter State Budgets; State Responses Could Slow Recovery," *Center on Budget and Policy Priorities*, February 25, 2010, p. 1.

[2] Ibid., p. 1.

[3] No Author, "Cities Balking at New DPS Crime Lab Fees," *The Arizona Republic*, November 5, 2008.

[4] Fran Spielman and Dave McKinney, "Chicago Cops May have to Patrol Expressways," *Chicago Sun Times*, March 24, 2010.

[5] Christopher W. Hoene, "City Budget Shortfalls and Responses: Projections for 2010–2012," National League of Cities, Washington, D.C., December 2009, p. 1.

[6] WSLS10 (Television), Angela Hatcher, "Losing Troopers: Virginia State Police Hit Hard by Budget Cuts," on-line access, p. 3, WWW2.WSLS.com, November 11, 2008.

[7] WTVI-Fox News, George Sells, "Salaries Slashed for East St. Louis Firefighters and Police," on-line access, March 16, 2010, Fox2Now.com

[8] Todd South, "Police Satellite Precincts Closing," *Chattanooga (TN) Times Free Press*, on-line access, February 4, 2010, TimesFreePress.com

[9] Jeff Brady, "Facing Budget Gap, Colorado City Shuts Off Lights," National Public Radio, February 14, 2010, on-line access, NPR.org

[10] Matt Bartosik, "Police Station: Sorry, We're Closed," NBCChicago.com, on-line access, July 29, 2009.

[11] Arlington (VA) Proposed Fiscal Year 2011 Budget Proposal.

[12] Maxine Bernstein, "Portland Police Propose Cutting Mounted Patrol and Leaving Some Positions Vacant to Balance Budget," PortlandLive.com, on-line access, January 14, 2010.

[13] In Minnesota alone in the past few decades, more than 100 small towns have disbanded their police department, merged with another one, or turned to their sheriff for services," See Tom Robertson, "Cass Lake Abolishes Police Force, Seeks Enforcement Deal with County," MPR News Q: Minnesota's On-Line News Source," August 1, 2008, on-line access, August 1, 2008.

[14] See Vicki Wilson, "Being Prepared for Disasters," Government Finance Review, Vol. 23, No. 6, December 2007, pp. 22–26 and Timothy McKeon, "Lessons from Recent Natural Disasters," *Municipal Finance Journal*, Vol. 27, No. 4, Winter 2007, pp. 27–53.

[15] Roland N. McKean, *Public Spending* (New York: McGraw-Hill, 1968), p. 1.

[16] Kathy Kiely, "'Tea Partiers' Flood Streets of Capital," *USA Today*, April 16, 2010.

[17] Robert J. Landry III and Cynthia S. McCarty, "Causal Factors Leading to Municipal Bankruptcies," *Municipal Finance Journal*, Vol. 28, No. 1, Spring 2007, p. 21.

[18] Aaron Wildavsky, *The Politics of the Budgetary Process,* 2nd ed. (Boston: Little, Brown, 1974), pp. 1–4.

[19] See David R. Shock, "Capital Budgets: The Building Blocks for Government Infrastructure," *Government Finance Review,* Vol. 23, No. 3, June 2007, pp. 16–22.

[20] Robert D. Lee, Ronald W. Johnson, and Philip G. Joyce, *Public Budgeting Systems* (Boston: Jones and Bartlett, 8th Edition, 2008), p. 17.

[21] Ibid, p. 53.

[22] Because sheriffs are elected and police chiefs appointed, there are some differences in city and county budgeting because as an elected official, a sheriff would be more independent. See LaFrance T. Casey and MaCherie, "Sheriffs' and Police Chiefs' Leadership and Management Decisions in the Local Law Enforcement Process," *International Journal of Police Science and Management,* Vol. 12, issue 2, Summer 2010, pp. 238–255.

[23] Police Chief Bruce G. Roberts, letter to the city of Ft. Lauderdale Commission, April 1, 2004.

[24] Robert D. Lee and Ronald Johnson, *Public Budgeting Systems* (Gaithersburg, Md.: Aspen, 1998), p. 265.

[25] These ideas are taken from David Nice, *Public Budgeting* (Belmont, Calif.: Wadsworth, 2002), pp. 104–110.

[26] See Jeffrey C. Steinhoff, "Forensic Auditing: A Window to Identifying and Combating Fraud, Waste, and Abuse," *Journal of Government Financial Management*, Vol. 57, No. 2, Summer 2008, pp. 10–18.

[27] The organizational placement of procurement, purchasing, payment of invoices, and property control varies. They may be clustered in a F/FSD or spread out over several departments. In very small units of government, one or two people working in the same office may perform these functions. For purposes of this text, we use a F/FSD that encompasses all of these functions, although in actual practice there are many variations.

[28] Mark Schelker, "Public Auditors: Empirical Evidence from U.S. States," *Center for Research in Economics, Management, and the Arts* (CREMA: Basel, Switzerland), 2008, p. 9.

[29] No Author, *Conducting Performance Audits in Accordance with the Yellow Book* (San Diego: Office of the City Auditor, 2009), pp. 4–6.

[30] Allen Schick, *Budget Innovation in the States* (Washington, D.C.: Brookings Institution, 1971), pp. 14–15.

[31] A. E. Buck, *The Budget in Governments of Today* (New York: Macmillan, 1945), p. 5.

[32] In 1913, Ohio became the first state to adopt the executive budget.

[33] No Author, *Purpose and Methods of the Bureau of Municipal Research* (New York: Bureau of Municipal Research, 1907), p. 25.

[34] For additional background on program budgeting, see David Novick, *Origin and History of Program Budgeting* (Santa Monica: Rand Corporation, 1966).

[35] In 31 states the requirement is expressed legislatively and in the remaining 16 states by executive order. See Dongsung Kong, "Performance-Based Budgeting: The U.S. Experience," *Public Organization Review*, Vol. 5, 2005, p. 93.

[36] Gilbert Geis, "Editorial Introduction," *Criminology and Public Policy*, Vol. 7, No. 2, 2008, p. 215.

[37] John Worrall, *Asset Forfeiture* (Washington, D.C.: Center for Problem-Oriented Policing, 2008), p. 5.

[38] Julissa McKinnon, "Forfeited Assets Help Bridge Gaps In Police Department Budgets," *The Press Enterprise*, Riverside, California, February 21, 2010.

[39] Asset Forfeiture, p. 3.

[40] Henry Hyde, Forfeiting Our Property Rights: Is your Property Safe? (Washington D.C.: Cato Institute, 1994), as cited in Ibid, p. 3.

[41] Ibid., pp. 21–25.

[42] Ibid., p. 7.

[43] Asset Forfeiture, pp. 9–10.

[44] Ibid., p. 11.

[45] John Burnett, "Seized Drug Assets Pad Police Budgets," National Public Radio, June 16, 2008.

[46] Ibid.

[47] This section is a brief synopsis of Howard Witt, Highway Robbery? Texas Police Seize Black Motorists' Cash, Cars, Chicago Tribune, March 10, 2009 and Lisa Sandberg, "Property Seizure by Police called 'Highway Piracy,'" *Houston Chronicle*, February 7 2009.

[48] Pamela Delaney and Donald Carey, "Police Foundations: Partnerships for the 21st century," *The Police Chief,* Vol. 74, No. 8, 2007, p. 1 of on-line copy.

[49] Ibid., p. 2.

[50] Adam Lynch, "Police Foundation Eyeing Safe City Role," *Jackson (Miss) Free Press*, March 31, 2010.

[51] Television station KREM (Seattle, Washington, KREM.com), December 9, 2009.

[52] San Diego Mayor Jerry Sanders, Press release, March 18, 2010.

part four
Organizational Issues

This concluding section deals with three enduring concerns in law enforcement agencies: stress, legal aspects of administration, and organizational change.

Stress is, like morale, a fluctuating condition that can affect individual and organizational performance. It is the subject of Chapter 13, which examines various stressors and how to deal with them.

Law enforcement officers have a keen understanding of criminal law, but are less familiar with the civil liability which may arise out of their actions, particularly in high liability risk areas such as the use of force and high speed pursuits that transcend reasonableness and violate the rights of citizens. Chapter 14 provides a grounding in these concepts.

It is said that the only thing that is constant is change. Law enforcement agencies are criticized by some as being tradition bound, archaic bureaucracies. The reality, as documented in earlier chapters, is that over the last three decades they have been very nimble in adopting and adapting new operational philosophies. Chapter 15 examines forces pushing agencies toward change, conditions unfavorable for change, change models, and related topics.

13

Stress and Police Personnel

If, under stress, a man goes all to pieces, he will probably be told to pull himself together. It would be more effective to help him identify the pieces and to understand why they have come apart.

— *R. Ruddock*

Objectives

■ Describe the three stages of physiological response to stress as defined by Hans Selye.

■ Discuss diseases of adaptation and recent medical findings.

■ List the major characteristics of the type A personality, the type B personality, and the workaholic.

■ Explain why police officers are more prone to stress than are individuals in many other occupations.

■ Analyze what the potential psychological effects are on a police officer when he or she is forced to take a life in the line of duty.

■ Discuss the ways alcohol-related problems manifest themselves in police officers.

■ Describe some of the issues that police administrators must deal with in terms of drug use by police.

■ Discuss some of the negative consequences associated with the use of steroids.

■ Discuss some of the typical warning signs that indicate an officer might be contemplating suicide.

■ Explain the supervisor's responsibilities regarding suicidal officers.

■ Identify the sources of work satisfaction as a stress reducer.

■ Discuss what police departments can do to curtail incidents of domestic violence among their officers.

- Identify the steps police supervisors must take if they notice a pattern of controlling or abusive behavior in an officer.

- Discuss stress reduction techniques.

- Describe the range of services that can be made available to police officers who are involved in domestic violence incidents.

OUTLINE

Introduction

For the past 35 years, the topic of stress and its relationship to police work has been extensively studied by both the social science community and the police profession. As a result, there is now an abundance of police stress-related information available to the law enforcement executives to assist them in fully understanding and developing programs designed to reduce stress among their personnel.[1] Police administrators should be aware of the following stress-related information: (1) how stress is defined by the medical and social science community, (2) the relationship between diseases of adaptation and job-related stress, (3) the ways in which personality type can impact positively or negatively upon job performance, (4) why the use of deadly force by police officers is consistently listed as the number one stress inducer, (5) the negative physical and psychological impacts of alcohol, drugs, and steroids on police performance, (6) the multiple aspects of police suicide and what can be done to prevent it, (7) the aspects of police work that are not stressful, (8) police domestic violence and the ways in which police departments can and should react to it, (9) stress reduction techniques, and (10) the functions and value of an employee assistance program.

What is Stress?

Hans Selye, the researcher and theorist who pioneered the physiological investigation of stress, defines **stress** in the broadest possible terms as anything that places an adjustive demand on an organism. Identified as "the body's nonspecific response to any demand placed on it," stress can be either positive (eustress) or negative (distress; see Table 13.1).[1] According to this distinction, many stressful events do not threaten people but provide them with pleasurable challenges. The excitement of the gambler, the thrill of the athlete engaged in a highly competitive sport, the deliberate risk taking of the daredevil stunt man—these are examples of stress without distress. For many people, this kind of stress provides the spice of life.

Biological Stress and the General Adaptation Syndrome

Selye has formulated what he calls the **general adaptation syndrome (GAS)** to describe how stress, on the biological level, can incapacitate an individual. The GAS encompasses three stages of physiological reaction to a wide variety of stressors: environmental agents or activities powerful enough in their impact to elicit a reaction from the body. These three stages are:

- Alarm
- Resistance
- Exhaustion

The **alarm stage**, sometimes referred to as an emergency reaction, is exemplified on the animal level by the so-called fight-or-flight syndrome. When an animal

Table 13.1
CHANGES TO THE BODY AT THE ALARM STAGE

Heart rate increase	Blood flow increases to heart, lungs, and large muscles
Blood pressure increase	Perspiration, especially to palms
Large muscle groups tense	Digestive secretions slow
Adrenaline rush	Dry mouth due to saliva decrease
Increase blood sugar	Bowel activity decreases
Hypervigilance	Extremities become cool
Pupils dilate	Sphincters tighten
Increased hearing acuity	More white blood cells enter the bloodstream
Increased blood clotting	Cholesterol remains in the blood longer
Increased metabolism	Dilation of the lung passages and increased respiration

Source: Wayne Anderson, David Swenson, and Daniel Clay, *Stress Management for Law Enforcement Officers*, 1st edition, © 1995, p. 37. Adapted by permission of Pearson Education, Inc., Upper Saddle River, NJ.

encounters a threatening situation, its body signals a defense alert. The animal's cerebral cortex flashes an alarm to the hypothalamus, a small structure in the midbrain that connects the brain with body functions. A powerful hormone called ACTH is released into the bloodstream by the hypothalamus and is carried by the bloodstream to the adrenal gland, a part of the endocrine, or ductless gland, system. There, ACTH triggers the release of adrenaline, which produces a galvanizing, or energizing, effect on the body functions. The heart pounds, the pulse races, breathing quickens, the muscles tense, and digestion is inhibited. The adjustive function of this reaction pattern is readily apparent—namely, preparing the organism biologically to fight or to run away. When the threat is removed or diminished, the physiological functions involved in this alarm, or emergency reaction, subside, and the organism regains its internal equilibrium.

If the stress continues, however, the organism reaches the **resistance stage** of the GAS. During this stage, bodily resources are mobilized to deal with the specific stressors, and adaptation is optimal. Although the stressful stimulus may persist, the symptoms that characterized the alarm stage disappear. In short, the individual seems to have handled the stress successfully.

Under conditions of prolonged stress, the body reaches a point where it is no longer capable of maintaining resistance. This condition characterizes the **exhaustion stage**. Hormonal defenses break down, and many emotional reactions that appeared during the alarm stage may reappear, often in intensified form. Further exposure to stress leads to exhaustion and eventually to death.[2]

Diseases of Adaptation and Recent Medical Findings

There is considerable agreement that some types of stress can worsen the symptoms of almost any condition, but recent medical research suggests there is little evidence that stress is the exclusive or the principal cause of any disease. For decades it was accepted by the medical community that stress led to the overproduction of stomach acid, which caused duodenal ulcers. Stress does increase the amount of acid produced in the stomach, and there is no doubt that, once a person has a duodenal ulcer, acid makes the ulcer hurt. However, medical science has determined the ulcer is not caused by stress but rather by a bacterial infection, curable with antibiotics. Doctors also once believed that the inflammatory bowel diseases—Crohn's disease and ulcerative colitis—were caused by stress. They now know these diseases are caused by inherited tendencies toward abnormal inflammation in response to gut bacteria. Also, there is little evidence that stress causes asthma, although some patients have flare-ups more often at times of stress.[3]

It is the role of stress in heart disease that has received the most attention over the years, and with good reason. Like our ancestors, we all occasionally face the single, sudden, and extreme stressors that the stress response has evolved into in order to protect us from dangerous situations. However, unlike our primitive ancestors, the acute stressor is not caused by an approaching wild animal's intent on devouring us or the belief that we will soon be dead because we have been hexed by the local witchdoctor. Instead, it might result from a car that has run a red light and is hurtling toward us or perhaps someone is attempting to forcibly enter our home. Our response to such sudden and extreme stressors can protect us, but it can also trigger a powerful hormonal release that can have dire consequences if a person already has heart disease.

Perhaps even more important are the persistent, chronic, low-grade stressors experienced by almost everyone in a modern society, such as the recurring tension in dealing with an unpleasant supervisor, co-worker, spouse, or child; or worrying about how to pay the bills this month. These chronic stressors, like sudden and acute stressors, can also affect the most common and lethal form of heart disease we face—atherosclerosis, sometimes called "hardening" of the coronary arteries.

Coronary atherosclerosis deforms artery walls and can ultimately block blood flow, starving the heart muscle of the oxygen it needs. Plaques of atherosclerosis cause symptoms in two ways. First, if the plaques grow large enough to significantly obstruct the flow of blood, the heart will not get the blood supply it needs when it is forced to work harder—for example, by exercise or by anger or fear. The heart is not actually damaged, but pain can occur whenever the heart is again forced to work hard. Second, plaque can rupture, either when the heart is working hard or even when a person is at rest and at peace. Plaque rupture causes a blood clot to form that suddenly and often completely stops the flow of blood through the artery.

Chronic stressors also contribute to heart disease indirectly if they lead us to overeating, under-exercising, or smoking. Stress is a toxic emotional and physical response; anger, hostility, depression, and anxiety are examples of such toxic responses. Anxiety, for instance, involves apprehension combined with palpitations, fatigue, and shortness of breath. Some people respond to chronic stressors with remarkable equanimity. Others spend a substantial fraction of their day experiencing one or more of the toxic reactions. This is influenced in part by our genes, but is also controllable with stress-management techniques (discussed later in this chapter). In addition, if these toxic reactions are not controlled, there is growing evidence that heart disease is more likely to occur and at an earlier age.[4]

Sudden, major stressful life events can sometimes cause catastrophic results in people with underlying heart disease—including heart disease they did not know they had because it had never before caused symptoms. This could then result in the sudden outpouring of adrenalin resulting from a specific highly stressful event such as a police officer responding to an officer in need of assistance, or a felony in progress call. This can cause a plaque of atherosclerosis to rupture, which in turn can generate dangerous heart rhythms and sudden death.

In a paper published nearly 40 years ago in the *Annals of Internal Medicine*, internist and psychiatrist George Engel reconstructed the events in the hours before 170 people died suddenly. Particularly for women, Engel found that the most common trigger for sudden death was a major loss—of a spouse or self-esteem. For men, sudden danger (a constant companion for law enforcement officers) more often was a trigger. Subsequent evidence supports Engel's thesis. For example, sudden deaths increased immediately following the Northridge earthquake in southern California in 1994, and after September 11, 2001—and not just in New York City.

Interestingly and surprisingly, Engel found that sudden death could also follow a triumph or a happy ending to a long struggle. He reported the sudden deaths of a number of individuals, including a just-released prisoner upon returning home, a man who had just scored his first hole in one, and an opera singer who was receiving a standing ovation. Even joy can disrupt silently diseased arteries. This is not meant to suggest that individuals should avoid things that give them pleasure, but the Engel study suggests that, whenever feasible, people should pursue these things in frequent, but small, doses, rather than in rare surges of ecstasy.[5]

Stress and Personality Type

Friedman and Rosenman identified certain distinctive personality types and the relationship among these personality types, stress, and coronary heart disease.[6]

Type A Personality (Higher Risk)

- Under constant stress, much of which is self-generated
- Continuous pressure to accomplish
- Hostile and demanding
- Always in a hurry; sense of time urgency
- Continuing impatience
- Intense and ambitious
- Believes time should be used "constructively"

- Has difficulty relaxing and feels guilty when not working
- Compelled to challenge, and not understand, another type A personality

The qualities underlying type A characteristics include the following:

- Constant state of being "on guard"
- Hypermasculinity
- Constantly working against time
- Lack of insight into one's own psychological needs

The physiological implications are as follows:

- Seven times as likely to develop heart disease
- Higher cholesterol and triglyceride (blood fat) levels (sudden stress increases triglyceride; prolonged stress increases cholesterol)
- Clotting elements have greater tendency to form within coronary arteries
- Excess accumulation of insulin in blood

Type B Personality (Lower Risk)

- Less competitive and less rushed
- More easygoing
- Better able to separate work from play
- Relatively free of a sense of time urgency
- Ambitions are kept in perspective
- Generally philosophical about life

Workaholic (Higher Risk)

- This phrase was coined in 1968
- Similar to type A
- Has an addiction to work
- When absent from the job, may experience withdrawal symptoms similar to those of withdrawal from other addictions
- Is agitated and depressed when not working
- May account for up to 5 percent of the working world
- Typical workaholics
  - Readily buck the system; often bucked by the bureaucracy
  - Display well-organized hostility toward the system's imperfections
  - Obsessed with perfection in their work
  - Haunted by deep-seated fear of failure; will "play to win" at all games
  - Prefer labor to leisure
  - Constantly juggle two or more tasks (called multitasking)
- Many are overachievers and "get things done"
- Takes its toll and may result in:
  - Gastrointestinal problems
  - Cardiovascular disease
  - Divorce

The Consequences of Police Work Addiction

The following is a cautionary tale based upon an actual case, using a fictitious name, which describes the pitfalls of being a workaholic.

Great leaders lead by example, and Police Chief William Smith was no exception. He was totally selfless and always available, arriving at work each morning before 8:00 and not leaving until everyone else had gone home. It was not uncommon to find him working on Saturday or Sunday. The deputy chief told those assembled at the church that he was actually reluctant to leave each night before the chief. Everyone felt sad that Chief Smith left a young family and even sadder that he should pass away in the prime of his life.[7]

Certainly, police officers are expected to put aside all other needs when duty calls, and, without question, duty does call. Commanders and officers alike must sustain an endless capacity to meet this demand. Communities hold fast to the expectation that the police will do all that can be humanly done and, at times, much more than should be expected of mere humans. Therein lies the great challenge for law enforcement officers and supervisors—maintaining a healthy balance in meeting *reasonable* responsibilities to the job, to themselves, and to their families.

Perhaps Chief Smith represents an extreme example of the dangers inherent in the work-addicted lifestyle. However, literature on work addiction asserts that work constitutes the drug of choice for some 30 percent of the population, for whom working is so vital to their emotional well-being that in fact they have become addicted to it.[8] While the actual mortality rate for work addiction may be low, the social lethality of this behavior proves overwhelming. These unfortunate individuals are predisposed to involve themselves—and their families—in a life not unlike that of Chief Smith's. Clearly, work addicts (or workaholics, the more common descriptor) cannot assess what is important in healthy lifestyle choices and, thus, experience a diminished quality of life. Regrettably, they do not suffer alone. They unwittingly share this pain with their families and colleagues alike.

Workaholics are married to their work. Their vows to love and honor their spouses above all "others" no longer hold meaning or possibility. No spouse and no family can compete with this all-consuming obsession.

Workaholics themselves are a key contributor to the unhealthy family patterns resulting from work addiction for a number of reasons. First, they may have grown up in a dysfunctional family system where role models taught unhealthy patterns of relating to others. Research indicates that the family origin contributes greatly to the development of the workaholic, and the roots of the workaholic's perfectionism often lie in childhood experiences.[9] In these dysfunctional homes, families reward children for good performance, not for who they are. They give praise and conditional love whenever children perform a certain way or meet certain high expectations. In adulthood, this same need for perfection is the basis for the obsession for work—everything must be done properly and always at a very high level of competence and perfection.

Second, the need for workaholics to feel dominant and "in control" may make them less able to relate to peers. They may interact more easily with older and younger people or those of lower status or socioeconomic level than themselves. This need for continually being in control of themselves and in charge creates tension in family relationships. The one constant involved in this work mind-set devalues the quality of social interactions. Loved ones have a reasonable expectation that time spent together is time well spent and, therefore, they should not be made to feel that such time comes at the expense of personal productivity. Loved ones can sense when the workaholic is "just going through the motions." The same holds true for relationships with peer groups and clients. People have a strong sense for those who are too busy to make time to properly address issues. Conflict becomes inevitable, and everyone "gets drawn into the act by waltzing around the workaholic's schedule, moods, and actions."[10]

The self-imposed behavior of work addiction also causes physical symptoms. Excessive pumping of adrenaline resulting in abnormal blood pressure, heart trouble, stomach sensitivity, nervousness, and the inability to relax under any circumstances are commonplace. Workaholics report feeling pressure in their chests, dizziness, and light-headedness.[11] Obviously, any long-term stress that manifests such symptoms as these can result in dangerous health consequences of many types. Chief Smith's protracted work addiction led to serious illness and his ultimate, untimely death.

Those people obsessed with work share the traits of others with such addictions as substance abuse, food dependencies, or sexual compulsions. A classic definition of a workaholic describes "a person whose need for work has become so excessive that it creates noticeable disturbance or interference with bodily health, personal happiness, and interpersonal relations, and with smooth social functioning."[12] The unique difference between work addiction and other addictions, however, is that supervisors often sanction work addiction. Supervisors and peers admire this so-called work ethic, and it can be both financially and professionally rewarding.

Workaholics become gradually more emotionally crippled as they become embroiled with the demands and expectations of the workplace. They are "addicted to control and power in a compulsive drive to gain approval and success."[13] The obsession with work grows out of the workaholic's perfectionism and competitive nature. As with other addictions, work is the "fix," the drug that frees the workaholic from experiencing the emotional pain of the anger, hurt, guilt, and fear in the other areas of the workaholic's life. Workaholics constantly focus on work, seeking to meet their personal emotional needs through their professions.

With this information in mind, law enforcement supervisors must understand the dangers that work addiction presents (see Table 13.2). These supervisors also must remember that they have an ethical responsibility to intervene when they observe the telltale signs of the work-addicted personality.

Perhaps the poet Robert Frost had Chief Smith in mind when he observed, "By working faithfully 8 hours a day, you may eventually get to be boss and work 12 hours a day." Certainly, expectations run high in the law enforcement profession. Establishing and maintaining relationships creates tremendous demands on time, resources, and energy; life balance easily becomes lost. The wise boss must understand and accept this reality.

Table 13.2
WORK-ADDICTION RISK TEST

To find out if you are a workaholic, rate yourself on each of the statements below, using a rating scale of 1 (never true), 2 (sometimes true), 3 (often true), or 4 (always true). Put the number that best describes your work habits in the blank beside each statement. After you have responded to all 25 statements, add up the numbers for your total to determine if you are or not a workaholic.

____ 1. I prefer to do most things myself, rather than ask for help.

____ 2. I get impatient when I have to wait for someone else or when something takes too long.

____ 3. I seem to be in a hurry and racing against the clock.

____ 4. I get irritated when I am interrupted while I am in the middle of something.

____ 5. I stay busy and keep many irons in the fire.

____ 6. I find myself doing two or three things at one time, such as eating lunch, writing a memo, and talking on the telephone.

____ 7. I overcommit myself by accepting more work than I can finish.

____ 8. I feel guilty when I am not working on something.

____ 9. It is more important that I see the concrete results of what I do.

____ 10. I am more interested in the final result of my work than in the process.

____ 11. Things just never seem to move fast enough or get done fast enough for me.

____ 12. I lose my temper when things do not go my way or work out to suit me.

____ 13. I ask the same question again, without realizing it, after I already have received the answer.

____ 14. I spend a lot of time mentally planning and thinking about future events while tuning out the here and now.

____ 15. I find myself continuing to work after my coworkers have stopped.

____ 16. I get angry when people do not meet my standards of perfection.

____ 17. I get upset when I am in situations where I cannot be in control.

____ 18. I tend to put myself under pressure from self-imposed deadlines.

____ 19. It is hard for me to relax when I am not working.

____ 20. I spend more time working than socializing with friends or on hobbies or leisure activities.

____ 21. I dive into projects to get a head start before all of the phases have been finalized.

____ 22. I get upset with myself for making even the smallest mistake.

____ 23. I put more thought, time, and energy into my work than I do into my relationships with loved ones and friends.

____ 24. I forget, ignore, or minimize celebrations, such as birthdays, reunions, anniversaries, or holidays.

____ 25. I make important decisions before I have all the facts and a chance to think them through.

For clinical use, scores on the test are divided into three ranges. Those scoring in the upper third (67–100) are considered highly workaholic. If you scored in this range, it could mean you are on your way to burnout, and new research suggests that family members may be experiencing emotional repercussions as well. Those scoring in the middle range (57–66) are considered mildly workaholic. If you scored in this range, there is hope. With acceptance and modifications, you and your loved ones can prevent negative long-term effects. Those scoring in the lowest range (25–56) are considered not workaholic. If you scored in this range, you are probably an efficient worker instead of a workaholic and have no need to worry that your work style will negatively affect yourself or others.

Source: B. E. Robinson, *Chained to the Desk* (New York: New York University Press, 1998), pp. 52–54. Minor editorial revisions have been made to several test items.

Figure 13.1
A police officer weeps as he enters a church to attend the funeral service for a fellow officer who was killed in the line of duty.
(Courtesy of The Image Works)

Stress in Law Enforcement

Police work is highly stressful—it is one of the few occupations in which an employee is asked continually to face physical dangers and to put his or her life on the line at any time. The police officer is exposed to violence, cruelty, and aggression and is often required to make extremely critical decisions in high-pressure situations.

Police Stressors

Violanti and Aron distributed a 60-item Police Stress Survey (PSS) to a random sample of 110 officers in a large New York State police department.[14] Ninety-three percent of those sampled (N =103) completed the PSS and returned it. Table 13.3 displays the results of this survey. The single-most-potent stressor was killing someone in the line of duty. The empathy police officers have for victims is revealed by the fact that the fourth-most-potent stressor was handling child abuse cases, which ranked ahead of other well-known stressors, such as engaging in high-speed chases, using force, responding to felony-in-progress calls, and making death notices.

The stressors in Table 13.3 can be factored into two components: those that are organizational/administrative and those that are inherent in the nature of police work. Within these stressors, there were some variations. Sergeants in charge of substations reported the most organizational/administrative stress, while detectives reported the least. For officers in the 31- to 35-year-old range, the single most powerful stressor was shift work. However, for officers over 46 years of age, the mean values of all stressors dropped. This is probably due in part to the accommodations that such officers have learned to make as well as the nature of the jobs that people more senior in their careers hold. For African Americans, the highest-ranking stressor was inadequate support by the police department.

The Use of Deadly Force as a Major Source of Stress

It is apparent from Table 13.3 that killing someone in the line of duty is the single event that causes the greatest degree of stress for law enforcement officers. Available data indicate that about 600 criminals are killed each year by police officers in the United States.[15] Some of these killings are in self-defense, some are accidental, and others are to prevent harm to others. The sources of stress attached to an *officer-involved shooting* (OIS) are multiple, and include the following:

- The officer's own psychological reaction to taking a life
- The responses of his or her law enforcement peers and the officer's family
- The rigorous examination by departmental investigators and administrators
- The possible disciplinary action or change of assignment
- The possibility of criminal prosecution
- The possibility of civil litigation
- Unwanted media attention.[16]

Table 13.3
POLICE STRESSORS RANKED BY MEAN SCORES

Stressor	Mean Score	Stressor	Mean Score
Killing someone in line of duty	79.38	Excessive paperwork	43.15
Fellow officer killed (see Figure 13.1)	76.67	Court leniency	42.65
Physical attack	70.97	Disagreeable regulations	42.27
Battered child	69.24	Ineffective judicial system	42.00
High-speed chases	63.73	Family demands	41.84
Shift work	61.21	Politics in the department	40.64
Use of force	60.96	Inadequate supervision	40.11
Inadequate dept. support	60.93	Public criticism	39.52
Incompatible partner	60.36	Assigned new duties	39.22
Accident in patrol car	59.89	Ineffective corrections	39.08
Insufficient personnel	58.53	Inadequate salary	38.45
Aggressive crowds	56.70	Rapid change from boredom to high stress	38.06
Felony in progress	55.27	Making arrests alone	37.23
Excessive discipline	53.27	Personal insult from citizens	36.67
Plea bargaining	52.84	Negative public image	36.17
Death notifications	52.59	Increased responsibility	33.03
Inadequate support (super.)	52.43	Exposure to pain and suffering	33.01
Inadequate equipment	52.36	Exposure to death	32.06
Family disputes	51.97	Second job	31.51
Negative press coverage	51.80	Lack of participation in decisions	31.10
Court on their day off	51.06	Public apathy	29.50
Job conflict with rules	50.64	Promotion competition	29.46
Fellow officers not doing their job	49.02	Promotion or commendation	28.79
Lack of recognition	48.10	Nonpolice tasks	27.94
Physical injury on the job	47.10	Demands for high morality	26.14
Making quick decisions	45.82	Politics outside the dept.	25.48
Restrictive court decisions	44.82	Strained nonpolice relations	23.60
Getting along with supervisors	44.48	Boredom	23.25
Disagreeable duties	43.90	Minor physical injuries	23.23
Mistreatment in court	43.50	Racial conflicts	22.53

Source: Reprinted from the *Journal of Criminal Justice* 23, no. 3, John M. Violanti and Fred Aron, "Police Stressors: Variations in Perceptions among Police Personnel," p. 347, Copyright © 1995, with permission from Elsevier.

Perceptual, Cognitive, and Behavioral Disturbances Resulting from the Use of Deadly Force

Many police officers who have been involved in a deadly force shooting episode have described one or more alterations in perception, thinking, and behavior that occurred during the event,[17] and these are similar to those reported in military personnel following a firefight. Most of the following reactions can be interpreted as natural adaptive defensive reactions of an organism under extreme emergency stress:

- *Distortions in time perception* are most common, with the majority of officers recalling the shooting event as occurring in slow motion, although a smaller percentage reported experiencing the event as speeded up.

- *Sensory distortions* are also common and most often involve *tunnel vision,* in which the officer is sharply focused on one particular aspect of the visual field, typically the suspect's gun or weapon, while blocking out everything in the periphery. Thus, such distortions are also very common for officers who are engaged in high-speed pursuits. Similarly, "*tunnel hearing*" may occur, in which the officer's auditory attention is focused exclusively on a particular set of sounds, most commonly the opponent's voice, while background sounds are excluded. Sounds may also seem muffled or, in a smaller number of cases, louder than normal. Police officers have reported not hearing their own or other officers' gunshots. Thus, overall perceptual clarity may increase or diminish.

- *A sense of helplessness* may occur during the shooting exchange, but this may be underreported due to the potential stigma attached. A small proportion of service members report they "froze" at some point during the event: again, either this is an uncommon response or personnel are understandably reluctant to report it, especially in a culture like law enforcement, which places a premium on physical courage and disparages those who show any degree of timidity in the face of danger. In a series of interviews with police officers,[18] it was found that most of these instances of "freezing" really represented the normal *action-reaction gap* in which officers make the decision to shoot only after the suspect has engaged in clearly threatening behavior. In most cases, this brief evaluation interval is a positive precaution, to prevent the premature shooting of someone who does not pose a threat to the officer. But in situations where the ostensibly prudent action led to a tragic outcome, this cautious hesitation by an officer may well be viewed retrospectively by him or her as a fault: "If I hadn't hesitated to shoot, maybe my partner would still be alive."

- *Disturbances in memory* are commonly reported in shooting exchanges. About half of these involve impaired recall for at least some of the events during the shooting; the other half involve impaired recall for at least part of the officer's own actions; this, in turn, may be associated with going-on-automatic response. More rarely, some aspects of the event may be recalled with unusual clarity, sometimes characterized as a *flashbulb memory.* Over a third of the cases involve not a total loss of recall but a distortion of memory, to the extent that the shooter's account of what happened differs markedly from the report of other observers at the scene; in such cases, they might be unfairly accused of lying.

Five Basic Phases of the Post-Shooting Reaction

1. The first phase occurs prior to the shooting itself and consists of *concern about being able to pull the trigger* when the time comes and not freezing up and letting one's fellow officers down.
2. The second phase is the *actual killing experience*, which is often done reflexively, with officers describing themselves as "going on automatic."
3. The third stage is that of *exhilaration* that comes from having been able to put one's training into action. This exhilaration, fueled by the release of huge amounts of adrenalin, can create a high or rush, which in some cases can give rise to what the military has characterized as "combat addiction." It has been described as the kind of "adrenalin overdosing" that can negatively impact a police officer's nervous system and lead to adverse reactions later on (i.e., hesitating to use deadly force when it is clearly justified or overreacting to situations that do not justify the use of deadly force).[19]
4. The fourth phase[20] is what police psychologists[21, 22] have called the *recoil, remorse and nausea* phase. This follows the rush of exhilaration and is often associated with a close-range kill; this is the more common type of response experienced by police officers who tend to confront their adversaries in close quarters, rather than from a distance, which is often the case with military personnel.

For police officers, feelings of guilt or self-recrimination may be especially likely in cases where the decision to shoot was less than clear-cut or where the suspect's actions essentially forced the officer into using deadly force, such as botched robberies, violent domestic disputes, or suicide-by-cop (SbC)[23] (discussed later in this chapter).

During the recoil/remorse phase, law enforcement service members may seem detached and preoccupied, going through the motions of their job duties, and operating on what could be characterized as "behavioral autopilot." In addition, they may be hypersensitive or even annoyed to well-meaning probing and congratulations by peers who make comments such as "Way to go, killer—the dirt bag deserved it."

Also, during this recoil phase, a variety of posttraumatic symptoms may be seen, most of which will resolve themselves in a few days or weeks.[24] Some of these will represent general posttraumatic reactions similar to those experienced by psychological trauma workers.[25] This reaction is typically classified as **posttraumatic stress disorder (PTSD)**, while others will have a specific law enforcement line-of-duty shooting focus. The most common symptoms of PTSD are:

*   Headaches
*   Stomach upset
*   Nausea
*   Weakness and fatigue
*   Muscle tension and twitches

- Changes in appetite and sexual functioning
- Sleep impairment, with frequent awakenings and often nightmares
- Intrusive imagery and flashbacks may occur
- Distorted memories
- Anxiety and depression
- Panic attacks
- Unusual and disorienting feelings of helplessness, fearfulness, and vulnerability
- Self-second-guessing and guilt feelings

5. The fifth phase,[26] *rationalization and acceptance*, can be a long process, and many law enforcement officers wrestle with this single event for a lifetime. As the officer begins to come to terms with the shooting episode, a similar resolution or acceptance phase may ensure, wherein the officer assimilates the fact that the use-of-deadly-force-action was necessary and justified in this particular instance. Even under the best of circumstances, resolution may be partial rather than total, and psychological remnants of the experience may continue to haunt the officer periodically, especially during future times of crisis. But in most cases the officer is eventually able to return to work with a reasonable sense of confidence.[27]

However, in the worst cases, sufficient resolutions may never occur, and the officer enters into a prolonged posttraumatic phase, which may effectively end the officer's law enforcement career. In less severe cases, a period of temporary stress disability allows the officer to seek treatment, to eventually regain his or her emotional and professional bearings, and to ultimately return to the job. Still other officers return to work right away, but continue to perform marginally or dysfunctionally until their actions are brought to the attention of superiors.[28]

Suicide by Cop

On hearing the term **suicide by cop (SbC)**, the average person could mistakenly think of officers who take their own lives. However, to law enforcement officers, this refers to an individual who wishes to die and uses the police to affect that goal. Even when such shootings are clearly justified, the event is often quite stressful for the officers involved. The following case of an attempted suicide by cop serves as an example of this phenomenon from both the officers' perspective and the offenders' perspective.[29]

Case Study

Case #1: The Officer's Perspective Two officers were dispatched to an apartment building in response to a woman yelling for help. On arriving at the location, they observed a female standing on the front steps. She waved them inside and then entered the apartment, leaving the door open behind her. As the officers approached the doorway, they could hear a male yelling and then saw him standing in the kitchen area. As the male observed the officers enter the apartment, he produced a large butcher knife. He held the blade of the knife firmly against his stomach with both hands and appeared highly intoxicated, agitated, and angry. The officers drew their service weapons and ordered the man to put down the knife. The offender responded by stating, "[Expletive] you, kill me!" He turned toward the kitchen counter, put the handle of the knife against it with the blade touching his stomach, and grabbed the counter with both hands as if to thrust himself fully onto the knife. The officers attempted to talk to the offender, who responded by turning around and slicing himself severely on his forearm, bleeding profusely. The officers repeatedly asked him to drop the knife. One officer aimed his service weapon at the offender while the other pointed a chemical spray container at him. Still armed with the knife, the offender advanced closer to the officers. This caused the officers to retreat to a position where they attempted to use the kitchen door frame as cover.

As this was occurring, a backup unit arrived on the scene. The offender repeatedly told officers to shoot him while continually ignoring commands to drop the knife. From a distance of approximately 12 feet, he raised the knife in a threatening manner and charged the officers. One officer fired two .45-caliber rounds from his service weapon. Both struck the offender in the chest but seemed not to have any effect, except to make him angrier. The officer then fired two more rounds at which point the weapon jammed. One of these rounds had struck the offender in the hand, passing through it and lodging in his groin. The second round hit him in the chest. The offender continued to charge both officers as they retreated down the hallway and out of the front door. As the offender arrived at the front door, he received another .45-caliber gunshot wound to the groin, fired by the second officer. He dropped the knife and backed up against the wall inside the doorway but remained on his feet. The officers entered the premises, removed the knife, took the offender into custody, and called for an ambulance. The offender was transported to the hospital and survived the incident. The officer who fired the initial four rounds stated, "It was my life or his, and it became his. I was upset that this guy put us in a position where I had to do something like this. I was upset with the fact that this guy kept pushing the issue and had made the decision himself, where I didn't have a decision."

Case #1: The Offender's Perspective In the morning, the offender had a serious argument with his wife, one that would only escalate if he remained in the apartment. The previous day, he had a disagreement with several friends, which resulted in a fistfight. He stated that "the argument with my wife increased the pressure on me." He left the apartment and went to several bars. He drank liquor for approximately 7 hours and got extremely intoxicated. A relative helped him home, where he and his wife continued to argue.

While standing in the kitchen, he observed two police officers enter the apartment. The mere presence of the officers further enraged him. When asked if

Figure 13.2
A man, armed with what police would later learn were unloaded guns, confronted Chicago police officers. When the man refused to drop his guns and threatened to kill the officers, he was shot and killed.
(AP Photos)

he had wanted the officers to end his life for him, the offender said, "Quickly, I figured when they seen the knife that would have been enough. It would have been all over. But it didn't end up that way." When asked about specific thoughts during the confrontation with the officers, the offender stated, "I never thought about suicide. Never in my wildest years. I'd take a beating before I'd commit suicide. But, at the time and at that particular moment, the pressure was so great; the common reality wasn't there anymore. It was gone. I didn't care. I didn't care about nothing that was standing before me. I just wanted out." After advancing on the police officers, he was shot five times. The offender stated the first of several rounds that struck him "felt like bee stings" and only tended to enrage him. But by the time he reached the front of the building, he had become incapacitated. While being transported to the hospital, the offender told emergency medical technicians, "Let me die; don't try to save me." He pled guilty to several counts of assault on a police officer while armed and was sentenced to a short prison term.

Suicide by Cop and Police Officers as Victims

Harvey Schlossberg, retired director of psychological services for the New York Police Department, indicates that an SbC shooting is often tantamount to a "psychological assault" on the officer involved in the shooting. When an officer determines the suspect's weapon is inoperative or the suspect is otherwise responsible for a confrontation to bring about his or her death at the hands of the authorities, the officer may question his or her own reactions to this confrontation.

Society may be quick to identify a dead SbC suspect as the victim in this incident, when the real victim is the officer forced into the situation by a suicidal person. The department must provide the support needed by the victim officer in such circumstances and the officer must be made to understand that his or her actions were correct and professionally justified.[30]

Alcoholism and Police Officers

Alcohol problems among police officers manifest themselves in a number of ways: a higher than normal absentee rate before and immediately following the officer's regular day off, complaints of insubordination by supervisors, complaints by citizens of misconduct in the form of verbal and physical abuse, intoxication during regular working hours, involvement in traffic accidents while under the influence of alcohol on and off duty, and reduced overall performance.

It has been suggested further that policing is especially conducive to alcoholism. Because police officers frequently work in an environment in which social drinking is commonplace, it is relatively easy for them to become social drinkers. The nature of police work and the environment in which it is performed provide the stress stimulus.

Traditionally, police departments adhered to the "character flaw" theory of alcoholism. This outdated philosophy called for the denunciation and dismissal of the officer with an alcohol problem. Today, police departments attempt to rehabilitate officers, and typically they are separated from the service only after such attempts have failed. Police departments now have a broad mix of employee assistance programs to assist officers with their drinking problems, including self-assessment checklists (see Table 13.4), peer counseling, counseling with in-house psychologists and those on retainers, and support groups.

Departmental Programs

There is no single best way for a department to assist its officers with a drinking problem, but some agencies have enjoyed a fair degree of success for their efforts. For example, the Denver Police Department has used its closed-circuit television system to teach officers who are problem drinkers and encourage them to join the in-house program. A major portion of the in-house program was designed to persuade the problem drinker, after having been exposed to a sufficient amount of the educational component, to enter the Mercy Hospital Care Unit and achieve the status of a recovering alcoholic.[31]

It is the responsibility of the individual police agency and its administrators to act on the fact that alcoholism is a disease and to create a relaxed atmosphere and an in-house program for the dissemination of information relative to this problem. As indicated earlier, the objective of such a program is ultimately to persuade individual officers to enter a care unit for treatment. The combination of unsatisfactory performance, excessive costs, and the almost certain progressive deterioration of the individual officer to the point of unemployability, if the illness goes unchecked, creates a situation that conscientious chiefs of police or sheriffs should neither tolerate nor ignore. If drinking affects an officer's health, job, or family, immediate action is essential—the officer is probably an alcoholic.

Table 13.4

ALCOHOL SELF-ASSESSMENT CHECKLIST

Each of the following conditions or behaviors has been found to be associated with alcohol abuse or problem drinking. Check the ones that apply to you. This exercise will sensitize you to what to look for when evaluating a person for alcohol abuse potential.

____ 1. Drinking alone regularly.

____ 2. Needing a drink to get over a hangover.

____ 3. Needing a drink at a certain time each day.

____ 4. Finding it harder and harder to get along with others.

____ 5. Memory loss while or after drinking.

____ 6. Driving skill deteriorating.

____ 7. Drinking to relieve stress, fear, shyness, insecurity.

____ 8. More and more family and friends worrying about drinking habits.

____ 9. Becoming moody, jealous, or irritable after drinking.

____ 10. "Binges" of heavy drinking.

____ 11. Heavy weekend drinking.

____ 12. Able to drink more and more with less and less effect.

None of these alone or in combination means an individual has an alcohol abuse or drinking problem. However, the more of the items that are checked off, the greater the likelihood of an alcohol abuse problem.

Source: Theodore H. Blau, *Psychological Services for Law Enforcement,* p. 198. © 1994 by Theodore H. Blau. Reprinted by permission of John Wiley & Sons, Inc.

Reports by the Denver Police Department indicate that the organization has benefited in the following specific ways since the implementation of its alcohol abuse program:

- Retention of the majority of the officers who had suffered from alcoholism
- Solution of a set of complex and difficult personnel problems
- Realistic and practical extension of the police agency's program into the entire city government structure
- Improved public and community attitudes by this degree of concern for the officer and the officer's family and by eliminating the dangerous and antisocial behavior of the officer in the community
- Full cooperation with rehabilitation efforts from the police associations and unions that may represent officers
- The preventive influence on moderate drinkers against the development of dangerous drinking habits that may lead to alcoholism; in addition, an existing in-house program will motivate some officers to undertake remedial action on their own outside the scope of the police agency program.[32]

Drug Use by Police Officers

Drug abuse by police officers has garnered a great deal of attention.[33] A national study of 2,200 police officers found that 10 percent had serious drug problems.[34] As a result of this condition, police administrators have had to grapple with such issues as the following:

- What positions will the employee unions or other employee organizations take if drug testing is proposed?
- Who should be tested for drugs? Entry-level officers? Regular officers on a random basis? All officers before they are promoted? Personnel assigned to high-profile units, such as bomb disposal and special tactics and response?
- When does a supervisor have "reasonable suspicion" of a subordinate's drug use?
- Who should collect urine or other specimens and under what conditions?
- What criteria or standards should be used when selecting a laboratory to conduct the police department's drug testing program?
- What disciplinary action is appropriate when officers are found to have abused drugs?
- What duty does an employer have to rehabilitate employees who become disabled as a result of drug abuse?[35]

In recent years, issues concerning the testing of sworn officers for drugs have been debated and litigated. In the early days of such litigation, court rulings were sometimes wildly contradictory, with most courts striking down such requirements, typically on the basis that it was an unwarranted intrusion into officers' constitutional right to privacy.[36] Nevertheless, three major principles have emerged from the many random drug cases decided by the courts. The first is that drug testing—both on the basis of reasonable suspicion and when conducted on a random basis—does not violate the federal Constitution. The second is that, although drug testing may not violate federal Constitutional rights, it may not be permissible under the constitutions of some states. The third principle is that, in states that have granted collective bargaining rights to police officers (see Chapter 11, Labor Relations), drug testing cannot be unilaterally implemented by the employer. Instead, it must be submitted to the collective bargaining process.

The selection of officers for drug testing must be truly random and part of a clearly articulated drug testing policy. The courts will not support the police department's operation of a non-random drug testing program except when there is reasonable suspicion to test for the presence of drugs.[37]

Anabolic Steroids

When police administrators consider the use of illegal drugs by their personnel, they typically think of the traditional illegal drugs, such as marijuana, cocaine, heroin, amphetamines, and barbiturates. However, one class of drugs that is abused more than many police administrators realize are **anabolic steroids**.

For example, the U.S. Bureau of Customs investigated the smuggling of anabolic steroids into this country.[38] Their investigation led them to certain health clubs in North Carolina, where it was determined that state patrol officers were illegally using anabolic steroids. The North Carolina State Patrol joined the investigation, and subsequently three troopers were terminated. In Miami Beach, Florida, a physical training sergeant noticed one of his female charges was "bulking up" too fast. She also displayed street behavior that led a department supervisor to recommend she be assigned to nonstreet duties. It was subsequently established she had been using anabolic steroids. In addition to using steroids themselves, officers in New York have been convicted of selling anabolic steroids.

Adverse Health Impact

There are recognized medical uses of anabolic steroids. Among the conditions for which anabolic steroids may be therapeutically appropriate are deficient endocrine functioning of the testes, osteoporosis, carcinoma of the breast, growth retardation, and severe anemia.[39]

The use of anabolic steroids, as summarized in Table 13.5, is associated with a number of potential outcomes that are adverse to an individual's health. These risks are even greater when anabolic steroids are taken under the direction of a self-appointed "roid guru" or when users self-dose because the typical usage under these and related circumstances is 10 to 100 times greater than typical medical dosages.[40] Further complicating the nontherapeutic use of steroids is self-treatment with preparations not legally available in the United States, and veterinary preparations, such as Boldenone (Equipose), for which it is difficult to estimate dosage equivalency,[41] virtually ensuring that dosages well beyond those recognized as medically appropriate will be taken.

Unknown or less-well-known to anabolic steroid abusers than the previously noted risks are certain affective and psychotic symptoms. Charlier[42] maintains that "aggressive behavior is almost universal among anabolic steroid users." There are documented case histories of severe depression, visual and auditory hallucinations, sleep disorders, thoughts

---

Table 13.5
ADVERSE EFFECTS OF ANABOLIC STEROIDS

Men	Women	Both Sexes
• Breast enlargement	• Breast diminution	• Increased aggression, known as "roid rage"
• Testicular atrophy with consequent sterility or decreased sperm count	• Clitoral enlargement	• Increased risk of heart disease, stroke, or obstructed blood vessels
• Impotence	• Facial hair growth	
• Enlarged prostate	• Deepened voice	• Acne
	• Menstrual irregularities	• Liver tumors, jaundice, and peliosis hepatitis, (blood-filled cysts)
	• Excessive body hair	
	• Baldness	• Pre-teens and teenagers: accelerated bone maturation, leading to permanently short stature

Source: C. Swanson, L. Gaines, and B. Gore, "Use of Anabolic Steroids," *FBI Law Enforcement Bulletin* 60, no. 8 (1991): 19–23.

of suicide, outbursts of anger, anorexia, psychomotor retardation, and irritability. In a survey of health club athletes who used steroids, 90 percent reported steroid-induced aggressive or violent behavior, and there is also considerable evidence to show that this applies to law enforcement officers as well.[43] The following actual case illustrates this point.

Several years ago, a uniformed deputy sheriff in Oregon was on his way to work in his personal car when it started to overheat. He stopped at a nearby feed store and requested assistance from the proprietor in getting some water for the radiator. She told him where the water was. After filling his radiator he asked her if he could use her telephone in order to call the sheriff's department, because he was going to be late to work. (This was a time before cell phones were as readily available as they are today.) He called his supervisor to advise him he was going to be late because he was having car problems. When he completed the phone call the proprietor told him in a sarcastic way, "I should start charging you cops because of all the times you come in here to use my phone." The deputy became angry at her for what he perceived as her sarcastic and disrespectful comment but left without saying anything. The following day, still angry about her comment, he returned to the feed store. At this time he was off duty, on his way to the gym and wearing workout clothes. As would later be learned, he was a heavy user of steroids and at the time of this incident was experiencing what is characteristically referred to as "**roid rage**." He was also armed with his .357 magnum service revolver. He confronted the woman about her sarcastic remarks the day before and then forced her at gunpoint into his personal car. After the officer drove a short distance, the women tried to escape and the deputy shot her in the back. He dumped her injured body from the car onto the street. When members of his agency interviewed the assaulted woman she told them what had happened and who shot her. The deputy was arrested shortly thereafter and one of the first things he said upon being arrested was "It was those steroids. It was those steroids." Prior to this incident the deputy had a perfect work record and there was absolutely no evidence of any anger management issues on his part. However, a blood test revealed he had been using heavy doses of three different types of very powerful steroids and had 50 times the level of the male hormone testosterone that would normally be expected to be found in the male body. He was subsequently found guilty at trial and sentenced to 20 years in prison. As a result of the gunshot wound, the victim's spinal cord was irreparably damaged and she remains today a wheelchair-bound paraplegic.

Although not physically addicting, steroids can cause a psychological dependence that can be divided into three stages: the initial stage of exploration, a continuing stage of regular usage, and cessation from use. People are attracted to steroid use for a variety of reasons, all of which center on developing a more domineering physique. Initial users are generally "turned on" to the drugs by other abusers or seek them out at health clubs or gyms, where such drugs are commonly abused. The continuation stage occurs after initial use, when subjects have experienced some success with the drug. Thereafter, subjects become obsessed with their larger physiques, increased strength, or sexual appeal. Exercise becomes easier whenever steroids are used, and pain and a lack of strength appear when the drugs are discontinued. This process may continue until subjects are confronted with difficulties that result from their drug dependency. Cessation of usage will come only when the subjects become disinterested or are confronted with their problems.

Anabolic Steroids: The Legal Environment

The Drug Enforcement Administration (DEA) has the major responsibility for enforcing the federal Controlled Substances Act (CSA), which is intended to minimize the quantity of drugs available for illegal use. The CSA places a substance into one of five schedules on the basis of such factors as potential for abuse and whether there is a recognized medical use of the substance. Most over-the-counter (OTC) and prescription drugs do not fall within one of the CSA schedules, and the responsibility for enforcement efforts relating to them rests with the Food and Drug Administration (FDA) and state agencies. The FDA determines whether a substance falls within the OTC or prescription category; each state then has the legal power to determine who can legally prescribe and dispense OTC and prescription substances. The federal Anti-Drug Act of 1988—also referred to as the Omnibus Drug Abuse Initiative—created a special category of anabolic steroids within the prescription class, and all violations involving the sale or possession with intent to distribute anabolic steroids are now felonies.

Even before the passage of the Anti-Drug Act, it was illegal to possess anabolic steroids without a prescription in all 50 states. Thus, all officers in this country using anabolic steroids without a prescription are committing an illegal act.

Awareness of the nature and impact of illegal anabolic steroid use is seen in litigation. "Anabolic steroid-induced rage" has been used as a defense in sexual assault cases; in one instance, the judge accepted this argument as a mitigating factor when sentencing a defendant in a sexual assault. Liability is one of the most critical issues regarding steroid usage. It is only a matter of time before it will be alleged in a state tort or federal civil rights lawsuit that "but for the failure of the police department to conduct a proper background and drug screening, the anabolic steroid-induced violent assault on my client would never have occurred" (negligent selection) or that "but for the failure of the police department to properly train its supervisors on how to identify the manifestations of anabolic steroid abuse, the physical trauma to Mrs. Johnson would not be an issue before this court today" (failure to train and failure to supervise). Although there are almost limitless liability scenarios, there is only one inescapable conclusion: If administrators do not confront this issue quickly, harm will be done to citizens, officers, families, and public treasuries.

Administrative Concerns and Anabolic Steroids

In research on administrative attitudes toward steroid use, people in the internal affairs, public information, and command positions as well as staff psychologists of 30 police departments across the country were interviewed. With few exceptions, the response was "That's not a problem in this department, and we've never had a problem with it." Yet, replies of that nature are deceiving. For example, a departmental representative who had stated in the morning that steroid abuse was not a problem called back in the afternoon, saying, "I've been thinking. . . . One of our retired officers runs a gym frequented by our officers and some of them have gotten very muscular awfully quick." Police officials readily recognize cocaine or marijuana abuse as a police personnel problem, but for the most part they still are not aware of the seriousness of steroid abuse. If this situation is not corrected soon, departments will be confronted with increasing numbers of steroid-related problems. Some agencies have decided to deal with this problem by randomly testing their officers for anabolic steroid use.

Police Suicide

Considerable difficulty exists in studying police suicide.[44] Researchers often find that either information on officer suicide is not collected or departments are reluctant to allow access to such data.[45]

In addition, the results of an ongoing study of police suicides over a 40-year period indicate that nearly 30 percent of police suicides may have been intentionally misclassified as accidental or undetermined deaths. Because police officers traditionally subscribe to a myth of indestructibility, they view suicide as particularly disgraceful to the victim officer and to the profession.[46] The police represent a highly cohesive subculture whose members tend to "take care of their own." The desire to shield victim officers, their families, and their departments from the stigma of suicide may lead investigators to overlook certain evidence intentionally during the investigative process, plus in some cases there can be some insurance/beneficiary implications if the death is ruled a suicide. One study of the Chicago Police Department estimated that as many as 67 percent of police suicides in that city had been misclassified as accidental or natural deaths.[47]

Why Police Officers Commit Suicide

One of the most comprehensive studies ever undertaken to examine police suicide was conducted by the New York City Police Department. The study revealed that, while New York City police officers are more likely than the general public to commit suicide, they do respond positively to training programs that offer them avenues of help.[48]

The study's recommendations included the further development of confidential counseling resources within the New York Police Department; additional training in handling depression, problematic interpersonal skills, and recognizing the effects of alcohol and drugs; and police academy training in officer "life-saving"—how and when to seek help for oneself or a fellow officer when necessary.

"Police officers are trained from day one not to show weakness, and officers believe discussion of problems or feelings is evidence of weakness," said Andre Ivanoff, an associate professor at the School of Social Work at Columbia University. "Training in the future must incorporate the idea that it's okay to ask for help and talk about negative feelings."

After viewing a film and participating in an in-service training session on police suicide, officers surveyed by questionnaire expressed a greater willingness to seek help for themselves and for fellow officers. Ivanoff conducted the research and trained officers who led the discussion groups.

Responses to the survey indicate that police view interpersonal problems, depression, and the use of alcohol and other drugs as the primary reasons for suicide, not the generalized stress of police work, popularly cited in mental health journals. Of 57 police suicides reported by the department over a 9-year period, relationship problems and depression were the leading factors in cases in which a contributing factor was identified.

Methods of Suicide by Police Officers

The method most used by officers committing suicide is the service weapon, according to the NYPD police department statistics. Among the 57 reported police suicides, all but 4 were committed with the officer's gun.

The goals of the Police Suicide Project were to increase knowledge about both the myths surrounding suicide and the actual risk factors linked to suicide, such as depression; to impart positive attitudes about getting help for problems that seem beyond control; and to publicize the department's counseling programs. "The project met and surpassed its initial objectives," Ivanoff said. "Attitudes toward getting help, specifically toward the use of helping resources for oneself and for others, improved dramatically."

Studies of other police departments have revealed that suicides are more common among older officers and are related to alcoholism, physical illness, or impending retirement.[49] Other clues have been cited to help explain the high rate of self-inflicted death among police officers: the regular availability of firearms, continuous-duty exposure to death and injury, social strain resulting from shift work, inconsistencies within the criminal justice system, and the perception among police officers that they labor under a negative public image. In addition, research confirms a higher propensity for suicide among males, who dominate the police profession.[50]

A study of the Detroit Police Department found that the vast majority of police officers who took their lives were white, young, male, high school educated, and married. Alcohol abuse was fairly common among the sample (42 percent), as was a formal diagnosis of psychosis (33 percent). However, marital difficulties appeared to be the most prevalent problem among the Detroit sample.[51]

Among the occupational factors surrounding police suicide, frustration is often cited as particularly important. Almost unfailingly, officers enter policing with high ideals and a noble desire to help others. Over time, this sense of idealism can transform into hard-core cynicism.

The roots of frustration emanate from the central irony of American policing: Society charges police officers with the task of regulating a public that does not want to be regulated. For individual officers, the resulting frustration is exacerbated by a largely unsympathetic press, a lack of community support, and a criminal justice system that values equity over expediency. A sense of social isolation often ensues, compelling officers to group together in a defensive stance. When an officer feels that the frustration is no longer tolerable or that no coping alternative is available, suicide may become an attractive option.

Access to Firearms

Another factor that distinguishes police officers from the general population has been implicated in the high number of police suicides. That is, most law enforcement officers carry or have access to firearms. An ongoing study of police suicides in the United States reveals that 95 percent involved the use of the officer's service weapon.[52]

Another study compared suicides in New York City and London. While the police suicide rate in New York City was twice that of the general population, the police suicide rate in London, where officers do not carry firearms, was similar to that of the city's civilian population.

The police firearm holds special significance for officers. It is a very potent symbol of the power of life and death. Society entrusts law enforcement officers with the authority to use their weapons and to take the life of another person in certain situations. In police suicides, officers in effect are claiming the right to take their own lives. After all, the weapon has been issued as a means to stop misery and to protect others from harm. Despondent officers may view suicide in such a way (see Figure 13.3).

Alcohol Abuse

Alcohol abuse, discussed earlier in this chapter, has also been implicated as a significant contributing factor in police suicides. Administrators should be aware that alcoholism may lead to other work problems, such as high absenteeism, traffic accidents, or intoxication on duty. Given the established correlation between alcoholism and suicide, these symptoms should not be ignored. They should be considered indications of a larger problem.

Figure 13.3
Sylvia Banuelos, whose husband, Ernesto, shot and killed himself, holds his service badge at the grave site. Ernesto Banuelos was an Orange County, California, sheriff's deputy. Behind her are her children, Matthew (left), Adam, Andrew, and Justin.
(Photo by Bob Riha, Jr., *USA Today*)

Fear of Separation from the Police Subculture

As officers near the end of their law enforcement careers, another potential threat appears: separation. To individual officers, retirement may mean separation from the camaraderie and protection of police peers. During their years of service, officers may have clustered with other officers because of a general isolation from society and its prejudices toward the police. On retirement, these officers must enter the very society they perceive as alien and hostile.

While the benefits of retirement may be viewed positively by the majority of officers, separation from the police subculture can be a frightful and devastating prospect for others. Fear, coupled with increasing age (a definite suicide risk factor), loss of friends, loss of status as a police officer, and loss of self-definition, leaves some retiring officers vulnerable to suicide. One study found a tenfold increase in risk of suicide among police retirees.[53]

Recognizing the Warning Signs

Identifying at-risk officers is the first step toward helping them.[54] Is there any common pattern to be found in police suicidal behavior? In truth, any member of a department can become depressed and commit suicide under certain circumstances. However, a long trail of evidence typically leads to the final act. Many suicidal people have mixed feelings about dying and actually hope to be rescued. About 75 percent give some kind of notice of their intentions.[55] If recognized and taken seriously, these early warning signs make prevention and intervention possible.

When officers who have consistently been good performers begin to fail to perform at the optimal level for an extended period of time, the problem might be related to a major depressive episode. Clinicians agree that depression can be so serious that it sometimes results in a homicide, typically of a spouse or significant other, followed by suicide.

Supervisory Responsibility in Suicide Prevention

It is quite clear that police managers and supervisors can play a very important role in suicide prevention. For example, supervisors should schedule interviews with officers who appear depressed, sad, hopeless, or discouraged. During this interview, the supervisor should check the officer's body language, look for sad facial expressions, and be alert to a flat mood. The officer might complain of feeling down, not having any feelings at all, or being anxious. Complaints about bodily aches and pains might be reported to cover the officer's true feelings.[56]

The twin feelings of hopelessness and helplessness indicate a high risk of suicide. Officers who think and speak in these terms feel that their lives are devoid of hope, or they see themselves as unable to meaningfully alter their situations. When they reach this point, they often take action. The finality of suicide might be seen as a technique to restore feelings of former strength, courage, and mastery over the environment.[57] Supervisors should listen carefully for expressions of these feelings.

Suicidal officers might have negative influences in their personal lives as well. Supervisors should look for histories that include suicidal behavior, mental illness, chronic depression, multiple divorces, and alcoholism. Losses in an officer's life, drug abuse patterns, and stress overload also contribute to the problem. Older officers might experience physical problems or face impending retirement and feel that they will become socially isolated.[58] Such physical and social losses can generate the destructive feelings of hopelessness and helplessness.

It is important for supervisors to ask specifically whether officers are having thoughts of hurting themselves. Many may find it difficult to ask such a basic question, but it must be done. Officers who indicate they are having suicidal thoughts must not be left alone. All threats must be taken seriously. Other people might not have heard their pleas for help. Supervisors should plan their intervention so that it leads to a professional referral. The specific methods of intervention must be thought out as carefully as possible in order to avoid violence directed inward or outward at other employees. Without careful plans in place, officers confronted by supervisors might react unpredictably. Because their thought processes are confused, they might strike out at coworkers, supervisors, or family members, resulting in a homicide followed by suicide. Even if that does not occur, the danger of suicide exists at the point of intervention.

Supervisors should refer officers to a certified mental health professional, even setting appointments and making arrangements for the officers to be there. The department's responsibility does not end there, however. Supervisors should monitor the situation to ensure that officers are evaluated and receive continued support and counseling.

Sources of Work Satisfaction as a Stress Reducer

Thus far, we have focused on the aspects of police work that are negative and stress-inducing. However, it is very easy to find numerous police officers who would readily admit that there are many aspects of the job that are truly rewarding, believe it is the greatest job in the world, and leaves them with a tremendous sense of satisfaction. A number of years ago, a comprehensive study was conducted by Herzberg, Mausner, and Snyderman in part to determine the sources of work satisfaction for police officers.[59] The following examples were provided to them by police officers who responded to their research questions.

Providing Assistance to Citizens

The contributions that appear most valued by officers are those calls involving citizens who are manifestly helpless. One such category is that of elderly people, who may be demonstrably fearful, lonely, or confused:

> *Example 1:* An elderly man passed away, and naturally his elderly wife didn't exactly know what to do, right? So after the ambulance crew and the fire department left, we . . . sat down at the table and found out if her husband had any wishes as to which particular funeral home he wanted to handle his funeral services. Once we found out which one it was we called the funeral director, and then started helping her out by calling her relatives. Some of her family who had

arrived by then thanked us for helping her out because she didn't know what to do or who or call. That made me feel good at least because I was able to help this woman who didn't know up from down in this kind of stressful situation. Any decent person would do something like that, but we get paid for doing that.[60]

Most of the officers proudly recalled giving assistance to children. These included situations of child neglect and circumstances in which services were arranged or brokered by the officers. In some instances, the officers reported they had followed up to make sure that the problem was solved:

> *Example 2:* About 4 years ago my partner and I responded to a call where there were accusations being made that a young kid had been kept in his room against his will for approximately 2 years. He was being let out briefly, maybe once or twice a month, to attend school, just to show up. So we went there, and we investigated. . . . It was obvious he had been kept in there for an extended period of time. We found out the windows were all boarded up. There were buckets in there [where] he could defecate and urinate, and we investigated that along with the state. After doing some research we were able to find out this kid had some mental problems and was also quite aggressive. His mother had come to this country a couple years ago and wasn't aware of the types of services that were available to her in the United States, such as child counseling and so forth. We were able to get help for the family, for the kids, and now today when I see this kid he always recognizes me. I see the difference in him and I am very much aware of how he could have been. The mother also expressed her appreciation for everything we were able to do for her. We stayed on it for about a good 4 or 5 months, and finally the outcome was that they got a better house and they got turned on to state agencies. Counseling was made available, the mother got employed and the kid got put into a special school system along with the other kids. It was gratifying to know they benefited from our help.[61]

Exercising Interpersonal Skills

Although policing is often equated with the use of legal power or force, officers appear to take great pride in their ability to resolve delicate situations through exercises of verbal ingenuity. In both human services and crime-related incidents, the deployment of interpersonal relations skills was clearly valued:

> *Example 3:* We were able to talk a guy out of his house who had a gun. We took the gun away from him when he exited the house and fortunately nobody got hurt. I felt good about this because we could have killed the guy, but we chose not to. I had several situations like that with people with weapons. If you want to take this as an opportunity to shoot people you can but I didn't and because I didn't I felt good. I'm glad we didn't do that. You know we walk into a lot of potentially violent situations but sometimes through discussion you can convince people to come out of the houses or put knives down and not hurt their spouse or kids. It's a good feeling to know when you have diffused a tense situation and were able to help people.[62]

Getting Feedback

A source of feedback to officers is any change or positive result that citizens attribute to their influence or to actions they have taken:

> *Example 4:* An older woman, I think she was 82, had her car stolen. She was getting her hair done someplace in the middle of the city. She comes out and finds her car is gone. She was very upset. She was so sweet, so we put her in the back of the patrol car and said, we were going to give her a ride home. "Oh, you would do that for me?" and we said, sure. We took the report, drove her home, and you wouldn't believe it, the best part is that two hours later we found her car and were able to return it to her. She was so grateful she wanted to make us cookies and coffee. "Oh please, you're so sweet," and when we found her car it was a good feeling to know we were able to help someone like that. It is just nice to get a thank you once in awhile; unfortunately, too often we don't get much respect for the job we do.[63]

Receiving Peer-Group Support

The officers cited two sources of satisfaction that had to do with peer support. One focused on the solidarity and loyalty of the police force, the other on relationships with partners and other work associates. The following example highlights rewards having to do with belongingness, solidarity, and support:

> *Example 5:* What really gives me a sense of satisfaction is the people I work with. The camaraderie that they have; it is a really tight-knit group. These are probably some of the closest friends I have ever had in my life, even in such a short period of time. You have a common bond. You all deal with the same situations, occasionally dangerous situations, and you kind of have an understanding of what the other one goes through. I found the degree of loyalty and friendship on the job that I didn't know existed when I was young. I found no matter what kind of background I had or what color I was, there was a sense of loyalty because we were all in the same profession.[64]

Police Domestic Violence

Given the stressful nature of police work, it is not surprising that officers sometimes have difficulty keeping what happened to them at work separate from their home lives. "Leave it at the office" is a common admonition to officers. While the intent of this message is clear, it is often hard to do so consistently and sometimes results in domestic violence.[65]

The International Association of Chiefs of Police (IACP) Model Policy on Police Officer Domestic Violence defines it as follows:

> It is any reported, founded, and/or prosecuted incident of domestic violence wherein a sworn police officer is the suspected offender. It is also an act of violence (threatened or actual) perpetrated by a police officer (on or off duty) or any police department employee upon his or her intimate partner. "Partner" refers to any individual (opposite or same sex) the officer has dated, cohabitated with, married, and/or has a child in common.[66] These definitions may be limited

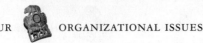
to the definitions in the law of each state. While not the focus of this policy, other forms of family violence (for example; child and elder abuse) should be addressed in a parallel manner.[67, 68]

It is not known how many acts of **domestic violence** police officers commit in their own homes. The reasons for the nonreporting of such incidents include victims with low esteem who think they "got what they deserved," threats from their attackers of more severe physical harm if the victims do call the police, and the belief that fellow officers will not take action against "one of their own."

Early Warning and Intervention

Of critical concern to departments is how to screen and select new officers to minimize the risk of hiring officers who may engage in domestic violence.[69] To understand the connection among the various forms of family violence, it is essential to investigate whether a candidate has a history or likelihood of engaging in child abuse, domestic violence, or elder abuse. The process of investigating candidates must be handled in two stages: (1) pre-employment screening and investigation and (2) postconditional offer of employment.

Pre-employment Screening and Investigation

All candidates should be asked about any history of perpetrating child abuse, domestic violence, or elder abuse and past arrests or convictions for such crimes. They should be asked whether they have ever been the subject of a civil protective order. If the candidate answers positively to any of these questions or the department uncovers any information in the background check that indicates a history of violence, the candidate should be screened out of the hiring process.

During the background investigation, a check should be made for restraining orders issued in any jurisdiction where the candidate has lived.

Postconditional Offer of Employment

If the candidate's background investigation does not indicate a history of child abuse, domestic violence, or elder abuse, the department should proceed with a psychological examination, which should include indicators of violent or abusive tendencies. This portion of the screening process should be conducted by an experienced clinical psychologist or psychiatrist. (See Chapter 9 Human Resource Management for a more detailed discussion.)

Zero Tolerance Policy

Departments must make it clear to all officers that the department has a zero tolerance policy on domestic violence, and the department should share this information with family members of the officer. Departments should look to develop a line of communication directly with the domestic partners of recruits and officers. For example, a department can hold a family orientation day prior to graduation from the police academy. Family members should be provided with instructions on whom to contact within the department if any problems arise. The dual purpose of establishing such contact is

IN THE NEWS Tacoma Police Department Develops Domestic Violence Program in the Face of Tragedy

The Tacoma, Washington Police Department was forced to examine its policies pertaining to domestic violence among officers when its chief of police, David Brame, killed his wife and then himself during a dispute in 2003. The new policy is divided into five sections, including response to domestic violence calls involving officers, prevention of abuse, investigations, examination of applicants to the police department, and assistance for victims. The program differs from other police domestic violence programs in that it focuses attention on the victim and ensures that he or she is put in touch with authorities other than the police department. According to the department, this is important because police responding to the call may know the officer perpetrating the violence and should not be privy to information regarding the location of the victim.

Tacoma's program also requires that the supervisors of all officers, including the police chief, be notified immediately of any domestic violence incidents and initiate both criminal and administrative investigations of the officers. However, the program is not considered a zero tolerance policy. Although the International Association of Police Chiefs recommend a zero tolerance program, Tacoma officials believe that zero tolerance puts the victim at risk by exacerbating stress on the offender, sending the officer back to commit further acts of violence.

Tacoma's policy also focuses extensively on weeding out potential abusers during the hiring process, as well as on providing education on the effects of police work on relationships. Although Tacoma officials believe the new policy provides a full spectrum of domestic violence responsiveness, some critics argue that domestic violence is merely a symptom of other problems, such as depression and posttraumatic stress disorder, and should be treated as such to maximize prevention.

Source: "Tacoma Unveils New Focus on DV by Officers," *Law Enforcement News,* April 2004, 10 and 14.

to underscore the department's zero tolerance policy, even with the police chief, and to provide victims with an avenue for direct communication with a department employee who is trained in handling such calls.

Department Responsibilities

An individual or a family member of an officer may recognize early indicators of potential violence, such as issues of power and control. The power and control might take the forms of restricting contact with family and friends, requiring the partner to turn over his or her paycheck, and limiting activities outside the home. Victims may communicate their concerns "informally" at first, such as with calls to an officer's supervisor. These informal contacts must be treated with care, since this is a critical opportunity for a department to provide intervention using early intervention and prevention strategies. The model policy calls for a formal system of documenting, sharing, and responding to information from concerned partners and family members.

Departments need to provide officers and their families with nonpunitive avenues of support and assistance before an incident of domestic violence occurs. Departments must establish procedures for making confidential referrals to internal or external counseling services with expertise in domestic violence. These referrals can be made on the request of an officer or family members or in response to observed warning signs.

Officers will not be entitled to confidentiality anytime they or family members disclose to any member of the department that an officer has engaged in domestic violence. Confidentiality should be extended to partners or family members who report an officer as a matter of safety. A report of such criminal conduct must be treated as an admission or a report of a crime and investigated, both criminally and administratively.

Departments must understand that other officers may become involved in domestic violence situations by engaging in inappropriate activities that interfere with cases against fellow officers who are engaged in such acts as stalking, intimidation, harassment, or surveillance of victims, witnesses, and/or family members of victims or witnesses. If this occurs, these officers must be investigated and sanctioned and/or charged criminally where appropriate.

Supervisory Responsibilities

Typically, an abusive person engages in certain patterns of behavior. These may include repeated actions of increasing control directed at his or her partner preceding an incident of physical or criminal violence.

The early indicators of potential violence are not limited to home life; the department may detect warning signs in an officer's behavior prior to a domestic violence incident. Supervisors must receive specific training on warning signs and potential indicators of violent or controlling tendencies. Warning signs that may indicate a likelihood of violent behavior include increased use of force in arrest situations, drug/alcohol problems, frequent tardiness or absences, verbal disputes, physical altercations, and other aggressive behavior.

When supervisors become aware of a pattern of controlling or abusive behavior exhibited by officers, the supervisors have a responsibility to document the information and notify their immediate ranking supervisor, who will then inform the chief in accordance with the department's chain of command. After making proper notification, supervisors should inform officers that the behaviors have been documented. A recommendation can be made to officers that they participate voluntarily in a counseling or support program to address the identified issue or behavior.

In cases in which behavior violates departmental policy, a department can seize the opportunity to mandate participation in a batterer intervention program in addition to any appropriate sanctions.

Early prevention and intervention strategies employed by a department at this phase of the continuum have tremendous potential not only to reduce future violence but also to save victims' lives and officers' careers. The services that can be made available include the following:

- Employee assistance program referral (discussed later in this chapter)
- Internal professional counseling (police psychologist)
- External professional counseling (contract/referral)
- Advocacy support from local agencies
- Peer support program (with clear reporting and confidentiality guidelines)

The department will need to ensure that the quality and expertise of these resources are sound. Collaboration with local domestic violence victim advocacy organizations is recommended.

Police Officer Responsibilities

As part of a department's zero tolerance policy, all officers need to understand their responsibility to report definitive knowledge they have concerning domestic violence on the part of an officer. Departments must be prepared to investigate and possibly sanction and/or charge criminally any officer who fails to report such knowledge or to cooperate with an investigation.

In addition, all officers need to know they will be investigated and sanctioned and/or charged criminally if they engage in activities such as stalking, surveillance, intimidation, or harassment of victims or witnesses in an attempt to interfere with investigations of other officers accused of domestic violence.

In the event that an officer is the subject of a criminal investigation and/or a protective or restraining order, the officer is responsible for informing his or her supervisor and providing copies of the order and timely notice of court dates regardless of the jurisdiction.

Incident Response Protocols

A department's response to 911 calls involving police officer domestic violence immediately sets the tone for how a situation will be handled throughout the remainder of the continuum. Further, the unique dynamics between the offending and responding officers (e.g., collegiality and rank differential) often make on-scene decisions extremely difficult.

A department must take the following actions, all of which are critical steps in responding to allegations of domestic abuse by police officers:

Communications officer/dispatcher documentation—When a call or report of domestic violence involves a police officer, the dispatcher should have a standing directive to document the call and immediately notify both the on-duty patrol supervisor and the chief of police. This directive ensures that key command personnel receive the information and prevents the call from being handled informally.

Patrol response—Any officer arriving at the scene of a domestic violence call or incident involving a police officer must immediately request the presence of a supervisor at the scene, regardless of the involved officer's jurisdiction.

On-scene supervisor response—The on-scene supervisor has responsibilities for the following:

- Securing the scene and collecting evidence
- Ensuring an arrest is made where probable cause exists
- Removing weapons in the event of an arrest
- Considering victim safety
- Notifying the police chief or sheriff if the incident occurs outside the officer's jurisdiction

The on-duty supervisor must respond to the call and assume all on-scene decision making. Leaving the decision making to officers of lesser or equal rank to the suspect officer puts the responding officer in a difficult situation. The presence

of a ranking officer on the scene resolves this problem. The policy recommends that, in police officer domestic violence cases, no fewer than two officers, with at least one of senior rank to the accused officer, be present. This is also the case when serving arrest warrants and civil protective orders.

Crime scene documentation—Recanting or reluctant witnesses and victims are not uncommon when domestic violence occurs. Police on the scene of a 911 call must take specific actions to document all evidence, including color photographs/videotape of injuries, overturned/damaged furniture, interviews of neighbors and family members, and threats from the officer. Documentation of this evidence will be essential to the successful prosecution of the case with or without the victim's presence in court.

Arrest decisions—Policies on arrest for domestic violence incidents vary among state, county, and local jurisdictions. In all cases, responding officers should base arrest decisions on probable cause. When a crime has been committed, an arrest will be made, as in all other cases. The on-scene supervisor is responsible for ensuring an arrest is made if probable cause exists or for submitting written documentation to explain why an arrest was not made. All officers need sufficient training to enable them to determine which party is the primary (i.e., dominant) aggressor in domestic violence situations. Every effort should be made to identify the primary aggressor to avoid the unwarranted arrest of victims.

Weapon removal—If an arrest is made, the on-scene supervisor will relieve the accused officer of his or her service weapon. Some police officers may have several weapons at their home. Where multiple weapons are present, removing only the service weapon of the officer leaves the victim entirely vulnerable to further violence. While federal, state, and local laws vary on how and when such weapons can be removed, police have broad powers to remove weapons in certain circumstances, particularly if an arrest is being made. Where application of the law is questionable, the on-scene supervisor should suggest that the officer in question voluntarily relinquish all firearms. The supervisor can also simply ask victims if they want to remove any weapons from the home for safekeeping by the department. When no arrest has been made, the on-scene supervisor should consider removing the accused officer's weapon as a safety consideration.

After weapons are removed, decisions need to be made about how long they will or can be held. Where court orders of protection are in place, these orders may also affect decisions on gun removal or seizure.

When the accused officer is the chief, director, or superintendent of the department, a specific protocol must be in place to document and report the incident to the individual who has direct oversight for the chief, director, or superintendent.

When police respond to a domestic violence incident involving an officer from another jurisdiction, all responding officers, investigators, and supervisors will follow the same procedures to be followed if responding to a domestic violence complaint involving an officer from their own department. The on-scene supervisor will notify the chief of police from the accused officer's department verbally as soon as possible and in writing within 24 hours of the call.

Departments may be faced with domestic violence situations where the victim is a police officer. If this occurs, standard domestic violence response and investigation procedures should be followed. The department should take steps to protect the privacy of the officer and make referrals to confidential counseling services. The department should not allow the reported incident to impact negatively on the assignments and evaluation of the victimized officer.

If both the victim and the offender in a domestic violence situation are police officers, the protocols established by the department should remain substantially the same. Safety of the victim should be the paramount concern. In the event that an order of protection has been issued, a department will need to make careful decisions concerning work assignments for accused officers pending administrative and criminal investigations. Gun removal in this situation becomes extremely complex. In the development of the policy, individual departments should seek legal guidance to ensure that the rights of all concerned are protected.

> *Department follow-up*—The department or supervisor should require a debriefing of all officers involved in a response to the scene of a police officer domestic violence case and may include communications officers. At the debriefing, the department's confidentiality guidelines should be reviewed. In addition, a command-level **critical incident** management review of every domestic violence case involving an officer should be conducted.

The department must take responsibility for conducting an assessment to determine the potential for further violence on the part of the accused officer. A specifically trained member of the command staff should review a checklist of risk factors with the accused officer. In addition, the evaluation should be supplemented by interviews with the victim, witnesses, and family members. Information gained from the assessment should be used to determine appropriate sanctions, safeguards, and referrals. The command officer assigned as the victim's principal contact should discuss the risk factors with the victim as part of safety planning.

Stress Management Techniques

Some police officers think that stress is just "a fairy tale—something that those who can't hack it can blame for their problems." Thus, the first step is for officers to recognize that unchecked stress can cause them to be sick more frequently, to engage in self-destructive behaviors (such as substance abuse or suicide), to live life less fully, to lose their families, and simply to be more uncomfortable every day than they need to be. The second step for officers is to monitor their own bodies and actions for stress, even though this capacity for self-awareness and introspection is difficult for some people to develop. Simply put, officers need to be in touch with what they are feeling, to think about what they have said and done, and to ask, "Why?" The final step is to eliminate or reduce stress by engaging in the so-called **stress inoculation activities**:

- Exercise rigorously for 20 to 30 minutes at least three times per week
- Maintain a proper diet, including minimizing the intake of foods high in salt and cholesterol
- Develop leisure interests and hobbies, such as hiking, tying fishing flies, rock climbing, gardening, collecting stamps, writing poetry and fiction, learning a foreign language, and photography—in other words, learning new things that excite and refresh the mind
- Meditate and pray
- Avoid maladaptive responses to stress, such as smoking and drinking
- Establish support groups
- Develop a network of friends, including people outside the department
- Monitor yourself; refer yourself for help before you have to be referred; you will avoid some problems, reduce others before they become entrenched, and get more out of the helping process
- Use relaxation techniques, such as biofeedback, yoga, progressive muscle relaxation, tai chi, imagery, and breathing exercises
- Make sure your career and other expectations are consistent with your actual situation[70]

Sleep Deprivation as a Stress Inducer

Although sleep deprivation is often not thought of as a stress factor, it can be a significant factor in the creation of stress. For example, sleep deprivation can cause the following to occur in police officers:

- Increased mood swings
- Impaired judgment
- Decrease in adaptability to certain situations
- Heightened sense of threat
- Increased anxiety or depression
- Increased chances of mental illness (e.g., officers may develop post-traumatic stress disorder or bipolar disorder)
- Reduced eye-hand coordination
- Weight gain
- Pain (e.g., backaches, headaches)
- Inability to relax (e.g., cause restless sleep, provoke heightened alert response)
- Gastrointestinal problems (e.g., loss of appetite or abdominal distress)
- Damage to the cardiovascular system (e.g., causing heart disease, arteriosclerosis or congestive heart failure)
- Use of more sick leave
- Inappropriate uses of force more frequently
- More vehicle accidents

- More accidental injuries
- Greater difficulty dealing with the community members and other law enforcement agencies
- Higher likelihood of dying in the line of duty[71,72]

Deprivation Is Comparable to Excessive Drinking

A sleep deprivation study found that not sleeping for 17 hours impaired a person's motor skills to an extent equivalent to having an alcohol toxicity of 0.05 percent. Not sleeping for 24 hours was equivalent to a toxicity level of 0.10 percent.[73] This level of deprivation would impair speech, balance, coordination, and mental judgment.

Sleep Deprivation Can Cause Work-Related Accidents

A study found that four out of eight officers involved in on-the-job accidents and injuries were impaired because of fatigue.[74] Such accidents include automobile crashes that were due to officers' impaired eye-hand coordination and propensity to nod off behind the wheel. Other work-related injuries come from accidents that occur when officers have impaired balance and coordination.

Despite the impact of fatigue, many officers continue to work double shifts, triple shifts, and second jobs. Some work well over 1,000 hours of overtime a year. Excessive work with inadequate rest over a long period of time can make officers sleep-deprived—53 percent of officers report an average of 6.5 hours of sleep or less.[75]

Employee Assistance Programs

Although their evolution has been slow in development, a variety of employee assistance services are currently available within police departments.[76] The growth of **employee assistance programs (EAPs)** in the law enforcement field can be traced back to the early 1950s.[77] Many programs, such as those initiated in Boston, New York, and Chicago, were created to deal primarily with alcohol abuse.

In the 1970s, agencies such as the Los Angeles Sheriff's Office, the Chicago Police Department (see Figure 13.4), and the San Francisco Police Department expanded their programs to include problems not related to alcohol. In 1980, mental health professionals began providing personal and job-related counseling services to FBI personnel. Mental health professionals were also used to assist FBI managers with a variety of employee-related matters. By 1986, many of the largest police departments in the United States had formed "stress units" or other sections to provide help for officers having personal or occupational difficulties. In the early 1990s, the U.S. Customs Service provided stress-management training for both its supervisory and its nonsupervisory personnel throughout the country.[78] The majority of law enforcement agencies with 100 or more officers now have written policies regarding providing counseling assistance services for their officers.[79]

CHICAGO POLICE DEPARTMENT'S
Professional Counseling Service
Employee Assistance Program

FOR FURTHER INFORMATION
CALL 747-5492 or
747-1371 (24 hours)

Professional Counseling Service
407 South Dearborn–Suite 800
Chicago, IL 60605

CONFIDENTIALITY

Officers and/or their family members may wonder if counseling sessions or contacts with our program are completely confidential, or will they become part of some department record which can be used against them in the future. The answer is **NO**.

All contacts with the Professional Counseling Service/Employee Assistance Program are held in the strictest confidence based on state and federal guidelines, related to client confidentiality and client privilege. (Rule 501 of the Federal Rules of Evidence, 13 June, 1996.)

Unlike facilities which rely on insurance payments, we are not required to record session notes or retain records for any purpose.

WHY SEEK COUNSELING?

Do you feel tense all the time? Is there someone you love who drinks too much? Are you experiencing marital problems?

You are not alone

Job pressures . . . finances . . . death of a loved one . . . marital difficulties . . . gambling . . . your son or daughter experimenting with drugs. There are countless factors which add stress to your life and may lead to these difficult situations in different ways.

Many people attempt to escape from their problems by turning to alcohol. Others begin to lose their temper and punch walls . . . or someone they love. Still others withdraw, feel it just is not worth it anymore, and sink into a deeper depression.

These responses don't relieve the problems—they create other, more serious ones.

But remember, you are not alone.
There is help.

THE PROFESSIONAL COUNSELING SERVICE

EMPLOYEE ASSISTANCE PROGRAM

The Chicago Police Department recognizes the unique demands placed upon its members, their families, and the connection between personal and professional life.

Thus, the Professional Counseling Service–Employee Assistance Program was established to provide all Department members and their families who desire assistance a *confidential* means to find solutions to a variety of problems.

The Professional Counseling Service–Employee Assistance Program is here to assist you.

SERVICES PROVIDED

The Professional Counseling Services–Employee Assistance Program offers a variety of assessment and counseling services including:

- INDIVIDUAL
- MARITAL
- FAMILY
- COUPLES
- REFERRAL FOR FINANCIAL COUNSELING
- STRESS MANAGEMENT TRAINING
- REFERRALS FOR DEATH AND BEREAVEMENT GROUPS
- FAMILY VIOLENCE ISSUES
(Physical, Emotional and Verbal Violence)
- COUNSELING, ASSESSMENT AND REFERRAL FOR "TROUBLED TEENS"
- TRAUMATIC INCIDENT DEBRIEFING PROGRAM

Figure 13.4
Chicago Police Department's information brochure for its employee assistance program.
(Courtesy of Superintendent Terry G. Hillard and Sergeant Robert J. Delaney, Chicago Police Department.)

ALCOHOL ASSISTANCE UNIT

Alcoholism is a devastating, progressive, fatal illness which can take a tremendous toll on the individual and their family members. The Alcohol Assistance Unit was established to provide a viable alternative, and linkage with treatment programs to effectively confront this disease and other addictions.

Trained sworn personnel are available to assist in every aspect of recovery.

The unit affords Department members and their families who have alcohol problems with a *confidential* objective and nonjudgmental resource to which they can go voluntarily for advice and assistance.

The Department recognizes alcoholism as an illness which negatively affects the major areas of a person's life such as health, family situations and work.

If any part of your life is negatively affected by alcohol or drugs, take advantage of this service.

Do it for yourself and those you love!

TRAUMATIC INCIDENT DEBRIEFING PROGRAM

The first thing that needs to be said about "trauma debriefing" is that *it is not counseling*. Officers do not need counseling for doing their job.

Trauma is a response to events which occur during an officer's tour of duty, which is shocking and disturbing. It does not mean that the officer's judgment is being called into question or that he/she is "falling apart."

What it does mean is that the officer should be paying special attention to how they are being affected by the impact of vulnerability to Post-Traumatic Stress Disorder, to which our officers may be prone to experience.

This service is also offered to members of an officer's family should they choose to participate. As with other services, there is

NO CHARGE

WHO IS ELIGIBLE?

This free confidential service is available to all active Chicago Police Department members and their family members as well as retired sworn personnel.

Contacts with our office may be made anonymously for those seeking information about the program or any services but not yet ready to reveal their identity.

It is important to remember that if someone you care about has a problem, you also have a problem and should seek assistance for yourself.

Figure 13.4 (Continued)

CONCLUSION

It has been our objective throughout this chapter to present clear and straightforward discussions of the major areas of stress in police work that can be read with profit and interest by police administrators who do not necessarily possess a scientific background or training.

CHAPTER REVIEW

1. Describe the three stages of the general adaptation syndrome, as described by Hans Selye.
2. According to recent medical findings, what is the relationship between diseases of adaption and stress?
3. What are the major characteristics of a type A personalities, type B personalities, and workaholics?
4. What are the sources of stress attached to an officer-involved shooting (OIS)?
5. What are the five basic phases of the post-shooting reaction?
6. Alcohol-related problems manifest themselves in police officers in a number of ways. What are they?

7. Describe some of the issues that police administrators must deal with in terms of drug use by police officers within their agencies.

8. What are the three general principles defined by the courts in relation to random drug testing?

9. What are some of the physical and psychological effects of steroid use?

10. What are the most common factors related to police suicide?

11. What are some of the typical warning signs that an officer might be contemplating suicide?

12. What are a supervisor's responsibilities regarding suicidal officers?

13. What sources of work satisfaction are stress reducers?

14. What are some things police departments can do to curtail incidents of domestic violence among their officers?

15. If a police supervisor notices a pattern of controlling or abusive behavior in an officer, what steps should be taken?

16. What range of services can be made available to police officers who are involved in domestic violence incidents?

17. What are some examples of so-called stress inoculation activities?

18. What are some of the benefits of an employee assistance program (EAP) to employees?

KEY TERMS

alarm stage: the component of general adaptation syndrome that puts the body on a "fight-or-flight" alert by releasing hormones that produce an energizing effect on the body.

anabolic steroids: a group of synthetic hormones usually derived from testosterone, that promote storage of protein and the growth of muscle tissue.

critical incident: a crisis situation, often involving human suffering beyond the normal range, that causes emergency personnel, family members, or bystanders to experience a strong physical, mental, or emotional reaction that interferes with usual coping skills.

domestic violence: acts of violence by one family or household member against another.

employee assistance programs (EAPs): programs made available by employers to help employees having personal or occupational difficulties.

exhaustion stage: the point in general adaptation syndrome when resistance can no longer be maintained and the body's defenses against stress begin to break down.

general adaptation syndrome (GAS): the biological and physiological reactions, caused by stress, that may eventually incapacitate an individual.

posttraumatic stress disorder (PTSD): a psychological reaction that occurs after experiencing a highly stressful event outside the range of normal human experience.

resistance stage: the second step in general adaptation syndrome, exemplified by specific responses to continued stress by the body in order to optimize adaptation.

roid rage: an outburst of violent or aggressive behavior caused by taking large doses of anabolic steroids.

stress: anything that places an adjustive demand on the organism.

stress inoculation activities: activities that help eliminate or reduce stress.

suicide by cop (SbC): a situation involving an individual who wishes to die and uses the police to affect that goal.

type A personality: the personality type characterized by an intense and ambitious mindset, which puts the person under constant stress and physiological strain.

type B personality: the personality type characterized by a more easygoing state of mind than the type A personality.

workaholic: the personality type similar to a type A, which can result in serious physical and psychological consequences.

ENDNOTES

[1] H. Selye, *Stress without Distress* (Philadelphia: Lippincott, 1974), p. 60.

[2] Ibid., pp. 35–39.

[3] Anthony L. Komaroff, "The Usual Suspect," *Newsweek,* 25 (February 2009), pp. 52–53.

[4] Ibid.

[5] Ibid.

[6] Meyer Friedman and Ray Rosenman, "Type A Behavior Pattern and Its Association with Coronary Heart Disease," *Annals of Clinical Research* 3, no. 6 (1971), p. 300.

[7] Gerard J. Sloan and Jean M. Casey, "Police Work Addiction: A Cautionary Tale," *FBI Law Enforcement Bulletin* (June 2003), pp. 13–17. (This discussion of workaholics was adapted from this article.)

[8] B. E. Robinson, *Chained to the Desk* (New York, NY: New York University Press, 1998), p. 3.

[9] B. Killinger, *Workaholics: The Respectable Addicts* (Buffalo, NY: Firefly Books, 1991).

[10] Supra note 1, 75.

[11] Supra note 2.

[12] W. E. Oates, *Confessions of a Workaholic* (New York, NY: Abingdon Press, 1971), p. 4.

[13] Supra note 2, 6.

[14] John M. Violanti and Fred Aron, "Police Stressors: Variations in Perceptions among Police Personnel," *Journal of Criminal Justice* 23, no. 3 (1995), pp. 287–294.

[15] "An Interview with Dr. Lorie DeCarvalho," *The Crisis Management and Traumatic Stress Report* 1, no. 1 (Summer/Fall, 2008), pp. 15–17.

[16] C. Baruth, "Pre-critical Incident Involvement by Psychologists," in *Psychological Services for Law Enforcement*, eds. J. T. Reese and H. A. Goldstein (Washington DC: USGPO, 1986), pp. 413–417.

[17] Alexis Artwohl, "Perceptual and Memory Distortion During Officer-Involved Shootings," *FBI Law Enforcement Bulletin* (October, 2002), pp. 18–24. (This discussion was adapted from this article.)

[18] Ibid., pp. 18–24.

[19] Bruce A. Rodgers, *Psychological Aspects of Police Work: An Officer's Guide to Street Psychology* (Springfield, IL: Charles C Thomas, 2006).

[20] D. A. Grossman, *On Killing: The Psychological Cost Of Learning to Kill in War and Society* (New York: Little, Brown, 1996).

[21] E. Nielsen, E. "Traumatic Incident Corps: Lessons Learned," in *Critical Incidents in Policing,* eds. J. Reese, J. Horn & C. Dunning (Washington DC: US Government Printing Office, 1991), pp. 221–226.

[22] M. B. Williams. "Impact of Duty-related Death on Officers' Children: Concepts of Death, Trauma Reactions, and Treatment," in *Police Trauma: Psychological Aftermath of Civilian Combat,* eds. J. M. Violanti & D. Paton (Springfield: Charles C Thomas, 1999), pp. 159–174.

[23] D. B. Kennedy, R. J. Homant, and R.T. Hupp, "Suicide by Cop," *FBI Law Enforcement Bulletin* (August, 1998), pp. 21–27.

[24] W. Anderson, D. Swenson, and D. Clay, *Stress Management for Law Enforcement Officers* (Englewood Cliffs: Prentice Hall, 1995).

[25] M. A. Borders and C. H. Kennedy, "Psychological Interventions After Disaster in Trauma," in *Military Psychology: Clinical and Operational Applications*, eds. C. H. Kennedy and E. A. Zillmer (New York: Guilford, 2006).

[26] Grossman, *On Killing*.

[27] L. Miller, *Practical Police Psychology: Stress Management and Crisis Intervention for Law Enforcement* (Springfield, IL: Charles C Thomas, 2006).

[28] L. G. Bender and others, *Critical Issues in Police Discipline: Case Studies* (Springfield, IL: Charles C Thomas, 2005).

[29] A. J. Pinizzotto, E. F. Davis, and C. E. Miller III, "Suicide by Cop: Defining a Devastating Dilemma," *FBI Law Enforcement Bulletin* (February 2005): p. 14 (This discussion was adapted from this source.)

[30] Clinton R. Vanzandt, "Suicide by Cop," *Police Chief* (July 1993), pp. 29–30.

[31] L. Dishlacoff, "The Drinking Cop," *Police Chief* 43, no. 1 (1976), pp. 32–39.

[32] Ibid., 39.

[33] On this point, see Mary Niederberger, "Random Drug Test for Police Opposed," *Pittsburgh Press*, April 6, 1989; Rob Zeiger, "14 Fired Officers Returned to Duty," *Detroit News*, July 22, 1988; Shelly Murphy, "Court Upholds Drug Tests for Hub Cops," *Boston Herald*, May 13, 1989; Marilyn Robinson, "Drug Use Cuts Police Recruits by Nearly 50%," *Denver Post*, July 15, 1983; and David Schwab, "Supreme Court Backs Drug Tests for South Jersey Police Officers," *Newark Star-Ledger*, April 4, 1989.

[34] J. J. Hurrell and R. Kliesmet, *Stress among Police Officers* (Cincinnati: National Institute of Occupational Safety and Health, 1984), p. 12.

[35] *Newlun v. State Department of Retirement Systems*, 770 P. 2d 1071 (Wash. App. 1989). Relatedly, *McElrath v. Kemp*, 27 Govt. Emp. Rel. Rep. (BNA) 605 (D.D.C. 1989), deals with an alcoholic employee who had relapses after being treated and was terminated but was reinstated later.

[36] Will Aitchison, *The Rights of Police Officers*, 3rd ed. (Portland, Ore.: Labor Relations Information System, 1996), pp. 228–233, is the source of the information in this paragraph, with restatement by the authors.

[37] *Delaraba v. Nassau County Police*, 632 N. E. 2d 1251 (N.Y. 1994).

[38] C. Swanson, L. Gaines, and B. Gore, "Use of Anabolic Steroids," *FBI Law Enforcement Bulletin* 60, no. 8 (1991), pp. 19–23.

[39] A. G. Gilman et al., *Goodman and Gilman's The Pharmacological Basis of Therapeutics* (New York: Macmillan, 1985), pp. 1440–1458.

[40] Harrison G. Pope and David L. Katz, "Affective and Psychotic Symptoms Associated with Anabolic Steroid Use," *American Journal of Psychiatry* 145, no. 4 (1988), p. 488.

[41] Ibid.

[42] Charlier, "For Teens, Steroids May Be Bigger Issues Than Cocaine Use," *Wall Street Journal*, October 4, 1988.

[43] Pope and Katz, "Affective and Psychotic Symptoms," pp. 187–190.

[44] J. M. Violanti, "The Mystery within: Understanding Police Suicide," *FBI Bulletin* (February 1995), pp. 19–23.

[45] J. H. Burge, "Suicide and Occupation: A Review," *Journal of Vocational Behavior* 21 (1982), pp. 206–222.

[46] J. Skolnick, *Police in America* (Boston: Educational Associates, 1975), p. 21.

[47] J. M. Violanti, "Police Suicide on the Rise," *New York Trooper*, January 1984, pp. 18–19.

[48] Andre Ivanoff, "Police Suicide Study Recommends Additional Training, Counseling," *Columbia University Record* 20, no. 2 (September 16, 1994), www.columbia.edu/cu/record/record2002.14.html

[49] J. Schwartz and C. Schwartz, "The Personal Problems of the Police Officer: A Plea for Action," in *Job Stress and the Police Officer*, ed. W. Kroes and J. Hurrell (Washington, D.C.: U.S. Government Printing Office, 1976), pp. 130–141.

[50] S. Labovitz and R. Hagehorn, "An Analysis of Suicide Rates among Occupational Categories," *Sociological Inquiry* 41 (1971), pp. 67–72; see also Z. Nelson and W. E. Smith, "The Law Enforcement Profession: An Incidence of High Suicide," *Omega* 1 (1970), pp. 293–299.

[51] B. I. Danto, "Police Suicide," *Police Stress* 1 (1978), pp. 32–35.

[52] P. Friedman, "Suicide among Police: A Study of 93 Suicides among New York City Policemen 1934–40," in *Essays of Self Destruction*, ed. E. S. Schneidman (New York: Science House, 1968).

53 C. W. Gaska, "The Rate of Suicide, Potential for Suicide, and Recommendations for Prevention among Retired Police Officers" (doctoral diss., Wayne State University, 1980).

54 T. E. Baker and J. P. Baker "Preventing Police Suicide," *FBI Law Enforcement Bulletin*, October 1996, pp. 24–26.

55 See, for example, J. M. Violanti, J. E. Vena, and J. R. Marshall, "Disease Risk and Mortality among Police Officers: New Evidence and Contributing Factors," *Journal of Police Science and Administration* 14 (1986): 17–23; and K. O. Hill and M. Clawson, "The Health Hazards of Street Level Bureaucracy Mortality among the Police," *Journal of Police Science* 16 (1988), pp. 243–248.

56 Thomas E. Baker and Jane P. Baker, *Preventing Police Suicide* (October 1996): www.fbi.gov/publications/leb/1996/oct966.txt

57 P. Bonafacio, *The Psychological Effects of Police Work* (New York: Plenum, 1991).

58 J. Schwartz and C. Schwartz, *The Personal Problems of the Police Officer: A Plea for Action* (Washington, D.C.: U.S. Government Printing Office, 1991), pp. 130–141.

59 F. Herzberg, B. Mausner, and B. B. Snyderman, *The Motivation to Work* (New Brunswick, N. J.: Transaction, 1993) as cited in H. Toch, *Stress in Policing* (Washington, D.C.: American Psychological Association, 2004), pp. 26–46.

60 Ibid.

61 Ibid.

62 Ibid.

63 Ibid.

64 Ibid.

65 L. D. Lott, "Deadly Secrets: Violence in the Police Family," *FBI Law Enforcement Bulletin*, November 1995, pp. 12–15. This discussion was adapted from this article.

66 Police Officer Domestic Violence, Concepts and Issues Paper, Developed by the International Association of Chiefs of Police, April 1999.

67 These definitions may be limited to the definitions in the laws of each state. While not the focus of this policy, other forms of family violence (for example: child and elder abuse) should be addressed in a parallel manner.

68 In order to access the Model Policy on Police Officer Domestic Violence, as well as the accompanying Concepts and Issues Paper log onto www.theiacp.org and click on Publications (under Information Resources) then scroll down to "Police Officer Domestic Violence Information," this will lead you to links to each of the two documents.

69 André Ivanoff, "Police Suicide Study Recommends Additional Training, Counseling," *Columbia University Record* 20, no. 2 (September 16, 1994): www.columbia.edu/cu/record/record2002.14.html

70 Many of these factors are identified in Robert W. Shearer, "Police Officer Stress: New Approaches for Effective Coping," *Journal of California Law Enforcement* 25, no. 4 (1991), pp. 97–104.

71 B. J. Vila and D. J. Kenney, "Tired Cops: The Prevalence and Potential Consequences of Police Fatigue," (pdf, 6 pages) *National Institute of Justice Journal* 248 (2002), pp. 16–21.

72 U.S. Department of Justice, Office of Justice Programs, "How Fatigue Affects Health" (Washington, D.C: National Institute of Justice, The Research, Development, and Evaluation Agency of the U.S. Department of Justice, January 6, 2009) accessed 5 May 2010; available from http://www.ojp.usdoj.gov/nij/topics/law-enforcement/stress-fatigue/health.htm

73 D. Dawson and K. Reid, "Fatigue, Alcohol and Performance Impairment," *Nature* 388 (1997), p. 235.

74 B. J. Vila, *Tired Cops: The Importance of Managing Police Fatigue* (Washington, DC: Police Executive Research Forum, 2000).

75 D. J. Dijk, D. F. Neri, J. K. Wyatt, J. M. Ronda, E. Riel, A. Ritz-De Cecco, R. J. Hughes, A. R. Elliott, G. K. Prisk, J. B. West, and C. A. Czeisler, "Sleep, Performance, Circadian Rhythms, and Light-Dark Cycles During Two Space Shuttle Flights," *American Journal of Physiology* 281 (2001), pp. R1647–R1663.

76 Max Bromley and William Blount, "Criminal Justice Practitioners," in *Employee Assistance Programs*, ed. William R. Hutchison, Jr., and William G. Emener (Springfield, Ill.: Charles C Thomas, 1997), p. 400.

77 J. T. Reese, *The History of Police Psychological Service* (Washington, D.C.: U.S. Department of Justice, 1987).

78 C. Milofsky, E. Astrov, and M. Martin, "Stress Management Strategy for U.S. Customs Workers," *EAP Digest* 14, no. 6 (1994), pp. 46–48.

79 Bromley and Blount, "Criminal Justice Practitioners," p. 401.

14

Legal Aspects of Police Administration

Law is order, and good law is good order.
—*Aristotle*

Objectives

- Explain the three general categories of torts. How do they differ?

- What does "acting under the color of state law" mean? How does this statement relate to Section 1983 actions?

- What is a *Bivens* action?

- List and describe the negligence theories applicable to police supervision and management.

- What is procedural due process? Substantive due process?

- What is a Brady violation?

- When might rules infringing on the free speech of officers be upheld?

- Under what circumstances can an officer use deadly force?

- What four elements must be proven in order to sue the police for negligence in a high-speed pursuit?

- What are a department's responsibilities in reducing liability in high-speed pursuits?

- What is the focus of most training programs regarding emotionally disturbed persons?

- What is the balancing test as referred to in alcohol and drug testing in the workplace?

OUTLINE

Introduction

One of the primary characteristics of our nation's law is its dynamic nature. Rules of law are developed by legislation, regulation, and by court decision. In this chapter, we talk about the fluid nature of our lawmaking system as it applies to police and police executives. It is important to understand the legal aspects of police administration because: (1) Police officers understand criminal law because they deal with it on a daily basis; however, they have a relatively poor understanding of civil law; (2) civil law addresses private injuries that lead to liability and subsequent monetary damages due to negligence; (3) the major areas of litigation against the police fall under Title 42, U.S. Code, Section 1983 and usually involve negligent hiring, negligent assignment and retention, negligent supervision, and/or negligent training; (4) police officers have Constitutional rights that are enjoyed by all citizens within the United States including the rights and liberties that address privacy, free speech, search and seizure, and self-incrimination; and (5) most civil actions against the police arise from the misuse of firearms and deadly force, use of force, high speed pursuits, and police handling of emotionally disturbed persons. Finally, police officers are held to a different and higher standard of conduct both on and off the job. Even when their actions do not arise to the level of a criminal complaint, they still might receive discipline that can result in termination and loss of career. These types of behaviors and officer actions most often violate departmental policy addressing conduct unbecoming of an officer, sexual conduct, residency requirements, religious beliefs or practices, moonlighting, and alcohol and drug testing.

The reader should view the material that follows as instructive background rather than as an authoritative basis for action. Police administrators should always seek qualified legal counsel whenever they face a problem or a situation that appears to have legal ramifications. A primary objective of this chapter is to make police administrators more capable of quickly determining when they face such a problem or situation.

Liability for Police Conduct

One of the most troubling legal problems facing police officers and police departments in recent years has been the expanded impact of civil and criminal **liability** for alleged police misconduct. It is commonplace to hear police spokespersons complain that law enforcement officers are widely hampered by the specter of being undeservedly sued for alleged improper performance of duty. Although one can argue that the magnitude of police misconduct **litigation** may be overstated, the amount of litigation appears to be increasing and is apparently accompanied by a movement toward larger monetary damage awards.

Basic Types of Police Tort Actions[1]

Law can be divided into two parts: criminal law and civil law. Police officers and other criminal justice practitioners are generally more familiar with criminal law because they deal with it on a daily basis. Each "piece" of the law addresses a specific type of action. For instance, criminal law focuses on crimes, whereas civil law applies to torts.

Barrineau defines a crime as a public injury, an offense against the state, punishable by fine and/or imprisonment. It is the violation of a duty one owes the entire community; the remedy for a breach of such duty is punishment (fine or imprisonment) imposed by the state. Crimes are exemplified in the FBI Crime Index (murder, assault, robbery, rape, burglary, larceny, auto theft, and arson), wherein each crime is composed of specific elements and has an affixed penalty.

On the other hand, a **tort** is a private injury inflicted on one person by another person for which the injured party may sue in a civil action. Such action may bring about liability that leads to an award of money damages. Tort actions encompass most personal injury litigation. The injured party initiates the lawsuit and is called the **plaintiff**. The sued person is called the **defendant** and is often referred to as the *tort feasor*.[2]

One example of a tort action brought against police officers is an allegation of criminal behavior, such as assault and battery (police brutality). More commonly, they are civil actions brought about by claims of false arrest, false imprisonment, invasion of privacy (through illegal search and seizure), negligence, defamation, or malicious prosecution.[3] Most of the suits against police officers fall into three general categories: negligence torts, intentional torts, and constitutional torts.[4]

Negligence Torts   AGRAVIO

Our society imposes a duty on individuals to conduct their affairs in a manner that does not subject others to an unreasonable risk of harm. This responsibility also applies to criminal justice practitioners. If a police officer's conduct creates a situation recognizable as dangerous by a reasonable person in like circumstances, the officer will be held accountable to those injured as a result of his or her conduct.

In **negligence** suits, defendants are not liable unless they foresaw or should have anticipated that their acts or omissions would result in injury to another. The key in negligence suits is the standard of the reasonably prudent person, also referred to as **reasonableness**. Was the care provided at the same standard that a reasonably prudent person would observe under a given set of circumstances?[5] Examples of negligence involving police officers often arise from pursuit driving incidents in which the officers violate common traffic laws, such as speeding, running a stop sign, or failing to control their vehicles, resulting in the injury or death of another person.

Intentional Torts

An intentional tort is the voluntary commission of an act that to a substantial certainty will injure another person. It does not have to be negligently done to be actionable. Intentional torts are therefore *voluntary* and *deliberate* acts, such as assault, false arrest, false imprisonment, and malicious prosecution.

Constitutional Torts

The duty to recognize and uphold the Constitutional rights, privileges, and immunities of others is imposed on police officers and other criminal justice practitioners by statute, and violation of these guarantees may result in a specific type of civil suit. Most of these suits are brought under Title 42, U.S. Code, Section 1983, in federal court.

In our system of government, there are court systems at both federal and state levels. However, federal courts are intended to be courts of somewhat limited jurisdiction and generally do not hear cases involving private, as opposed to public, controversies unless a question of federal law is involved or the individuals involved in the lawsuit are residents of different states. Even then, the suit can be decided in a state court if both parties to the controversy agree to have the dispute settled there. As a result, most tort suits have been brought in state courts.

Title 42, U.S. Code, Section 1983

A major trend in the area of police misconduct litigation is the increase in the number and proportion of these suits that are being brought in federal court. The most common legal vehicle by which federal courts can acquire jurisdiction of these suits is commonly referred to as a **1983 action**. This name derives from the fact that these suits are brought under the provisions of Section 1983 of Title 42 of the U.S. Code. This law, passed by Congress in the aftermath of the Civil War and commonly referred to as the Civil Rights Act of 1871, was designed to secure the civil rights of the recently emancipated slaves. It prohibits depriving any person of life, liberty, or property without due process of law. Specifically, Section 1983 states:

> Every person who, under color of any statute, ordinance, regulation, custom, or usage of any State or Territory, subjects, or causes to be subjected, any citizen of the United States or any other person within the jurisdiction thereof to the deprivation of any rights, privileges, or immunities secured by the Constitution and laws, shall be liable to the party injured in an action at law, suit in equity, or other proper proceeding for redress.[6]

After 90 years of relative inactivity, Section 1983 was resuscitated by the U.S. Supreme Court in the landmark case *Monroe v. Pape* (1961).[7] In this case, the Court concluded that, when a police officer is alleged to have acted improperly (for example, in conducting an illegal search), that officer can be sued in federal court by alleging that he or she deprived the searched person of his or her Constitutional right under the Fourth Amendment to be free from unreasonable searches and seizures. A critical element of Section 1983 is that the violation must have occurred while the officer was acting "under color of State law"—that is, while the officer was on duty and acting within the scope of employment as a sworn police officer. Unless there is direct personal participation by police supervisory personnel, they are not generally liable for Section 1983 damages, even if there are broad allegations of failure to properly train and supervise police officers who are liable in the Section 1983 lawsuit.[8]

Bivens Action

Section 1983 is the primary civil rights statute involved in litigation against munici-pal and state police officers. However, the statute rarely applies to federal agents (such as officials of the FBI, Secret Service, and Drug Enforcement Administration) because its terms require that the plaintiff be acting under "color of State law." Federal officials can be sued under one of two complaints. The first is a ***Bivens* action** for a violation of constitutional rights. The *Bivens* action applies only to the individual, not to the government. The second is a tort action against the United States under the Federal Tort Claim Act (FTCA).[9] Both actions can be combined into one lawsuit.

Essentially, a *Bivens* action is a judicially created counterpart to a Section 1983 tort action. The Supreme Court has permitted suits against federal officials (not, how-ever, against the United States) for violations of Constitutional rights that would oth-erwise be the subject of a Section 1983 action against a state or local officer. Its name is derived from the landmark case *Bivens v. Six Unknown Federal Narcotics Agents* (1971), wherein the Supreme Court held that a cause of action for violation of the Fourth Amendment (search and seizure clause) can be inferred from the Constitution itself.[10] Hence, federal courts have jurisdiction to hear federal question cases involving suits against federal employees in their individual capacities.[11]

In summary, there are three basic types of tort actions that can be brought against police for misconduct: traditional state law torts, Section 1983 torts, and *Bivens* torts. It is important to understand these classifications because the type of tort action brought will determine who can be sued, what kind of behavior will result in liability, and which immunities might be available to the defendants.

Who Can Be Sued?

At common law, police officers were held personally liable for damage caused by their own actions that exceeded the boundaries of permissible behavior. This rule applied even if the officer was ignorant of the boundary established by the law. As unjust as many of such results may seem, the rule establishes one of the traditional risks of policing.

A more difficult question concerns whether the supervisors of the officer and/or the government unit by which he or she is employed can be sued for that individual's misbehavior. Generally, an effort to impose liability on supervisors for the tortious conduct of their employees is based on the common-law doctrine of *respondent supe-rior*. That doctrine, also called **vicarious liability**, developed along with the growth of industrial society and reflected a conscious effort to allocate risk to those who could afford to pay for the complaint of damages.[12]

As could be expected, the growing area of negligence as a Section 1983 cause of action has caused concern within police supervisory ranks. The courts have supported several negligence theories applicable to police supervision and management. The fol-lowing is a discussion of important negligence cases and subsequent legal development in this area.[13]

Negligent Hiring

The law enforcement administrator and the local government entity have a duty to "weed out" those obviously unfit for police duty. Further, the courts have held that an employer must exercise a reasonable standard of care in selecting persons who, because of the nature of their employment (such as policing), could present a threat of injury to members of the public.[14] Further, in 1997 the Supreme Court held that law enforcement and government entities could be held liable under Section 1983 if the plaintiff's injury was an obvious and direct consequence of a bad hiring decision on the part of an agency. In this case, an officer was hired by a local police department *after* it was discovered that the officer had lied on his original application and had been convicted of a felony, barring him from police service under state regulatory agencies.[15]

Negligent Assignment, Retention, and Entrustment

Police administrators who know or should have known of individual acts or patterns of physical abuse, malicious or threatening conduct, or similar threats against the public by officers under their supervision must take immediate action. If an internal investigation sustains an allegation of such serious conduct by an officer, appropriate action by a police chief could be suspension—followed by assignment to a position with little or no public contact—or termination. A police chief failing to take decisive action when required could be held liable for future injuries caused by the officer. In addition, entrustment of the "emblements of office" (e.g., a badge, a gun, or a nightstick) subjects a municipality and appropriate administrators of a municipal agency to liability whenever injury results from the known misuse of such emblements. In other words, administrators and supervisors have a duty to supervise errant officers properly.[16]

Negligent Direction and Supervision

The administrator and/or supervisor have the duty to develop and implement appropriate policies and procedures. Therefore, a written manual of policies and procedures is an absolute must. This manual must provide clear instruction and direction regarding the position of police officer, be widely disseminated, and be accompanied with training so that all officers understand the significance of the manual.[17] Further, the courts have held that supervisors must "take corrective steps" where evidence indicates that official policy is being abridged and/or the public is being placed at an "unreasonable risk" because of the actions of a police officer. Inaction on the part of the police supervisors and/or administrators is enough to establish negligence if there is a pattern or custom of police abuse and accession to that custom by police supervisors and/or administrators.[18] For example, the failure of a police sergeant to order the termination of a high-speed pursuit of a minor traffic violator through a congested downtown business area that results in serious personal injuries or deaths to members of the public is sure to bring litigation based on an allegation of failure to supervise (see Figure 14.1).

Figure 14.1
As described in Chapter 2, community policing places additional responsibility on the supervisor to instruct and direct officers during routine incidents. Neighborhood disturbances are often characterized by high emotion and potentially violent confrontations that may require the presence of a supervisor at the scene. The failure to provide such direction and/or supervision can result in a negligence tort action.
(© Dnavarrojr/ Dreamstime.com)

Negligent Training

The local unit of government and the administrator or supervisor of a police department have an affirmative duty to train their employees correctly and adequately. In a recent landmark case (*City of Canton v. Harris*), the Supreme Court limited the use of inadequate police training as a basis for Section 1983 actions. The Court held that inadequate police training may form the basis for a civil rights claim "where the failure to train amounts to **deliberate indifference** to the rights of persons with whom the police come in contact" and that such official indifference amounts to "policy or custom." Therefore, it is incumbent on the plaintiff to prove that the training program is inadequate as to the expected duties of an officer and that the deficiency of training is closely related to the ultimate injury.[19]

The two areas of negligence that have been the greatest sources of litigation under Section 1983 in recent years have been negligent supervision and negligent training. Incidents arising out of the use of deadly force and use of force, and pursuit driving, have certainly raised significant questions regarding training and are covered later in this chapter.

A second difficult question with respect to who may be sued for damages caused by police misconduct concerns the liability of the police department and the government unit of which the department is a part.[20] Individuals pursuing damage claims under Section 1983 against local government officials and state officials who are sued in their individual rather than official capacities will have to overcome the defense available to such parties of "qualified, good-faith immunity." Such official immunities are not creatures of Section 1983; they arose from traditional, common-law protections that were historically accorded to government officials. Basically, the good-faith immunity doctrine recognizes that public officials who exercise discretion in the performance of their duties should not be punished for actions undertaken in good faith. Imposing liability on public officials in such situations would inevitably deter their willingness to "execute . . . [their] office with the decisiveness and the judgment required by the public good."[21]

Over the years, the courts have struggled to develop a test for good faith. In 1975, the Supreme Court articulated such a test that considered both the official's state of mind when he or she committed the act in question (the subjective element) and whether the act violated clearly established legal rights (the objective element).[22]

However, 7 years later, the Supreme Court decided that the subjective element of the text should be dropped, leaving only the standard of **objective reasonableness**.[23] Now a court must determine only whether the law at issue was "clearly established" at the time the challenged action occurred. Furthermore, if the plaintiff's allegations do not show a violation of clearly established law, a public official asserting good-faith immunity will be entitled to dismissal of the lawsuit before it proceeds further.[24]

The immunities available to state and local officials are generally designed to protect individuals from liability arising out of the performance of official acts. With the Eleventh Amendment providing similar protection to the states, the question of the immunity of a local government was raised. Initially, the Supreme Court concluded that Congress had not intended to apply 42 U.S.C. 1983 to municipalities, thereby giving municipalities what is called "absolute," or unqualified, immunity from suit.[25] On reexamination of this issue in the 1978 case *Monell v. Department of Social Services*,[26] the Court decided that Congress had intended for Section 1983 to apply to municipalities and other local government units. The Court further concluded that, although certain other immunities were not available to a municipality in a Section 1983 lawsuit, the municipality could not be held liable solely because it employed an individual who was responsible for Section 1983 violations. The Court made it clear that local government entities will be liable under Section 1983 only when that government's policies or official procedures can be shown to be responsible for the violation of federally protected rights.

Unfortunately, the *Monell* decision did not fully articulate the limits of municipal liability under Section 1983. The result has been considerable litigation to establish when a deprivation of federally protected rights actually results from enforcement of a municipal policy or procedure and at what point an official's actions can be fairly treated as establishing the offending policy.[27]

More recently, the Supreme Court has held that "single acts of police misconduct" do not, by themselves, show that a city policy was involved in the alleged tortious act.[28] Generally, a plaintiff must show a pattern of negligence or deliberate indifference by the agency.[29]

Scope of Liability

In general, state tort actions against police officers provide a greater scope of liability than do the Section 1983 and *Biven* suits. That is, in tort actions under state law, a greater range of behavior is actionable.

The types of torts under state law that commonly are brought against police officers can be categorized as intentional or negligence torts. An intentional tort is one in which the defendant knowingly commits a voluntary act designed to bring about certain physical consequences. For example, the tort of assault is the purposeful infliction on another person of a fear of a harmful or offensive contact. If X points an unloaded pistol at Y, who does not know the pistol is unloaded, X has created in Y an apprehension that Y is about to experience a harmful contact from a bullet. X voluntarily lifts the pistol and points it at Y, fully expecting that it will cause Y to be apprehensive about being hit by a bullet. Thus, X is liable to Y for the intentional tort of assault.

The tort of negligence involves conduct that presents an unreasonable risk of harm to others that, in turn, is the proximate cause of an actual injury. Whereas in an intentional tort the consequences following an act must be substantially certain to follow, in the tort of negligence the consequences need only be foreseeable. When X drives through a stop sign, even if unintentionally, and hits the side of Y's car, X's behavior presents an unreasonable risk of harm to others and is the proximate cause of the damage to Y's car. Although X would have been negligent for "running the stop sign" even without hitting the other car, he or she would not have committed the tort of negligence in that no injury was caused.

The Supreme Court has limited the scope of liability in reference to negligence as an element of deprivation of Constitutional rights in Section 1983 and *Bivens* actions. In *Daniels v. Williams* (1986), the petitioner sought to recover damages as a result of injuries sustained in a fall caused by a pillow negligently left on the stairs of the city jail in Richmond, Virginia. The Court held that the petitioner's Constitutional rights were "simply not implicated by a negligent act of an official causing *unintentional* loss or injury to life, liberty, or property."[30] This case has had a profound impact on limiting Section 1983 and *Bivens* actions to intentional torts; hence, the sheer volume of such cases has significantly decreased in past years. It is important to note, however, that the Supreme Court "has not changed the rule that an intentional abuse of power, which shocks the conscience or which infringes a specific constitutional guarantee such as those embodied in the Bill of Rights," still implicates serious liability.[31]

As noted earlier in this chapter, many lawsuits against police officers are based on the intentional torts of assault, battery, false imprisonment, and malicious prosecution.[32] Suits against police officers for intentional torts can be brought as state tort actions, Section 1983 suits, or *Bivens* suits. Although suits against police officers for negligence torts can be brought as state tort actions, the issue is not so clear-cut with regard to Section 1983 and *Bivens* suits.

Generally, damages assessed in civil litigation for negligence are ordinary (compensatory) damages that are paid by the employing government entity (or its liability insurance carrier) on behalf of the defendant officer. Therefore, as a general rule, the individual employee is not required to pay ordinary damages that result from a civil negligence suit. This is so because, normally when government employees are performing their duties within the scope of employment, they are deemed to be the agents or representatives of the employing agency and therefore not personally liable for their

Figure 14.2
When police officers use wholesale "roundup" procedures on gang members without probable cause to arrest or search, they may run the risk of being sued under the Section 1983 tort claims of harassment, false imprisonment, and malicious prosecution. (Robert Nickelsberg/ Getty Images)

acts. However, where punitive damages are assessed for conduct that is grossly negligent, wanton, or reckless, individuals who have been responsible for such acts are personally liable and, generally speaking, these assessments are not absorbed by the employing government entity or by liability insurance. Thus, law enforcement employees who act in reckless, wanton, or grossly negligent manners will be subject to and personally liable for punitive damage awards (see Figure 14.2).

In this constantly changing area of the law, the Supreme Court has established a rule that police are entitled to "qualified" immunity for acts made in good faith that can be characterized as "objectively reasonable." In *United States v. Leon*,[33] the Court focused on the objectively ascertainable question of whether a reasonably well-trained officer would have known that the act committed was illegal. Subsequently, following that logic the Court held that, if police personnel are not "objectively reasonable" in seeking an arrest warrant, they can be sued personally for many damages, despite the fact that a judge has approved the warrant. In fact, the Court stated that a judge's issuance of a warrant will not shield the officer from liability if a "well-trained officer in [his] position would have known that his affidavit failed to establish probable cause and that he should not have applied for the warrant."[34] However, the Court modified its position in a later case when an FBI agent conducted a warrantless search of a resident's home for a fugitive by holding that an alleged unlawful warrantless search of an innocent third party's home does not create an exception per se to the general rule of qualified immunity. The Court held that the relevant question is whether a reasonable officer would have believed the search lawful once the clearly established law and the information possessed by the agent were taken into consideration and, if the answer is yes, whether the agent is protected by qualified immunity from civil liability.[35] This standard was upheld in 2001 and 2009.[36]

As with many areas of the law, lower courts have somewhat modified this landmark decision. In 1987, a U.S. district court found that qualified immunity protects all but the plainly incompetent or those who knowingly violate the law.[37] And in 1992, a federal court ruled that law enforcement officers are protected by immunity from "bad guesses in gray areas" but are liable for "transgressing obviously bright lines of law,"[38] essentially leading the way for protective immunity for officers honestly attempting to do their job. This was affirmed again in *Pearson et al. v. Callahan* in 2009.[39] Still, whereas public officials exercising discretion (e.g., judges and prosecutors) have absolute immunity for their unreasonable acts, the only person in the system left to sue for damages for a wrongdoing will be the police officer, unless his or her acts can be attributed to the policy or procedural custom established by the employing government agency.

Trends in Tort Liability for Police Supervisors and Administrators

Although there has been a reluctance to hold police supervisors and administrators liable for the misbehavior of their subordinate officers, some courts have been increasingly willing to extend liability to these officials where the plaintiff has alleged negligent employment, improper training, or improper supervision.[40]

Under negligent employment, a police official can be held liable for his or her failure to conduct a thorough investigation of a prospective employee's suitability for police work if he or she hires an applicant with a demonstrated propensity "toward violence, untruthfulness, discrimination or other adverse characteristics."[41] Of course, under this theory, the injuries suffered by the plaintiff would have to have been the result of the negative trait that had been demonstrated by the individual before employment as an officer. If the negative trait is not demonstrated until after employment, a party injured by the officer may be able to sue a police official successfully for negligently retaining the officer or otherwise failing to take appropriate remedial action. In some circumstances, the official may not be able to dismiss an officer who has demonstrated unfitness, but the official still might be found liable if he or she negligently assigns the unfit officer to duties where the public is not protected adequately from the officer's particular unfitness. Finally, the official is potentially liable for negligently entrusting a revolver to an officer who has a history of alcohol or other drug abuse or the misuse of a weapon.

Suits alleging that police officials have improperly trained a police officer have been particularly successful where firearms were involved in inflicting the injury. Courts have stressed that the "law imposes a duty of extraordinary care in the handling and use of firearms"[42] and that "public policy requires that police officers be trained in the use of firearms on moving and silhouette targets and instructed when and how to use them."[43] Suits alleging lack of necessary training are also becoming increasingly

Figure 14.3
Police officers responding to hostage and/or barricaded suspect situations often require specialized training in crisis negotiations and the use of firearms. In this case, a man was taken hostage at a local television station while the suspect shouted demands from the control room. After hours of skilled negotiations by local detectives, the hostage was released without harm, avoiding potential liability stemming from the incident.
(AP Photo/Roberto Pfeil)

successful in cases involving the use of physical force to overcome resistance, the administration of first aid, pursuit driving (see Figure 14.3) and false arrest.[44]

Another emerging theory of recovery against police officials is an allegation of failure to properly supervise or direct subordinate officers. This type of suit is typically brought where officials have failed to take action to rectify a recurring problem exhibited in the conduct of police operations by subordinates.[45] An interesting development in this area concerns the situation in which the police department issues a written directive that establishes a policy more stringent than the law requires. In several cases involving such a situation, the courts have held that the written directive establishes a standard of conduct to which police officers must conform or face the possibility of civil liability for their actions.[46]

The last area to which courts have given increased attention concerns cases in which it is alleged that the police officer failed to provide needed medical care to people with whom the officer came in contact.[47] Although the incidents giving rise to such allegations can occur in a variety of situations, they seem to occur with greatest frequency when the plaintiffs have been in custody or have been mistakenly thought to be intoxicated when they actually were suffering from a serious illness. These cases are based on four categories of recovery: (1) failure to recognize and provide treatment for injury, (2) failure to provide treatment on request, (3) failure to provide treatment on recognition of an injury, and (4) negligent medical treatment. Suits in the first three categories may allege either negligent conduct or intentional behavior. Court rulings suggest that police officers who ignore classic signs of illness, such as a heart attack, are depriving arrestees of their Fourteenth Amendment right to receive medical care as a pretrial detainee. To prove that an officer is subject to liability because he or she failed to provide medical treatment requires a showing that the officer acted with deliberate indifference to the serious medical needs of an arrestee.[48] Recent cases have affirmed that holding.[49] Some courts have held that police officers do not have a duty to care for injured persons with whom they come in contact,[50] although such a holding is not likely to occur when the injured person is in their custody.

Misuse of Firearms and Deadly Force

The past two decades have been witness to an enormous increase in the number of lawsuits filed against police departments for wrongful deaths. In the vast majority of these cases, the issue is not that an officer injured an innocent third party while shooting at a "bad guy" but rather that the "bad guy" should not have been shot in the first place.

Unfortunately, in the past, police officer training has too often focused on the issue of how to shoot and not when to shoot. Many times when a problem does arise relating to the use of deadly force, it is not that the officer failed to qualify at the police pistol range or that the weapon malfunctioned but that the officer made an error in judgment.

The police chief and his or her legal counsel must question whether this error in judgment was merely a human error resulting from the pressure of the moment or whether the police department failed to provide proper guidelines to the officer. If proper guidelines were made available to the officer, did the police department incorporate these guidelines into its formal training program?

Let us examine what areas a use-of-deadly-force policy should cover and the formalized mechanisms by which officers can be trained to understand this policy.

Tennessee v. Garner (1985)

Until 1985, the courts nationwide had not established a standard of law regarding the use of deadly force. Likewise, law enforcement agencies had not developed a standard, written directive that would establish national guidelines. While most larger police agencies had established use-of-deadly-force policies, those policies certainly were not consistent in form or content.[51]

On March 27, 1985, all this started to change when the Supreme Court ruled unconstitutional a Tennessee law that permitted police officers to use deadly force to effect an arrest.[52] The Tennessee statute on the police use of deadly force provided that if, after a police officer has given notice of an intent to arrest a criminal suspect, the suspect flees or forcibly resists, "the officer may use all the necessary means to effect the arrest."[53] Acting under the authority of this statute, a Memphis police officer shot a juvenile, Garner, as he fled over a fence at night in the backyard of a house he was suspected of burglarizing. The officer ordered him to halt, but he failed to stop. The officer then fired a single shot and killed him. The officer used deadly force despite being "reasonably sure" that the suspect was unarmed and believing him to be 17 or 18 years old and of slight build. The suspect's father subsequently brought an action in federal district court, seeking damages under 42 U.S.C.S. 1983 for asserted violations of his son's constitutional rights. The district court held that the statute and the officer's actions were unconstitutional. The court of appeals reversed and the Supreme Court affirmed the Court of Appeals' decision.

The Supreme Court held that the Tennessee statute was unconstitutional insofar as it authorized the use of deadly force against, as in this case, an apparently unarmed, nondangerous, fleeing suspect. Such force may not be used unless necessary to prevent the escape and the officer has probable cause to believe that the suspect poses a significant threat of death or serious physical injury to the officer or others. The Court's reasoning was as follows:

1. Apprehension by the use of deadly force is a seizure and subject to the Fourth Amendment's reasonableness requirement. To determine whether such a seizure is reasonable, the extent of the intrusion on the suspect's rights under that amendment must be balanced against the government interests in effective law

enforcement. This balancing process demonstrates that, notwithstanding probable cause to seize a suspect, an officer may not always do so by killing him or her. The use of deadly force to prevent the escape of all felony suspects, whatever the circumstances, is constitutionally unreasonable.

2. The Fourth Amendment, for purposes of this case, should not be construed in light of the Common-Law rule allowing the use of whatever force is necessary to effect the arrest of a fleeing felon. Changes in the legal and technological context mean that the rule is distorted almost beyond recognition when literally applied to criminal situations today.

   Whereas felonies were formerly capital crimes, few felonies are now. Many crimes classified as misdemeanors or nonexistent at Common Law are now felonies. Also, the Common-Law rule developed at a time when weapons were rudimentary. The varied rules adopted in the states indicate a long-term movement away from the Common-Law rule, particularly in the police departments themselves; thus, that rule is a dubious indication of the constitutionality of the Tennessee statute. There is no indication that holding a police practice, such as that authorized by the Tennessee statute, will severely hamper effective law enforcement.

3. While burglary is a serious crime, the officer in this case could not reasonably have believed that the suspect—young, slight, and unarmed—posed any threat. Nor does the fact that an unarmed suspect has broken into a dwelling at night automatically mean he or she is dangerous.

Evaluation of Written Directives

As suggested earlier, when an alleged wrongful death case is being evaluated, the adequacy of the police department's policy must be considered. Generally speaking, an adequate policy addresses the following topics: defense of life and fleeing felons, juveniles, shooting at or from vehicles, warning shots, shooting to destroy animals, secondary guns, off-duty weapons, and registration of weapons (see Figure 14.4).

Defense of Life and Fleeing Felons

State laws and departmental policies still remain fairly diverse even after *Garner*, although with narrower bounds. No longer can these provisions leave officers virtually untethered, as in the extreme case of one small American town whose only gun guidance to its officers was the homily "Never take me out in anger; never put me away in disgrace."[54]

The range of firearms policies hereafter is likely to be from the "defense-of-life" regulations, which permit shooting only to defeat an imminent threat to an officer's or another person's life. At the other extreme, a minimal compliance with the *Garner* rule permits shooting at currently nonviolent, fleeing suspects who the officer reasonably believes committed a felony involving the threat but not the use of violence. Both approaches are currently employed by many large police departments.

The defense-of-life approach significantly reduces the possibility of wrongful death allegations.

Figure 14.4
Officers enter a suspected drug house during a search warrant execution. Police firearms regulations should provide direction during incidents in which the probability for the use of deadly force is high.
(© Mikael Karlsson/Alamy)

Juveniles

For the most part, police departments do not instruct their officers to make a distinction between adults and juveniles in using deadly force, unless it is readily apparent that the individual is a juvenile. This is not based on a callous disregard for youthful offenders; rather, it is based on the pragmatic view that an armed juvenile can kill with the same finality as an armed adult. Further, it is often difficult, if not impossible, to tell if an offender is a juvenile or an adult.

Shooting at or from Vehicles

The trend in recent years has been to impose severe limitations on police officers shooting at or from vehicles except as the ultimate measure in self-defense or the defense of another when the suspect is using deadly force by means other than the vehicle.

Some of the reasons presented against shooting at or from vehicles are difficulty in hitting the target, ricochets striking innocent bystanders, population densities, difficulty in penetrating the automobile body and steel-belted tires, inability to put a stop to the vehicle's momentum even when the target suspect is hit, damage that might result from causing the vehicle to go out of control, difficulty in hitting a moving target, and striking of an innocent passenger in the fleeing vehicle.[55]

There is little question that, if a motorist is trying to run a police officer down and the officer has no reasonable means of escape, then the officer has every right to defend his or her life. What often happens, however, is that the officer starts shooting at a vehicle when he or she is no longer in danger. For example, if a vehicle attempts to run a police officer down and the officer is able to take evasive action and get out of harm's way, under the provisions of many police departments' policies, the officer is no longer permitted to shoot at the vehicle because the officer is no longer in danger.

Naturally, if the driver turns the vehicle around and goes back toward the officer, the officer once again has the right to protect his or her life.

Warning Shots

There seems to be a general consensus among administrators that department policies should prohibit warning shots, as they may strike an innocent person. Privately, however, officials might fear something else: that officers shooting at and missing a suspect may claim that they were merely firing a warning shot and attempt to avoid answering for their actions. In addition, police officials point out that warning shots rarely accomplish their purpose, especially if suspects know that officers will not or cannot shoot them.[56]

Shooting to Destroy Animals

Police departments generally allow their officers to kill an animal in self-defense, to prevent substantial harm to the officer or others, or when an animal is so badly injured that humanity requires its relief from further suffering. A seriously wounded or injured animal may be destroyed only after all attempts have been made to request assistance from the agencies (i.e., humane society, animal control, or game warden) responsible for disposal of animals. The destruction of vicious animals should be guided by the same rules set forth for self-defense or the defense and safety of others.[57]

Secondary Guns

Police officers in the United States are all conspicuously armed with a revolver or semiautomatic handgun. This fact is recognized and for the most part approved by our citizenry. A second fact not commonly known is that many police officers also carry a concealed secondary weapon. There are stated reasons for the practice: Officers are concerned about being disarmed (with sound justification) during a confrontation, officers are less likely to be caught off guard when confrontation is not anticipated, and officers can less conspicuously be prepared to protect themselves during routine citizen stops. Regardless of the rationale, the practice is considered acceptable by knowledgeable police officials but treated by many police administrators as something understood but not formally admitted.

A major criticism of backup weapons is that they may be intended as "throwaways" in the event an officer shoots an unarmed suspect. In order to protect the officer from such allegations, it is generally recommended that there be a strict policy of registering all backup guns with the department.[58]

Off-Duty Weapons

The rationale for officers to be armed while off duty is based on the assumption that police officers within their own jurisdictions are on duty 24 hours a day and are therefore expected to act in their official capacity if the need to do so occurs. This, for the most part, was the policy of many police departments. Until recently, an officer who failed to comply with this regulation was subject to disciplinary action if a situation occurred that needed police action, such as responding to a robbery in progress, and the officer could not respond because he or she was unarmed.

Many police departments now make being armed while off duty optional but still compel their officers to register with the department any weapons they choose to wear off duty and to qualify regularly with the weapons. Most police departments also designate the type of ammunition the officers may carry in all weapons they use, regardless of whether they are used on duty or off duty.[59]

Registration of Weapons

Most police departments require their officers to use only department-approved weapons on and off duty and further require that the weapons be inspected, fired, and certified safe by the departments' armorers. Further, the firearms must be registered with the departments by make, model, serial number, and ballistics sample.[60]

Familiarization with the Department's Policy

It does a police department little good to have an adequate use-of-deadly-force policy if its officers are not familiar with all aspects of that policy. Following are some examples of formalized administrative means by which officers can become familiar with their agencies' policies:

- *Recruit training*—Instructions dealing with the deadly-force policy should be incorporated into the unit of instruction dealing with firearms training. As suggested earlier, the judgmental aspects of using deadly force are as important as the hands-on skill development of police officers in firearms training. Such a unit of instruction should involve a discussion of the numerous situations that officers will typically encounter and what course of action would keep these officers in strict compliance with their departments' policies and minimize wrongful deaths.

- *Field training officer*—The field training officer to whom a rookie officer is assigned immediately upon graduation from the police academy is responsible for continuing the training process started by the police academy and for evaluating the suitability of the rookie for police work. Such programs frequently incorporate training features designed to reinforce topics covered in the formal classroom setting of the academy. This component of the training program should be examined to be certain it deals with the topic of police use of deadly force.

- *Roll-call training*—A part of this training, which typically occurs just prior to the officers going on patrol, can be spent in reviewing newly developed departmental policies, procedures, and regulations, including those dealing with the use of deadly force.

- *In-service training*—In-service training classes typically range from one to five days (see Figure 14.5). It is quite clear that the *Garner*[61] decision has resulted in many police departments rethinking and rewriting their use-of-deadly-force policies. The importance of the *Garner* decision will not be fully appreciated if a

police department merely rewrites its policy and hands it out to its officers with no explanation. It is imperative that some explanation be provided, preferably by legal counsel, so that there is no misunderstanding about what this policy means. This familiarization and orientation can occur in conjunction with the firearms requalification training that officers have to go through regularly, or it can be treated within the context of an in-service training course.[62]

Police Use of Force and Less-Lethal Weapons

Law enforcement agencies must walk a careful line in American society. While police officers are responsible for maintaining peace and order, this is complicated by a multitude of factors unique to each and every situation. When an officer responds to a call for service or reacts to observed criminal behavior in the field, that officer must either quell the disturbance or apprehend a suspect, sometimes through the use of force. Police use of force is most often justifiable and legal, particularly when overcoming resistance during arrests or in course of protecting themselves or others from harm.[63]

Figure 14.5
Police use of deadly force requires extensive training in firearms techniques that can be validated and documented by qualified personnel.
(© Kathy McLaughlin/The Image Works)

There is a general, usually unrealistic, societal expectation of increasingly more technical and sophisticated weapons available to police agencies. This is propagated in the entertainment industry. Television and big-screen productions tend to display deadly force in black and white; the evil doer misses or inflicts minor wounds while heroes are incredibly accurate and kill painlessly and from great distances. Less-lethal weapons in the entertainment arena can be viewed through a similar lens. The public, raised on science fiction like Star Trek©, expects phaser-like weapons that can incapacitate without causing permanent harm or death. Viewers watch as the fictitious recipient is usually rendered unconscious from a single application of a less-lethal weapon and recovers almost immediately. This creates a massive discrepancy between reality and the portrayal of **less-lethal weapons** in popular media. In reality, they are, as their name reflects: less than lethal. Less-lethal weapons are used without the intent to cause permanent injury or death. While they have the potential to cause death or serious injury, these weapons are considerably less harmful than the projectiles fired from firearms.[64] Common less-lethal weapons used in policing include chemical weapons such as oleoresin capsicum (OC) or pepper spray, bean-bag guns, net guns that shoot a web around suspects, and controlled energy devices (CEDs).

Tasers®

A controlled energy device (CED) is a device designed to deploy electricity throughout the body of the target to temporarily cause loss of muscle control. Throughout the history of law enforcement in America there have been many devices that loosely fit this description, including "cattle prods" or "stun guns." Such devices allow electricity to be deployed on contact with the skin or within close distances. Over the past several years, the technology for these devices has become more advanced, allowing the user to apply the device more accurately and from greater distances. Although greatly accepted as a less-lethal weapon option by many local, county, state, and federal police agencies, they have also been met by community concerns about safety, misuse, and overuse. TASER® International[65] is the company best known for producing CEDs. Their product has become so well-known that the name "TASER®" has become synonymous with "CED," much like the name "band-aid" is to a plastic bandage.[66]

According to the Government Accounting Office, TASERS® are now used by more than 10,000 law enforcement agencies across the United States.[67] TASERS® shock a person with 50,000 volts and create intense pain and discomfort by involuntary constrictions of skeletal muscles in order to gain compliance on the part of the suspect. A person being shocked or "tased" is conscious and the event is designed to last for 5 seconds or less; however, the newest version of the weapon is designed to produce up to three cycles of 5 seconds (15 seconds). While application of the electrical current is possible by contacting the end of the device to the skin, the uniqueness of the TASER® weapons lies in its ability to be applied from greater distances. Powered by high-pressure air probes that are similar to darts, the probes are fired while tethered to the handheld device on wire that can reach from 15 feet to 31 feet. However, in order for the device to be effective in gaining compliance, both probes must strike the target, preferably with a spread of about 1 foot between the probes.

Liability and Less-Lethal Weapons

While empirical research on police use of force has increased over the last 50 years, only limited attention has been paid to use-of-force encounters wherein the police used "less-lethal weapons" generally, and the TASER® specifically. Alpert and Dunham have focused on use of force encounters and police injuries and have demonstrated that the greatest likelihood of officer injury occurs when they

Figure 14.6
The use of a TASER on a young spectator caught by the national media during the 2010 World Series raised public debate about police use of less-lethal weapons. (Steven M. Falk/ Philadelphia Daily News/MCT)

attempt to control a suspect by punching, kicking, take-down, wrestling, and joint locks.[68] These types of incidents account for almost 70 percent of injuries. Research findings also reveal a higher likelihood of injury to the suspect when officers use canines, bodily force, and impact weapons (e.g., batons, riot sticks) as well. Generally, research reveals that few problems occur when healthy subjects are shocked or "tased" for less than 15 seconds.[69] Even though the bulk of research shows that the use of less-lethal weapons reduces injury, there have been several highlighted incidents across the nation that have peaked interest in the use of such weapons and influenced public opinion (see Figure 14.6).[70]

Most departments using TASERS® place the weapon within their continuum of force policy and provide extensive training on the use of the weapon. Most importantly, recent research[71] using data from 12 local police departments representing more than 24,000 incidents found that the use of physical force (e.g., striking, wrestling, come-along holds) by police increased the odds of injury to both suspects and officers. Conversely, the use of less-lethal weapons (such as OC spray or TASERS®) decreased the odds of injury to suspects and officers. When used appropriately as trained, and controlled through use-of-force policy, the employment of less lethal weapons (such as OC spray and TASERS®) against healthy suspects reduces injury overall; by reasonable extension, the use of less-than-lethal weapons also reduces the number and severity of potentially successful liability claims brought against the police.[72] To further reduce liability, officers should follow many of the suggestions designed to reduce liability during use of deadly force encounters as proscribed above, be well-trained on each type of less-lethal weapons, be familiar with policies relating to their use, and receive periodic in-service training to update their skills and the usage of such devices.

One of the most litigious areas against the police under 42 USC, Section 1983 are lawsuits alleging excessive use of force. Individuals have a clear constitutional right to be free from excessive use of force when they are being arrested. In *Graham v. Connor* (1989), the Supreme Court established a guideline to examine claims of excessive force during an arrest. The Court established that excessive force claims should be analyzed under the Fourth Amendment's Objective Reasonableness Standard. That is, was the force used in a given instance "reasonable" under the Fourth Amendment perspective of seizing a "free citizen" by the police? The Court emphasized that the overriding function of the Fourth Amendment is to protect an individual's personal privacy and dignity against unwarranted intrusion by the police. Thus, to be successful in stating a claim for excessive force under the Fourth Amendment, the claimant must show that the force was unreasonable by showing that the force resulted in an injury to the plaintiff, that the force was clearly in excess of the force needed to effect the arrest, and that such excessiveness was objectively unreasonable. The Fourth Amendment's objectively Reasonableness Standard is made on a case-by-case basis and in light of the facts and circumstances of each incident, not 20-20 hindsight. It is not a subjective standard relating to an officer's thoughts, which are irrelevant. The Court went on to discuss a number of important criteria in balancing whether the use of force was appropriate to the need of the state to apprehend or arrest an individual. For instance, what was the severity of the crime at issue, what was the relative threat to the officer or others, and was the subject fleeing from arrest or actively resisting arrest? In looking at the "totality of the circumstances" of an event, the Court concluded that the real issue in each case in whether the officer's actions were objectively reasonable in light of the facts and circumstances confronting him or her, at that moment, without regard to their underlying intent or motivation.

As a result, many agencies have developed policies that provide officers with a variety of force options based on the specific event or situation at hand. With a very strong emphasis on using the minimum amount of force necessary to effect an arrest, prevent an escape, or overcome resistance by an unruly subject, officers are trained to communicate and be flexible in their attempt to deescalate a use-of-force situation. Note the emphasis that the Los Angeles Police Department places on reporting incidents where officers use force other than verbalization in confronting a subject.

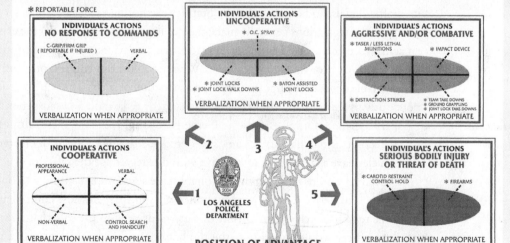

Source: Graham v. Connor, 109 s. Ct. 1865, 1872 (1989).

Police Liability and High-Speed Pursuit

The legal theory underlying most pursuit-related lawsuits is that the police were negligent in conducting a pursuit.[73] A negligence action is based on proof of the following four elements: (1) the officer owed the injured party a duty not to engage in certain conduct, (2) the officer's actions violated that duty, (3) the officer's negligent conduct was the proximate cause of the accident, and (4) the suing party suffered actual and provable damages.[74] Negligence litigation focuses on the alleged failure of an officer to exercise reasonable care under the circumstances.

Duty Owed

Courts first determine the duty owed in a pursuit situation by examining the officer's conduct in light of relevant laws and department regulations. With the exception of some police departments that prohibit all pursuits, police officers have no duty to refrain from chasing a criminal suspect, even when the risk of harm to the public arising from the chase is foreseeable and the suspect is being chased for a misdemeanor.[75] In *Smith v. City of West Point*,[76] the court stated that police "are under no duty to allow motorized suspects a leisurely escape."[77] However, police do have a duty of care with respect to the manner in which they conduct a pursuit. This duty is derived from state statutes, court decisions defining reasonable care, and departmental pursuit policies.

Statutes in most jurisdictions confer a special status on police and other authorized emergency vehicles, exempting them from certain traffic regulations, such as speed limits, traffic signals, and a right of way.[78] Statutes exempting emergency vehicles from ordinary traffic regulations generally make the privilege conditional on (1) the existence of an actual emergency, (2) the use of adequate warning devices, and (3) the continued exercise of due care for the safety of others. Whether a government unit or its officers can be held liable depends in large part on the construction of such statutes. As a general rule, police drivers are not liable for negligence as a matter of law solely because they disregard a traffic regulation during an authorized emergency run. However, these statutes provide no protection against liability for an officer's reckless driving. Drivers of emergency police vehicles have a statutory duty to drive with due regard for the safety of others.

Court decisions defining the reasonable care standard constitute a second source from which to derive a duty owed by police pursuit drivers. Most courts have translated the reasonable care standard into a duty to drive with the care that a reasonable, prudent officer would exercise in the discharge of official duties of a like nature.[79] "Reasonable care" is a relative term depending on the exigencies of the situation and the degree of care and vigilance reasonably dictated by the circumstances of the chase.

A third source from which to derive a duty owed by police pursuit drivers is department policy. A law enforcement organization's policies, procedures, and training material concerning high-speed pursuits are generally admissible as evidence in lawsuits against the department or its officers for the negligent operation of a pursuit vehicle.[80] For example, in order to ascertain the standard of care applicable to a particular pursuit situation, a court could admit into evidence a police department regulation defining the proper speeds at which police cars responding to emergency calls were supposed to enter intersections when proceeding against red traffic signals. Depending on the jurisdiction involved, departmental pursuit policies may be merely a guideline to assist juries in determining the reasonableness of pursuit conduct, or they may actually constitute a duty owed, the violation of which would be considered negligent.

Proximate Cause

Liability must be based on proof that police conduct in breaching a duty owed was the **proximate cause** of a pursuit-related accident. Proximate cause is difficult to establish in cases involving the intervening negligence of other drivers, such as a case in which a fleeing motorist collides with an innocent person. In such cases, some courts impose liability on the officer and the department if the accident was a foreseeable consequence of police negligence.[81] For example, if police pursue without activating their lights and siren and an innocent citizen enters an intersection without being warned of the pursuit and collides with the pursued vehicle, the police may be liable because the accident was the proximate and foreseeable result of their failure to adequately warn other drivers of the pursuit. In *Nelson v. City of Chester, Ill.*,[82] the court held that the city's breach of its duty to properly train its police officers in high-speed pursuit might be found to be the proximate cause of the pursued driver's death, notwithstanding the contributing negligence of the pursued driver.

Legal barriers to civil actions, such as immunity, have been removed in many jurisdictions by a combination of legislation and judicial decisions, even though the extent of immunity continues to vary.[83] Statutes in most states have limited sovereign immunity to discretionary as opposed to ministerial decisions. Accordingly, the decision to pursue is viewed as discretionary, rendering the public entity immune, but the manner of pursuit is a ministerial decision for which there is no general grant of immunity. *Rhodes v. Lamar*[84] used this bifurcated approach to hold that the decision to institute a pursuit is a discretionary decision for which a sheriff enjoyed sovereign immunity, but liability was not precluded if the pursuit was conducted in a manner that violated a reasonable duty of care. In *Fagan v. City of Vineland*, the Court of Appeals allowed the municipality to be sued directly under Section 1983 when the pursuit causing a constitutional tort was pursuant to municipal policy or custom. Furthermore, the court allowed the municipality to be held liable for lack of training its officers in high-speed pursuit even if none of the officers involved in the pursuit at issue violated the Constitution.[85]

Federal Civil Rights Act

Pursuit-related liability under the federal Civil Rights Act, 42 U.S.C. 1983, requires proof that an officer's conduct violated a constitutionally protected right.[86] In *Cannon v. Taylor*,[87] the Court of Appeals for the 11th Circuit concluded that "a person injured in an automobile accident caused by the negligent, or even grossly negligent, operation of a motor vehicle by a police officer acting in the line of duty has no Section 1983 cause of action for violation of a federal right."[88] The Supreme Court in *County of Sacramento v. Lewis* decided that a police officer does not violate the Fourteenth Amendment's guarantee of substantive due process "by causing death through deliberate or reckless indifference to life in a high-speed automobile chase aimed at apprehending a suspected offender."[89] The only violation of substantive due process occurs when there is a purpose to cause harm unrelated to the arrest. Automobile negligence actions are grist for the state law mill, but they do not rise to the level of a constitutional deprivation.[90] The common thread running through the cases is that negligent conduct during a pursuit does not suffice to trigger jurisdiction under 1983. However, a municipality can be held liable under Section 1983 if there was no or inadequate high-speed pursuit training for its officers, even when the officers involved with a pursuit were not individually negligent.[91]

Certain techniques employed by police during a pursuit may raise constitutional issues cognizable under 1983. For example, in *Jamieson By and Through Jamieson v. Shaw*[92] the court held that the constitutionally permissible use-of-force standard set forth by the Supreme Court in *Tennessee v. Garner*[93] was violated when a passenger in a fleeing vehicle was hurt when the vehicle hit a so-called deadman roadblock after officers allegedly shined a bright light into the driver's eyes as the vehicle approached the roadblock. In *Bower v. County of Inyo*,[94] a high-speed pursuit of over 20 miles ended when the fleeing suspect was killed when his vehicle hit a tractor-trailer that police had placed across the road as a roadblock. The Court of Appeals held that police use of a roadblock could constitute a constitutional violation of substantive due process if it was designed as an intentional deathtrap where the approaching driver does not have a clear option to stop because the roadblock is concealed around a curve or inadequately illuminated. The Supreme Court went further in stating that the deceased driver was unreasonably "seized" when the roadblock was placed completely across the highway in a manner likely to kill the driver and that the police officers were liable under the Fourth Amendment and Section 1983 for the use of excessive force.[95]

Factors Determining Liability

Pursuit-related litigation usually involves an inquiry into whether the manner in which the pursuit was conducted was reasonable under the circumstances of that case. Each pursuit situation is different and requires a particularized assessment. Following is a brief discussion of certain factors that most frequently determine the extent of pursuit-related liability.

Purpose of Pursuit

This factor relates to the need or reason for a pursuit. Does the purpose of the pursuit warrant the risks involved? What is the nature and seriousness of the suspected offense? Is the fleeing motorist suspected of committing a serious crime or only a misdemeanor? Was the motorist already operating the vehicle in a reckless and life-threatening manner before the pursuit started, or had the motorist committed a minor, nonhazardous traffic violation prior to the pursuit but then started driving in a reckless and life-threatening manner after the pursuit was initiated? Is there a need for immediate apprehension, or has the suspect been identified so that apprehension at a later time is possible?

Driving Conditions

This factor involves a general assessment of equipment, the weather, roadway and traffic conditions, and the experience and personal ability of the drivers involved in the chase.

Use of Warning Devices

The use of adequate visual and audible warning devices, such as flashing lights and a siren, not only is a statutory mandate for most pursuit situations but also ensures to the greatest extent possible that other vehicles and pedestrians are alerted to approaching emergency vehicles and to the need to yield the right of way.

Excessive Speed

Whether a particular speed is excessive depends on the purpose of the pursuit, the driving conditions, and the personal ability of a police driver to control and effectively maneuver the vehicle. Speed when crossing an intersection against a light or sign is an especially critical consideration, since statistics suggest that most pursuit-related collisions occur at intersections.[96] Liability may be based on the failure to sufficiently decrease speed when approaching an intersection so that a complete stop can be made to avoid a collision.

Disobeying Traffic Laws

Pursuit vehicles are statutorily obligated to use due care for the safety of others when disobeying traffic laws, such as operating a vehicle on the wrong side of the road, passing on the right, going the wrong way on a one-way street, passing in a "no passing" zone, or proceeding against a traffic signal. These dangerous and high-risk driving situations should be avoided because police are generally held liable for any resulting accidents.[97]

Roadblocks

Special care is required when using roadblocks to ensure that innocent persons are not placed in a position of danger and that the fleeing motorist is afforded a reasonable opportunity to stop safely.[98] To reduce the risk of liability, it is recommended that roadblocks be used only when authorized by a supervisor and only as a last resort to apprehend a fleeing motorist who is wanted for a violent felony and who constitutes an immediate and serious threat. Although the Supreme Court stated that a roadblock could be a Fourth Amendment unreasonable seizure granting Section 1983 liability,[99] the Court of Appeals for the First Circuit qualified the definition of "seizure" to apply to roadblock accidents constituting a "misuse of power" as opposed to the "accidental effects of otherwise lawful governmental conduct."[100]

Termination of Pursuit

Every police department's pursuit policy has a provision dealing with termination of pursuit. When officers are expected to terminate varies considerably, depending on the agency's philosophy. Some agencies allow their officers very broad latitude, while others greatly restrict officers' actions. Policies generally fall into one of three models:[101]

1. *Judgmental*—Allowing officers to make all major decisions relating to initiation, tactics, and termination
2. *Restrictive*—Placing certain restrictions on officers' judgments and decisions
3. *Discouragement*—Severely cautioning or discouraging any pursuit, except in the most extreme situations

However, despite these variations in department policies, a noticeable trend has been emerging. Increasingly, police departments are permitting their officers to pursue only individuals who are known to have committed dangerous felonies—that is, murder, felonious assault, rape, robbery, kidnapping, and so on. This trend is occurring because it is becoming increasingly difficult to justify pursuits that result in injuries and the death of innocent third parties, as well as the injuries and death of police officers. Another reason for the dramatic shift in these policies has been because of the enormously high monetary judgments imposed by juries for injuries to innocent third parties.

Alpert[102] and Beckman[103] show that the vast majority of pursuits are for traffic violations and/or misdemeanors and not felonies. The issue of when the violator would eventually stop was addressed by Alpert.[104] He interviewed 146 inmates who had fled from the police and who were confined to jails in three cities: Omaha, Nebraska; Miami, Florida; and Columbia, South Carolina. Over 70 percent of the suspects said they would have slowed down "when I felt safe" whether the pursuit was on a freeway, on a highway, or in a town. The phrase "when I felt safe" was interpreted by the respondents as outdistancing the police by 2.2 blocks on surface streets, 2.3 miles on highways, and 2.5 miles on freeways. Fifty-three percent of the suspects responded that they were willing to run at all costs from the police in a pursuit, and 64 percent believed that they would not be caught; however, 71 percent said they were concerned with their own safety, and 62 percent stated they were concerned with the safety of others while engaged in a chase.[105]

Thus, law enforcement agencies that allow their officers broad discretion in pursuit can expect a greater number of arrests of violators who flee. However, they can also

---

Quick
FACTS ▸▸ Dallas Institutes a Restrictive Vehicle Pursuit Police

The Dallas Police Department has one of the most restrictive vehicle pursuit policies in the United States, and the policy appears to be saving officers' and citizens' lives. Since the policy was enacted at the beginning of 2007, individual officers and the police unions have been critical, indicating that the policy is "soft on criminals" and encourages traffic violators not to stop for the police. Several officers indicated that the policy actually undermined their ability to "catch criminals." However, after a review in July 2010, Dallas officers now see the wisdom of the policy: No officer or citizen has died in the city of Dallas in the last 3 years as the result of a police vehicle pursuit, and crime rates are the lowest in Dallas for decades. The policy was overwhelming supported by officers in a series of focus group discussions regarding the possibility of change.

Note that the policy places the entire decision on the officer. The highlighted area indicates that the officer must be able to immediately articulate why he or she is engaging in a chase, and that the immediate need to apprehend the offender (via a police pursuit) outweighs the safety of other members of the community who might be endangered by the chase.

Dallas Police Department General Order
301.00 Emergency Vehicle Operation

Revised 09/18/09

301.07   Vehicle Pursuits

A. Purpose - The purpose of this policy is to establish guidelines for making decisions with regard to vehicular pursuits.

B. Philosophy - General Order 906.01 B., states "protection of human life is a primary goal of the police department; therefore, police officers have a responsibility to use only the degree of force necessary to protect and preserve life." Initiating or participating in a vehicular pursuit presents a danger to the officers involved, the suspect, and the general public. Accordingly, the decision to initiate a pursuit must be based on the pursuing officer's conclusion that the immediate danger to the officer, public and suspect created by the pursuit is less than the immediate or potential danger to the public should the suspect remain at large.

C. Definition - A Pursuit is defined as an active attempt by an officer in an authorized emergency vehicle to apprehend a fleeing suspect in a motor vehicle who is attempting to elude the officer. A suspect is considered to be fleeing upon making any overt action intended to avoid arrest. For the purpose of this order, violators who follow all traffic regulations after an officer initiates a traffic stop and are merely failing to yield to the authorized emergency vehicle are not considered to be fleeing. The term "Chase" will be considered synonymous with "Pursuit".

D. Decision to Initiate Pursuit

   1. The decision to pursue must be based upon facts and circumstances known to the officer.

   2. In deciding whether to pursue, an officer must take the following pursuit risk factors under consideration:

      a. road, weather and environmental conditions.

      b. population density, vehicle and pedestrian traffic.

      c. relative performance capabilities of both the authorized emergency vehicle and the suspect's vehicle.

      d. seriousness of the offense.

      e. presence of other persons in the police vehicle.

      f. age of offender.

      g. whether or not the offender's identity is known, and

      h. any circumstance under which the pursuing officer will be unable to maintain control of the emergency vehicle.

   3. An officer may initiate a pursuit under the following circumstances:

      a. When the officer has probable cause to believe that a felony involving the use or threat of physical force or violence has been, or is about to be, committed, and the officer reasonably believes that the immediate need to apprehend the offender outweighs the risk to any person of collision, injury or death, or

      b. to assist another law enforcement agency that has initiated a pursuit under the same circumstances.

      c. All other pursuits are prohibited.

   4. Officers will not pursue a motorist whose only offense is driving while intoxicated if the actions of the driver escalate beyond merely failing to yield to the emergency vehicle.

E. Manner of Operation While in Pursuit

   1. The emergency warning lights, siren, and emergency vehicle headlights will be used at all times while operating Code 3.

   2. Only police vehicles equipped with operable emergency warning lights and sirens will participate in the pursuit of a fleeing vehicle.

   3. Unmarked vehicles without roof mounted emergency warning light systems will not become involved in a pursuit. Supervisors in unmarked vehicles will follow the chase using a Code 1 response.

   4. If a pursuit is initiated by a motorcycle, the motorcycle will abandon the pursuit when a four-wheel unit with roof mounted emergency warning light systems joins the pursuit.

   5. Vehicles with passengers (prisoners, witnesses, suspects, complainants or other non-police personnel who have not signed a waiver of liability) will not become engaged in pursuits.

   6. Paddy Wagons will not become engaged in pursuits.

expect to have more uninvolved third parties injured or killed, as well as more police officers injured and a greater number of lawsuits. Conversely, those departments that have more restrictive policies can expect more conservative results. The final decision is ultimately left to the chief administrator of the agency.

Departmental Responsibility for Liability Reduction

To reduce the risks and liability associated with vehicular pursuits, law enforcement organizations must carefully evaluate their pursuit policies, training, supervision, and postincident evaluations. Liability reduction is accomplished through sound management controls and a reduction in the number of pursuit-related accidents.

Policy Development

The function of a well-written pursuit policy is to state the department's objectives, establish some ground rules for the exercise of discretion, and educate officers as to specific factors they should consider when conducting a vehicular pursuit. Where feasible, a comprehensive policy statement should give content to terms such as "reasonable" and "reckless" and provide officers with more particularized guidance. A policy should be tailored to a department's operational needs, geographical peculiarities, and training capabilities. A written policy also provides a basis for holding officers accountable for their pursuit-related conduct.

Training

Lack of adequate training may contribute to many pursuit-related accidents. The natural tendency for many police drivers is to become emotionally involved and therefore lose some perspective during a pursuit. They are also required to drive different police vehicles with unique handling characteristics under various road and weather conditions. It is easy to lose control of a vehicle that is driven beyond its or the driver's capabilities, and law enforcement organizations can be held liable for failing to provide adequate driver training to prepare officers to handle vehicles safely in pursuit situations.[106] The extent and type of training required depend on a department's operational needs and objectives. A minimal level of cost-effective training can be accomplished by emphasizing defensive driving techniques and carefully instructing officers about departmental pursuit policies and relevant state regulations concerning the operation of emergency vehicles.

Supervision

Police departments are responsible for providing adequate supervision of officers involved in a pursuit. Experts who have studied the emotionalism and psychology associated with pursuits recommend that, as soon as possible after a pursuit has been initiated, a supervisor who is not in any of the pursuit vehicles be tasked with the responsibility of supervising the pursuit.[107] The supervisor who is not immediately involved is in a better position to oversee objectively the pursuit and decide whether it should continue and under what circumstances. The supervisor should track the location of the pursuit, designate the primary and secondary pursuit vehicles, and maintain tight controls on the desire of other officers to get involved or parallel the action. Effective communication between the pursuing vehicles and the supervisor is essential.

The failure to transmit information concerning the location of a pursuit or the condition of the pursued driver may contribute to a subsequent accident.

Evaluation and Documentation

Law enforcement organizations should provide for an ongoing process of evaluation and documentation of pursuit-related incidents. All pursuits, including those successfully terminated without an accident, should be routinely critiqued to determine whether departmental policy was followed and the extent to which any policy modification, training enhancement, or other remedial action is warranted.

Liability and Emotionally Disturbed Persons

Forty percent of persons suffering from serious mental illness will be arrested at least once during their lifetime. For this reason, it is imperative that progressive law enforcement agencies assume responsibility for evaluating potentially dangerous situations and recognizing those individuals suffering from various forms of mental illness. These individuals are commonly referred to as **emotionally disturbed persons (EDPs)**.[108]

Police responses to emotionally disturbed persons are determined to some degree by the manner in which the contact is initiated. The largest percentage of police officer contacts with EDPs are a result of on-the-street observations of bizarre, disruptive, or abnormal behavior. These encounters often end in an arrest of the subject for a relatively minor charge (e.g., disturbing the peace, disorderly conduct, vagrancy, or loitering), especially if alcohol use can be easily detected (see Figure 14.7). In other cases, the police receive complaints on an EDP as a result of a family disturbance or

Figure 14.7
A New York City police officer asks a homeless woman, who was sleeping on the floor at New York's Penn Station, to move along.
(AP Photo/Joe Cavaretta)

IN THE NEWS Portland Police and Oregon Try to Impact Police Handling of Emotionally Disturbed Persons

Amid a rash of highly controversial shootings throughout the state of Oregon, the legislature passed Senate Bill 111 (SB 111) in late 2007, to be in force by the end of 2008. The law requires each county in the state to develop a plan regarding the use of deadly physical force by law enforcement officers. The purpose of the committee composed of various law enforcement executives within each of Oregon's 36 counties was to develop a deadly physical force plan to meet specific criteria:

- Develop proper training on the use of deadly force for police officers on a local and state-wide basis.
- Provide mechanisms for support for officers, civilians, and families of a community involved in a deadly force incident.
- Develop a specific process or protocol for investigating a deadly force incident.
- Determine whether the use of deadly force complied with applicable federal, state and local law as well as the individual police department police.
- Stimulate research and interest on the issue of police use of deadly force.

Unfortunately, Oregon continues to suffer under the specter of questionable police use of deadly force. On January 29, 2010, an unarmed Aaron M. Campbell was shot in the back by members of the Portland Police Bureau SWAT team as he exited his apartment complex. Campbell, a person with a violent past including weapons charges and resisting arrest, had reportedly been suicidal after the death of his sister. During a bungled communication, officers mistakenly believed that Campbell made threatening gestures and the ensuing 50 rounds fired by the police was caught on video and widely dispersed on YouTube (see:— http://www.youtube.com/watch?v=_iwyd4ZHBUc).

The questionable shooting sparked an outrage in the city, with numerous public demonstrations and the firing of Chief of Police Rosie Sizer on May 12, 2010, in part for $1.6 million settlement for yet another questionable police-involved death. James A. Chasse, a skid-row bum with a history of mental illness was chased by police after allegedly urinating on the street. Witnesses indicated that police officers tackled, tased, and kicked Chasse as he laid defenseless on the ground. He died in the backseat of a police cruiser from injuries that included 26 breaks to 16 ribs and a punctured lung.

It is precisely these types of questionable incidents that cause significant strain between the police and public, and demand that police act appropriately in handling emotionally disturbed persons.

Source: See http://www.leg.state.or.us/07reg/measpdf/sb0100.dir/sb0111.c.pdf (Retrieved July 20, 2010). See also, 'Why James Chasses' Story Matters to Portland,' *The Oregonian*, May 11, 2010; "Man Shot and Killed by Police, KPTV.com (February 1, 2010) see http://www.kptv.com/news/22383908/detail.html

neighborhood problem. In either event, officers are often confronted by an individual with whom they have had prior contact (perhaps multiple prior contacts) and one who might unexplainably burst into a violent confrontation, endangering everyone at the scene. As a result, many police departments are beginning to address this issue through basic and advanced training. For example, the Washington State Criminal Justice Commission has developed a unique curriculum focused on five key areas:

1. Recognizing abnormal behavior and mental illness (neuroses, psychoses, and psychopathic/sociopathic behavior)
2. Dealing with suicidal subjects (true versus parasuicidal behavior)
3. Developing crisis intervention skills (legal considerations in subject committal, tactical responses to handling the EDP, and responses to mental disturbance calls)
4. Developing awareness and knowledge of community services (interim facilities, hospital and emergency services, community care homes)
5. Recognizing and caring for Alzheimer's patients (physical cues and behavior)[109]

Other departments have also developed specialized in-service courses designed to provide more information to officers. The Monterey County Police Chief's Association has developed a Crisis Intervention Team (CIT) Academy in San Jose, California. The academy has distinguished itself through community collaboration and is well respected as a training model by the legislature and law enforcement community in California. The CIT Academy provides a 40-hour intensive training course that includes role playing, interactive participation of people with mental illness (consumers), identification of various symptoms and signs of medication use by consumers, crisis negotiation skills and tactics, panel discussions and feedback, visits to interim-type housing facilities, suicide and crisis training, and a constant review of all countywide protocols and incident procedures.[110] The training focuses on developing the most useful tool available to officers on the street: the ability to communicate in a nonthreatening manner.

The effective training of police officers in dealing with EDPs should result in two significant changes. First, there should be fewer incidents in which the use of force is necessary, thereby increasing officer safety. Second, effective training will provide a strong defense to litigation, should the department become entangled in litigation arising from the handling of an emotionally disturbed person.

Administrative Discipline: Due Process for Police Officers

The Fifth and Fourteenth Amendments to the Constitution state that "no person shall be . . . deprived of life, liberty, or property, without **due process** of law."

Liberty and Property Rights of Police Officers

There are two general types of situations in the disciplinary process in which an employee of a law enforcement agency can claim the right to be protected by the guarantees of due process.[111] The first type involves those situations in which the disciplinary action taken by the government employer threatens **liberty rights** of the officer. The second type involves a threat to **property rights**.

Liberty rights have been defined loosely as rights involving the protection and defense of one's good name, reputation, and position in the community. It has, at times, been extended further to include the right to preserve one's future career opportunities as well. Thus, when an officer's reputation, honor, or integrity is at stake because of government-imposed discipline, due process must be extended to the officer.[112]

It should be noted that the use of the "liberty rights" approach as a basis for requiring procedural due process has proven extremely difficult. The Supreme Court further restricted the use of this legal theory by holding that it can be utilized only when the employer is shown to have created and publicly disseminated a false and defamatory impression about the employee.[113]

The more substantial and meaningful type of due process guarantee is that pertaining to the protection of one's property. Although the general concept of property extends only to real estate and tangible possessions, the courts have developed the concept that a person's property also includes the many valuable intangible belongings acquired in the normal course of life, such as the expectation of continued employment. However, not all employees are entitled to its protection.

The courts have consistently held that an employee acquires a protected interest in a job (property interest or right) only when it can be established that there exists a justifiable expectation that employment will continue without interruption except for dismissal or other discipline based on just or proper cause. This expectation of continued employment is sometimes called "tenure," or "permanent status."[114]

Federal courts have been inclined to read employment laws liberally so as to grant property rights whenever possible. For example, the Fifth Circuit Court of Appeals found that a city employment regulation that allowed termination "only for cause" created a constitutionally protected property interest.[115] A federal district court held that a Florida statute (Section 112.532), known as the "Law Enforcement Officers' and Correctional Officers' Bill of Rights," created a property interest in employment because of its disciplinary notice provisions.[116] That approach is consistent with those of other jurisdictions in which state statutes have been interpreted to give property interests in a job to local government employees.[117]

Once a liberty or property right has been established, certain due process guarantees attach to protect the employee. The question becomes, What process is due?

The question of due process for police officers falls into two categories: **procedural due process** and **substantive due process**. The former, as its name implies, refers to the legality of the procedures used to deprive police officers of status or wages, such as dismissal or suspension from their job. Substantive due process is a more difficult and elusive concept. Simply, substantive due process is the requirement that the basis for government disciplinary action be reasonable, relevant, and justifiable.

Procedural Due Process

One of the 20th century's preeminent administrative law scholars, Kenneth Culp Davis, identified 12 main elements of a due process hearing:

> (1) timely and adequate notice, (2) a chance to make an oral statement or argument, (3) a chance to present witnesses and evidence, (4) confrontation of adverse witnesses, (5) cross-examination of adverse witnesses, (6) disclosure of all evidence relied upon, (7) a decision based on the record of evidence, (8) a right to retain an attorney, (9) a publicly-compensated attorney for an indigent, (10) a statement of findings of fact, (11) a statement of reasons or a reasoned opinion, (12) an impartial deciding officer.[118]

The courts have not examined all the trial elements in the context of the police disciplinary process. However, some cases have held that police officers must be informed of the charges on which the action is based,[119] be given the right to call witnesses,[120] be confronted by the witnesses against them,[121] be permitted to cross-examine the witnesses against them,[122] be permitted to have counsel represent them,[123] have a decision rendered on the basis of the record developed at the hearing,[124] and have the decision made by an impartial hearing officer.[125]

A question that has proven particularly troublesome for the courts is whether due process requires that an evidentiary hearing be held before the disciplinary action being taken. In *Arnett v. Kennedy*, a badly divided Supreme Court held that a "hearing afforded by administrative appeal after the actual dismissal is a sufficient compliance with the requirements of the Due Process Clause."[126] In a concurring opinion, Justice Powell observed that the question of whether a hearing must be accorded before an employee's removal "depends on a balancing process in which the government's interest in expeditious removal of an unsatisfactory employee is weighed against the interest of the affected employee in continued public employment."[127] In *Mathews v. Eldridge*, the Supreme Court set forth the competing interests that must be weighed to determine what process is due: (1) the private interest that will be affected by the official action; (2) the risk of an erroneous deprivation of such interest through the procedures used and the probable value, if any, of additional or substitute procedural safeguards; and (3) the government's interest, including the function involved and the fiscal and administrative burdens that the additional or substitute procedural requirement would entail.[128]

In 1985, the Court further clarified the issue of pretermination due process in *Cleveland Board of Education v. Loudermill*.[129] The Court found that public employees possessing property interests in their employment have a right to "notice and an opportunity to respond" before termination. The Court cautioned that its decision was based on the employees also having an opportunity for a full posttermination hearing. Therefore, assuming that a public employee will be able to challenge the termination in a full-blown evidentiary hearing after the fact, pretermination due process should include an initial check against mistaken decisions—essentially, a determination of whether there are reasonable grounds to believe that the charges against the employee are true and support the proposed action. The Court went on to describe an acceptable pretermination procedure as one that provides the employee with oral or written notice of the charges against him or her, an explanation of the employer's evidence, and an opportunity to present his or her side of the story. The Court reasoned that the government interest in the immediate termination of an unsatisfactory employee is outweighed by an employee's interest in retaining employment and the interest in avoiding the risk of an erroneous termination.[130] In 1997, the Court ruled that public employees do not have the right to a hearing before suspension without pay as long as the suspension is short, the effect on pay is insubstantial, and the employee is guaranteed a postsuspension hearing.[131]

Thus, it is clear that public employees who can legitimately claim liberty or property right protections of due process for their jobs are guaranteed an evidentiary hearing. Such a hearing should be conducted before disciplinary action is taken unless the prediscipline protections just mentioned are provided, in which case the full-blown hearing could be postponed until afterward.

For administrators with a collective bargaining relationship with their employees, where minimal procedural safeguards are provided in contractual grievance provisions,

that avenue of relief may provide an acceptable substitute for constitutionally mandated procedural rights.[132]

Substantive Due Process

As mentioned earlier, due process requirements embrace substantive as well as procedural aspects. In the context of disciplinary action, substantive due process requires that the rules and regulations on which disciplinary action is predicated be clear, specific, and reasonably related to a valid public need.[133] In the police environment, these requirements present the greatest challenge to the commonly found departmental regulations against conduct unbecoming an officer or conduct that brings discredit on the department.

The requirement that a rule or regulation be reasonably related to a valid public need means that a police department may not intrude into the private matters of its officers in which it has no legitimate interest. Therefore, there must be a connection "between the prohibited conduct and the officer's fitness to perform the duties required by his position."[134] In addition, the conduct must be of such a nature as to adversely affect the morale and efficiency of the department or have a tendency to destroy public respect for and confidence in the department.[135] Thus, it has been held that a rule prohibiting unbecoming conduct or discrediting behavior cannot be applied to a police officer's remarks that were highly critical of several prominent local figures but were made to a private citizen in a private conversation in a patrol car and were broadcast accidentally over the officer's patrol car radio.[136]

The requirements for clarity and specificity are necessary to ensure (1) that the innocent are not trapped without fair warning, (2) that those who enforce the regulations have their discretion limited by explicit standards, and (3) that where basic First Amendment rights are affected by a regulation, the regulation does not operate unreasonably to inhibit the exercise of those rights.[137]

The courts' applications of these requirements to unbecoming conduct and discrediting behavior rules have taken two courses. The first course, exemplified by *Bence v. Breier*, has been to declare such regulations unconstitutional because of their vagueness. In its consideration of a Milwaukee Police Department rule that prohibited "conduct unbecoming a member and detrimental to the service," the court found that the rule lacked

> inherent, objective content from which ascertainable standards defining the proscribed conduct could be fashioned. Like beauty, their content exists only in the eye of the beholder. The subjectivity implicit in the language of the rule permits police officials to enforce the rule with unfettered discretion, and it is precisely this potential for arbitrary enforcement which is abhorrent to the Due Process Clause.[138]

The second course taken by the courts has been to uphold the constitutionality of the regulation because, as applied to the officer in the case at hand, it should have been clear to him that his behavior was meant to be proscribed by the regulation.

Under this approach, the court is saying that there may or may not be some circumstances in which the rule is too vague or overbroad, but the rule is constitutional in the present case. Thus, it should be clear to any police officer that fleeing from the scene of an accident[139] or making improper advances toward a young woman during the course of an official investigation[140] constitutes conduct unbecoming an officer or conduct that discredits the police department.

Many police departments also have a regulation prohibiting neglect or dereliction of duty. Although on its face such a rule seems to possess some of the same potential vagueness and overbreadth shortcomings characteristic of the unbecoming conduct rules, it has fared better in the courts because the usual disciplinary action taken under neglect-of-duty rules nearly always seems to be for conduct for which police officers could reasonably expect disciplinary action. The courts have upheld administrative sanctions against officers under neglect-of-duty rules for sleeping on the job,[141] failing to prepare for planned demonstrations,[142] falsification of police records,[143] failure to make scheduled court appearances,[144] failure to investigate a reported auto accident,[145] and directing a subordinate to discontinue enforcement of a city ordinance.[146] The courts have refused to uphold disciplinary action against a police chief who did not keep 8-to-4 office hours,[147] and against an officer who missed a training session on riot control because of marital problems.[148]

Damages and Remedies

In determining an employee's entitlement to damages and relief, the issue of whether the employer's disciplinary action was justified is important. For example, when an employee's termination was justified but procedural due process violations occurred, the employee can recover only nominal damages in the absence of proof of actual compensable injuries deriving from the due process violation. On proof of actual injury, an employee can recover compensatory damages, which would include damages for mental and emotional distress and damage to career or reputation.[149] However, injury caused by the lack of due process when the termination was justified is not compensable in the form of back pay.[150]

Constitutional Rights of Police Officers

Police officers have the same individual rights that all citizens within the United States are afforded under the U.S. Constitution. Even though they have been given significant training, held to a higher standard of conduct, and are subject to public and legal scrutiny, they still enjoy the same protections afforded to everyone else in our society.

Free Speech

The First Amendment of the U.S. Constitution prohibits Congress from passing any law "abridging the freedom of speech." It has been held that the due process clause of the Fourteenth Amendment makes this prohibition applicable to the states, counties, and cities as well.[151]

Although freedom of speech is one of the most fundamental of all constitutional rights, the Supreme Court has indicated that "the State has interests as an employer in regulating the speech of its employees that differ significantly from those it possesses in connection with regulation of the speech of the citizenry in general."[152] Therefore, the state may place restrictions on the speech of its employees that it could not impose on the general citizenry. However, these restrictions must be reasonable.[153] Generally, disputes involving the infringement of public employee speech will be resolved by balancing the interests of the state as an employer against the employee's constitutional rights.[154]

There are two basic situations in which a police regulation or other action can be found to be an unreasonable infringement on the free speech interests of an officer. The first is when the action is overly broad. A Chicago Police Department rule prohibiting "any activity, conversation, deliberation, or discussion which is derogatory to the Department" was ruled overly broad because it prohibited all criticism of the department by police officers, even if the criticism occurred in private conversation.[155] The same fate befell a New Orleans Police Department regulation that prohibited statements by a police officer that "unjustly criticize or ridicule, or express hatred or contempt toward, or . . . which may be detrimental to, or cast suspicion on the reputation of, or otherwise defame, any person."[156]

The second situation in which a free speech limitation can be found unreasonable is in the way in which the government action is applied. The most common shortcoming of police departmental action in this area is a failure to demonstrate that the statements by the officer being disciplined adversely affected the operation of the department.[157] Thus, a Baltimore police regulation prohibiting public criticism of departmental action was held to have been applied unconstitutionally to a police officer who was president of the police union and who had stated in a television interview that the police commissioner was not leading the department effectively and that "the bottom is going to fall out of this city."[158] In this case, no significant disruption of the department was noted. However, when two officers of the Kinloch, Missouri Police Department publicly complained of corruption within city government, the court held that the "officers conducted a campaign . . . with complete disregard of chain of command motivated by personal desires that created disharmony among the 12-member police force."[159] Because the allegations were totally unfounded and were not asserted correctly through channels instituted by state "whistle-blower" procedures, the dismissals were upheld.

A more recent basis for enforcing employees' First Amendment freedom of speech is that of public policy. The Court of Appeals for the Eighth Circuit held that discharging an employee who violated the police department's chain of command by reporting misconduct to an official outside of the city violated the employee's First Amendment rights. The court reasoned that the city's interest in maintaining discipline through the chain-of-command policy was outweighed by the public's vital interest in the integrity of its law enforcers and by the employee's right to speak out on such matters.[160] Generally, speech about corruption or criminal activity within the officer's law enforcement agency is very likely to be given protection under the First

Amendment, especially when such speech is protected by a state "whistle-blower statute."[161] Central to a successful claim under a whistle-blower statute is that the employee show that discipline resulted from the employee's reporting of a violation of the law. Essentially, there must be an element of retaliation against the employee for publicly reporting illegal conduct.[162] The employee need only have a reasonable belief that illegal conduct has occurred and need not have absolute proof of the illegality.[163]

It appears that one's right to speak openly about the policies of a police department may well depend on four important factors: (1) the impact of the statements on the routine operations of the department, (2) the truth of the statements, (3) the manner in which the statements are made regarding existing policy orders involving chain-of-command and state whistle-blower regulations, and (4) the position occupied by the officer. For instance, statements made by dispatchers, clerks, and first-line officers in a large department that have relatively little impact might be given much more tolerance than supervisory or command personnel complaining of departmental policy because the degree of influence, validity, and credibility significantly increases with rank.

Other First Amendment Rights

A basic right of Americans in our democratic system of government is the right to engage in political activity. As with free speech, the government may impose reasonable restrictions on the political behavior of its employees that it could not impose on the citizenry at large. It is argued that, if the state could not impose some such restrictions, there would be a substantial danger that employees could be pressured by their superiors to support political candidates or causes that were contrary to their own beliefs under threat of loss of employment or other adverse action against them for failure to do so.[164]

At the federal level, various types of partisan political activity by federal employees are controlled by the Hatch Act. The constitutionality of that act has been upheld by the Supreme Court.[165] Many states have similar statutes, which are usually referred to as "little Hatch" acts, controlling political activity by state employees. The Oklahoma version of the Hatch Act, which was upheld by the Supreme Court,[166] prohibited state employees from soliciting political contributions, joining a partisan political club, serving on the committee of a political party, being a candidate for any paid political office, or taking part in the management of a political party or campaign. However, some states, such as Florida, specifically prohibit local governments from limiting the off-duty political activity of their employees.

Nonpolitical associations are also protected by the First Amendment. However, it is common for police departments to prohibit officers from associating with known felons or other persons of bad reputation on the basis that "such associations may expose an officer to irresistible temptations to yield in his obligation to impartially enforce the law, and . . . may give the appearance that the community's police officers are not themselves honest and impartial enforcers of the law."[167] Sometimes the prohibition is imposed by means of a specific ordinance or regulation, whereas in other instances the prohibition is enforced by considering it conduct unbecoming an officer. Of course, if the latter approach is used, the ordinance or regulation will have to overcome the legal obstacles discussed earlier, relating to unbecoming conduct or discrediting behavior rules.

As with rules touching on the other First Amendment rights, rules prohibiting associations with criminals and other undesirables must not be overly broad in their reach. Thus, a Detroit Police Department regulation that prohibited knowing and intentional associations with convicted criminals or persons charged with crimes except in the course of an officer's official duties was declared unconstitutional because it proscribed some associations that could have no bearing on an officer's integrity or the public's confidence in an officer. The court cited as examples an association with a fellow church member who had been arrested on one occasion years ago and the befriending of a recently convicted person who wanted to become a productive citizen.[168]

The other common difficulty with this kind of rule is that it is sometimes applied to situations in which the association has not been demonstrated to have had a detrimental effect on the performance of the officer's duties or on the discipline and efficiency of the department. Thus, one court has held that a police officer who was a nudist but was fully qualified in all other respects to be a police officer could not be fired simply because he was a practicing nudist.[169] On the other hand, another court upheld the firing of a police officer who had had sexual intercourse at a party with a woman he knew to be a nude model at a local "adult theater of known disrepute."[170] The court viewed this behavior as being of such a disreputable nature that it had a detrimental effect on the discipline and efficiency of the department. In 2005, the Supreme Court determined that the police department could terminate an officer for selling a sexually explicit videotape of himself, in which he identified himself as a police officer. The Court ruled that, even though the activities of the officer took place outside the workplace, the department "demonstrated legitimate and substantial interests of its own that were compromised by the officer's speech" and the activities did not fall under free speech protections.[171]

The First Amendment's protection of free speech has been viewed as protecting means of expression other than verbal utterances.[172] That issue as it relates to an on-duty police officer's personal appearance was addressed by the Supreme Court decision in *Kelley v. Johnson*,[173] which upheld the constitutionality of a regulation of the Suffolk County, New York Police Department that established several grooming standards for its male officers. The Court in *Kelley* held that either a desire to make police officers readily recognizable to the public or a desire to maintain an esprit de corps was a sufficiently rational justification for the regulation. The issue of personal grooming and style continues to be a subject of hot debate in departments across the nation, particularly as officers move closer to their constituencies through community policing endeavors.

Searches and Seizures and the Right to Privacy

The Fourth Amendment to the U.S. Constitution protects "the right of the people to be secure in their persons, houses, papers, and effects, against unreasonable searches and seizures." This guarantee protects against actions by states and the federal government.[174] Generally, the cases interpreting the Fourth Amendment require that, before a search or seizure can be effectuated, the police must have **probable cause** to believe that a crime has been committed and that evidence relevant to the crime will be found at the place to be searched. Because of the language in the Fourth Amendment about "persons, houses, papers, and effects," for years the case law analyzed what property was subject to the amendment's protection. However, in an extremely important case in 1967, the Supreme Court ruled that the amendment protected individuals' reasonable expectations of privacy and not just property interests.[175] Interestingly, 21st-century technology has brought forth a number of key Fourth Amendment issues regarding privacy, especially involving private communications (cell phones, e-mail, and text messaging) and wiretaps. In a case involving a police officer suspected of gambling, the Supreme Court held that the use of a pen register did not require the same constitutional safeguards as those surrounding a wiretap. The pen register uses a "trap-and-trace" device that records phone numbers and the duration of each call but does not capture any type of communication between parties. The Court reasoned that no warrant or probable cause was needed, as the Fourth Amendment was applicable to captured communication only and that there was no reasonable expectation to privacy regarding the actual phone number.[176]

The Fourth Amendment usually applies to police officers when at home or off duty as it would to any other citizen. However, because of the nature of their employment, a police officer can be subjected to investigative procedures that would not be permitted when an ordinary citizen is involved. One such situation arises with respect to equipment and lockers provided by the department to its officers. In this situation, the officer has no expectation of privacy that merits protection.[177] Officials can search private lockers without a warrant. Further, in a landmark case in 2010, the Court ruled unanimously that a search of a police officer's personal, and sometimes sexually explicit, text messages on a city-owned pager was constitutional, even though it was conducted without a warrant.[178] By extension of previous case logic, cell phone communications and e-mail on a city-owned cell phone or computer would also not be protected material and the officer does not have a constitutional right to privacy regarding these devices. Again, there appears not to be an expectation of privacy for officers when using government-owned devices or equipment.

Another situation involves the ordering of officers to appear at a lineup. Requiring someone to appear in a lineup is a seizure of his or her person and, therefore, would ordinarily require probable cause. However, a federal Appeals Court upheld a police commissioner's order to 62 officers to appear in a lineup for the purpose of identifying officers who had allegedly beaten several civilians. The court held that, in this situation, "the governmental interest in the particular intrusion (should be weighed) against the offense to personal dignity and integrity." Because of the nature of the police officer's employment relationship, "he does not have the full privacy and liberty from police officials that he would otherwise enjoy."[179]

To enforce the protections guaranteed by the Fourth Amendment's search-and-seizure requirements, the courts have fashioned the so-called *exclusionary rule*, which prohibits the use of evidence obtained in violation of the Fourth Amendment in criminal proceedings. However, in a series of cases, the Supreme Court has redefined the concept of "reasonableness" as it applies to the Fourth Amendment and the exclusionary rule. In *United States v. Leon* and the companion case of *Massachusetts v. Sheppard*, the Court held that the Fourth Amendment "requires officers to have reasonable knowledge of what the law prohibits" in a search.[180] In essence, *Leon* and *Sheppard* began to develop the concept of "totality of circumstances" confirmed in *Illinois v. Gates*—that is, that evidence cannot be suppressed when an officer is acting "under good faith" whether or not a warrant issued is good on the surface.[181] These cases have far-reaching implications in civil actions against police officers, in that officers enjoy the benefits of qualified immunity when they are acting in good faith and under the belief that probable cause does exist.[182] Indeed, the Court has held that only a clear absence of probable cause will defeat a claim of qualified immunity.[183]

Finally, the exclusionary rule and the previously mentioned cases have an important bearing on disciplinary hearings involving the police. In *Sheetz v. Mayor and City Council of Baltimore*, the court held that illegally seized drugs in the possession of an officer could be used in an administrative discharge proceeding against that officer.[184] The Court reasoned that only a bad-faith seizure would render the evidence inadmissible because the police are not motivated to seize illegally for the purpose of use in an administrative discharge proceeding; hence, the exclusionary rule was not applicable, and the officer's firing was upheld.

Right Against Self-Incrimination

On two occasions, the Supreme Court has addressed questions concerning the Fifth Amendment rights of police officers who are the subjects of investigations. In *Garrity v. New Jersey*,[185] a police officer had been ordered by the attorney general to answer certain questions or be discharged. The officer testified, and the information gained as a result of his answers was later used to convict him of criminal charges.

The Fifth Amendment protects an individual from being compelled "in any criminal case to be a witness against himself."[186] The Supreme Court held that the information obtained from the police officer could not be used at his criminal trial because the Fifth Amendment forbids the use of coercion of this sort to extract an incriminating statement from a suspect.

In *Gardner v. Broderick*,[187] a police officer had declined to answer questions put to him by a grand jury investigating police misconduct on the grounds that his answers might tend to incriminate him. As a result, the officer was dismissed from his job. The Supreme Court ruled that the officer could not be fired for his refusal to waive his constitutional right to remain silent. However, the Court made it clear that it would have been proper for the grand jury to require the officer to answer or face discharge for his refusal, as long as the officer had been informed that his answers could not be used against him in a criminal case and the questions were related specifically, directly, and narrowly to the performance of his official duties. The Court felt that this approach was necessary to protect the important state interest in ensuring that the police officers were performing their duties faithfully.

In its ruling, the Supreme Court set forth a basic standard for disciplinary investigations of police officers. Referring to *Garrity*, the Court ruled that although a police agency can conduct an administrative investigation of an officer, it cannot in the course of that investigation compel the officer to waive his or her privilege against self-incrimination. As it has been interpreted, *Garrity* requires that before a police agency can question an officer regarding an issue that may involve disciplinary action against the officer for refusal to answer questions, the agency must do the following:

1. Order the officer to answer the questions
2. Ask questions that are specifically, directly, and narrowly related to the officer's duties
3. Advise the officer that the answers to the questions will not be used against the officer in criminal proceedings[188]

If the officer refuses to answer appropriate questions after being given these warnings and advisement, then he or she may be disciplined for insubordination.

As a result of these cases, it is proper to discharge police officers who refuse to answer questions that are related specifically and directly to the performance of their duties and who have been informed that any answers they do give cannot be used against them in a criminal proceeding.[189]

Historically, it was not uncommon for police departments to make use of polygraph examinations in the course of internal investigations. The legal question that has arisen most frequently is whether an officer can be required to submit to such a procedure under threat of discharge for refusal to do so. There is some diversity of legal authority on this question, but the majority of courts that have considered it have held that an officer can be required to take the examination.[190]

An Arizona court overturned a county merit system commission's finding that a polygraph examination could be ordered only as a last resort after all other investigative efforts had been exhausted and held that:

> a polygraph is always proper to verify statements made by law enforcement officers during the course of a departmental investigation as long as the officers are advised that the answers cannot be used against them in any criminal prosecution, that the questions will relate solely to the performance of official duties, and that refusal will result in dismissal.[191]

The use of polygraph examinations as a viable tool for internal affairs investigations was further strengthened by a state court in 2008.[192] The Massachusetts appeals court found that the Plymouth police department did not violate the state's statute by requiring a police officer who was accused of sexually molesting two minors to take a polygraph test for suspicion of criminal misconduct. After refusing to take the examination, the officer was terminated for "just cause."

On the other hand, a more recent decision of the Florida Supreme Court held that the dismissal of a police officer for refusing to submit to a polygraph test constituted "an unjust and unlawful job deprivation." Further, the court recognized that granting to public employers a carte blanche authority to force employees to submit to unlimited questioning during a polygraph test would conflict with the employees' constitutional right of privacy and would abrogate their protection against self-incrimination.[193]

Further, the use of a polygraph test to screen job applicants for police jobs has fallen under severe criticism. In 1987, a federal judge declared the test to be both unconstitutional and unreliable and ordered the city of Philadelphia to reconsider the applications of individuals denied positions because of their failure to pass a polygraph test. Conversely, the court of appeals reversed the district court holding and stated that the use of polygraph tests for pre-employment screening did not violate either equal protection or substantive due process.[194]

As a result of these cases and the resulting ambiguity concerning polygraph testing and the Fifth Amendment, most jurisdictions have limited the use of the polygraph by statute and/or administrative regulation. Also, most agencies have developed extensive internal policies to limit the use of the polygraph and to expressly detail circumstances in which the test may be used to corroborate officer statements.

Other Grounds for Disciplinary Action

Although police officers enjoy the same constitutional rights as other citizens within the United States, they are clearly held to a different standard of conduct both on and off the job. In many cases, their actions do not rise to the level of a criminal complaint yet still become the grounds for disciplinary actions that may result in termination and loss of career.

Conduct Unbecoming an Officer

By far, the largest number of police disciplinary cases arise under rules prohibiting conduct unbecoming an officer. These rules have traditionally been vague and overly broad in order to control officers both on and off duty.[195] Most "conduct unbecoming" regulations have been challenged for being unconstitutionally vague.[196] The basis of this claim rests in the concept of reasonableness as applied to the misconduct.[197] In a leading case, the California Supreme Court held that the permissible application of a "conduct unbecoming" regulation turns on whether the officer could reasonably anticipate that his or her conduct would be the subject of discipline:

> We construe "conduct unbecoming" a city police officer to refer only to conduct which indicates a lack of fitness to perform the functions of a police officer. Thus construed, [the rule] provides a sufficiently specific standard against which the conduct of a police officer in a particular case can be judged. Police officers . . . will normally be able to determine what kind of conduct indicates unfitness to perform the functions of police officer.[198]

A wide variety of conduct has been held to fall appropriately within the scope of a "conduct unbecoming" regulation. It is important to note that the regulation must reasonably warn the officer of what type of conduct would be considered unbecoming and that said conduct would tend to affect the officer's performance of his or her duties adversely or cause the department to fall into public disrepute.[199] Some of the activities that commonly fall within the scope of a "conduct unbecoming" regulation and that have been upheld by the courts include associating with crime figures or persons

IN THE NEWS   Police Officers Lose the Battle to Show Their Tattoos and Wear Beards

Officer Mike Riggs, a police officer with the City of Fort Worth, Texas, lost his suit against the city, alleging that he was subjected to discriminatory treatment when the department forced him to wear long sleeves and long pants during his duties in the bike unit. Riggs was hospitalized for heat exhaustion in 2001, and he blamed his illness on having to wear the clothing in the extreme Texas heat. Other officers in the unit were allowed to wear shorts and short-sleeved shirts on duty, but the department claimed that the tattoos were excessive to the point of unprofessionalism. Riggs's tattoos were not racist or obscene in any manner and included a Celtic tribal band, a Celtic design that included his wife's name, a mermaid, a family crest, the cartoon character Jessica Rabbit, and a 2-foot by 2-foot, full-color rendering on his back of St. Michael spearing Satan.

In a similar suit, Sgt. Shelby Stewart and three other officers with the Houston Police Department sued the city for a policy that banned beards and/or goatees. The city's response for the policy was that beards and goatees prohibit effect use of gas masks, which officers are required to wear during a WMD attack. In each case, the district courts sided with the city, indicating that the departmental policies were not discriminatory.

In yet another case, Connecticut police officers were also ordered to cover spider-web tattoos on their arms that are sometimes associated with racist groups and white supremacists. The officers insisted that they picked their tattoos merely because they liked the designs and not because they were linked with any type of ideology.

Much like the Texas case, the district court and circuit court ruled against the officers, as the department had a legitimate interest in requiring that the tattoos, beards and goatees be covered.

In addition to covering tattoos, police departments often have rules and policies that effect officer appearances and personal grooming habits. Some of the areas that are noted from police departments around the United States include:

- Hair must be combed, neatly maintained, and tapered on the sides and neck; in some instances, hair must be above the ear. Women's hair must not extend beyond the bottom of a shirted collar; no hair ornaments.
- Facial hair is often prohibited. However, where allowed, mustaches must be neatly trimmed and cannot extend beyond the corner of the mouth; no handlebar mustaches.
- Sideburns must be neatly trimmed and must not extend beyond the bottom of the ear; no flared sideburns.
- Fingernails must be clean, not painted, and may not extend beyond one-quarter inch past the finger.
- Rings are limited to one per hand; no necklaces or other jewelry is allowed; small stud earrings are allowed for women, but no earrings for men.
- Make-up for female officers must be conservative and not gaudy.
- No facial or tongue piercings are permitted; no facial tattoos are allowed.

Sources: Riggs v. City of Fort Worth, 229 F.Supp.2d 572 (N.D. Tex. 2002); *Inturri v. City of Hartford,* #05-2114, 165 Fed. Appx. 66, 2006 U.S. App. Lexis 2538(2d Cir., Jan 31, 2006); "Grooming and Appearance Rules for Public Safety Workers," *AELE Monthly Law Journal* (January 2007); "Houston Delays Vote on Battle of the Beards" *KHOU.com Local News* (July 10, 2008); and "Police, Undercover," *Dallas Morning News* (July 23, 2009), p. 14A.)

with a criminal record,[200] verbal abuse and swearing,[201] off-duty drinking and intoxication,[202] criminal conduct,[203] dishonesty,[204] fighting with coworkers,[205] insubordination,[206] and a number of improprieties involving sexual activity, including promiscuity and fraternizing with known prostitutes (see Figure 14.8).

One of the more interesting and recent cases involving "conduct unbecoming an officer" involved the Federal Bureau of Justice in 2009. In *Doe v. U.S. Department of Justice*,[207] Doe argued that the FBI failed to show that his off-duty misconduct affected the "efficiency of the service" of his employment. The Office of Responsibility for the FBI developed an investigation revealing that Doe had videotaped his personal sexual activities with women, including two women in his division, and that he might have done so without their consent. Doe was terminated for "unprofessional conduct"—conduct unbecoming an agent of the Federal Bureau of Investigation. Although an external review by the Merit Systems Protection Board supported the FBI's decision to fire Doe, the Federal Circuit Court of Appeals ruled that the FBI failed to address how Doe's off-duty and personal conduct negatively impacted the agency's "ability to perform" its mission. Further, the court ruled that the FBI failed to point out a violation of a specific internal policy that fit the circumstances of the conduct. Consequently, the MSPB's decision was reversed and remanded, and John Doe continues to be a Special Agent with the FBI. The case appears to reaffirm the concept that cases resting on "conduct unbecoming an officer" must not be overly vague, must indeed violate specific policies, and the behavior must be shown to negatively impact the agency in some manner.

Brady Violations

In a landmark 1963 case (*Brady v. Maryland*),[208] the U.S. Supreme Court ruled that the suppression of any evidence by the prosecution favorable to the accused violates the due

Figure 14.8
Employment discrimination on the basis of age, gender and/or race is prohibited by federal law.
(Jonathan Kirn/ Photolibrary)

process clauses of the Fourth and Fourteenth Amendments of the Constitution. As a result, prosecutors were compelled to disclose to the defense any and all evidence that might be exculpatory for the accused—meaning any evidence that could possibly clear the suspect must be presented to the defense. Such evidence could include physical evidence, fingerprints, DNA, photographs, and the alike, that conflicts with the prosecutor's evidence, and any evidence that could impeach the credibility of a prosecution witness.

More importantly for police administrators, in a follow-up case, *Giglio v. United States* and other Brady progeny cases,[209] the Court extended that obligation to share exculpatory information with the defendant to include information concerning the credibility of the prosecution's witnesses, including individual police officers. As a result, police agencies must disclose to the prosecution, who must disclose to the defense, any exculpatory or impeachment evidence that demonstrates that a witness is lying about specific facts in a case, or is generally unworthy of belief. Evidence of this nature is often referred to as "Brady material." Failing to disclose such evidence is a "Brady" violation that can lead to dismissal of the criminal case and civil (U.S. Code 42, Section 1983) cases brought against the individual prosecutor, the police department, and the officer for violation of the suspect's constitutional rights.

Lying

Brady cases have had a dramatic effect on the credibility of individual police officers as witnesses. Because the prosecution is bound to reveal any possible impeachment evidence regarding its own witnesses, an officer's internal affairs records and any documented report where the officer lied or was untruthful must be presented as Brady material. Such officers simply cannot testify in court without being impeached; hence, their ability to work as a police officer is seriously compromised. For this reason, many police departments now have policies that terminate an employee for lying.

Social Network Sites

Although past incidents of lying and untruthfulness form the basis for impeaching the individual officer under Brady, there are indeed other issues that warrant discussion. Postings on social network sites have recently been entered into evidence in successful attempts to discredit police officers. Take, for example, officers who have posted racy and/or nude photos of themselves on their Facebook page, or pictures of officers taking drugs or drinking excessively on YouTube, or statements by officers that are offensive, racist, and show extreme bias on Twitter or a local blog. These examples show not only poor judgment on the part of the officer, but in the worst case, provide potential evidence for impeachment during a trial. While the behavior does not comport to Brady technically, this type of material can still be used to impeach the officer's credibility. As a general rule, the following "tips" are offered for police using social networking sites:

- *No nudity or sexually explicit pictures*—This includes pictures of you or you with a friend who is disrobed. Understand that your Facebook pictures and YouTube videos can easily be presented in court.

- *No drug taking or excessive alcohol postings*—Keep private "partying" photos to a minimum.
- *No gun glorification*—Keep your weapon and other police equipment off your social networking sites, and keep pictures of you in uniform off your social network sites.
- *Avoid bashing the department and keep rumors quiet*—Not only does this alleviate issues previously discussed that may indeed "interfere with the official business of the department," but also protects you from potential civil actions if the statements are found to be untrue.
- *Restrict personal information and manage your privacy settings*—Remember that suspects use the computer as well and that personal information relating to your address and family may place you in harm's way.[210]

Sexual Conduct and Sexual Orientation

The cases in this area tend to fall into two general categories: cases involving adultery and cases involving homosexuality. Most cases are in general agreement that adultery, even though committed while the police officer is off duty and in private, created a proper basis for disciplinary action.[211] The courts held that such behavior brings adverse criticism on the agency and tends to undermine public confidence in the department. However, one case involving an Internal Revenue Service agent suggests that to uphold disciplinary action for adultery, the government would have to prove that the employing agency was actually discredited; the court further stated that the discreditation would not be presumed from the proof of adulterous conduct.[212]

More recently, the Supreme Court justices appeared to be divided on the issue of extramarital sexual activity in public employment. In 1984, the Court of Appeals for the Sixth Circuit held that a Michigan police officer could not be fired solely because he was living with a woman to whom he was not married (a felony under state law). In 1985, the Supreme Court denied review of that decision over the strong objection of three justices who felt the case "presented an important issue of constitutional law regarding the contours of the right of privacy afforded individuals for sexual matters."[213]

In cases involving sexual improprieties that clearly affect an officer's on-the-job performance, the courts have had far less controversy. In a series of cases, the courts have consistently supported the disciplinary action attached to the department's "conduct unbecoming" regulation, including cases in which officers were cohabiting or in which the sexual activities were themselves illegal (e.g., public lewdness, child molestation, sexual activity with prostitutes, and homosexuality).[214] In fact, the courts have upheld internal regulations barring the employment of spouses, in part because of the concern for an officer's work performance.

The issue of homosexual activity as a basis for discharge was presented to the Supreme Court. Oklahoma had a law permitting discharge of schoolteachers for engaging in "public homosexual activity." The lower court held the law to be facially overly broad and therefore unconstitutionally restrictive. The Supreme Court affirmed the decision.[215] Another federal court held that the discharge of a bisexual guidance counselor did not deprive the plaintiff of her First or Fourteenth Amendment rights.

The counselor's discussion of her sexual preferences with teachers and other personnel was not protected by the First Amendment. Her equal protection claim failed because she did not show that the heterosexual employees would have been treated differently for communicating their sexual preferences.[216]

In an equally important federal case involving 13 lesbian deputies terminated from the Broward County, Florida Sheriff's Department, the Supreme Court held that homosexuals are not a suspect class accorded strict scrutiny under the equal protection clause and, therefore, the dismissal did not deprive the plaintiffs of any constitutional or equal protection right.[217] However, in 2003 the Supreme Court ruled that state sodomy laws are unconstitutional,[218] nullifying many police departments' argument that homosexuality is a criminal violation that is a viable basis for discharging a police officer. Amid recent debates regarding police harassment within the gay, lesbian, bisexual, and transgender (GLBT) communities, many larger departments (e.g., New York, Los Angeles, San Francisco, and Seattle) have developed recruiting and hiring programs aimed at attracting GLBT officers. Unfortunately, research on police agencies in Texas and Georgia reveal that recruitment efforts have been unsuccessful and that the 2003 landmark case (*Lawrence v. Texas*) has had little impact on the hiring and retention of GLBT officers in policing.[219]

Residency Requirements

A number of local governments have established requirements that all or certain classes of their employees live within the geographical limits of the jurisdiction. These residency requirements have been justified by the governments imposing them as desirable because they increase employees' rapport with and understanding of the community. When police officers were concerned, it has been asserted that the presence of off-duty police has a deterrent effect on crime and results in chance encounters that might lead to additional sources of information.

Before 1976, challenges to the legality of residency requirements for public employees dotted the legal landscape. In 1976, the Supreme Court, in *McCarthy v. Philadelphia Civil Service Commission*, ruled that Philadelphia's residency requirement for firefighters did not violate the Constitution.[220]

Since the *McCarthy* decision, the legal attacks on the residency requirements have subsided. The cases now seem to be concerned with determining what constitutes residency. The most obvious means of attempting to avoid the residency requirement (by establishing a second residence within the city) appears doomed to failure unless the police officer can demonstrate that he or she spends at least a substantial part of his or her time at the in-city residence.[221] A strong argument has been made that in areas where housing is unavailable or prohibitively expensive, a residency requirement is unreasonable.[222] In upholding the application of such requirements, courts have focused on the issues of equal enforcement and the specificity of the local residency standard.[223]

Moonlighting

Traditionally, the courts have supported the authority of police departments to place limits on the outside employment of their employees.[224] Police department restrictions on moonlighting range from a complete ban on outside employment to permission to engage in certain endeavors, such as investments, rental of property, teaching of law enforcement subjects, and employment designed to improve the police image. The rationale in support of moonlighting prohibitions is that "outside employment seriously interferes with keeping the [police and fire] departments fit and ready for action at all times."[225]

However, in a Louisiana case, firefighters offered unreputed evidence that moonlighting had been a common practice before the city banned it; during the previous 16 years, no firefighters had ever needed sick leave as a result of injuries suffered while moonlighting, there had never been a problem locating off-duty firefighters to respond to an emergency, and moonlighting had never been shown to be a source of fatigue that was serious enough to impair a firefighter's alertness on the job. Under these circumstances, the court ruled that there was not a sufficient basis for the prohibition on moonlighting and invalidated the ordinance.[226]

It is important to note that, in several cases involving off-duty, moonlighting officers (as private security guards or store detectives), the same legal standards imposed on sworn officers acting in the capacity of their jobs apply. The Court has held that off-duty officers act "under color of State law" and are subject to Section 1983 liability while working in a private security or "special patrolman" capacity.[227] Therefore, it follows that police agencies and departments may be liable under the same ramifications, opening up a new wave of future litigation involving police officer off-duty employment.

Alcohol and Drug Testing

It is common for police departments to require that their officers not be under the influence of any intoxicating agent while on duty. Even in the absence of such specific regulation, disciplinary action has been upheld when it was taken against an officer who was suspected of being intoxicated while on duty by charging him or her with neglect of duty or violation of a state law.[228]

Regulations that prohibit being under the influence of an intoxicating or mind-altering substance have been upheld uniformly as reasonable because of the hazardous nature of a police officer's work and the serious impact his or her behavior or misbehavior is sure to have on the property and safety of others. The necessity to require a clear head and rational action, not confused by alcohol or drugs, is clear.[229] A Louisiana court upheld a regulation that prohibited an officer from consuming alcoholic beverages on or off duty to the extent that it caused the officer's behavior to become obnoxious, disruptive, or disorderly.[230]

Effective enforcement of regulations against an officer's being under the influence of drugs or alcohol will occasion situations when a police supervisor or administrator will order an officer to submit to one or more tests to determine the presence of the prohibited substance in the subject's body. It has been held that a firefighter could be ordered to submit to blood sampling when reasonable grounds existed for believing that he or she was intoxicated and that it was permissible to discharge the firefighter for his or her refusal to comply with the order.[231] More recently, the courts have also been asked to review police department policies that require officers to submit to urinalysis for the purpose of determining the presence of drugs or alcohol. In *United States v. Jacobsen*, the Supreme Court defined the concept of search and seizure:

> A "search" occurs when an expectation of privacy that society is prepared to consider reasonable is infringed. A "seizure" of property occurs when there is some meaningful interference with an individual's possessory interests in that property.[232]

According to the Supreme Court, removing urine from an individual's body is a search within the meaning of the Fourth Amendment. Consequently, when a government agency tests an employee's urine, due process must be applied, which involves providing probable evidence of illegal activity. In the case of public employer drug testing, the search is justified from the beginning, when "reasonable grounds exist for suspecting that the search will turn up evidence of work-related drug use."[233]

A reasonable search depends on a "balancing test" set forth by Justice Sandra Day O'Connor:

> A determination of the standard of reasonableness applicable to a particular class of searches requires balancing the nature and quality of the intrusion on the individual's Fourth Amendment interests against the importance of the governmental interest alleged to justify the intrusion. In the case of searches conducted by a public employer, we must balance the invasion of the employee's legitimate expectations of privacy against the government's need for supervision, control, and the efficient operation of the work place.[234]

The Supreme Court has ruled on two cases that have become landmarks for drug testing in the public sector. In *Skinner v. Railway Labor Executives' Association*, the Court upheld a mandatory drug testing program in cases in which the government had no reasonable suspicion about any particular public employee but had a substantial interest in maintaining public safety.[235] In a case even more important to police agencies, the Court considered in *National Treasury Employees Union v. Von Raub* whether the U.S. Customs drug testing program was constitutional. The customs service drug-tested employees who sought a promotion to positions that required seizing or safekeeping illegal drugs, carrying firearms, or handling classified documents. The Court held that such employees have a "diminished expectation of privacy" and that drug testing is a minimal intrusion that is far outweighed by the government's interests to keep the public and citizenry safe.[236]

The prevailing view appears to be that totally random, unscheduled drug testing is unacceptable but that particular officers can be required to submit to urinalysis if there exists a "reasonable suspicion" that the officer has been using a prohibited substance or is involved in an incident involving citizen safety.[237] For instance, in 2007, the New York Police Department instituted a new drug and alcohol policy regarding critical incidents involving the police. If an officer fires his or her weapon either on or off duty, or is involved in a traffic accident that causes injury or death, a portable breathalyzer test is automatically given as a condition of employment. If the breathalyzer test concludes a blood alcohol level of 0.08 or greater, the officer is immediately placed on administrative leave and an Internal Affairs investigation is opened.[238] More importantly, advanced alcohol and drug testing is then conducted through blood tests or urinalysis. The results of such compulsory tests are appropriate evidence for introduction in administrative discharge proceedings.[239]

Decisions involving other government employees and similar kinds of personal intrusions (e.g., strip searches of prison guards) seem to support the view that random testing is unreasonable under the Fourth Amendment.[240] However, without a definitive decision from the Supreme Court on random drug testing, lower federal court decisions concerning public agency personnel appear to allow random drug testing without reasonable suspicion of individual drug abuse if (1) an employer knows that drugs are used in the workplace, (2) the testing will not totally disrupt the employee's privacy expectation, and (3) the jobs are "safety-sensitive" in nature.[241]

In an attempt to skirt the issue of mandatory or random testing, some departments have incorporated drug testing as a "usual and customary" part of a required medical examination. For instance, the Philadelphia Police Department requires a medical examination for all individuals attempting to secure employment under the following conditions: (1) when an officer is first hired, (2) when an officer is transferred to a "sensitive" position (i.e., vice and narcotics division, SWAT, and hostage negotiation teams), (3) when an officer is promoted to a higher rank, and (4) when an officer returns to duty after an extended period of time (e.g., long illness, disability, or suspension). Drug abuse is viewed as a medical malady and is subject to disclosure, similar to the findings of other tests that show spinal problems, poor vision, hearing loss, and the like. Hence, drug testing can be viewed as a routine part of the medical examination for pre-employment to a new position.

In Arlington, Texas, all police officers are required to take an annual medical examination and perform acceptable physical agility tests that "qualify" them for continued employment. The department links these tests to "insurability" through policies and regulations. Officers with physical disabilities (including alcohol and drug addiction) cannot be insured through the city of Arlington. An important note regarding both the Arlington and the Philadelphia police departments is the attitude expressed about officer drug abuse. Each department views the problem as a medical issue; therefore, extensive programs for counseling and rehabilitation have been established. Although these regulations have *not* been court tested, it appears reasonable that a comprehensive look at the issue of drugs in the workplace will support drug testing as a routine part of a medical examination.

CONCLUSION

The legal aspects of police administration are complex and varied. While most administrators are somewhat protected under qualified, good-faith immunity clauses, liability is not absolved when executives deliberately or knowingly allow unreasonable actions on the part of officers under their command. Successful Section 1983 lawsuits against the police most commonly occur during incidents involving deadly force, use of force, pursuit driving, and handling emotionally disturbed persons. To reduce liability, departments should develop written directives and policies regarding police procedures, make sure that officers are familiar with these policies, train officers on these policies and procedures at both the recruit and in-service academies, and routinely update officers on new techniques and procedures as they evolve.

Police officers enjoy the same constitutional rights as other members of our society. However, they are often held to a higher standard of conduct. Police officers who engage in a variety of behaviors either on or off the job, such as associating with crime figures or persons with a criminal record or persons engaged in criminal activity such as drug dealing and/or prostitution, verbal abuse and swearing, excessive drinking and intoxication, criminal conduct, dishonesty and lying, fighting with coworkers, insubordination, and dereliction of duty are subject to discipline. Officers can be terminated for such activities for "conduct unbecoming an officer." In addition, officers run into trouble whenever they conduct illegal activities or commit crimes. Officers can be required, as a condition of their employment, to submit to polygraph examinations, breath analysis, urinalysis, and blood analysis whenever drug or alcohol use is suspected. The results of these tests can be used in administrative hearings that may end in discipline and/or termination for the officer.

CHAPTER REVIEW

1. What are the three general categories of torts?
2. Explain the meaning of "acting under the color of state law" as it relates to U.S. Code 42, Section 1983 actions.
3. What is a *Bivens* action?
4. What are the primary negligence theories applicable to police supervision and management?
5. Describe procedural and substantive due process.
6. Identify when department rules and policies might infringe on the free speech of officers.
7. What is a Brady violation?
8. Describe the circumstances when an officer can use deadly force.
9. Identify the four elements that must be proven in order to sue the police for negligence in a high-speed pursuit.
10. Describe a police department's responsibility in reducing liability in high-speed pursuits.
11. Identify the desired outcomes of effective training of police officers in dealing with emotionally disturbed persons.
12. Describe the "balancing test" as referred to in alcohol and drug testing in the workplace.

KEY TERMS

1983 action: a tort action by which federal courts obtain jurisdiction of suits that involve the deprivation of any rights, privileges, or immunities secured by the Constitution by an individual acting under color of any statute, ordinance, regulation, custom, or usage of any state.

***Bivens* action:** a judicially created counterpart to a 1983 action that gives the federal courts jurisdiction over torts involving federal officials.

defendant: the person or organization being sued; also called a tort feasor.

deliberate indifference: a legal standard that involves more than negligence; the conscious or reckless disregard of the consequences of one's acts or omissions.

due process: a guarantee of fairness in legal matters that requires that all legal procedures set by statute and court practice must be followed for every individual, so that there is no prejudicial or unequal treatment.

emotionally disturbed persons (EDPs): individuals suffering from various forms of mental illness that may complicate interactions with police officers.

less-lethal weapon: As their name reflects, less-lethal weapons are used without the intent to cause permanent injury or death. Common less-lethal weapons include chemical weapons such as oleoresin capsicum (OC) or pepper spray, bean-bag guns, net guns that shoot a web around suspects, and controlled energy devices (CEDs) like Tasers.

liability: legal responsibility for a person's or an organization's acts or omissions.

liberty rights: rights involving the protection and defense of one's good name, reputation, and position in the community.

litigation: a lawsuit or another question to the court that resolves a legal matter or question.

negligence: the failure to exercise the care toward another person that a reasonable person would do in the same circumstances; also includes taking action that a reasonable person would not take; negligence is accidental.

objective reasonableness: A court-developed standard imposed under the Fourth Amendment "reasonableness" inquiring as to whether an officer's actions are "objectively reasonable" in light of the facts and circumstance of a specific incident. Would a reasonable officer confronted with the same or similar circumstances make the same decisions and conduct the same actions under review? The "objective reasonableness" test acknowledges that police officers are often forced to make split-second decisions under highly stressful conditions relating to the amount of force necessary in a particular incident.

plaintiff: the injured party that initiates a legal action.

probable cause: Arising from the Fourth Amendment, probable cause is the standard by which a police officer has the authority to make an arrest, conduct a personal or property search, or to obtain a warrant for arrest; a set of facts and circumstances that would lead a reasonable person to believe that a crime has occurred and that a specific person is responsible for that crime.

procedural due process: the legality of the procedures used; in this case, to deprive police officers of status or wages.

property rights: rights involving the protection of one's property; in some cases, an individual's right to his or her job is considered a property right.

proximate cause: an event that directly results in another event, particularly injury due to negligence or an intentional, wrongful act.

reasonableness: a standard applied to many legal questions in which it must be determined if conduct or action was reasonable in the eyes of the court.

substantive due process: the requirement that the basis for government disciplinary action be reasonable, relevant, and justifiable.

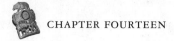

tort: a private injury inflicted on one person by another person, for which the injured party may sue in a civil action.

vicarious liability: a legal doctrine also known as "respondent superior" imposing liability on supervisors and managers for the tortious conduct of their employees.

ENDNOTES

1 Much of this section is taken, with some addition, from H. E. Barrineau III, *Civil Liability in Criminal Justice* (Cincinnati: Anderson, 1987), pp. 3–5.

2 Ibid., p. 3.

3 False arrest is the arrest of a person without probable cause. Generally, this means making an arrest when an ordinarily prudent person would not have concluded that a crime had been committed or that the person arrested had committed the crime. False imprisonment is the intentional illegal detention of a person. The detention that can give rise to a false imprisonment claim is any confinement to a specified area and not simply incarceration in a jail. Most false arrests result in false imprisonment as well, but there can be a false imprisonment after a valid arrest also, as when the police fail to release an arrested person after a proper bond has been posted, the police unreasonably delay the arraignment of an arrested person, or authorities fail to release a prisoner after they no longer have authority to hold him or her. "Brutality" is not a legal tort action as such. Rather, it must be alleged as a civil (as opposed to a criminal) assault and/or battery. Assault is some sort of menacing conduct that puts another person in reasonable fear that he or she is about to have a battery committed on him or her. Battery is the infliction of harmful or offensive contact on another person. Harmful or offensive contact is contact that would be considered harmful or offensive by a reasonable person of ordinary sensibilities. See Clarence E. Hagglund, "Liability of Police Officers and Their Employers," *Federation of Insurance Counsel Quarterly* 26 (summer 1976), p. 257, for a good discussion of assault and battery, false arrest, false imprisonment, and malicious prosecution as applied to police officers.

4 Although a fourth category (strict liability tort action) does exist in the wider body of law, such a general category is rare in police officer litigation. Therefore, for the purposes of this book, strict liability actions are not discussed. Under strict liability, one is held liable for one's act, regardless of intent or negligence. The mere occurrence of certain events will necessarily create legal liability. A good example of such cases is often found in airplane disasters in which the air transportation company is strictly liable for the passengers' health and well-being, regardless of other factors.

5 *Black's Law Dictionary*, 4th ed. (St. Paul, Minn.: West, 2004), p. 470.

6 Title 42, U.S. Code Section 1983.

7 See *Monroe v. Pape*, 365 U.S. 167, 81 S. Ct. 473 (1961). The plaintiff and his family sued 13 Chicago police officers and the city of Chicago, alleging that police officers broke into their home without a search warrant, forced them out of bed at gunpoint, made them stand naked while the officers ransacked the house, and subjected the family to verbal and physical abuse. The court held that the definition of "under color of State law" for Section 1983 purposes was the same as that already established in the criminal context and concluded that, because Section 1983 provides for a civil action, the plaintiffs need not prove that the defendants acted with a "specific intent to deprive a person of a federal right" (365 U.S. at 187). The court also held that municipalities (such as the city of Chicago, in this case) were immune from liability under the statute, although the Supreme Court later overruled this part of *Monroe v. Pape*, holding that municipalities and other local governments are included among "persons" open to a Section 1983 lawsuit. See *Monell v. Dept. of Social Services of the City of New York*, 436 U.S. 658, 98 S. Ct. 2018 (1978). (Citations to case opinions give the volume number in which the opinion is located followed by the name of the reporter system, the page number, the court if other than the Supreme Court, and the year in which the opinion was rendered.)

8 The resuscitation of Section 1983 hinges on the misuse and abuse of power imbued to individuals acting as police officers. All municipal and county law enforcement officers take an oath to uphold and enforce the laws of a specific state in which their municipality resides. Therefore, municipal police officers are squarely within the confines of Section 1983. "Misuse of power," possessed by virtue of state law and made possible only because the wrongdoer is clothed with the authority of state law, is action taken "under the color of

law." *United States v. Clasic*, 313 U.S. 299, at p. 326, 61 S. Ct., 1031, at p. 1043 (1941) as quoted in *Monroe v. Pape*. Thus, private citizens cannot be sued under Section 1983 unless they conspire with state officers. (See *Slavin v. Curry*, 574 F. 2d 1256 [5th Cir. 1978], as modified by 583 F. 2d 779 [5th Cir. 1978].) Furthermore, if a state officer has immunity to a Section 1983 lawsuit, private citizens who conspired with him or her do not have "derivative immunity" to the lawsuit. (See *Sparks v. Duval County Ranch Co., Inc.*, 604 F. 2d 976 [5th Cir. 1979], at p. 978.) In addition, see *Sanberg v. Daley*, 306 F. Supp. 227 (1969), at p. 279.

[9] Most tort actions against the U.S. government must be brought under the FTCA. The FTCA is a partial waiver of sovereign immunity, with its own rule of liability and a substantial body of case law. Federal employees can be sued for violation of constitutional rights and for certain Common-Law torts. For more information, see Isidore Silver, *Police Civil Liability* (New York: Mathew Bender, 1987), section 1.04, from which this material is taken.

[10] See *Bivens v. Six Unknown Federal Narcotics Agents*, 403 U.S. 388, 91 S. Ct. 1999 (1971). See also Silver, *Police Civil Liability*, section 8.02.

[11] Silver, *Police Civil Liability*, Section 8.02.

[12] See William L. Prosser, *Handbook of the Law of Torts*, 4th ed. (St. Paul, Minn.: West, 1971), p. 69, for a good discussion of the philosophical basis for and development of the doctrine of vicarious liability.

[13] Although this list does not include all types of negligence theories regarding 1983 action against police supervisors and managers, it does provide a starting point in understanding this issue. This part has been adapted from Barrineau, *Civil Liability*, pp. 59–60.

[14] See *Peter v. Bellinger*, 159 N.E. 2d 528 (1959); *Thomas v. Johnson*, 295 F. Supp. 1025 (1968); *McKenna v. City of Memphis*, 544 F. Supp. 415 (1982), affirmed in 785 F. 2d 560 (1986); *McGuire v. Arizona Protection Agency*, 609 P. 2d 1080 (1908); *Di Cosal v. Kay*, 19 N.J. 159, 450 A. 2d 508 (1982); *Pontiac v. KMS Investments*, 331 N.W. 2d 907 (1983); and *Welsh Manufacturing Div. of Textron, Inc. v. Pinkertons, Inc.*, 474 A. 2d 426 (1984).

[15] See *Board of the County Commissioner of Bryan County v. Brown*, 117 S. Ct. 1383 (1997).

[16] See *Moon v. Winfield*, 383 F. Supp. 31 (1974); *Murray v. Murphy*, 441 F. Supp. 120 (1977); *Allen v. City of Los Angeles* (No. C-9837), LA Sup. Ct. (1975); *Stengel v. Belcher*, 522 F. 2d 438 (6th Cir. 1975); *Dominguez v. Superior Court*, 101 Cal. App. 3d 6 (1980); *Stuessel v. City of Glendale*, 141 Cal. App. 3d 1047 (1983); and *Blake v. Moore*, 162 Cal. App. 3d 700 (1984).

[17] See *Ford v. Breiser*, 383 F. Supp. 505 (1974); *Dewel v. Lawson*, 489 F. 2d 877 (10th Cir. 1974); *Bonsignore v. City of New York*, 521 F. Supp. 394 (1981), affirmed in 683 F. 2d 635 (1st Cir. 1982); *Webster v. City of Houston*, 689 F. 2d 1220 (5th Cir. 1982), reversed and remanded on the issue of damages in 739 F. 2d 993 (5th Cir. 1984); and *District of Columbia v. Parker*, 850 F. 2d 708 (D.C. Cir. 1988), cert. denied in 489 U.S. 1065, 109 S. Ct. 1339 (1989).

[18] See *Marusa v. District of Columbia*, 484 F. 428 (1973); *Webster v. City of Houston*, supra note 22; and *Grandstagg v. City of Borger*, 767 F. 2d (5th Cir. 1985), cert. denied in 480 U.S. 917, 107 S. Ct. 1369 (1987).

[19] *City of Canton v. Harris*, 389 U.S. 378, 103 L. Ed. 412, 109 S. Ct. 1197 (1989), at pp. 1204–5; *Merritt v. County of Los Angeles*, 875 F. 2d 765 (9th Cir. 1989); *Owens v. Haas*, 601 F. 2d 1242 (2nd Cir. 1979), cert. denied in 444 U.S. 980 (1980).

[20] Prosser, *Handbook of the Law of Torts*, pp. 977–978.

[21] *Scheuer v. Rhodes*, at p. 240.

[22] *Wood v. Strickland*, 420 U.S. 308, 95 S. Ct. 992 (1975).

[23] *Harlow v. Fitzgerald*, 457 U.S. 800, 102 S. Ct. 2727 (1982).

[24] *Mitchell v. Forsyth*, 472 U.S. 511, 105 S. Ct. 2806 (1985).

[25] *Monroe v. Pape*, supra note 7.

[26] 436 U.S. 658, 98 S. Ct. 2018 (1978).

[27] See, for example, *Rookard v. Health and Hospitals Corp.*, 710 F. 2d 41 (2d Cir. 1983).

[28] *Oklahoma City v. Tuttle*, 471 U.S. 808, 105 S. Ct. 2427 (1985); but see *Pembauer v. Cincinnati*, 475 U.S. 469, 106 S. Ct. 1292 (1986).

[29] M. S. Vaughn et al., "Assessing Legal Liabilities in Law Enforcement: Police Chief's Views," *Crime and Delinquincy* 47, no. 1 (January 2001): 22.

[30] *Daniels v. Williams*, 474 U.S. 327, 106 S. Ct. 662 (1986).

[31] *New v. City of Minneapolis*, 792 F. 2d 724, at pp. 725–26 (8th Cir. 1986). See also *McClary v. O'Hare*, 786 F. 2d 83 (2nd Cir. 1986).

[32] Hagglund, "Liability of Police Officers," p. 257.

[33] *United States v. Leon*, 468 U.S. 897, 104 S. Ct. 3430 (1984).

[34] *Malley v. Briggs*, 475 U.S. 335, 106 S. Ct. 1092 (1986).

[35] *Anderson v. Creighton*, 483 U.S. 635, 107 S. Ct. 3034 (1987).

[36] *Saucier v. Katz*, 533 U.S. 194, 121 S. Ct. 2151 (2001). See also *Pearson et al. v Callahan*, 07-751 (494 F3d 891) (January 21, 2009).

[37] *Malley v. Briggs*, 475 U.S. 335, 341 (1986).

[38] *Maciarello v. Summer*, 973 F. 2d 295, 298 (1992).

[39] *Pearson, et. al. v Callahan*, 07-751 (494 F3d 891) (January 21, 2009).

[40] Schmidt, "Recent Developments."

[41] Ibid., p. 198.

[42] *Wimberly v. Patterson*, 183 A. 2d 691 (1962), at p. 699.

[43] *Piatkowski v. State*, 251 N.Y.S. 2d 354 (1964), at p. 359.

[44] Schmidt, "Recent Developments," p. 199.

[45] *Fords v. Breier*, 383 F. Supp. 505 (E.D. Wis. 1974).

[46] *Lucas v. Riley*, Superior Court, Los Angeles County, Cal. (1975); *Delong v. City of Denver*, 530 F. 2d 1308 (Colo. 1974); *Grudt v. City of Los Angeles*, 468 P. 2d 825 (Cal. 1970); *Dillenbeck v. City of Los Angeles*, 446 P. 2d 129 (Cal. 1968).

[47] *AELE Law Enforcement Legal Defense Manual*, "Failure to Provide Medical Treatment," Issue 77-6 (1977).

[48] *Watkins v. City of Battle Creek*, 273 F. 3d 682, 685–86 (6th Cir. 2001).

[49] *Carter v. City of Detroit*, 480 F. 3d 305, 310, 311 (6th Cir. 2005).

[50] *AELE Law Enforcement Legal Defense Manual*, "Failure to Provide Medical Treatment."

[51] Kenneth James Matulia, "The Use of Deadly Force: A Need for Directives in Training," *The Police Chief*, May 1983, p. 30.

[52] Kenneth James Matulia, "A Balance of Forces: Model Deadly Force and Policy Procedure," *International Association of Chiefs of Police*, (1985): 23, 24. See also *Tennessee v. Garner*, 471 U.S. 1, 105 S. Ct. 1694 (1985). While this citation is relatively old, many of the basic positions held here are reiterated in the Commission on Accreditation for Law Enforcement Agencies (CALEA), Model Policy for Use of Force and Use of Deadly Force (2010).

[53] *Tennessee v. Garner*, supra note 17.

[54] *Tennessee v. Garner*, supra note 179.

[55] Matulia, "A Balance of Forces," p. 72.

[56] Catherin H. Milton, Jeanne Wahl Halleck, James Lardnew, and Gray L. Albrecht, *Police Use of Deadly Force* (Washington, D.C.: Police Foundation, 1977), p. 52.

[57] *Matulia*, "A Balance of Forces," p. 52.

[58] Ibid., p. 77.

[59] Ibid.

[60] Ibid., p. 78.

[61] 471 U.S. 1, 105 S. Ct. 1694 (1985).

[62] Matulia, "A Balance of Forces," p. 78.

[63] C. Mesloh, M. Henych, and R. Wolf, Conducted Electrical Weapons and Resolution of Use of Force Encounters. In M.W. Kroll, J.D. Ho (eds.) *Taser® Conducted Electrical Weapons: Physiology, Pathology and Law* (New York: Springer Science and Business Media, 2009). Much of this section on TASERS and the Police Use of Less-Lethal Weapons has been adapted from Ross Wolf, "TASERS and Electronic Control Devises," LETN Video: *Electronic Control Devices* Courseware 111-0510 (Carrollton, TX: Critical Information Network, 2010).

[64] C. Mesloh, R. Wolf, M. Henych, and F. Thompson, "Less Lethal Weapons for Law Enforcement: A Performance-Based Analysis." *Law Enforcement Executive Forum* (2008) 8(1), pp. 133–149.

[65] See TASER International at: www.taser.com

[66] Ross Wolf, "TASERS and Electronic Control Devises," LETN Video: *Electronic Control Devices* Courseware 111-0510 (Carrollton, TX: Critical Information Network, 2010).

[67] U.S. General Accounting Office, TASER Weapons: Use of TASERS by Selected Law Enforcement Agencies (Washington, D.C.: USPO, 2005).

[68] Geoffrey P. Alpert and Roger G. Dunham, *Understanding Police Use of Force: Officers, Suspects, and Reciprocity* (Cambridge, NY: Cambridge University Press, 2004). See also Geoffrey P. Alpert, "Police Use-of-Force, Less Lethal Weapons, and Injuries: Findings from a National Study," *Police Quarterly*, Forthcoming, 2010.

[69] Ibid.

[70] Incidents involving TASERS that have caused death and serious injury continue to dot the newspapers across the United States and Canada. For a discussion of concerns involving less-lethal weapons and a description of specific highlighted events, see a series of reports by Amnesty International (London: Amnesty International) at — www.amnestyusa.org: 1) "USA Amnesty International's Continuing Concerns about TASER Use (2006); Excessive and Lethal Force? Amnesty International's Concerns About Deaths and Ill-Treatment Involving Police Use of TASERS (2004); USA: Police Use of Pepper Spray—Tantamount to Torture (1997) and the American Civil Liberties Union (ACLU) at—www.aclu.org: 1) Pepper Spray Update: More Fatalities, More Questions (1995) and 2) Stun Gun Fallacy: How the Lack of TASER Regulation Endangers Lives (2005).

[71] See John M. MacDonald, Robert J. Kaminski, and Michael R. Smith, "The Effect of Less-Lethal ON Injuries in Police Use-Of-Force events," *American Journal of Public Health*, 99:12 (December 2009), pp. 2260–2274 and M. R. Smith, R. J. Kaminski, J. Rojek, G. P. Alpert, and J. Mathis, "The Impact of Conducted Energy Devices and Other Types of Force and Resistance on Police and Suspect Injuries," *Policing: An International Journal of Police Strategies and Management*, 30 (2007) pp. 443–426.

[72] Geoffrey P. Alpert, "Police Use-of-Force, Less Lethal Weapons, and Injuries: Findings from a National Study," *Police Quarterly*, Forthcoming, 2010.

[73] Daniel L. Schofield, "Legal Issues of Pursuit Driving," *FBI Law Enforcement Bulletin*, May 1988, pp. 23–30. This discussion was adapted from this source.

[74] Richard G. Zivitz, "Police Civil Liability and the Law of High Speed Pursuit," *Marquette Law Review*, 70, no. 237 (1987), pp. 237–279.

[75] *Jackson v. Olson*, 712 P. 2d 128 (Or. App. 1985).

[76] 457 Do. 2d 816 (Miss. 1985).

[77] Ibid., at p. 818.

[78] See generally Annotation, "Emergency Vehicle Accidents," *American Jurisprudence, Proof of Facts* (St. Paul, MN: West, 1985), p. 599.

[79] See *Breck v. Cortez*, 490 N.E. 2d 88 (Ill. App. 1986).

[80] See generally Annotation, "Municipal Corporation's Safety Rules or Regulations as Admissible in Evidence in Action by Private Party against Municipal Corporation or Its Officers or Employees for Negligent Operation of Vehicle," *American Law Review*.

[81] See *Fiser v. City of Ann Arbor*, 339 N.W. 2d 413 (Mich. 1983).

[82] 733 S.W. 2d 28 (Mo. App. 1987).

[83] For a general discussion of immunity, see David Charlin, "High-Speed Pursuits: Police Officer and Municipal Liability for Accidents Involving the Pursued and an Innocent Third Party," *Seton Hall Law Review* 16, no. 101 (1986). While this citation is relatively old, many of the basic positions held here are reiterated in the Commission on Accreditation for Law Enforcement Agencies (CALEA), Model Policy for Police Pursuits (2010).

[84] 490 So. 2d 1061 (Fla. App. 1986).

[85] *Fagan v. City of Vineland*, 22 F. 3d 1283 (3rd Cir. 1994).

[86] 42 U.S.C. 1983 provides in relevant part: "Every person who, under color of any statute, ordinance, regulation, custom, or usage, of any State of Territory, subjects or causes to be subjected, any citizen of the United States or other person within the jurisdiction thereof to the deprivation of any rights, privileges, or immunities secured by the Constitution and laws, shall be liable to the party injured in an action at law, suit in equity, or other proper proceedings for redress."

[87] 782 F. 2d 947 (11th Cir. 1986).

[88] Ibid., at p. 950.

[89] See *County of Sacramento v. Lewis*, 98 F. 3d 434 (1998).

[90] Ibid.

[91] See *Allen v. Cook*, 668 F. Supp. 1460 (W.D. Okla. 1987). See also *Fagan v. City of Vineland*, supra note 202.

[92] 772 F. 2d 1205 (5th Cir. 1985).

[93] 471 U.S. 1, 105 S. Ct. 1694 (1985). The Supreme Court held that the use of deadly force to apprehend an unarmed fleeing felon was an unreasonable seizure which violated the Fourth Amendment.

[94]   817 F. 2d 540 (9th Cir. 1987). In *City of Miami v. Harris*, 490 So. 2d 69 (Fla. App. 1985), the court held that a city can be liable under 1983 for a pursuit policy that is adopted with a reckless disregard of whether such policy would cause loss of life without due process.

[95]   *Brower v. County of Inyo*, 489 U.S. 593, 109 S. Ct. 1378 (1989).

[96]   A discussion of empirical studies regarding pursuits is set forth in Geoffrey P. Alpert, "Questioning Police Pursuits in Urban Areas," in *Critical Issues in Policing: Contemporary Readings*, ed. R. G. Dunham and G. P. Alpert (Prospect Heights, Ill.: Waveland Press, 1989), pp. 216–229.

[97]   *Jackson v. Olson*, supra note 192.

[98]   See Annotation, "Municipal or State Liability for Injuries Resulting from Police Roadblocks or Commandeering of Private Vehicles," 19 *American Law Review* 4th 937.

[99]   *Brower v. County of Inyo*, supra note 212.

[100]   *Horta v. Sullivan*, 4 F. 3d 2 (1st Cir. 1993), at p. 10.

[101]   Edmund Fennessy, Thomas Hamilton, Kent Joscelyn, and John Merritt, *A Study of the Problem of Hot Pursuit by the Police* (Washington, D.C.: U.S. Department of Transportation, 1970).

[102]   Geoffrey P. Alpert, "Questioning Police Pursuit in Urban Areas," *Journal of Police Science and Administration* 15 (1987), pp. 298–306.

[103]   Eric Beckman, "Identifying Issues in Police Pursuits: The First Research Findings," *The Police Chief* (July 1987), pp. 57–63.

[104]   Geoffrey P. Alpert, *Police Pursuit Policies and Training* (Washington, D.C.: U.S. Department of Justice, Office of Justice Programs, National Institute of Justice, May 1997), pp. 1–8.

[105]   Ibid.

[106]   See, for example, *Nelson v. City of Chester, Ill.*, 733 S.W. 2d 28 (Mo. App. 1987); *Biscoe v. Arlington County*, 738 F. 2d 1352 (D.C. Cir. 1984).

[107]   Alpert, "Questioning Police Pursuits in Urban Areas," pp. 227–228.

[108]   International Association of Chiefs of Police, *Dealing with the Mentally Ill: Concepts and Issues* (Alexandra, Va.: IACP Law Enforcement Policy Center, December 1, 1997).

[109]   Washington Criminal Justice Training Commission (WCJTC), *Crisis Intervention Skills: Abnormal Behaviors, Mental Illness, and Suicide* (Seattle: WCJTC. 2000).

[110]   Michael Klein, "Law Enforcement's Response to People with Mental Illness," *Law Enforcement Bulletin* (February 2002), pp. 12–16.

[111]   See, generally, Joan Bertin Lowy, "Constitutional Limitations on the Dismissal of Public Employees," *Brooklyn Law Review* 43 (summer 1976): 1; Victor G. Rosenblum, "Schoolchildren: Yes, Policemen: No—Some Thoughts about the Supreme Court's Priorities Concerning the Right to a Hearing in Suspension and Removal Cases," *Northwestern University Law Review* 72 (1977), p. 146.

[112]   *Wisconsin v. Constantineau*, 400 U.S. 433, 91 S. Ct. 507 (1970); *Doe v. U.S. Department of Justice*, 753 F. 2d 1092 (D.C. Cir. 1985).

[113]   *Codd v. Velger*, 429 U.S. 624, 97 S. Ct. 882 (1977). See also *Paul v. Davis*, 424 U.S. 693, 96 S. Ct. 1155 (1976), which held that injury to reputation alone does not constitute a deprivation of liberty. See also *Swilley v. Alexander*, 629 F. 2d 1018 (5th Cir. 1980), where the court held that a letter of reprimand containing untrue charges that was placed in an employee's personnel file infringed on his liberty interest.

[114]   See *Board of Regents v. Roth*, 408 U.S. 564, 92 S. Ct. 2701 (1972); *Perry v. Sinderman*, 408 U.S. 593, 92 S. Ct. 2694 (1972); *Arnett v. Kennedy*, 416 U.S. 134, 94 S. Ct. 1633 (1974); *Bishop v. Wood*, 426 U.S. 341, 96 S. Ct. 2074 (1976). Also see Robert L. Rabin, "Job Security and Due Process: Monitoring Administrative Discretion through a Reasons Requirement," *University of Chicago Law Review* 44 (1976), pp. 60–67, for a good discussion of these cases; see also *Bailey v. Kirk*, No. 82-1417 (10th Cir. 1985) and Carl Goodman, "Public Employment and the Supreme Court's 1975–76 Term," *Public Personnel Management* 5 (September–October 1976), pp. 287–289.

[115]   *Thurston v. Dekle*, 531 F. 2d 1264 (5th Cir. 1976), vacated on other grounds, 438 U.S. 901, 98 S. Ct. 3118 (1978).

[116]   *Allison v. City of Live Oak*, 450 F. Supp. 200 (M.D. Fla. 1978).

[117]   See, for example, *Confederation of Police Chicago v. Chicago*, 547 F. 2d 375 (7th Cir. 1977).

[118]   Davis, *Administrative Law*, p. 242.

[119]   *Memphis Light Gas & Water Division v. Craft*, 436 U.S. 1, 98 S. Ct. 1554 (1978).

[120] *In re Dewar*, 548 P. 2nd 149 (Mont. 1976).

[121] *Bush v. Beckman*, 131 N.Y.S. 2d 297 (1954); *Gibbs v. City of Manchester*, 61 A. 128 (N.H. 1905).

[122] *Morrissey v. Brewer*, 408 U.S. 471, 92 S. Ct. 2593 (1972).

[123] *Goldman v. Kelly*, 397 U.S. 254, 90 S. Ct. 1011 (1970). See also *Buck v. N.Y. City Bd. of Ed.*, 553 F. 2d 315 (2d Cir. 1977), cert. denied in 438 U.S., 98 S. Ct. 3122 (1978).

[124] *Morrissey v. Brewer*, supra note 70.

[125] *Marshall v. Jerrico, Inc.*, 446 U.S. 238, 100 S. Ct. 1610 (1980); *Hortonville J.S.D. No. 1 v. Hortonville Ed. Assn.*, 426 U.S. 482, 96 S. Ct. 2308 (1976); *Holley v. Seminole County School Dist.*, 755 F. 2d 1492 (11th Cir. 1985).

[126] 94 S. Ct. 1633, 416 U.S. 134 (1974), at p. 157.

[127] Ibid., at pp. 167–68.

[128] 96 S. Ct. 893, 424 U.S. 319 (1975), at p. 335.

[129] 105 S. Ct. 1487, 470 U.S. 532 (1985).

[130] Ibid., at p. 1494.

[131] See *Gilbert v. Homar*, 520 U.S. 924 (1997).

[132] *Gorham v. City of Kansas City*, 590 P. 2d 1051 (Kan. S. Ct. 1979); *Winston v. U.S. Postal Service*, 585 F. 2d 198 (7th Cir. 1978).

[133] *Bence v. Breier*, 501 F. 2d 1185 (7th Cir. 1974), cert. denied in 419 U.S. 1121, 95 S. Ct. 804 (1975).

[134] *Perea v. Fales*, 114 Cal. Rptr. 808 (1974), at p. 810.

[135] *Kramer v. City of Bethlehem*, 289 A. 2d 767 (1972).

[136] *Rogenski v. Board of Fire and Police Commissioners of Moline*, 285 N.E. 2d 230 (1972). See also *Major v. Hampton*, 413 F. Supp. 66 (1976), in which the court held that an IRS rule against activities tending to discredit the agency was overbroad as applied to a married employee who had maintained an apartment for illicit sexual liaisons during off-duty hours.

[137] *Grayned v. City of Rockford*, 92 S. Ct. 2294, 408 U.S. 104 (1972), at pp. 108–109.

[138] *Bence v. Breier*, supra note 81, at p. 1190.

[139] *Rinaldi v. Civil Service Commission*, 244 N.W. 2d 609 (Mich. 1976).

[140] *Allen v. City of Greensboro, North Carolina*, 452 F. 2d 489 (4th Cir. 1971).

[141] *Petraitis v. Board of Fire and Police Commissioners City of Palos Hills*, 335 N.E. 2d 126 (Ill. 1975); *Haywood v. Municipal Court*, 271 N.E. 2d 591 (Mass. 1971); *Lewis v. Board of Trustee*, 212 N.Y.S. 2d 677 (1961). Compare *Stanton v. Board of Fire and Police Commissioners of Village of Bridgeview*, 345 N.E. 2d 822 (Ill. 1976).

[142] *DeSalvatore v. City of Oneonta*, 369 N.Y.S. 2d 820 (1975).

[143] *Marino v. Los Angeles*, 110 Cal. Rptr. 45 (1973).

[144] *Guido v. City of Marion*, 280 N.E. 2d 81 (Ind. 1972).

[145] *Carroll v. Goldstein*, 217 A. 2d 676 (R.I. 1976).

[146] *Firemen's and Policemen's Civil Service Commission v. Shaw*, 306 S.W. 2d 160 (Tex. 1957).

[147] *Martin v. City of St. Martinville*, 321 So. 2d 532 (La. 1975).

[148] *Arnold v. City of Aurora*, 498 P. 2d 970 (Colo. 1973).

[149] *Carey v. Piphus*, 435 U.S. 247, 98 S. Ct. 1042 (1978).

[150] *County of Monroe v. Dept. of Labor*, 690 F. 2d 1359 (11th Cir. 1982).

[151] *Gitlow v. New York*, 268 U.S. 652, 45 S. Ct. 625 (1925).

[152] *Pickering v. Board of Education*, 88 S. Ct. 1731, 391 U.S. 563 (1968), at p. 568.

[153] *Keyishian v. Board of Regents*, 385 U.S. 589, 87 S. Ct. 675 (1967).

[154] *Pickering v. Board of Education*, supra note 100.

[155] *Muller v. Conlisk*, 429 F. 2d 901 (7th Cir. 1970).

[156] *Flynn v. Giarusso*, 321 F. Supp. 1295 (E.D. La. 1971), at p. 1299. The regulation was revised and later ruled constitutional in *Magri v. Giarusso*, 379 F. Supp. 353 (E.D. La. 1974). See also *Gasparinetti v. Kerr*, 568 F. 2d 311 (3rd Cir. 1977), cert. denied in 436 U.S. 903, 98 S. Ct. 2232 (1978).

[157] *In re Gioglio*, 248 A. 2d 570 (N.J. 1968); *Brukiewa v. Police Commissioner of Baltimore*, 263 A. 2d 210 (Md. 1970); *Kannisto v. City and County of San Francisco*, 541 F. 2d 841 (9th Cir. 1976), cert. denied in 430 U.S. 931 S. Ct. 1552 (1977). Compare *Magri v. Giarusso*, supra note 104; *Hosford v. California State Personnel Board*, 141 Cal. Rptr. 354 (1977); and *Simpson v. Weeks*, 570 F. 2d 240 (8th Cir. 1978).

[158] *Brukiewa v. Police Commissioner of Baltimore*, supra note 105.

[159] *Perry v. City of Kinloch*, 680 F. Supp. 1339 (1988).

[160] *Brockell v. Norton*, 732 F. 2d 664(8th Cir. 1984).

[161] See *Perez v. Agostini*, 37 F. Supp. 2d 103 (D.P.R. 1999); *Dill v. City of Edmond, Oklahoma*, 155 F. 3d 1193 (10th Cir. 1998); *Cahill v. O'Donnell*, 7 F. Supp. 2d 341 (S.D.N.Y. 1998); *Hadad v. Croucher*, 970 F. Supp. 1227 (N.D. Ohio 1997); *Saunders v. Hunter*, 980 F. Supp. 1236 (M.D. Fla. 1997); *Forsyth v. City of Dallas, Texas*, 91 F. 3d 769 (5th Cir. 1996); and *Glass v. Dachel*, 2 F. 3d 733 (7th Cir. 1993).

[162] Adapted from Will Aitchison, *The Rights of Law Enforcement Officers*, 4th ed. (Portland, Ore.: Labor Relations Information System, 2000), p. 298.

[163] See *Lytle v. City of Haysville*, 138 F. 3d 857 (10th Cir. 1998), and *Frederick v. Department of Justice*, 73 F. 3d 349 (4th Cir. 1996).

[164] *Broaderick v. Oklahoma*, 413 U.S. 601, 93 S. Ct. 2908 (1973), and *Reeder v. Kansas City Bd. of Police Comm.*, 733 F. 2d 543 (8th Cir. 1984).

[165] *United Public Workers v. Mitchell*, 330 U.S. 75, 67 S. Ct. (1947): *U.S. Civil Service Commission v. National Association of Letter Carriers*, 413 U.S. 548, 93 S. Ct. 2880 (1973).

[166] *Broaderick v. Oklahoma*, supra note 112.

[167] *Sponick v. Detroit Police Dept.*, #15396, 49 Mich. App. 162, 211 N.W.2d 674 (Mich. App. 1973).

[168] *Sponick v. City of Detroit Police Department*, 211 N.W. 2d 674 (Mich. 1973), at p. 681. But see *Wilson v. Taylor*, 733 F. 2d 1539 (11th Cir. 1984).

[169] *Bruns v. Pomerleau*, 319 F. Supp. 58 (D. Md. 1970). See also *McMullen v. Carson*, 754 F. 2d 936 (11th Cir. 1985), where it was held that a Ku Klux Klansman could not be fired from his position as a records clerk in the sheriff's department simply because he was a Klansman. The court did uphold the dismissal because his active KKK participation threatened to cripple the agency's ability to perform its public duties effectively.

[170] *Civil Service Commission of Tucson v. Livingston*, 525 P. 2d 949 (Ariz. 1974).

[171] *City of San Diego v. John Roe*, 543 U.S. 77, 125 S. Ct. 521 (2005).

[172] See, for example, *Tinker v. Des Moines School District*, 393 U.S. 503, 89 S. Ct. 733 (1969).

[173] 425 U.S. 238, 96 S. Ct. 1440 (1976).

[174] *Mapp v. Ohio*, 367 U.S. 643, 81 S. Ct. 1684 (1961).

[175] *Katz v. United States*, 389 U.S. 347, 88 S. Ct. 507 (1967).

[176] *Smith v. Maryland*, 442 U.S. 735, 99 S. Ct. 2577 (1979), and *Chan v. State*, 78 Md. App. 287, 552 (1989). The "expectation to privacy" clause was developed in *Katz v. United States*, supra note 12, a case that involved warrantless electronic surveillance of a public telephone booth. The Court said that "the Fourth Amendment protects people, not places. What a person knowingly exposes to the public, even in his own home or office, is not subject to Fourth Amendment protection. But what he seeks to preserve as private, even in an area accessible to the public, may be constitutionally protected. . . . There is a twofold requirement, first that a person have exhibited an actual expectation of privacy, and second that the expectation by one's society is prepared to recognize it as reasonable/legitimate."

[177] See *People v. Tidwell*, 266 N.E. 2d 787 (Ill. 1971).

[178] See Ontario v. Quon 529 F.3rd 892 (2010).

[179] *Biehunik v. Felicetta*, 441 F. 2d 228 (2nd Cir. 1971), cert. denied in 403 U.S. 932, 91S. Ct. 2256 (1971).

[180] *United States v. Leon*, 468 U.S. 897, 104S. Ct. 3430 (1984), and *Massachusetts v. Sheppard*, 468 U.S. 981, 104 S. Ct. 3424 (1984).

[181] *Illinois v. Gates*, 462 U.S. 213, 103 S. Ct. 2317 (1984).

[182] The concept of the "good faith-reasonable belief" defense as either a qualified or an absolute immunity has significant case history. See Isadore Silver, *Police Civil Liability* (New York: Matthew Bender and Company, 1987), chapters 4 and 7.

[183] See *Floyd v. Farrell*, 765 F. 2d 1 (1st Cir. 1985); *Malley v. Briggs*, 475 U.S. 335, 106 S. Ct. 1092 (1986); *Santiago v. Fenton*, 891 F. 2d 373 (1st Cir. 1989); and *Hoffman v. Reali*, 973 F. 2d 980 (1st Cir. 1992).

[184] *Sheetz v. Mayor and City Council of Baltimore, Maryland*, 315 Md. 208 (1989).

[185] 385 U.S. 493, 87 S. Ct. 6126 (1967).

[186] The states are bound by this requirement as well. *Malloy v. Hogan*, 378 U.S. 1, 84 S. Ct. 489 (1964).

[187] *Gardner v. Broderick*, 392 U.S. 273, 88 S. Ct. 1913 (1968).

[188] These procedural rights in police disciplinary actions have often been referred to as the "Garrity Rights." They were developed through a series of cases; see *Lefkowitz v. Turley*, 414 U.S. 70, 94 S. Ct. 316 (1973),

and *Confederation of Police v. Conlisk*, 489 F. 2d 891 (1973), cert. denied in 416 U.S. 956, 94 S. Ct. 1971 (1974). Further, as the rights appear here, see Aitchison, *The Rights of Law Enforcement Officers*, p. 118.

[189] See *Gabrilowitz v. Newman*, 582 F. 2d 100 (1st Cir. 1978). Cases upholding the department's authority to order an officer to take a polygraph examination include *Eshelman v. Blubaum*, 560 P. 2d 1283 (Ariz. 1977); *Dolan v. Kelly*, N.Y.S. 2d 478 (1973); *Richardson v. City of Pasadena*, 500 S.W. 2d 175 (Tex. 1973); *Seattle Police Officer's Guild v. City of Seattle*, 494 P. 2d 485 (Wash. 1972); *Roux v. New Orleans Police Department*, 223 So. 2d 905 (La. 1969); *Coursey v. Board of Fire and Police Commissioners*, 234 N.E. 2d 339 (Ill. 1967); *Frazee v. Civil Service Board of City of Oakland*, 338 P. 2d 943 (Cal. 1959); and *Hester v. Milledgeville*, 777 F. 2d 1492 (11th Cir. 1985). Cases denying the department's authority include *Molino v. Board of Public Safety of City of Torrington*, 225 A. 2d 805 (Conn. 1966); *Stape v. Civil Service Commission of City of Philadelphia*, 172 A. 2d 161 (Pa. 1961); and *Farmer v. Fort Lauderdale*, 427 So. 2d 187 (Fla. 1983), cert. denied in 464 U.S. 816, 104 S. Ct. 74 (1983).

[190] *Eshelman v. Blubaum*, supra note 141, p. 1286.

[191] *Farmer v. City of Fort Lauderdale*, supranote 141.

[192] *Furtado v. Town of Plymouth*, 451 Mass. 529, 888 N.E.2d 357 (Mass. 2008).

[193] *Faust v. Police Civil Service Commission*, 347 A. 2d 765 (Pa. 1975); *Steward v. Leary*, 293 N.Y.S. 2d 573 (1968); *Brewer v. City of Ashland*, 86 S.W. 2d 669 (Ky. 1935); *Fabio v. Civil Service Commission of Philadelphia*, 373 A. 2d 751 (Pa. 1977).

[194] *Anderson v. City of Philadelphia, Pennsylvania*, 668 F. Supp. 441 (1987), reversed by 845F. 2d 1216 (3rd Cir. 1988).

[195] See Aitchison, *The Rights of Law Enforcement Officers*, pp. 58–62.

[196] See *Bigby v. City of Chicago*, 766 F. 2d 1053 (7th Cir. 1985), cert. denied in 474 U.S. 1056, 106 S. Ct. 793 (1986); *McCoy v. Board of Fire and Police Commissioners* (Chicago), 398 N.E. 2d 1020 (1979); *Davis v. Williams*, 588 F. 2d 69 (4th Cir. 1979); *Parker v. Levy*, 417 U.S. 733, 94 S. Ct. 2547 (1974); *Bence v. Brier*, 501 F. 2d 1184 (7th Cir. 1974), cert. denied in 419 U.S. 1121, 95 S. Ct. 1552 (1977); and *Gee v. California State Personnel Board*, 85 Cal. Rptr. 762 (1970).

[197] Whether or not reasonable people would agree that the conduct was punishable so that an individual is free to steer a course between lawful and unlawful behaviors is the key to "reasonableness." See *Cranston v. City of Richmond*, 710 P. 2d 845 (1986), and *Said v. Lackey*, 731 S.W. 2d 7 (1987).

[198] *Cranston v. City of Richmond*, supranote 148.

[199] See *City of St. Petersburg v. Police Benevolent Association*, 414 So. 2d 293 1982, and *Brown v. Sexner*, 405 N.E. 2d 1082 (1980).

[200] *Richter v. Civil Service Commission of Philadelphia*, 387 A. 2d 131 (1978).

[201] *Miller v. City of York*, 415 A. 2d 1280 (1980), and *Kannisto v. City and County of San Francisco*, 541 F. 2d 841 (1976), cert. denied in 430 U.S. 931, 97 S. Ct. 1552 (1977).

[202] *McIntosh v. Monroe Police Civil Board*, 389 So. 2d 410 (1980); *Barnett v. New Orleans Police Department*, 413 So. 2d 520 (1982); *Allman v. Police Board of Chicago*, 489 N.E. 2d 929 (1986).

[203] *Philadelphia Civil Service Commission v. Wotjuski*, 525 A. 2d 1255 (1987); *Gandolfo v. Department of Police*, 357 So. 568 (1978); *McDonald v. Miller*, 596 F. 2d 686 (1979).

[204] *Monroe v. Board of Public Safety*, 423 N.Y.S. 2d 963 (1980).

[205] *Redo v. West Goshen Township*, 401 A. 2d 394 (1979).

[206] *Brase v. Board of Police Commissioners*, 487 N.E. 2d 91 (1985).

[207] See *John Doe v. U.S. Department of Justice*, 565, F.3d 1375 (Fed Cir. 2009)

[208] See *Brady v. Maryland*, 373 U.S. 83 (1963).

[209] See *Giglio v. United States*, 405 U.S. 150 (1972) and expansion of the *Brady* duty in *United States v. Agurs*, 427 U.S. 97 (1976), *United States v. Bagley*, 473 U.S. 667 (1985), *Kyles v. Whitley*, 514 U.S. 419 (1995), and *Youngblood v. West Virginia*, 547 U.S. (2006).

[210] Adapted from Richard Weinblatt, "Top 10 Social Networking Tips for Police," Policeone.com (August 25, 2009). Retrieved on July 24, 2010.

[211] *Major v. Hampton*, 413 F. Supp. 66 (1976).

[212] *City of North Muskegon v.* Briggs, 473 U.S. 909 (1985).

[213] *National Gay Task Force v. Bd. of Ed. of Oklahoma City*, 729 F. 2d 1270 (10th Cir. 1984).

[214] See *Whisenhund v. Spradlin*, 464 U.S. 964 (1983), and *Kukla v. Village of Antioch*, 647 F. Supp. 799 (1986), cohabitation of officers; *Coryle v. City of Oil City*, 405 A. 2d 1104 (1979), public lewdness;

Childers v. Dallas Police Department, 513 F. Supp. 134 (1981); and *Fout v. California State Personnel Board*, child molesting; *Fugate v. Phoenix Civil Service Board*, 791 F. 2d 736 (9th Cir. 1986), sex with prostitutes; and *Doe v. Commonwealth Attorney*, 425 U.S. 901, 96S. Ct. 1489 (1976), *Smith v. Price*, 616 F. 2d 1371 (5th Cir. 1980), and *Bowers v. Hardwick*, 478 U.S. 186, 106 S. Ct. 2841 (1986), sodomy as a state law prohibiting homosexuality.

[215] *Bd. of Ed. v. National Gay Task Force*, 729 F. 2d 1270 (10th Cir. 1984), affirmed in 470 U.S. 903, 105 S. Ct. 1858 (1985).

[216] *Rowland v. Mad River Sch. Dist.*, 730 F. 2d (6th Cir. 1984), cert. denied in 470 U.S. 1009, 105 S. Ct. 1373 (1985).

[217] *Todd v. Navarro*, 698 F. Supp. 871 (1988).

[218] *Lawrence v. Texas*, 539U.S. 558, 123 S. Ct. 2472 (2003).

[219] Ibid., and see Eric Coleman and Sutom Cheurprakobkit, "Police Hiring and Retention of Sexual Minories in Georgia and Texas after Lawrence v. Texas." *Journal of Criminal Justice* 37, (2009), p. 256.

[220] *McCarthy v. Philadelphia Civil Service Comm.*, 424 U.S. 645, 96 S. Ct. 1154 (1976).

[221] *Miller v. Police of City of Chicago*, 349 N.E. 2d 544 (Ill. 1976); *Williamson v. Village of Baskin*, 339 So. 2d 474 (La. 1976); *Nigro v. Board of Trustees of Alden*, 395 N.Y.S. 2d 544 (1977).

[222] *State, County, and Municipal Employees Local 339 v. City of Highland Park*, 108 N.W. 2d 544 (1977).

[223] *Hameetman v. City of Chicago*, 776 F. 2d 636 (7th Cir. 1985).

[224] *Cox v. McNamara*, 493 P. 2d 54 (Ore. 1972); *Brenkle v. Township of Shaler*, 281 A. 2d 920 (Pa. 1972); *Hopwood v. City of Paducah*, 424 S.W. 2d 134 (Ky. 1968); *Flood v. Kennedy*, 239 N.Y.S. 2d 665 (1963). See also *Trelfa v. Village of Centre Island*, 389 N.Y.S. 2d 22 (1976). Rules prohibiting law enforcement officers from holding interest in businesses that manufacture, sell, or distribute alcoholic beverages have also been upheld. *Bock v. Long*, 279 N.E. 2d 464 (Ill. 1972); *Johnson v. Trader*, 52 So. 2d 333 (Fla. 1951).

[225] Richard N. Williams, *Legal Aspects of Discipline by Police Administrators*, Traffic Institute Publication No. 2705 (Evanston, Ill.: Northwestern University, 1975), p. 4.

[226] *City of Crowley Firemen v. City of Crowley*, 264 So. 2d 368 (La. 1972).

[227] See *Rojas v. Alexander's Department Store, Inc.*, 654 F. Supp. 856 (1986), and *Reagan v. Hampton*, 700 F. Supp. 850 (1988).

[228] *Reich v. Board of Fire and Police Commissioners*, 301 N.E. 2d 501 (Ill. 1973).

[229] *Krolick v. Lowery*, 302 N.Y.S. 2d 109 (1969), at p. 115, and *Hester Milledgeville*, 598 F. Supp. 1456, at p. 457, n. 2 (M.D. Ga. 1984), modified in 777 F. 2d 1492 (11th Cir. 1985).

[230] *McCracken v. Department of Police*, 337 So. 2d 595 (La. 1976).

[231] *Krolick v. Lowery*, supra note 229.

[232] 466 U.S. 109, 104 S. Ct. 1652 (1984), at p. 1656.

[233] *National Federation of Federal Employees v. Weinberger*, 818 F. 2d 935 (1987). See also related cases: *National Treasury Employees Union v. Von Raab*, 816 F. 2d 170 (1987), and *Lovvorn v. City of Chattanooga, Tennessee*, 846 F. 2d 1539 (1988).

[234] *O'Connor v. Ortega*, 480 U.S. 709, 107 S. Ct. 1492, (1987).

[235] 489 U.S. 602, 109 S. Ct. 1402 (1989).

[236] Supra note 195.

[237] *City of Palm Bay v. Bauman*, 475 So. 2d 1322 (Fla. 5th DCA 1985). Officers can be required to submit to urinalysis if there is a "reasonable suspicion" that the officer has been using a prohibited substance (including alcohol), see *Jackman v. Schembri*, 635 NYS.2d 30 (A.D. 1995)[1996 FP72].

[238] The New York Policy was challenged and upheld in *Lynch v. City of New York*, 589 F.3rd 94 (2d Cir. 2009).

[239] *Walters v. Secretary of Defense*, 725 F. 2d 107 (D.C. Cir. 1983).

[240] *Security of Law Enforcement Employees, District Counsel 82 v. Carly*, 737 F. 2d 187 (2d Cir. 1984); *Division 241 Amalgamated Transit Union v. Suscy*, 538 F. 2d 1264 (7th Cir. 1976) cert. denied in 429 U.S. 1029, 97 S. Ct. 653 (1976); *McDonnell v. Hunter*, 612 F. Supp. 1122 (S.D. Iowa 1984), affirmed in 746 F. 2d 785 (8th Cir. 1984).

[241] For a comprehensive review of the cases in this area, see Gregory P. Orvis, "Drug Testing in the Criminal Justice Workplace," *American Journal of Criminal Justice* 18, no. 2 (spring 1994), pp. 290–305.

15

Organizational Change

Change is not made without inconvenience, even when moving from worse to better.
—Richard Hooker (1554–1600)

Trying to change the federal bureaucracy has the same effect as punching a curtain.
—President John F. Kennedy (1917–1963)

Nothing is more difficult . . . more uncertain of success . . . than introducing change.
—Niccolo Machiavelli (1469–1527)

Objectives

- Identify eight recurring reasons that explain why change occurs in law enforcement agencies.

- Discuss five situations when change should not be initiated.

- Analyze Kurt Lewin's three-step model in organizational change.

- Discuss the role of the rank and file in organizational change.

- Define *organizational development*.

- Analyze the relationship between politics and organizational change.

- Explain why organizational change sometimes fails.

- Describe how to make organizational change succeed.

OUTLINE

Introduction

In the operational climate surrounding complex organizations today, questioning whether change will occur is irrelevant because organizational change is constant, ubiquitous, and often a purposeful reality. The appropriate questions address both how and when change will occur and what the consequences of this change will be.

There are certain positive as well negative aspects of organizational change that police administrators must be aware of in order to successfully affect organizational change. It is also important for police administrators to be aware that a failure to understand the hazards involved in planned change can result in their dismissal, and in the case of sheriffs, a failure to be re-elected. To understand the many facets of the organizational change, process police administrators should possess the following information: (1) the most common reasons why police departments change, (2) when it might be neither appropriate nor politically feasible to affect organizational change, (3) the various successful change models, (4) the positive and negative roles that politics can play in organizational change, (5) the important role that rank-and-file officers can play in organizational change, (6) some of the most common reasons why organizational change efforts fail, and (7) what the police manager needs to accomplish in order to have a successful organizational change.

Why Change Occurs

While any number of factors can be the catalyst for change, there are several recurring themes that lead to it in police agencies; among these are:

1. A single catastrophic event, often followed by civil liability litigation, leads to the chief of police being replaced. Illustratively, "Chief Jones" had come up through the ranks in his hometown 45-member police department of "Georgetown." A war hero as a young man, he was well liked by all segments of the community, largely because he had coached Little League baseball for years and knew many parents and was active in the local high school football boosters club, where he was well liked by the town's "movers and shakers." A town resident was raped and beaten; a second rape occurred within a few days, and this victim was cut multiple times with a knife. In both crimes the suspect was identified as a local man with a teardrop-shaped tattoo under one eye. An arrest warrant was issued for his arrest. There was considerable fear that, if not rapidly apprehended, the suspect might kill his next victim because of the increase in the level of violence between the first and second rapes. Both crimes were given considerable publicity in which the suspect was identified.

   One evening, a detective received a call from a citizen, reporting that as he drove down a road he saw the rape suspect entering a home outside the city limits in the county. This and other information from the caller, who was unknown to the detective, was never critically evaluated. The speed limit in this area was 55 MPH, the house was set nearly 40 yards from the highway, and there were no street lights in the area; it was dark and the porch light was off. Moreover, if the suspect was entering the house, his back would have been to the highway and, even if it was not so momentarily, how did the citizen, who did not know the suspect, see a small tattoo of a teardrop at that distance in the dark?

   The detective rapidly went through the building, asking, "Who wants to go get this son of a bitch?" Without a search warrant for the home the suspect was alleged to be in and without requesting the assistance of the county sheriff's office, approximately eight officers went to the home, which was dark inside, broke into it, and shot and killed the 70-year-old homeowner, who fired two shots at shapes charging into his house.

   The state investigative agency's report on the shooting found that the department's policies and procedures were nonexistent or inadequate, there was no raid plan or briefing, the "raid team" had never trained together, there was no attempt to verify the information the detective received before acting on it, and the suspect was not only not at the home but had never been there. The shooting took place two days before Christmas, leading citizens to ask, "Whose house are the police going to break into next and kill someone?" The city council concluded there was a massive failure of leadership and newspaper editorials called for and resulted in the chief's dismissal. In the wake of these events, Georgetown hired a professional from outside the community to head the police department, and he came in with a mandate for sweeping reforms.

2. A new mayor is elected and the current chief is replaced with one of the newly elected mayor's own choosing. The new mayor may bring his or her own vision of how the agency should be organized and operated;[1] alternatively, the new chief is selected with the understanding that he or she has a mandate to implement certain changes that are consistent with the new mayor's political and philosophical vision of governance.[2] (See Chapter 4, Politics and Police Administration for a more detailed discussion of this subject.)

For example, one of the nation's foremost police administrators, William J. Bratton, was selected to head the Los Angeles Police Department in October 2002 and served in that position until 2009 when he left to go to work for a private security firm. He was the 54th chief of the Los Angeles Police Department (LAPD) and was formerly commissioner of the New York City Police Department (NYPD). As commissioner, he represented the classic "change agent" in policing, and as commissioner of the NYPD, he introduced the Compstat system of tracking crime and holding police executives accountable for strategies to reduce crime in specific areas. He went on to develop a real-time police intelligence computer system, which became the first fusion center in the United States at the local level and began the emergence of intelligence-led policing. In Los Angeles he was charged with changing the internal dynamics of the LAPD. Formerly, under a Federal Consent Decree issued in November 2000, arising in part from the Rampart Precinct corruption scandal in the late 1990s and a series of excessive force, false arrest, and unreasonable search and seizure complaints, the LAPD faced significant internal policy changes from the past. To his credit, Chief Bratton was able to totally revamp the department's Internal Affairs Division and reduce complaints relating to police brutality. At the same time, violent crimes in LA were lowered.

3. A key political figure suffers a major embarrassment and feels the law enforcement agency is to blame, resulting in the chief being forced out. For example, a governor who was a competent fixed-wing, multi-engine pilot with an instrument rating was being flown around his state in the state patrol helicopter. When the governor wanted to fly the helicopter, the aircraft commander, who was a sergeant, refused to allow him to do so, citing a lack of training and safety concerns. One version of this is that the governor gracefully accepted this, while the other version is that there was a "nasty confrontation" about it. Subsequently, this story was covered by the news media and the governor felt not only had the event been blown out of proportion, but "someone at the state patrol had been talking out of school." When reportedly pressured by a member of the governor's staff, the state patrol director refused to discipline or transfer the pilot, resulting in additional bad publicity for the governor. Shortly thereafter, the state patrol's director quietly retired.

4. A chief of police retires, takes another position, or is fired. A consultant is hired to conduct an evaluation of the department[3] and the report is given to the new chief as a blueprint for change in the department. A few consultants seem to specialize in "headhunter" type of reports meaning city managers desiring to get rid of chiefs have been known to hire such consultants, as opposed to using ones who are more

even-handed and balanced in writing their reports. At the risk of oversimplification, the headhunter type of report is filled with negative statements, while the more professional consultant notes both the department's strengths and its weaknesses. While the latter type of report may lead to the chief's dismissal, it is on the basis of a fundamentally fair summation of present conditions in the department.

5. A new sheriff is elected and implements the changes that were part of the platform on which he or she ran. In one county, the defeated sheriff had insisted on buying a helicopter; its purchase price and operating costs were considerable for that county. As a candidate, the new sheriff promised he would get rid of the helicopter and "get back to basics, putting officers where they were needed, namely on the street instead of using a pie in the sky strategy."

6. A sheriff decided to remove his legal advertising from the town's daily newspaper and run it in the town's small, weekly newspaper after the daily newspaper wrote some critical editorials about the way the sheriff was running the department. Also, shortly thereafter, instead of continuing to buy the department's cars from the large dealer used for a number of years, the sheriff awarded the contract to a smaller, competing dealer (state law did not require him to obtain bids). Later, the sheriff publicly said he was just trying to be fair in the distribution of the car contracts, although privately he conceded perhaps he should have simply bought some cars from both dealers. The large dealership owner was a generous contributor to local politicians and had access to influence and power. The daily newspaper became more critical of the sheriff's office and subsequently supported his opponent, whose campaign centered on "returning to doing basic things well." In the background, the large dealership owner also worked against the incumbent, who was defeated in the next election.

   What the defeated sheriff failed to appreciate is that over time, expectations build up for how an organization operates and that to some degree it becomes "captured" by these expectations of other organizations. The large dealership owner expected he would routinely get the contract for the cars and the newspaper believed it could influence how the sheriff's office operated. When major expectations are abruptly not honored, serious conflict invariably follows. The sheriff also violated one of the most important tenets of elected office: don't get into a fight with newspapers—they buy their ink by the barrel.

7. The chief's conduct or style becomes an issue that leads to his or her dismissal. In one instance, a chief arrived at the department's annual police officers' ball when he already had been drinking heavily. As the evening wore on, he got progressively more drunk and refused to allow his staff members to drive him home, electing to stay at the party, where he got into several major confrontations with members of his department and one of their spouses. His dismissal was predicated on a public debate: "He is supposed to be a model for others; if he cannot control himself, how can he lead others?"

8. Morale in the police department is low, too many things seem to be going wrong, the present administration is always reacting to problems for which it seems no thought has been given or preparation has been made, or citizen groups are vociferous in their criticisms of the department. In such situations, police unions or associations may also

oppose the chief and have given him or her a vote of no confidence (discussed in greater detail in Chapter 11, Labor Relations). In such environments, complaints against police officers may be on the upswing, the use of sick leave by officers is excessive, the turnover rate is high and the level of experience in the department is dangerously low, the agency has difficulty attracting quality candidates or cannot even fill vacancies with the minimally qualified, the use of force incidents are increasing, and the crime rate is climbing while clearance levels are dropping out of sight.

Paradigm Shifts

As we learned in Chapter 2, Policing Today, paradigms are ways or models of doing things and they often have an accompanying set of rules and procedures. Max Weber's bureaucratic model can be thought of as a paradigm; when new paradigms are developed, they may have significant potential for causing significant organizational change. It is possible that the three most important paradigm shifts in the last 30 years of policing have been: (1) individual identification by DNA, which has created demands for new skills, training, and procedures in investigation, especially in the areas of evidence identification, collection, preservation and processing, as well as quantum leaps in clearing decades old cold cases and exonerating those who were erroneously convicted; (2) the shift from the traditional policing model, responding to incidents, to the widespread adoption of the community policing model; and (3) the development of fusion centers in the wake of the multiple terrorist attacks on September 11, 2001, such as the San Diego Regional Threat Assessment Center, which is creating significant new roles for local law enforcement agencies. However important these new roles are, they have exacerbated already existing staffing shortages in state and local law enforcement agencies. Prior to the implementation of fusion centers, many police agencies had difficulties recruiting and retaining officers and were also experiencing staffing shortages from sworn members in Reserve or National Guard units being called up for extended active military service. Moreover, even with federal funding to assist with the creation of the fusion centers, a number of officers being reassigned to them are only being made available by stripping personnel from lower-priority functions; for example, by reducing the number of investigators in nonviolent crimes units.

Historically, there have also been other paradigm shifts. For example, in many jurisdictions up until the mid to late 1960s, two officers walked high-crime area beats together. However, a large number of agencies concluded that this was unnecessary when personal handheld Motorola radios became available; a lone officer would call for backup if it was needed and the other officer was freed for other duties.

When Change Should Not Be Made

Because change is a perilous process, some thought should be given to whether it should be undertaken in the first place. Among the conditions that indicate contemplated change should be delayed are:

1. The knowledge, skill, or other resources needed to carry out the change effectively do not exist inside the department.
2. An appropriately experienced external **change agent** is not presently available.

3. The effort of making the change is greater than any benefits to be derived. Former Georgia Governor Zell Miller expressed this as "the juice isn't worth the squeezing." This principle can also be stated as "all motion isn't progress; some of it is just thrashing around."

4. Collateral damage, such as abandonment by key supporters or significant union opposition, may lead chiefs to use their limited stack of "political chips" on another issue of greater concern to them and the community.

5. Too much change is already underway in the department and the nature of the change is not sufficiently important to make now, versus its potential for personnel to feel confused about priorities or conclude that the organization is becoming unstable.

Two Organizational Change Models

There is an old story about a boy who wanted his dog to have a short tail. But rather than hurt the dog by cutting the tail off all at once, the boy sliced an inch off at a time. This story illustrates what is described as "pain level" associated with gradual and radical change strategies in public organizations. One camp maintains it is better to implement change swiftly (radical change) and get the upheavals that follow done and over with; the other camp wants to implement changes incrementally over time (gradual change) so that personnel have an opportunity to adjust to new realities and requirements. Proponents of radical change argue that when change is gradual, unanticipated events can derail the effort before it can be completed and that it gives opponents time to organize themselves to thwart further implementation. Figure 15.1, Kurt Lewin's three-step model on organizational change is a general model of the likely impact on police members when authoritarian and participative strategies using wide input and involvement are used as the basis for gradual radical organizational change. Regardless of whether change is

Figure 15.1
Kurt Lewin's three-step model on organizational change.

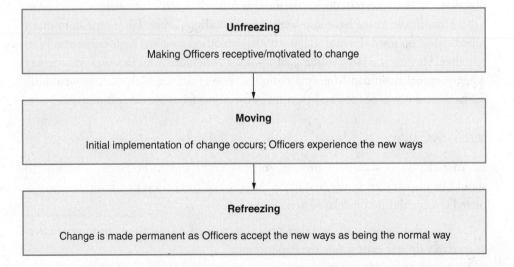

gradual or radical, the chief cannot sit passively on the sidelines to see how it turns out—he or she must actively help lead the change; as noted in Chapter 7, Leadership is not a spectator sport.

While some changes can be accomplished through the pronouncement by chiefs, especially in very small departments, larger departments are more complex and therefore require greater planning, the use of more sophisticated techniques, and wide involvement to garner crucial input and support before moving forward to the implementation phase. This often involves the use of organizational development (OD). In Chapter 5, Organizational Theory, the OD process was defined and described. To briefly review, OD is an applied behavioral science method of changing organizations through long-term efforts designed to improve the work culture and work processes.

In this section, two models of **directed change** are presented. The first one, **Lewin's three-step model**, was selected because it is one of the oldest, simplest, and yet, the most durable. The second model, the **traditional action research model**, represents a fairly typical change process. If the second one seems somewhat familiar, it may be due to the fact that planning was covered in an earlier chapter (see Chapter 8, Planning and Decision Making). The traditional action research model is simply a special type of planning. Both Lewin's three-step model and the Traditional Action Research Model rely on the use of organizational development (OD).

Kurt Lewin's Three-Step Model on Organizational Change

This model involves three sequential steps (see Figure 15.1):

1. *Unfreezing*—Officers, like all other people, get into their "comfort zones." Before change can occur, they have to be "unfrozen" from the perceptions and behaviors that are presently part of who they are and how they approach their jobs. Often, this is accomplished by creating a sense of urgency that the present way of doing things is deficient in some way and that a shift to some new procedures will produce better results more efficiently. This tactic is known as "disconfirmation" because, to some degree, it invalidates what is presently being done. The heart of unfreezing is making people be receptive to change.

2. *Moving*—This is a transitional phase in which officers actually experience the changes that were planned; there will be less resistance if officers are, to the maximum extent possible, included in the planning process and feel that they have some impact in shaping events. While chiefs do make top-down decisions that constitute major change, such as to begin using Compstat, there is ample room to involve sworn and civilian personnel from across the agency on the details of implementation, such as the design of forms to capture data and what types of data are most useful for planning various types of operations. The use of officers on task forces or committees cannot be symbolic or gratuitous; such motives will be "sniffed out" immediately and provoke an unpleasant set of dynamics for the chief to preside over.

3. *Refreezing*—The purpose of this phase is for officers to make permanent the changes they experienced in the previous phase, part of the normal way in which they see things, think about them, and behave. Some of the refreezing can be accomplished by appealing to the professionalism of officers—"When we get this thing fully up and running, everybody in the state will be looking at us, wondering how we got so far ahead of them." However, drawing upon the lessons learned from the shift from traditional policing to community policing, resistance tapered off and refreezing occurred faster when departmental awards were realigned with community policing goals, such as recognition for enrolling 25 businesses in a crime prevention program. Thus, as part of any large-scale change process, the use of awards to reinforce the desired behaviors should be carefully considered.

Traditional Action Research Model

There are many organizational development (OD) change models; however, most of them approximate the traditional action research model with the following five steps (see Figure 15.2):

1. *Recognizing the need for change*—Without this awareness, it is simply "business as usual" for police agencies. The change awareness may come from the need to implement the provisions of a Supreme Court decision or a consent decree entered into in partial settlement of a civil liability suit. The department's planning and research unit may have identified lapses in performance that need to be addressed or unusual opportunities on which to capitalize, such as the availability of federal grants to implement community policing programs or to upgrade crime scene investigation capabilities. Individual officers, supervisors, command staff members, or the union may make written recommendations in the form of memos or completed staff work that leads to change. Additionally, any of the situations discussed in the earlier section "Why Change Occurs" can take place, such as a new chief being hired with a mandate to make specific changes in the department's operating philosophy, organizational structure, programs and policies, and procedures.

2. *Assessing/diagnosing the situation*—Two fundamental tasks in assessing the situation must be executed flawlessly: (a) determining the opportunity or the problem—care must be taken to make sure that attention is given to the real problem and not a symptom of it, and (b) determining the gap or difference between what is now happening and what the department would like to have happen. In order to accomplish these twin objectives, data must be gathered. Sources of such data include 911, training, and other records, surveys of personnel and clients, and reviews of disciplinary records and litigation trends.

3. *Action planning*—The gap or difference between what is happening and what is desirable is the zone of impact, where meaningful change can occur if something significant is selected to work on. The chief must decide who will be in charge of the change process. Internal candidates for this responsibility know the organization, its capabilities, and its personnel but may lack the necessary skills to lead an effective intervention or may not have the time to devote to the change

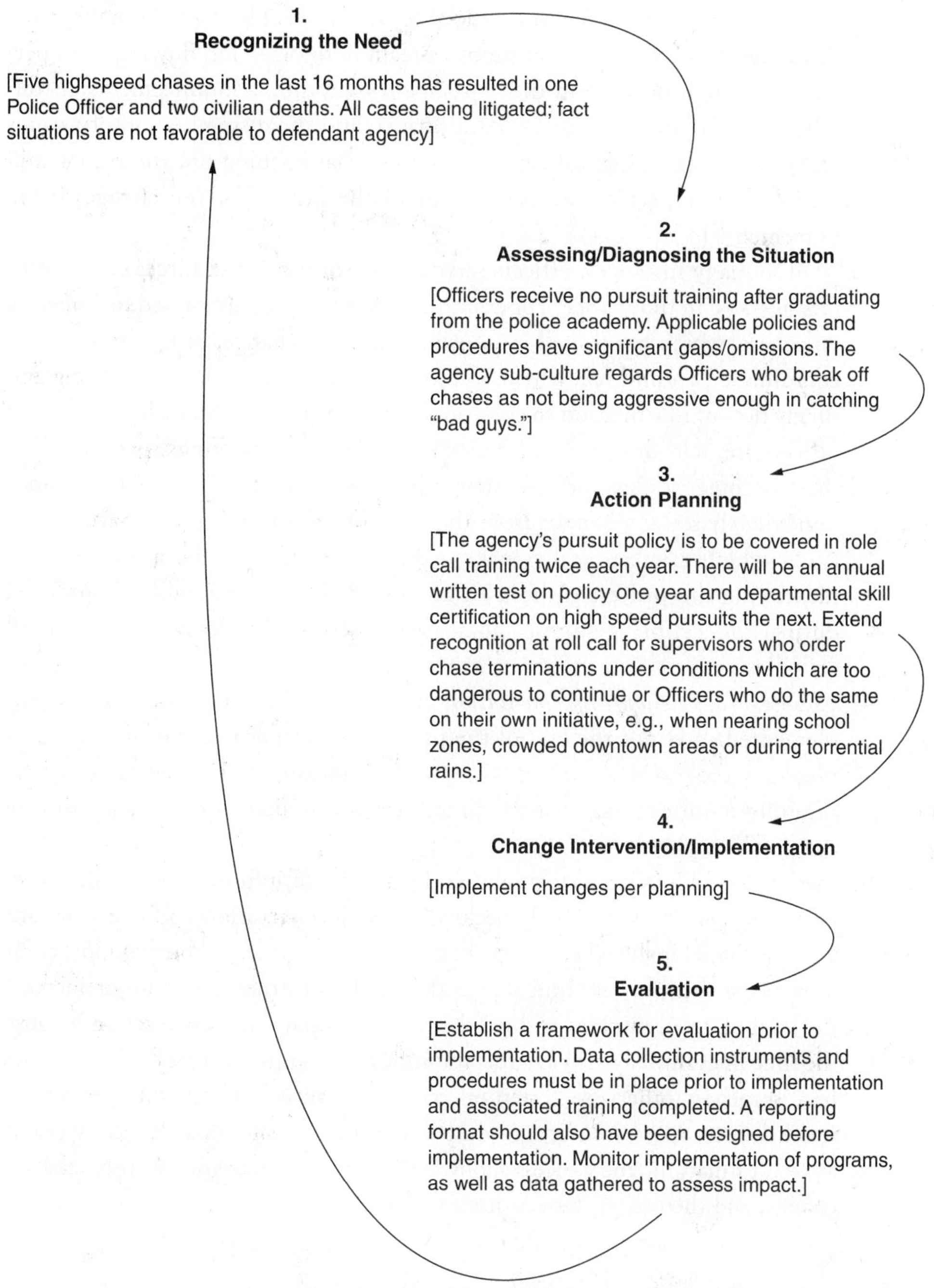

1.
Recognizing the Need

[Five highspeed chases in the last 16 months has resulted in one Police Officer and two civilian deaths. All cases being litigated; fact situations are not favorable to defendant agency]

2.
Assessing/Diagnosing the Situation

[Officers receive no pursuit training after graduating from the police academy. Applicable policies and procedures have significant gaps/omissions. The agency sub-culture regards Officers who break off chases as not being aggressive enough in catching "bad guys."]

3.
Action Planning

[The agency's pursuit policy is to be covered in role call training twice each year. There will be an annual written test on policy one year and departmental skill certification on high speed pursuits the next. Extend recognition at roll call for supervisors who order chase terminations under conditions which are too dangerous to continue or Officers who do the same on their own initiative, e.g., when nearing school zones, crowded downtown areas or during torrential rains.]

4.
Change Intervention/Implementation

[Implement changes per planning]

5.
Evaluation

[Establish a framework for evaluation prior to implementation. Data collection instruments and procedures must be in place prior to implementation and associated training completed. A reporting format should also have been designed before implementation. Monitor implementation of programs, as well as data gathered to assess impact.]

Figure 15.2
Traditional action research model.

effort. External consultants don't have any "baggage" because people in the department typically don't know them, but they lack the depth of knowledge about the department an insider would have. Although outsiders come with a certain amount of instant credibility, any missteps they make are often judged harshly with biting comments such as "If he's the expert and making big bucks, how come we've got such a mess on our hands?"

As mentioned earlier, it is crucial to involve people from throughout the department and to have a continuous stream of information flowing to all personnel through posting on the department's intranet, announcements at roll-call, information posted on bulletin boards, and the dissemination of memos and newsletters. When officers don't know what is going on, the rumor mill works overtime, seldom to the benefit of the process or the changes being implemented.

In many instances, officers serve on one or more task forces or committees involved in the change. For example, officers may be appointed to a steering task force, which has overall responsibility for the change, or the information coordination committee, which is charged with providing the continuing and timely flow of information to everyone in the department. Many lower-ranking officers are field-oriented and may chafe at being in meetings, particularly if they become restless at the slow progress being made initially, cannot immediately see any benefit from the work of the committee, or have doubts about whether it can really make a difference.[4] Ultimately, a written plan identifying the process to be used and the results desired will be produced during the action planning phase, with responsibilities assigned for all activities.

4. *Change Intervention/Implementation.* This is when the action plans are implemented. It is not the end of the process but rather the end of the beginning. As the various activities are set in motion, their progress must be carefully monitored against the time lines and standards established during the previous phase.

5. *Evaluation.* This is best accomplished by a series of informative, scheduled reports and periodic personnel checking through observation and conversations with personnel involved at various levels of the department. The two most common needs during this time are (a) the need to further articulate or increase the level of detail in plans and (b) the need to initiate corrective action because the time lines initially set were too ambitious and cannot be met or the activities have somehow otherwise gotten off track (e.g., an equipment supplier cannot make delivery as previously agreed upon). As the decision makers receive evaluative information, the process loops back to step 1, recognizing the need for change, and the process repeats itself.

Politics and Organizational Change

As discussed in detail in Chapter 1, The Evolution of Police Administration, we know that politics is neither inherently "bad" nor "good"; instead, its character is derived from how it is used. The larger an organizational change, the more likely politics will inevitably come into play. In many instances, political figures want to champion important changes in police departments. By consistently voicing their support in front of the audiences they address, politicians can be a potent adjunct to the change process, helping underscore both its significance and the backing it has. This is critical in preparing the organization for change and in helping it to maintain its focus and drive, so the changes can be successfully implemented.

Conversely, politicians can be a barrier to change when they want to make unneeded modifications to the scope of the change or attempt to micro-manage implementation details. However well intended, some politicians end up being an impediment when they attempt to become too involved with change. They must learn to trust the people charged with leading the police department and not attempt to substitute their judgment for that of the chief's and the command staff and to hold them accountable for the results or lack thereof.

Personal politics are typically at work during large-scale organizational changes in law enforcement agencies. This is normal and should be expected. Senior police officials seek to have those they have mentored for many years either promoted or assigned to desirable commands. Personnel on promotional rosters will seek to be among those selected to fill openings created by a reorganization of their department. The fact that people work to have themselves promoted during a reorganization should surprise no one. However, it is unsavory and kills morale when unqualified or marginally competent people with unbridled ambition successfully use politics to their personal advantage at the considerable expense of others or when the use of politics interferes with the timely and effective implementation of the changes. This actual case study that follows illustrates this point.

"Boss Town" had a strong mayor form of government and a police department with 500 sworn officers. For 18 months the department worked on a major reorganization; as part of this effort, 63 new positions were created, into which people had to be promoted. The ranks involved ranged from corporal and lieutenant, ranks new to the department, to one deputy chief/colonel position. It was widely known that the brain power behind the changes was "Major Thompson," perhaps the most highly able and respected of the senior commanders. Everyone in the department considered it a foregone conclusion that he would get the newly created deputy chief position. "Major Handshake" had come up through the ranks, but at every level, exceptions to the regular promotional process were made so that he could be advanced. His most recent promotion was just 10 months previous, when he had been promoted to major. Because the department's probationary period for supervisory positions was 12 months, Major Handshake was still on probation for another 2 months and was not eligible for promotion to the newly created deputy chief position.

At this point, politics, in the worst sense, was relied upon by Major Handshake to enhance his career. The mayor's son served on the state road board and was up for reappointment by the governor. It was personally important to the mayor that his son be reappointed and it was an economic development asset to the region for the son to continue to serve, so that he could funnel additional funds to the region for improved road systems. Major Handshake's uncle was not only a member of the governor's cabinet but also a close personal friend of the governor. The mayor received a call from the state capitol, expressing interest that Major Handshake be promoted to deputy chief. To ensure his son's reappointment, the mayor froze the implementation of the police reorganization for 60 days, at the end of which Major Handshake was off probation and promoted to deputy chief.

One cost of this delay was that the promotions, additional pay, and growth in seniority in grade for over 60 people were nonstarters for 2 months. Another cost was that a group of 7 very highly regarded detectives and sergeants informally met to discuss what it meant when the most qualified and professional person in the department could not get the promotion he deserved. What did that mean or suggest in terms of their own futures? Four members of this group subsequently resigned and went on to distinguished careers elsewhere. Of the three who stayed, one ultimately became the chief, who privately lamented in later years the substantial loss of talent caused by the promotion of Major Handshake.

Various Levels of Change

Not all change is momentous. However, the wider the scope of the change and the greater the number of people significantly impacted, the more difficult it is to implement, sustain, and institutionalize it. For example, assume that historically in a department the ranking patrol supervisor at the scene of a serious crime was in charge of the scene. A new policy is issued, stating whenever detectives are dispatched to the scene of a serious crime, they are in command of all aspects of conducting the on-site investigation. Usually, this would affect the job of patrol sergeants and, although they would grouse at the loss of authority, the change would be implemented without any significant turbulence or opposition. In fact, some sergeants would simply say, "It's fine by me; it's one less thing I have to worry about." But when there is large-scale directed change, "more people are going to be ticked off and eating Rolaids." While some policy changes can be made without controversy, others will provoke opposition; an excellent example of this is when an agency goes to a very restrictive high-speed chase policy and rank-and-file officers feel that their "hands are being tied when it comes to catching bad guys."

When automobiles started becoming more commonplace, police chiefs assigned their best officers to traffic duty because they would be coming into contact with the wealthy and professionals who could afford the cars. In a sense, police professionalism had its first modest start in traffic units; officers assigned there considered themselves elite. Once in a while, that leftover manifestation of this fact still appears.

Recently, a consultant finished a major organizational study of a police department with 200 sworn officers. One of his recommendations was that the traffic division (TD) be eliminated and all personnel from the traffic division be transferred to the patrol division. However, in order to maintain a high level of ability to investigate serious personal injury and fatality accidents, each patrol division shift would be assigned several of the best qualified TD accident investigators, who would continue to specialize in the same jobs they formerly held. The rest of the TD officers would be assigned to patrol duties. The reason for the recommendation was that the traffic division, whose members considered themselves the elite of uniformed officers, had become increasingly dysfunctional over a period of years. Among the indicators of this was that no traffic unit worked past 10:00 P.M., meaning that TD officers were not working during some of the prime hours for driving while intoxicated (DWI) enforcement. Moreover, compared with similarly sized cities, the TD officers generated fewer cases, despite having more personnel, used more sick leave than other officers in the department, and were often antagonistic to personnel in other divisions. They were often characterized as prima donnas by other officers in the department because of their reluctance to handle any other types of police incidents other than traffic accidents and traffic law enforcement. The change was implemented, but not without great upheaval. Some TD officers and supervisors attempted to have the change killed before it was implemented by visiting politicians who began to voice various concerns, pro and con, about the change. Some experienced TD officers left to take jobs in police departments in several nearby, smaller municipalities. The chief, who had risen through the ranks internally and had only recently been appointed, felt that the "change was long overdue, but messy." The mayor, who had appointed the chief, dismissed the controversy by noting that "You can't make an omelette without breaking a few eggs; we can't have a few malcontents trying to make policy." Slowly, things changed. DWI arrests went up because there were more officers working during the prime enforcement hours for them, response times to calls for service improved slightly because there were more patrol officers on duty to answer calls, and the number of traffic accidents declined marginally each month.

As the positive aspects of the change were "kicking in," a radical shift occurred that no one had foreseen. After some discussion and study, the city's voters approved merging their police department under the sheriff's office, which had a traffic unit. The benefits of the city police department having gone through a hard, large-scale organizational change were lost when the two agencies actually combined operations 18 months later. Under the sheriff, the former TD officers remembered who had supported the elimination of their division and made life difficult for them whenever they could, although slowly that behavior seemed to lessen over time. Thus, in large organizational change, there can be some lingering unanticipated difficulty for years beyond when the change actually happens.

The Role of the Rank and File in Organizational Change

The dominant mindset of police departments, police reformers, appellate judges, and criminal justice scholars—in short, of nearly everyone who thinks about policing and its problems–is, and always has been, that policing needs strong, top-down management. But in many ways police officers necessarily collaborate in the shaping of their work environment.[5] Partners assigned to the same patrol car discuss how they should spend their time and the best ways of responding to known problems in familiar places. Teams of officers plan undercover stings. At a more indirect level, police officers have a say in organizational planning and policy making through strongly supported police unions as well as identity-based caucuses of police officers' groups such as minority officers, women officers, or gay or lesbian officers. And even without pressure from below, wise sergeants, lieutenants, and captains—like wise supervisors in any occupation—find ways to enlist the rank and file in the process of cooperative problem solving. Arguments for systematically involving frontline employees in workplace decision making have gained extraordinarily broad currency over the past several decades, in the public sector and the private sector alike—but not in policing. This is so despite the increasing frequency with which police executives speak in terms of team management, shared organizational outcomes, and aligning police managerial systems with the private sector employment relations practices.[6,7]

Three overlapping arguments are commonly made for involving rank-and-file officers in the decision-making process:

- It heightens morale and commitment.
- It develops democratic skills and habits.
- It makes for better decisions.

Scholars addressing this issue emphasize how police decision making could be improved by securing what is called *diffused and seminal intelligence* of the police rank and file, *craft knowledge, street knowledge*, or *context-specific knowledge*.[8] It includes not only the kind of micro-level sociological understanding all good officers acquire about their beats, but also, a hands-on feel for best practices, innovative ideas for improving those practices, and a thorough, nuanced understanding of their fellow offices—who can be trusted, who shirks responsibility, who cuts corners, who is prone to violence. Thus, line officers can collectively offer not only richer and more nuanced *answers* to central problems of policing, but also distinctive and important *questions*—questions different than, and complementary to, the ones typically posed by police executives and typically pursued by scholars.

In addition, if the policy is strongly opposed by the rank-and-file members of the agency, they could decide to flex their political muscle in opposition to it as reflected in the following news article.

IN THE NEWS   Change Successfully Blocked by Rank-and-File Officers Labeling It a "Quota System"

The Ogden (Utah) City Council decided to drop a controversial police performance evaluation plan that included 18 factors, including a score for the number of traffic tickets given. This followed a period during which the wife of an officer who drove a van used to display signs critical of the traffic quota and Mayor Godfrey. Within hours, the officer was placed on administrative duty, although the police chief maintains this was due to other alleged actions by the officer. A 2-day "blue-flu" was also used, with officers calling in "sick" during it. The city's administration has agreed to meet with officers to identify and discuss issues; the meetings will be led by a professional mediator to keep them on track.

Source: "Ogden Rescinds Ticket Quota for Police," The Associated Press and Local Wire, August 16, 2006.

Why Organizational Change Efforts Sometimes Fail

While organizational change is ubiquitous and necessary, it is also tenuous. As any organization prepares itself to manage the challenge of a planned change, it must be aware of the various threats that might be present that could inhibit the success of the change effort. Despite proper strategy selection, elaborate planning and resourcing, and strong administrative commitment, evaluation research shows that many attempts at major organizational change fail.[9]

Threats to the success of a planned organizational change can take many forms, both internal and external to the organization. External threats to change initiatives can present themselves as budgetary setbacks, a lack of support or misunderstandings from citizens, or opposition by a newly elected politically powerful official. Internal threats to change initiative also come in many forms. These include, but are not limited to, a lack of leadership commitment, a conflicting organizational culture, or as earlier suggested in this chapter, a lack of support or understanding from the employees involved in the change.[10]

Models Regarding Change

There are three models regarding officer receptivity to planned organizational change:

1. A life experiences/life chances model
2. An officer/organizational subculture model
3. An organizational/structural model

The first model, the life experiences/life chances model, examines the influence of officers' ascribed and achieved status attributes, as measured by their socio-demographic and work experience characteristics. Although sparse, the extant literature suggests that some officer socio-demographic and work experience characteristics (race, gender, education, and years of service) are associated with their receptivity to change[11] and that female, minority, college-educated, and less-experienced officers are more open to organizational changes. Because policing has traditionally been a field dominated by White males and not requiring a college degree, the presence of women, minorities, and college-educated officers among the more recent recruits to the profession constitutes a form of organizational change aimed at diversifying and professionalizing the ranks. Such officers tend to

---

Quick FACTS ▸▸ Up to 80 Percent of Changes Fail

Just how hard is organizational change? Research suggests that between 50 and 80 percent of the time, the major results that were anticipated are *not* produced. Smith interviewed 210 managers who reported a change failure rate of over 75 percent.

Source: M. E. Smith, "Implementing Organization Change: Correlates of Success and Failure," *Performance Improvement Quarterly*, 15, no. 1 (2002): 67–83.

be less wedded to more traditional models of policing and, likewise, are less integrated into the police subculture.[12]

The second rival model, the subculture of policing model, addresses the effects of officers' work orientation on their receptivity to planned organizational change. In particular, the influence of officer cynicism, traditionalism, as well as their crime-control and service work orientations. Those officers who most adhere to elements of the subculture of policing (i.e., have high scores on measures of cynicism, traditionalism, and a strong crime control orientation) are least receptive to organizational change, especially those that involve service activities and partnerships with community members to solve noncrime-related social problems. Conversely, those who hold a strong social orientation are most receptive of such change.

The final model, the organizational/structural model, asserts that officers' receptivity to change is a function of their perceptions of the extent to which their agency is prepared for such a change. This model also examines the association between officer receptivity to change and their perceptions of agency readiness with regard to the adequacy of officer training, administrative commitment, resource distribution, and reorganization.

Ways to Make Organizational Change Successful

To accomplish organizational change, the police manager needs a combination of will and skill to seize the opportunity to make the needed changes. The basic recommendations that follow can help managers seize opportunities for change in their departments.

Use Coaching as a Tool to Facilitate Organizational Change

Coaching, when provided by a carefully selected peer or supervisor, can be an invaluable tool for assisting officers in accepting change. If done properly it can provide officers with increased awareness and information about the benefits of the change (i.e., requiring a 2-year college degree for promotion to sergeant and a 4-year bachelor's degree for a promotion to the rank of lieutenant and above). It can also give officers an opportunity to express any negative emotions they might be feeling about the change and provide them with the opportunity to express precisely why they are opposed to the new policy.[13] If properly handled, coaching can give the officers inclined to resist the change an opportunity for self-evaluation and a chance to consider how the organizational change could affect them in a very positive way.

Once an administrator has made a decision to implement a change and has moved into an action stage, carefully selected coaches who support the change process should work with potentially resistant individuals as they move through the change process. The coach can provide social and emotional support for the change process and can help the individual being coached accept the change in such a way as to make it easier to be implemented.

Individual and group coaching is just one tool for facilitating the change process in organizations; however, it should be given serious consideration. The organization as a whole must find ways of informing its employees about the benefits of the new program, ways of raising an awareness of the pros and cons of changing or not changing, and ways of reinforcing and supporting employees as they go through the change process.[14]

Coaching can be a critical part of this change process becaue it focuses on the individual's own agenda. It can also provide an effective process to assist officers in dealing with all the other changes they or their police organizations feel necessary to implement.[15]

Set Flexible Priorities

Police managers should plan their reform agendas very carefully but be prepared to change plans quickly. Effective managers always juggle their plans, putting some on hold while pursuing others. Priorities may vary with the manager's personal interests, the recent political history of the department, or new pressures being put on the department. They may also vary with issues largely unrelated to the police, such as a municipal election that has resulted in a shift in political power. There are reform agendas that will improve police performance, agendas that will heal community conflicts, and agendas that will advance personal careers. These are not always the same.

In any given situation there may be issues that police managers feel are very important but they have found that their ideal goals are strategically impossible to accomplish. Thus, police managers should set potentially achievable goals. This is not to advocate timidity in setting such goals but merely to counsel against overreaching folly.[16]

Assemble Resources

In order to effect successful organizational change, police managers should accumulate political and other resources to strengthen their credibility and persuasiveness. It is important to have as many allies as possible. How these resources are accumulated, and which ones are chosen, depend very much on the personal style of the players in question. Police chiefs, for example, are often faced with the choice of whether to build support in the community, in the department, with local elected officials, or some combination. Because community coalitions shift, however, it is important to seek a broad base of support from citizen leaders, media, prosecutors, state legislators, and others.[17]

Seize Opportunities

With priorities set and resources in line, a police manager should be ready for a wide range of opportunities for change. These opportunities can be defined as events that can throw the spotlight on police policy and provide a "case in point" justification for an organizational change proposal.

Ironically, opportunities often come disguised in crises, and managers must resist the initial impulse to think first of damage control. In some cases it may be advantageous for managers interested in change to embrace a crisis and make the most of it. Several generic kinds of events provide opportunities to capitalize on crises to achieve reform.

For example, dramatic tragedies can sometimes provide an opportunity for making needed improvements in department procedures. In one department, the death of an officer who employed an improper tactic in a traffic stop led to the development of a training course on traffic stop safety, as well as expanding the training on other officer survival skills. Other crime-related crises can also be used to bolster requests for additional police officers and financial resources. The dramatic death of an officer or uninvolved innocent third party during a high-speed pursuit for a minor traffic violation may provide an opportunity for a chief law enforcement officer who supports a more conservative pursuit policy to impose restrictions that had been heretofore resisted by rank-and-file officers.

Local or nationwide studies of a police department or policing in general on similar related issues can provide support for the chief's reform agenda. Even if a report is critical, the chief may be able to use its conclusions for the benefit of the department.

Budget crises and fiscal restraint—even layoffs—provide opportunities for questioning traditional practices and making hard choices. As a matter of fiscal necessity, for example, many departments have reordered their priorities, adopted various forms of call screening, and started to refer some kinds of calls to nonpolice organizations. For a chief who has long argued that the police cannot do everything, dramatic news about city tax shortfalls which have become endemic in recent years can provide the political opportunity to make needed changes.[18]

Create Opportunities

No matter how skillfully a police manager seizes opportunities, major items on the reform agenda may still have to be left unaddressed because of political or other reasons. The times may be so sensitive or so complex that no naturally occurring event opens a window for them. However, in some rare cases, police reformers have created their own opportunities by initiating publicity concerning police problems. However, such actions should be undertaken only after consultation with the local government manager or mayor to avoid having important individuals being publically "blindsided" or "embarrassed."

In highly publicized situations, police at various ranks have tried to create public debate through leaks or whistle blowing, with attendant press coverage. More quietly, some top executives have sought to freshen their agencies by airing out some of their own dirty laundry in order to provoke the press into demanding reforms sought by the executives themselves. Another way to call attention to departmental problems is to launch an internal investigation or commission a study. Clear proof of misconduct provides a firm excuse for radical changes, and investigations are often the best way to produce that proof. Studies can be used to make people remember an old problem or to demonstrate the existence of a new one.[19]

Follow Through

In all these seized and nurtured opportunities, reform depends on more than just a single press conference. Announcing a planned change or signing an executive order is not usually enough to make change happen. Without a concerted follow-up effort, many or most reforms may die.[20]

CONCLUSION

The objectives of any police executive contemplating change should be to do so in a manner that offers the greatest possibility of success, does not result in a reduction of the quality and quantity of service to the public, and does not polarize the organization and the community into warring factions. In this chapter we have set forth many ideas and suggestions that should help the enlightened police administrator to implement organizational change successfully.

CHAPTER REVIEW

1. Identify eight recurring reasons why change occurs in law enforcement agencies.
2. State five reasons when change should not be made.
3. What are the three steps in Kurt Lewin's model on organizational change?
4. What are the five steps in the traditional action research model?
5. What are the most common overlapping arguments commonly made for involving employees in workplace decision making?
6. Why do organizational change efforts sometimes fail?
7. What are the three models regarding officer receptivity to planned organizational change?
8. What are ways to make organizational change succeed?

KEY TERMS

change agent: an individual or a group from within or outside the police department that stimulates, guides, facilitates, and stabilizes the change process.

directed change: a carefully planned, formal action designed to bring about a new condition.

Lewin's three-step model: a change model that has three sequential steps: (1) unfreezing, (2) moving, and (3) refreezing.

traditional action research model: a five-step change model consisting of the following: (1) recognizing the need for change, (2) assessing/diagnosing the situation, (3) action planning, (4) the intervention, and (5) evaluation.

ENDNOTES

[1] In Citrus Heights, California, the main reasons given for selecting a new chief were his "organizational skills and fresh approach to law enforcement." See David Richie, "Citrus Heights Names Top Cop," *Sacramento Bee*, November 30, 2005.
[2] See Robert Rogers, "Rialto, Police Lay Blueprint for Future," *Inland Valley Bulletin*, April 17, 2006.

[3] For example, see Ivan Moreno, "Littleton PD Morale Rated Low; Consultants Find Distrust, Fear Expensive Turnover." *Rocky Mountain Times*, September 13, 2006.

[4] Hans Toch and J. Douglas Grant, *Police as Problem Solvers* (Washington, D.C.: American Psychological Association, 2005), p. 342.

[5] David Alan Sklansky and Monique Marks, "The Role of the Rank and File in Police Reform," *Policing and Society 18*, no. 1 (March 2008), pp. 1–6. (This discussion was adapted with permission from this source.)

[6] E. McLaughlin and K. Murji, "Resistance Through Representation: 'Storylines,' Advertising and Police Federation Campaigns," *Policing and Society* 8, no. 4 (1998), pp. 367–399.

[7] M. Silvestri, "'Doing' Police Leadership: Enter the 'new smart macho,'" *Policing and Society* 17, no. 1 (2007), pp. 38–58.

[8] H. Toch and J. D. Grant, *Police as Problem Solvers: How Frontline Workers Can Promote Organizational and Community Change*, 2nd ed. (Washington, DC: American Psychological Association, 2005).

[9] John K. Cochran, Max L. Bromley and Matthew J. Swando, "Sheriff's Deputies' Receptivity to Organizational Change," *Policing: An International Journal of Police Strategies & Management 25*, no. 3 (2002), pp. 507–529. (This discussion was adapted from this source.)

[10] R. Aragon, "Community-Oriented Policing: Success Insurance Strategies," *The FBI Law Enforcement Bulletin* 66 (1997), pp. 8–18.

[11] A. J. Lurigio and W. G. Skogan, "Winning the Hearts and Minds of Police Officers: An Assessment of Staff Perceptions of Community Policing in Chicago," *Crime and Delinquency* 40, no. 3, (1994), pp. 315–330.

[12] John K. Cochran, Max L. Bromley and Matthew J. Swando, "Sheriff's Deputies' Receptivity to Organizational Change," *Policing: An International Journal of Police Strategies & Management 25*, no. 3 (2002), pp. 507–529.

[13] Richard C. Lumb and Ronald Breazeale, "Police Officer Attitudes and Community Policing Implementation: Developing Strategies for Durable Organizational Change," *Policing and Society 13*, no. 1 (2002), p. 99.

[14] Ibid.

[15] Richard C. Lumb and Ronald Breazeale have developed a training program to prepare supervisors to address and resolve problems before they affect either employees or the organizations. The results of this study can be found in Ibid., pp. 100 and 101.

[16] Lawrence W. Sherman, Albert M. Greenfield Professor of Human Relations in the Department of Sociology and director of the Fels Center of Government, University of Pennsylvania, and Anthony V. Bouza, former chief of police, Minneapolis, Minnesota, in *Local Government Police Management*, 4th edition (Washington DC: International City/County Management Association, 2003), p. 440.

[17] Ibid., p. 440.

[18] Ibid., pp. 440, 441.

[19] Ibid., p. 441.

[20] Ibid., p. 441.

Index